A UNIQUE YORKSHIRE VILLAGE

THE HISTORY OF INGLETON

John Bentley

[signature: John Bentley]

INGLETON PUBLICATIONS 2008

ISBN 978-0-907911-05-0 Cardback
978-0-907911-06-7 Hardback

Copyright J.I.BENTLEY
Typeset in 10 point Times New Roman by Mike Gill

PRINTED BY FRETWELL PRINT & DESIGN
Healey Works, Goulbourne Street, Keighley, Yorkshire, BD21 1PZ

CONTENTS

ACKNOWLEDGEMENTS

I thank Stan Lawrence of Austwick, late headmaster of Burton School for stimulating my interest in the local history of the Ingleton area during his classes at the Ingleborough Community Centre in 1975. Thanks go to Mike Howarth of Ingleton for editing this volume. With his wide career in teaching English and his interest and knowledge of the Ingleton area he was the perfect man for the job. His Ingleton credentials are especially solid as his father was born at Greenwood Leghe. Mike Gill has played a great part by setting up the text and illustrations on computer ready for printing and by compiling the index. As co-author of *Ingleton Colliery* and Recorder of the Northern Mine Research Society he has acquired a wide knowledge of Ingleton especially of the coalfield and quarries. It was Mike who recommended the printers, Fretwell Print and Design of Keighley. Des Fretwell of Keighley is thanked for all assistance and printing.

I must thank W.R. Mitchell, MBE, Hon. D.Litt., better known as Bill Mitchell to his many admirers and numerous readers of the *Yorkshire Dalesman* which he edited for so many years. His foreword to this volume is much appreciated. Thomas Tomlinson author of *Our Tomlinson Family History* has been helpful with information, assistance in scanning illustrations into the computer and solving many computer problems. The Tomlinsons were numerous in Ingleton over several centuries. Thanks also go to Bernard Bond who has kept me in touch with things going on at Ingleton and has been a constant source of information and advice. His home is a hive of local history activity and he has made many important discoveries of maps, photos, documents and artefacts relating to the village. Much of his material has been used in this book.

Illustrations have come from a wide number of people. The Tommy Sydney collection came to me from his wife. Photographs have also been loaned by Arthur Bateson from his superb collection of photographs and post cards. Stan Frankland allowed me to copy a selection of his photographic collection only months before his death this year. I thank Eric Guilliam for his advice on Ingleton photos over the years and the colour photo used on the front cover; Richard & Lillian Randel for photo of Ingleton Colliery; Donald Binns for permission to use photographs from his railway publications; Mary Sagar for the photo of girls exercising at Storrs School, and David Johnson for his photograph of the Hoffmann kiln at Ingleton. I thank my wife Carol for several drawings.

Thanks go to Anthony Brown for loan of mill deeds and documents, Phil Hudson for his research on Ingleton's mills and Frances Lincoln Publishers for permission to use excerpts from *Wainwright in the Limestone Dales*. Gordon Barker is thanked for use of his grandfather, James Barker's, papers and other information, the late Anthony Perry for information on the Shireburns of Stonyhurst and Twistleton and Noel Crack for information on the Lancaster Richmond Turnpike. Thanks also go to Margaret Dickenson for much information on the Moore and Harling families and Dave Weedon for his work on Ingleton photographers. Ingleton Parish Council is thanked for access to parish records and David Butters warden of Ingleborough Community Centre for being ever helpful.

Thanks also go to Margaret Butler, Richard Barker, Dorothy Baines. Lauraine Palmeri of Prospect Cottage, June Mullinder, Andrew Lynn, Adrian Brown, Malcolm Cullshaw, Dr Ralph Tomlinson, Robert White, Peter Harling, Jean Boardman of Ingleton Hall, Prof Richard Hoyle, Graham Lee, Mrs Ann Pybus for RAOB material which belonged to her father Joseph Walker, Robin Gill for National School documents, Beryll Morphet, Margaret Butler of Skipton, Robin Hainsworth, Carol A. Howard, George Redhead and Bill Dootson. Also thanks to the late Bob Brown, Jack Redhead, Tommy Sydney, Dennis Moore, Mrs Dawson of Blue Hall, Margaret Sutton, Rose Thornton, and Jim Lambert,

Thanks go to the Lancashire Record Office, Bow Lane Preston; North Yorkshire County Record Office Northallerton; Cumbria Record Offices at the Castle Carlisle and Kendal; the West Riding Archive Service; Lancaster University; the Yorkshire Archaeological Society Leeds; Borthwick Institute of Archives York and the Public Record Office in London. The Lancaster library, Skipton library and the Yorkshire Dales National Park Authority were also very helpful.

Finally I should thank you – the person I know I might well have missed who loaned me a photograph or gave me information.

FOREWORD
by
W.R. (Bill) Mitchell, MBE, Hon. D.Litt.,

Forty years ago, when John Bentley began to jot down notes about Ingleton, the task of writing local history must have seemed relatively easy. He had been familiar with the village since boyhood. An inquiring mind led him to fill a multitude of notebooks.

In an impressive feat of mental concentration, he copied and printed all the entries about Ingleton from the Lancaster press, between 1800 and 1940, rounding off the job by binding them into five volumes. He has presented his material – clearly, objectively – in no less than thirty-two sections.

From the first, John was working to a grand plan. Here are two sections. The first deals with the broad sweep of history in well-defined historical periods, from the Brigantes to our contemporaries. The second section elaborates important aspects of that history, such as mills – four mills, no less, their stories elaborated over eight large pages, plus meticulous references. Coal mining, a subject of which John and several friends are authorities, is recorded in satisfyingly fine detail.

To a casual visitor, the most picturesque view of Ingleton takes in a railway viaduct (now more ornamental than useful), an Anglican church (on an unstable site above a gushing river) and, of course, Ingleborough, described by young Laurence Binyon, in the first of many poems, as "the big blue hill." These are the obvious sights, as are the Twiss and Doe, those sprightly rivers that the modern tourist might safely explore on paths and bridges. Ingleton has long since prized its scenery.

Hard facts about industrial projects are off-set by a chapter showing that Ingleton is rich in its literary and artistic connections. To Thomas Gray, a visitor in 1769, the two rivers were "torrents", with great stones instead of water rolling along their beds. The diaries of Victorian Anthony Hewitson, guide book writer, which now repose in the Lancashire Record Office, deal with minor facts and gossip – the small change of rural life.

I was delighted to see references to the local works of Frederick Riley, who I knew well. And a substantial section based on local references in Southey's strange little novel called *The Doctor* (1848 edition). Herein are tales of Chapel-le-Dale. I once heard a passage read at a wedding in the little chapel in the dale while the happy couple signed the registers.

The success of John Bentley's substantial, ever-interesting book rests not on the fancies of visitors – of which there have been many – but on hard facts about such local industries as quarrying and mining. A host of Ingleton men were slaves to industry. We have facts, figures and tales about roads, railways, tourism and much more. To the author, Ingleton is unique. It is a conclusion a reader reaches long before he or she has attained the last page of this splendid local history.

INTRODUCTION

Ingleton has always fascinated me because of the variety of its history and I have researched it for over forty years. So many Yorkshire villages are very attractive, but with little more than a basic agricultural background. They have a church, perhaps an old inn or two, or a lead mine, but Ingleton has such a wide breadth of history. With the pre-historic settlement on Ingleborough and the Saxon tun below, it has a wealth of both agricultural and industrial heritage. Many aspects of Ingleton's past have not been easy to find. Records for Yorkshire are spread amongst so many record offices and depositories including Northallerton, Wakefield and Leeds. Not a great deal had been written on Ingleton's history and Balderstone's *Bygone and Present,* although fascinating, contains precious little historical information.

Ingleton was a colliery village for several centuries, the centre of a large wood trade, and had a vast lime industry that supplied many Victorian towns with lime for their building development. With the coming of the industrial revolution, mills were developed for spinning and weaving. One mill was transformed into a brewery in the Victorian period and Ingleton became a brewery town. Then from the eighteenth century the tourist trade developed and grew with the coming of the railway and today it still provides walks, caving, camping and a host of caravan sites for town and city folk to escape to.

Most town and village histories are either written chronologically or thematically, but this has both and is written in two sections. The first chapters follow the village's history through the ages from the prehistoric to the twentieth century. The second part looks at important aspects of the township's history, church and chapel, tourist industry, collieries, inns, and many other topics.

This book is not extravagantly referenced, but I hope that the sources of the main material that the reader may want to follow up will be noted. I made notes on Ingleton long before I ever intended writing a history of the place so references were often not made. There are also many things that I simply know about Ingleton and have no reference to offer. If a month and date are given for events then the Lancaster or Craven press were probably the source. In preparation for writing this history I copied and printed all the entries about Ingleton from the Lancaster press from 1800 to 1940 and bound them in five volumes.

I know the accepted method of writing dates is '16 January 1885' and in my previous publications I have conformed to this dating system although I have never liked it. In this volume dates are written 'January 16th 1885' and sometime 'the 16th of January 1885'. Up to 1751 the new year began on Lady Day, March 25th. From 1751 the new year began on January 1st as it does today. Years in this volume are usually given as we would give them today. You will find no Early Modern in this book - Tudor period yes, Georgian yes, but Early Modern when was that ? Some historian said, 'I am committed to the concept but can't tell you when it began or ended.' Well I am committed to the Tudor Period and Georgian Period and I can tell you exactly when they began and when they ended.

A great disappointment is the fact that in spite of evidence from The Ingleborough Archaeological Group, the Ingleton Angling Association, myself and others the Ordnance Survey have refused to change the rivers names at Ingleton back to as they were some forty years ago. The evidence we presented should have even convinced a court of law, but we were turned down. Sadly the confusion will now continue and readers must be warned that the river names in this book do not correspond with the Ordnance Survey. I ask readers to read the chapter on rivers and draw their own conclusion.

Ingleton has always been a place that welcomed me, I have always felt a relaxation on entering the village, the promise of friendly meetings, good rest, and good food and drink. Ingleton has been a place of escape for much of my life. In researching a history there is always a promise of more information to be found, but if this book is not written and published now it may never be completed. So if you find things that are missing, as there surely are, please forgive me and enjoy what is there. The research has often been exciting, new discoveries have always been a delight, but writing and putting this book together has been damned hard work.

John Bentley 2008.

BRIGANTES AND ROMANS

The names Ingleborough and Ingleton have the same name origin-the mountain and the settlement at its feet. Ingleborough had its hill fort in pre-Roman times when the Brigantes were the tribe controlling the area, but of course its name is of a much later date and came when the settlers of Ingleton probably gave the names to the mountain and village at the same time. However, the mountain was predominant and named Ingleborough while the town echoed that name. 'Ingle' has been associated with fire as in inglenook and in the past this has been the predominant explanation for the origin of Ingleborough, the fire fort. This explanation has been the more readily accepted and popular because Ingleborough was known to be the site of an ancient beacon and important in the chain of beacons that crossed the country to give warnings in time of invasion and crisis. Ingleborough was also the site of a massive hill fort which gave rise to the borough part of its name. Balderstone in his *Ingleton Bygone and Present* calls Ingleton the fire, or beacon town. He says that the 'ingle' in Ingleborough and Ingleton comes from the Scotch 'ingle' meaning fire.

Joseph Carr, a noted Ingleton authority of the Victorian period, gave a different origin to Ingleborough and Ingleton.[1] He argued that as the name 'Ingle' came up so many times where it was not associated with fire as in Ingleton in County Durham, Ingleby in Lincolnshire, Ingleby Greenhow and others, that there was another origin. He says the meaning was English borough and English town. Baines in his history of Yorkshire says that all Danish bys with the prefix 'ingle' mean English town. This explanation sounds reasonable as Ingleton was an Anglian settlement.

A third explanation is one that was suggested by Ekwall, an expert in place name origins. He pointed out that that there was an Old English word 'ing' meaning 'peak,' which would explain a series of difficult place names. Such as Ingleborough and Ingleton. Ingon, Inglewood and Inkpen. In most of these names the meaning 'peak' is topographically appropriate. This explanation was held by A.H. Smith in *The Place Names of the West Riding of Yorkshire.* Ingleborough means the fortified peak and there is no doubt that is what Ingleborough was. Robert Gambles in his *Yorkshire Dales Place-Names* writes 'Ingleborough: Ingelburh 1165 Old English ing-hyll + Old English burh. The fort on the hill.' This last explanation of origin is most probably the correct one.

Yorkshire at the time of the Roman invasion was a part of Brigantia, the wide tribal land of the Brigantes. They were a loose federation of people whose land stretched from sea to sea and covered much of northern England. The Prehistoric remains on Ingleborough are of a massive size and covered some fifteen acres the whole of the level platform of the summit of the mountain. The area was surrounded by a rampart of stone some three-thousand feet in length. In places it was hardly necessary, due to the natural rock edge, which would have made the ascent difficult. There are openings on the north, the south west and the east. Placed irregularly within the fort are traces of some nineteen circular foundations of what were considered to be hut dwellings.

This chapter can not be completed without looking at the recent work of Yvonne A. Luke. In her study *Rethinking Ingleborough* produced in 2003 for an MA in Field Archaeology. Yvonne Luke examines the prehistoric site on Ingleborough and redefines it a ceremonial and ritual site from the 2nd Millenium BC. The monument has been long described as an Iron Age hill fort comprising a stone built rampart enclosing about twenty round houses. However, recent studies have shown that there are no signs of hearths in the round houses and there is no proof that they were ever roofed houses for occupation. They could be described as hut circles or possibly ring cairns, but Yvonne Luke thinks they are better described as 'ring

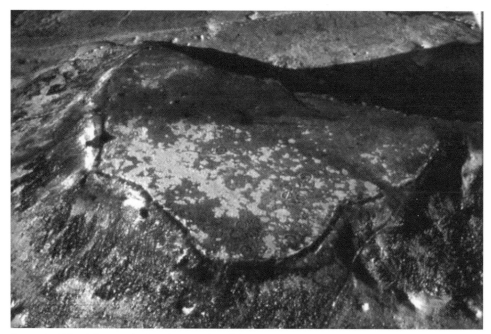

Summit of Ingleborough showing traces of ring structures.

structures.' She reasons that once you have taken the ramparts and other defensive names out of the site then it become easier to see it as a ritual site.

Yvonne Luke's approach is convincing and her study has already changed the way in which the remains on Ingleborough summit are interpreted. Ingleborough is a massive and commanding feature of the landscape and must have overwhelmed prehistoric man. He would have been driven to climb the mountain and to put it to some purpose. To live there all the year round appears very unlikely and a ritual site seems very plausible. Yvonne Luke comments, 'Inevitably the evaluation is incomplete and the interpretation must be provisional, but if I had to describe the new model in a phrase, it would be a holy mountain, a sacred place.'

The Romans invaded Britain and conquered most of the country, subduing the natives and building roads and forts to establish their new colony. The nearest Roman fort to Ingleton was at Bainbridge. This fort was built on a hillock at the edge of the present township and its Roman name was Virosidum, meaning High Seat, which was very apt for its situation. The first fort at Bainbridge was built by Agricola (AD 78-84) but re-built several times and occupied until the end of the fourth century. The Brigantes initially accepted Roman occupation and Queen Cartimandua co-operated with them. However, in AD 51 after Cartimandua handed over Caractacus, a British guerrilla leader, to the Romans, her husband Venutius gathered anti-Romans together and caused a revolt. The Romans put down the revolt and re-established the queen's position. Then in AD 69 Cartimandua divorced her husband, Venutius, and took up with his armour-bearer, Vellocatus. Civil war broke out in the area and the Roman emperor Vespasian formerly ended the client-state relationship and sent Petillius Cerialis with the IX legion and other troops to annex Brigantia to Roman Britain. Venutius made his stand at Stanwick near Richmond and was there defeated by disciplined Roman troops. Venutius disappeared after the Brigantes were subdued and was heard of no more.

What concerns us as far as Ingleton is concerned is that the Roman fort at Bainbridge is supposed to have been connected by road westwards via Ingleton to Lancaster. This route can still be followed over Cam fell and past Ingleborough. There is then a question as to the route it takes. Of recent years a route down through Twistleton has been favoured. This route enters Ingleton from Chapel-le-dale through Mealbank between the two rivers. It is said that the Hawes road out of Ingleton as far as Chapel-le-Dale was a new route, inferring that it was cut by the Lancaster Richmond Turnpike Trust in the eighteenth century. However the road down through Twistleton was little more than a pack-horse track until 1795 when the local authorities had it widened to five yards and walled.

It seems doubtful that the Romans would have allowed themselves to be caught between two rivers which were so often in flood. It would have meant that they could easily have been trapped by an enemy and had little chance of escape. The only other possible route would have been along the base of Ingleborough approaching the river crossings as the road through Ingleton presently does and this seems to be the most sensible route for a Roman road. The mound on which the church was later built was most likely used as a fort to protect the river crossing and could have been used as such from Roman times. Control of the river crossings would have been necessary and a place to camp would have been needed especially when the rivers were in flood.

Sadly no evidence of Roman occupation has been found in Ingleton township, no altars, no gravestones, no milestones. It is unlikely that any road the Romans may have used through Ingleton was a Roman road as most people know it. It would have been a fairly narrow rough road and not made according to the text book Roman road. Eventually in the late fourth century the Romans withdrew from Britain as their troops were needed to defend Rome itself. Britain was left to defend itself as best it could and following the Roman departure Angles and Saxons invaded the country and settled along the coast before moving further inland. A group of these invaders, most probably Angles, eventually founded the settlement at Ingleton.

REFERENCES

1. *Recollections of Ingleton* 1896, J. Carr , 1896 ed. J.I. Bentley, Ingleton Pub., 1991, p.10.
2. *Yorkshire Dales Place-Names,* R. Gambles, Dalesman Publishing 1995. p.52.

ANGLO-SAXON SETTLEMENT
AND NORMAN MANOR

The first settlement of Ingleton as we know it today took place on the lands on the east bank of the river Greta known as the demesne lands. Here the first 'ton' was probably set up, a small settlement surrounded by a ditch and palisade. It was an Anglian rather than Saxon settlement being in the area it was, but Anglo-Saxon is the term in general use. The ditch was probably filled with water from an early date as it was near to a spring which provided water for a moat and part of that moat survived as a moat to around 1830.[1] Part of the drained moat still survives on the south side of Ingleton Hall to this day. It is the only obvious sign left to show that here stood an early moated settlement and later a moated manor house which survived several centuries. Within the protection of the ton the Anglo-Saxon founders of Ingleton build their chief's hall and lived and kept their animals in huts around it. They needed protection from both marauding humans and animals. Of course as the rule of law developed and kingdoms were established, families spread out from the ton and settled in areas nearby and began to shape the village of Ingleton that we know today.

There were small settlements in the Ingleton area long before the Romans came and most would be affected by the Roman occupation. There was also Norse infiltration into the area as shown in the names Braida Garth and Moorgarth and the Ingleton fells settlements of Southerscales, and Winterscales. Viking style long huts are to be found at Ribblehead and at Braida Garth in Kingsdale. The Norse 'township' had its homes spread out over a wide area. The Danes had divided Yorkshire into Ridings and the Ridings into Wapentakes. In each Wapentake there was a central meeting place. Here they held courts in which twelve thegns acted in the same way as the later twelve men of the jury who were derived from them. Ingleton before the Norman Conquest lay in the kingdom of Northumbria, a Viking kingdom. It was part of the wapentake of Ewecross.

Ingleton is recorded in the Domesday Book as the village of Inglestune with six carucates of land. Before Norman occupation the land belonged to Earl Tosti who was the last Saxon to hold the area. Tosti was chief minister to Edward the Confessor and brother of King Harold. Tosti had the reputation of tyranny and cruelty when he was ruler of Northumbria, but he was killed at the battle of Stamford Bridge on September 25th 1066. Only three weeks later his brother, King Harold, was killed during the Battle of Hastings. Then William the Conqueror came to the throne. In 1084 William commissioned the recording of the state of the nation, this record of land ownership and land use known as the Domesday Book was mainly intended as a guide to levying taxes.

The Domesday Book recorded the following for the Ingleton area:-

Manor, in Witetune, Earl Tosti had six carucates of land to be taxed. In Neutone two carucates; Ergune (Arum or Arkholme) six carucates; Ghersinctune two carucates; Hotum (Hutton) three carucates; Cantesfelt three carucates; Irebi three carucates; Borch (Overburrow) three carucates; Lech three carucates; all in Lancashire.
Boretune four carucates; Bernulfswic one carucate; Inglestune (Ingleton) six carucates; Castretune three carucates; Berebrune (Barbon) three carucates; Sedberge three carucates; Tiernebi, six carucates.

All these villages belong to Witetune

This excerpt from the Domesday Book is rather bare compared with many areas. There is no mention of the inhabitants and no mention of a church at Ingleton, but entries do vary very much. At this time Ingleton was part of the manor of Whittington and the area seems to have been spared the worst of the harrowing of the North by William the Conqueror and his knights. Ingleton with six carucates of arable land had more land under the plough than most of the other local villages. A carucate or hide was the amount of land that could be ploughed in a year by one man with family support. It was between 60 and 180 acres in modern measure and we could say that Ingleton had roughly 600 acres under cultivation. The area was granted to the Abigni family who later married into the Mowbray family, and even adopted the latter family name as its own. In Ewecross the Mowbray lands extended from the north-west of Craven to the borders of Westmorland, and Burton-in-Lonsdale was the head and stronghold of the western barony. The meaning of Burton is the 'castle ton' and the site of the castle is still plain to see at the roadside though now only a grass covered hill. The Mowbrays let the manor of Ingleton to a sub-lord and he had to pay homage at the court in Burton.

The manorial system which had begun in Anglo-Saxon England was further developed by the Normans. It was not until many centuries later that the system became know as the 'feudal system'. At Ingleton the people were under the control of the lord of the Manor. They relied on the manor court for justice and the running of routine affairs. They had to grind their corn at the lord's mill and give labour service on his demesne lands as part payment for their tenancy. The demesne lands, pronounced demain, were the lands in the manor which were allocated for the lord himself. These demesne lands at Ingleton were much the same in 1306 as they were in 1066, but they had grown by 1653 due to additions by enclosure and purchase.

However, the High Demesne and Low Demesne were the same in 1306 as in 1653 [2] some fifty three acres between them. The Tithe Award of 1847 records the High and Low Demesne as a total of fifty-seven acres. Ingleton Hall, the Hall meadow, the Low Demesne and High Demesne would have appeared much the same on a map of 1100 as they appeared in 1847. The lord of the manor gained money from rents and charges in the court. Fines had to be paid for collecting wood, for brewing ale and for marriage. On the death of a tenant his holding could pass to his son, but only on payment of an 'heriot', once again a fine or payment had to be paid to the lord of the manor.

Right up to the end of the Norman period the inhabitants of Ingleton were tenants of the lord of the manor and worked the strip fields in the surrounding countryside. They had no legal right to leave their holdings and to the lord of the manor they were serfs - unfree men. Freemen were few and far between, fewer than in Anglo Saxon times. However, many of the people of Ingleton, as in other manors, were always ready to advance themselves, to gain extra freedom and extra benefits in life. We will see that over the next two centuries they slowly and surely achieved this.

REFERENCES.

1. *Ingleton Bygone & Present*, R. & M.Balderstone, p.114.
2. PRO Close Roll (Chancery) 1653 Part 43.No. 9.

LATE MEDIEVAL INGLETON
c.1200 – 1484

A povre widow, somedeel stape in age
Was whilom dwelling in a narrwe cottage,
Beside a grove, standing in a dale.
GeoffreyChaucer

In the year 1297 Ingleton folk were taxed on their farm animals and goods. This was the Yorkshire Lay Subsidy of Edward I, instituted in the twenty-fifth year of his reign. Animal stock and goods were to be 'well and loyally' valued and when this was done one ninth had to be paid in tax. Clothes and personal ornaments were exempt and no one was to be taxed whose goods amounted to less than nine shillings. The valuation was as at Michaelmas Day in 1297. Tax returns should always be looked at suspiciously whether in 1297 or 1997. Local collectors can shield their area and individuals can, and do, falsify their returns and sometimes evade taxation altogether.

The West Riding was the poorest area of Yorkshire and there were no goods valued except cattle and corn. Hay is mainly missed and farm carts hardly mentioned. Money is shown in Roman numerals in documents up to around 1700. £3 6s 8d becomes iij li. js viijd. The letters i and j were interchangeable until the eighteenth century and the j is always used where the value ends in a single penny or shilling, vd for five pence, but vjd for sixpence. Li stood for pounds, s for shillings and d for pence – the origins being libra, solidus and denarius from the Roman monetary system. The tax return was in Latin as usual for the time and is set out below:-[1]

WAPENTACHIUM DE YUKCROS
INGELTON

Taxacio villate de Ingelton.
Taxatores-Rogerus le Rede Johannes le Calvehirde, Thomas de Askebaldstorths, Hugo filius Gilberti Prat.

Adam Hogg' habet in bonis duos boves, precium bovis vs; duas vaccas, precium vacce, iijs. vjd; unum juventum, precium iijs; iiij[or] oves, precium cujuslibet vjd; iiij[or] quart aveni, precium quart. xijd; unum quart. ordei, precium xijd; unam bigat' feni, precium xd. Summa bonorum, xxxjs ixd, unde ix[us] den.iijs vj o.

Johannes Carpenter habet in bonis j bovem, precium vs; j vaccam, precium vs; j vaccam, precium iijs vjd; unum quart. avene, precium quart. xijd; j bigat' feni, precium xd. Summa bonorum, xs iiijd, unde ixus den. xiiijd 0.

Nicholas filius Miles habet in bonis j bovem, precium vs; j vaccam, precium ijs vjd; unum quart avene, precium xijd; bigat' feni, precium xd. Summa, xs iiijd, under ix[us] den. xiijd o.

Stephanus fil Gilberti habet in bonis j bovem, precium vs; tria quart. avene, precium quart. xijd; dim. quart. ordei, precium xijd; j bigat' feni, precium xd. Summa, ixs xd, unde ix[us] den. xiijd q.

6

Adam del Bank' habet in bonis j bovem, precium vs; duas vaccas, precium vacce iijs vjd; iiij^{or} oves, precium ovis vjd; tria quart avene, precium quart. xijd; dim quart. ordei, precium xijd. Summa bonorum, xviijs, unde ix^{us} den. ijs.

Nigellus Skot habet in bonis j vaccam, precium iijs vjd; j juvencam, precium xviijd; viij oves, precium cujuslibet vjd. Summa, ixs, unde ix^{us} den. xijd.

Elias de Skales habet in bonis duas vaccas, precium vacce iijs vjd; duo animalia juniora, precium cujuslibet ijs; xx^{ti} oves, precium oves vjd; unam bigat' feni, precium xd. Summa, xxjs vjd, unde ix^{us} den. ijs vd q.

Walterus Waules habet in bonis duas vaccas, precium vacce iijs vjd; iiij^{or} oves, precium oves vjd; j bigat' feni, precium xd. Summa, ixs xd, unde ix^{us} den. xiijd q.

Henricus Pynder habet in bonis duas vaccas, precium vacce iijs vjd; iiij^{or} oves, precium ovis vjd; j bigat' feni, precium xd. Summa bonorum, ixs xd unde ix^{us} den. xiijd q.

Ricardus filius Merwyn habet in bonis j bovem, precium vs; j vaccam, precium ijs vjd; duo quart, avene, precium quart. xijd. Summa, xs vjd, unde ix^{us} den. xiiijd.

Thomas filius Thome habet in bonis j bovem, precium vs; j vaccam, precium iijs vjd; j bigat' feni, precium xd. Summa ixs iiij^{or}d, unde ixus den., xijd o.

Laurencius de Skiront habet in bonis j bovem, precium vs; j vaccam, precium iijs vjd; iiij^{or} oves, precium ovis vjd; j quart. avene, precium xijd; j bigat' feni, precium xd. Summa xijs iiijd, unde ix^{us} den. xvjd o.

Thomas Russel habet in bonis duos boves, precium bovis vs; vj oves, precium ovis vjd; j quart. avene, precium xijd; j bigat' feni, precium xd. Summa, xiiijs xd, unde ix^{us} den. xixd o.q.

Walterus de Caldecotes habet in bonis j bovem, precium vs; j vaccam, precium iijs vjd; j bigat' feni, precium xd. Summa, ixs iiijd, unde ix^{us} den. xiid o.

Reginald de Tweselton' habet in bonis j bovem, precium vs; j vaccam, precium iijs vjd; v^{que} oves, precium ovis vjd; duo quart. avene, precium quart. xijd; j bigat' feni, precium xd. Summa, xiijs xd, unde ix^{us} den. xviijd o.

Johannes le Mawer habet in bonis duas vaccas, precium vacce iijs vjd; duo animalia juniora, precium utriusque iijs. Summa, xs unde ix^{us} den. xiid q.

Adam Stodhirde habet in bonis j bovem, precium vs; j vaccam, precium iijs vjd; unum jumentum, precium iijs; j quart. avene, precium xijd. Summa, xijs vjd; unde ix^{us} den. xvjd o. q.

Ricardus Wade habet in bonis duas vaccas, precium vacce iijs vjd; j juvencam, precium xviijd; j bigat' feni, precium xd. Summa ixs iiijd, unde ix^{us} den. xiid o.

Ricardus del Mire habet in bonis j bovem, precium vs; tria quart. avene, precium quart. xijd; dim. quart. ordei, precium xijd; j bigat' feni, precium xd. Summa, ixs xd, unde ix^{us} den. xiid o. q.

Nicholaus le Mercer habet in bonis duas vaccas, precium vacce iijs vjd; j juvencam, precium xviijd; j quart. avene, precium xijd; j bigat' feni, precium xd. Summa, xs iiijd, unde ix^{us} den. xiijd o. q.

Ricardus filius Walteri habet in bonis duas vaccas, precium vacce iijs vjd; unum boviculum trium annorum, precium iijs; j juvencam, precium xviijd. Summa xxjs vjd, unde ix^{us} den. xvjd o.

Adam filius Ricardi del Mire habet in bonis duas vaccas, precium vacce iijs vjd; j animal duorum annorum, precium xviijd; j bigat' feni, precium xd. Summa, ixs iiijd, unde ix^{us} den. xijd o.

Wilhelmus filius Tille habet in bonis duas vaccas, precium vacce iijs vjd; iiij^{or} oves, precium ovis vjd. Summa, ixs, unde ix^{us} den. xijd.

Randulphus filius Johannis habet in bonis j bovem, precium vs; j jumentum, precium iiijs. Summa, ixs, unde ix^{us} den. xijd.

Dominus Willelmus de Tweselton' habet in bonis iiij^{or} boves, precium bovis vs; tres vaccas, precium vacce iijs vjd; tria animalia juniora, precium cujuslibet xviijd; duo jumenta, precium jumenti iijs; xiiij oves, precium ovis vjd; v^{que} quart. aveni, precium quart. xijd; j quart. ordei, precium ijs. Summa lvjs viijd, unde ix^{us} den. vjs iiijd o. q.

Adam Yowehirde habet in bonis viiijto quart. avene, precium quart. xijd; j quart. ordei, precium ijs. Summa, xs unde ix^{us} den. xiijd o.

Thomas de Yreby habet in bonis duos boves, precium bovis vs; j vaccam, precium iijs vjd; j animal duorum annorum, precium xviijd; duo quart. avene, precium quart. xijd; dim. quart. ordei, precium xijd; j bigat' feni, precium xd. Summa, xviijs xd, unde ix^{us} den. xxvd q.

Rogerus Godyoman habet in bonis duas vaccas, precium vacce iijs vjd; vj oves, precium vjd. Summa, xs, unde ix^{us} den. xiijd q.

Summa totalis bonorum de Ingelton xixli viijs iijd.
Summa summarum tocius None.   xlviijs jd o. q. cum taxatoribus.

(Bovis-oxen, vaccus-cow, ovis-a sheep, juventum-horse, avene-oats, ordeum- barley, fenum-hay, aimalia junoria-young animals.)

Twenty-eight people are taxed, all men, and with a rough estimate of five to a family that would give a population of one hundred and forty. Including those not taxed and other odd folks, perhaps a total of one hundred and fifty people were living in Ingleton in 1297. Most of the inhabitants appear to have owned only a few animals. The only person with a larger number is William of Twistleton, the lord of the manor of Twistleton. He was lord of Twistleton on the payment of one penny rent. The Manor of Twistleton had been a separate Manor from Ingleton from time immemorial, though still part of Ingleton township. William had inherited Twistleton Manor from his father Adam, who had inherited from his father John who was living in 1256.

All the inhabitants would be involved in farming, but many would also have occupations of builder, carpenter, pinder, shopkeeper and others which were needed to keep a village running. John Carpenter certainly suggests that he was a local carpenter and Henry Pinder would have been looking after the pinfold which was most probably at the top of the Back Gate where it remained over many centuries. Nicholas le Mercer was a dealer in textiles so it is likely that weaving was going on in the area.

Surnames have not yet become fixed and might well have changed if the person changed his trade or moved to another location. He might be John son of Richard one day and John le Smith the next. Thomas Russel or Red is possibly an ancestor of the Redmans and Redmaynes who came later. It will be noted that some surnames such as Stodhirde and Yowhirde, come directly from agricultural occupations. The majority of Christian names appear remarkably modern, Richard, John, Adam, Nigel, Stephen, Thomas, William, Lawrence and Nicholas.

INQUISITION POST MORTEM

An inquisitions post mortem was held when a tenant holding land directly from the crown died, or a landowner whose position might be of concern to the royal government. A writ was sent to the sheriff of the county and the answers to the following questions were asked. What land did the deceased hold at the time of his death? Who did he hold it from? What was its annual value? What services were due for holding the land? Who was his heir and what was his age? These documents begin in the middle of the thirteenth century and are valuable for the information they give. If a man held land directly from the Crown then he was termed a tenant-in-chief.

The Inquisition often gives a description of the manor the deceased held which is termed an 'extent' Such a manorial extent is given in the Inquisition below, which was held at Ingleton on January 13th 1306. It was held due to the death of John son of Hugh who was lord of the manor of Ingleton.[2] A jury of twelve men stated:-

That John son of Hugh held nothing in chief, but he held the manor of Ingleton in tail of Hugh son of Henry and his heirs, by the service of paying 10li. a year to Hugh and his heirs, of the grant of the said Hugh, and by doing on behalf of the same Hugh and his heirs to the chief lord of the fee, that is, to the lord of Burton in Lonesdale, 22s. a year for a certain ferm called Burton male, and 17s for the fine of the wapentake, and by doing to the same lord of Burton forinsec service as much as belongs to six carucates of land where 17 carucates make a knight's fee. Hugh held the manor with other tenements before the grant of the lord of Burton by homage, and service, and suit at the court of Burton every three weeks. In demesne, 70° acres of arable land (12d.) Sum 70s. 6d. Meadow in demesne, 22 acres (12d) Sum 22s. Divers tenants holding 22 bovates (15s.) Sum 16li. 10d. Divers tenants holding 21 cottages (12d) Sum 21s. An assart called Skyrhouth, 69s. 7°d. An assart called Souterschales, 61s. 10d. A water mill, 106s. 8d. A fulling mill, 18s. In the hamlet of Bentham 3° bovates of land... Free tenants of the same manor Geoffrey of Upsale holds the hamlet of Caldecotes by the service of 3s. and doing forinsec service. Master William of Twyselton holds the hamlet of Twyselton by the service of 1d. and doing forinsec service. Adam de Mirewra holds a bovate of land by the service of 3s. 1d. and by doing forinsec service. John de Bentham holds a moiety of the hamlet of Bentham by forinsec service only.[3] Perquisites of the halmote of the said manor, by estimation 6s. 8d. Sum of the whole besides the service due outside, 29li. 4s. 0°d. Henry son of John son of Hugh is his nearest heir, and was aged 3 years at the feast of St. Edmund the King and Martyr last past (20 November 1305).

This document shows the lord of the manor of Ingleton had died quite young. It shows that he held the manor from the chief lord of Burton-in-Lonsdale and gave money and services to the chief lord for the manor. The document gives the acreage of demesne land and that land would be the area of Ingleton later known mainly as the High and Low Demesne, names which still remain to this day. We can see that already Twistleton and Coldcotes have become separate entities and that Twistleton was a manor in its own right and so it remained. Already there is a link with Bentham and we shall see that later in the Tudor period the two are linked in both manor and parish. Of considerable importance is the recording of two mills at Ingleton, a water corn mill and a fulling mill. The fulling mill was on the Greta in the Bottoms and the corn mill on Ingleton Beck a few hundred yards above Ingleton Bridge.

By this time we can also see there are at least twenty-one cottages in the manor of Ingleton and can imagine that they are situated on the Main Street, the Bank and Back Gate thus forming a rear collection of small gardens and crofts where their cattle can be safely kept. John de Mowbray was the lord of Burton at the time and being under age he was a ward of the king. His father Roger de Mowbray had recently died but his mother Roysia was still living. John son of Hugh, or John Fitzhugh, as he was known had married Isabella the daughter of Michael de Ryhill and held lands through her as well as from his father.

In 1290 Parliament granted a tax for the marriage of the King's eldest daughter. The tax was not collected for twelve years but the money paid by Ingleton and Bentham is recorded as follows:- [4]

INGLETON.
De Johanne filio Hugonis pro tribus car. Terrae in Ingleton, unde xviij car., etc. vjs viijd. q.

BENTHAM
De eodem Johanne pro tribus car. Terrae in Bentham, unde, ut supra vjs viijd. q.

The *Nomine Villarum,* of Edward II, a return of wapentakes and hundreds taken by sheriffs, lists who were the lords of the manor in 1315. It records that Henry Fitzhugh held the two vills of Bentham and Ingleton and also the two vills of Dent and Sedbergh in the wapentake of Ewecross.[5] This shows that the manors of Ingleton and Bentham were connected from an early date. In 1204 'Ingleton et duabus Bentham' is mentioned in the Furness Coucher Book, being Ingleton and the two Benthams.

SCOTTISH RAIDS
After their victory at Bannockburn in 1314 the Scottish raids over the border increased. In late November 1319 the Scotch rebels burned the towns of Gisburn in Craven, Settle and Giggleswick. They penetrated as far south as Castleford calling at Settle again on return journey. Both Settle and Barbon were nearly wiped out. The Scots burned churches and houses, carried off cattle and behaved brutally to men, women and children. Because of these raids a remission of taxes was granted by Edward II in the 13th year of his reign. This remission included Sedbergh, Burton, Thornton, Twistleton, Ingleton, Clapham, Austwick and Bentham. The Scottish armies travelled light and travelled swiftly and frequently English armies with armoured knights and all their baggage were no match for them. The Ingleton area must have suffered greatly from their raids and the people had little warning.

To make matters worse the early fourteenth century was a time of bad harvests and famine. 1315 was called the first year of the great famine. Heavy rain through July and August caused a total failure of crops. The situation was aggravated by cattle plague. There was a heavy mortality of humans and livestock. 1316 was another famine year and this grievous famine affected England for several years.

POLL TAX 1379

In 1379 in the time of Richard II a poll tax was set.[6] It was a graduated tax from ten marks, at which the Duke of Lancaster was charged, down to four pence for each ordinary individual above the age of sixteen. Church ministers were excluded from the tax. The tax rolls for the West riding of Yorkshire survive and cast a considerable light on the population of the time. We see the gentry, the trades-people and merchants and the common people. Merchants were charged one shilling, carpenters, butchers and other tradesmen six pence, innkeepers two shillings and most others four pence.

INGLETON

Johannes Shedhyrd & ux	iiij.d.
Robertus Kyng & ux	iiij.d
Robertus de Overend & ux	iiid.d.
Johannes de Redmane, Armatus	vj.s viij.d.
Willelmus filius Ricardi, Spicer & ux	xij.d.
Johannes Wetherhyrd, Faber & ux.	xij.d.
Willelmus Grundolf & ux	iiij.d.
Thomas de Ellerbeck & ux.	iiij.d.
Johannes Page & ux.	iiij.d.
Thoma Browne & ux.	iiij.d.
Johannes de Craven & ux	iiij.d
Thomas de Skyrhow & ux.	iiid.d.
Thomas Kyd & ux.	iiij.d.
Johannes Dawson & ux.	iiij.d.
Robertus Chephyrd & ux.	iiij.d.
Willelmus de Cowpland & ux.	iiij.d.
Johannes Morehall & ux.	iiij.d.
Willhelmus de Scales & ux.	iiij.d.
Johannes filius Willelmi & ux.	iiij.d.
Johannes Mort & ux.	iiij.d.
Johannes Crawer & ux.	iiij.d.
Randulphus Smith, Faber & ux.	vj.d.
Robertus Dykson & ux.	iiij.d.
Gilbertus Baynbryg & ux.	iiij.d.
Johannes filius Nicholai & ux.	iiij.d
Ricardus Scot & ux.	iiij.d.
Willelmus Walker & ux.	vj.d.
Hugo Denyson & ux.	iiij.d.
Thomas de Hall & ux.	iiij.d.
Johannes filius Ellote & ux.	iiij.d.
Johannes filius Ricardi & ux.	iiij.d.
Hugo de Holme & ux.	iiij.d.
Laurencius Tomson & ux.	iiij.d.
Johannes de Wod & ux.	iiij.d.

Johannes Husband & ux	iiijd
Thomas Lauson & ux.	iiij.d.
Stephanus Hog & ux.	iiij.d.
Johannes Cittson & ux.	iiij.d.
Johannes de Bank & ux.	iiij.d.
Willelmus Smeth, Faber, & ux.	vj.d.
Johannes de Lese & ux.	iiijd.
Thomas Bene & ux	iiijd.
Edmundus filius Thome & ux.	iiij.d.
Johannes Cowper & ux.	iiiij.d.
Robertus Pynder & ux.	iiij.d.
Servient-Thomas Jonson Wetherhird	iiij.d.
Johannes filius Galfredi	iiij.d.
Agnes Kyd	iiij.d.
Magota de Wyterscale	iiij.d.
Emma Harwod	iiij.d.
Agnes ux. Ricardi Sariant	iiij.d.
Agnes Schephyrd	iiij.d.
Alicia Cowper	iiij.d.
Hugo Bateman	iiiij.d.
Elena serviens Willelmi	iiij.d.
Robertus de ffreklyngton	iiij.d.
Galfridus Spenser, de Ingleton	iiij.d.

Summa xxvij.s. ij.d.

Firstly you will note the names were Latinised, but it is easy to see William, John, Stephen and the rest. Saxon and Norman French had now blended into an English language, but many official documents remained in Latin for several centuries. You will note the popularity of the names John and William. It is interesting to see that surnames have arrived although far from all have a regular surname at this time. Several of the surnames denote the jobs they do, Randolph Smith was a blacksmith (faber) as was William Smith. William Walker was a walker or cloth fuller and he would have worked in the fulling mill by the river. The existence of a fulling mill indicates the presence of woollen handloom weaving in the area at least from the fourteenth century. Robert Pynder would be the village pinder looking after the pinfold where all stray animals were impounded until claimed and paid for by their owners. Whether John Shepherd and Agnes Shepherd were still shepherds is a question that we cannot answer. There was also a spicer, a seller of herbs and spices.

Several surnames tell us where the people lived and show that those places were already settled with farms and cottages. These include Skirreth, Scales, Winterscales, and the Bank. Other surnames show where the people originated such as Bainbridge, Frecklington, and Scotland. Surnames were slower to be adopted in the north of England than the south and several Ingleton folk were known simply as William son of Richard, John son of William and Elena servant of William. So we can see that surnames are by no means fully settled. The highest payment in Ingleton was paid by John Redmayne who paid six shillings and eight pence. He was a knight and probably lived at Ingleton's moated manor house where he was standing in for the lord of the manor. The Redmayne family were a notable family in the area over several centuries.

We should now consider population. There are forty-five married couples noted in the tax return and taking an average family as four or five, a population of around two hundred would be a good estimate. We must remember that this tax was only some thirty years after the Black Death when almost half the population of England died of the plague. So we are looking at a small village with some thirty to forty cottages clustered on the Bank, the main street and the Back Gate, with outlying farms. We know that they had a corn mill and fulling mill, a moated manor house and a church. Sadly we cannot identify the minister, as the clergy were exempt from this tax. We see the names of a few servants, but certainly all Ingleton's population were now free, there were no slaves as there had likely been in Anglo Saxon times, and no unfree men forced to work on the lands of the lord of the manor as there had been in Norman and later manorial times.

What else can we gain from these names and taxation details? Where is the butcher, the baker and the candlestick maker? The trades are remarkably absent. Above all there is no innkeeper which seems remarkable, but had there been one he would have surely been noted and have had to pay his two shillings tax. The village must have had a source of ale and probably some of the cottagers acted as small alehouses selling ale. Otherwise it appears Ingleton folks would have had to have travelled further afield for a proper inn. There are two blacksmiths and they would be needed for a variety of work including shoeing horses and making iron implements. However, they are also signs of passing traffic, of travellers on the road, and perhaps the roads through Ingleton are already becoming busy with people on their way from Keighley to Kendal or Lancaster to Richmond. Travellers would need repairs to carts and wagons. Later we will see that blacksmiths were attached to at least two inns in Ingleton.

We also need to have a glance at the Tax returns for the neighbouring villages of Burton and Bentham. Burton was smaller than Ingleton and only one inhabitant paid more than sixpence and that was Thomas de Lond who paid one shilling. In Bentham only thirty-six households were recorded and there were certainly no knights or gentry. Again it is strange that neither Burton or Bentham listed an innkeeper. The peasants' revolt followed the Poll Tax in 1381 and caused trouble throughout the country.

An Inquisition held at York in 1415 recorded that, Thomas Rolleston had died and that he had held the manor of Ingleton from Henry Lord Fitzhugh.[7] He had paid a yearly rent of £10 and other services to Henry and paid ' yearly to Lord de Moubray, lord of Burton in Londesdale, by way of fee farm for the said manor 22s. It is worth 20 marks a year, and the advowson of the church 13s.' Thomas also held land and buildings in Bentham which belonged to the manor of Ingleton. It appears from this record that the sub-lord Henry Fitzhugh was also sub-letting Ingleton Manor. Thomas Rolleston had inherited the manor from his wife Beatrice, who had inherited from her brother Robert who had in turn inherited from his father John Haulay, chivaler. Thomas' daughters, Margaret the wife of John Tirwhit, and Ellen the wife of Christopher Conyers, inherited the manor: Margaret was sixteen years old and Ellen fifteen and they had both married before the death of their father.

The lords, and sub-lords, of the manor of Ingleton continued their rule although most had little contact with the place and there is no trace of them having lived at Ingleton and the running of the manor would be left to a steward. Renting and sub renting was common and the descent of the Manor of Ingleton is most complicated up to the Tudor period. By the end of the fourteenth century tenants were exchanging their field strips to amalgamate their holdings and they were also selling land. Working for the lord of the manor was mainly changed to payments in money rather than work. However, military service was still a must and service for forty days could be demanded. Manor Rolls would have recorded all the manor transactions, but these have not survived.

REFERENCES.

1. *Yorkshire Lay Subsidy 1297, YAS Record Series* Vol. XVI, Ed. W. Brown, 1894.
2. *Yorkshire Inquisitions Vol.4. YAS Record Series,* Vol.37. Ed. W. Brown, Leeds, 1906. pp. 98-99.
3. Forinsec service – service due outside demesne or manor to chief lord.
4. *Craven and the North West Yorkshire Highlands,* H. Speight, Smith Settle, 1989, p.209.
5. ibid
6. *Lay Subsidy 2 Richard II, Poll Tax 1379.* The YA & T Journal, YA & T Association, Vol. VII. London 1882. p.174.
7. *Yorkshire Inquisitions* Vol.4. YAS Record series, Vol.37. Ed. W. Brown, Leeds, 1906. p.105.

TUDOR TIMES
1485-1603

After Richard III's death at Bosworth Field, Henry Tudor became king of England. He is said to be the first business man to sit on the throne of England and he certainly took interest in the royal estates to derive the full income he could from them. The Tudors also brought better organisation to the country through local government, which Henry VIII put on a firmer footing by means of Justices of the Peace and the parish vestry. It was fairly efficient and was done on the cheap as most did their work for nothing apart from basic expenses.

More documents survive for this period so we can learn more about Ingleton in the Tudor period. A great source of information is the wills Ingleton folk made before their deaths and the inventories of their goods which were drawn up following their deaths. In the Tudor period Ingleton was in the Parish of Bentham in the Deanery of Lonsdale. Lonsdale was one of the five western deaneries of the Archdeaconry of Richmond. The Archdeaconry of Richmond was part of the new See of Chester formed by Henry VIII in 1541. Due to the fact that most of Lonsdale Deanery was in Lancashire, the deanery records are to be found in the Lancashire Record Office at Preston. The documents were kept at Lancaster until 1851 when they were moved to Somerset House, from there they were finally moved to Preston in 1954.[1,2]

The probate records of the Western Deaneries have not been well treated in their long history. Some early wills are in deplorable condition. They are written on paper and have suffered from both damp and vermin. By luck some hundred and thirty documents have survived for the Parish of Ingleton in the Elizabethan period. They vary from the labourer leaving only a few shillings to the prosperous yeoman leaving valuable cattle

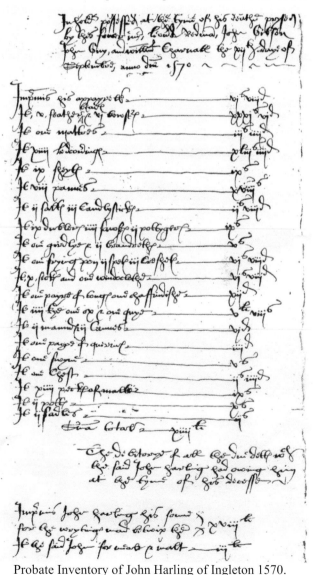

Probate Inventory of John Harling of Ingleton 1570.

15

stocks and goods. After the testator's death, and usually on the day of the death, his goods and chattels were listed and valued by four sworn men, usually friends, neighbours or relatives, and an inventory was made. The probate inventory was a document required by the ecclesiastical court before a will could be proved.

Tudor wills occasionally tell us the trades that people had and give us further insight into the village activities. However, most men were farmers, the more substantial farmers titled yeomen or small tenant farmers known as husbandmen. The following occupations were noted in wills: curate, innkeeper, miller and weaver. They were likely noted as they were full time occupations. Ingleton would need the work of many tradesmen and craftsmen – the blacksmith, mason, carpenter, tailor, shoemaker, tanner, cooper, butcher, miller and all these would be represented in Tudor Ingleton.

John Harling who made his will in 1570 was an innholder or innkeeper and his inventory listed the obvious materials of his trade, including table ware, kitchen ware and brewing vessels. In 1598 a second John Harling made his will and he had a large brewing vessel suggesting that he was perhaps the son of the first John Harling and also an innkeeper. Agnes Sproat, the widow of Thomas Sproat, made her will in 1589. She had obviously some standing in the community as the three witnesses to her will were Robert Fish, parson of Bentham; Thomas Bateson vicar of Thornton; and George Williamson curate of Ingleton. After her death her inventory listed pots, pans and pewter and beer and cider barrels. She had twenty pairs of sheets and it appeared that she was running an inn or boarding house. This is confirmed in the debts owing to her. 'Item in the hands of the administrators of James Procter for the tablinge of a boye, for one year and a half year xl^s, and for haye for a horse for ij years in the winter tyme and for a sheet wherein the sayde James Procter was wounde and buryed in.' We could further speculate that Agnes was also engaged in laying out the dead for burial, for her sheets had obviously other uses than just for bed linen. One of those valuing her goods was John Harling, another hint that she was an innkeeper. Agnes had a small personal chest in which she kept her precious things including a gold Elizabethan half crown and a silver spoon: gold and silver were rare in Ingleton.

Many of the folks in Ingleton were involved in domestic industry. Inventories show that over half were involved in some form of textile work. Only one testator owned a loom, and that was William Day who was a weaver at Moorgarth. In 1583 William left all his weaving gear to his son-in-law, Richard Balderston. The loom was called 'a pair of studdles', a loom was usually referred to as a pair of looms. Although this was the only loom shown in inventories there would have been other looms in Ingleton and the area. We know there was a fulling mill on the river at Ingleton in 1305 and in 1711 so there is no doubt a fulling mill was working in Tudor times. There at the fulling mill newly woven cloth was beaten by large wooden hammers to mesh the warp and weft in one of the final processes of cloth making.

Ingleton's Elizabethan inventories also reveal other items of woollen textile equipment. Spinning wheels, wool combs and wool cards appear frequently in inventories and show evidence of woollen yarn production. Some yarn would have been used locally but other yarn may have been spun for collection by outsiders. Other yarn from rough wool could well have been used in the knitting industry. There was wool by the stone in Elizabethan inventories. Thomas Foxcroft had twelve stones in 1588; William Procter had six stones in 1599; and Leonard Wetherhead had sixteen stones in 1592. The problem lies in where the wool went. Situated where Ingleton is on the Keighley Kendal road, it would seem natural that much went to the weaving trade in Kendal.

Though wool played a considerable part in Ingleton's domestic industry far more people were involved with the growing, preparing and spinning of hemp and flax. The production of coarse linen cloth and ropes from flax and hemp had been a domestic industry in the Fylde and Lancashire plain from the middle ages.[3] Ingleton borders upon Lancashire and was involved in this flax and hemp cultivation and probably had been for centuries.

Growing hemp was regarded as a labour consuming but quite profitable occupation for poor villagers and this would seem to be the case in Ingleton.[4] Hemp and hemp seed occur in the poorer inventories and Agnes Pearson had six pounds weight of hemp in 1577. Thomas Battersby had 'twenty seven heyes of harden yarn' and Leonard Craven's inventory listed a 'heckle' which was a metal comb used for pulling through flax, or rippling flax to remove the seed capsules. In 1584 William Greenbank had wheels, combs and cards and hemp and hemp seed. This appears to suggest that the spinning wheel and other equipment was used for hemp and not for wool. The spinning of flax was a widespread home industry outside the woollen areas. In the case of Ingleton it also seems to have been widespread in an area which was also concerned with wool.

No one testator had much value in hemp and flax and typical entries in the Ingleton inventories are: 'linen yarn 4s', 'hempe and line 1s 8d', 'hempe lyne and yarn 5s 4d', 'hemp 2s', 'hempe and lyne 1s 4d', and 'hemp 1s'. Ingleton still has a memory of this industry in a field area called Hemplands and there is little doubt that hemp and flax were grown fairly widely in Tudor Ingleton. Hemplands was a four acre field between Laundry Lane and Red Ash Lane.

At her death in 1589 Agnes Sproat had 'hempe and lyne on the earthe' to the value of four shillings. Agnes probably an innkeeper, as well as growing hemp and linen also had both hemp and woollen yarn, and in her household goods linen tow sheets. We have only a fraction of the jig-saw and it is hard to put the pieces together. Perhaps linen was being woven in the township or perhaps only yarn was being prepared and then passed on to other areas for weaving. The Preston area got some of it raw flax and yarn from as distant as London and Ireland at this time.[5] Although many were involved in some domestic industry there appears no sign of a really profitable and vigorous domestic activity which could raise the standard of living sufficiently to provide some of the luxuries of the time. The domestic industry in Ingleton, apart from a few exceptions, gives a picture of the poor struggling to earn a few extra pence.

Now we look at the things that are listed in the inventories of Tudor Ingleton folk. Almost all inventories include furniture and through the Tudor period items of furniture appear fairly standardised. Much of the furniture seems very basic and worth only a few pence, especially in second hand value. The stool and form or bench were the main items of seating. The form, a long backless seat, had been the common form of eating at table since medieval times. Chairs only appear on a few of the lists and usually occur in those with more wealth. William Hird (1593) had chairs, but their value is unknown as they were listed with other items of furniture: arks chistes, bordes, chayres and bedstocks.

Tables appear in many but not all inventories. However, boards are frequently listed and it is likely that these were loose boards which were laid on trestles as a temporary table. Many of the Elizabethan farm tables would have been of massive construction, the tops being planks held together by cross battens on the underside. Dish boards are also mentioned and it would appear that these were also boards on trestles used as side tables or 'side boards' upon which to keep dishes and tableware.

When storage was needed the ark and chest were the items used and they were very common. There were great meal arks kept in the barn or cellar to store meal, malt and other cereals. Chests were also used for storing sheets in the bedroom and small chests or coffers were used for personal items. Cup boards were originally side tables for serving food- hence the word 'cup-board.' A few inventories including that of William Greenbank (1580) record an aumbry. The aumbry was an early cupboard which could be used for either vessels or food. Where it was used for food there were frequently latticed fronts to allow for ventilation.

Usually the most important item of furniture in the household, and the most expensive, was the bed. Although there are many beds and the term bedstocks is the most common term in use there is no direct evidence that four-poster beds were in use. They are supposed to have been in general use from about the year 1550. However, the term bedstocks or bedstead does not indicate any size, and some beds mentioned may well have been four-poster beds. Mattresses are frequently mentioned and sometimes the material from which they were made. John Harling had feather beds, bolsters, and mattresses and sheets; some were for personal use and some for clients at the inn. John Walker (1587) had a chaff bed, that is a mattress stuffed with straw, and there were many more chaff beds among the poorer folk of Ingleton. Being poked by sharp pieces of straw was one of the unpleasant sides of sleeping in Tudor times. Most people would have straw filled beds and feather beds were thought by Tudor writer, William Harrison, to be one of the luxuries 'weakening the fibres of the English people'. Harrison wrote in 1567, 'Our fathers yea and we ourselves have lain full oft upon straw pallets, covered only with a sheet, undercoverlets made of dagswain or hop harlots.' Hop harlots were large sacks.

The bed and its accompanying bedding were often the most expensive items of domestic property. Thomas Battersby (1572) had bedding worth £1 16s. Rarely is a bed listed at under one pound and Thomas Foxcroft (1586) had the most expensive bed which was valued at £3 5s 4d. The main furniture is usually shown as low value and was most likely of the home-made or country craft variety. Items would have been constructed for use and wear rather than beauty of appearance. The pictures of Elizabethan furniture often shown in antique books would give the wrong impression. In Ingleton plain boards and plain furniture would have been the rule. The use of cushions, though infrequent, does show that some attention was being paid to comfort. John Foxcroft (1599) had four cushions to make his furniture that little more comfortable.

Cattle and sheep were listed, but will be dealt with under agriculture. Husbandry gear was listed and accounted for ploughs, spades and other tools and equipment. Food was listed from beef and bacon to butter and cheese and meal and malt. Cooking was usually done on a large open fire and cauldrons, pots and pans are listed. Reckan-crooks from which cooking vessels were suspended appear in most inventories. The reckan-crook was fixed to the stone fireplace and was hinged to swing out. Spits were in general use and many lists included a dripping pan to catch the dropping fat under the spit. Iron brandreths are common and these iron tripods sat on the fire so that pans and other cooking vessels could be placed on them. Frying pans were common and appear in many inventories. Chafing dishes were used to keep food warm and were small portable grates which were filled with hot charcoal.

Much table ware was still made of wood. Treen had been in use for centuries and although pewter and brass vessels were becoming more common, wooden vessels still remained in most Elizabethan Ingleton houses. Platters were large wooden plates, and large wooden tubs were used for salted beef and were called 'Salting or powdering tubs.' Pewter was more evident in the wealthier households. Pewter doublers, salts and candlesticks are listed along with general pewter vessels.

Drinks would be limited to a small selection of water, milk and beer. Brewing equipment is mentioned on many lists and the knop and gylling vat or gylle vat were the common vessels. They were mainly made of wood, but occasionally it is noted that a brewing vessel is made of lead, which would not have been very healthy. Pewter also contained lead and the use of pewter probably caused lead poisoning. The diet appears adequate and no doubt was in times of good harvests, but there were many years in Tudor times when harvests were bad. Following poor harvests men and animals would be liable to suffer.

When the valuers came to list clothing they usually dealt with the whole of the testator's clothing as one item. However, there are two main occasions when clothing is listed in detail. If clothing was being bequeathed then it was described in detail to help the executors identify it. Secondly, as in the case of Richard Coop, the village miller, his clothing is listed in detail as sadly he had little else to put in the inventory.

Men had doublets, which were the principal main male garment down to 1660. Jerkins and jackets are frequently mentioned and these were usually worn over the doublet. Shirts were worn under the doublet. Richard Wetherhead (1558) had a black jacket, a pair of hose or netherstocks which were worn with short trunk hose or breeches. William Guy had similar

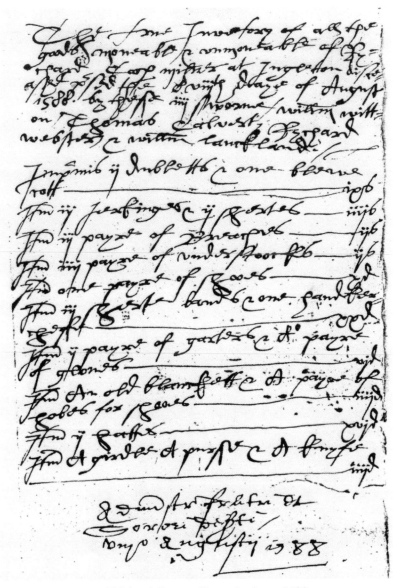

Probate Inventory of Richard Coop miller at Ingleton 1588.

19

clothing with the addition of a cap. George Tatham (1595) had a best coat and a doublet which he left in his will along with a white doublet, his best hat, and everyday clothing.

Women had more colour to their clothing and their clothes were probably finer, even in the austerity of Tudor Ingleton. Isabel Craven had a red coat and a brown coat as well as three white petty coats and linen clothes. Her sister Alice had two red coats and other clothing. The clothes of only two persons are given in detail and both are men. The first, Richard Coop, was Ingleton's miller who died in 1588. Apart from on old blanket his sole possessions were his few clothes. His total possessions were valued at only £1 2s 0d. He had two doublets, three jerkins, two shirts and three pairs of breeches. He also had four pairs of understocks to go with the short breeches and he had garters and gloves. He owned only one pair of shoes, but also had a pair of hobbs, which were wooden platforms worn with shoes to protect them from rough roads and mud. Richard also had two hats, a girdle, a handkerchief, a purse and a coif. Several folks had 'pantables' which were open toed slippers probably for use around the house.

The second inventory to itemise clothing is that of James Procter of Bruntscar who died in 1587. Where Richard Coop was one of the poorest of the population James Procter was very close to being the wealthiest. Without doubt he was one of the best dressed men in Elizabethan Ingleton, his clothes were those of a gentleman. He had several suits of clothing, shirts and hats. He had two pairs of boots, most probably knee length in soft leather. His suits were valued at £1 each, his boots at 6s 8d and his shirt at 9s. James also had a cloak and white hat and to complete the picture a sword and gold ring. On his valuable bay horse he must have been a noted figure in the township.

A multitude of other items are noted in inventories from stone and timber for building to manure. Whatever a man or woman owned was listed in the inventory. Household goods were often valued together under the collective term, 'hustlements.' Farming equipment was often listed collectively as 'husbandry gear.'

WIDOWS' RIGHT AND CHILD PORTIONS

'My wife to have her third part or widow right according to the custom of the manor', was a common component of Tudor wills where a widow was left. In 1551 Roger Iveson of Ingleton bequeathed to his wife, 'her widow right according to the custom of the countrie.' The 1592 court decree reinforced this in stating, 'the widow of every tenant of all and every or any of the Customary Lands or Tenements within the said Manor shall quietly have and enjoy during her life, if she live so long sole and unmarried, a full third part of all the Customary land, tenements and Heriditaments.' This formula varies in only two cases. In 1576 Robert Procter left half his tenement to his wife and when Christopher Lupton made his will in 1593 he left his wife the whole tenement and directed that after her death it should go to their daughter Agnes.

It appears to have been the custom of Ingleton manor that the eldest son was left the land holding and it was not split up. A result of this system of primogeniture was that some provision has to be made for the other children and this was done through child portions. In Ingleton wills there was usually a provision for younger sons and daughters in the form of child portions to be paid out of the estate in instalments over several years so that the estate was not impoverished. The children frequently shared the goods of their father, but usually child portions appear to represent a share of the tenancy – the real estate rather than personalty, that is goods and chattels.

Occasionally the child portion comes purely from the personalty as when Leonard Batty of Twistleton (1583) requested his son William to pay daughters Elizabeth and Agnes 'so mutche owte of my goods & cattells to either of theyme as shall amount to theyre Childe part or porcion.' At that time the word either meant each. Occasionally the stipulation is made that if the child part is not paid on time then property or land can be claimed in lieu. When Robert Procter, in 1576, ordered his heir, Richard Procter, to pay twenty marks to younger son William, he added that if this was not paid then William was to have a half share of the tenement.

The younger children of a family had either to stay and work on the farm where they would have a low wage and little chance of marriage or move into the village or farther afield and take up a trade or labouring work. From time to time there was a special case as when in 1587 Peter Procter of Bruntscar stipulated that his eldest son William should pay his son John ten pounds when he came to the age of twenty-four. This payment was on condition that John regained his health. If he did not then John was to be kept in meat, drink, clothing and bedding for the rest of his life. In this will four daughters were each left five pounds. In general the amount paid to daughters was considerably less than that paid to sons: this reflected both the inequality of the sexes and the fact that girls would have to rely on the finances of their future husbands.

ELIZABETHAN MUSTER ROLL

In 1539 a Muster Roll was taken in the country and the returns have survived for the Wapentake of Ewecross which of course includes Ingleton.[6] The roll lists all males between the ages of sixteen and sixty who were due to give military service. It also shows those who at the time for one reason or another were unable to serve. The rolls also show what arms the men could bring with them when they were called for military service. They were marked as B for billmen, A for archers or N/A for not able.

YNGLETON

Constables there Thomas Wedyrhurde
Geffray Stevyson

B	James ffalsecrofte	a jacke, a salett and a byll
B	Lawrence Sprott	horse & harness
B	John Guye	
B	Richard Walker	harness for a man
B	Leonard Cravyn	harness for a man
B	John Balderston	horse & harness
B	John Cravyn	a byll
B	Gyles Redman	harness for a man
B	Richarde Gybson	
B	Jamys Middleton	a byll
N/A	Matthewe Harlyn	a byll
B	John Walker	a byll
N/A	Thomas Guye	a jacke & a salett
B	Leonard Siggeswyk	
B	John Harlyn	a jakke
N/A	Ranold Benyson	a byll
B	James Tatham	horse & harness
A	Thomas Walker	a byll
N/A	Thomas Wylson	a byll
B	John Sprott	a byll
B	Richard Harlyn	a byll
A	William Redman	a bowe

B	James Balderston	a jacke, a salett, a byll
B	Edward Alanson	
B	Leonard Walker	
N/A	Thomas ffregleton	
B	John ffregleton	
B	Richarde Redman	
A	Leonard Cravyn	
A	Gyles Cravyn	
B	Geffray ffirthbanke	
N/A	Richard Johnson	
N/A	William Hirde	
B	Edmunde Slater	
B	William Calverte	
A	Leonard Cravyn	
N/A	Alex Gray	horse. Harness & byll
B	Richarde Cravyn	horse & harness
B	John Stevynson	a jake, a salett & a byll
B	Christopher Craven	a byll
B	Rafe Sprott	
B	Leonard Canncefield	
B	Roger Gybson	a jake & a byll
N.A	Thomas Cravyn	
B	John Stevynson	
B	John Taytham	
N/A	Thomas Proctor	
B	John Hirde	a jakke
B	Thomas Baytman	a salett
B	Thomas Baytman	a salett
B	Anthony Baytman	
B	William Cravyn	horse & harness
B	Edmunde Langton	
A	John Battersby	a bowe
B	Thomas ffalscrofte	a byll
A	William Gregson	a bowe
B	Richard Gregson	a jake, a salett, a byll
B	Leonarde Redman	
B	William Wyldemen	
B	John Deny	
N/A	Thomas Waydell	
N/A	Jamys Waydell	
B	William Fregylton	
B	Matthewe Whytton	
N/A	Robert Sprotte	
B	William Cravyn	
B	William Deny	
B	John Gybson	a jake
B	William Balderston	
B	John Balderston	
A	Lawrence Siggeswyke	a bowe
B	Christopher Cravyn	horse & harness
B	William Proctor	
A	Geffray Proctor	

B	Christopher Lupton	
A	John Redman	
B	Thomas Beamonde	
B	Christopher Redman	a byll
B	Jamys Beamonde	a byll
B	William Cosyn	
B	John Guye	
N/A	John Beamonde	
N/A	John Beamonde	
N/A	John Beamonde	
A	Rowlyn Mason	a bowe
B	William Wedyrhirde	
B	Christopher Wedyrhirde	
A	Anthony Wedyrhirde	a bowe
A	William Wedyrhirde	a bowe
N/A	Edmonde Petye	
A	Robert Petty	a bowe
B	Thomas Guye	a byll, a horse & harness
B	Robert Remyngton	
A	Alex Guye	a bowe
A	Alex Sprott	
A	Thomas Sprott	
B	Thomas Jackson	a byll
A	John Sprott	a bowe
A	John Gregson	a bowe
A	Leonarde Proctor	a byll
A	John Gregson	a bowe
B	Thomas ffoster	a byll
N/A	Thomas Benyson	
B	John Proctor	a byll
B	Richard Harlyn	a byll & a jake
B	Matthewe Siggeswyke	a byll
A	Christopher Gybson	a byll
A	John Redman	a byll
A	John Cravyn	a byll
N/A	John Balderston	a byll

We can see that of ninety-one men listed for service nineteen are unfit or unable to serve for other reasons. Many of those unfit have no weapons, but some have good equipment and must have served in the past. Many have weapons and armour while others have nothing and will have to rely on county supplies. They were expected to provide arms according to their means. The bill was a long pike, combining axe blade and lance point, similar to a halberd. A sallett was a simple metal hat for head protection in battle. A jack was a leather or canvas jerkin covered with small metal plates.

It is interesting to note how surnames had changed since 1379 when so many had no fixed surname at all. The names in this list Craven, Foxcroft, Procter, Redman, Gibson, Guy and Mason are all names that come into the early Parish Registers. Now surnames are well established many surnames listed in the muster roll carry on through the following centuries and some survive to the present day. Ingleton at this time could put twenty-three bowmen into the field and archers were such an important part of English armies especially when we think of Crecy and Agincourt. Ingleton men were still carrying out regular practice with their long bows in some field in the village in 1539. In 1590 the Privy Council decreed that long bows should never again be issued as weapons of war. From then on they continued in use, but only for sport.

Several Ingleton men had arms and armour listed in their inventories at death and several had swords and daggers. Richard Gibson (1554) states, 'I will that my son Christopher have my jacke, a pair of splyntes, a sconce, a yoke and bowes.' A jacke was a defensive jacket or doublet quilted with leather for body protection. Splyntes or splents were plates for protecting the inside of the arms and a sconce was a metal skull-cap or head piece without a visor. In 1603 Alexander Guy left his 'armour and harness' to his son. Alexander also had two bills which were similar to halberds.

LORD OF THE MANOR & LITIGATION WITH INGLETON TENANTS

The wealthy men who became Lords of the Manor frequently bought the manor as a business investment to raise money. They then lived in a comfortable manor house from the rents and dues of the manor. Wealthy families often owned several manors while others owned and lived in the one manor. If they could they raised rents and if necessary evicted tenants. This was especially true at Ingleton where hard lords of the manor gave the tenants a hard time. In 1522 Dame Margaret Pickering is noted as, 'Cheif their, The lorde Mounteagle Stuarde their.' In 1529 the Lord of the Manor of Ingleton was Sir William Pickering Knt. Later in the century Ingleton manor came into the hands of Sir Richard Cholmley and later still his son Richard Cholmley.

In Tudor times the power of the Manor Courts were waning, but the Lord of the Manor still had jurisdiction as to whom he allowed to take property in the manor and be entered in the manor court books. When the minister of Ingleton, Michael Farthwaite fell out with the lord of the manor he was unable to continue living in the 'Over Gate' in Ingleton Manor and had to move across the river into Twistleton. There he built cottages at Bridge End and lived in one of them. We know this because he recorded the story in his will, explaining that building the cottages was the reason for his financial problems. He also explained that he later made it up with the lord of the manor.[7]

When Thomas Battersby of Ingleton made his will in 1572 he left his title and 'tenant-right' to his son Anthony. Thomas Battersby's is the first surviving will to use the word 'tenant-right' to describe the system of land tenure. It is ironic for his son Anthony Battersby was the first to lose his tenant-right and his very tenement, in standing up to the Lord of the manor in a tenancy struggle. Conditions of tenancy were important for Ingleton's Tudor farmers. A 'tenant at will' could be displaced at the lord's will whereas a 'customary tenant' had security of tenure. Customary tenure was common in the north of England and the system of tenant-right was a special variety of it. Tenant-right was known mainly in the northern areas close to the Scottish border. The main characteristic of tenant-right was that the tenant had the power to dispose of his farm by deed or will, usually with, but occasionally without the license of the lord of the manor. This security of tenure had been historically linked to the liability for military service along the Scottish border.[8] A further characteristic was the right to pass the estate in the family so long as there was an heir of the same blood to inherit. When William Hird made his will in 1593 he stated, 'I will that the tenant-right of my tenement for want of heirs shall remain to the next of my blood.'

Many of the northern rebels who grouped at Doncaster in 1536, in the Rising of the North, had disagreed with their landlords over the terms of their tenure and their chief claim was that, 'lands in Westmorland, Cumberland, Kendal, Dent, Sedbergh, Furness and Abbey lands in Mashamdale, Kirkbyshire and Nidderdale should be held by tenant-right and that the customary payment for entry fines should be two years rent'.[9] Sedburgh and Dent both border on Ingleton and there would be no doubt that Ingleton tenants would be concerned with the same question at that time.

During the second half of the sixteenth century the lord of the manor of Ingleton, Sir Richard Cholmley, claiming that his tenants in Ingleton were tenants at will, increased fines and harassed them in an attempt to put the manor on the same footing as many other Yorkshire manors where landlords had managed to get rid of customary tenants and the restrictions which their kind of tenancy involved. Richard Cholmley wished to confirm that the Ingleton tenants were tenants at will and thus held their tenancies for a term of years or for life.[10] After Richard Cholmley died in 1587 his son Richard succeeded him and continued his attacks against the Ingleton tenants causing a greater breakdown in relations than before. The matter was eventually taken to court by the aggrieved tenants. They claimed that they had given Richard Cholmley a 'Benevolence' of £400 on the promise that he would treat them better than his father, but he had not done so. They accused him of taking tenants to court and impoverishing them by having to sell their stock for their defence. Cholmley had thrown out one of the customary tenants, Anthony Battersby, and his poor wife and children and demolished their house. They said they used to have 'four-score draught oxen' and now had few and that where they used to be able to supply a hundred equipped men for military service they would soon be hard pressed to find any.

In his defence Cholmley fell back on the relation of tenantright to military service against the Scots. He stated that the tenants were not bound to any military service, 'in time of Warrs upon the Boarders of England against Scotland', as were those able to claim tenant-right in Cumberland and Westmorland. They were, he said, liable only to the military musters and military service as were the rest of the people of England. He also claimed that the Lord of the manor of Ingleton had always been able to place or displace tenants at his will, and that they were therefore tenants at will holding their property for a term of years or for life.

A Chancery decree in the tenants favour was made in the year 1592. It was in the tenants' favour in that it confirmed their tenant-right – the right to pass on their holdings to their heirs, but in other aspects it favoured the Lord of the manor, Richard Cholmley. He was allowed to raise rents and gain extra payments when tenancies were transferred. Although Cholmley agreed to his tenants having full tenant-right, he still refused to take back Anthony Battersby or Thomas Foxcroft as manorial tenants. The tenants were impoverished by the strife and Cholmley, although apparently gaining increased rents, still died in impoverished circumstances. There was no doubt that neither side got their own way and the final results were not that final: litigation began again soon after. Richard Cholmley died in 1599 or 1600 and his son, another Richard Cholmley, sold the manor to a Lowther relative who again stirred up strife with the Ingleton farmers.

BOUNDARIES OF THE MANOR OF INGLETON AND BENTHAM

In the 34th year of Elizabeth I (1591-92) a document was drawn up giving the boundaries of the manor of Ingleton and Bentham.[11] At this time Ingleton and Bentham came under the same Lord of the Manor.

The Bounders of the Manors of Ingleton & Bentham
within the County of York parcele of the Inheritance
of Sr Richd Cholmley Knt in manner & forme
followinge.

ffirst the Ld (Lands) are bounden by … that is to say beginning at Cawdwell knott & to little Ingleburrow and as Heaven water divideth and to Grastone and to Knotberry hill end & so to Bruertreehalls & to Bodwell and to Todedub and then to Blinderwell at Bleakebanke yeat & down the sike as the water runneth to Goatgap & from thence to Meerbanke & then to Sandyforde & by the double dike to Threapaw & to the Graystone at Meargill head and down Southward as the water runneth to the water of Wenninge as the course of the sd water runneth to a place called Wreakbeck and up Southward the sd beck as the water runneth to a place called Whitebanke compassing certain grounds Cloudesbanke & descending into the water of Wenning as afsd & so from thence as the course of ye sd water of Wenning runneth to a place called Appletreehead & then to the Raven crosse dike & so and by the sd dike to Angestongill dividing the counties of Lancaster & Yorkshire & then to the water of Greeta and up the water of Greeta North to the water of Daw to ravenrath & then to a place called the Nabbe of the Shawe & then to Miafould and so to a Stone called Mossy Stone & then to the standing stone & up the ffoulsike north east to the Hole in the ff(?) and then to the height of Whernside & as the Heaven water divideth & then down east to the meerewall to Ellerbecke dike & thence to ffreardike as the water runneth & from thence to ffrearcrag & thence up to Wolsey yeat & as the water runneth to a place called Toddabb and then by ffrearwood South east to a place called mearewall ascending directly up the meargill unto the sd Bounder called Cawdwell knott aforesaid. ffinis.

This manor document acceptable as law as part of manor records shows that the river Doe ran as the boundary between Ingleton and Thornton and shows the error of the Ordnance Survey in changing the river names about twenty years ago, just when, after a century or more, they had finally got them right.

PLAGUE AND FAMINE

Sick in body but of good and perfect remembrance is a standard phrase in the early part of most Elizabethan Ingleton wills. It both explains the reason for the will being made and certifies the sanity of the person making it. There is only one specific variation in the will and that is where some begin, 'sick of the visitation of almighty God.' There are twelve such wills in the ones that survive for Ingleton in the Tudor period. Visitation was a term frequently used in association with plague although it is difficult to pin down to plague and plague alone rather than other epidemics of sickness.

Most studies of the plague have been based on parish registers, but these are not available for Ingleton in the Tudor period having been lost or destroyed from 1538 to 1607. North West England was subject to periodic outbreaks of plague during the Tudor period. 1557-1559 brought heavy mortality, 1586-1588, 1592, and 1596-1602 are notable years when plague is mentioned, but in looking at many sources it becomes apparent that the plague was never really absent from the north of England during the last quarter of the 16th century It is interesting to compare the year's of Ingleton visitation deaths with the known plague epidemics and many correspond.

Death usually took place within a few days when a person developed plague. Lawrence Harling made his will on November 18th and died on the 23rd; Joan Beaumond made her will January 19th 1595 and died a few days later; Thomas Wetherhead made his will on July 2nd 1595 and his inventory was made on July 12th; Alexander Guy made his will on July 7th 1603 and was dead in about two weeks; and Margaret Guy died the same day as she made her will January 28th 1601. All these could well have been victims of the plague. Margaret Guy's was an interesting case. Hers is the only nuncupative will found at Ingleton, that is to say a will made by word of mouth rather than written. The will records, 'First of all a neighbour's wife came to visit her and said Margaret what will you do with your goods?' Margaret gave her will by word of mouth and though only recorded later after her death, it was accepted as a legal will.

There is no doubt that there is a connection between the plague years and the years of poor harvests. Obviously in times of near starvation people would be more susceptible to plague or any other epidemic. The country experienced three bad harvests in 1557, 1558 and 1559. Bad harvests were also recorded in 1597, 1598 and 1599 the years we suspect Ingleton people died of plague. There is no doubt that the makers of the twelve 'visitation' wills were making a point that these wills were not being made in the normal course of old age or routine sickness. Whatever other epidemics might have been involved many did die of the plague. Many others in Ingleton probably died of plague and never made a will. There was a special order issued by the West Riding Justices in 1598, for the purposes of preventing the spread of the plague in the north. 'In regard to the p'sent Sickness in the North country; Yt is ordered that ev'y Constable w'thin this division shall sett 2 or three to watche and ward within their Constabulary, and shall see the same dulie kept as well in towns as hamletts. And that from henceforthe household'rs themselves shall keep the watche and ward according to their course and not hirelynges as heretofore hath bene accustomed'.[12]

REFERENCES

1. The records of the Western deaneries of the Archdeaconry of Richmond. LRO Report, 1954. p. 11.
2. *Elizabethan Ingleton,* J. Bentley, Ingleton Publications 1990.
3. *The Cotton Trade of Industrial Lancashire,* A.P. Wadsworth & J. de L. Mann, Manchester, 1931, p.25 & map.
4. *Agrarian History of England & Wales, 1500-1640,* R.J. Thirsk , Vol.IV Oxford, 1967, p.220.
5. *The Lancashire Textile Industry in the Sixteenth Century,* N. Lowe, Chetham Society, Vol.XX Third Series, Manchester, 1972, p.7.
6. Tudor Muster Roll
7. L.R.O. Lonsdale Wills, Michael Farthwaite, 1583.
8. *Agrarian History of England & Wales, 1500-1640,* R.J. Thirsk, Vol.IV, Oxford, 1967, p.220.
9. Ibid.
10. P.R.O. Chancery Proceedings , C2/Eliz/47.
11. Y.A.S Leeds. BRA.910 DD123. Ingleton Mining Docs. (This document is not original 16th century, but a copy made later and placed with the Ingleton Colliery documents.)
12. *YAS Record Series* Vol.2. p126.

STUART PERIOD
1602 – 1714

This was certainly a century of dramatic events both national and local; famine and plague; a civil war in which the king was executed; the Commonwealth period when the country was run by Oliver Cromwell; the return of monarchy; and finally the throwing out of the last Catholic king, James II, and in 1689 the 'Glorious Revolution', with the crowning of William, a new Protestant king from Holland. Ingleton folk would have been well aware what was going on and many would have been called to serve as soldiers. However, the main concern of Ingleton folk would have been getting enough food, avoiding disease and starvation, keeping their heads down during the civil war and where possible escaping taxation such as the Hearth Tax introduced in the last quarter of the seventeenth century.

FAMINE IN 1623

In Tudor times we have seen that there were outbreaks of plague, typhus and many other diseases and that people were more likely to catch these diseases if they were weakened by starvation. This situation continued into the seventeenth century. By far the worst year came in 1623 during the early years of the Stuart period. The fact that there was a serious problem is evident from the entries of deaths in Ingleton parish registers.[1] The deaths in the registers from 1618 are shown below. The first numbers are of the year January to December: the numbers in brackets are for year as calculated at the time, March 25th to March 25th:-

1618	36 (24) burials	1622	32 (35) burials
1619	26 (23) burials	**1623**	**52 (59) burials**
1620	16 (22) burials	1624	34 (27) burials
1621	36 (35) burials	1625	20 (19) burials

The rise in deaths can be seen in 1621 and 1622 culminating in the very high death rate of 1623. This same rise in deaths can be seen in many other parishes throughout Lancashire, the West Riding of Yorkshire and the north of England generally. Agricultural records show that 1622 was a poor harvest year followed by a hard winter.[2] This is the first hint that this problem was basically one of famine. The people of Ingleton had to provide food for their population from the cultivable land in the parish. That land was limited and if the population grew beyond a certain point then there was hardship and hunger. The population remained relatively static at this period checked by famine and accompanying diseases. The local government or sworn men of the parish had little enough charitable money to give out and could not give out food if there was none to be had.

The parish clerk at Ingleton has not left us many clues as to this terrible year, but there is mention that one or two of those buried are poor folk from other parishes of Horton and Kendal. The neighbouring parish of Thornton-in-Lonsdale did not suffer as much, but the parish clerk was more observant. In 1623 the clerk at Thornton recorded:-[3]

April 21st An unknown woman being a Crepell & carried of a Carre speechless but only that she said shee would have been in Westmerland she came from Ingleton & died in Maysingill at the howse of Thomas Gibson then being the towneship.

June 27th Alice d. of Ricd Wilson of Langridge in the parish of Rybchester in the Countie of Lanc., dyed in the howse of Leonard Cravens in Thornton fyeld the day here underwritten.

August 24th Jane d. of Thomas Burrowe of the parish of Beeethome.

October 28th Roberte s. of Robt Tomson of the parish of Skailbee weste from Carlyle in the Countie of Cumberland.

November 13th A Crepell was browghte by the Connstable of Ingleton shee was a younge woman to the howse of Roger Cansfeld of Thornton Connstable who dyed presently & never spoke one worde & therefore we cannot sett downe her name nor the parish where she was borne she was buried in the Churchyard at Thornton by Roger Cansfeld & Joan als Jennett Procter.

February 25th 1623/4 Xpofer Grayme borne beyond Carlyell as he sayethe dyed at the howse of Thomas Cherneley in Westhowse.

The above accounts tell us that this was a year of famine and people were wandering the roads. When food and money dried up many thought that they had a better chance of survival be moving away from their own parish in the hope of begging or finding work in other parishes in areas that perhaps had not been so hard it. In many cases their journey was futile and they died of starvation in some strange parish. In many cases where they had children with them the children died first. In November 1623 we are told that the Ingleton constable brought a young woman to Roger Cansfield the constable of Thornton. She was crippled and died without speaking one word. As soon as this woman appeared in Ingleton the constable would have arrested her and immediately passed her on to the neighbouring parish so that Ingleton did not have to feed her or look after her in any other way. This was the harsh reality of life and the Ingleton constables were strict in their enforcement, where possible they whipped or carried strangers out of the parish to die somewhere else. We also see that at this time children and the handicapped starved and died first in these times of famine.

In 1616 twenty-nine children were baptised at Ingleton, in 1617 there were twenty-one, in 1618 thirty-one and 1619 twenty-nine. In the famine year of 1623 there were only seventeen and the following year eighteen and for some time the numbers remained low. We know that starvation stops a woman's ability to conceive a child. This and the fact that many of the dead were men between the ages of twenty and fifty explains the low birth rate of 1623, 1624 and the following years into the 1630s.

Throughout the Stuart period there were outbreaks of plague from time to time throughout the country and we all know of the Plague of London which came in 1665. The death of some gave an opportunity for others. When parents died their children could marry earlier and take over the farm. Without famine and plague they might well have had to wait until their thirties or forties to be able to marry and have a place to live and support them.

THE LOWTHER FAMILY OF INGLETON

At this point we must consider the Lowthers' interest in Ingleton. Gerard Lowther had bought the manor of Ingleton from a relative, Richard Cholmley, around the year 1605. It is said that Lowther wanted to help Richard Cholmley, his insolvent son-in-law, by taking Ingleton Manor off his hands for a reasonable price and that he also hoped to overturn the decree of 1592 claiming that the decree against Richard Cholmeley was not binding on him.[4]

However, there is a further reason in that the Lowther family had been interested in minerals in the areas under their influence for many years and they were almost certainly aware of the coal deposits in the Ingleton and Bentham Manor. 'It was the Lowthers who made the biggest contribution to the growth of coal mining in Cumberland. For over two centuries the family worked continuously and profitably the coal under their own lands – and got other landowners to follow suit'.[5] The Lowthers also had estates at St Bees and were involved in coal mining there. '16 Apr 6 Car.I. W. Lowther of Ingleton, his son & heir Richd Low^r joyn in Conveying the Estates at St Bees to Sr John Lowther of Lowther in Considerat^n of £2450.' The Lowther involvement with coal at Ingleton will be discussed in the later chapter on Ingleton coalfield and collieries.

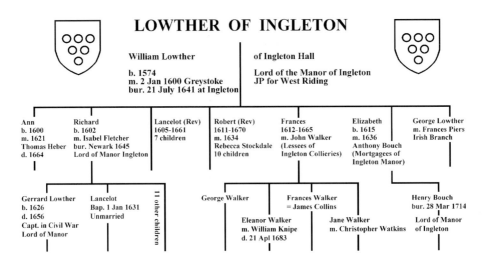

This pedigree shows the family connections of the Lowther, Walker and Bouch families who were involved in the Ingleton mines saga.

Pedigree of the Lowther family of Ingleton.

Gerard Lowther felt that as a lawyer he would be able to overturn the 1592 decree on the grounds that it was not binding on him. He began attempting to eject tenants who returned to Chancery Court. Lowther's claims were turned down and a decree issued against him in 1604. Gerard Lowther admitted that his motive in buying the manor had been to overturn the Chancery decree against Richard Cholmley. When Gerard was appointed a judge in Ireland he passed the manor and manor house to his younger brother, William Lowther, to manage. In 1610 William Lowther moved with his family to live at Ingleton Hall. William had married Eleanor Wellbury at Greystoke in Cumberland on January 2nd 1600 and the couple had spent the first years of their married life at Hackthorpe near Lowther, in a house built by his brother, Christopher Lowther, and where their first six children were born. William and Eleanor had a further child while they lived at Skirmingham.

At Ingleton William and Eleanor had nine more children who were baptised in Ingleton church. In total the couple had sixteen children and nine lived to become adults, four sons and five daughters. Eleanor Lowther died in childbirth of her sixteen child and was buried on August 22nd 1620 in the choir of the church at Ingleton. William's brother, Gerard, the Irish judge, visited Ingleton to see his brother and while visiting in 1619 his wife Anne died and was buried in Ingleton church on October13th. Sir Gerard Lowther died in Ireland in 1624 aged sixty two years and left lands to his nephew Richard Lowther of Ingleton by will. William Lowther died on July 21st 1641 aged 67 and was also buried in the church choir with his wife.

After Gerard Lowther's death, William Lowther continued litigation against the Ingleton tenants. In 1620 he acted on the King's proclamation, of July 1620, against tenant right. The proclamation ordered all litigation over tenant right to cease and instructed the lords to let all tenant right land by indenture only. William Lowther offered his Ingleton tenants new leases which they all refused to accept. Lowther then made writs of ejection against them. The tenants once again banded against the Lord of the manor and he moved a bill in Chancery against four Ingleton tenants citing their refusal to take leases as instructed by the proclamation. Chancery placed no weight on the proclamation and dismissed Lowther's case as vexatious.[6] This would appear to be the end of serious litigation between landlord and tenant at Ingleton.

THE SHIREBURNS OF TWISTLETON

The manor of Twistleton and Ellerbeck had been a separate manor from at least the thirteenth century. In 1565 Richard Shireburn of Stonyhurst bought it from William Redmayne to add to his many possessions in Lancashire and Yorkshire: 'Manor of Twyselton and 20 messuages and 2 watermills with land in Twyselton and Ingleton'.[7] Sir Richard Shireburn was a wealthy man, prominent in the government of Lancashire, being one of Her Majesty's Deputy Lieutenants of the County of Lancaster. He was also master forester of Bowland. Sir Richard was Catholic by religion, which at the time was referred to as papist. However, he still attended the Anglican Church occasionally so that he was not fined the £20 per month levied on absentees. A report of 1591 clearly said that he and his family were recusants, that they seldom went to church and when they did they stopped up their ears with wool to prevent themselves hearing the service. It was also said that Richard had brought a priest to hear his wife's confession when she was ill.[8] When lists of recusants were made there were always a good number at Twistleton and that may well be due to the Shireburn support.

We know from Richard Shireburn's rental accounts in 1571 that he had recently bought Twistleton manor and demesne on the south side of Ingleborough.[9] The Hall itself, with orchard, garden and demesne was rented out for £30 a year. The name of the tenant was not mentioned. Richard Shireburn also had land in Dent and at Greystonegill near Bentham. At Twistleton each of Sir Richard's sixteen tenants had to give two days' reaping, two days' harrowing and three days' mowing each year, and each was responsible for six cartloads of peat. Christopher Waller at Twistleton was in charge of collecting rents and dues.

Sir Richard Shireburn died in 1593 and was buried under an impressive monument at Mitton church. Twistleton passed to Thomas Shireburn and he and his wife had several children. Thomas died in 1607 and the Twistleton Manor went to his eldest son, Richard, who lived there for some years. The Diocesan Visitation of 1633 records Richard Shireburn and his wife Margaret as recusants.

The first mention of the family in the Ingleton parish register comes in 1626 with the entry in the baptisms:- 'Thomas filius Richard Shearborne Esquire de Twistleton 17 September.' A daughter Anne was baptised in October 1627. In September 1630 Richard Shireburn buried a daughter Anne at Ingleton and in 1631 he buried two further children, Katheren on April 20th and Richard on the 4th of May. His son Robert died in 1633 and daughter Elizabeth in November of the same year. Elizabeth's burial was the last mention of the Shireburns in the Ingleton parish registers and the loss of five children in three years was probably sufficient for the family to move. Like the Lowthers, the Shireburns had litigation with their tenants. The aim was to raise rents and bring about land enclosures. The Twistleton litigation was ended by a decree in 1625. 'Richard Sherborne of Twistleton in the County of

York Esqr, Lord of the said manor of the one part and John Greenbank of Twistleton, Leonard Greenbank, the Brother of the said John, Richard Batty, Thomas Greenbank, William Greenbank, Thomas Calvert, John Craven, Willm Wood, Leon^d Weatherhead, Willm Batty, Peter Foster, Marie Herd – widow, on behalf of her daughter Jennet – William Tatham, Willm Comeinge, Thomas Charneley, Leonard Weatherhead of Scales and Leonard Procter of Ellerbeck and Alexander Procter of Skirreth in the said County, husbandmen on the other part'.

The decree stated that there had been differences between the lord of the manor and the tenants, but that these had been settled. The tenants were confirmed in their tenancies and manorial rights and they were no longer required to do free manorial labour, or boon work for the lord of the manor. This work was replaced by a small financial payment. New rents and other charges were agreed for the future. Richard Shireburn was allowed to enclose ninety acres of land for his own use and the tenants were allowed one-hundred and ninety acres to improve and enclose for themselves.

CIVIL WAR

The Civil War came in 1642 and affected the whole country. The Craven gap had a great strategic importance. In the campaigns of Marston Moor (1644), Preston (1648) and Worcester (1651) much depended on the speed of moving troops from one side of the Pennines to the other. The principal road lay well to the south by Skipton, Gisburn and Clitheroe, but the road through Settle and Ingleton was often taken by those making for the north and wishing to avoid an enemy. After his defeat at Marston Moor Prince Rupert brought his men through Ingleton on their way to Hornby on July 10th 1644. They then continued through Garstang and Preston to Liverpool. There would be a constant coming and going of armed groups through the area and one good example is given by Royalist, Sir Henry Slingsby in his memoirs, 'On the 10th of September 1644 wee set forwards on our march for Skipton, and, by marching in the night, passed through the enemy that lay on every side. We had but one stop which was at a bridge near Ingleton where the enemy had set a guard; but we soon made our passage, with the loss of one lieutenant of horse, who was shot in the body and died on the way as he was carrying.'

Richard Lowther, lord of the Manor of Ingleton, rode off to join the Royalist army soon after Civil War began. He is first noted when as Colonel Richard Lowther he became governor of Pontefract Castle. His son Gerrard, a Captain of horse, served with him and his brother Robert Lowther was chaplain. Not long after he left to fight, Ingleton Hall was taken over by Major Rippon and his soldiers. Brayshaw in his history of Giggleswick records that Richard Horsfall of Storthes Hall in Giggleswick claimed damages after having livestock taken by the Parliamentarians. 'I had a bullocke and a heffer taken per John Paley Agent when Major Rippon's soulgers kept Ingleton Hall to the value of sevven pounds.'[10]

Richard Lowther had a difficult time at Pontefract where he underwent two sieges by the Parliamentarian Army. It was the first time that the defences of the castle had been put to the test. The first siege of Pontefract began on Christmas Day 1644 although it was not until January 1645 that the Parliamentarian gun batteries began an intense bombardment. The first siege ended in March 1645 when the Royalist forces under Sir Marmeduke Langdale drove off the Parliamentarian army and relieved the castle.

The victory was short-lived, as within a couple of weeks a second siege was in position. This time the besiegers were more effective in blocking off all exits from the castle. The castle was under continuous bombardment and the attacker's starvation strategy was eventually successful. On July 19th 1645 Richard Lowther made an honourable surrender to General Poyntz and was allowed to throw down his weapons and march off to join the nearest Royalist group at Newark. Not long after arriving at Newark Richard Lowther collapsed and died after the strain he had suffered. His son Gerard had to arrange his burial and then return alone to his home Ingleton Hall. Richard Lowther was buried in the graveyard of the church of St Mary at Newark on August 15th 1645. The burial register reads, 'Collonell Lowther Governor of Pontefract.' He had survived the ordeal of two sieges only to die a short time later; he was forty-three.

The Civil War ended the following year and young Gerard returned to his home and family at Ingleton Hall in Upper Gate. During the war Ingleton Hall had been occupied by parliamentary soldiers under Major Rippon and was much damaged. Gerard Lowther and his father had been Royalist heroes, but now his father was dead and Gerard was declared a 'delinquent' for having taken up arms against Parliament. Royalist Composition papers record the following:-

His delinquency that he was in arms against the Parliament and at Newark at the surrender and is to have the benefit of those articles: he took the covenant before Robert Windle minister at Preston in Yorks 20 July 1646 and Again before William Barton and the oath here 27 February 1646. He is seized in the Manor of Ingleton in the Parish of Bentham of the yearly value of £10 yearly rent of £120, in rents in Ingleton and in a colliery worth £20. He craves an allowance of £80 per annum to be paid for 7 years whereof 2 years are rent June yet to come and for £1000 to be paid at the feasts of Pentecost which shall be in 1649 for which the manor of Ingleton is charged by deed made by Richard Lowther father of the compounder 18 June 18 Car (1643) if the said manor be redeemed then the mother of the compounder is to have her thirds. He is indebted £1000 R. Gurdon, D. Watkins March 1646.

On March 23rd 1646 a fine of £400 was imposed on Gerard Lowther. So we see that not only was Gerard fined, but that the Manor of Ingleton was mortgaged. Gerard and his mother, Isabella, had a further problem in that when Richard Lowther died his personal goods were valued at £227 10s 4d, but his debts were valued at £428 4s 0d. However, by January 1649, only a year before her death, Isabella had paid off her husband's debts. The inventory of Richard Lowther's goods and chattels drawn up after his death is dated January 17th 1646. It lists his cattle, horse, corn and hay and the usual household goods from his silver plate and books to a broken clock. However, it also lists, 'In husbandrie gear & Coole pit.' and 'Worke towles,' both items being valued at £3 6s 8d.

As Gerard Lowther needed a considerable amount of money he leased all coal mines and rights to mine to his aunt, Francis Walker. The lease dated 1648 was for one hundred years and the amount £2,100. Francis Walker was already a widow and this was an investment for herself and her family. In 1653 Gerard and his brother, Lancelot, mortgaged the Manor of Ingleton to Anthony Bouch of Cockermouth. Anthony Bouch was their uncle, who had married Elizabeth Lowther at St. Leonard's, the Parish Church in Ingleton, on Jan 23rd 1634. The indenture dated September 14th 1653 is an interesting one which lists Ingleton Manor House, its demesne lands and the manorial mill on Ingleton beck. Anthony Bouch paid the Lowther brothers £1,800.[11]

There was an uneasy truce between the village and their Lord of the Manor, Gerard Lowther, as he had been put in his place as a 'delinquent.' He no longer harassed his tenants for extra rents or attempted to eject them and most had little contact with him. He still rode up the Back Gate into town to visit the blacksmith, the village mill and on Sunday to take his place in church. However, it was not long before his uncle Anthony Bouch came down from

Cockermouth in 1660 to claim the manor and Ingleton Hall as Gerard Lowther had not paid his mortgage. From this year the Lowther family departed from Ingleton.

The one thing the Puritans were successful at was stopping people having a good time: they spoiled people's simple pleasures – they banned Maypole dancing, singing and music in churches and even Christmas celebrations. They destroyed stained glass, ornate brasses, carved wood screens, marble tombs and statues in churches. These offended Puritan beliefs and were seen as papist and open to attack and destruction. Luckily the fanatics were in a minority and many churches were saved by people who valued their heritage, but thousands of churches were ruined. Ingleton church had no real problem, a poor church in a poor village in one of the poorest counties in the country, Ingleton had no marble tombs, no ornate woodwork, no brasses and few religious effigies.

Of the very few items that might have disturbed the Puritans one was the ornate carved Norman font. Perhaps this was the time the old font at Ingleton church disappeared to be become whitewash container and relegated into the tower storeroom. The Puritans were led by strict religious fanatics and tried to extinguish even the small pleasures that the villagers enjoyed. This was why in the end the people of the country welcomed back King Charles II in 1660 in spite of the fact that, for many, he stood for all that they had fought against in the Civil War.

In the archives of Carlisle Castle is a letter dated November 27th 1649 from Richard Lowther to his nephew Sir John Lowther.[12] He wrote:-

> As for Ingleton and the men of Ingleton I will never have more to do with either. I have lost by Grandfather father and sonne, losses and Injuries intaylde upon me from them…I that never bought the inheritance of anything but only 2 lyme kilnes will not now, being without issue bye lande with trouble. At 66 itt is bedd tyme with me and that bed is the grave.

We most certainly know that Richard Lowther's feelings were reciprocated by the people of Ingleton. This Richard was only a relation of the Lowther family of Ingleton. Born in 1584 he died in 1659 and was MP for both Berwick and Appleby. His father was Sir Christopher Lowther and his grandfather Sir Richard Lowther and the full extent of their relationships with Ingleton we do not know, but we do know that it led to a mutual hostility. After marrying into the Lowther family, Anthony Bouch, bought considerable land in Ingleton, so that when he took over Ingleton Hall as lord of the manor he already had land there apart from the lands of Ingleton Manor. Anthony had married Elizabeth Lowther at Ingleton on January 23rd 1634 and returned to live at Cockermouth. He came to live with his wife and son Henry in Ingleton Hall in 1660. Anthony had only about twelve years at Ingleton for he died in February 1673 and was buried in the east choir of the St Mary's Church. His son Henry took over as Lord of the Manor and things appear to have run smoothly apart from Henry's litigation with the colliery owners. Henry married Sarah the daughter of Sir William Fleming in 1689. Sarah died shortly afterwards in childbirth and a daughter Sarah was also lost. Henry married again into the Fleming family, his second marriage being to Mary the daughter of Sir Daniel Fleming. Henry and Mary Bouch had a daughter Catherine who married Edward Parker of Browsholme near Clitheroe on November 1st 1688. The marriage is recorded in the parish registers at Ingleton, 'M[r] Edward Parker & Catherine daughter of Henry Bouch Esq[r]'.

HEARTH TAX

The Hearth Tax was a short lived and very unpopular tax, but the records of this tax provide us with some interesting information on the village of Ingleton and its inhabitants.

The tax was introduced shortly after the Restoration in 1660 to provide more finances for Charles II. Assessments were made from 1662 to 1688 but the tax never really succeeded in raising sufficient money and was repealed by William and Mary in 1689. Every householder who owned property worth more than twenty shilling a year was liable to an annual charge of two shillings for every hearth in his house. Returns were made by the constables to the Justices listing those who had to pay and how many hearths they had. The return was delivered to the Justices of the Peace at Quarter Sessions. The constables were empowered to enter a house and search for the hearths if they thought a false declaration had been given.

The documents show the names of inhabitants along with the number of hearths in their house. We must remember that these lists show only those who are property owners and not those who are renting property. It is more likely to show the better off members of the village. Paupers who were excluded from the tax are often not listed. The charge of 2s per hearth was paid equally at Lady Day and Michaelmas.

The following is Ingleton's Hearth Tax record for Michaelmas 1672.[13]

INGLETON

Anthony Bouch	14
Richard Gibson	1
Leonard Lamb	1
Thomas Lamb	1
Robert Geldart	1
John Sedgwicke	1
Robort Clarke	1
Willm Prockter	2
Thomas Guy	2
John Hazlam	2
Richard Wilcocke	2
Thomas Hodgson	4
John Redman	1
Willm Wilcock	2
Lancelott Dawbikin	3
Edmond Sanderson	2
Thomas Sedgwicke	2
William Witton	1
Edward Lamb	1
Richard Redman	3
Leonard Redman	1
James Richardson	2
Widdow Babthorpe	2
Elizabeth Tatam	1
The heirs of James Simpson	1
John Redman	1
Thomas Prockter	2
Elizabeth Craven	3
Thomas ffirbanke	2
John Cockin	2
Robert Walker	1
Richard Walker	2
Henry Wigglesworth	1
ffrancis Croft	1

Isabell Craven	3
Christro Thurnbancke	1
John Hall	1
Robert Wilkinson	2
Robert Balderston	3
James Skirreth	1
Thomas Walker	1
Christo Oldfield	1
Anne Redman	1
Leonard Hird	1
John Richmond	2
Charles Smith	1
Gyles Redman	1
Christopher Walker	2
William Lamb	2
Willm Craven	2
Christopher Hird	1
Marmaduke Johnson	1
John Witham	1
Thomas Wilson	1
Anthony Prockter	1
Thomas Wilson	1
Anthony Prockter	1
Thomas Hall	1
	100
Empty & no distress to be had	
Luar: Butterfeild	1
Omitted by reason of poverty	19

INGLETON FELL QUARTER

Stephen Moore	1
Miles ffoxcroft	4
Gyles ffoxcroft	3
Nathaniell Parker	1
ffrancis Wetherell	1
Thomas Wetherell	1
William ffoxcroft	1
Richard Battersby	2
Thomas Calvert	2
John Johnson	1
Widdow Batty	1
Leonard Prockter	1
Thomas Prockter	1
Stephen Atkinson	1
Thomas Prockter	3
Leonard ffoxcroft	1
Tho ffoxcroft	1
John Cansfeild	1
Anthony Prockter	2
Alexander Prockter	1
William Wetherhead	2

John Prockter	1
William Bentham	1
Edmond Litton	1
John Burton	1
Anthony Leake	1
Mr Baines	4
James Burton	2
James Wetherell	1
Thomas Prockter	1
Stephen Battersby	1
Anthony Calvert	1
Leonard Calvert	1
Jeffrey Leake	1
Thomas Howson	2
John Langstrath	1

Richard Pickard Collector
James Burton Constable

TWISTLETON AND COLD COTES QUARTER

Mr Anthony Bouch	6
Mr Richard Beesley	6
Anthony Prockter	2
Simon Downey	2
Andrew Bricke	2
Thomas Greenbanck	2
Leonard Greenbanck	2
Isabell Craven	1
John Wood	1
Elizabeth Weatherhead	1
Robert Nicholson	4
John Prockter	2
Hugh Armistead	2
Richard Butterfield	2
Thomas Braithwaite	2
Christo Remmington	1
Geo Huginson	1
Thomas Gregson	1
Alice Banckes	1
Rowland Glover	2
Henry Greenwood	2
Willm Thirnbecke	1
Thos Redman	1
Adam Paley	1
John Redman heires	2
James Remmington	2
Anthony Battersby	1
Robert Laburne	1
	54

Robt Husband Collector
Marmaduke Redman Constable

There is a printed version of the Hearth tax for Lady Day 1672 and that includes the names of those excluded through poverty. Sadly the work has some transcription errors and for that reason has not been used. It is available in Ingleton library.[14]

In the Hearth Tax we can see that the Lord of the Manor, Anthony Bouch, had the most hearths with fourteen and he lived at Ingleton Hall. Of the rest only four of the population had four hearths, one being Mr Baines, who was denoted as Mr to show his status. Seven people had three hearths and the rest had two or one. Mr Beesley at Twistleton had six hearths and is given the respected title of Mr in spite of being a Catholic recusant. The list also shows that a good number of the village population were recorded as paupers judged to be without the means to pay the tax. The returns show the relative wealth of the people according to the number of hearths. We can also see the surnames in the township and see who were incomers and who were the long standing families. The returns illustrate how the population was continually changing, with new people coming into the area and others leaving.

PROBATE RECORDS - WILLS & INVENTORIES

The wills of Ingleton folk in the Stuart period from 1603 to 1714 give an interesting insight into people, their occupations, their way of life, their family relationships and their possessions. Austen Allen of Twistleton whose will is dated 1608 had two cows, a horse and six sheep. His house had 'stooles and chaires, chestes and bedstocks.' He had wool and a spinning wheel but few personal possessions. Life would have been quite bleak at Twistleton at this time. The total value of his possessions was only ten pounds apart from money owed to him. At the end of the period John Armitstead of Skirwith died in 1702. He is titled husbandman although his possessions would suggest yeoman rather than husbandman. A husbandman was usually more of a tenant farmer without a great deal of wealth or influence. Yeomen were usually recognised as being from established families, owning property, having considerable possessions and having influence in the community. John Armitstead had six cows, four oxen, five heifers, two steers, one bull, seven calves, three horses and seventy three sheep. The bull is significant as few owned a bull at this time. His house would have been less spartan than Austen Allen's as he had brass and pewter and plenty of furniture. He also had considerable farming equipment. His father, Hugh Armitstead, had farmed Skirwith before him and John also had a son Hugh who was left to provide for his sisters. John owned an estate at the Cross in Ingleton.

John Armitstead's brother Thomas was a woollen weaver in Ingleton and he also died in 1702. Thomas had some cattle, and owned a few fields, but the main interest is in his looms, shears, and other 'warke towles' for his trade as weaver. The fact that he had shears for cropping the nap of the cloth after weaving and fulling meant that he was able to prepare fine cloth. Thomas would likely have had wool combs for preparing yarn for the finer cloth. Hand cards were used for fluffing up the wool prior to spinning yarn to be used for more ordinary cloth. The fulling mill was available in the bottoms at Ingleton and then the finished cloth would either be sold locally or sent by pack horse to Kendal or the Yorkshire markets. It is likely that other members of the family assisted in the cloth-making process, either spinning or handloom weaving.

Thomas Lamb made his will in 1664, died in 1668 and was buried in Ingleton Church on December 7th. Thomas lived on the Bank at Ingleton where he had a fire house, barn, garden and garth. He was a cooper and his inventory shows that he had iron implements and tools and plenty of timber for making his barrels. However, like most tradesmen of the time he was also a farmer and had animals, carts, ploughs and other farming equipment. His wife was Jane and he had children Thomas, Mary, John, Robert and Leonard. He left his son-in-law Warth Closc in the Townfield and he had other property in Ingleton village and at Fell End.

Henry Lamb died in 1672 and was buried at Ingleton on February 22nd. He was also a cooper by trade and likely related to Thomas. Henry had a 'ffire house, barn garden and grassgarth' in Ingleton. His wife Isobel, son Edmund and daughter Barbara inherited his property. Among other things he left his wife 'all that piece of ground called the Clod lying in the Lordship of Twistleton.' Henry also had cattle.

John Lamb was a third member of the Lamb family who was a cooper by trade. John had not made a will and when seriously ill and close to death on December 17th 1674 he 'did declare by words his will & mind to Marmaduke Johnson & Elizabeth Adison these words first he said that his debts should be paid with his goods and what as his goods would not pay his ground should make forth and all the rest of his ground his wife & his daughter should have it equally betwixt them witness out hands.' There was also an inventory which plainly shows his tools and wood for his trade as a cooper.

Coopering, making barrels, was a craft practised in most villages. The casks produced were used to store and carry everything from wine and beer to fish and crockery. The cooper's tools remained much the same over centuries, axe, adze, knife, brace, auger and hammer. The cooper had a bench for his tools and he worked at the block, which in a village workshop would probably be an old tree stump. In Ingleton the Lambs' coopering workshop was probably on the Bank close to where they lived.

Myles Layfield made his will in 1651. He lived at Moorgarth and was a tanner by trade. Myles had an interesting inventory which included books, a sword and musket and a silver spoon. He had hand cards for carding wool and spinning wheels for spinning the carded wool. He had linen yarn and linen cloth and members of his household seem to have been involved in both wool and linen cloth production. He kept bees, had a yoke of oxen and other farm animals and farming equipment and yet his will describes him as a tanner. Perhaps he carried out his tanning on his farm at Moorgarth or perhaps worked in premises by the river in the Bottoms at Ingleton where tanning was carried out through the nineteenth century.

There had been a corn mill at Ingleton from early times and a miller was always needed. Richard Foster the miller at Ingleton died in 1650. Richard left his house to his eldest son John and bequests to his wife and other children. Once again he had books in his inventory which did not occur in the previous century. He was also an educated man as he signed his will. The mill had always been connected to the Manor of Ingleton and he was most likely employed by the lord of the manor. This connection is supported by the list of those owing him money. He was owed by Gerard Lowther Esq, Robert Lowther gent, Richard Lowther, gent, and finally by Lancelot Lowther gent: only two others, John Balderston and Leonard Walker, owed him money. Gerard Lowther was the Lord of the manor at that time and the others were members of his family.

There were two Ingleton men in the Stuart period who came into contact with the majority of the people of Ingleton. They were Robert Atkinson, butcher, and John Batty, the main village blacksmith. Robert Atkinson lived in the early part of the seventeenth century and died in June 1632. He was not only a butcher, but was also dealing in wool and yarn and had cards for preparing raw wool ready to make yarn That he supplied the leading families in Ingleton with meat we know from the list of those owing him debts on his death. The first in the list was Richard Lowther, son of the Lord of the Manor of Ingleton and the second was Richard Shireburn, Lord of the Manor of Twistleton. Then follow the names of Thomas Wetherhead, Alexander Redman, William Tatham, John Tatham, Thomas Balderston, Thomas Walker, and Thomas Guy, all leading figures in the village.

John Batty died in 1629 at Ingleton where he had been a blacksmith for many years. His inventory lists his bellows, vice and all other things in the smithy. Once again it is the list of debts owed and owing that interest us. The first on his list of debtors was William Lowther,

Lord of the Manor, followed by his son Richard Lowther. Then followed Richard Shireburn of Twistleton Hall, John Redman, Ann Redman, Thomas Wetherhead, Symon Boddy, Alexander Procter, Peter Procter, John Bentham, John Johnson, Thomas Procter, Richard Cansfield, Thomas Waller, Leonard Walker, William Tatham, Richard Ustonson, Lawrence Dowbigging, Thomas Wilson, John Sigswicke of Seedhill, John Walker, Edward Brotherton, Christopher Battersby, Marmaduke Redman, Robert Procter, Alexander Redman, Alexander Swanne, William Skarth, John Guy, William Greenbank, Alexander Hird, Anthony Batty, Brian Hodgson and others. John Batty had done metal work for most of the village and most of them owed him money. Where John Batty had his forge we do not know, but it is likely to have been next to the Wheat Sheaf or on the Bank near the Three Horse Shoes, two old smithy sites of Ingleton blacksmiths.

He had peat or turves in his inventory. They were digging turf on Ingleborough and at other places in the township for fuel. Turf or turves appear in many inventories and the scented smell of burning peat would have been a feature of seventeenth century life.

At the end of the Stuart period life was getting better in Ingleton, the plague had gone, never to return, new land was being farmed, the civil war was a distant memory, the puritan days were over and village festivities were enjoyed once again. Houses were slowly becoming better furnished, chairs were replacing benches and stools, and clocks and books were appearing in several households.

REFERENCES

1. *The Parish Registers of Ingleton & Chapel-Le-Dale 1607-1812*, The Yorkshire Parish Register Society 1933.
2. *Agricultural Records A.D.220-1977*, J.M. Stratton, Baker, London 1969.
3. *The Parish Register of Thornton-in-Lonsdale 1576-1812*, The Yorkshire Parish Register Society, 1931.
4. *Lords,Tenants, and Tenant Right in the Sixteenth Century*, R.W. Hoyle, Northern History, Vol. XX, 1984.
5. *West Cumberland Coal*, 1600-1982, Oliver Wood, Cumberland & Westmorland Antiquarian & Archæological Soc. Extra series XXIV.
6. PRO, C78/493, no 7.
7. YAS Record Series Yorkshire Fines 1. Vol.II. Feet of Fines Tudor Period. 1887.
8. Cal. State Papers Domestic Eliz., 1591-4, p.159.
9. *The Rental and Accounts of Sir Richard Shireburn, 1571-1577* W.F. Rea Hist Soc Lancashire and Cheshire, Vol. 110, 1958.
10. *A History of the Ancient Parish of Giggleswick*, Brayshaw & Robinson, 1932, p.81.
11. PRO Close Roll (Chancery) 1653, Part 43. No. 9.
12. CRO,Carlisle Castle. D/Lons/L1/1/8 D/Lons/LI/l/8.Lowther-Ingleton.
13. PRO Hearth Tax, E179/210/418
14. *The Hearth Tax Lists for Staincliffe and Ewecross Wapentakes, West Riding of Yorkshire, Lady Day 1672*, 1992, Ripon History Society and Ripon, Harrogate and District Family History Group, pp.32,33 & 59.

GEORGIAN TIMES
1714-1830

Parts of this period are often referred to as 'The Age of Elegance', but at Ingleton that was one thing it never was. There was no elegance in the church, and little if any in Ingleton Hall, which was so dilapidated it was demolished by the Parker family around 1770. There was no elegance in the inns, shops, or cottages: this age of elegance, in the main, missed Ingleton. Things were rough and ready at Ingleton, things were done with no frills, only necessities were provided, everything that could be repaired and re-used was: this was not a throwaway society. The church had been re-built in 1745 but was still a barn-like, plain structure, and the Parker's replacement for Ingleton Hall can still be seen today.

Ingleton Church as restored in 1743. No elegance here.

Farming was being improved, plague had gone and housing was getting better. Roads were being improved and travel made easier as was the distribution of goods from the port of Lancaster such as wine, timber and flax. As we saw in the Stuart period peat was being cut and burned in Ingleton homes and the practice continued through the Georgian period, even though coal was being mined and was readily available for the cottage fire. The farmers cut their peat on Ingleborough for centuries and in that time unearthed prehistoric remains including bronze axe heads. The peat once stacked and dried was brought down by cart when necessary to be used on the farm and cottage fire. As coal became more plentiful that was preferred, as peat, though cheap, was labour intensive to produce.

During this period the population of England was growing and the population of Ingleton grew too. Many factors contributed to this, there was more food production due to better farming, the plague had disappeared, there was more employment in town and country, poor law improved the life of the poor and medical techniques were improving. The population of England in 1714 was estimated to be about five and a half millions. Although many towns in Yorkshire and Lancashire were growing, the majority of people in England lived in rural villages like Ingleton. The population of Ingleton was never static and individuals and families were moving in and out throughout the period.

One family that came into Ingleton at this time was the Greenwood family. Isaac Greenwood was the son of David Greenwood of Greenwood Leghe at Heptonstall in Calderdale.[1] He was baptised at Luddenden in 1699 and business brought him to Ingleton where he decided to settle. Isaac lived in a house on the Bank where he died in 1763 and was buried at Ingleton on March 27th and was registered as a 'householder' in other words a man of some substance.[2] He left cattle, horses and carts and he considered himself a yeoman. Just what he did we do not know, but he laid the foundations for his family to prosper. Within two years of his father's death David Greenwood, his only son, had re-built the house and named it Bank Hall and the date stone of 1765 tells us that the work was done by David and Jane Greenwood. You will see that the date stone says D and I G, but the I and J were still interchangeable at this time.

David began buying land and farms at Ingleton and soon the family became looked upon as the local squires. David Greenwood married Jane Hodgson, the daughter of Robert Hodgson, the Vicar of Thornton, at Thornton-in-Lonsdale church on May 12th 1765. The couple had many children, Esther, Robert Hodgson born 1768, Ann 1770, Isaac 1772, James born 1772, John, William 1776, Wrightson 1778 and Jenny. Esther and Jenny died young. Robert Hodgson Greenwood went to Hawkshead Grammar School where he was a school fellow of William Wordsworth. Robert became a scholar and Senior Fellow of Trinity College at Cambridge. He never married and returned to Ingleton each summer to relax in his native village. David Greenwood died in 1799 and his son James Greenwood and his wife lived at Bank Hall with their son Christopher Jackson Greenwood who became a surgeon. Robert Hodgson Greenwood died in 1839 and was buried at Ingleton.

The Greenwoods were slowly growing to rival the lord of the Manor who lived at Ingleton Hall. Henry Bouch inherited the manor and Ingleton Hall from his father Anthony who was buried in Ingleton Church on February 5th 1673. Henry himself died in 1714 and was succeeded by Edward Parker who had married Henry Bouch's daughter, Catherine. Edward was the son of Thomas Parker of Browsholme Hall in the Trough of Bowland and the family's Ingleton connections stretched back many centuries as an early ancestor had married a Redmayne from Thornton parish. A stained glass window with the name Ingleton still survives at Browsholme as a memento of these Ingleton connections. Edward and Catherine had a son Thomas who died in 1728. After Catherine's early death Edward married Jane the daughter of John Parker of Extwistle Hall near Burnley. Edward and Jane had three sons and a daughter. Edward Parker died in 1721 and the inheritance passed through his son John to his grandson, Edward Parker, who continued as Lord of the Manor of Ingleton.

Edward Parker had an estate book drawn up with maps and lists of all the Parker family holdings of farms and land.[3] The estate book contains one of the earliest maps of Ingleton. The map shows the site of three mills in Ingleton, the meal mill in Twistleton, Ingleton old corn mill and the fulling mill in the Bottoms. It also shows fields and roads. The fields will be discussed under local agriculture. The roads were narrow and dirty round Ingleton and there were plenty of them due to ancient connections with Burton and Bentham and the new coal roads made for convenience whenever necessary. The Ingleton and Thornton bridges were narrow and at an odd angle to each other. They were fit only for pack horses, carts and foot travel. However, in this Georgian period they were both widened to double width, one was widened on the left and the other on the right so that the road was straightened at the same time as being widened. If you walk under the bridges, which is not easy, and look at the arches you can still see the original arch, the new arch and the joining line in the middle.

The eighteenth century brought improvement of the roads: the Keighley to Kendal and Lancaster to Richmond roads were both turnpiked and both passed through Ingleton. With road improvements cart and coach traffic increased and more travellers passed through Ingleton. Some of these were the earliest tourists and included the Rev John Hutton and the poet Thomas Gray, who will be discussed later under Ingleton's literary connections.

CRAVEN MUSTER ROLL

The Craven Muster Roll was drawn up in 1803 as a result of the Napoleonic Wars between England and France that lasted until 1815.[6] It gives us the names and occupations of all men in Ingleton between the ages of seventeen and fifty-five. The men marked with an asterisk were volunteers.

Class 1.

James Balderstone*	Gentleman
Robert Kidd*	Farmer's son
Matthew Carter*	Weaver
Richard Farraday*	Yeoman's son
Edward Wilcock*	Servant
William Thornton*	Yeoman's son
John Hutchinson*	Servant
William Dent*	Joiner
Edmund Harrison*	-do-
John Hodgson*	Carpenter
Edmund Carr*	Butcher
Thomas Walker*	Yeoman's son
John Bowker*	Weaver
Christr. Oldfield*	Yeoman's son
Richard Lund*	Farmer's son
William Atkinson	Servant
Roger Cookson	Farmer's son
William Green	Slate River
Lawrence Lambert*	Servant
William Haresnape	Carpenter
Edmund Leeming	Collier
John Lund*	Slater
Abraham Tayler	Servant
Stephen Hammerton*	Labourer
Thomas Hammerton*	-do-
Christr. Jackson*	Weaver
James Metcalf*	Servant
Thomas Pounder	Collier
Edward Langstroth	Labourer
John Langstroth	Labourer
John Thistlethwaite*	Weaver
Robt. Thistlethwaite* Jnr.	-do-
Christr. Smith	Labourer
Benjn. Ellis*	Cotton Merchant
Willm. Greenwood*	Labourer

James Thompson*	Blacksmith
John Bond*	-do-
Bryan Dugdale	Blacksmith
William Carr	Shoemaker
James Bullock*	-do-
William Scott	
Samuel Ellis*	Servant
John Ellershaw Jr*	Innkeepers' son
John Scott*	Collier
Joseph Dawson*	-do-
Adam Brown	Blacksmith
Joseph Brown*	Butcher
Francis Cragg*	Servant
Jacob Pounder	Collier
Anthony Metcalf	Farmer's son
Marmaduke Shepherd*	Servant
George Shepherd*	-do-
Edmund Lund*	-do-
John Lund*	-do-
Thomas Bentham*	-do-
Miles Taylor*	-do-
John Metcalf*	Yeoman
Richard Procter*	Farmer's son
Cuthbert Kidd*	Yeoman's son
Christr. Lund*	Servant
Thomas Town*	Apprentice
John Temp*	Labourer
Robert Wilcock*	Apprentice
John Hebden*	Farmer's son
James Cragg	Servant

Class 2.

Richard Procter	Farmer
James Bayliff	Labourer
Ralph Green*	Servant
Nicholas Battersby	-do-
Adam Thompson	Weaver
William Herd	Shoemaker
William Fairbank	Farmer
Richard Taylor*	Badger
Anthony Clapham	Butcher
Stephen Carr*	Fidler
John Edmundson	Labourer
John Kidd*	-do-
John Foster	-do-
Marmaduke Clark*	Collier
John Foxcroft Morton*	Yeoman's son
Thomas Lindsay*	Tailor
John Parker*	Farmer's son
Marmaduke Thornton*	Farmer
William Procter*	Labourer
Robert Shepherd*	Farmer

Francis Moore*	Servant
George Metcalf	Farmer
Francis Whaley	Yeoman
Robert Moore	-do-
Francis Metcalfe*	Farmer

Class.3.

Robert Atkinson*	Collier
John Richardson*	Cotton Spinner
Richard Atkinson*	Collier
Richard Harrison*	Cotton Spinner
William Foster*	Labourer
William Rimington	Yeoman's son
Robt Richardson Atkinson*	Farmer
John Hodgson	Farmer's son
Leonard Hodgson*	Shopkeeper
Christr. Wise*	Labourer
Richard Yeadon*	Farmer
Robert Procter*	Steward
James Middlebruff*	Blacksmith
William Carr*	Farmer's son
John Robinson	Labourer
John Watling	-do-
John Richardson*	Collier
Edward Wildman*	Farmer
Daniel Birket	Servant
Lawrence Baynes	Labourer
William Jackson*	Servant
Richard Thornton*	Yeoman
Christr. Down*	Farmer
William Metcalf*	-do-
Thomas King*	-do-
Anthony Lister	-do-
John Metcalf	-do-
Joseph Bentham*	-do-
Ottuel Lodge	Innkeeper's son

Class.4.

Richard Balderston	Gentleman
James Richardson	Shopkeeper
John Hodgson	Yeoman
Stephen Carr	Farmer
Willm. Houghton*	Collier
John Walker	Yeoman
Joseph Grime	Farmer
Gamaliel Briscoe	-do-
John Smith	-do-
John Marsden	-do-
Robert Oldfield	Yeoman
Thomas Redmayne	Farmer
James Robinson	Auctioneer
Richard Armistead	

Joseph Slinger	Farmer
Benjamin Battersby	-do-
Septimus Wildman	-do-
John Robinson	Servant
Stephen Sidgswick	Weaver
George Johnson	Collier
John Herd*	Shoemaker
William Marriner	Shopkeeper
Christr. Wilson	Labourer
John Greenbank	-do-
John Haresnape*	Carpenter
Joseph Radcliffe	Collier
John Wilkinson	-do-
Thomas Guyers	Slater
David Leeming	Collier
George Yeadon	-do-
Simon Slinger	Weaver
James Hammerton	Cinder burner
John Simpson Howson*	Collier
Anthony Tomlinson*	-do-
Joseph Anthistlewaite*	-do-
Thomas Parrington*	-do-
William Bowker	-do-
George Atkinson*	Cotton Spinner
Francis Grime*	Collier
William Tomlinson	Limeburner
Edward Tomlinson*	Collier
William Baynes*	-do-
William Adamset	-do-
Thomas Atkinson	Labourer
Edward Peel	Collier
James Sewart*	-do-
Christr. Harrison*	-do-
Robt. Rimington	-do-
William Dixon*	Chairbottomer
Anthony Tempest	Collier
James Peel*	Cotton Spinner
Samuel Foster	Labourer
John Harrison	Cotton Spinner
Richard Speddy*	Weaver
John Ellis*	Joiner
Paul Berry*	Cotton Spinner
Richard Harrison*	Collier
William Winn*	Labourer
James Greenwood*	Carrier
Lodge Herd	Servant
William Fawcett	-do-
Joseph Yeadon*	Blacksmith
Richard Howson	Shopkeeper
Edmd. Foxcroft Lodge	Surgeon
John Metcalf	Butcher
Robert Stackhouse*	Blacksmith

John Nelson	Shoemaker
Thomas Walker	-do-
William Lister	Labourer
Thomas Douthwaite*	Innkeeper
William Wilcock*	Clocksmith
Robert Smith*	Collier
John Raws	Tailor
Christr. Hodgson	Breadbaker
James Wildman*	Collier
William Newton*	-do-
Robert Chapman	Joiner
Charles Kay	Schoolmaster
Edward Moore*	Collier
Thomas Lambert	Waggon driver
Nathaniel Fawcett	Servant
William Langstroth	Labourer
John Whaley Willan*	Farmer
James Parker	-do-
Robert Metcalf*	Yeoman
Thomas Borrowdale*	Servant
Christr. Lund	Innkeeper
Thomas Atkinson	Shoemaker
John Bentham	Farmer
Miles Atkinson	Labourer
Revd. Henry Ellershaw	Clergyman
William Whaley	Yeoman's son
Thomas Armistead*	Farmer
Richard Metcalf	Farmer
William Lister	Innkeeper
John Sanderson	Farmer
William Bentham	Labourer
Richard Renison	Servant
Thomas Moore*	Shoemaker
John Parker	Farmer
John Moore	-do-
George Willis	Blacksmith
William Wildman	Schoolmaster
Richard Metcalf*	Farmer
Richard Wilcock	-do-
Richard Wildman*	Yeoman
John Taylor*	Farmer
Christr. Wildman*	-do-
John Lambert	-do-
James Lund	-do-

Totals	1st Class	65
	2nd Class	25
	3rd Class	29
	4th Class	110

Total of all Classes   229

This Muster Roll shows us that there were 229 men of military age in the Ingleton population of 1,101 leaving around 880 women, children and old men. The men in class one were under thirty with no children under ten; class two were unmarried men between thirty and fifty; class three were married men between seventeen and thirty with not more than two children under ten; and class four included all the other men up to the age of fifty-five. It is interesting to note the high number of volunteers. Out of sixty-five men in class one forty-eight were volunteers.

The roll shows that there were four innkeepers who kept four inns. Thomas Douthwaite kept the Bay Horse, John Ellershaw, senior, kept the Black Bull, and the other two William Lister and Christopher Lund must have kept the Wheat Sheaf and the Three Horse Shoes. The Ingleboro' Hotel had not been built, the Craven Heifer, Oddfellows Arms and Masons Arms were not yet open. We can see the differentiation between yeoman and farmer. Farmer can be equated with husbandman, but yeoman suggests an influential farmer owning rather than renting his farm and being a man of means and standing in the community.

Only two men in the roll are deemed worthy of being called gentlemen. There is one surgeon, two schoolmasters and one clockmaker. The one mentioned clergyman was not the minister at Ingleton, for that position was held by John Waller who is not listed as he was over sixty-five years of age. The slate quarries were working in the falls at Ingleton as witness William Green a slate river and two other slaters. The butcher, the baker but not the candlestickmaker are also there. The main groups of men fall into four categories: farmers, labourers, colliers and servants. The farmers and yeoman we would expect in a rural area; the colliers we expect because we know Ingleton had a considerable coalfield and labourers are always needed. The fourth large group is that of servants. At this time not only the wealthy had servants. People with a modest income could keep one servant to undertake all the general housework. Many of the servants were sons and daughters of neighbours' families. Many single women and widows were glad of food and board and little else in exchange for their domestic labour.

There is a cotton merchant and the workers he employed, six spinners and nine weavers. There are eight blacksmiths showing that with the colliery and growing traffic Ingleton needed extra blacksmiths. Four shopkeepers tend to show that there were few shops in Ingleton. The eight shoemakers would be more than needed for making the villagers' shoes and they would be employed, especially in winter, on the farms of Ingleton Fells, making shoes for town merchants. One man, Richard Taylor, was a badger which was a term used for travelling pedlars and chapmen.

RIDING THE BOUNDARIES

Before the days of maps, boundaries were passed down in manor rolls, by word of mouth, and by 'beating the bounds'. This walking or riding the boundary of the parish or manor was an essential part of parish and manor court business. Everyone was then clear of the parish and manor boundaries, especially the parish officers. After Ordnance Survey maps came in, the custom became entirely unnecessary as boundaries were then fixed on maps for all to see. However, some villages still carry out the ancient ritual to this day. Ingleton's manor boundaries were written in the court rolls in 1592 and are recorded in the Tudor chapter.

The following is an account of a riding of the boundaries of the Manor of Ingleton by the Lord of the Manor, Edward Parker, and a group of local men in September 1754 as recorded in Ingleton Manor Court records.[7]

The Boundaries of the Manor of Ingleton in the West riding of the County of York rid on Friday the twentieth day of September one thousand seven hundred fifty and four pursuant to notices before published in the several Parish Churches within and next adjoining to the said Manor by Edward Parker Esq Lord thereof accompanied by the several persons whose names hereto subscribed.

Beginning where Thornton River called Doe runs into and meets Ingleton River called Greet and down said river until Parks on an old Watercourse there to the river again and down said river and then westward by Grayholme (Guyholme?) to Greeta Gill and up said Greeta Gill to Sharps House and through part of it and on Past by John Howson's of Gill on the East side of Rawsons Close to the river Wenning and so up the said River to Mill Air and on the south side of the Fence said Mill Air to the River again and up the same to Eska Beck and Eska Lane by the backside of Eska House to the Boundary stone on Beckwith down Beckwith Sike to the River Wenning and up said river to Mere Gill and up same to the Common called Bentham Moor to the Graystone on Whitestone Green and the East side of Sharp ? How to the road leading between Bentham and Settle and on the same to Sandy Fore (Yore) by the Double Dike to Goat Gap and on the East side thereof up a Rivulet running cross to the Highway to Blindfield Well and so on Bleakebank by the Fence on the West side thereof to the Common and so straight up to a hurdle of Stones on the Grey Scarrs and to the Road Dubs and from thence upwards to a hurdle of Stones upon Green Plate so to Guy Sike head and to the Hurdle of Stones on Little Ingleborough and on the East side of Limestone Lode and Cross Ingleborough down Fair Weather Sike to Meir Gill down same to Bold Haw and up the river Wease to the Chapel and Weather Coat clough and by Gill Head to the Stone in the Mere up a Clough in Ellerbeck Ground and by a Gill to the top of Wherrnside then to the Hole in the ? in the Fell End so to Brocklosback (Brockaslack) in a direct line to the Standing Stone through Green Barn to Ravenray and then down the River Doe where it runs into and meets the Ingleton River where began.

Edwd Foxcroft	Robert Smith	Leonard Herd
Will Guy	John x Foxcroft	Joseph Shaw
Robt Hodgson	Thos Topham	Robert Richardson
Chas Waller	John Craven	John Jackson
Richard Balderston	Will Craven	Edwd Oddie
John Oddie	Wm Carus Steward of the Court	Richard Baynes
W^m x Bryans	Robert Smith	Miles Dixon
Richard Brennand	James Lund	

THE INGLETON SETTLE CANAL

The Georgian era was a great canal building period. Following Brindley's construction of the Bridgewater Canal, begun in 1759, canals became popular throughout the country and the following fifty years saw numerous canals planned and built. It was in this period that a canal was planned in the Ingleton area to serve the collieries, flag quarries, slate quarries and lime industry which both Ingleton and Burton had at this time. In 1780 R. Dickenson surveyed a canal to go from Parkfoot Bridge at Ingleton through Ingleton and Clapham to Settle.

Brindley reasoned that a contour canal, winding as it did, would serve more places and bring more trade. The trouble with the planned Ingleton canal was that it did not go far enough for taking lime to Settle was like taking coal to Newcastle. Ingleton colliery's main markets were in the villages and towns and villages up to Kendal. It doesn't appear to have been a viable commercial enterprise, however whether it was or not it didn't get the necessary

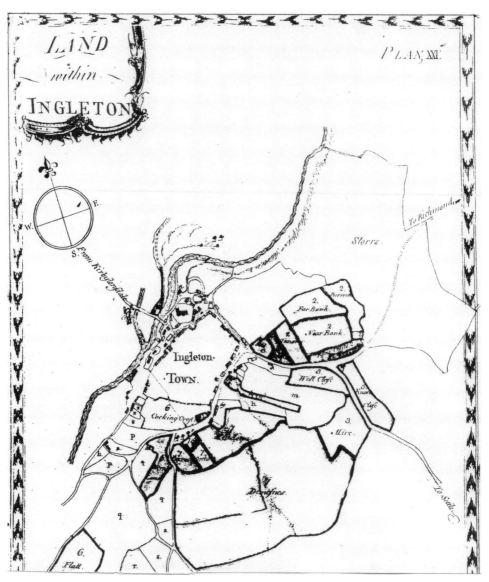

Section of map from the Estate Book of Edward Parker 1765.

financial and other backing. However, the owners of Ingleton Colliery would certainly have
been interested in the scheme.

The plan shows the length, rise and fall, and position of locks on the waterway. Ten locks
were needed to bring the canal towards Ingleton before it turned towards Clapham. A further
fifteen locks were needed to raise the canal out of Ingleton up to Whinneymire, but from then
on the contours favoured the canal to Clapham and beyond.[8] A branch canal was planned to
take the waterway into a canal basin on the Bank at Ingleton not far from the Church. Had the
canal been built, Ingleton may well have had a marina to add to its tourist attractions today.
A second canal was planned to connect the Ingleton canal with the River Lune at Lancaster
and receipts for a guinea towards the survey survives at Lancaster Library signed by Sam
Simpson. It was also planned that from Settle a canal should be constructed to link up with

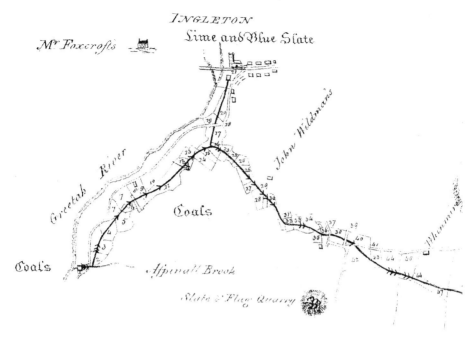

Plan of a proposed canal from Parkfoot Ingleton to Settle 1780.

the Leeds & Liverpool Canal at Foulridge, near Colne in Lancashire. Without sound financial backing, and for better or for worse, none of these projected canals were ever built. Until the arrival of the railway, Ingleton coal, slate and lime continued to be delivered by the traditional horse and cart.

REFERENCES

1. *Lancaster Guardian* January 13th 1894. We know from a speech made by William Norman Greenwood at his 21st birthday celebration that Greenwood Leghe at Ingleton had been named after Greenwood Leghe at Heptonstall in the ancient Parish of Halifax and that Isaac Greenwood was the first member of the family to settle in Ingleton.
2. LRO Lonsdale Wills, Isaac Greenwood 1763.
3. LRO, DDB 84/1 1763.
4. Ingleton Parish Council, The first Township Book, Vol 1, 1721 – 1845. (NYRO)
5. *Lancaster Guardian* June 1st 1895.
6. *The Craven Muster Roll*, 1803, North Yorkshire County Council 1976.
7. NYRO, Ingleton Manor Court Rolls 1692-1801 ZUC 3/1, MIC 1181.
8. YAS. MS1186. Plan of proposed canal from Parkfoot to Settle 1780.

VICTORIAN INGLETON

The Victorian period saw great developments in Ingleton. The population was growing and the people were better educated. People in Ingleton gained more information about the outside world through the press and many became eager to progress socially, economically, religiously, and politically. They began to question all that their fathers and grandfathers had accepted. Many rebelled against the church and became nonconformists. Some rebelled against Church rates levied on them whether they attended church or not. They questioned the power of the church minister, whether he was also a Justice of the Peace or not, but if he was a JP, then he was even more suspect.

THE PRESS

This Victorian advert for the *Lancaster Guardian* reveals a great deal. It is interesting to note that the paper was established in the very first year of Victoria's reign. The advertisement goes on to stress that it intends 'to keep its readers well informed on the political, general, and literary news of the week.' This the people of Ingleton had not had before and what is more they had their own village correspondent to put their own news in the press. This was an information revolution. There had been a few Yorkshire newspapers such as the *Leeds Mercury* which had been published from the eighteenth century, but their reporting of Ingleton news was negligible.

THE LANCASTER GUARDIAN
ESTABLISHED 1837.   PRICE 1d.

The *Guardian* is distinguished by the accuracy and fulness of its LOCAL REPORTS, by its complete record of DISTRICT INTELLIGENCE, and it seeks to keep its readers well informed on the POLITICAL, GENERAL, and LITERARY NEWS OF THE WEEK.

TO ADVERTISERS.—Having been established over 40 years, the *Guardian* has gained a very eminent position as a Family Newspaper and an influential medium for Advertisements Its circulation has now so largely increased in all directions, and amongst all classes, that it has been recognised as THE BEST ADVERTISER in North Lancashire, the adjoining districts of Westmorland and the West Riding of Yorkshire, and particularly in Lunesdale, Craven and Ribblesdale.

The *Guardian* is issued at an earlier hour on Friday, in order to permit its despatch by the afternoon trains, but subsequent editions will be issued when required by the arrival of Later News and Local Reports.

Guardian Office, Church Street, Lancaster.

The *Lancaster Guardian* was Liberal and Nonconformist, but there was also the *Lancaster Gazette,* which was Tory and Church of England. Both these papers gave considerable news from a wide variety of villages in their area, including Ingleton. Ingleton news also featured in the *Craven Herald* which was based at Skipton. Few things are thrown away as soon as newspapers, but luckily the publishers usually kept back copies for reference and these were eventually bound. Today they have been microfilmed and are available for us to research. Initially newspapers were heavily taxed, but in 1855 the stamp duty was repealed and this helped the sale of newspapers in the latter part of the nineteenth century. The second half of Victoria's reign saw a great burst of provincial newspapers though many did not survive for long. The *Lancaster Observer, Lancaster Standard, Lancaster Times* and *Lancaster Herald* were all published for a time in the Victorian period.

The Lancaster press gave a wide variety of national and local news and has been invaluable for the writing of this history. To increase sales they were always ready to report on murders, suicides and general disasters, but they also reported on the mundane events of village life. Feature articles are a great source of information with reports on the opening of a railway station, the events of a village fair and the visit to the local colliery. The press gave the people at the time a great amount of information and stimulation and they have left for us a window through which we can look back in time.

Local press correspondents used the press not only to report village news, but to press for change and report their complaints and the complaints of others. In Ingleton they pressed for reading room facilities, fairer distribution of charities, better housing, improvement of roads, the ending of Church Rates, reform in local government and hundreds of other things. Most of these subjects will be recorded in the later pages of this volume.

PHOTOGRAPHY

Photography developed in the nineteenth century and it became an important part of Ingleton life. Photographers came here to work because of the tourist industry and sold their photographs and albums in the village. Mostly they were photographs of the walks and falls, but many village events were photographed. Sadly the majority of these early photographs were lost. The photographers sometimes moved away or retired to the coast and took their boxes of glass photographic slides with them, usually never to be seen again. We know from press reports that photos were taken of the Bay Horse Inn before it was demolished and we know that in 1871 a large bull was photographed outside the Wheat Sheaf before walking to Ribblehead where it was to supply Christmas dinner for the navvies who were building the Settle Carlisle Railway, but neither photograph has survived.

The entrance to Ingleton from Thornton in 1900.

EMIGRATION

In the 'hungry forties' when small farmers were at a low ebb many were driven to look to the colonies for a way out of their problems and hopefully a way to gain a better life. At that time it was certainly a great leap to consider going off to Australia, New Zealand or America. In May 1846 two families from Chapel-le-Dale having raised enough cash for their journey set off for 'the wilds of North America.' The note in the press recording this, added, 'We understand that others from the village are preparing to follow their example.' In March 1849 several Ingleton folk were preparing to leave Ingleton for the United States of America.

Sadly no one recorded their names, but just gave a short notice in the press under the heading 'Adieu my native land adieu.'

In 1878 two Ingleton miners, George Gillbanks and William Bell, heard about New Zealand being a fruitful land and just the place for able bodied working men to make their fortunes.[1] They decided to pack up and go to this land of promise and plenty and sailed on June 26th on the 'Waitangi' for Lyttleton where they arrived on September 25th. There were twenty-five saloon, twenty-four second cabin and 183 third class cabin passengers on board the ship and there was no sickness worth mentioning during the eighty-nine days sail. The young men from Ingleton did not find things as they expected and in writing home to Ingleton they warned others not to follow at the moment. The following is a portion of the letter George Gillbanks sent home:-

Dear father, brothers and Sisters, We landed all safely and well at Port Lyttleton on the 25th of September. We had some very bad weather, and there was a great deal of seasickness. I was not sick, nor any of the children on board the ship. The children came off best. On board we lived mainly off salt beef and pork. When we landed a daily paper was given to each passenger, and on the next day a similar gift was repeated. The people were very kind to us. The government gave us a pass to go 55 miles up country to a railway. I cannot tell you what wages we shall get, as I do not know whether it will be piece or day work. Trade is very bad here and work hard to get. We are living in tents and all the country is covered in snow. The Wicha pass surpasses the Settle and Carlisle line, and it is a dreadful cold place. Tell Dick this is the place for a gun, as wild pigs, ducks, and geese are very plentiful. I have not seen a rabbit yet, but there are lots of wild pigs near our tent. Some of our party shot one and killed another within 100 yards of our tent. They weighed 300 pounds each. There are hundreds of wild ducks, and they are so very tame that they will sit until we get close to them. Today, Sunday, is a very rough day. On Monday the 6th of October I went out with some of our passengers with guns and they shot wild boar. Six shots were fired and they all took effect. I saw it skinned and the skin was about an inch thick. We saw fifteen wild pigs altogether and the one that was shot weighed about nine score pounds. The flesh of these wild pigs is very good. When alive they are very dangerous animals to deal with. Sheep are from 3s to 5s each. We have a quarter of one in the tent, which weighs 22lbs. Mutton is from 2° to 3d; candles cost 10d; onions 4d; bread 2d; salt 3d; butter 1s 8d; and tobacco 5s per pound. I have seen no beef. Please give my compliments to Mr W...... and J..... and tell them they had better wait until I hear more about work. I asked the foreman what wages we should get, but he did not know. Trade is very bad and it is rumoured that the natives are about to rise. I will tell you more in my next letter.

With love to all and all enquiring friends, from your affectionate son, Joseph George Gillbanks.

George Gillbanks probably did write a further letter or two and then contact ceased. In the years that followed the families of George Gillbanks and William Bell had no address to contact the young men and did not know whether they were alive or dead. George's mother and father died as did many of William Bell's family. Advertisements were put in New Zealand and English newspapers and eventually, after eleven years, contact was made. In April 1894 Mrs Matthewman, George Gillbanks' sister, received a letter from William Bell. The following was the story he told:-[2]

Today, February, 1894, a young man told me that he had seen in a newspaper George Gillbanks and William Bell advertised. He thought it was the *Liverpool Mercury.* He was living about twenty miles from my place and it was well he knew me and my friend Gillbanks. Though he was a careless fellow , who said he had either lost the paper or torn it up, and I could not be sure whether he was telling the truth or not, still I decided to write that night to Gillbanks' father, or some of his relations. Gillbanks lives 70 or 80 miles from where I live. I cannot explain much of our ups and downs in New Zealand, and Gillbanks will be better able to tell you this. I can tell you a few things you wish to know. George is in good health and strength, and I am proud to say about seven or eight years ago he settled down on a bit of land about 49 acres so that he is able to make a living without working for other people. The beginning of farming was rather a tough job, as I do not think he had five shillings to start with. It is bush land, and a man can not get it cleared quickly for cropping without he has a few pounds to begin with, but anything is better than working for masters, or bosses, as they are called, even if we can only get a spuds or potatoes, milk, oatmeal and fish. Well I am pleased to say that for seven or eight years George has been a staunch blue ribbon man, or Good Templar. New Zealand has a beautiful climate, and it is very favourable for health and strength, and for a productive soil. As to myself, in temper and strength I am all right, but as to my finances, I am not worth five shillings, only that I have got 133 acres of good bush land at the same place as that of Gillbanks. I have done nothing to it yet as I wish to get a few pounds to start with.

William Bell went on to say that he had worked in the gold mines and invested money in them which was lost as he had been unlucky. He only wished he had invested it in land earlier. He had bought a little house and stocked it with everything only to have it burned down with the loss of all his goods and even the things he had brought from Ingleton. He said that they had decided that it was better not to write home than to send bad news, and they had nothing but bad news to send. They were both still bachelors. He said that although George Gillbanks only lived about seventy miles away it took a letter about a month to reach him and another month to get a reply. He concluded:-

If any of my friends are grieved that I have kept them so long in suspense as to whether I was living or not they must forgive a poor penitent sinner. I would very much like to know whether my uncle Edward Tomlinson is living as I should like a few lines from him. I should like to know whether my mother is alive or dead, and my cousin Anthony Singleton and his father and mother. I should like to hear from any of my relatives and friends, and if they write I will not fail to reply in return. Address William Bell, care of H. Lowe, Walmangaros, near Westport, West Coast, New Zealand.

This rather sad story is made all the worse by the fact that George Gillbanks' family would have been quite willing and able to help him improve his land. Some of Ingleton's emigrants were lucky and made a good living in the United States and returned to Ingleton for a visit. Others like George Gillbanks and William Bell struggled and success did not come until later generations. As to the majority we have no idea what happened to them, but there is no doubt that their descendants are now spread across the globe.

MEDICAL
In Victorian times Ingleton was lucky to have a series of well-trained and active doctors. They were certainly needed, as having a colliery and other industries, accidents were a regular

feature of village life. In the early days victims of accidents were put in a cart and taken to their home to recover or die. They were not taken to hospital and their life was in the hands of the local doctor who also was usually a surgeon. It was only in later Victorian period after the coming of the railway that victims could be taken to hospital in Leeds or Lancaster.

A measles epidemic spread through Ingleton in 1845 and hardly a family was not affected. In two cases the infection proved fatal. There were other epidemics through the period from scarlet fever to typhus fever. Typhus fever made its appearance in Ingleton in 1847, but although affecting many people they all recovered. Smallpox, the most feared infection, reared its ugly head from time to time. In 1871 during the building of the Settle Carlisle Railway it became prevalent especially in some of the huts at Sebastopol and Jericho on Blea Moor. In one hut at Sebastopol a mother and three children died. An isolation hospital was made at Batty Green to keep the epidemic under control. People in Ingleton became afraid of contact with anyone from the railway works.

This terrible infection was conveyed to healthy areas by thoughtless persons anxious to get to their home or to friends when they felt ill. A case of this kind occurred at Ingleton in July 1871. A young man who had been working at Barrow returned to his family at Ingleton when he was suffering from smallpox. Luckily the news spread fast and Mr Exton, the superintendent of police, immediately took action to have him removed to the smallpox hospital at Batty Green which had been constructed for the railway workers and their families who succumbed to the disease. The Rev. Richard Denny, as a JP, signed the removal order and the same day the man's clothes, bed and bedding were all burned and the house disinfected. This prompt action stopped the spread of the disease.[3]

In spite of fevers and disease Ingleton was considered a healthy village and locality. In 1860 Ingleton claimed to be one of the healthiest of villages in the country. This was said to be due to the mountain air and the good supply of excellent water. The land was also generally dry and the lie of the land was good for drainage. In that year with a population of 1,300 inhabitants there had been no deaths between August and December.[4]

Joseph Carr, when correspondent of the *Lancaster Guardian,* was always keen to emphasise this healthy claim, probably as part of his plan to attract tourists to Ingleton. In his *'Recollections of Ingleton'* one article was entitled, 'How the Lancaster Guardian was the first to make known the salubrious climate of Ingleton'. In the article he told countless stories of men, women and children coming to Ingleton in a poor state of health who fully recovered their health after a short stay. They usually ended up climbing Ingleborough and that to him was the test of recovered health. All these stories can be read in his memoirs.

INGLETON'S DOCTORS

Dr *John Sellers* was doctor cum surgeon at Ingleton well before Queen Victoria came to the throne. Dr Sellers was born at Hornby about the year 1790. He had been a ship's surgeon on a man-of-war and as such had travelled the world. He had settled at Ingleton with his wife Ann and lived in the main street. He was known for his eccentric behaviour. He would only attend certain families and some people who were quite wealthy he would not go near, however urgently they asked for his services. For most he would give the promptest attention and do everything he professionally could for their welfare. Almost every evening he would slowly make his way to an inn at the centre of the village and there, in the front room, he might be seen smoking a long white clay pipe and enjoying a glass of gin. In old age he had a round rosy face and rotund figure.[5] Dr Sellers died in September 1861 aged seventy-one.

One Doctor who served his time with Dr Sellers was Dr Burrow who went to practice in Upper Bentham about 1821. Other surgeons also operated in Ingleton when the local doctor was unavailable. Sometimes they came from Bentham and sometimes people were attended by the railway surgeon. Dr Sellers dealt with many colliery accidents and with the typhus fever epidemic which broke out in December 1847. In March 1849 when some boys were playing near machinery at Ingleton Mill, one boy, Thomas Barnes, was caught in the machinery and received a dreadful wound. Fortunately he was quickly rescued and Dr Sellers attended him to dress the wound. In April 1849 John Annan, a labourer on the North Western Railway, was seriously injured when two railway wagons broke loose at Ingleton and ran over his legs. His leg was amputated on a table in the Mason's Arms by the railway surgeon Mr Ellertson.

Dr Frederick Griffiths, who was born in Huntingdon, came to Ingleton in 1858 to practice as a doctor. Before that he had been the assistant railway doctor based in Sedbergh, but having taken a liking to the Ingleton area he came to Ingleton to practice, on the death of Dr Sellers. For many years he was also the parish doctor for the Bentham district of the Settle Union. The Settle Union was a public authority representing around thirty villages set up to support the poor under the Poor Law Amendment Act of 1834. Dr Sellers was a churchman and Liberal and was connected with the gas company until the streets were lit with electricity. At one time he was a governor of the National School at Ingleton. In his later years he lived in the Square at Ingleton.

In July 1900 Dr Griffiths attended court in London as a witness for the Greenwood family in their case against James Barker. While in court he was seized with paralysis and had to be brought back to Ingleton, the strain of the court case had been too much for him. He died on November 25th after a few months illness at the age of sixty-three. He was known for his untiring medical work and his generosity in providing free advice and medicine to the poor. Many said that it was difficult to get a bill from him for medical treatment.[6]

He was buried in Ingleton cemetery where his grave tells us that he was surgeon at Ingleton for forty-two years. 'The Late Dr Griffiths-An Appreciation' was written in the press:-

> By the time these lines are published the grave will have closed upon all that is mortal of one of the oldest and best loved inhabitants of Ingleton… With untiring constancy for many years he might be seen riding at all hours, and in every weather, through our wildest dales and over our roughest country to visit his far scattered patients, bringing comfort and sympathy to all. Of late years with unabated devotion and energy he was to be met in his gig, driving up and down in all directions, still bent on some errand of help or mercy; not only giving freely of his time and skill to the very poorest, but carrying with him material help, nourishing food, or some dainty to tempt the appetite of some humble sufferer. Many a time he would also suggest to his friends in the neighbourhood of his poorer patients how best by timely help they might be the means of saving some valuable life, of restoring strength to a poor man on whom a family depended, or some poor mother and her little children. No one will know all the deeds of kindness and goodness done by him.

Another Doctor who practised in Ingleton in the late Victorian period was Dr Grime, but all that is know of him is that, according to Joseph Carr, he had a weak chest and benefited from Ingleton's climate. Dr William Metcalfe also practised at Ingleton for several years. He had a surgery at Field House where he lived. He died at Field House in April 1895. He was certainly nowhere near as well known, or as popular, as his contemporary Dr Frederick Griffiths. Dr Griffiths was followed by Dr Mackenzie who came to live at Broadwood in Thornton Parish right at the end of the Victorian period.

Doctor Frederick Griffiths

LORDS OF THE MANOR

The Lord of the Manor was still of some standing and importance. In 1810 the Hornby family of Kirkham bought Ingleton Manor from the Parker family of Browsholme, most probably from Thomas Lister Parker who sold the advowson of Bentham Church to James Farrar of Clapham in the same year. The Hornbys were flax manufacturers in Bentham and were not closely connected to Ingleton. They moved the flax and tow trade from Kirkham to Bentham and Hornby and Co was a thriving business. Hornby Roughsedge, a relative of the Hornby family, bought High Mill in Bentham in 1814. He later became a joint Lord of the Manor of Ingleton. In 1844 the Lords of the Manor of Ingleton were Hornby Roughsedge, Hugh Hornby and Joseph Hornby and they held their Court Baron and Customary Court at the Wheat Sheaf.

Hornby Roughsedge was the son of the Vicar of Liverpool and came to Bentham as the successor of Charles Parker. He was of an aristocratic family and bearing and showed little friendly disposition towards working people. He drove a carriage and pair, kept a coachman, footman and other servants and stayed aloof from those he considered below him. Hornby Roughsedge was the main promoter and builder of the hospice on Ingleborough and his attitude may well have been the reason that his hospice was destroyed, for Ingleton miners would have had little respect for him or his hospice. Most people in Ingleton had no contact with the Lords of the Manor who were irrelevant to them. It was only at times when the leading men of the village wished to have a site for a public service building such as a reading room that they had to deal with the Lords. Usually they got little help as in the case of the reading room

Manor Courts still continued to be held throughout the Victorian period. The Customary Court was held at the Wheat Sheaf where the business of fines and dues were dealt with before a jury. Following this there was always an excellent dinner provided for the tenants and specially invited guests. It became an event of the season. In December 1884 the guests at the manorial dinner were General Bracken, Richard Brown, and Dr Griffiths. Toasts were proposed and drunk to the success of business in Ingleton. By 1888 the Lords of the Manor of Ingleton were Thomas Dyson Hornby, Charles Edward Hornby and Hugh Frederick Hornby. In 1889 the Manor Court and dinner was held at the Ingleboro' Hotel. Nine deeds were presented to the court, passed and entered onto the court rolls.

In August 1884 Ingleton Manor Court was held in the Ingleboro' Hotel before the deputy steward Mr H. Vant. The jurors included T.T. Quinlan, J. King, W. Dixon, E. Danson, J.R.T. Parker, T. Cookson, T. Moore, R. Ormrod, T. Redhead, J. Thistlethwaite and R.W. Cragg, all well-known Ingleton men. In the records of the Court the jurors say, 'We find and present a deed and conveyance dated 20 June 1884, and enrolled at this court for the Right Honourable Thomas Taylour, MP, (commonly called Lord Bective), to John Morphet, of Chapel-le-Dale, Ingleton Fells, in the West Riding of the County of York farmer'. The deed transferred parts of The Scales Estate. The court also registered the death of William Willis, late customary tenant of the manor, and transferred his property at Goat Gap to his wife. The Rev. J. Turner, vicar of Ingleton, the Rev. Samuel Hartley, vicar of Sawrey, and General Bracken dined with the deputy steward Mr Vant.

In August 1900 the Customary Court of Henry Hugh Hornby, Rev. Charles Edward Hornby, Richard Cortazzi Hornby, and Mrs Matilda Theresa Madden, lords and lady of the Manor of Ingleton was held at the Ingleboro' Hotel. The business of the court was lengthy due to the death of Hugh Frederick Hornby, one of the lords of the manor. The Hornby family were settled in Liverpool and involved in trade with the east and would rarely visit Ingleton leaving everything in the hands of their steward.

The end of the manor courts came by Act of Parliament in 1922 when the Law of Property Act extinguished all manorial rents. At this time those paying manorial rents had to pay a final rent equal to several years payment. The descendants of the Hornby family held the manor until May 1989. The title of Lord of the Manor of Ingleton went to an American who bought the lordship as a status symbol, but wished to remain anonymous.

TWISTLETON MANOR

The Lord of the Manor of Twistleton and Ellerbeck continued to hold his manor court in Twistleton, usually at a house near the mill, and then adjourn to the Ingleboro' Hotel or one of the other inns in Ingleton for a sumptuous dinner. On one occasion the court was held in the mill itself. The lordship of Twistleton extended over Scales Moor and included much of Ingleton Fells or Chapel-le-Dale. In June 1873 the court opened at John Lord's house near the mill and J.R. Picard, solicitor of Kirkby Lonsdale and new steward of the manor, then adjourned the meeting to the Ingleboro' Hotel. Twistleton Manor had just come into the hands of John Seddon of Westhoughton, Bolton, Lancashire.

The court book only dates back to 1772 and the first court recorded was in 1772 when Walter Fletcher was Lord of the Manor and James Robinson was steward. The next court baron was 1777 and the third recorded was 1790. At this court the lordship was passed into the hands of the Rev. John Hutton and John Oddie who became joint lords. John Oddie was the son of Christopher Oddie and the family came from Cold Weather House near Gisburn. Christopher Oddie died in 1785 aged 86 and is buried near the tower on the south side of Ingleton Church.[7]

John Oddie, always spoken of as Lord Oddie, died in 1822 aged 87. Lord Oddie was rather eccentric and had a high opinion of his dignity and influence. 'I am all your masters at Ingleton' he used to say and the people humoured him. When men met him fishing in the river Doe he would ask, 'What do they say about me at Ingleton?' and the reply was sure to be, 'Oh they say you are all their masters.' This pleased him so much that he would invite them back to Twistleton Manor House for bread, cheese and ale. Lord Oddie's favourite at Ingleton was the wife of Dr Lodge. He called her 'Chitter Lily' and always enquired about her.

In 1800 the Rev. John Hutton retired as one of the lords of the manor and from that time the lordship was jointly held by John Oddie and Agnes Hutton, spinster. By 1814 Agnes had married and her husband, Captain John Johnson, became a joint lord. In 1822 on John Oddie's death, his nephew the Rev. William Oddie took his place and by 1826 was sole lord of the manor. In 1851 William Oddie died and his trustees took over until 1853 when Harriet Ann Leslie became lady of the manor. Barrington Price became the next lord and in the summer of 1872 the Manor House estate and the lordship of the manor were offered for sale at the Ingleboro' Hotel. It became obvious that the title was more attractive than the rents of the estate and the two main bidders were Lord Bective and John Seddon. John Seddon was the highest bidder and became lord of the manor.

John Seddon continued the traditional court meetings, where transfers of land were made and other manorial business done, followed by sumptuous dinners at Ingleton. He also continued the tradition of inviting local dignitaries to speak on these occasions. In 1873 Mr R. Chapman, Mr Towler, Mr Bentham, Mr R. Brown and Brian Waller of Masongill and Edinburgh University were among the guests. The chairman's toast was 'Success to the inhabitants and trade of Ingleton.' In 1876 W. Remmington died having been a juror at the Twistleton Manor Court for thirty-five years. John Seddon was eighty-two years old and continued as lord of the manor until his death in 1884. His widow, Mrs Seddon, took over at the June court in 1885 and the dinner following was held at the Three Horse Shoes.

In June 1890 when the manor court was held there was no business to present and it was simply a matter of the tenants, jury, and invited guests making their way to the Ingleboro' Hotel for the annual dinner. This is a good example of how manor courts had fallen from being all important courts to simply an excuse for a yearly feast and celebration. These annual court meetings and dinners continued into the twentieth century.

THE GREENWOODS OF GREENWOOD LEGHE

As the influence of the Lords of Ingleton Manor decreased, and as they rarely showed themselves in Ingleton, so the power and influence of the Greenwood family of Bank Hall and Greenwood Leghe grew. As the lords of the manors of Ingleton and Twistleton had become mere figureheads the power and influence of the Greenwood family had been established on the growth of the land and property they owned. By the mid-Victorian period they were the local squires. David Greenwood had died in 1799 and his son James had lived at Bank Hall for several years. James married Ellen Jackson and their son, Christopher Jackson, became a surgeon in Lancaster. Then David's younger son, William Greenwood, inherited Bank Hall. Late in life, at the age of sixty-nine, William married Elizabeth Hollies and when she came to Bank Hall, her brother Moses, and sister Dorothy, came to work as servants. The couple had three children, Ada, William Norman and Janet. William died in August 1857, aged eighty, leaving Elizabeth a wealthy widow.

On Friday October 14th 1870 William Norman Greenwood came of age. It was a day of great rejoicing in Ingleton for the young man's 21st birthday. The press quoted 'rejoicing on so extensive a scale on such an occasion is a rare thing in a village like Ingleton and it is likely that centuries have passed away since similar jubilant manifestations occurred in the neighbourhood.' There were processions, school children's parties, a party for the elderly and the Greenwood's tenants were invited to a dinner at the Three Horse Shoes. The Ingleton Brass Band came to play at his door at midnight and the church bells of St Mary's rang all day from four thirty in the morning. Flags were flown on the church tower and the National

School. Later in Jan 1873 when William Greenwood gave a treat to the Ingleton bell-ringers, his work people and a few friends it was reported that 'the health of the young squire was drunk.'

William Norman Greenwood married Isabella Balderstone, daughter of R.R. Balderstone, son of the Rev. Robert R. Balderstone late of Ingleton. Isabella was born in Port Natal near Durban in South Africa. The couple had four children: William, Harold, Percy and Oscar. They built a new and large mansion in 1874 on the site of Rigghill House, on the Clapham road, calling it Greenwood Leghe after their ancestral home near Heptonstall. Then on November 11th 1876 the *Lancaster Guardian* announced 'Sudden death of W.N. Greenwood. On Tuesday about 10pm Mr. William Norman Greenwood, of Greenwood Leghe died very suddenly, in the 28th year of his age. He was the eldest child and only son of the late William Greenwood, and nephew of Dr Greenwood of Lancaster. His sudden death has caused much excitement in the neighbourhood, and it has been the general topic of the inhabitants.' He was buried in Ingleton churchyard on Saturday November 11th.

Greenwood Leghe the home of the Greenwood family.

A few years later Isabella Greenwood married Alfred S. Kirk and they had one son Gerald. Gerald Kirk was a well-liked and talented young man who was killed in World War I. The Greenwood sons grew up at Greenwood Leghe and were well educated. The eldest son William Norman came of age in January 1894 and once again there were considerable celebrations in the village. Later we shall hear of William's exploits when he served in the Boer War. Before Greenwood Leghe was built there were old coal shafts on the site and there were other pit shafts on Greenwood land. However, in 1900, when James Barker, the Ingleton Colliery owner brought an embankment across their fields and built a tramway across the road near Greenwood Leghe they objected and took him to court. The Greenwoods won the court case as they used their money and influence to good effect, however both sides lost a great deal of money on the court case and the ill-feeling lasted many years. The

Greenwood estates were largely sold in the 1930s. The Greenwood family at Ingleton died out with the death of Oscar Greenwood: his grave in Ingleton churchyard records that he died March 30th 1960 aged eighty-two years. The graves of the Greenwood family all lie together in front of St Mary's Church at Ingleton.

ENTERTAINMENT

There was little entertainment in Victorian Ingleton and so when a circus or wild beast show came to the village there was a great excitement. In September 1851 Wombwell's Menagerie arrived at the Bridge Inn. The event was considered of such importance that many, especially the miners, took a holiday. The colliers had a great respect for Wombwell's Show. The *Lancaster Guardian* recorded:-

> At an early hour in the forenoon the inhabitants of Ingleton were on the move, and large numbers of young and old went on the Bentham Road to give the strangers a hearty welcome. The day, which was ushered in by thunderclouds and strong gales, eventually became very wet and stormy, that it was late in the evening before the anxious multitude could be given a view of the rare animals in the menagerie. It may be recorded to the praise of a few kind individuals that through their liberality the boys and girls of the Church Sunday and Day Schools of Ingleton and Thornton-in-Lonsdale were admitted gratuitously to the exhibition.[8]

George Wombwell's Travelling Menagerie of Wild Beasts toured the country and became one of the largest and most popular shows of the time. They were usually accompanied by their own band of musicians. Members of the Wombwell family organised different shows in the Victorian period. Later with a family marriage Bostock and Wombwell's Menagerie came into existence. The shows usually staged their performance in the Bridge Inn Croft behind the Bridge Inn. This three acre field was sufficient for the wagons and animals and could easily accommodate a large circus tent. It was handy for Ingleton village and also for others coming by road from Westhouse, Thorton-in-Lonsdale and beyond. Swallow's celebrated circus also visited Ingleton.

In July 1864 Robert Child of Leeds came to Ingleton to give 'A Phantasmagorical Entertainment.' By means of a magic lantern he gave a series of comic views. He also spoke about London Sharpers and tricksters and cautioned the youths of the village to beware of such people. However, the speaker did not practice what he preached for having hired the room for a quarter of his takings he left Ingleton the following morning on an early train without making any payment to the owners of the room.

In September 1874 Bostock and Wombwell's Menagerie came to Ingleton and exhibited their animals and other attraction on the hill in the centre of the village. The reported of the occasion said, 'The people of Ingleton love to attend circuses, especially wild beast shows, so that the proprietors of such establishments long since put the place down in their memorandums as a place where they can always replenish their coffers'.[9] Bostock and Wombwells Menagerie were still visiting Ingleton in 1896 towards the end of Victoria's reign. One writer in the press complained that there was no money to repair the church clock, repair the roads or bring better street lighting, but 'Let auctioneers, cheap Johns, travelling quack doctors, wild beast shows, comic and sentimental singers, living skeletons and the rest come to the village, they are sure to be patronised by the money commanding people of Ingleton'.

SOME EVENTS

These are not particularly special events, but simply the recording of some of the things that were happening in Victorian Ingleton. Civil Registration came in 1837, the year Victoria came to the throne, but the legislation was made in the time of William IV. From that time all births, marriages and deaths had to be registered with a registrar. Ingleton Church parish registers continued to be used, but from 1837 civil certificates gave much more detail. In March 1842 the Ordnance Survey officers left the area after completing their surveys. The results were the first Ordnance Surveys maps of the area. Unfortunately they made an error in the river names which has caused problems from that day to this.

In January 1868 the tan-yard at Ingleton caught fire. How the fire on James Preston's premises started was not known, but the river Greta being nearby there was plenty of water available and the fire was soon put out. One Saturday in September 1869 Arthur Fishwick went collecting nuts on the Helks and had an accident. The news that 'Old Fishwick is lost on the Helks,' spread round the village and people came out with lanterns and accompanied by the village bellman with his bell they began a search. They searched in vain until near midnight before going home. On Sunday morning the old man, aged eighty-four, was found in Swilla Bottom where he had fallen down a slope. He was cold, exhausted and injured, but recovered once he was rescued.

On Whit Monday 1871 the usual Old People's Tea Party was held. The old people, several of them in their eighties, enjoyed themselves. However, the after tea chairman, James Thompson from Wray, was not very tactful in saying that he was reminded of the following lines:-

> Like crowded forest trees we stand,
> And some are marked to fall:
> The axe will smite at God's command,
> And soon will smite us all.

In February 1876 Mr Atkinson tried to clean his chimney with gunpowder, 'as it had been the custom in Ingleton from time immemorial to fire chimneys when they were thickly bearded with soot, the visits of chimney sweeps are few and far between.' Unfortunately he caused much damage to both the house and himself.

William Thomas Kenyon of Meal Bank Cottage was a labourer at Meal Bank Quarry. One night in January 1879 he had been drinking in the Marton Arms and went with a friend to Thornton Station taking a ride in the guard's van back across the viaduct. When he got across to Ingleton he jumped out of the guard's van. Unfortunately as it was dark, and as he was drunk, he had not realised that the guard's van was still on the viaduct and he fell sixty feet to his death. The verdict of the coroner's court was 'accidentally killed.' Kenyon was only nineteen years of age.

George Merry, a coal miner, was brought before the magistrates at Ingleton on Wednesday October 17th 1884. He was charged with stealing money from the Wheat Sheaf on the 15th. Samuel Worthington had suspected Merry of taking money from the bar till previously and had got some silver coins marked by the blacksmith next door. The money was later left in the till when Merry was in the bar and when it disappeared Merry was arrested in the street and his pockets searched. He claimed that someone must have put the coins in his pocket, but the magistrates sentenced him to three months hard labour. On March 15th 1885 the parish verger was buried. William Banks was a miner at Ingleton and held no office at the colliery other than a working man, still by his good conduct and quiet demeanour he won the good word of his fellow workmen. As church verger he gained the esteem of all persons: it was a sudden death.

Old Jemmy Forbes, a hawker and rag gatherer, was well-known in Ingleton. He lived alone in a one-roomed home up a narrow passage in the Back Gate. One Thursday morning in January 1886, at about 7am, it was discovered that his house was on fire. Neighbours came put out the fire and gained entrance, but it was too late, old Jemmy Forbes had burned to death in bed.

Mary Richardson of Ingleton was charged with stealing George Boardman's cash box from his shop in Bell Horse Gate in February 1891. In court George Boardman said, 'I was sitting in the kitchen about 9pm when I heard my desk lid snap down. I ran into the shop and on entering saw the shop door swing to. I at once ran out and saw the prisoner run down Bell Horse-gate. I followed her and when I came up to her she handed me the box.' PC Ayrton said he received the prisoner into custody about half past nine o'clock. He charged her with stealing seven shillings and a box, the property of George Boardman. On being asked whether she would have her case decided by the magistrates or be taken to a higher court she asked for her case to be summarily dealt with. Her sentence was one month's hard labour- justice was swift and firm in Victorian times.

Celebrations for Queen Victoria's Jubilee in June 1897.

When John Atkinson died in May 1895 his obituary told how he had gone to Chicago after the disastrous fire there and helped in re-building the city. He followed the trade of his father and grandfather as a builder. He had built the bridge for the Craven Lime Company. On the 25th and 26th of July 1895 Ingleton had its worse floods in living memory. Both rivers burst their banks and caused considerable flooding.

In 1899 Richard Brown was called upon by the Parish Council to provide proper toilets for some cottages he owned in Ingleton. He denied that the cottages were his, but the tenants all said that they paid him their rent. Then as he did not comply with the order the council did the work and charged him with the cost of £9 1s 6d. Richard Brown appealed to the Local Government Board and questioned both the council's right to do the work as well as the cost.

Brown said a fairer price for the work was £6 13s 9d, but offered to split the difference and the council accepted the offer. Richard Brown, a quite wealthy manufacturer, lived on the Bank. He tried to show himself as a gentleman and churchman in Ingleton, but by these actions he showed that he really was - a miserly landlord with little regard for the truth.

VICTORIA'S REIGN

People in Ingleton came to have a better life during Queen Victoria's reign. They gained shorter working hours, they began to acquire Sunday clothes and to think more about modernising their houses. The church was happy to continue in the old way with church rates and church power, but the Nonconformists in general, and Joseph Carr in particular, were exerting a great challenge to the power of the church in the village. Democracy came to Ingleton with the new Parish Council and we shall hear more of the development of local government. Industry flourished with saw mills, cotton mills, quarries and colliery and a thriving tourist industry developed. The turnpike roads were thrown open and the railway came to the village. For the first time there was a civic pride in the village and to a great extent it was shared by all levels of society.

Ingleton in 1900 showing Tom Capstick's photographic shop on the right and the Co-op drapers on the left. The man posing is butcher, John Willie Lambert.

REFERENCES

1. *Lancaster Guardian*, Nov. 29th 1879.
2. *Lancaster Guardian*, May 5th 1894.
3. *Lancaster Guardian*, July 29th 1871.
4. *Lancaster Guardian*, December 29th 1860.
5. *The Story of My Village*, A. Hewitson , Ed J.I. Bentley, 1982, p.21.
6. *Lancaster Guardian*, December 1st 1900. The press said Dr Griffiths was 71 years old, but his grave records 63 and this is confirmed by census returns.
7. *Lancaster Guardian*, June 14th 1873.
8. *Lancaster Guardian*, September 25th 1858.
9. *Lancaster Guardian*, September 26th 1874.

INTO THE TWENTIETH CENTURY

In 1900 the new century was seen in at St Mary's Church and the bells rang out until midnight. Then locals assembled in the Square to listen to the Ingleton band play in the new year with a number of popular tunes including 'Hail Smiling Morn' and 'Soldiers of the Queen'. This was a yearly event and the assembly dispersed after giving three cheers for the Queen. This chapter is mainly composed of items from the local press which were significant in the lives of the people of Ingleton.

The Ingleton Brass Band played in the new century.

Victoria was still on the throne as the twentieth century dawned. The first notable thing that happened at Ingleton was that Thomas Calverley who had been a signalman at Ingleton, being a reservist, was called to serve in the Boer War. He was accompanied from his house to the station by railwaymen and following them the Ingleton Brass Band playing 'Soldiers of the Queen' and around two hundred people. As the train left the station the crowds cheered and a fusillade of fog signals were set off. However, the Boer War made little impact on the vast majority unlike the two major wars which were to follow it later in the century.

William Norman Greenwood of Greenwood Leghe was a volunteer in the Boer War and served as an officer with the Duke of Cambridge's Yeomanry. He was captured by the Boers and spent some time in a Boer prison. His welcome home to Ingleton in November 1900 was an impressive event with a procession, public banquet, concert and ball. The Greenwoods of Greenwood Leghe were still a family of considerable influence in Ingleton, though we shall see not long into the century the effigy of one of the members of the Greenwood family was on show in a Cardiff waxworks exhibition as a notorious poisoner.

Many local folk were more interested in the football match on New Year's Day when Ingleton played Settle at Ingleton. Ingleton scored in the first five minutes and before half time added three more goals. The final score was Ingleton 14 Settle 0. For those who wanted more excitement there was pigeon shooting at the Station Inn at Ribblehead. This was a limited success due to the darkness and the shortage of pigeons – live pigeons were used then and continued to be used for much of the century.

Ingleton went into the twentieth century with good trade prospects. The Craven Lime Company was doing a brisk trade at Meal Bank and the Granite Quarry was reported to be doing well. Ingleton Colliery was at a low ebb, but there were rumours of extensive developments soon to come and they did eventually come early in the second decade of the century. The Ingleton scenery was still attracting a large number of visitors and visitors who came for the scenery brought much needed cash to the village. Farming was never the cause of much excitement, but agriculture continued to be an important part of village economy.

Queen Victoria died early in the century and Ingleton Church was crowded for her memorial service. There was a procession led by the village band with children, members of the Oddfellows and others. Ingleton folks queued to see the Queen's funeral at the Wheat Sheaf Pavilion where Harry Hibbert of Bradford gave a cinematography exhibition. The new King was proclaimed in the square at Ingleton in front of a large crowd on Saturday February 9th 1901. Once again it was procession time with the brass band, but Ingleton was unsure of what it should do to celebrate King Edward VII's coronation. It was decided to have a fire on Ingleborough and a Coronation meal – one for adults and another for the children of the village. But then Edward was taken ill with appendicitis and the coronation had to be postponed. Ingleton waited and held their late celebrations in July. There was a grand firework display and then everyone turned their eyes to Ingleborough for the beacon fire, but the mountain was covered in dense mist which never lifted. However, the beacon fire was eventually lit a few days later and was reported as a grand sight.

In August 1902 active service volunteers returned from the Boer War. Cpl John Miller, L.Cpl William Thomas Clapham and Pte Lonsdale were each given an illuminated address. Electric lighting had come to Ingleton in 1900, but many were still cutting peat on Ingleborough for burning on their home fires. There was no real problem except when they left unsightly holes. One of the main areas for digging was Crina Bottom.

In October 1904 Ingleton Mill burned down. It had been built on the same site as the previous mill which had burned down in 1854. The gas company's works were next to the mill and there were fears of a gas explosion, but this was solved by letting some of the gas escape and cutting the connections. Later in November the onset of severe winter storms caused the gable end of the mill to collapse and tons of stone were thrown onto Mill House demolishing an outhouse and closet, as well as breaking slates and causing other damage. After the mill fire the remains of the mill were left towering over Mill House in a very threatening position. The gas works manager, Edward Barlow, narrowly escaped death as he was repairing a damaged gas pipe in the mill and was rendered unconscious.

In 1905 a steam laundry opened at Ingleton near the old brewery buildings and Brewery Lane eventually became Laundry Lane. The laundry flourished and became an important part of Ingleton's business and social activities, the laundry ball became one of the main social events of the year.

In March 1906 Thomas Redhead, fellmonger and wool dealer, died in his sixty-eighth year. Originally from Lancaster he had settled at Ingleton as a fellmonger and eventually taken over from Mr Preston. He was also a director of the Gas Company and a member of the Oddfellows. In April the same year Robert Balderston Cragg died. He was only fifty-two years old and had been a solicitor at Ingleton although he later moved to Skipton to practice. He was well known as the author of *Legendary Rambles-Ingleton & Lonsdale*.

Ingleton mill fire brought out the spectators in October 1904.

A review of 1907 reported that the print works was busy, visitors were still rolling into Ingleton, the laundry was doing well, the Granite Works had a prosperous year, but the Craven Lime Company had seen a fall in sales and no new houses had been built. In May 1908 John Inman Tomlinson died at the age of sixty-one. He had been caretaker of the National School for quarter of a century and verger at St Mary's for a similar period: he was a man who could be relied upon. He was a native of Ingleton and began work at Ingleton Colliery when he was seven years of age. In June 1907 Kenelm Vivian Sigismund Clegg took over at the Bridge Inn. In October Sam Worthington pointed out to the Council that there was a shortage of public conveniences in Ingleton. It was voted to erect 'a suitable convenience at a suitable place' and £50 was allocated for the work.

In 1909 there was concern over the township's debts. They had borrowed £1,915 for sewage works and this would be paid off in 1910. A second sum of £450 would be paid off in 1917. In 1879 £2,000 had been borrowed for the Water Works and that would be paid off by the end of 1909. In 1882 a further £150 was borrowed and that would be paid off in 1910. In 1902 a further £180 was borrowed and that would be paid off in 1932. In 1882/3 £1,000 was borrowed for the new cemetery and this would be entirely paid off in 1912. The Council were pleased to say that they were not much indebted at all. In November 1909 there were complaints that Brewery Lane was a quagmire: the laundry had been in operation since 1905, but it was still Brewery Lane.

By 1910 there was renewed activity at the New Ingleton Colliery Company. Many new men had been taken on and trouble broke out between rival groups. The matter ended up in court and several miners were charged and convicted of intimidation of fellow workmen. Jack Higson, Alf Higson, Clement Melbourne and Robert Wilkinson were all heavily fined. Being unable or unwilling to pay, all the men went to prison to serve hard labour. In June 1910 it was reported that the weir at Ingleton was getting in a bad state. Today you will be lucky to find one of the massive stones still in place in the river.

Following the death of Edward VII on May 6th 1910 the proclamation of King George V took place in the square at Ingleton on Saturday May 21st 1910 at 3.30 pm. The proclamation was read by W. Rhodes JP of Lund Holme. Then came the coronation of George V on the 22nd of June 1911 and the village celebrated in loyal fashion. There were many decorations with arches, Union Jacks, and bunting. There was a procession through the streets, starting at the National School and ending up at the Parish Church. The procession was led by Superintendent Warburton followed by the Ingleton Brass Band, the local territorials under Lt Clapham, the local cadets under Captain A. Barker and Lt J. Barker, the Ingleton Fire Brigade, the Coronation Committee, Parish Councillors, Ingleborough Oddfellows, Rechabites, Good Templars, British Women's Temperance Association, the school children, and the rear was brought up by the general public. A halt was called in the square to sing hymns, give a royal salute and sing the National Anthem.

Celebrations for the Coronation of George V in June 1911.

Coronation mugs and cups and saucers were given to the children who were also provided with a tea in the National School and Literary Institute. Around a hundred old folks were given tea at the Wheat Sheaf and the Oddfellows held a dinner. Over two hundred folks enjoyed the dancing in the Wheat Sheaf in the evening and Sir John Scott entertained his employees at the Granite Quarry to a dinner at the Ingleboro' Hotel.

However, there were many people in Ingleton who sought for a better life and one outside Ingleton and outside England. In April 1912 thirteen families sailed for Canada. Shortly before this around sixty people had already emigrated to Australia, New Zealand and other parts of the British Empire.

In 1913 the Ingleton Colliery was coming back to life and in December of that year land was purchased to build a New or Model Village for the incoming colliers. This added a new dimension to Ingleton and brought in families from Lancashire, Scotland, County Durham and other parts of Yorkshire. 1913 was a good year for the laundry, but Meal Bank Quarry was lying idle. Then in 1914 World War I broke out and Ingleton's Territorials were mobilised. Charles Littlefair, postman between Ingleton and Chapel-le-dale, turned up for work and found his calling up papers telling him to report at once to the Tower of London to join his regiment. By early 1915 one hundred and twenty-seven men from Ingleton were serving in the forces. Ingleton's population was only 1,672 and that included men, women and children. Ingleton had the first place in Yorkshire villages and the fifth place in the country for the number of men mobilised in relation to the population.

Some returned quickly like T. Metcalfe who lost a leg at Mons. By early 1915 Belgian refugees had started to arrive in Ingleton and by the end of the year Blue Hall had been taken over to accommodate them. In May the Duke of Wellington's West Riding Regiment came to recruit at Ingleton. The latest recruits were William Routledge and Edward Tomlinson, both over fifty, both grandfathers, and both with three sons already serving in the forces. Edward Tomlinson was back to grave digging at Ingleton cemetery by the end of the year having been discharged from the Duke of Wellington's Regiment due to age and ill health. At Ingleton the main street, the Bank and a few other streets were tarred for the first time. Other road improvements took place and in December 1915 the Council set out an official list of names for all the streets and roads in Ingleton.

WWI ended in November 1918 and stories of awards and service will be recorded in later chapter on military matters. There were many sad events in Ingleton and one took place in January 1919 with the burial of L.Cpl. D. Routledge at Ingleton cemetery with full military honours. Not all served in the war and Ingleton did have some problem with deserters, but mainly they were from other areas and not Ingleton. In May 1918 Arthur Saunders, a deserter from the army 5th Machine Gun Corps, was arrested in the Model village: he had also deserted his wife and children. He was found with papers in the name of Richard Kirkham and was looking for work at Ingleton Colliery. George Dring a miner at Ingleton, was also arrested as an absentee in May 1918, and remanded to await an escort. In 1919 at the end of the war came the great influenza epidemic which affected Ingleton along with the rest of Europe and killed more people in a few months than the war had done in several years.

Trade during the war was usually good and often due to the war itself and the demand for food and materials. It certainly guaranteed Ingleton Colliery a good price for its coal, much of which went to Barrow in Furness for the war effort. The Granite Quarry had been closed for a few years during the war and opened again in 1920. The Meal Bank Quarry, however, had gone for good and many found this especially difficult to accept as there had been a strong demand for lime during the war. Peace celebrations came in July 1919 and Ingleton celebrated with great enthusiasm. Local soldiers and sailors were given a dinner at the Wheat Sheaf Pavilion and around two hundred attended.

With the end of the war the tourist trade was revived and Ingleton once again was crowded with visitors, a sight which had not been seen since 1914. In February 1919 there were several property sales in Ingleton. The five Strand Cottages were sold for £565, that is for the complete row. Three cottages in Bell Horse Gate, complete with bakery, outbuildings and land sold to Sam Worthington for £350.

In October 1920 the foundations were put in for an addition to the New Village. These twenty-six houses, built with concrete blocks and steel girders, were erected by contractor Frank Hopkinson of Worksop. On Sunday 14th of November the War memorial was unveiled at 2.30pm. It was an impressive ceremony though held in 'pitiless rain'. Also in 1920 Harold Greenwood, one of the Greenwood family of Greenwood Leghe was charged with murder. He was alleged to have poisoned his wife with arsenic. He was working in Kidwelly in Wales as a solicitor and was charged at Llanelli Court. The jury at the inquest said, 'We are unanimously of the opinion that the death of the deceased, Mabel Greenwood, was caused by acute arsenical poisoning as certified. And that the poison was administered by Harold Greenwood.' A great crowd outside the court booed as he was taken away by two warders. He pleaded not guilty and was able to afford the services of Sir Edward Marshall Hall, KC one of the most notable advocates of the day. To the amazement of everyone he was found

Impressive peace celebrations at Ingleton in July 1919.

not guilty. Harold Greenwood's effigy was placed in the 'Chamber of Horrors' at Cardiff wax works exhibition, but he won £50 damages in a court case against them.

In 1920 further property was sold in Ingleton. All the Pemberton cottages brought £300 as a lot and New Winning with land and two cottages was bought by W. Bargh of Ingleton for £1,100. 1921 brought the coal strike to Ingleton and gas supplies were cut off in May. Miners worked on the outcrop in the local river. Other colliers riddled the tips for coal and sold it by the bag. In July George Peck, an Ingleton miner, was found drowned in Kingsdale. The inquest reported that he was a steady man but was out of work because of the coal strike. On Tuesday morning he went to the colliery to look at the sheet to see who was needed for work and not finding his name he went home. His son had just gone out to Australia a week before. He didn't drink and hadn't appeared depressed: verdict – 'found drowned'. The year 1921 was remembered as a black year for Ingleton mainly due to the coal strike.

The year 1923 saw a soup kitchen being opened at Ingleton to alleviate distress caused by continual unemployment. Gifts of vegetables and meat were given and tickets were issued by Dr Mackenzie and Nurse Dodgson to the needy, especially miners' children. Following the Maltby Mining Disaster in 1923 a team of Ingleton miners led by manager, A.B. Hewitt, promptly responded to the call. In March 1924 Ingleton colliery resumed work after being closed for well over two years. In January 1924 two cottages were pulled down to widen the road at Hollin Tree corner, the site of many accidents. In 1925 Ingleton was undecided what to do about the 'German gun'. They had accepted the gun as a war trophy and placed it at the Cross, but now it was becoming a nuisance and looking neglected. People in Ingleton were tired of the thing: the Parish Council decided to retain 'the honour' of having it.

To toll out the old year and ring in the new had always been a custom at Ingleton. Usually a large crowd assembled in the square and danced the New Year in to the strains of Ingleton Brass Band and the choirs of the Church and Wesleyans. In 1926 all this changed and there was only a perfunctory tolling of the bells shortly before midnight. In April George Walling complained about the poor manner in which the church bells were rung and the church wardens were instructed to have the church bells put in order and to get a team of bell-ringers together. In April Ivy Cottage in the Bottom sold to H. Redhead for £185.

1926 brought the General Strike. The Trades Union Congress had promised to support miners over the extending of their hours of work and the cutting of their pay and they did so. Ingleton Colliery was closed again and by July one hundred and fifty miners' children were being given two meals a day by a 'Canteen Committee' at Ingleton. Subscriptions in money and kind came from all quarters. The Trade Union Congress came to terms with the government, but miners were far from happy. At Ingleton miners were drifting back to work in October 1926 to work extended hours for less pay. Colliery management and local magistrates took it out on miners for the inconvenience that had been caused in the General Strike. Miners were charged for poaching rabbits and petty matters. Miners T. Lee, S. Brown, William Hutton, Albert Brocklehurst, Edward Bagot and John Jenkins were all taken to court for stealing a tree trunk from the colliery tip. The tree had been blown down in a gale and had been stripped of its branches and thrown aside. The men were short of fuel at home and sawed it up in full view of the colliery manager who said nothing at the time. They were given a heavy lecture by JPs who said, 'this kind of thing would have to be put a stop to.' In November there were still some miners at Ingleton who stood behind the Miners' Federation and stated that they were not going back to work.

In 1927 the New Year was ushered in quietly at Ingleton, the Church bells were not even rung. In January miner James Bragan was charged for stealing coal from the sidings worth four pence and taken to court: he was fined five shillings. On Good Friday 1928 the Ribble Motor Service began to run a bus between Lancaster, Kirkby Lonsdale and Ingleton. Buses also were to run from Lancaster and Kendal to Ingleton, Hellifield and Skipton. It was also proposed to run a service between Kendal and Manchester running through the district. It had already been reported that in 1926 that Ingleton was well served with bus services and that it was no problem to reach Skipton, Lancaster, Kendal, Settle and Kirkby Lonsdale at regular times. The latest company to enter the field was Lancashire & Westmorland Motor Services Ltd.

In July 1928 two Ingleton miners, Fred Rhodes and James Morris, were charged in court with stealing a wagon cover said to be worth £4 from the LMS Railway. James Morris had used it to cover a hen hut, but Fred Rhodes had taken it. Fred Rhodes was sentenced to four months in prison with hard labour. Morris was fined £3 or one month's prison with hard labour as a receiver of stolen property. In August Robert Balderston, the author of *Ingleton Bygone and Present,* died within a few months of his eightieth birthday and was buried in Ingleton cemetery. In 1929 it came to the notice of the Parish Council that the village lamplighter was only ten years old. As no one under fourteen years should have been employed he was sacked. The lad got to know who reported him and said, 'I have one in for thee.' A branch of Martin's Bank opened at Ingleton on July 2nd 1929. It opened Tuesdays and Fridays from 12.30pm to 3pm.

1930 brought the opening of Ingleton's new school by Sir Percy Jackson. The old National School was repaired inside by the County Council and outside by the Church. It was intended to use it as a Sunday school when it has been refurbished. Because of subsidence the New Bridge at Ingleton was closed and traffic re-routed through the village. In May J.T. Marsden, proprietor of the Ingleton Picturedrome, bought Bank Cottage and began converting it into a cinema. In August the newly formed Ingleton detachment of the 4th Border Regiment of Territorials went to train with the Battalion at Rhyl.

The Laundry Ball, in February 1931, was one of the events of the year in Ingleton. In September of that year a maternity child welfare centre was set up in the Blue Hall. It was not until January 1933 that work began on the New Road Bridge over the Greta although it had been three years since the old bridge showed signs of collapse. The new bridge was constructed of steel. In March 1933 at the height of a snowstorm the Church of St Oswald at Thorton-in-Lonsdale was burned out and left as a shell in spite of the efforts of Settle Rural District Fire Brigade. People from Ingleton were able to see the blaze. 1933 saw the building of Ingleton's open air swimming pool which was opened in 1934 and provided a new amenity for the village. In June 1935 a restoration fund was started for the Church of St Mary due to the foundations giving way. There were rumours that the Ingleton Colliery was going to close down, but the press reported in August 1935 that, 'the fact that a conveyor which is being installed will itself cost £1,000, should dispel any fears in that direction.' However, there was soon a stoppage due to a roof collapse and then a dispute between management and miners. By the end of the year miners were leaving Ingleton to find work elsewhere.

1936 was another sad year for Ingleton, the colliery was silent by April and by the end of the year Ingleton had officially been placed on the government's list of distressed areas. The Ingleborough Mountain Race to the summit of Ingleborough, usually held on Whit Monday, was cancelled because of the colliery closure. In April Percy Greenwood died at Bank Hall aged 59. He was one of the last of the Greenwoods of Greenwood Leghe. Only Oscar Greenwood now remained. In September 1936 Ingleton finally got rid of the unwanted German gun and it was placed in the scrap yard having been bought for ten shillings.

1937 was another bleak year of unemployment. Allotments for the unemployed were started and there was a move to try to landscape the colliery tip near the New Village. Edward VII abdicated and George VI came to the throne. In April and May Reg Hainsworth and a small band of helpers carted fifteen tons of material to the summit of Ingleborough for a coronation bonfire. Horses pulled sledges and even a thirty horse power car was driven to the summit, though it did get stuck. The coronation date was May 12th and Ingleton's bonfire was set for Saturday the 14th. There was a heavy mist on the night that the fire should have been lit so the event was postponed until Saturday May 21st. However, it was a success as around five hundred people climbed Ingleborough for the occasion.

At Ingleton, as elsewhere in the country, the depression years of the 1920s and 1930s continued until WW2. War with Germany was declared in September 1939 and Ingleton men were soon serving throughout the world. At home in Ingleton Captain Farrer took charge of the Home Guard and he was ably supported by Sgt. Redhead, Cpl. Slinger and many others. At the end of the war Youth Hostels were revived and people came back to Ingleton to get away from the towns and cities and the dull routine of work.

In the 1950s and 1960s cavers, pot-holers and campers in general flowed into Ingleton. Few people had cars and most came by bicycle, motor bike or on foot. They slept near the inns in sleeping bags and many camped on Storrs Common and anywhere else they could find, often to the annoyance of villagers. One Ingletonian said, 'If you judged by the milk bottles they left in the summer, we had week-enders from Wigan and Warrington, on the one hand, and Darlington on the other. Liverpool lads have been coming up here for years'.

In 1954 there were only four or five caravans in Ingleton, but ten years later there were two-hundred and ninety-seven registered. In fact the majority of these caravans were across the river in the parish of Thornton-in-Lonsdale, but for decades the lower areas of Thornton had been called Ingleton. Most of Ingleton glens and water falls are also in Thornton, but once again most visitors knew only that they had been at Ingleton. Caravan sites sprung up at Broadwood, the Marton Arms, the Trees, Greenwood Leghe and Parkfoot.

The car came to Ingleton and at first Ingleton coped well with adequate parking space, but then the increase in car use brought problems. In 1954 Ingleton lost its railway and the station became derelict and remained so for several years until the Ingleborough Community Centre was built on its site with a large new car park.

In the twenty-five years following WWII the standard of living of most people in this country did not just improve, but was transformed. In general it was a period of mass prosperity. Employment was available, wages rose and a great range of technical improvements brought the luxuries of record players, televisions, fridges, freezers and many other items. Ingleton changed in character, especially in its inhabitants, who came from all over, and to a great extent worked outside the village. People could now live in Ingleton and work in Lancaster and farther afield. Ingleton was now only a shadow of the agricultural village that it had been at the beginning of the century.

POPULATION

The population of Ingleton is of interest and here are listed both estimated and exact population figures at various times in Ingleton's history from 1066 to 1951.

1066	c.85	1623	c.650	1871	2,541
1297	c.150	1700	c.750	1901	1,671
1379	c.200	1801	1,106	1931	2,235
1530	c.450	1851	1,390	1951	1,892.

The population of 1871 was swelled by those working on the Settle Carlisle Railway who lived in the township. The high for 1931 was due to the colliery being in full swing. The growth of the population of Ingleton is in no way related to the growth of the country. Ingleton always remained a slow growing village.

LOCAL GOVERNMENT

The Manor Courts held the power of local government in Ingleton for many centuries. The manor of Ingleton ran the affairs of all the township except Twistleton which had been held as a separate manor. There was also a part of Ingleton Township at Ingleton Fells which came under the Manor of Newby. The manor courts organised everything in the village from choosing the village constables to making sure that the inhabitants kept the roads and hedges in good condition.

By Tudor times the manor courts were still active, but their power had much declined and the power of the independent parish was growing. The Tudor years saw the establishment of the parish as the basic unit of local government; local government, but directed by national government. The parish vestries were empowered not only to select churchwardens, but also village constables, surveyors of the highways and overseers of the poor. All these parish officers had to give their services free for one year at a time and were chosen from the property and land-owning members of the village – the ratepayers.

This system put in place by the Tudors was cheap and it lasted for several centuries. The whole system was supervised by Justices of the Peace who were mainly selected from the local gentry and the clergy. They also served for basic expenses. At the local level the JPs had to approve those selected to be constables and overseers. Although the power of the manor was limited, the manor courts still met at Ingleton well into the twentieth century when manorial rents were finally extinguished by Parliament

In Tudor times Ingleton was represented by the 'twenty-four sworn men' who are mentioned in varied documents. It would appear that they administered legacies, had the village 'stock' or funds and ran the general affairs of the village. It is interesting to note that the twenty-four sworn men may relate to the double jury of twenty-four sworn men who sat to decide important questions at manor courts. By the 1720s, when the Ingleton township books first give us an insight into village government, the twenty-four sworn men are called the 'chosen men' or 'principal inhabitants of the township', but often the number fell far short of twenty-four.

PARISH RECORDS

The first official records of Ingleton Township date from 1721.[1] What happened to the previous records and minute books is unknown. Perhaps they were lost, burned in a fire or disappeared with some absconding parish official. Certainly a new book had to be started in 1721 to record parish business. This volume began on March 14th 1721 and closed April 9th 1847. The first page has two entries:-

'May 17. 1723
Whereas Mr Christopher Bateson and Christopher Procter were appointed Assistants to the officers of the Township in the Difficulties of their business for the year 1722 they having done their Endeavour for that year for the ensuing do with the Consent of the other sidesmen now make Thomas Parker esquire or whom he pleases to depute, and John Cockin to succeed them in that necessary affair.

April 24. 1724
Richard ffoxcroft and John Cockin with the Consent of all Sidesmen do nominate ffrancis Moore of Winterscales and Thomas Wildman of Coldcotes to succeed them in 'the matters above'.

There is no word of what 'the matters above' were. There is no mention of the special difficulties in the Township that necessitated extra men being drafted in to help. These items were written on page one and dated 1723 and 1724, and yet on page two we find material dated 1722. Anyway things got off to a new start in a new Township Book.

The Chosen men of Ingleton or Principal Inhabitants set out a few rules which were to be followed by parish officers in future. These were set out on April 25th 1722:-

Whereas notice was given in the parochial Chapel of Ingleton that the Chosen men and parochial Officers should appear to give and take in accs at this Day we the persons then appearing have agreed that these Rules following shall start precedents for future years.

Imps
That the Chapelwardens and Overseers of the Township of Ingleton shall yearly prepare and bring in their Accts at this Day and the Constables to do likewise.

2nd That all the Charges in repairing rebuilding and beautifying the Parochial Chapel of Ingleton shall be raised by the whole Chapelry including Ingleton ffell and that the Charges belonging to the Chapel of Ingleton ffel, shall be raised by the inhabitants of that Chapel of Ease only.

3rd. That the Bell-Ropes be preserved as long as useful, and then sold towards buying new ones.

4th That the Constables make their monethly Searches at their own Charge.

If we think of questioning the priorities of the Chosen Men of Ingleton, especially about their third priority, we should remember that the Church was the centre of village life and the meeting place of the village's ruling group. The Church bells had a great importance and the bell-ringers and bell-ropes had a reflected importance. The bells brought the congregation to church for clocks were rare and inaccurate, they rang for weddings, tolled for funerals and celebrated national festivals and victories. The upkeep of the bells and bell-ropes demanded constant expenditure. Preserving bell ropes for as long as possible and then selling them towards buying new ropes was also a question of economy and they were keen on that. Any spending came from the rates and the Twenty Four Sworn Men were the biggest ratepayers in the township and had the most to lose.

SETTLEMENT

At a meeting on March 14th 1722 the Chosen persons of Ingleton agreed that they get orders from two Justices of the Peace to remove several inhabitants of Ingleton to the place of their legal settlement. The 1662 Act of Settlement empowered Overseers of the Poor to remove strangers who had come into a village without prospects of work. A stranger coming in to help with harvest had to bring a certificate from his own parish guaranteeing to take him back. After forty days the stranger could claim that he was entitled to a settlement. Later a settlement in Ingleton could only be got by being born there, by renting property worth £10 a year, working a full year as a hired servant, or serving a full apprenticeship in the village. This settlement system continued well into the second half of the nineteenth century.

In March 1721 Ingleton wanted to be rid of the following people:-

Richard Harrison and his wife and three children to the Parish of Claughton.
William Millers and his wife to Cancefield.
William Bullock and his wife and one child to the township of Lawkland.
James Leeming his wife and several children to Ashton
Matthew Jackson his wife and several children to Langcliffe.
Peter Wildman his wife and one child to Burton.
William Clapham his wife and one child to Burton.

In such cases it was custom for the Justices of the Peace to confirm their removal at Quarter Sessions. Once the magistrates had confirmed the expulsions Ingleton quickly removed the unwanted paupers who were escorted out of the village by a parish officer. In 1772 the Chosen Men announced that, 'Every person who has not produced a Proper Certificate nor gained a Lawful Settlement in our Township of Ingleton' would have action taken to remove them from the village.

Removals of men women and families from Ingleton continued into the second half of the nineteenth century. In 1848 the Vestry, 'ordered that John Kitchen be removed to his last legal place of Settlement.' In November 1849 the Overseers gave orders 'to remove William Windle a pauper now chargeable to the Township, to his legal place of Settlement'. The overseers paid for William Marsden to be assisted to Bradford where he had found employment. However, he was soon back in Ingleton as a pauper. In 1851 the overseer, George Coward, was ordered, 'to take such course as he think best to get William Marsden and family to Liverpool, and that he see them shipped for America.' Ingleton hoped that by that action they would be rid of the family for ever. In 1847 Isabella Smith was escorted from Ingleton to Liverpool and put on board ship for America. The township records state, 'that six pound ten shillings be allowed to Isabella Smith to Emegrate to America'.

There were times when Ingleton often had to accept paupers back from other towns and villages and this they did not like. In June 1856 Magistrates ordered that James Preston along with his wife and seven children should be removed from Burrow with Burrow to Ingleton. A meeting was called at Ingleton on June 9th and it was unanimously resolved to appeal against the decision. Solicitor George Hartley of Settle was appointed to conduct the case. In August 1847 the township books record a list of thirty-one people who had gained a right to settlement by having lived in the village for five years. They included Esther Robinson a notorious vagrant, who was eventually killed in a shot gun accident, and William Boardman, a pauper barber born in Rotherham, who eventually set up a successful business in the village and whose descendants eventually came to live in Ingleton Hall.

PARISH APPRENTICES

Under the Elizabethan Poor Law the children of poor parents could be apprenticed by being compulsorily farmed out to ratepayers of the parish. After 1691 when serving as an apprentice in a parish for forty days was one of the ways in which a person could gain a legal settlement, the vestry often made sure that the poor children were apprenticed to someone outside the parish. However, those outside the parish could not be forced to take apprentices and fees had to be paid. Ingleton's authorities usually apprenticed poor children to those in the parish because they could not refuse and also because no payment was necessary.

The Ingleton vestry allocated apprentices to those with the largest estates in the township and usually made a note of those who had not had any apprentices before, or as they put it in the eighteenth century, 'Which have never had any since the memory of man.' In 1884 there were still many apprenticeship indentures in the Ingleton Church vestry cupboard which have since been destroyed or lost as they were not there when an archive list was compiled in 1970.

Ingleton's apprentices were sometime difficult to control. Richard Haslem, who was obviously a restless soul, led the parish a merry dance in the eighteenth century and the Township books record:-

Richard Haslem bound himself apprentice by indenture to John Gibson of Kirkby Lonsdale, for four years and one half, which indenture was dated two years and a half before the real time of his service, which began in the year 1749. He stayed with his said master only one year and a half, when he broke his leg and went home to his mother in Ingleton, which was about May 1750, lived with his said mother until about Martinmas when he made a verbal agreement with his said master to serve the remainder of his time with Stephen Maudsley, in Ingleton aforesaid, with whom he had lived only about 7 months, when he had his indentures given up to him and went to Thomas Walker's at Leck, and stayed there one month, and then went to John Shepherd's and stayed there ten weeks, and then went to Robert Marshall's and stayed there ten weeks, when he went and hired himself for one whole year with Nic Hugganson, Tatham-cum-Ireby, in the parish of Thornton and County of Lancaster, for six pounds wages, and served with Hugganson that year, except about three weeks he went to work at his mother's by his master's consent, for which he abated a proportional share of his wages; then hired with Thomas Caton about nine months, then lived with said Caton about eleven months, then hired with the said Hugganson about six months, after which service he returned to his mother and lived with her about three years. In 1765 he hired with John Jackson of said Ingleton for 5s to serve the office of chapel-warden for him, and in the year 1768 he hired for Robert Tennant, of said Ingleton, to serve the office of chapel-warden for him, and received the like sum of 5s for such service, which said service was not for himself nor in his own right, neither in the said Haslem's name, inserted in any of the town's books as chapel-warden, but the person's name who hired him who was appointed chapel-wardens, and were accountable to the township for the rates assessed the same years.

Richard Maudsley was bound to John Newton for Mr Parker's estate at Twistleton; Richard Balderston had an apprentice bound to him on April 28th 1764; Nathaniel Armistead was bound apprentice to Thomas Kidd for James Balderston's estate at Coldcotes in the year 1801 and also in 1801 Charlotte Wildman was bound to Francis Kidd for his pasture in Twistleton. In 1802 J.W. Willan was fined £10 for refusing an apprentice for Francis Metcalfe's estate in Twistleton which shows that there was no way to refuse a parish apprentice without incurring a heavy fine. On one page in the Township books there is a list of fifty-one farmers and landowners who had had apprentices put out to them.

BASTARDY

One of the problems facing the church vestry was illegitimate children. The first thing the overseers tried to do was to get the name of the father. Once this was done pressure was put on him to marry the girl or at least pay for the upkeep of the child. In July 1796 it was recorded that Stephen Smithies of Kirkby Lonsdale had paid £5 10s to the churchwardens and overseers of the poor for Ingleton for an illegitimate child born to Mary Harrison. On September 8th the same year when Stephen Smith and Mary Harrison were married at Kirkby Lonsdale the money was returned to him. The Ingleton authorities would no longer have to pay for the upkeep of Mary Harrison or her child.

In 1801 Thomas Hambleton of Leck was charged in a similar fashion when Alice Newton had an illegitimate child in Ingleton. He paid £20 to the poor of Ingleton and also £20 for the maintenance of the child. The overseers at Ingleton obviously succeeded with him, but others had no money to make any payment.[2]

THE POOR

One of the greatest problems of the vestry at Ingleton was dealing with the poor. In the sixteenth and early seventeenth centuries there was no poor house or workhouse in Ingleton. This is shown by all expenditure on the poor being made in allowances for their support. The allowance for the poor for the year 1723 is given below as shown in the Township Book:-

Elizabeth Atkinson	1-12-00	Grace Carter	0-12-06
Jonas Dixon	2-00-00	Isabel ffoxcroft	0-15-00
John Bentham	2-12-00	Anthony Leaks 2 children	4-15-00
Ann Procter	0-17-04	Leonard Wetherhead	1-10-00
William Redmayne	3.00-00	Barbara Walker	0-10-00
Alice Leech	0-17-06	Elizabeth Remmington	0-12-00
Thomas Calvert	2-12-00	Anne Lamb	0-12-00
Elizabeth Cansfield	2-05-00	Elizabeth Waring	2-12-00
Agnes Redmayne	1-12-06	William Carter	2-12-00

These were people the township could not throw out of the village. These were the village's own poor to be supported within the community as there was no poor house or workhouse at this time. These lists continue each year for many years and some names appear with regularity. It is interesting to note the names and we see that families such as the Redmaynes, who

Cross Farm for many years Ingleton's workhouse in the eighteenth century.

usually had a high social standing, were not exempt from becoming destitute. Family deaths, illness and other misfortunes brought many into the ranks of the paupers.

On April 21ˢᵗ 1738 the Township book records:-

> At a vestry Meeting it is agreed by all ye principal Inhabitants and Land Holders within the Township of Ingleton Whose hands are hereunto subscribed that their shall be for ye ensuing year a Work House Erected and sett up to Employ and maintain ye poor within ye said township as ye act of Parliament directs for that purpose and for the better establishing of the same we do appoint James Redman, Thomas Waller, Giles Redman & William Metcalf along with ye overseers to be directors and Governors of ye same and what Ever Rules or ye majority of them do or they make for the Regulation and Government thereof the will be agreeable too as Witness our hands.

The Workhouse Act of 1723 had empowered parishes to erect workhouses. Ingleton did not consider the idea for many years, but eventually in 1738 obviously thought it would be a good idea. However, it is doubtful whether they actually carried it out, but found it easier to use a farm already in existence. They eventually set up the workhouse at Cross Farm and brought Ingleton's paupers together.

In 1773 there were only five persons in the poor house at Cross Farm, Miles Dawson, John Simpson Jnr, Ralph Thompson, Esther Wilson and Hannah Berry. The workhouse at Cross Farm continued for many years, but in December 1807 it was proposed, 'to build a workhouse for the Accommodation of the Poor living in the Township of Ingleton'. This new poorhouse was built on the edge of Storrs Common on the Lancaster to Richmond turnpike road and became known as Mount Pleasant. The paupers where possible were given employment and they grew vegetables in their own garden. The able bodied men were probably set to work on the ground opposite Storrs Hall breaking stone for the repair of the roads. The stone breaking yard was later turned into tennis courts for Storrs Hall School.

Many people supplied the Storrs poorhouse with food and goods. The Ingleton Township accounts show the buying of milk and butter, meal and flour and Joseph Brown the Ingleton

The original building at Storrs Hall was Ingleton's workhouse.

butcher supplied beef and bacon. Shoes were mended and cotton bought for sewing. In 1826 a new bed was bought for three shillings and in 1827 Thomas Moore was paid for supplying a chaff bed. Paul Berry, the parish clerk, was paid six shilling for shaving the male inmates. Thirty yards of cloth was bought in 1827 and was probably used to make clothes. Coal was supplied to the workhouse for both cooking and heating. Wool was bought in, either raw for carding or knitting wool for inmates to produce knitwear. Inmates who were able to work would be kept busy.

Storrs workhouse continued until Poor Law Amendment Act of 1834, following which a new Union Workhouse was opened at Giggleswick to cover the Settle Union District and all Ingleton's paupers were moved there. The Settle Union was composed of thirty townships and included Settle, Austwick, Bentham, Burton-in-Lonsdale, Clapham, Giggleswick, Hellifield, Horton, Ingleton, Kirkby Malham, Long Preston, Malham, Stainforth and Thornton-in-Lonsdale. As the workhouse at Storrs had been paid for in part by charity money, when the building was sold by the Settle Union, Ingleton received money which was distributed to the poor. When the new workhouses were built they were termed by some, 'palaces for paupers'. Many were impressive buildings with fine internal fittings, but all this was negated by the separation of the sexes, separation of children, basic food and rigid rules. The harsh regime was deliberately developed to make sure that people would not see workhouses as an easy option and would try their best to avoid them. Following the grouping of villages to administer poor law relief these collective Boards of Guardians soon came to control water, health and much more.

Prior to 1819 the authorities at Ingleton had called themselves the 'chosen men' and the 'principal inhabitants, but following the Sturges Bourne Act of 1819 they became a Select Vestry to administer poor law relief. This meant they were elected annually by the ratepayers of the township. The Ingleton Vestry adopted the term Select Vestry and used the term until the coming of the Parish Council. The schoolmaster of the day was usually pressed into acting as the clerk for the Vestry and for this he was paid one pound each year.

PARISH COUNCIL

A great change came to Ingleton following the Local Government Act of 1894 also known as the Parish Councils Bill. Here was Ingleton's opportunity to get rid of the old Select Vestry controlled by the Church and presided over by the minister. Non-conformists had long hoped for such a day. The Rev. H.W. Smith of Lancaster wrote in the *Lancaster Guardian*, 'The Parliamentary Act is the most democratic measure the country has ever known. It is the village for the villagers. Home Rule for each parish in England and Wales… Nonconformists must realise that their day has come'. He warned people to beware of letting the vicar slide back into the position of chairman just because he was the vicar.

At Ingleton the first meetings were still presided over by the vicar. However, by the end of 1895 a Parish Council was elected and installed and the vicar was relegated to church matters only. All parish documents were handed over to the new council in January 1896. From that time the Church and its vestry were severed from control of the village and the work of local government was carried on in a business-like way by elected members of the community.

REFERENCES

1. Ingleton Township Book 1721-1847. Deposited in NYRO 2007.
2. *Lancaster Guardian,* May 13th 1893, also Township Book 1721-1847.

LAW AND ORDER

In manorial times the Manor Court organised law and order in the village. Misdemeanours were reported at the Manor Court and the culprit was dealt with in court being fined or otherwise punished. If a man was unable to pay it was 'taken out of his hide' in other words he was whipped. At the age of twelve all males accepted adult responsibility in the manor and swore an oath which included that they would neither be a thief nor harbour a thief and they were attached to another older member of the village for security. It was a system that worked and crime rates were fairly low.

Later the organising of village constables came under the jurisdiction of the township. They were chosen from the village ratepayers in rotation and JPs and ministers were exempt. Each person had to serve a year and be responsible for his area. He was paid no salary, but he was paid basic expenses if he had to escort some villain to the local prison or pass on some beggar or pauper to another parish. In 1842 a vestry meeting was held in the Church at Ingleton to make a return of those persons qualified to be appointed to be parish constables according to the recent statute. Laws were frequently changed and amended throughout the years, but the system remained much the same for centuries. The constables appointed were William Hodgson, George Coward, William Thompson, John Barrett, joiner, and John Procter. They served for the various areas of the township from Chapel-le-Dale to Coldcotes.[1] Some served voluntarily, but others only served if they could not get out of it.

In the eighteenth century a person nominated to be constable could hire someone in his place, especially if he was a busy or wealthy man, or both. If the person nominated was acceptable to the vestry meeting then that person served as constable. If the paid constable did a good job then the next nominated person to be constable might well let the hired constable continue and so the paid constable came into being. William Thompson became the paid constable at Ingleton in the mid-nineteenth century and was the last paid constable for the village, for in his time the Yorkshire Constabulary came into being and county police came to Ingleton.

The Ingleton Court House was held in an upper room of the Wheat Sheaf Inn and it was entered by stone steps from the outside. Here the magistrates met and court cases were heard not only for Ingleton, but also for the surrounding villages. There were problems in that sheep were slaughtered in the area and the magistrates complained that the steps to the court house were often covered with blood and the entrails of sheep. The problem was eventually solved when a new court house was constructed in the village in 1859.

The County Police Act of 1839 and the County and Borough Police Act of 1856 led to the formation of a West Riding police force. Ingleton was chosen as the head quarters for the Wapentake of Ewecross and therefore had a police superintendent appointed. Superintendent Exton was the first and came to Ingleton in January 1853 where he made his presence felt by stopping 'varied unlawful practices at Ingleton' and by committing several vagrants to Wakefield House of Correction. The Police Division of Ewecross came into being and included the villages of Ingleton, Clapham, Burton-in-Lonsdale, Thornton-in-Lonsdale and Austwick. Two detachments of Yorkshire Rural Police were sent to Ingleton, the second contingent arriving on January 23rd 1857. When the Yorkshire Police Force was instituted and spread throughout the County the constables were referred to by many as 'the plague of blue locusts!' Superintendent Exton had already made his present felt and the excesses of the Ingleton miners in both drinking and fighting began to be controlled. In 1855 the superintendent gave his police statistics for the Ewecross Division as follows:-[2]

APPREHENDED

Assault with intent to murder	1
Arson	1
Rape	1
Burglary	2
Larceny	5
False Pretences	1
Aggravated Assault	1
Assault on Constables	2
Common Assault	2
Breach of Peace	2
Malicious Injury	1
Drunkenness	6
Profane Swearing	2
Vagrancy	11
Arrears in Bastardy	6
Total	45

SUMMONED

Aggravated Assault	1
Assault on Constable	1
Common Assault	6
Breach of Ale House Act	3
Breach of Beer House Act	2
Drunkenness	20
Sporting without game certificate	3
Trespass in pursuit of game	4
Breach of Highway Act	2
Trespass on Property	2
Malicious Injury	2
Profane Swearing	1
Bastardy	6
Non Payment of Church Rates	5
Non Payment of Poor Rate	9
Permitting nuisance	2
Total	69

Superintendent Exton concluded his report by saying that he was happy to say that wandering vagrants and sturdy beggars are now rarely seen in the area. Although the official West Riding police force were now at Ingleton in February 1855 a meeting at the National School selected the constables for the year. The following were elected:-

James Sedgwick	Ingleton Fells	Farmer
William Willis	Ingleton Fells	Farmer
William Lund	Moorgarth	Farmer
John Barrett	Ingleton	Joiner
Thomas Baines	Moorgarth	Farmer
Stephen Downham	Twistleton	Farmer
Alexander Robinson	Rareber Top	Butcher
John Harrison	Ingleton	Coal miner
Richard Robinson	Cold Cotes	Farmer
Joseph Lupton Smith	Ingleton	Grocer
Richard Atkinson	Ingleton	Grocer

The Wheat Sheaf Inn once the Court House for Ewecross.

The above constables continued their watch and ward in their own areas confident in their authority from the township and probably suspicious and resentful of the newly appointed outside police constables. The official well- trained police force on the other hand looked on the local constables as blundering amateurs. However, the two separate bodies of constables survived together for several years. In May 1854 William Thompson arrested James Smith in the act of begging and took him before W.G. Bell JP of Melling Hall. Smith was committed under the Vagrancy Act and sent to the House of Correction at Wakefield for twenty-one days hard labour. In 1858 village constables were again appointed, William Thompson being the only paid constable at £5 per year. The local Vestry still continued to appoint and pay William Thomson as Ingleton village constable.

In February 1863 there was a Vestry Meeting to select 'eight men good and true, to keep Her Majesty's peace, and watch and ward in their several districts.' At this meeting the chairman said that the inhabitants were a lot of fools to pay either £5 or 5 farthings, as a village constable was no manner of use now that there were members of the Yorkshire police force at Ingleton. At a following meeting of ratepayers, Joseph Carr proposed the following motion, 'That there shall be no paid constable for the following year'. The motion was passed unanimously and the parish stopped paying William Thompson at once and the old position of village constable became redundant. The appointment of local village constables was never mentioned again at Ingleton after 1863.

The new police force was certainly better trained and more efficient. William Thompson, a long serving paid village constable, was noted for the way that he kept out of trouble. While street disturbances were going on at fair time he would be sitting in his usual corner set in the public house. One old Ingletonian remembering his youth in Ingleton recounted:-

One Sunday morning, when my father and I were waiting at George Coward's until the bells chimed, a gang of navvies trooped into the square immediately in front of

84

the window. They formed a ring round two of their number who were stripped to the waist. One was a great Goliath of a fellow and the other was a little fellow of around twenty. It was David and Goliath all over again. But Goliath was not very sober so that at the beginning of each round the youth rushed in and knocked him down offhand. While the 'battle', as Ingleton people call such affairs- was progressing, Master Thompson, the constable, who lived in a cottage abutting the square, came out in a state, truncheon over one shoulder, head erect, chest out, and in addressing the rioters cried out in a loud voice – 'I command you to desist in the Queen's name'. The navvies paid no more attention than if it had been a tomtit chittering, whereupon Master Thompson, who had been a schoolmaster at an earlier period, having done his duty marched back again'.[3]

The new West Riding Court House at Ingleton was opened in November 1859 with a large attendance. Everyone was happy with the new building which was constructed by local contractor, Joseph Bentham. The court was divided into three compartments. The first was the magistrates bench room which was 16ft 9in by 12ft 9ins. There was an attached retiring room 12ft 9ins by 8ft. The second part was the court itself measuring 88ft 5ins by 13ft and was provided with table, seats for magistrates, clerk and attorneys. There were boxes for witnesses and prisoners, and seats with backs for about fifty persons. The third part was an open space for spectators measuring some 35 feet by 12 feet and had a stove for heating.

The new building which was fully opened in 1860 also included a superintendent's residence, police office, and two cells for prisoners. The site cost £75 and the building, including all extras cost just £1,000.[4] Previously if a thief was apprehended and had to be imprisoned, Ingleton had no lock up and the person had to be taken to Bentham. In 1849 the authorities at Ingleton were still discussing the idea of building a lockup, but appeared never got around to it. Suggestions had been that a lockup be erected in the pinfold or in the Strands. The problem was solved when the new court house was built with its two cells. The JPs were happy with their rooms and no longer had they to hold court in a small room over the Wheat Sheaf. Warnings were given by the police superintendent to tobacco chewers at Ingleton. There were complaints that men stained the floor of the court house by spitting jets of tobacco juice onto the floor.

Petty Sessions which had been held at the Wheat Sheaf were now held at the new court house. Petty crime was dealt with under the jurisdiction of two of Her Majesty's Justices of the Peace. These JPs came from Ingleton and the surrounding area and made up the Ingleton Bench. None of the JPs distinguished themselves in any way and most were from the local lesser gentry. They were quite severe, arrogant and generally disliked by the local population, yet they kept the legal show running cheaply in Petty Sessions and in Quarter Sessions, which were held four times a year at central places such as Skipton and Wakefield. The main exception was JP John Thomas Coates (1810-1898) who ran Ingleton Mill for many years. It was said that as a magistrate 'he was remarkably accessible to working men and the poorest of the poor'.[5] Brewster Sessions were also held at the court house. These were held annually, usually in the first fortnight in February. They met to licence all landlords and deal with inns and ale-houses. In 1876 when licenses were renewed at Ingleton Court House the list of inns and alehouses and their landlords for the township of Ingleton was as follows:-[6]

INNS

Ingleboro' Hotel	Ellen Powell
Wheatsheaf	Thomas Redmayne
Three Horse Shoes	Gamaliel Briscoe

Bridge Inn	John Dumoney
The Hill Inn	Richard Swinbank
Newby Head	Richard Lodge
Gearstones	Francis Yates
Travellers Rest	George Jackson

BEERHOUSES

Oddfellows Arms	John King
Craven Heifer	John Tomlinson
Masons Arms	Joseph Gillbanks

The police at Ingleton had an annual inspection. In July 1862 it was carried out by Lt.Col. Woodford, Her Majesty's Inspector for the Northern Division. He inspected the men in the yard of the court house. The force consisted of one superintendent, one sergeant and seven constables. The inspection was reported to be highly satisfactory. Col. Woodford also inspected the police books and was satisfied by the way they were kept. Col. Cobb who accompanied the HMI, inspected the court house and offices which were undergoing considerable alterations and he was also perfectly satisfied with what he saw.

At the police station in Ingleton there was a gang chain which was used to take prisoners to Leeds or Wakefield. In May 1869 it was needed for two prisoners charged with robbery, three for vagrancy, and one for being drunk and riotous. These men had been committed to the House of Correction at Wakefield and sent by train from Ingleton. At Clapham station another prisoner was added to the gang. So many prisoners bound by one chain attracted the attention of rail passengers, and most said they had never seen so many prisoners in one gang.[7] By the end of the century the leg irons had been taken out of use and they disappeared. Ingleton had always enjoyed a privileged position with having the court house for the area in their township. Prisoners were brought here, JPs came for sessions and the Ingleton public could easily be spectators in interesting cases. In 1892 that position was threatened when there was a proposal to remove the Petty Sessional Court to Bentham. The locals looked upon this as an injustice to Ingleton and called a meeting at the National School in December 1892. The vicar, the Rev. J. Turner chaired the meeting which was a crowded one. He said he did not know what led in the first instance to Ingleton being chosen for the Petty Sessions, but no doubt the authorities had good reasons for selecting Ingleton as the most suitable place in the Division. Ingleton had not altered, it stood now as it did then, and his opinion there was no other place in the Ewecross Division more suitable.

It was thought that alterations were necessary in the court house, but the meeting expressed the opinion that it would be cheaper to carry out alterations than to erect a new court house at Bentham. Letters were written to the County Council and to local JPs to solicit their support. Some said Ingleton was chosen a the centre for administration of justice because it was central. Bentham, however was not; it was only a mile or so from Lancashire and magistrates and others coming from places including Sedbergh and Dent would be inconvenienced. The meeting set up a small committee to draft a petition and also elected people to visit local villages to gain support and test opinions. The protests were kept up for several years and were still going on seven years later in 1899, but eventually the threat was seen off and Ingleton retained its courthouse.

The JPs who worked at Ingleton Court came from a fairly wide area and were usually local gentry. Ministers of the Church of England were also accepted as JPs. However, by accepting such a position ministers put themselves in an awkward position as to many the work of a JP could not be reconciled with a minister of God. Those who officiated at Ingleton included, W.A.F. Saunders of Wennington Hall, J.W. Farrer and O. Farrer of Ingleborough House Clapham, E.M. Fenwick and T.F. Fenwick, of Melling Hall, E. Tatham, R.W. Waitman, and C. Ingilby. The Rev. Fisher was a JP as was the Vicar of Ingleton the Rev Richard Denny. John Thomas Coates of Ingleton Mill also served many years as a JP.

The Ingleton band on one occasion stopped to play at Wennington Hall and after playing, one of the members knocked at the door. The door was opened by the brusque, local magistrate W.A.F. Saunders:-

The man who had knocked then said, 'Please sir remember the band' But instead of remembering the band, his majesterial highness made the band remember him for some years afterwards: instead of handing out something pecuniary consoling, or inviting the musicians into the house to partake of refreshments, as they had fully anticipated, he just looked straight at them, said in a loud voice, 'Go to the devil and shake yourselves', and then shut the door. The musicians mightily stunned by such an order, did not, I hardly need say, make any attempt to obey it, but walked away at once, and long recollected the welcome here accorded to them'.[8]

With the police head quarters for the Division of Ewecross being at Ingleton there was a superintendent in control. The first superintendent was Mr Exton who came around 1856 and left for service in Skipton in May 1875. Mr Exton was a very popular man and was recalled to Ingleton in August 1875 to be presented with a gold watch and chain by the village in recognition for his services. He was replaced by Superintendent Horn who died at Ingleton on July 26th 1888 at the age of sixty-two. He had served fourteen years at Ingleton and was buried at Skipton. The third police chief was Superintendent Lamb who served at Ingleton from 1888 to around 1893.

Mr Lamb was followed by the notorious Superintended Gunn who served until 1897. In June 1897 he led the Jubilee procession in full military costume, but by the end of the year he had retired. When he left Ingleton most we pleased to see the back of him as he had caused so much trouble and strife in the village. Mr Gunn was followed by Major Hammond. Major Hammond was followed by Superintendent Haynes who ran the Ewecross Division in 1903 with two sergeants and seven constables. Superintendent Haynes left for Rotherham in 1908 and Inspector Barraclough took his place. Superintendent Warburton came to Ingleton next and was transferred to Otley in 1909.

The court house at Ingleton fell into disuse in the twentieth century and was only kept on as a police station. Then the police station itself was closed and eventually sold and turned into a private residence. Responsibility for law and order is no longer an Ingleton affair.

REFERENCES

1. *Lancaster Gazette,* November 5th 1842.
2. *Lancaster Gazette,* January 20th 1855.
3. *Lancaster Guardian,* December 20th 1902.
4. *Lancaster Guardian,* November 12th 1859.
5. *Lancaster Guardian,* October 14th 1898.
6. *Lancaster Guardian,* September 2nd 1876.
7. *Lancaster Guardian,* May 29th 1869.
8. *The Story of my village-Ingleton,* A. Hewitson, Ed. J.I. Bentley, Ingleton Publications 1982.

CHURCH AND CHAPEL

The church of St Mary at Ingleton is delightfully situated on a prominent position overlooking the river valley below. The old tower stands only a few feet away from the slope down to the river and from here there is a picturesque view. There is every possibility that the site of Ingleton Parish Church was once a fortified position overlooking the river crossings in the valley below and designed to secure and protect them. When churches were built many centuries ago their builders often placed them in or on ancient earthworks or at sites of early pagan religions. This was done to show that the Christian Church was taking over the physical and spiritual power of the site.

> In the name of god amen the viij days of Julie in the years of the Reigne of our Lord god a thousande fyve hundreth Seventie and three I William Dennye of felende beinge of hole mynde & in good and perfect remembrance laude and prase be unto almightie god make & ordayne this my present testament containing herein my last will in manner & forme followinge that is to say fyrste I commend my soule unto almightie god my maker & redeemer & my bodie to be buried in the parish church of saint Leonard at Ingleton.

This introduction to the last will and testament of William Denny of Fell End at Ingleton is dated 1573. It was made a generation or so following the establishment of the Church of England and the break up of the Catholic Church by Henry VIII. The first important thing it shows is that the Parish Church of Ingleton was originally dedicated to St Leonard and not St Mary. In the Tudor period Ingleton lay in the parish of Bentham in the Deanery of Lonsdale. Lonsdale was one of the five western deaneries of the Archdeaconry of Richmond. The Archdeaconry of Richmond became part of the new See of Chester formed by Henry VIII in 1541. Due to the fact that most of the Lonsdale deanery was in Lancashire, the records of the deanery of Lonsdale, along with the other four western deaneries, are to be found in the Lancashire Record Office. The documents remained in the local registry at Lancaster until 1858 when they were moved to Somerset House in London, from where they were finally taken to the Lancashire Record Office in Preston in October 1954.

However, one odd will had got amongst Yorkshire records and a nineteenth century local historian found it. It was the will of Richard Gibson of Ingleton made in 1554 and when he saw that the testator wished to be buried in the church yard of St Leonard at Ingleton he jumped to the wrong conclusion. He knew that the parish church at Ingleton was dedicated to St Mary and so he came to the conclusion that Richard Gibson must have lived in the Chapel-le-Dale area and that the church there must be St Leonard's. Far from it!! If he had seen the many other Ingleton wills of the period all wishing to be buried at St Leonard's he would have realised that St Leonard's was then the Ingleton Parish Church and that there had been a change in the dedication from St Leonard to St Mary. Had he also looked at the parish registers he should have seen at this time in the sixteenth century there were no burials at Ingleton Fells.

The misinformed researcher passed his information to the minister at Chapel-le-Dale who accepted it and eventually 'St Leonard's' was inscribed on the church notice board thereby compounding the error. This error has been repeated in local histories of the area. Chapel-le-Dale being a small chapel-of-ease was never dedicated to any particular saint and certainly not to St Leonard. Originally it was Weasedale Chapel and later Chapel-le-Dale. The change of dedication at Ingleton, from St Leonard, the patron saint of prisoners and pregnant women, whose emblem was a link of chains, to St Mary was probably made sometime in the seventeenth century. St Leonard, who was a hermit, was one of the most popular saints in the later middle ages. A change of dedication was often made when a church was rebuilt. Why the change was made at Ingleton is not known. When the Rev. James Raine MA, Canon of York wrote *The Dedications of Yorkshire Churches* in 1873, the old dedication of Ingleton Church was given as St Leonard and the modern dedication was left blank.

The second thing that William Denny's will shows us is that the old Catholic religious declarations used in the introductions to will were being dropped. However, some still stuck to the old and when we see a will still mentioning the virgin, the saints or angels we know that the testator very likely had Catholic beliefs. John Harling, an Ingleton innkeeper was one of the last to use the specifically catholic introduction to his will when he died in 1570 and left his soul to the blessed lady Saint Mary and to all the holy company of heaven.

ROMAN CATHOLIC - RECUSANTS

Having noted that the parish church at Ingleton was originally Catholic and from 1536 Church of England, it must be remembered that the Catholic religion never died out in the area. Ingleton had many Catholic 'recusants' in the seventeenth century who were listed, often fined and sometimes persecuted. A recusant meant a 'refuser' in that they refused to attend the parish church. Twistleton was a stronghold for the old religion as lists show and the reason could well be connected with the fact that the Lord of the manor of Twistleton was a Shireburn a member of the Catholic family of Shireburns from Stonyhurst in Lancashire.

In 1604 catholic recusants were listed and Bentham had two, Giggleswick one, Horton one, Kirkby Lonsdale two, but Ingleton had seven.[1] The magistrates at Skipton listed Popish recusants in the area in 1678 and 1679 and those from Ingleton are listed below:-

1678 Ingleton
Thomas Baynes Isabell his wife.
Widow Calvert
Jeffrey Leake Cicilly his wife
Anth Leak Agnes his wife
Thomas Leak & Eliz his wife
Richard Beesley, Agnes his wife
John Taylor, Isabell his wife, Richard his son, Agnes his daughter

1679 Ingleton
Thomas Baines & Issabell his wife
Widow Calvert
Jeffrey Leak Cicilly his wife
Anthony Leak Agnes his wife
Wife of Thomas Leake
John Taylor& Isabell his wife, Richard & Agnes their children

The recusants had to report to Skipton, but John Lodge the minister at Ingleton spoke up on behalf of John Taylor explaining that, 'John Taylor is sick and likely to die and his wife near delivery and not able to travel.' This activity by magistrates in Skipton was a result of the 'Popish Plot' of 1678 divulged by Titus Oates which caused hundreds to be arrested, tortured and many executed, in spite of it being completely untrue. The plotters, Titus Oates said, planned to assassinate the King and put his Catholic brother on the throne. Anti Catholic feelings ran high through the country and Catholics were called in to sign an oath of allegiance.

In July 1691 the Chief Constable again issued orders for Papists to be brought to judges to take oaths. It was also ordered that they should be disarmed and that horses they had over £5 in value should be seized and sold. Any guns they owned should be taken for his majesty's service. Those papists recorded at Ingleton in 1691 were, 'Richard Beesley of Twistleton Gent and Agnes his wife, Isobell Taylor, Isobell Redmayne, Thomas Leake and Elizabeth his wife and Agnes Leake widow'. It must be remembered that Catholics could not attend university, be Members or Parliament, join the civil service or be officers in the military and that they were barred from many other appointments. Priest hunting and the harassment of recusants died down in the mid-eighteenth century, but Catholic emancipation did not come until 1829 with the Catholic Emancipation Act.

ORIGINS OF INGLETON CHURCH

St Leonard's at Ingleton was first built in the Norman period. Many churches in this country are built on prehistoric sites especially burial mounds. In fact Pope Gregory in a letter of 601 to Abbott Mellitus, who later became the Bishop of London, instructed that pagan temples should be sanctified with holy water and new churches erected on their site to usurp the early religious connections. This allowed converts from paganism to keep a connection with the old site and also allowed the new Christian church to show that it had triumphed over the old site of religious or military power. In Ingleton's case the church was built on the site of a possible early fortification that commanded the river crossings at Ingleton. Walk round to the church tower at Ingleton and look into the valley and you will have little doubt that this commanding position was used as an early fortification.

Ingleton Church came under Bentham and the Rector of Bentham was the parson. The minister at Ingleton was a curate and Ingleton was a chapelry until Ingleton became a parish in its own right in the late nineteenth century. However, in this book the church at Ingleton is always referred to as the Parish Church and the man in charge as the minister. When Ingleton was divided from Bentham the Rector of Bentham claimed the advowson of Ingleton Church, that is the right of choosing the minister, and had to pay £40 annually towards his salary.

MINISTERS AT INGLETON CHURCH

William Walker	1548	
William Redman	1555	
Richard Baines	1557	died
Thomas Fieldhouse	1558,1562	
Michael Farthwaite	1577	died 1583
George Williamson	c.1588-1618	
Edmond Atkinson	1623	died
Francis Robinson	1624	died (probably of plague)
William Nodale	1629	died
Christopher Frankland	1642	died 1642
John Ashton	1654	Commonwealth period
Leonard Walker	1654	High Registrar
William Smith	c.1660 d.1675	(Also Rect of Lowther)
Christopher Lupton	1665	(died)
John Brockbank	1667	
John Wells	1675	
John Lodge	1679	
John Spark	1688-1690	

William Thornton	1691	died 1694
John Wetherhead	1697	
Robert Clarke	1684-1699	(possibly longer)
Anthony Backhouse (Bachus)	1707	(buried Skipton April 28th 1713)
James Redmayne	1707	
Thomas Bowes	1711-1730	
J. Jackson	1731-1739	
Robert Hodgson	1740-1763	
Lawrence Moore	1763-1764	
John Waller	1764-1805	
William Waller	1805-1843	
Robert Richardson Balderston	1843-1844	(Acted for W. Waller Rev. Pooley. during his illness.)
Richard Denny	1844-1874	
Thomas Dodd Sherlock	1874-1879	
Charles Reay Pughe	1880-1883	
James Turner	1884-1907	
John Llewellyn	1907-1917	
D.J. Davies	1917-1921	
Henry J. Lockett	1921-1934	
S.N. Livesey	1934-1937	
Gordon Charles Ashbee	1938-1944	
Norman Vincent Dinsdale	1945-1950	
Harold John Croft	1950-1957	
William Simpson	1958-1964	
William Ruck	1964-1980	
Christopher Wray	1980-1986	
Roger Joseph Hamilton Fry	1987-1995	
Tim Ashworth	1996-2003	
Charles Ellis	2004	

William Walker

William Walker was named as 'clerk', that is minister, in John Foxcroft's will in 1548. As John Foxcroft lived in Ingleton and wished to be buried in Ingleton churchyard the first witness William Walker Clerk is most likely to have been the minister of Ingleton at the time. William Walker is also witness to Roland Jenson's will in 1553. He is not noted after this time and may well have been removed when Mary Tudor came to the throne in 1553 and restored the Catholic faith.

William Redman

This was the time of Mary Tudor and having brought back the Catholic religion, wills brought back mention of 'owre Ladye Sainte Marye and all the Blessed Company in havene'. Ministers had to be careful as over three hundred Protestants were burned by 'Bloody Mary'. William would have been a practising Catholic. He was associated with Robert Margerison who is noted in the wills of sisters, Isabel and Alice Craven, in 1556. Isabel requests him, 'to pray for me and to say a whole trental.' A trental was a set of thirty daily masses for the dead usually said on consecutive days. Alice left five shillings for him to pray for her soul and say half a trental. Robert Margerison would seem to have been Catholic priest in the Ingleton area at that time, but he is not mentioned again.

Richard Baines

Sir Richard Baines of Ingleton made his will at Ingleton in 1557 wishing to be buried in the Churchyard of St Leonard the Parish Church. He was certainly Catholic in his religion and his shown by his will which states, 'I bequeathe my Soule to almightie God his Blessed mother Oure Lady Saynte Mary & to all the holy Companye in heaven and my body to be buried in the Churche of Saynte Leonard at Yngleton and there to be eyarthed at the Syghte of William Proctor of the hylle and Leonard Wederheade of Southerscales.' No doubt William Procter and Leonard Wetherhird were also good Catholics.

Thomas Fieldhouse

Thomas Fieldhouse is a witness to the will of Richard Wetherhead in 1558. The will names, 'Sir Thomas Fieldhouse curate'. The Rector of Bentham at the time was Richard Fieldhouse and from a will we know that Thomas had a brother. The likelihood is that Richard Fieldhouse the Rector of Bentham was Thomas' brother and put him in as curate at Ingleton. As Thomas Fieldhouse runs past 1558 when Mary Tudor died we must suppose that he was the new Protestant minister and likely to have set Ingleton back once again on a Protestant course.

Michael Farthwaite

In 1578 there was a Visitation of the Chester Diocese Commissioner. The church was recorded as being in a poor state and the minister was heavily criticised.[2]

> They have not Service done in dew time. Ther parson kepeth no house nor Releveth the poore; he is not diligent in vysitinge the sicke. And lately kept in his hous a noughty woman, he teacheth not the cathechisme they have no sermons he himself fornycateth without doing any penaunce and he maketh a donge hill in the churchyard.
> – and he hathn kepte a Typlinge house.

The Commissioner obviously did not like Michael Farthwaite and to mention such things as the curate having once kept an ale house and there being a midden in the churchyard suggest this was a deliberate attempt to find every item to denounce him. Most churchyards would have had a midden at that time. The answer may lie in the minister's religious beliefs. and his disputes with the Lord of the manor. The commissioner was incorrect in his report because the minister at Ingleton was a curate and not a parson and he makes no mention of the dedication. This appears to be Michael Farthwaite the minister who died five years later and who explained his problems in his will.

Michael Farthwite died in October 1583 and his will made on July 18th of the same year survives and tells an interesting story. He explains that he disagreed with the Lord of the Manor Sir Richard Cholmley who would not allow him to live in a house in the Manor of Ingleton. So Michael Farthwaite built a cottage at Bridge End just over the river in Twistleton Manor and lived there. The inventory attached to the will addresses him as Sir Michael Farthwaite as it was the manner of the period that ministers were addressed as Sir. Sadly his wife was left to pay more debts than the value of his goods.

The commissioner who criticized Michael Farthwaite said that he neglected visiting the sick. The will of Alexander Beaumond of Ingleton tells a different story. Michael Farthwaite was sole executor of the will of Alexander Beaumond in February 1581. Alexander asks his forgiveness for trouble over the deeds to two cottages. He also acknowledges Michael Farthwaite's great troubles and costs during his sickness for which he left him some payment. So here was a minister criticised by the diocese but praised by the parishioners.

George Williamson

George Williamson was minister at Ingleton in difficult times and had to administer to many who were dying of the plague. He was called into their houses to witness their wills and must have been put at considerable risk. However, he survived through the plague of the 1590s and was mentioned as witness on the will of John Beaumond in October 1613.

Edmond Atkinson

When Edmond Atkinson was buried at Ingleton on September 26th 1623 the entry in the burial register recorded 'Edmond Atkinson Clarke' which meant that he was a minister. Only his inventory survives and this says he was of Fell End, a farm just above Ingleton. As 1623 was a bad year for the plague he most probably fell victim to this or to some associated disease. His inventory shows few goods and no livestock: the total value of his goods and chattels was only twelve shillings although he was owed considerable debts by people from Hutton Roof, Rathmell, Clapham and Ingleton.

Christopher Frankland.

Christopher Frankland was curate at Ingleton until his death in March 1642. He was criticised in the Archbishop's Visitation Records for 1633, 'for not reading praier upon the Eves of Sundaies & holi dayes, nor upon Wednesdays & Freidayes and for omitting to weare the surplice at some time in reading divine service & for cathechiseing but once a moneth.' Christopher was buried in the church at Ingleton on April 1st 1642. His inventory shows that he had few possession apart from his clothes and books. He did have a horse which he would have used for travelling through the parish. In 1640 he was remembered in Thomas Battersby's will and left 10shillings.

Leonard Walker

'Leonard Walker of Ingleton in the said County husbandman being Chosen by the Inhabitants & householders of the parish of Ingleton to bee theire parish Register came before mee the Fift day of Novemb[r] 1653 And was by mee approved on to bee theire said parish Register & to have the keeping of this booke. And be sworn according to the Act (of Parliam[nt] of the xxiiij[th] of August Last) in that case made and provided. John Assheton'.[3] This was the Commonwealth period when the puritans ruled the roost. Christmas celebrations were abolished as were so many other things like maypole dancing. Stained glass windows were removed from many churches and plain glass used in its place.

Leonard Walker, chosen in 1654 to keep the parish registers, was likely to have been sacked pretty quickly at the Restoration. Presbyterians and other puritans were cleared out from churches across the country. After the restoration the registers would have come back into the keeping of the minister as this had always been considered to be one of the minister's main tasks. Fairs and dances, Christmas and other festivals, would have come back to Ingleton and Leonard Walker and his friends would have had to make the best of it. Leonard Walker died in 1674 and his probate record says, 'Clerk de Ingleton', but he was certainly not still minister at that time.

William Smith

William Smith was Curate at Ingleton as well as Rector of Lowther. His son the Revd Joseph Smith became a distinguished divine and writer. William Smith was Rector of Lowther in 1657, but at that time Ingleton was controlled by Cromwell's men and William would have been unable to serve as minister at Ingleton. He most probably served somewhere between 1660 and 1670 after the Commonwealth Period when Charles II came to the throne at the Restoration. William Smith died in 1675.[4] There is the possibility that William Smith held the position of curate of Ingleton, but actually remained at Lowther and only visited occasionally, having a stand-in running Ingleton chapelry. This is suggested as William Smith does not appear to be mentioned in the parish registers or any Ingleton wills.

John Brockbank

On April 25th 1667 the marriage register at Ingleton records, 'Johannes Brockbank minister de Ingleton et Maria Willon filia Thomae Willon de Kirkby Lonsdale in conjugio juncti sunt per publicatorem.' The register says that the marriage was at Kirkby Lonsdale. The baptism register shows that he had a son John who was baptised on February 25th 1668. A letter from him exists dated November 25th 1677. The letter is in possession of Bill Dootson a collector of Ingleton Postal History. It was sent – 'To M[r] Edward Wilson this give att Parkhouse, or else where, with verve and speed. Leave this at Geo. Yeatts his house att Cowinge Bridge to be sent wth speed as is directed.' It reads:-

Sir, This night I am informed by Mr. Knipe that the Parishioners of Beethom doe expect me at Beethom the next Lords day and that they have notice of my coming then, which makes me wonder much, for neither by word nor writtinge I ever as yet promised to come there, yet notwithstandinge seeing the Parish doe depende upon my commeinge there I would have come: But that I have already promised to be at Weasdale Chappell then which is a Chapple belonginge to us: So, S[r] I pray excuse my

Will of minister William Thornton who died 1694.

94

not comeing then. But if the Churchwardens will be pleased to appointe a time when I may come, and give me Sufficient Notice if it be att or before Christmas then (God wilinge) I will come, and do yr Parish what I can, that I may be (as Mr. Knipe informes me) kept harmless. Pray Sʳ give the Churchwardens notice of this that they may provide for the day that yʳ Parish may not be disappointed and by so doeing you shall much oblige your servant to command. Jo Brockbank'.

William Thornton.

William Thornton, Curate at Ingleton, died in November 1694. His inventory of his goods and chattels contained only his clothing, his books and a box with other small items. His possessions were valued on November 20ᵗʰ 1694 by Thomas Baynes, the curate of Bolton, and three others. His purse and clothing was valued at £8, his books at £7 and the rest of his goods at £1, making the total value of his possessions £16.

Thomas Bowes 1711-1730.

Thomas Bowes was curate at Ingleton and is noted in the parish registers. He was made a Freeman of City of Lancaster in 1723. He married Mrs Jane Stout at Ingleton on November 25ᵗʰ 1717. He served at Ingleton from around 1711 to 1730. During his ministry many marriages of folks from Lancaster Parish, Sedburgh and other places appear in the Ingleton Marriage Register. At times there are more outsiders marrying at Ingleton than locals and as they were not coming for the beauty of the church. Thomas Bowes must have been very well known over a wide area. After a long succession of short serving ministers Thomas Bowes remained minister for nineteen years. Nothing is known of J.Jackson who followed Thomas Bowes and served until Robert Hodgson came to the church in 1740.

Robert Hodgson 1740-1763. (1716-1800)

Robert Hodgson the son of James Hodgson was baptised at Ingleton on April 7ᵗʰ 1716. He served as minister at Ingleton for over twenty years eventually moving to become vicar of Thornton-in-Lonsdale in 1763. He and his family were close to the Greenwood family of Bank Hall, and shortly after his move to Thornton his daughter, Jane, married David Greenwood at Thornton Church in May 1765. His grandson Robert Hodgson Greenwood became a Cambridge academic and friend of William Wordsworth.

Robert Hodgson was vicar at Thornton for thirty-seven years and died on March 10ᵗʰ 1800, the same day and same month as he was born in 1716. He was buried on March 13ᵗʰ within the altar rails at Thornton Church.

John Waller 1764-1804

John Waller was a member of family that came to the Ingleton area in the sixteenth century or earlier. When William Waller made his will in September 1598 he left his daughter one dwelling house, 'in Towne and fields of Compton in County of Bedford.' This shows that the family still had connection from the south of England from where they came. The Wallers had been an educated and influential family. Edmond Waller went to Parliament at seventeen, was a famous poet, and personally worked with Charles I, Cromwell, Charles II and James II in his long and eventful life. Ingleton Wallers claimed descent from the same family. Their earliest notable member was Sir Richard Waller who captured the Duke of Orleans at the Battle of Agincourt and added the Duke's coat of arms to his own. Some Ingleton Wallers in the nineteenth century still claimed that same coat of arms.

'The Reverend John Waller upwards of forty years Incumbent Curate of this Chapel he died March the 6ᵗʰ aged sixty-five years.' So records the Parish Burial Register March 10ᵗʰ

1805 when he was buried. He was baptised on April 4th 1743 at Ingleton church the son of Christopher Waller. He came as curate to Ingleton in 1764 and remained there the rest of his life. As chairman of Ingleton Vestry meetings he played an important part in the running of the village.

William Waller 1805-1843 (lived 1760-1844)

The Rev. William Waller BD took over as minister at Ingleton shortly following his father's death. Between them they served eighty years at Ingleton Church. In the 1830s William Waller taught at Ingleton's Churchyard School and was known for his short temper and heavy-handed punishment. This was remembered by Anthony Hewitson in his memoirs. Hewitson also tells us that the Rev. Waller was a person of considerable learning much above the average of country ministers and that he was an admirable preacher. However, sometimes while in church he would stop preaching for a moment or two to take a sip of wine from a fairly large goblet which he had on a shelf within the pulpit. When the congregation were leaving church, comments were often made on the service and they were invariably full of praise.

William Waller could have had a more successful career, but he chose to stay at Ingleton where he was contented. His father had served Ingleton Church for life and he also served for a lifetime. Their record of service has not been equalled before and certainly not since. The story of how he helped a William Tomlinson a youth who lost his leg in an accident is told in the last chapter of this book and certainly shows that he was both compassionate and generous. William Waller died on October 10th 1844 aged eighty.

Richard Denny JP - the Clerical Magistrate 1844 -1874

The Rev. Richard Denny BA, of Trinity College Dublin, continued the tradition of long service at Ingleton. He came following the death of William Waller and remained for twenty-nine years. He gained a great attachment to Ingleton going so far as to name a son James Ingleton Denny. However, he sought the position of JP and having become a JP used his power in the parish as both minister and JP. This made him unpopular to many in the village because of some harsh decisions he made both as a vicar and magistrate.

He was typical of Cruikshank's clerical magistrate. Vicars had considerable power, but when they were magistrates as well, their status could be formidable and was not usually used to the benefit of their parishioners and other village folk. When the Rev. Denny was ordained by the Bishop he was asked, 'Will you be diligent in prayers-laying aside the study of the world and the flesh? He said he would. He was asked by the Bishop, 'Will you maintain and set forwards, as much as lieth in you, quietness, peace, and love among all Christian People?' He said he would. There was a rising tide amongst reformers

Cruikshank's Clerical Magistrate.

96

again such 'clerical magistrates' and William Hone, writer and satirist (1780-1842) wrote his Clerical Magistrate poem from which some lines are quoted below.

> He though vowing 'from all wordly studies to cease',
> Breaks the Peace of the Church to be Justice of Peace;
> Breaks his vows made to Heaven-a pander for Power,
> A Perjuror – a guide to the People no more,
> On God turns his back, when he turns States Agent;

Rev. Denny was autocratic. During the Church Rate controversy when Joseph Carr and W. Dent Thompson were due to have a debate at the National School, at the last minute Rev. Denny gave orders that Joseph Carr was not to be allowed to speak. A platform had been set up and the room was crowded. Joseph Carr went outside and spoke in the village square. Mr Hunter, one of the school trustees, who was there, said he had not the slightest objection to Mr Carr speaking. It is surprising that Joseph Carr gave up so easily, but perhaps he saw the futility of opposing Denny at this point

Another example of Denny's nasty work was when he imprisoned a man for using his field as a toilet and had him taken to the lock up at Bentham. He did this in spite of the fact that the man had a young boy with him who was then left wandering in the village alone. There was no mercy from the vicar, but some of his parishioners had mercy and they went to Bentham, paid the fine and had the man freed and brought him back to Ingleton and united him with his son. This episode was recounted in the *Lancaster Guardian* in August 1869. Of course his nonconformist opponents relished in telling this story and also recounting that in his position as JP Denny had dismissed cruelty cases against animals.

Even when the Rev. Denny carried out good works such as giving out village charities as he did at Christmas each year there was negative side. He only gave charities to church-people and usually ignored others. He chaired township and vestry meetings and served on the bench in Ingleton Court House. In 1859 he was chairman at the founding of the Ingleton Angling Organisation, but here his motive appears to have been to control fishing in the rivers and to stop the local working man from poaching. In 1860 a local rifle corps was founded at Ingleton and not only was the Rev. Denny the chairman of the inaugural meeting, but it was reported that he was one of the 'moving spirits of the meeting.' This would appear unusual activity for a clergyman.

There is a stained glass window to his memory which reads, 'In Dutiful and Loving Memory of Richard Denny BA for 29 years the faithful pastor of this parish. The founder of the school and the special friend of its youth. This window is inscribed by his affectionate family born 1813 died 1888.' However, we must remember that this memorial window was put up by members of his own family. The Rev. Denny's case at Ingleton illustrates that a vicar was unwise to be a JP, but so frequently in Victorian times many were. William Denny died in 1888 and was buried at Ingleton.

Thomas D. Sherlock 1874-1879

The Rev. Sherlock was the nephew of the Rev. Edgar Sherlock Rector of Bentham and through his uncle's influence came to be minister of Ingleton Church. We know of three Sherlock brothers, Edgar Rector of Bentham, Cornelius architect of Liverpool and Randal Hopley Sherlock newspaper proprietor in Liverpool, and they all come into our Ingleton story. Thomas Sherlock was the only son of Randal Hopley Sherlock. The Sherlocks were conspicuous enough in Ingleton for Conan Doyle, who knew Ingleton well, to adopt the name Sherlock for his famous detective.

Thomas Sherlock moved along with the church restoration and did at least propose a good architect, his uncle Cornelius. On Sunday November 9th 1879 Rev. Sherlock gave his farewells at Ingleton Church. He left to become a minister in London. Thomas Sherlock died in 1893 and in his will left £500 to the living of the parish and £50 to the poor of Ingleton for immediate distribution. Before Thomas Sherlock came to Ingleton the previous four ministers had served close to one hundred and thirty years. From Sherlock's time all ministers at Ingleton, with the exception of James Turner, have been relatively short serving ministers and sixteen ministers together have only served as long as the previous four.

Charles Reay Pughe 1880-1883

Ingleton was a popular place for vicars in Victorian times and when the Rev. Pughe was appointed in 1880 it was reported that there were over one hundred applications for the position. Pughe was not popular at Ingleton and appears to have done little except get the promise of a £1000 from his wealthy aunt towards the building of the new church. When he gave his last speech on leaving he said, 'When I look back I feel that were my time to come over again I might have done far more than I have done, but I trust what little I have done has not been in vain'.

After only a year in office he sacked the Parish Clerk saying that he would be clerk himself and a Parish Clerk would no longer be needed. This was a cruel act to a man who had served for many years and an act for which he was long remembered at Ingleton. Francis Bullock had worked for a pittance for thirty-two years and had served in the choir for over forty years and was cast aside for asking for a slightly larger salary.

One positive thing that the Revd Pughe did do was to bring surplices to Ingleton church choir, but he was democratic and asked the choir to vote on it and the vote was almost unanimously in favour. So in January 1882 the choir appeared for the first time in church wearing white surplices. Charles Pughe took his leave of Ingleton to go to Castle Heaton in Wiltshire in December 1883 having served only three years.

James Turner 1884- 1907

James Turner was born in Peshawar North West India. He was MA of Gonville and Caius College Cambridge. He came to Ingleton from Headingly at Leeds and was inducted on Thursday the 14th of February 1884 by Edgar Sherlock the Rector of Bentham. At his induction Rector Sherlock lectured James Turner on a clergyman's duties with some force; daily visiting, meeting all parishioner, making no distinction between rich and poor, visiting the sick, preaching, and being a godly example before the public. This might have been necessary for his predecessor Denny, but not for James Turner who well knew the duties of a clergyman and was ready to carry them out at Ingleton. James Turner gave his first sermon on Sunday the 17th of February 1884.

Rev. James Turner with his pet dog.

James Turner told church groups of one ancestor who was one of those imprisoned in the Black Hole of Calcutta in 1756. He was a man whose main concern was his parishioners and being a man of action he got on with the re-building of the parish church in a speedier manner than his predecessors and completed the work.

J. Llewellyn 1907-1917.

John Llewellyn came to Ingleton on the request of James Turner who resigned due to ill health in 1907. He served until 1917. D.T. Davis vicar of Burley, Leeds came to Ingleton to follow John Llewellyn.

Information on former ministers at Ingleton has come from a wide variety of sources. The parish registers themselves often note the minister and churchwardens in their pages. At other times the ministers are shown only in the burial register on their death. From the time of the Rev. Jackson in 1731 the list is more accurate. There has been no attempt to cover every minister especially as some ministers seem to have sunk without trace. However, this is the most comprehensive collection of information ever put together on the ministers who served at Ingleton. The early ministers of Ingleton were curates rather than vicars as Ingleton was a chapelry of Bentham Parish. However we must remember that up to the end of the nineteenth century they held considerable power in the village.

TITHES AND THE TITHE AWARD AT INGLETON

Tithes of one tenth were charged on all Ingleton farmers, but the tithes went to the Rector of Bentham and not to the minister of Ingleton. There was a tithe barn at Ingleton where tithes were collected and stored. By the mid- nineteenth century the old tithe barn had been demolished and the Tithe Award of 1839 stated, 'There is not any Glebe Land within the said township (Ingleton) except it be the site of an old Tithe Barn.' This was the only church land at Ingleton apart from the church and churchyard. The award does not mention where the barn had stood. However, Joseph Carr in his memoirs tells us that Harling Barn, 'was used in olden times for tithe corn.'

As a result of the Tithe Commutation Act of 1836 tithes in corn, pigs, lambs and other produce were turned into cash payments and became a rent charge on the land. The Commissioners met in Ingleton and finally produced a Tithe Map and Schedule. The map showed the land of the township and all fields and buildings were numbered. The schedule listed the owners and occupiers of that land and the rent charges they were due to pay. Just as there had been an outcry against church rates there was an outcry against church tithes and eventually they were ended. The Tithe Act of 1925 abolished the rent-charge and the Tithe Act of 1936 abolished tithes altogether. Copies of the Ingleton Tithe Award can be found in the North Yorkshire Record office at Northallerton, the West Yorkshire Archives at Leeds, and the Public Record Office in London.

THE PARISH REGISTERS

> Their names, their dates, are entered in a column,
> The unjust here embalmed beside the just:
> And in the pages of this dusty volume
> A second time they moulder into dust (D.L.J.)

Thomas Cromwell, Vicar General to Henry VIII, was responsible for the origin of parish registers. In 1538 he gave instructions that a book and chest with two locks should be provided in each parish and that a register should be kept of all baptisms, marriages and burials. The first registers were on paper and in 1598 parishes were ordered to use vellum in future and copy up the old paper register onto vellum. Many ministers were too lazy to bother and either got rid of the early register or just left it as a paper copy. Ingleton's parish registers begin in 1607. The first register is in well worn condition, the writing is uneven and often faded and stained. Information given is very basic. Below is the first entry of a baptism, marriage and burial from the Ingleton registers:-

> Anno Domini 1607
> Robert Wetherhird filius Matthei bapt fuit 28 June
> Richardus Balderston et Emma Hirde nupt. Fuerunt 8 July
> Leonardus Walker sepultus erat 5 Oct

Most registers were badly kept through the Civil War period and gaps occur in the Ingleton Registers. During the Commonwealth period JPs and not ministers solemnised marriages and those who were appointed were called Registers. The early entries were in Latin, but Latin was banned in parish registers in 1733. Up to 1751 the new year began on Lady Day, March 25th. December 31st 1721 was followed by January 1st 1721 and not 1722. Although before 1752 many people celebrated new year on January 1st, the legal year did not start till March 25th. Following the Calendar Act of 1751 from 1752 the new year began on January 1st as it does today.

In 1754 Hardwick's Marriage Act enforced better recording of marriages using a separate register. Standardised forms were used to record the status of those marrying, their parish of residence, the occupation of the bridegroom, and their signatures, if they could write, and their mark if they could not. Rose's Act of 1812 brought in separate printed registers for both baptisms and burials. Baptisms now included the names, addresses and occupations of the parents. The burial register included the age, address and occupation of the deceased.

In 1978 the Parochial Register and Records Measure ordered that all parish registers should be deposited in a secure record office usually the local County Record Office. Ingleton Parish Registers are now in the North Yorkshire County Record Office at Northallerton where they can be seen on microfilm. The church retains the current volumes only. The registers from 1607 to 1812 were printed by the Yorkshire Parish Register Society in 1933, but the volume is quite scarce today. Parish registers often included charities, they help with discovering who was minister at a given time and they are vital for researching family history. The registers also show that throughout the centuries the population was mobile with families coming and going. Sadly until the nineteenth century employment details were rarely given.

BURIED IN WOOLLEN.

By an act of 1666, to come in after March 25th 1666, people had to bury the dead in woollen cloth. As the act was not well observed a repeat act of 1678 was brought in making it necessary to swear an affidavit in front of a JP that the burial had been in woollen and the affidavit had to be shown to the minister at the church. The reason for the act was originally 'for the encouragement of the woollen manufactures, and the prevention of the export of moneys for buying and importing of linen.' There was a five pounds penalty for those disobeying the order. In September 7th 1678 James Craven is the first mentioned, 'wound in woollen according to the Act.'

At Ingleton on July 5th 1681 Anne the wife of Giles Foxcroft of Weathercote was buried and the register records in 'Linin'. There was no doubt she had requested to be buried in linen and was so buried in spite of the legislation. Whether her husband paid the five pounds penalty is not known. The act was suspended in 1814, but it had not been enforced for years.

CHILD MARRIAGES
In earlier centuries child marriages were often carried out where the bride and groom were as young as ten years of age. Some times this was done at night which shows there was some question of legitimacy attached to it. In one case the curate who performed the marriage was punished by the Archbishop of York for, 'marieng at inconvenient tymes and unlawful persons'. Before 1763 a girl could marry at the age of twelve or more and a boy fourteen or more. With a bishop's licence they could marry even younger. After 1763 a woman had to be twenty-one to marry unless she had consent of parents. Many of these marriages only come to light due to later divorce proceedings. Such is the case at Ingleton where Thomas Bentham and Ellen Bentham alias Bolton were married at Ingleton about 1552. The divorce case was held in February 1565.

This deponent says that Thomas Bentam and Elene Bentam were married together at Engleton above xij yeres passid, the said Thomas beinge at that tyme under xij yeres of age (12) and the said Ellin somewhat younger, and beinge askid whie they were married in their minoritie, he sais, that Richard Bentam, grandfather unto the said Eleine, was a very weathy man; and (it) was supposed that he wold have been good unto them, and bestowed somme good ferme upon her; but, ere he died, the said Thomas and Ellein disagreed, and she plaid many light points. The grandfather takinge displeasure, left her nothing.

Ellen said she married Thomas but how long ago she could not remember as she was very young, about ten years old or twelve at the most. She also said 'that after the said marriage they never lay together, nor dwelled together in one howse; but ever did dissent and were continualie ever asunder; she with her mother, and he x (ten) miles of'.' Ellen confessed to having had illegitimate children by other men and said she was sorry for her offences: a divorce was granted.[5]

INGLETON PARISH CLERKS
The parish clerk was normally appointed by the minister of the church. Quite frequently in early times he might well be in holy orders himself, but later he was usually a man with another occupation such as shoemaker, landlord or whatever. He led funerals and gave the responses at services. He also often acted as sexton digging graves, ringing the bells and doing odd jobs in the church. He was paid for services at feasts, weddings and baptisms.

Robert Clerk
Robert Clerk was the first noted parish clerk at Ingleton. He died in 1691 and the burial register records, 'Robb Clark ye Parish Clerk, in ye body of ye Church'

James Redmayne
James Redmayne was another parish clerk whose position was recorded when he was buried at Ingleton in 1723.

Robert Wilkinson
Robert Wilkinson was a parish clerk at Ingleton who died in 1750.

Paul Berry

Paul Berry was a long serving parish clerk and more is known about him than any other. He was born in 1762 in Yorkshire, but not Ingleton. His wife was called Elizabeth and although they did not marry at Ingleton they were in the village by 1790 when their first child, Grace, was baptised. Paul and Elizabeth had ten children baptised at Ingleton from 1790 to 1811. Paul probably came to the village for work and was working as a cotton spinner in 1803 at Ingleton mill. In that year he was shown as a volunteer in the local militia.

As he was said to have been parish clerk for over fifty years he must have begun around 1800 when he was working as a cotton spinner. It was usual that the position as parish clerk was a secondary occupation as it paid little. He is noted in the 1841 census return when he was seventy-eight years old, and living at Ingleton Bridge by the river and recorded as Chapel clerk. He was parish clerk when Anthony Hewitson was young in 1846 and Hewitson noted him in his memoirs in the following passages:-

The Parish Clerk whose business it was to read the responses and lessons and announce the psalms to be sung was a very antiquated, singularly-ramshackle individual. He would now and then fall fast asleep and require rousing to make his response or he would start up and say 'Amen' loudly at a point where it was unnecessary or he would give out the wrong psalm. Altogether he was a source of much astonishment, amusement and annoyance, but being an old church official he was allowed to remain at his post until at last age and infirmity entirely incapacitated him from clerking.

When a death occurred in the village Paul Berry, the old parish clerk, made the grave himself - if the interment had to take place in the churchyard. Many a time whilst doing such work he quite nonchalantly threw out, upon the side, a skull or sundry other osseous remains, which were afterwards deposited in the bone house- a weird walled in place at the north western corner of the church. The ground was very closely packed with bodies and this accounted for the finds which the clerk made. In the course of his excavations he now and then met with an entire corpse in a considerable state of preservation-so well preserved that he would be able to identify it. One day while digging a grave, he reached a coffin, and curiosity prompted him to have a peep into it, so he gently raised the lid and then beheld the face of a man whom he had buried numerous years before. He at once recognised the man and said the only difference he could see about him was that his beard and finger nails had grown a good deal.

Generally when a funeral was about to take place the same ancient official turned up at the house wherein the coffined corpse lay. The bulk, or a tolerable number of the neighbouring people, previously bid to the funeral, were also there. Warm ale or spirits was served out amongst them, as they stood about the door, and funeral cakes were likewise distributed. The closed-up coffin was then taken outside and placed upon the bier and the old clerk commenced singing a very plaintive psalm or hymn, after which the funeral party walked to church.

In was noted in the *Lancaster Gazette* in May 1847 that Paul Berry had sued Joseph Hodgson and Edward Tomlinson at the Ingleton petty Sessions in the Wheat Sheaf for not paying Easter Offerings known as smoke money or the smoke groat. The Parish Clerk was entitled to the 'smoke groat' at Whitsuntide, but Paul Berry complained that few now paid it. Earlier he had taken people to court for non payment. Originally, before the Reformation, the money went to the Pope. Then in many places it went to the priest. At Ingleton and other places it was given to the parish clerk. It was sometimes called 'smoke money' 'smoke silver' or 'smoke farthing'. It was paid by everyone having a fire in the house. Paul Berry died in 1851 and was buried in Ingleton churchyard on March 31st aged eighty-nine.

Francis Bullock

Francis Bullock followed Paul Berry as clerk at Ingleton Church. He was born at Tatham and came to live at Ingleton in his younger days. He served as parish clerk and sexton for thirty-two years and also for a time ran a shop in the village. In 1881 he asked for a rise in his salary. The Rev Pughe had only been in the village just over a year, but he not only refused to accept Francis Bullock's tender as parish clerk, but also stated that in future no parish clerk would be needed as he himself would do the job.

On April 28th 1881 the *Lancaster Guardian* reported that 'The income of the Parish Clerk was not large as he only got his fees at deaths and marriages and the smoke groat at Easter. The income from the smoke groat was small and uncertain. This year it yielded only 24 shillings and it was obtained with some difficulty. Many of the parishioners ceased to pay the smoke groat many years ago, and many of those who paid it did it more through respect to the Parish Clerk than from a sense that it was a just due. The clerk has been a member of Ingleton Church Choir for over forty years and now has resigned that membership.'

Francis Bullock resigned as clerk and sexton because they would not accept his tender. During his service he had dug 647 graves, and as parish clerk had attended 153 weddings. The church was stingy in the treatment of an old church servant who was 71 years of age and had served so well. Francis Bullock had obviously done much more for Ingleton Church than ever the Rev. Pughe did. To make matters worse the Rev. Pughe failed to do the job that Frances Bullock had done, he never dug a grave, never did churchyard work and probably passed many of the other duties to the churchwardens.

CHURCHYARD

The churchyard at Ingleton was used as a burial ground for many centuries. In the early centuries most bodies were buried simply wrapped and bound in cloth. In this way the natural decomposition was fairly quick and there was no problem of shortage of space. Coffins became more popular in fourteenth and fifteenth centuries, but did not come into regular use until the eighteenth century. Grave stones were less used in earlier centuries and often those used would be made were off wood and again decomposed over the years. The burial records of Ingleton church begin in 1607, the registers before that date being long lost. Between 1607 and 1812 4,459 people were buried in the churchyard. Thousands had been buried there from the building of the church to 1606 and from 1812 to the churchyard being closed in 1882 many more. An estimated total of around ten thousand people were laid to rest in that small plot. Naturally bones were turned up on new burials and were put in the charnel house or 'bone house' as Hewitson called it. The charnel house disappeared about the time the church was rebuilt in 1887.

Burials in the church very common in the sixteenth and seventeenth centuries and in quite alarming numbers, alarming to think decomposing bodies were lying under the pews and down the church isle and the vapours pervaded the air especially on warm days. Children were nearest to the unpleasantness and contamination if there was any. It was a time of smallpox and other fevers and most burials were of children. People liked to be buried near their own pew, some near the font and others in the choir. Probably those buried in the porch were buried there because they were unable to get into the church where it cost more. Burials inside Ingleton Church stopped about 1738 a few years before the re-building of church in

1745. The last burial inside the church was in 1742. From 1607 to 1742 a total of 759 bodies were buried inside Ingleton Church, which is quite an astounding number: some of these would have been victims of plague.

In September 1819 an order was made for changing the footpaths in the churchyard and the work was supervised by James Brunton and Joseph Brown surveyors of the highways for Ingleton. Over the years the footpaths were put in better order and the churchyard was walled to keep out hens and pigs. On August 11th 1754 the Ingleton Manor Court threatened that they would take action against all persons who kept hogs in the manor and did not ring and control them because they, 'grub up the holy place called the Church Yard,' and frequently lie in the streets. The present graves in the churchyard and most memorials in the church were recorded by the Lancashire Family History and Heraldry Society in 1996.

CHURCH RATES

The church vestry had the right to set and collect rates from all owners and occupiers of property in the township. The money raised was used to pay for the upkeep of the church buildings, church bells and bell ringers, the expenses of parish officers and a host of other things. While the inhabitants were predominantly Church of England there was no problem, but when dissenters came along in the form of Wesleyans and other chapel denominations then trouble started. They did not see why they should pay rates to a church they did not attend, as after all they had to pay for the running of their own church. The church rate was demanded with a threat that if it was refused the person's property would be seized and sold, or the person would be sent to prison for fourteen days.

This was a national problem and in some towns where nonconformists had great strength they forced the church into making the church rates voluntary. At Rochdale armed troops had to be brought in and the vicar kept under guard. The Prime Minister, Lord Melbourne, tried to bring in a Church Rates Bill in 1834, but it was dismissed by the King and the Lords. The Church saw the danger of the Church being brought into disrepute, but they were unwilling to give up the power they had held for centuries. There was also a growing movement for the complete separation of Church and State.

At Ingleton resistance to paying church rates came from the nonconformists in general and Joseph Carr in particular. Ingleton's minister at the time was the Rev Richard Denny and he being both a minister of the church and a JP was ready to put up a fight against this challenge from chapel folk. In 1858 a notice was posted as usual on the church door at Ingleton that there would be a meeting to levy a church rate on Friday the 25th. There was such a large attendance and as the vestry was too small the meeting was adjourned into the church itself. The chairman appealed for the meeting to run in a Christian spirit, but he knew that there would be problems. A proposal for the rate was made. When an amendment was proposed that the meeting be adjourned for a year, the chairman would not put the motion to the meeting. Then Joseph Carr proposed another amendment that no rate be made and the chairman again refused to put the vote to the meeting. Eventually the original motion for the rate was put to the meeting and carried by twenty-one against eighteen.

At the end of the meeting Mr R. Preston demanded a poll to which the chairman objected, not because he was worried about losing, but because he knew it would cause trouble in the village. Mr Preston repeated his demand and so a poll was arranged. This was the way the anti-church rate group kept up their opposition. As the 'church rate movement' grew, Ingleton, Bentham and neighbouring villages sent a signed petition to Parliament to support a bill for the total and unconditional repeal of church rates. There were even the signatures of some church people on the lists as they knew that the injustice of this annual religious tax could disturb the quietest locality and cause ill feeling amongst those who should be working together for the good of a village.

In May 1861 there was more confrontation when church rates were raised to provide six new church bells for Ingleton to replace the three they had. Then in 1862 the opposition were keen to watch that the church did not call a swift meeting to pass the rate before the opposition were organised. At the meeting in October when expenses were presented the opposition went through every item of expenditure even questioning payment to the Rev Denny for copying the parish register. Joseph Carr stirred up the meeting by saying that many paid the church rate because otherwise they might be evicted from their cottages. He again demanded a full poll in the village.

At the next meeting in June 1863 Joseph Bentham stood up and said that Joseph Carr should have no voice in the meeting as he had not paid the church rates last year. Joseph Carr replied that they had not been asked of him and refused to be silent. He then questioned every item of church expenditure from ringing the bells to washing the surplices: the anti church rate group harassed the meeting from beginning to end. Following this meeting the Rev Denny resolved to take firm action and took Joseph Carr to court for not paying the church rates. As Joseph Carr still refused to pay, in February 1864 four policemen entered his house and took some of his property for sale to raise the cash. They chose six painted rose wood chairs with cane bottoms, an armchair, an American rocking chair, a mahogany bookcase and a washstand. The JP who authorised the seizing of the property, W.A.F. Saunders, said that he was only doing his job..

The sale took place one Saturday afternoon in the village centre. A gentleman bought the first articles put up for sale for £3 1s and as this exceeded the debt the sale was stopped. The man in question then presented Joseph Carr with his own furniture and praised him for his brave stand. At this point Joseph Carr took advantage of the situation and standing on a chair made a plain and pointed speech on the injustices of church rates. It was a hard fight for Joseph Carr and the Wesleyans in Ingleton, as the church and gentry still held great power in the small isolated rural areas. Sadly the controversy soured local relationships and set church against chapel. However, the government eventually realised that the situation could not go on especially as police and military were frequently becoming involved in various parts of the country. In 1868 the Compulsory Church Rate Abolition Act was passed and church rates became no longer compulsory: the people of Ingleton were very relieved. Joseph Carr had stated, 'I believe in agitation rightly carried on, as the most effective method of redressing any wrong and of securing to the oppressed their rights'.

CHURCH REBUILDING

Ingleton church was partially rebuilt in 1743. 'Rebuilt and beautified' were the words used to describe the work, but some questioned this. Joseph Carr commented that it did not appear to have the least claim to beautiful architecture. He tells us in his memoirs that, 'In an article in the *Lancaster Guardian* I described it in appearance as looking like a barn with mill windows in it, and that no stranger would take it for a Church of England if it had not been for the ancient tower at its west end'. Balderstone in his book on Ingleton says, 'The old chapel was of such uncomely symmetry that a description of its ugliness had better be omitted from these pages.' A church historian of the nineteenth century wrote, 'The church is entitled to very little notice, except for its fine Norman font. The body seems to have been built in the 17th century, with vile square windows'. The building is illustrated in this volume and you can decide for yourself.

Exactly how much work was done in the 1740s is not known, but there is no doubt that it was done on the cheap. Rough stones, plain windows were the order of the day and by the

The old church at Ingleton on the day of the foundation stone laying for the new church Tuesday May 18th 1886.

1880s it looks to have been rendered in grey concrete. The interior was probably less changed than the exterior in this rebuilding. Ingleton church as rebuilt in 1743 was as plain inside as outside without any marble effigies, fine carved screens or works of art – it was a poor church in a poor village in one of the poorest counties of the country. The poorest counties were seven northern counties including Yorkshire, Lancashire and Northumberland.

By the late 1870s there was a call for a new church. The call came for two reasons, the first was that few people liked the appearance of the building, and the second was that there were dangerous problems with subsidence in the walls and foundations. One of the arches near the bell loft had given way and emergency action had to be taken.

When the first calls to action came Thomas Sherlock was minister, but finding little support for restoration he was discouraged and nothing happened as he was soon to leave Ingleton in 1879. He was replaced by Charles Pughe and things appeared to be more hopeful. His wealthy aunt, Mrs Ripley of Lancaster, promised a £1000 for the building fund, but still the scheme dragged on wearily during his incumbency. Then in 1882 a Grand Bazaar was organised at Ingleton in aid of the church restoration funds. The bazaar was held in the National School on two days in October 1882 and was a great success. It was opened by local MP Isaac Holden and supported by the ladies of Underley Hall: the Countess of Bective was in charge of the tea buffet. Everything was sold in the bazaar from Burton pottery to paintings, food and clothes. A novelty in the shape of a cage containing two little kittens was exhibited, and the cage bore the written request, 'Please buy me today or they will drown me tomorrow.' Hopefully the kittens were sold and hopefully the notice was only joking!!

Charles Pughe left Ingleton in 1884 having built up a restoration fund of £1,800 and having engaged Cornelius Sherlock of Liverpool as architect, but work was far from starting. The next minister was James Turner. He arrived in 1884 and found that there were suggestions that it was dangerous to ring the church bells and that there were plans to build the church on another site in the village. By 1885 Cornelius Sherlock had drawn up plans. He said, 'My

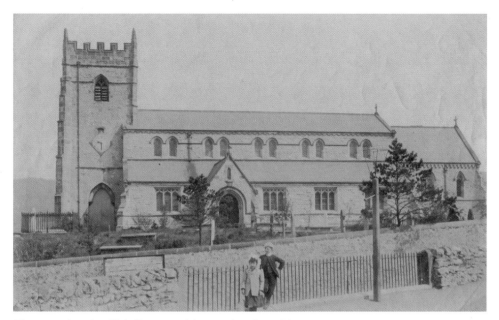

The new church officially opened September 21ˢᵗ 1887.

plans shew the new body of the church to be rebuilt on a very strong bed of concrete, up to, but entirely independent of the tower. So that should the tower subside there will be no injury to the body of the church.' Plans for building on another site were soon dropped partly because of the difficulty of finding one.

James Turner was keen to make progress, but it was not until a meeting on December 28ᵗʰ 1865 that it was decided to advertise for tenders. On Tuesday the 18ᵗʰ of May 1886 the foundation stone of the new church was laid by Dr John Gott the Dean of Worcester. Church lands in the Ingleton area had come under the Dean and Chapter of Worcester at the Reformation. John Gott was also no stranger to Ingleton for he was born in Yorkshire and first visited Ingleton when he was Vicar of Leeds. The main contractor was John Hewitson. Other contractors were Verity and Shuttleworth of Keighley for woodwork, Croft and Baines plumbers, W. Slinger slater and plasterer and G. Swift mosaics for the chancel floor. The exterior walls were built of blue limestone from Skirwith quarry and the facings came from Bentham.

Work began first on demolishing the old building and the only old relics found were bones. The bones of the hundreds of people buried in the church had been disturbed in 1743 and deposited under the west end flooring as the easiest means of dealing with them. Near the tower on the north side thirty-eight skulls were dug up from one square yard: the ground was literally paved with them. Over three hundred skulls were found in total. Some of the skulls were stolen by trippers and although the police tried to find them before the excursion trains left Ingleton they failed. Most of the smaller bones had probably been buried in a pit dug in the churchyard.

When Ingleton Church was rebuilt in 1886 away went the old pews, the sundial and the old church clock. The old gallery where the musicians played for the service had been removed many years before around 1858. The new church had an organ and the fiddler, the clarinet player and the rest became redundant whether they liked it or not. We know from Thomas Hardy's 'Under the Greenwood Tree' that villagers frequently took exception to the use of an harmonium or organ to replace musicians and a choir. Hewitson in his The Story of my

Village tells us that, 'The church choir, located in a clumsy, dingy, unsightly gallery at the west end of the church, amounted to a curiosity. The members of it consisted of the village schoolmaster, a shoemaker, a couple of joiners, one or two colliers and several lads. The instruments played comprised a clarinet, a cornopean, a bassoon, a flute and a base fiddle.'

With the coming of the organ churches may have gained in musical quality, but a great deal of history and character was lost. The musicians and old style choirs had popular appeal which the organ and surpliced choirs had not. Many complained that the vitality of church music had been replaced by the dull uniformity of the organ. Only in the last years of the twentieth century has the old style of music returned to churches and chapels alike, a necessity for continued evangelism, for the majority of people the organ and surpliced choir are still a turn off.

The new church was consecrated and formally opened for public worship in September 1887 by the Bishop of Ripon and had sitting accommodation for 450, that is 100 more than the old one. The new church was fifteen feet longer and five feet wider than the old one. Much of the stone for the new church came from Wellhead Quarry at Skirwith while other stone came from Bentham. The new church, unlike the one it replaced, was a credit to the village and was much admired.

FEATURES OF INGLETON CHURCH

Only some features of the church interior are listed here. Gerald Tyler's church guide gives more detail of the stained glass windows and other monuments.

The Norman Font

One of the most interesting items in Ingleton Church is the 'Norman' stone font. Like most Norman fonts it is round and heavy. It is not only interesting for its age, but also for the many stories told about it. The usual story told in many Ingleton guides and church histories is that in the Commonwealth period the font was thrown out of the church and rolled down into the river from where it was rescued some centuries later. How anyone can repeat such a story is unbelievable. Anyone who knows the rivers at Ingleton know that they move and grind rocks at an amazing rate. Once the weir at Ingleton lost a stone or two it was demolished in a few years and each stone was far larger and stronger than the font. They say being in the river caused the wear and tear.

The second story, told in the foreword of the printed Parish Registers says that the font was rolled down into the river probably in Commonwealth times, but rescued by the Rev. William Waller who rescued it and placed it in the belfry of the church where it was used as a pot for mixing whitewash.

The third story says that it was taken out of use and put in the tower where it was used for mixing lime for painting the church walls. This is a more plausible story and the lime may well have caused some corrosion to it. However, it could well have been rolled down the hill behind the church and remained half buried in rubbish, but certainly not in the river. The fonts in many churches were taken and used as cooking pots, washing tubs, and even pig troughs before being restored by the Victorians.

Ingleton's celebrated carved font.

108

The rescuing of the font is generally attributed to the historian and author Thomas Dunham Whitaker. 'The font when he found it, was thickly encrusted with lime, and had been used as a trough for mixing mortar, and afterwards as a whitewash bowl for daubing the arches and columns of the old church.'[6] This seems a reasonable explanation and following Dr Whittaker's intervention the font was cleaned up and returned into the church. However, Hewitson stated that he had found no proof of Dr Whittaker's involvement, 'on the contrary, the only reliable evidence we have been able to obtain goes to show that the font was restored at the instance of T. Lister Parker, Esq., and at his expense; that this took place about 1830, during the incumbency of the Rev. William Waller; and that after being cleaned it was placed on a small, common pedestal, in the north-western corner of the Church.' Eventually John Thomas Coates designed a base for it. Many said that the font showed the Madonna and child as the church was dedicated to St Mary. However, when the font was in use at Ingleton, the church was dedicated to Saint Leonard, not St Mary, making the story another red herring.

The font is carved with scenes depicting the story of the virgin Mary. They include the three kings bringing their gifts to the child in Mary's arms; murder of the innocents by Herod; Rachel weeping for her children, and the Holy family making their flight to Egypt. There are fourteen subjects depicted within interlaced arches and the carvings stand out in bold relief. It may be that the old font was thrown out at the reformation because of its decorative carvings which would have been suspect. Statues and sculptures were disfigured or removed, but unfortunately at Ingleton there are no surviving documents from the period to tell us what happened.

The Norman font at Ingleton is not only round and heavy, but it is deep as it was most probably used for baptism by immersion. In the early church infants were usually baptised by total immersion in holy water, emphasising the entry into Christian life. The Book of Common Prayer, 1559 and 1662, directs dipping as normal method. Only if the child was weak was water just poured onto it.

The Vinegar Bible

Ingleton possesses an interesting old church Bible dated 1717. It is known as the 'vinegar Bible' because of a misprint. It was bought for service as a lectern Bible long before it was realised that it was unusual. The heading for the parable of the vineyard, Luke 20, was printed as, 'The parable of the vinegar.' The Bible was produced by John Baskett at Oxford. The book contained many other misprints apart from 'vinegar' and became known as, 'A Baskett-full of Errors.' The Bible is now a rarity as copies are scarce and much sought after.

Pulpit Old and New

Ingleton Church had an old wooden three-tier pulpit before the re-building of the church in 1886. It was retained in the new church for a while, but then in 1888 it was replaced. What happened to it is not known, but it is remembered by Anthony Hewitson in his memoirs. He described it as, 'a heavy desk-fronted contrivance of the three-decker kind'. The new pulpit was in carved Caen stone with pillars of Connemara marble and was presented by Alfred and Isabella Kirk of Greenwood Leghe and is inscribed, 'To the glory of God. Presented by Mr and Mrs Alfred Kirk, of Greenwood Leghe, July, 1888.'

BELLS AND BELL-RINGING

Ingleton's church bells had been rung by bell-ringers from time immemorial. They were paid for the work and enjoyed celebrations at the Cross Keys Inn at Ingleton which was close to the church. From time to time they were treated to a meal, as in January 1873 when William Norman Greenwood of Greenwood Leghe gave a treat at the Three Horse Shoes to the bell-ringers and his work people. In 1861 Ingleton Church had six new bells fixed in the belfry and they were rung for the first time in November by the Hornby Bell Ringers and both bells and ringers gave great satisfaction. At the afternoon ringing one of the clappers fell and made such a noise in descent that ringers and visitors all rushed out fearing that the bells were coming down.[7]

The Church Vestry, under Rev. Denny chose the new steel bells because they were considerably cheaper than traditional bells. The bells were made by Naylor, Vickers and Co of Sheffield in 1861 at a cost of £317 7s 3d and the total cost after hanging the bells was £358 12s 8d. Naylor Vickers had obtained Riepe's German patent for casting steel bells in 1851 and soon they became very popular throughout the country. The large tenor bell was forty-eight inches in diameter and weighed 780 lbs. The small treble bell was thirty-one inches and weighed 540 lbs. The total weight of the six bells was around 5,000 lbs. The old bells were sold for scrap to raise funds towards the new ones. There were originally three bells at Ingleton inscribed as follows:-

1. Be it known to all men that SE Thomas Stafford of Penrith made me Ano Doni 1630 RF.

2. T.P.: ESQ.: T.B. CURATE. T.W. : H.C. : R.E. : C.W. : CHURCHWARDENS : I.R. : CLARK: C.B : T.R. : I.W. : C.I.: I.R. : T.B. : O.S. : P.N. : 1719 : I.G. :I.M. : C.O. (T.B. was Thomas Bowes the Curate and I.R. was James Redmayne the Parish Clerk.)

3. SOLI DEO GLORIA PAX HOMINIBUS 1779.

At a Vestry meeting on Thursday May 24th 1877 the attitude to bells and bell-ringers changed. T. Taylor put in a tender of £9 for ringing the bells, £5 for cleaning the church and £1 for winding up the clock. R. Foster tendered £9 for bell-ringing, and £4.10s for cleaning.

The interior of Ingleton Church c.1900.

Charles Beck tendered £5 for cleaning only. In the discussion that followed it was proposed that bell-ringers be dispensed with and a machine be procured for that purpose. At the meeting £18 was raised and a further £12 promised. The inventor of the bell-ringing machinery, a gentleman from Bradford, was invited to Ingleton. After inspecting the church tower he said that he could have the machinery installed and ready for operation in one month. The machine had sufficient power to ring the bell to the highest pitch and also to be regulated to chime in the softest tone. It was able to ring seventy-six changes and there would be no necessity to remove the bell ropes or bell tongues, so that should the machine break down the bells could be rung in the usual way. In early July the bell ringing machine was installed in the tower of St Mary's by Mr J. Saw & Sons. The six bells were rung on the first Sunday morning by a slender youth and the sound was thought to be equal to hand ringing.[8]

The cost of the machine was little more than the cost of bell-ringers and the wear and tear of bell ropes for two years. The one great advantage that was stressed was that the machine needed no priming with beer. A little oil was more to the machine's liking than a dozen bottles of ale. Nothing is recorded of what the bell-ringers thought of this change. However, the bell-ringers had the last laugh for within a few years the machine broke down, was not renewed and the bell-ringers were back in charge. In January 1886 the bell-ringers of the Parish church rang the old year out and the new year in. Then they went to Bonnick's where they were treated to an excellent supper.

CHURCH PLATE

Ingleton Church has no ancient silver plate. They have a cup with paten cover, salver and flagon, a set which dates from 1850. They were bought through Dobson's of Piccadilly, London and all bear the inscription, St Mary's Ingleton 1850.'

WESLEYAN METHODISTS

Many people have complained that the site of the Wesleyan Chapel at Ingleton is a poor one, too far from the road and shut off by other buildings and that some have had difficulty in finding it. When the Wesleyan Methodists first planned their chapel at Ingleton they had the chance of one of the choicest sites in the village with extensive and lovely views yet they deliberately decided to seclude themselves from the main streets. They had learned from painful experience that if they wished to worship in peace they must keep out of the main routes and notice of the village roughs. In one of the rooms where they used to worship before the chapel was built they had to endure many annoyances. Throwing in dead cats and stones amongst the worshippers occurred on several occasions. On one occasion cockle shells were fastened to the feet of a cat which was pushed into the room where they were worshipping. The perpetrators of the incident thought that the cockle shells would make a noise on the floor and divert the attention of the worshippers. Burton chapel was built in the main street and the consequence was that the Methodists were subject to constant annoyances, especially on winter nights. The roughs of the day loved to get hold of dead dogs, cats, hens, or anything of an offensive character to throw into the chapel amongst the worshipers.

The Ingleton Methodist Chapel was opened in 1838 and enlarged in 1884. as the memorial stone on the front of the building shows. Joseph Gillbanks the builder did the masonry work on the 1838 chapel for the cost of £20. Some Ingleton colliers who worked on the night shift helped at Storrs Quarry during the day and stone was carted free of charge for the building ensuring that the chapel was built for the least possible cost.

However, Methodism in Ingleton dates from 1816. It was firmly established in 1835 under the ministry of the Rev. A. Dernaly. Around this time the Methodists held evangelical meetings in the village of Ingleton. They were liked by few. The church with its vestry and

The Wesleyan Methodist Chapel at Ingleton.

churchwardens ran the village and they wanted no rivals. When the Methodists made a convert they were accused of using undue pressure and driving them mad. At that time to be called a 'Methody' was an insult and a cross to bear.

A memorial stone-laying service for a chapel extension took place on June 17th 1884. The Rev. S. Thies and Rev. W. Wilson conducted the service and money was raised towards the extension work. The work was carried out by Messrs Atkinson and Sons and was completed in June 1885.

REFERENCES

1. *List of the Recusants and Noncommunicants in Yorkshire in 1604,* from MSS in Bodleian Library, Trans. and Edited by E. Peacock FSA, 1872.
2. Borthwick Institute, Archbishops Visitation Records, Visitation 1578-9.
3. Ingleton Marriage register 1654.
4. *The Lowther Family,* H. Owen, Phillimore, 1990, p.125.
5. LRO, *Lancashire & Cheshire Child Marriages,* 1897, pp. 32, 33.
6. *Craven & the North West Yorkshire Highlands,* H. Speight, pp.213/4.
7. *Lancaster Guardian,* November 23rd 1861.
8. *Lancaster Guardian,* June 2nd & July 7th 1877.

CHARITIES AND BULL LAND

One of the first items in the Ingleton township records which begin in 1722 is a list of charities.[1] The way they are listed, without any dates and with no special order suggest they were written by asking the principal inhabitants what they remembered and by looking at entries in the parish registers, probably because they had lost an earlier book in which they were recorded. Like most villages Ingleton had several charities left by public benefactors over the years for the benefit of the poor and other purposes.

These charities were generally distributed by the clergy and churchwardens at Christmas, even when this was against the directions of the donors. The following is a copy of the Ingleton charities contained in that minute book.

'Charities to the poor of Ingleton by Severall Donors.'

'Twenty two pounds given by John ffoxcroft of the Cross in Ingleton to the poor of the said township, and the yearly Interest thereof charged upon little Dale Close belonging to Elizabeth Carr, of Skirrith to be distributed on St Mark's Day.'

'Ten pounds given by Agnes Procter of Bruntscar the Interest to be paid by Peter Procter her son and his Heirs.'

'ffifty pounds given by Henry Bouch Esq the Interest to be divided one half to the Schoolmaster of Ingleton and the other to the poor of the sd Township the Executors of the said Henry Bouch charged with the payment to be distributed March 25th yearly.'

'Five pounds formerly given by some Charitable hand not now remembered charged upon land lying on Rareber side and two hemplands now in possession of Joseph Vipond.'

'Thirty Four pounds given before the Memory of any of the present Inhabitants and let to Interest to Richard Bradley, John Bradley and the Bond taken in the names of Christopher Jackson of Cold Cotes, and Peter Procter of Bruntscar.'

'The sum of One pound in the Hands of Francis Kidd not acc[t] for above- Thos Sedgewick late of Bankend Left by will 20 pounds for the use of the Poor of which sum Fran Kidd pays interest for yearly.'

'Out of Green Slack John Howson, gave by will 10 shillings to be paid to the Chapel Wardens of the Township of Ingleton yearly to be laid out in White Bread or Loaves made of Wheat Flower to be Divided Equally amongst the poor of the said Township yearly.'

'John Bentham left by will £10 to be paid out of Gill Head Estate, and the Interest of the said ten pounds to be paid yearly for the use of the Poor.'

You will notice that no dates are given for any of the above charities. Ingleton Township did not keep its records well. There were at least two charities that were not recorded in the township books. One was the legacy of Richard Blackamore alias Hunte. He was around in

Ingleton in the late sixteenth and early seventeenth century. He was first noted in the charities entered in the Ingleton Parish Register as having left a charity to Ingleton. Perhaps he was a trader dealing in Ingleton or a shopkeeper or the landlord of an inn, sadly his will gives no profession. He was buried at Ingleton on May 14th 1611 by the evidence of the Ingleton burial register. His will is recorded at York and not with the Deanery of Lonsdale where most Ingleton wills were deposited. The following section of his will concerning the legacy was copied into the parish registers as a record:- [2]

> 'Legacie given by Richard Blackamore and payed by Thomas Chernley his executor unto the Swoorne-men and Church wardens at Ingleton on the fourth day of Auguste Anno Dm. 1611.
>
> The Tem[s] and forme of they wordes of the parti bequeathinge concerning the use of this legacie be theis I Richard Blackamore Doe give and bequeth to the parish Church or Chappelne of Ingleton the somme of ten pounds the which said Somme shall be payed by myne executor to they Swornemen and Churchwardens of the said parish of Ingleton, and to be putt furwarded yearlie from years to yeare by they Swornemen and Churchwardens for ever Provided all Wayes that the said ten pounds shall still remaine in Stocke to the said parish and such profites to be taiken yearlie for the same as they lawes will permitt and the said Yearlie profite to be yearlie bestowed, within the said parish to godlie uses and for the best relieffe of they poore As shall seme best and most convenient by the Swornemen and Church Wardens from tyme to tyme as aforsaid for ever.

He left £10 in 1611, a considerable sum at that time. This was given at an apt time for there were lean years from the 1590s and in 1623 there came the worst of all when many in the population were starving and the majority were short of food. His will tells us that he had a house in Ingleton, but was born in County Durham. He left money to the poor of his birthplace as well as to Ingleton, Bolton-by-Bowland, Newcastle-upon-Tyne, and Gateshead. The only family he mentions is a sister in Gateshead. However, he mentions several godchildren. The name Blackamore suggests the possibility that he was a Blackamoor or coloured man.

The second charity not recorded in the township books, but recorded in the parish registers, is a legacy given by Thomas Procter and paid by his executor on the 21st of September 1623:-[3]

> Item it is my will and I give unto the good of the poore of the parishe of Ingleton Ten poundes, And the said Ten poundes to Remaine for ever, And shall be delivered yearly of the ould Churchwardens unto the new, And the profites essuyinge and growinge out of the said ten poundes soe much as the law will suffer shall be distributed at the discretion of the old Churchwardens when they go forth of their office, And especially unto poore mens Children which goeth to trade or into the Country And I hope the twentie and fower men which is sworne for the good of the parishe will see this my guifte rightlye used.

One problem may have been solved. When the list of charities was written, the charity of John Knowles of Twistleton, who left property in 1704 to Peter Procter and Christopher Jackson and their heirs to administer the charity, was forgotten. The two men were sidesmen at Ingleton. This was most probably the £34 supposedly left before the memory of the present inhabitants.

When the sworn men made out the list in the township book around 1721 it is possible that the two legacies had been forgotten, but hopefully they were remembered at the right time by the churchwardens. Henry Bouch left two legacies in his will, made in 1712. The first legacy was twenty five pounds the interest from which was to be used towards assisting the poor of Ingleton. The second legacy was a further twenty five pounds the interest of which was to be allocated, 'for the use of the school and the master thereof at Ingleton.'

When the Rev. T.D. Sherlock came to Ingleton in 1874 he found that the charities had been for some time only given to church people and the poor who were nonconformists were usually overlooked. No one who ever left a legacy ever stated that it was only to be given to members of any particular church as at the time the legacies were made there was only the one village church. However, when nonconformist churches sprung up in Ingleton it became a different matter. The Rev T.D. Sherlock introduced a more Christian and liberal distribution of the township's charities.

In May 1895 Mr A. Cardew, barrister at law and Assistant Charity Commissioner, held an enquiry into Ingleton's charities at the West Riding Court House in Ingleton.[4] The minister, churchwardens, overseers and several of the Parish council were present. The Charity Commissioner said that the enquiry was part of a general enquiry that was being held in all the parishes of the West Riding and that the object was to get the full information on all charities which could be put on record as printed reports submitted to Parliament and issued as Parliamentary Papers.

It was stated that the charity money left by Henry Bouch of Ingleton Hall, Thomas Procter, Agnes Procter and an unknown donor had been laid out on building a poorhouse. The money was now invested 'in Consols' being represented by £118 17s which produced £3 5s 8d. The interest was distributed amongst the poor at Christmas.

The Charity Commission said that those who were receiving parish relief should not receive any charity money and that no charity money should be given to anyone who kept a dog. However, he said that the distribution of the charities could be safely left to the discretion of the trustees. The Rev. Turner said that there were not many people in Ingleton who were actually destitute. A further charity that came to light in this enquiry was Redmayne's Charity. This was money came from a rent charge on a field called Beck Crook paid by the tenant of Seed Hill. The money was distributed amongst widows who received one shilling each.

In the Charity Commission enquiry other charities came to light concerning Chapel-le-Dale. The sums of £5 10s and £3 had been left to Chapel-le-Dale Church with the exception of 2s 6d which was for the schoolmaster. This charity left in the hands of Abraham Kidd had been lost. Also £4 per annum for the repair of the church was lost. Then there was Rose's Charity, the sum of £80 left by Janet Rose by will dated October 1710. The money was for teaching poor children in Chapel-le-Dale. It was laid out in the purchase of three and a half acres land in Dent known as Baxen Ghyll. Part of the field belonged to the vicar, but the school's share was £12 per annum. William Bramley's Charity was also mentioned in which £80 had been left for the free education of nine families in Chapel-le-Dale.

Legacies continued to be left to church and chapel through to the present day. Hewitson in his *Guide to Ingleton* records the legacies of Alice Atkinson of Giggleswick, who died in 1879. She had a memorial window placed in the church in memory of her mother and Redmayne grandparents. She also left fifty pounds to the poor of Ingleton and a further five hundred pounds to Ingleton Church.

£22.10s was given to the taker to buy a suitable bull on condition that at the end of his term he would refund the same amount to the next person who provided the bull. A promissory note for money was held by the churchwardens.

The next letting of the Bull Lands and town bull should have been in 1810, but the next mention in the Township Book is in 1813 when the book records:- 'Vestry 9th February 1813. Proposals made by the churchwardens, overseers and inhabitants for the keeping of two good bulls for the use and benefit of the inhabitants interested in the Bull Lands and money viz., £22 10s.' At this meeting it was decided amongst other things that 'the taker provide for the term of four years to support, maintain and keep, for the use and benefit of the persons interested in the aforesaid, two good bulls, viz., one to be of the Dutch or short-horned breed, and the other a well-bred long-horned English bull.' William Howson was the taker and had to comply with the conditions such as keeping the bulls to the satisfaction of the inspectors, keeping the Bull Lands fences in good repair and paying all parochial rates and other assessments.

No further reference to the township bull and the Bull Land is made in the Township book between 1813 and 1860. In February 1860 the meeting was held in the Wheat Sheaf Inn and Richard Jackson was the chairman. The minutes of the meeting begin, 'Wheat Sheaf Inn, Ingleton, February 24th 1860. Pursuant to public notice duly given, a meeting was holden this day at the Wheat Sheaf Inn in Ingleton for the purpose of letting the finding and keeping of a bull or bulls for the benefit of the inhabitants of the hamlets of Ingleton and Moorgarth, subject to the following conditions.' Up to this time the bull had always been for the use of the township after all it was termed the township bull, but now this meeting limited it to Ingleton and Moorgarth. No reason was given as to why Twistleton, Cold Cotes and Ingleton Fells had been excluded: these three areas were all in the Township and Parish of Ingleton. There was no documentary evidence, no ancient custom or tradition to justify this meeting to limit the benefit of the township bull to Ingleton and Moorgarth. There was a great outcry, but nothing was done as no-one was willing to take the matter to court.

In December 1874 a meeting was held in the National School to let the town bull. The bull was now said to be let for two years and the person who 'took the bull', as it was termed received £18 from the last taker with which to buy a bull for the township's use, and then at the next taking should another candidate have more votes than he, he had to pay £18 to his successor. In 1874 Mr Bentham was chairman and the candidates were Richard Shaw, James Lord and James Briscoe. The votes were Lord nine, Shaw five and Briscoe three. It was also the custom to appoint three inspectors to see that the bull provided was kept in a healthy and proper condition. On this occasion Messrs Gawith, Mason and Metcalfe were elected inspectors. This was the meeting at which Joseph Carr was appointed to examine the records in an attempt to discover the origin of the bequest of Bull Land: Joseph Carr was unsuccessful.[6]

In December 1880 a meeting was held at The National School to let the bull lands and the town bull. James Lord of Skirwith who had kept the bull was leaving Ingleton and a new keeper had to be found. R.B. Ellershaw was chairman and it was proposed that Cold Cotes and Twistleton should be included in the scheme. The chairman said that Cold Cotes and Twistleton had an equal right to use the bull, but when a proposition was put to the meeting they voted 22 to 20 against allowing them to be included. Matthew Dinsdale was declared keeper of the bull for two years. In 1882 at the next bull letting the chairman Mr Danson said he thought that the fact that the bull money had been reduced from £22 10s to £18 may explain that some arrangements had been made between the different hamlets to give the sole rights to Ingleton and Moorgarth. This meeting appeared to make new rules as they went along. It was now decided that to be able to vote farmers must be cow keepers. William Bracewell was appointed as bull keeper for a term of two years.

In 1884 there was strong competition to take the bull by Thomas Mason of Raygill who said that his bull had received 2nd prize at Bentham Show, but had deserved the 1st. However William Bracewell still easily won the vote to continue as bull keeper. On the death of William Bracewell in 1885 the bull was taken up by Robert Preston and he was unanimously appointed to keep it in 1886. In 1888 Robert Preston no longer wished to keep the town bull and Robert Bradley of Ingleton Hall was appointed to take over. In 1888 it was proposed that a superior bull be obtained and the money to buy it be raised by charging a nominal sum to farmers to have their cows serviced. The proposal was lost by the casting vote of the chairman, Mr Danson.

Problems came when Ingleton gained a Parish Council in 1895. Firstly they got into trouble for allowing the Overseers to let the town bull rather than the Council. Then following floods the Parish Council fenced the Bull Land and the District Auditor refused to allow the cost, as the Bull Lands were considered a charity and repairs should be paid from the proceeds from the lands. The councillors were surcharged for the money they had spent. The money had to be repaid and the matter occupied the Parish Council for around three years. Eventually the matter was settled and the money refunded. Some blamed the Settle Sanitary Authority for conveying the Bull Lands to the Charity Commissioners when the sewerage works were done. In reality it all went back to the Ingleton Court House in 1895 when the Assistant Charity Commissioner listed the Bull Lands as a registered charity.

By 1919 Robert Bradley of Ingleton Hall had kept the town bull for twenty-five years and he continued as bull keeper for a few years longer. In 1928 there was a court case at Kirkby Lonsdale County Court over Ingleton town bull. John Baines of Nutgill farm at Ingleton took the Ingleton bull inspectors to court because they refused one of his cows access to the bull and he claimed damages of £5 15s. The reason for the refusal was that cow in question had been grazing with an animal suffering from tuberculosis. The judge dismissed the claim with costs, saying that he considered the bull-keeper had a right to be cautious.

Over the years the bull was less used as some farmers acquired bulls of their own. Eventually the Bull Charity had to be wound up and put to other uses. A new Bull Land Charity was registered on February 5th 1969 with the Charity commissioners as Main Charity 222586. The scheme was drawn up in October 1968. The area of benefit was the Parish of Ingleton and its objects were listed as follows:-

1. Any charitable purposes for the general benefit of the inhabitants of the Parish of Ingleton.
2. Relieving either generally or individually persons resident in the Parish of Ingleton who are in conditions of need, hardship or distress.

REFERENCES

1. Ingleton Township Book/Vestry Minutes 1721-1847 (Deposited NYRO 2007)
2. *The Parish Registers of Ingleton and Chapel-le-Dale, 1602-1812,* The Yorkshire Parish Register Society 1933, Transcribed by Col. W.H. Chippindall. p.284
3. Ibid.
4. *Lancaster Guardian,* June 1st 1895.
5. *Lancaster Guardian,* June 8th 1895.
6. *Lancaster Guardian,* December 5th 1874.

INGLETON FAIR

Ingleton Fair is coming on.
Lads and lasses plenty:
Every lad shall have a lass'
But I'll hae fower an'twenty.

Ingleton Fair was celebrated from medieval times on the feast day of Saint Leonard, the Patron Saint of Ingleton Church. This was the 6th of November and for centuries Ingleton folk celebrated their patronal feast on this date. Most of Europe went on to the Gregorian Calendar, but England stayed on the Julian Calendar until 1752 by which time we were ten days out of time with the rest of Europe. However, in 1752 when the Julian Calendar was abandoned and the Gregorian Calendar adopted in England, eleven days were cut out of the calendar from the third of September that year. Eleven days disappeared and all events moved forwards eleven days. The people of Ingleton realised that their Fair Day would not be a true celebration of their true fair day unless, in the future, they added on the lost eleven days and held it on November 17th and so that is just what they did.[1]

By 1752 Ingleton Church had been re-dedicated to St Mary, and St Leonard had been forgotten, but at least the old men could then say they still celebrated Ingleton Fair on the real anniversary. There was a lot of resentment at the time, many objected to losing eleven days, and others realised that they would never have a true birthday again unless they celebrated it eleven days late.

On the eve of the patronal festival a candle lit procession would be made to the church in honour of the saint to whom the church was dedicated. In the early centuries people celebrated the feast day with games and activities centred round the church: it was a day of general rejoicing. Ale and food were sold and entertainment was provided by local people and travelling players. Later the celebrations spread out from the church into the village, to a local field, to the inns, to the streets and village square. There were stalls with things for sale and it would certainly be an important day in the life of the village. It was a holy day, a holiday, a day of feasting, dancing and rejoicing and it offered a real attraction in the lives of the village people who lived a fairly harsh existence.

Then at Ingleton, as in many other places, over the years the patronal festival developed into a fair and became extended to several days with cattle sales and sports. In 1889 the government published two volumes entitled *Market Rights and Tolls* which looked at the history of fairs and markets. The report showed those fairs and markets noted in 1792 in Owen's *New Book of Fairs* and gave its own list for the year 1888. Ingleton is listed as having a fair in Owen's 1798 book and in the 1888 report, a fair, but no market.

Our first good description of Ingleton Fair comes from Anthony Hewitson who recounting his memories of Ingleton in the 1840s wrote:-[2]

Sometimes at the annual fair there appeared on the scene, in the centre of the village, a travelling menagerie, and the men in charge of the caravans seemed to think that they had the right to occupy and monopolise, without any payment, and quite irrespective of the claims of anyone else, the whole of the space there. When those who had put up stalls or booths in this central part heard that the menagerie caravans were entering the village, they would at once begin to clear out, the commotion was immense. All the innumerable articles and odds and ends previously placed in position for sale were packed up; trestles, wooden framework and canvas coverings were taken

120

down. A species of stampede was made to some other part of the village – any part available, and clear of that which was threatened. And then up would come the menagerie caravans, the horses champing and sweating, the drivers in charge shouting and cracking their whips, and, then when the central place of the village had been reached, if they found in it any booths or stalls which the owners had not removed, and which at all appeared likely to stand in the way of placing the caravans in close conjunction for show purposes, the men with the horses would drive full speed against them, upsetting or smashing everything in their line of progress, scattering nuts, oranges and everything in all directions, and so continuing in this rough, wild, clearing out fashion until the whole of the central ground was free for the absolute occupation of the menagerie. And there seemed to be nobody able or willing to officially check or interfere with this game of brute force and monopoly.

The only representative of law and order in the village was the parish constable William Thompson. A mild ponderously built middle-aged man, he was also schoolmaster and registrar. If hunted after and met with during fair day he would probably have been found snoozing serenely in the chimney corner at home, quite indifferent to all external ructions, or else comfortably smoking a long clay pipe, in a neighbouring public house, amid a company strenuously devoted to ale-supping and entirely averse to bothering with noisy, belligerent outside displays at such a season.

Anthony Hewitson describes the stalls which were set up at Ingleton fair, but there was more to the fair than that. There was an important cattle sale and sports were held. Moreover it was a time of general celebration and the people of the village celebrated in dancing and drinking in the village inns.

In November 1874 the annual Ingleton Fair was held on the 17th. It took up the Back Street and a large portion of Main Street. The road to Hawes and the road to Clapham were crowded with cattle and it was reported as the largest show remembered. One portion of the main Street used to be crowded with onion carts, and it was a common saying in Ingleton that they were buying their 'winter beef.' Only rain and the police cleared the streets after heavy drinking in the public houses. On Wednesday the drinking was kept up and there were sports behind the Wheat Sheaf. Trotting, foot races, quoits and high pole leaping were the main amusements.

That Fair Day a fuller article on Ingleton fair appeared in the *Lancaster Guardian* in 1874 entitled *A Ramble Through Ingleton Fair*:-

Some one may say, what is there in a country fair but what is known to everyone, and who can tell us more than we know about fairs? It is evident that all men do not know what goes on at fairs, and it was for this reason that a rambler took a stroll through Ingleton fair. The prompting cause of such an exploit was the words of the superintendent of police to the Ingleton bench of magistrates when a certain licensed victualler applied for lengthened hours for the sale of drink on fair night. The words will bear repeating. 'There is drunkenness in his house, and in all the public houses at fairs.' Whether it gave the bench a penchant to hear and see the doings in those houses they licence for the sale of intoxicating drinks is not my business, but it evoked a strong desire in me to see and hear what really did take place. Though there was a good deal of drinking the first day, most of the sensible business men left the town sober and in good time. Night was the time to see and hear the jolly sounds and strange antics of the disciples of John Barleycorn. Some of the public houses were not so throng between six and seven o'clock.

The dancing rooms were full, and they were jiggling it right merrily. They could not have done it with more spirit if they had been winning their bread by it. One young lady was so thoroughly absorbed with the pleasure of the dance, that in closing she said 'It was a shame and a sin to turn them out at ten o'clock.' One dancing room between nine and ten o'clock was crowded to the door and still more people were pushing in. Some young people who were pushing their way through the crowd exclaims 'It's warse than t'Shoe.' The fumes of tobacco and drink and animal exhalations was sickening. There were so many dancing at once that they whirled and capered from one side of the room to the other as well as they could do for the standing crowd.

Some of the male dancers were rather heavy in the head, and they were either bowing gracefully to their lady partners or they were nodding time to the fiddle. The companies on the second and third nights of dancing were not as select as on the first night, and there was a much greater proportion of young men. Some of the dancers and lookers on were smoking either cigars or pipes and the air was very much vitiated… People will dance, and the Rambler does not condemn them for it, but if we are to have public dancing rooms, let them for the sake of public health be spacious and airy. Such dances as these described lead to sickness and death, just as much a drinking unwholesome water and defective drainage.

The above was a good description of Ingleton's fair. There was dancing in the upper and side rooms of all the village inns, all through the day, and often right through the night until five or six o'clock in the morning. The music was nearly always provided by a fiddler and they were much in demand at fair time. The fiddler was independently paid for the music for every dance by one or more of the people participating in it. The dances consisted mainly of jigs and reels, interspersed with hornpipes. There was no limitation on drinking hours and little supervision. So long as people could drink, and so long as the innkeepers could supply it, the drinking went on.

As the years passed Ingleton Fair slowly became less of an event. Regular cattle markets were held in the area and the number of cattle showed dropped. As the event became less celebrated stall holders dwindled until there were only one or two stalls. In the early and mid-nineteenth century there were always many onion sellers at Ingleton Fair. The onion was often referred to as 'winter beef'. Housewives bought large quantities of onions in November to last through the winter. Historically onions were one of the few foods that did not spoil during the winter months. Boiled onions and onion soup formed an important supper dish during the winter months. Onions were tasty and nourishing and for many years they formed a winter standby, especially for the poor. In 1880 there was only one onion seller whereas at one time there was such a demand for them that one side of the Main Street was occupied with onion carts. Also in 1880 not so many country people attended and the day passed off without any noticeable drunken rows. However, two full days of sports were still held on the 18th and 19th of November. In 1882 it was noted that the Ingleton Fair had long been waning in the number of stalls and items for sale.

Cattle in good condition usually met with ready sale at Ingleton Fair. In 1864 prices were reported as follows:-

Calving cows £17 to £20; gelt cows from £12 to £16; young cows £7 to £12. Pigs were sold from 16s to 22s; Scotch ewes were 16s and wethers 18s to 20s. Onions were around 18 pence a stone.

The Three Horse Shoes one of the noisy and smoky inns on fair day.

The number of other stalls at the Fair varied from year to year, but onions, nuts, hardware, ginger-bread, children' toys and clothes were usually on sale.

From 1880 to the end of the century Ingleton fair continued, but with more ups and downs. The turn of the century passed and the fair came into the twentieth century. In 1904 the cattle show was one of the best in the area, but the sports held were only for children. The 1909 fair was noted for poor attendance and poor displays of cattle. In 1912 owing to restrictions on Irish cattle there was a thin show of animals. It was also reported that cattle dealers had been in the area well before the fair buying up all the cattle they could find. In 1913 it was stated that 'The establishment of Auction Marts have just about killed off old local fairs.' In 1917 the annual fair was not so well attended and the show of cattle was judged poor in both quality and quantity.

The end finally came in 1923 when the *Lancaster Guardian* reported, 'From time immemorial a cattle fair has been held at Ingleton on November 17th. On Saturday not a single animal was shown. Auction Marts have gradually done their work and snuffed this fair out of existence, but it was left to the foot and mouth disease to give it the final coup de grace.' From that mention in 1923 nothing more was heard of Ingleton Fair and it disappeared from the local calendar. It had survived for around seven hundred years, which in itself is quite remarkable. Had it been a summer fair then the sports might have continued on their own, but being held in November, and considering local weather, there was little prospect of its survival.

REFERENCES

1. Only the author's supposition, but everything fits. This is an example of where intuition as well as research can uncover the past.
2. *The Story of My Village Ingleton,* A. Hewitson, ed. by J.I. Bentley, 1982, p.8.

SCHOOLS AND EDUCATION

Ingleton certainly had a school and a schoolmaster in the Elizabethan period. This fact is shown by several wills where bequests are given to the schoolmaster and scholars. These bequests were usually for their presence at the funeral service where the scholars would sing. In 1566, Giles Redman left a penny to each scholar at his funeral and Richard Baines in 1557, left a penny to 'every scholar that can synge'. It was a custom in those Catholic times to leave bequests to priests and scholars to sing at funerals for the souls of the dead. Thomas Battersby made such a bequest in 1572. His will reads, 'I give unto the Schoolmaistre and his Scholers yf they be at my Buriall ijs to be given equally amongst theime'.[1]

Early schools were invariably connected with the church and often held there, and so it was at Ingleton. However, as time passed and the community grew, the presence of children continually in the church frequently became a nuisance and Churchyard schools were built. These schools in the churchyard were near enough for the schoolmaster, who was often the priest, to shuttle between church and school and yet distant enough to stop the children annoying the churchwardens and church vestry in the carrying out of their daily duties of running the church and parish affairs. William Brown was accused on a church visitation in 1633 for, 'teaching schoole in the Church.' On December 8th 1772 the Ingleton Vestry announced:- 'It is this day agreed by us whose hands are underwritten, that for the future no person be permitted to enter this chapel with intent to teach or make a school thereof'.[2]

Ingleton's churchyard school stood on the northern boundary of the churchyard with its windows facing the church. There is no record of whether it was founded by a charitable gift, erected by subscription, or built by the laying of a rate on the township. When it was built we do not know, but it was certainly an old building as it had been out of use and closed for some time before 1763. In 1772 the vestry were insisting that the school should be repaired and used. It was probably while the school was in disrepair that the school went back into the church and the children caused such annoyance as to make the vestry finally decide to keep them out for the future. The Churchyard School was probably built in the sixteenth century.

One thing is certain, the school belonged to the township and the power to elect schoolmasters and run the school was in the hands on the 'Principal Inhabitants', that self elected group who ran the township through the Church Vestry along with the churchwardens and overseers. In 1633 John Firbank was schoolmaster and in trouble for not presenting his licence. In 1700 John Farrer was schoolmaster. His son James was buried in April 1700 and by June John was also dead. In April 1735 James Jackson was elected schoolmaster. Not only had he to teach, but he had also to act as clerk to the township and even then his salary was low. On April 25th the vestry recorded, 'It is agreed publicly that Mr James Jackson schoolmaster, is to take in all accounts, viz: churchwardens, overseers and constables, and give accounts of the same to the principal inhabitants when they shall require it, and he is to have for the same one pound yearly as long as the parish think convenient.'[3] If the schoolmaster was not willing to sign to take over the parish accounts then he would not be employed as schoolmaster.

For many years the Rev. John Waller, the minister of Ingleton, was schoolmaster. He likely took over for several reasons. Firstly it would augment his salary, secondly he was fully qualified to do the job and thirdly he was on the spot. Perhaps there was the fourth reason that they were unable to get a master elsewhere. This is shown in 1788 when he gave up the school and township minutes record, 'yet he hath no successor.' Obviously John Waller had had enough and was resigning, successor or no successor. In 1714 Henry Bouch, Lord of the Manor, left £25, 'to be put to interest for the use of the school and the master thereof at

Ingleton and his successors'. The money was mainly used to repair the school and the schoolmaster was left with a pound a year and had to raise the rest of his salary by charging his pupils.

Ingleton school does not seem to have had a schoolmaster between 1788 and 1792 when Francis Brown was appointed. During this time the school had once again become dilapidated and was in need of repair and it had to be repaired before Francis Brown was able to take over his duties. A meeting was called on May 7th 1792, 'to consult about repairing the school for Mr Brown to teach in and for the benefit and advantage of the inhabitants'.[4] Francis Brown was appointed, 'to teach school within the school house at Ingleton provided that he undertake not to apply for a license thereto and to quit the same at any time whenever a majority of the principal inhabitants gave him notice so to do.' If he took a license to teach the school authorities were worried that he might rebel should they decide to sack him. The Vestry stated that, 'Mr James Redmayne, Mr John Barlow, Mr Richard Balderston and Marmaduke Morton do lay out the sum of five pounds in their discretion for the repair of the said school-house and that no part of Mr Bouch's charity be paid to the said schoolmaster till the sum is laid out'. This parochial decision was perhaps contrary to the intent of Henry Bouch's will, but no one could question the Vestry's decision. Still the poorly paid schoolmaster had to sign his name to the words, 'I do hereby agree to accept the said school subject to the above conditions as witness my hand.'

So here we have the minister and the principal inhabitants spending money on the repair of the school which Henry Bouch left 'for the use of the school and the master thereof at Ingleton.' Francis Brown did not last long at Ingleton for he was discharged in 1795, but no reason is recorded. The next schoolmaster was James Remington, but he also was dismissed after a short term. Then the Rev. John Garnett came to teach at the village school. The churchwardens and overseers were authorised to get the school repaired at the township's expense. John Garnett lasted about the same time as his predecessors at the Churchyard School before he too disappeared from Ingleton's history.

In 1801 John Wilson, said to be a good classical master, was appointed, 'to teach in the school at Ingleton a certain number of children not to exceed forty at any one time.'[5] The Vestry fixed the school fees which he was entitled to charge. 'Reading English only, 5s per quarter; Latin 7s 6d per quarter; writing 6d per week; and for accounts 1s per quarter is additional. The said master to be put in immediate possession of the school and to secure one pound on the 24th of December next, being the salary belonging to the school at Ingleton. The windows of the said school to be put in repair by the inhabitants of Ingleton and left in good repair by the master when he quits the school. That the said school and master shall be under the care and inspection of James Redmayne, Richard Balderston, Edmund Foxcroft Lodge and Robert Chapman'.[6] We see that the schoolmaster's salary was still one pound a year.

Thomas Kenyon also taught for some period at the Churchyard School around this time. Thomas Kenyon was a local man who was appointed to fill the position of schoolmaster until a regular master was appointed. Kenyon had intended to become a clergyman and was qualified in religious duties, but he was defective as a disciplinarian. He was too indulgent towards his scholars and made himself so familiar with them that he lost influence over them. He was often known to play at marbles with the children at school. A mother of one of the scholars came to visit one day and found the master and her boy playing at marbles. It was the master's turn to play and after the manner of the village boys he called out 'Knockie down to thee dimple hole'.[7] The mother was not impressed. There is no record as to when Thomas Kenyon left the township school, but later he taught privately in his house on the bank and also at the west end of the village. The 1803 Craven Muster Roll for Ingleton shows two schoolmasters, Charles Kay and Richard Wildman, but we do not know where they were teaching.

In 1811 a new master was appointed and the power for future appointments was taken out of the hands of the ratepayers and vested in eleven trustees. Paul Berry, the parish clerk, read the following notice in the Church on Sunday April 7th 1811. 'Notice is hereby given, that the proprietors and occupiers of land within the township of Ingleton are particularly requested to attend in the Vestry of the Chapel of Ingleton, on Wednesday next, precisely at four o'clock in the afternoon, for the purpose of appointing a schoolmaster, to teach school at Ingleton, and also for the purposes of appointing proper persons to be trustees of the said school'.[8]

At that Vestry meeting Samuel Butler Hodgson was appointed schoolmaster and the following trustees were also appointed:- Richard Balderston, William Herd, Adam Thompson, Thomas Walker, William Green, James Robinson, Robert Chapman, John Howson, Matthew Carter, Thomas Jackson and Thomas Yeadon. The new strategy must have succeeded for Samuel Hodgson remained at Ingleton for many years without dismissal or interference.

In February 1818 a son, Thomas, was baptised at Ingleton to Anthony Scott schoolmaster so we must give him mention here. William O'Connell also taught at the school and was a popular master. He resigned his mastership because of the illness of his uncle in Ireland who wished him to take charge of his affairs. He went to Ireland and following the death of his uncle returned to Ingleton. As the Churchyard School was then in the hands of another master he opened a private school in a cottage on the east side of the Back Gate. He was of a respectable family and was spoken of as an excellent teacher by most of those he taught. Eventually, after two or three years, his son and daughter came to visit him and persuaded him to return home to Ireland. He occasionally drilled his scholars in the street and on occasions held a brush handle by his right arm in place of a musket. When his military drill took place it caused considerable interest in the street and attracted many spectators.[9]

In September 1824 William Thompson of Aysgarth, at the age of twenty-three, was elected schoolmaster at a Vestry meeting on the following conditions. 'That he enter upon the said school at Ingleton situated in the Chapel yard and keep possession of it until such time as he received a written notice from the minister, chapel-wardens, and principal inhabitants in vestry lawfully assembled, to give up the said school.' William Thompson attached his name to the following bond. 'I William Thompson agree to accept the above school belonging to the township on the above conditions.' Having established himself financially and socially on February 12th 1831 William Thompson married Jane Dent at St Mary's Ingleton.

On December 24th 1837, after teaching for thirteen years, William Thompson resigned from his post and gave up the Churchyard School and started his own private school. In this way he got rid of the trustees and other interference and there was little difference as he had to collect fees in both the township school and his own private school. In his own school all the money was his and he could charge his own rates and not those set out by the township. Schoolmasters were usually well respected, but poorly paid and a second source of income was often necessary to earn a proper living. William Thompson found other methods of earning his living when he became Relieving Officer for the Bentham district. For thirty-six years he was also registrar of births, and deaths and vestry clerk. He also served as paid village constable over many years. He was also correspondent for the *Lancaster Gazette, Lancaster Observer and Kendal Mercury.* He was a zealous Conservative and churchman and remained in Ingleton until in old age he went to live with his son at Preston where he died aged seventy-five years in September 1876. Although born at Aysgarth, William Thompson became one of the notable personalities of Ingleton.

A Vestry meeting on January 4th 1838 decided to advertise in the *Lancaster* Gazette and the *Lancaster Guardian* for a new master. The advertisement read, 'Wanted a Schoolmaster for the township school of Ingleton, in the County of York, well qualified to teach English grammatically, writing and arithmetic and if classics so much more eligible. The income will principally arise from quaterage, as the salary is very small, but the chapelry is populous, and an attentive master would have a fair prospect of a sufficient number of pupils. Testimonials as to abilities and moral and religious conduct, to be sent by the candidate to the minister and chapel wardens (if by letter post paid) on or before Thursday the 25th day of January instant, on which day a vestry meeting will be held to consider the credentials of the different candidates and elect a schoolmaster.[10]

The day of appointment was January 23rd 1838 and of the several candidates Robert Danson, late school assistant to the Rev. William Newton of Over Kellett was chosen. On agreeing to take the job he subscribed to the following conditions:- 'Reading, English Grammar, and Geography 4s.6d per quarter; for Reading, English grammar, Geography and writing 10s; for Reading, English Grammar, Geography, Writing and Arithmetic, 13s per quarter. The hours for teaching shall be from the 25th day of March to Martinmas, from eight to twelve in the forenoon. In the afternoon from one till five. The rest of the year from eight to twelve in the morning and from one to four in the afternoon'. Saturday was to be a holiday and there were to be holidays at Whitsuntide, or Midsummer and Christmas. The vacations were to be two in the year of three weeks each. It was stressed that the Sunday School Society had to have possession of the school on Lord's day for teaching their children as usual and for accommodation for their books and forms, and the township shall hold their adjourned meetings in the school when they think proper.

John Waller had been minister and schoolmaster at Ingleton and his son William followed him as minister. In the 1830s when William Green was school superintendent, the Rev. William Waller took an interest in the school and also an active part in the teaching. He was a person of considerable learning, but he had a quick temper and now and then would flog scholars with a heavy hand. William Waller wore a wig and to the consternation of the scholars it once flew off while he was energetically whacking a boy.[11]

THE NEW NATIONAL SCHOOL 1848

During the 1830s and 1840s the population of Ingleton was rising and many more children were wanting an education. On Thursday September 11th 1845 a meeting was held in the Churchyard School, 'to consider several matters relating to a new school' At this meeting it was agreed that waste ground at the top of the village known as Ash Green should be acquired for the purpose of building a school and playground. The land had been had been offered by the Lord of the Manor and his jury at the last Ingleton Manor Court. Ash Green was used as a storage place by joiners and others and much of it was occupied with the wood and wagons of the village timber merchants. It was resolved that subscriptions should be sought so

Ingleton National School. Written on back, 'Lizzie Brown at school 1865.'

127

that the building could go ahead. On October 16th the Vestry appointed a committee to carry out the project. The Rev. R.Denny was chairman and the other members were John Thomas Coates, Joseph Hunter, Richard Brown, and William Metcalfe. It must be stressed that subscriptions were given by members of both the Church of England and nonconformists.

In May 1846 the *Lancaster Gazette* noted:- 'The ground for the foundation of the building for the new schoolrooms at Ingleton has been cut out during the past few days, and rapid progress is made in leading materials. It is expected to be completed towards the close of September. A large piece of ground is to be attached to it for the purpose of a playground. This building will not only be very useful, but will be an everlasting ornament to the village'. The masonry work on the school was contracted to Joseph Gillbanks. The suggestion of it being opened in October 1846 was premature. The school was officially opened in October 1848 when one hundred and twenty children paraded with the Ingleton Brass Band and were served with tea after the procession. Robert Danson was the first schoolmaster of the new school and he transferred with the children from the old Churchyard School. The old school was then sold and a substantial house was built on the site which was named Churchyard View.

Robert Danson the first schoolmaster at the new National School taught there until his sudden death in November 1855 when he was found dead in the road after falling from his horse near Farleton. What caused him to fall from his horse which cost him his life was never discovered. The inquest which was held at the Castle Inn at Hornby recorded a simple verdict of 'found dead'. His grave can still be seen in the churchyard at Ingleton. He was for some time a corespondent for the *Lancaster Gazette.* At Ingleton school he was succeeded by Samuel Hartley who was usher at the time of his death and was elected as a suitable successor by the school trustees. Samuel Hartley continued as schoolmaster until 1870. Following him George Cowburn taught from 1870 to 1875, Mr J. Lister from 1875 to 1877, Mr Kent 1878 and Mr Ireland 1879 to 1883. George Walling who was appointed in 1883 served as headmaster for forty years until his retirement in March 1924. He was well liked and respected in Ingleton and a fitting presentation was made.

George John Sergeantson the owner of Ingleton Collieries, gave a substantial sum towards the building of the new National School and many in Ingleton subscribed to the fund. The manager at the Ingleton colliery gave each man sixpence on New Years day and as the collection for the school was at its height he asked the men to add a further sixpence and give it to the school fund. The miners did so on the promise by a trustee of the school that it would be available for all public meetings by church-people and nonconformists alike. However, this promise was later broken by the Rev. R.Denny who had the trustees under his thumb. Nonconformists were also banned from being managers of the school as by the deed and foundation only people who were Church of England communicants could hold the office of managers. The vicar and churchwardens were ex-officio trustees of the school. In 1879 several men put forward for election as managers were rejected on that account. Nonconformists were allowed no say in the village school although they had helped to build it and in the main were responsible for the prosperity of Ingleton at that time. William Bracewell, the owner of Ingleton Collieries, was a keen Methodist as was Levi Towler of Ingleton Mill. Henry Robinson of Storrs Lime-works and Mr Wilson of Clark and Wilson of Meal Bank were also nonconformists. Joseph Carr was quick to point this out in the local press.[12]

From 1862 'payment by results' was brought in and Her Majesty's Inspectors inspected the schools each year to test the '3Rs, reading, 'riting and 'rithmetic'. It encouraged teachers to make greater effort, but it also encouraged 'parrot learning' of facts and figures. Up to twelve shillings per child was paid on the results of the examinations. Then came the 1870 Education Act which was one of the important milestones in the country's educational history.

INGLETON NATIONAL SCHOOL

COMMITTEE OF MANAGEMENT
REV.R. DENNY JOSEPH HUNTER ESQUIRE.
JOHN T. COATES, ESQUIRE. RICHARD BROWN,ESQUIRE.

MASTER
MR. S. HARTLEY.

ADMISSION OF PUPILS.

1. No pupil to be admitted under Three Years of Age.

2. Any Boy or Girl of that Age or upwards may be admitted by applying to the Master

3. The Rates of Payment (which are to be in advance and tendered each Monday Morning) are 2d., 3d., and 4d according to the Class in which the Pupil shall be placed by the Master.

4. Each Pupil to pay 6d per annum for Fuel. One Moiety on the first Monday in October and the other on the first Monday in February of each Year.

5. The Committee will supply Books, but the Stationery used in the School shall be purchased of the Master, and 3d. per quarter will be charged for Pens and Ink.

6. The Course of Instruction will embrace Reading, Writing, Arithmetic, Mensuration, the Elements of Algebra, Vocal Music, English Grammar, History, Geography, and the Holy Scriptures.

7. The School shall be open during summer at Nine O'clock in the Morning, and close at Twelve; open at Half-past One in the Afternoon, and close at Half-past Four

8. No Pupil shall be absent from School without leave, but if detained at Home by Sickness the Parent must Acquaint the Master

9. Any Pupil coming to School with dirty Hands, or uncombed Hair, or generally untidy, will be sent home again.

10. The Master shall have power to expel any Pupil, subject, however, to an Appeal to the Committee; and no payment shall be remitted to any Pupil who expulsion shall be confirmed.

11. There will be two Vacations of Two Weeks each, one at Midsummer and one at Christmas.

12. A Mistress will attend in the Upper School Rooms in the Afternoons to teach the Girls Needlework, but no additional charge will be made.

13. No Pupil shall be admitted into the School whose Parents do not express their willingness to observe these rules.

The idea of the 1870 act was to fill in the gaps in the voluntary system by local Board Schools set up by local School Boards. Nonconformists favoured Board Schools as they got an equal share in the running of the schools and were not excluded as they were at Ingleton. Education was not made compulsory until 1880 when all the gaps were filled and there were schools for all children to go to. At first school was compulsory to the age of ten years and this was extended to twelve in 1889. In 1891 education was made free for all.

In March 1879 attendance at Ingleton school was poor and the trustees requested the School Attendance Committee of the Settle Union to make bye-laws respecting the attendance of children at school under section 74 of the Elementary Education Act of 1870 for the township of Ingleton. Once the 1880 act came in Settle School Attendance Committee were fully empowered to take parents to court for non attendance at school and did so on a regular basis. In 1882 George Martindale, Edward Thistlethwaite, William Singleton, John Metcalfe and Thomas Charnley were all fined for not ensuring that there children attended school. Many excuses were given, the children were ill, they had no proper shoes or clothes to wear for school. Some claimed they could not afford the payment of 'school pence'.

The *Lancaster Guardian* reported the case of Jane Dewhirst of Ingleton, who was charged with failing to send her ten year old son to the National School. He had made only 57 attendances out of a total of 104. Mr Millington, the School Attendance Officer, said that some time ago the Poor-law Guardians for the township of Ingleton had paid the school pence for the boy, but on account of poor attendance the benefit was discontinued. The case was dismissed as the mother claimed that she had to go out to work as a charwoman and that the boy missed attending school unknown to her. In June 1884 John Briscoe was charged with not assuring that his son, John James Briscoe, attended school. His mother claimed that the boy had been ill. The boy himself said that his mother kept him off school to run errands: the parents were fined.

The only hope for Ingleton's Nonconformists was that the Church might not be able to raise the money for the extension and then a School Board would have to be set up and a nondenominational school formed. With the expansion of Ingleton Colliery by William Bracewell of Barnoldswick in Lancashire the mining population grew rapidly as miners came from various parts of the country with their families from 1872. An enlargement of the school became necessary to conform to the Educational Department's regulations. However, money was raised for the school extensions by the church and village without the need to form a School Board. The old portion of the school was greatly improved and a large addition made on the south side. The school was then able to accommodate from 180 to 200 children. The average attendance at the opening of the extensions in August 1876 was 170. The new additions cost between £300 and £400 and the school was able to continue without threat.

It was still referred to as the National School and there was a separate infants and senior department. However, when the infant's schoolmistress left through lack of funds in October 1878 there was an outcry that the little ones were wandering in the streets and a demand for the forming of a School Board. At a public meeting in Ingleton on Friday December 13th 1878 at the National School the proposal to form a School Board was rejected; there were 22 votes in favour and 86 against. One of the main reasons that the ratepayers of Ingleton voted against a School Board was the fear of the costs on the rates and few considered the educational factors involved, although church people wished to retain power over education to keep out nonconformists.

By 1880 the National School had improved and was getting a better Government grant. The report if the Inspector stated 'This school is orderly, well conducted and has made gratifying progress. The attainments of the scholars are now in a very satisfactory state'.[13] The total Government grant was £144 which was good considering that in 1877 the school only got £69. However the school was still short of money. The school had to pay staff, cleaners and buy materials. Apart from the Government grant they raised money by school pence and by gifts and donations. The school needed around £300 to run efficiently. With a grant of £150 and school pence raising £110 there is still a deficiency of £40. The government grant depended on attendances. When the school was short of money cash was raised by raising subscriptions and other activities. There was always the threat that the school might not be able to continue and a dreaded School Board would have to be formed and education taken out of the hands of the church.

In the early 1880s John Heaton taught school in his own house in Ingleton. The National School staff and governors were upset by this and labelled children who went to his school as absent from school. There was no other certificated school at Ingleton except the National School they told everyone. William Warrener, George Martindale, Thomas Charnley and John Robinson were prosecuted for non-attendance of their children at school.

John Heaton was a clever eighteen year old who had attended Collingwood Grammar School. Joseph Carr wrote a letter to support Heaton's School and asked the head of Collingwood School to testify that John Heaton was efficient to teach. The case against the parents and John Heaton was dismissed in court and John Heaton continued teaching for some time. There was much annoyance in Ingleton at the time of this prosecution especially as there were many children running about the streets of Ingleton who attended no school at all. John Heaton taught day and night school and is said to have taught at Meal Bank Cabin.

John Maudsley taught school in an upper room in a building once on the site of the Ingleborough. His family lived in Bentham and he daily walked between the two villages. John Maudsley only maintained the school for a short time. No doubt it was during the time he taught at Ingleton that he gave lessons in sacred music to the Ingleton Church choir. The family moved from Bentham to Lancaster about 1840.

Anthony Hewitson praised Robert Danson the headmaster of Ingleton school, and his successor, Samuel Hartley, for their education work and quoted some of their successful students to illustrate his point. 'The Rev. W.D. Thompson is now the vicar of St. Saviour's, Preston; the Rev. S. Hartley is the vicar of Sawrey in Westmorland: Mr. Richard Brown is one of the leading lawyers in Manchester; Mr. S. Rumney has held the mayoralty of the same city; Mr. A. Hewitson is the proprietor and editor of the Preston Chronicle; Mr. T. Harrison is the sub-editor of the Carlisle Journal; and Mr. Edmund Danson is the engineer of the Ingleton Collieries'.

Robert Danson was succeeded, at his untimely death in 1855, by Mr. Hartley, and brought a new list of successful pupils, 'Mr. James Leeming soon rose to a prominent post in the London Clearing House; Mr. James G. Brown is now one of the leading manufacturers in Rochdale; the Rev. J.M. Danson, in addition to graduation in honours from the University of Dublin, now occupies several posts of honour in the Scottish Episcopal Church; Mr. Armstrong, after passing through the training college at Chester, entered the Royal Military College at Chelsea; the brothers Thistlethwaite have been entirely successful in the scholastic profession; Mr. Thomas Bentham has taken high honours in the Mathematic Schools at Oxford; and several of the Harrison family have in their own sphere covered themselves with credit'.[14] It will be noticed that all the educational successes mentioned are boys, there is not a mention of a single girl as there was no equality of the sexes in education at Ingleton at this time.

BLUE HALL SCHOOL

The old National School continued into the twentieth century with additions from time to time. However, once again at the beginning of the twentieth century there was a growth in population and a growth in the number of children of school age. The New Ingleton Colliery

NATIONAL SCHOOL,
INGLETON.

MANAGERS:

REV. R. DENNY, B.A.   J. T. COATES, Esq.
R. BROWN, Esq.   J. HUNTER, Esq.

MASTER:

MR. S. HARTLEY.

THE FOLLOWING ARE

The Inspectors' Summaries
SINCE 1858:—

'59.—"Mr. Hartley teaches intelligently, quietly, and with great good sense."—TEMPLE.

'60.—"This School is decidedly good."—TEMPLE.

'61.—"The upper part of the School is in excellent order and very good state of attainment."—SHARPE.

'62.—"This is a very good School."—TEMPLE.

'63.—"This is an excellent School."—TEMPLE.

'64.—"The School has been taught with great care and spirit."—SHARPE.

'65.—"The School is thoroughly well taught."—SHARPE.

In consideration of the state of the School, as evidenced by the above Reports, Mr. HARTLEY's Certificate has been raised three divisions—the highest advance attainable at one time.

INGLETON
NATIONAL SCHOOL.

MANAGERS:

REV. R. DENNY, B.A.   J. HUNTER, ESQ.
J. T. COATES, ESQ.   R. BROWN, ESQ.
            WM. METCALFE, ESQ.

MASTER:

MR. S. HARTLEY.

Copy of Report
MADE
UPON INSPECTION IN APRIL, 1864
BY THE
REV. L. W. SHARP.

H.M. INSPECTOR FOR WEST RIDING OF YORKSHIRE:—

"This School is taught with great care and spirit, it is well classified and in good discipline. The Scripture knowledge is thoroughly well taught throughout. The elementary and general knowledge are good."

"The Infants are taught in the upper room, chiefly by the Senior Pupil Teacher, and an uncertificated Mistress, under the Master's superintendence. They are fairly taught, but require greater variety of lessons."

National School reports 1858-1864.

had opened and miners had flocked to Ingleton with their families. There was now a need to accommodate three hundred children. The war had postponed action from 1914 to 1918, but in 1919 action was taken and Blue Hall was bought to be fitted up as a temporary school. At the time of writing several people in Ingleton can tell of their education at Blue Hall. The school was opened in February 1919 when one hundred and seventy children moved from the National School. There was a large garden at the rear of Blue Hall for the boys to do gardening and the girls were given cookery lessons as a new innovation. Two hundred children were left in the junior and infants departments.

INGLETON'S NEW 'MODEL SCHOOL'

In the 1920s there was a call for a new and larger school to cater for the children of Ingleton as the use of Blue Hall was only supposed to be temporary. A good site in a central position was purchased for a new school as early as 1914, but work on the new school was postponed for various reasons. Eventually work was begun in the summer of 1928 by Messrs A. Gregory and Son of Castleford. Work progressed well and the school was opened by Sir Percy Jackson, Chairman of the West Riding Education Committee on January 11th 1930.[15]

Ingleton's new school was said to be a 'model school' and 'a new trend in education'. Education had often been difficult in the premises at Blue Hall and the old National School had been condemned as unfit for a school several years before. The new school cost £13,226 excluding the cost of the site. Accommodation was provided for four hundred scholars and separate rooms were allocated for domestic science, woodwork and chemistry. It was so constructed that necessary additions could be made without interfering with the running of the school and without marring the general appearance. In fact at the time of opening plans had already been made for two extra rooms to be built.

The school was built on the quadrangle system with ten classrooms, four rooms for the hundred seniors, and six rooms for the three hundred juniors and infants. There was a large hall, forty-five by twenty-five feet and also a combined manual instruction and science room filled with benches and sinks. There was also a domestic science and laundry room with wash tubs, sinks, and a hot plate gas oven. Windows were fitted with Vita glass and the building was heated with two Robin Hood boilers. Mr J.T. Bradley was appointed as caretaker. Mr Stevens was appointed headmaster and Miss Lister headmistress of the infants department.

The old National School was repaired jointly by the county Council and Ingleton Church, the former repairing the exterior and the latter the interior. When it was refurbished it was used as a Sunday school. The new school was soon extended and children began to come in from High Bentham, Low Bentham, Clapham, Newby, Tunstall, Ireby and Leck. Most were over eleven years old and were brought to Ingleton by bus. By mid 1930 the senior department had grown to 358 children with eight teachers.

STORRS HALL SCHOOL

Storrs Hall school was founded by Elizabeth Smith, the daughter of the Rev. R.M. Balderston of Ingleton. Born in 1815 she attended the Clergy Daughters' School at Cowan Bridge, founded in 1823, the same school which the Brontë sisters attended with such terrible consequences. Emily and Charlotte were withdrawn from the school in 1825 following the deaths of their sisters, Maria and Elizabeth, earlier the same year. There are the graves of more pupils in the graveyard at Leck. The appeal of Cowan Bridge School to the Rev. R.M. Balderston at Ingleton and Rev. Patrick Brontë at Howarth was the low fees of £14 per year. The rest of the running costs of the school were paid by Carus Wilson's charitable friends.

The head and founder of this infamous school was the Rev. William Carus Wilson who in 1832 moved the school to Casterton where it still prospers. Carus Wilson believed that strict

New Model School.

punishment and suffering even to death was good for children's' souls and those who attended his school certainly suffered. Some still say that he was not really a bad fellow at all, but quite caring, but read his writings in his *Children's Friend Magazine* and you will discover what a diabolical man he was. They are full of horrific deathbed stories of young children and gruesome tales of death and hell. One small boy of three when asked whether he would choose life or death, replies 'Death for me. I am fonder of death' When a child asks, 'Why do they whip us if they love us' he is told that they are whipped to save their souls. Charlotte Brontë put her experiences into the novel *Jane Eyre* where Cowan Bridge School became Lowood and Carus Wilson became the infamous Mr Brocklehurst. Elizabeth Balderstone, learning from her severe experiences, committed her life to more humane teaching.

After some years in the teaching profession Elizabeth Smith started a school for young ladies at Sandwood in Keighley. Her husband, George Smith, who was an accountant, also turned his hand to teaching. George and Elizabeth Smith had always enjoyed visiting Ingleton, as Elizabeth had been brought up in the village. They bought the old workhouse at Mount Pleasant and George Smith changed the appearance of both house and grounds so that it became a neat and respectable residence and an excellent holiday home.

Eventually the building at Storrs was developed and became Storrs Hall School for young ladies which opened in 1866. The main reason for moving the school from Keighley to Ingleton was that Keighley had become such a smoky industrial town. At Ingleton the school had more space and it was considered a much healthier location. Storrs School mainly took its pupils from the trades-people and lesser gentry of nearby Lancashire and Yorkshire towns and was a popular and efficient private school. A list of the girls attending the school in 1871 includes girls from the following places, Liverpool, Leeds, Horton, Ingleton, Kildwick, Malham, Colne, Haworth, Whitehaven and Nottinghill. One master at the school was Robert Balderston, a Cambridge undergraduate, who later settled in Ingleton and in later life wrote *Ingleton Bygone and Present.*

When Elizabeth Smith died quite suddenly in November 1872 it was a shock to the village. It was her custom to invite the elderly residents of Ingleton to a dinner on Christmas Day. She was a very charitable woman in many other ways and helped the poor of Ingleton. This was done mainly through a Dorcas Society run by her and the young ladies of the school which helped to provide clothing for the poor of Ingleton. The school was taken over by the

Misses Brown who continued it for many years well into the twentieth century. They were the daughters of Richard Brown of Bank Cottage in Ingleton. Margaret Greenwood Brown was the headmistress and her sisters Jane and Agnes were schoolmistresses. A fourth sister had retired from the school on her marriage to Mr Hopkinson of Huddersfield in October 1877. In 1891 Margaret, Jane and Agnes Brown were listed as joint head of the school.

The school had grown larger in numbers and five other teachers were employed. The girls came from as far away as Scotland, Portsmouth and Woolwich and as near as Bentham and Clapham. Over the years the local press recorded thousands of examination successes at the school. In July 1887 it was stated that Misses Brown had fifty examination successes. One of the Miss Browns would personally check the dormitories at lights out and the girls were expected to kiss her goodnight. Margaret Greenwood Brown died at Grange where she was just spending a few weeks before going to live at Harrogate: she had just retired on Thursday May 29th 1919 aged 74. Jane Brown enjoyed many years of retirement at Harrogate and died in her 82nd year in December 1930.

Miss Andrews succeeded the Misses Brown at Storrs Hall School. She managed the school for around five years and died in Ireland in July 1925 while visiting friends. Following her death Storrs Hall School soon closed.

DAME SCHOOLS

In Ingleton there were a couple of dame schools in the 1840s. One was run by Jenny Ellershaw, and the other by Jane Stackhouse, who was the wife of a miner. These women took in young children of nursery school age and were often little more than child minders. Anthony Hewitson in his *Story of My Village* tells us that he went to them both as a child, one following the other. Ingleton had such dame schools through the eighteenth and nineteenth centuries as there were always parents who wished their children to have some care and instruction in early life. Most of the dame schools were held in cottages in an area known as Lowergate. Some of these schools were for small boys and girls, in which they were taught their letters and easy reading before going on to the Churchyard School. From time to time there were a better class of dame school for girls in which knitting, sewing, and what was called sampler work was taught. Doing the last named was considered of great importance as it was a test of the dame's superior capacity for teaching and the pupil's for skill in needlework. Completed samplers were held in high repute and were as a matter of course framed and hung up in the home to be later handed down as heirlooms to future generations.

REFERENCES

1. Lonsdale Deanery Probate Records WRW/L, LRO Preston.
2. Ingleton Township Book/Vestry Minutes 1721-1847. (Deposited NYRO 2007)
3. ibid.
4. ibid.
5. ibid.
6. ibid
7. *Lancaster Guardian* June 17th 1893.
8. Ingleton Township Book 1721-1847
9. *Lancaster Guardian* June 17th 1893.
10. Ingleton Township Book 1721-1847
11. *The Story of My Village Ingleton,* A. Hewitson, Ed. J.I. Bentley, 1982, p.37.
12. *Lancaster Guardian* January 4th 1879.
13. *Lancaster Guardian* July 10th 1880.
14. *The Story of My Village Ingleton,* A. Hewitson, Ed. J.I. Bentley, 1982, p.43.
15. *Lancaster Guardian,* Jan 11th 1930.

Girls in class at Storrs Hall.

There was no shortage of space for physical exercise at Storrs Hall School.

INNS OF INGLETON

This chapter looks at the stories of the inns of Ingleton and the part they have played in village life over the centuries. The word 'inn' conjures up thoughts of refuge after a long journey, food and drink, warmth and rest for the weary traveller. These inns have been the public house, everyman's parlour, courthouse, dance hall, dining room, public meeting place, auction room, market and mortuary.

The earliest mention of Ingleton's inns come in the Quarter Sessions records of the seventeenth century. A General Session of Quarter Sessions at Wetherby on January 10th 1642 records that:-

> Forasmuch as this court is informed that William Skarth and Richard Ustonson of Ingleton have, since Easter last, kept very disordered alehouses, contrary to the forme of the Statute. Ordered that the said William Skarth and Richard Ustonson shall forthwith find sureties for their good behaviour, and to appear at the next general quarter sessions of peace to be holden at Skipton, then and there to answeare the premisses, and a warrant to be ordered to levye the penaltie of the law upon them as delinquentes.

William Skarth and Richard Ustonson were both innkeepers in Ingleton, but the names of the inns they ran are not recorded. From time to time the authorities clamped down on inns and the drinking and gambling that went on in them. On the whole, periodic activity of this sort did little to alter things and the inns and innkeepers carried on as usual.

THE BAY HORSE

> Who'er has travelled life's dull round,
> Where'er his stages may have been,
> May sigh to think he still has found
> The warmest welcome, at an inn.

> William Shenstone, 1714-1763.

The Bay Horse was said to be Ingleton's oldest inn. No pictures, drawings or photographs appear to have survived of this old coaching inn which was made into three shops in 1870 when the licence was transferred to a new hotel built across the road. For many years it was Ingleton's main coaching inn and had an excellent reputation for both food and service. It was here that the first meeting were held in 1767 to make plans for the enclosure of three thousand acres of Ingleton and Bentham Moor. At that time the landlord was John Barlow. In 1802 when the Bay Horse was let for a number of years, it was described as:-[1]

> All that commodious and well-accustomed Inn known by the name of the Bay Horse in Ingleton, with the gardens, stables, coach houses, granary and other buildings thereunto belonging, together with about five and a half acres of rich meadow and pasture land now in the occupation of Mr. John Hartley. The above inn is now in full business, being particularly well situated in the direct road from the whole of the West Riding of Yorkshire as well as from Hull and Scarboro to Kendal, Lancaster, Whitehaven etc., from Harrogate to the Lakes and in the middle road from London, and all parts of the south to the above mentioned places; also on the road from the

east part of Yorkshire and Durham to Lancaster; in a good line for posting, which has considerably increased throughout the country of late years.

By December John Hartley had left the Bay Horse and was settled at the Royal Oak in Kirkby Lonsdale. Thomas Dowthwaite came down from Kendal where he had been landlord of the Woolpack and took over the Bay Horse. Sadly he did not last long at Ingleton and was declared bankrupt in 1809. His bankruptcy led to the sale of all his possessions at the inn.[2]

> All the household goods and furniture of Thomas Dowthwaite, consisting of twelve good four post and camp bedsteads, with hangings, very good feather beds, and mattresses. Table and bed linen, carpets, pier and swing glasses. Mahogany dining and other tables, chairs, chests of drawers, a good clock and a variety of kitchen furniture, brewing utensils etc. Also a very good four wheeled carriage, four carriage horses, with harness, one good milch cow, Carts, cart gear, Horse harness and other farming utensils.

The inn was let again to Richard Brown and he was followed by Thomas Lindsay. When Thomas Lindsay died in 1818 he also was found to be bankrupt. So the story went on with Matthias Steele another landlord ready to come and try his luck. It is interesting to note that Thomas Dowthwaite's goods include brewing utensils and it is likely that he brewed most of his own beer. However, it would have been reasonable to expect the brewing equipment to be part of the inn and not the landlord's personal property. After the New Road was cut in 1823 many stage coaches stopped coming up Bell Horse Gate into the village.

Thomas Barker, William Hartley, Edward Wilcock, James Kitchen, John Harling and John Holme followed each other as landlords. In July 1857 the licence passed from John King to John Bland of Lancaster and he served as landlord until the Bay Horse closed. During the 1860s John Kidd, the owner of the Bay Horse, realised that with the coming of rail traffic the old Bay Horse coaching inn, with its low ceilings, was out of date and unable to cope with modern times. He decided to build a new hotel in Ingleton the like of which the village had not seen before, the Ingleboro' Hotel. Though no longer an hotel the building is still there for all to see dominating the top of the main street. The old inn was transformed into three shops. The license was transferred across the road, and the old landlord John Bland BA, went to live with his daughter at the Bridge Inn where died in May 1874.

THE WHEAT SHEAF

> There is nothing which has yet been contrived by man,
> by which so much happiness is produced as by a good tavern or inn.
> Dr. Samuel Johnson 1709.

The Wheat Sheaf is one of the oldest inns of Ingleton and some of the old photographs hanging on the wall show its age. A blacksmiths shop stood next door, Hodgson's Smithy, which was later added to the inn. Richard Brown was landlord to his death in 1812 when his son Joseph Brown took over and was landlord until he died in 1837. Richard Brown's son Adam inherited the blacksmiths premises next door to the Wheat Sheaf. When Joseph Brown died in 1837 he left a considerable amount of property. He owned Kirksteads, Dale House, an estate at Yarlsber, three cottages and a barn in Ingleton, half share in the Bridge Inn and a large amount of land. As a butcher and innkeeper he had certainly been successful in business.

Wheat Sheaf with landlord James Saul.

In earlier centuries many blacksmiths were also innkeepers and the smithy was next door to the inn. By 1843 Mrs Anne Whitham was in charge. In 1851 Christopher Foster was the landlord. It is interesting that Christopher gave his occupation as farmer of twenty acres rather than landlord. In August 1851 the annual license day was held at the Wheat Sheaf and all the licensed victuallers in Ewecross attended. Thomas Redmayne was a popular landlord from the 1860s to his retirement in 1882.

Before the building of the new Court House and Police Station at Ingleton the Court House for Ewecross was held in an upper room at the Wheat Sheaf Inn. Here the JPs met to renew licenses and here all petty crimes in the villages of Ewecross Division were dealt with. In September 1872 Superintendent Exton complained about the butcher's shop adjoining the Wheat Sheaf, as it was no unusual thing for sheep to be slaughtered in the street near the steps to the old magistrate's room and sheep's entrails were often left in the area. The landlord promised to put up a slaughterhouse behind the inn and end the nuisance.[3]

Not only were Petty Sessions held at the Wheat Sheaf but on many occasions the yearly Court of both the Manor of Twistleton and the Manor of Ingleton were held there. The Twistleton court usually assembled at a cottage near the mill which is in Twistleton and then adjourned to the Wheat Sheaf in Ingleton to complete their business and especially enjoy the sumptuous dinner which followed it.

Sadly a third type of court was often held in the inn. In May 1872 when James Mathers, Innkeeper of the Welcome Home at Batty Green, tried to stop a runaway horse and cart outside the Wheat Sheaf he slipped and the cart wheel passed over his neck killing him instantly. He was brought into the inn and his body laid out to await the arrival of the coroner from Skipton. The inquest was held at the inn which acted as both mortuary and Coroner's Court.

Over the years the Wheat Sheaf played an important part in the township's affairs as the landlord was usually one of the few people who could keep books and accounts. About a century ago some Ingletonians, especially Wesleyan Methodists, protested that too much township business was conducted in the Wheat Sheaf and that it was an insult that they had to go there to see the township's accounts.

On February 4th 1860 a meeting was held at the Wheat Sheaf 'for the purposes of letting the finding and keeping of a bull or bulls for the benefit of the hamlets of Ingleton and Moorgarth'. When dances were held at the Wheat Sheaf and they frequently were well into the twentieth century they drew people from far and wide and it was often reported that, 'Mr Thomas Moore gave tone and animation to the assembly by the stirring strains of his fiddle.'

Thomas Redmayne retired as landlord of the Wheat Sheaf in 1882 after many years and Sam Worthington came to take over. The Worthington family were to serve as landlords of the Wheat Sheaf and then run the falls walk at Ingleton. On the evening of November 2nd 1887 there was a considerable fire on the premises of the Wheat Sheaf. The fire originated in the stable or the hay loft which adjoin the inn on the east. When fire gained such a hold and smoke filled the inn and neighbouring cottage all people and furniture were evacuated. The fire engine from Bentham arrived at 1am, but by then the flames had been subdued.

The Inn was owned by Joseph Brown Metcalfe of Prince Edward County in Virginia and Elizabeth Metcalfe of Ingleton High Street, both descendants of Richard Brown who had been owner and landlord from the eighteenth century. In 1888 they sold to William Mitchell of Mitchell's Brewery in Lancaster.

In 1900 Sam Worthington had plans passed to build a dining room for the accommodation of summer visitors who flocked to Ingleton.[4] It was a permanent wooden building capable of holding three hundred people, in fact at times it was said to have held four hundred. It took the place of a large marquee which had previously been erected on the bowling green behind the inn. It contained cooking equipment and catered for visitors until the 1940s when it burned down. It was always known locally as 'the pavilion'.

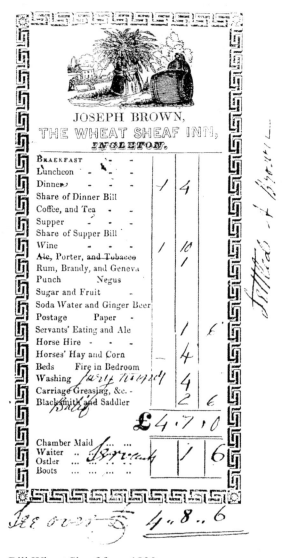

Bill Wheat Sheaf from 1830.
Probably from a Court meeting.

Sam Worthington handed over to James Saul in 1909 and after James Saul's death in 1916 Mrs Saul looked after the inn until 1922 when it was taken over by Joseph Thomas Procter a retired schoolmaster from Morecambe. He was followed by Captain James Richard Wilson in 1923. Extensive alterations were carried out by landlord John Henry Worden in 1927.

From time to time fights were organised in the field behind the Wheat Sheaf. In June 1913 Edward Buckham and John Filburn, two Ingleton pit-sinkers, fought a bare-fist fight. Buckam was sober, but Filburn was under the influence of drink. When they were later brought up before the magistrates the chairman asked, 'Was it a regular sort of prize fight?' and the constable told him that it 'was a made up affair'.

The story of the Wheat Sheaf is completed with the accident to William Foster. He was a miner from Ingleton Colliery and in November 1885 he did not survive his last visit to the inn. He had visited the toilet at the back of the building and on his return he fell down the cellar steps, was knocked unconscious and died the same night. The Coroner's Court was naturally held at the Wheat Sheaf. Joseph Bentham was a witness and told the coroner, 'He was not drunk, but a little fresh'. The unanimous verdict of the jury was accidental death. Historically in Ingleton it was the Wheat Sheaf and not the Wheatsheaf.

THE THREE HORSE SHOES

He that drinks and goes to bed sober,
Falls like the leaves fall and dies in October.
He that drinks and goes to bed mellow,
Lives as he ought to live, and dies a jolly good fellow.

This inn was also called the Horse Shoe Inn at times during the last century, but officially was probably always The Three Horse Shoes. It was, and still is, often referred to as either 't'Shoe' or simply 't'Shoes.' The Horse Shoe has always been a symbol of good luck and with the association of the mystic number three the idea is that the luck is multiplied. You well know that the horse shoe must be upright to hold the luck, and by superstition it should be held with three nails each driven in by three blows of the hammer.

There is also the suggestion of a connection with the blacksmith and the smithy and three horse shoes suggest a horse in need of a blacksmith. In 1822 the record of the first known landlord, George Yeadon, shows us that he was a blacksmith by trade as well as landlord and this may well have been traditional, just as we shall see that all last century the landlords of the Masons Arms were all masons. The 1851 census shows that the inn was being run by Margaret Metcalfe and she was still in charge twenty years later in 1871 at the age of seventy. Gamaliel Briscoe was a long time landlord from 1872 and he was still in charge in 1881.

The Greenwood family of Greenwood Leghe owned the inn for many years and usually chose the landlord who was often an estate worker. The inn could well have become The Greenwood Arms. The Greenwood family held their estate dinners there and it was there the family celebrated. On Friday October 14th 1870 William Norman Greenwood celebrated his twenty-first birthday and Ingleton was decorated with flags and the church bells were rung. Mr Greenwood's numerous tenants, with other invited guests sat down to an excellent supper at the Horse Shoes Inn. In January 1873 William Norman Greenwood gave a dinner for the church bell-ringers, his workpeople and a few friends. It is reported that the health of the young squire was drunk.

The Three Horse Shoes was sold to Yates and Jackson's Brewery at Lancaster in March 1889 for £1,715.[5] Thus ended the Greenwood Leghe connection with the inn - or did it?

141

Certainly after that date tenantry dinners were held at the Ingleboro' Hotel where the dining room was larger, but some connection was retained. In 1899 when the Greenwood family wanted a witness to say that Barker's tramway across the road was a 'nuisance' it was the landlord of the Three Horse Shoes, William Fisher, who made out an affidavit before magistrates to say that the crossing frightened his horses and was unsafe – that is in spite of the fact that it was completely safe and had been passed by the County Council.

In September 1911 John Walker landlord of the Three Horse Shoes, a sixty-six year old widower, died. He was a member of an old Ingleton family and for thirty years had been groom for the Greenwood family of Greenwood Leghe, so even at this date there was still some Greenwood connection. He had been landlord of the Shoes for nine years where he was very popular.

Many Coroner's Courts were held here, several in 1865. One was on the body of a cowman killed by a fall of planks in a hay loft, but others were of miners, for that was the risk industry in Ingleton for several centuries. The inn like many others was used as an auction room from time to time. In June 1875 a sale of property was recorded at, 'the Horse Shoe Inn'. A joiner's shop sold to Robert Kidd for £82; three cottages, barns and stable sold to George Boardman for £431; two old houses and garden near the National School sold to Joshua Howson for £208; and a plot of ground where Harling Barn once stood on the south side of the New Road was bought by Robert Atkinson for £51. The Oddfellows held their annual supper at the Three Horse Shoes in January 1878 and after dinner it is recorded that, 'Mr Thomas Moore gave tone and animation to the assembly by the stirring strains of his fiddle'.

During this century there have been many landlords here, John Walker, Jim Coates and Tommy Sydney who had a minah bird on the bar, are among those who are remembered. The inn has a low ceiling and fairly small rooms and was notorious especially on fair days for being smoky, noisy and crowded.

THE BRIDGE INN

> Long ago, at the end of the route,
> The stage pulled up and the folk stepped out.
> They have all passed under the tavern door,
> The youth and his bride and the grey three-score.

The Bridge Inn was built soon after the New Road was cut through Ingleton to save coaches on the Keighley Kendal Turnpike Road from having to negotiate Bell Horse Gate. Built about 1830 it was still called the New Bridge Inn in the 1840s. It stood close to the old stone bridge and the toll gate which spanned the road by the toll house. It soon became the stopping place for coaches on the new road. No longer did they call at the Bay Horse, but used the New Bridge Inn instead. From 1807 to 1843 the Union Coach from Leeds to Kendal regularly passed through Ingleton on Monday, Wednesday and Friday. It passed through Otley, Skipton, Settle, Ingleton and Kirkby Lonsdale. It returned from Kendal at 5am on Tuesday, Thursday and Saturday. Up to 1823 the coach stopped in the village, but from 1823 to its end in 1847 it dropped and collected passengers at the Bridge Inn.

The inn thrived and soon the Bridge Inn Croft was being used for a regular calf market which was attended by buyers from as far as Leeds, Liverpool and Manchester. In 1851 farmers around Ingleton and Thornton arranged with the landlord to hold a cattle market in addition to the weekly calf market. It began on Thursday May 12th 1851 and was held every alternate Thursday.

Bridge Inn, Ingleton's coaching inn on the New Road.

Robert Dickinson was landlord of the Bridge Inn during the early 1830s and died there in May 1834. The 1841 census shows that James Mattinson aged thirty-five was the landlord and lived there with his wife Alice and their children. By 1851 Alice had been widowed and had re-married Richard Farrer who was the new landlord. In 1853 John Holme was the landlord and died there on June 17th 1853. In 1856 Mr and Mrs Hutton were running the inn. By 1871 Thomas Gill was the innkeeper. It is interesting to note that in the nineteenth century landlords were also known as victuallers, ale drapers, and innkeepers. By 1877 the landlord was John Domoney, a cattle dealer from Hampshire, and he remained at the Bridge until his death in 1890. In 1877 John Dumoney opened the 'American Beef Shop' at the Bridge Inn to sell American beef as an agent of the American Fresh Meat Company. The Bridge Inn American Beef Shop was opened on March 3rd 1877 and the beef was said to be juicy and excellent by those who came to buy it. The cost of the meat varied from 6d to 9d per pound.

John Dumoney came down early one morning in June 1890 and hanged himself in the large assembly room at the Bridge Inn. Mrs Dumoney said her husband had drunk rather heartily since Whitsuntide of that year. A Coroner's Court was held and a verdict of 'temporary insanity' was reached. Mr Cartmell of Kendal cut the rope to let him down. He was sixty-four years of age and had been landlord of the Bridge for fifteen or sixteen years and also carried on the trade of cattle dealer. He was widely known and generally respected.

The Bridge Inn officially became the Bridge Hotel in February 1902 after the Petty Sessions at the Court House in Ingleton. At the time the title hotel was thought more fashionable than inn. To many it remained the Bridge Inn until it finally closed. In 1904 Charles Renshaw had come to the Bridge and was making alterations. Charles Renshaw completed his alterations, but he didn't last long as landlord. In 1907 he was found guilty of selling adulterated gin. Kenelm Vivian Sigismund Clegg became landlord of the Bridge in 1907 and was also soon in trouble with the police, but the case against him of selling adulterated liquor was dismissed. The most noteworthy thing about him was his impressive name.

Thomas Peers became landlord at the Bridge in 1920 and then in May 1922 he offered the hotel for sale with vacant possession. The bidding started at £1,000 but was withdrawn at

143

£2,600. From Thomas Peers, the inn eventually passed to Annie Gibbons. The Siddles were proprietors in the 1930s as motoring days developed and it became RAC and AA appointed. The inn became a tied house and then later in the 1970s returned to become a free house.

In 2003 the Bridge Inn was sold and the site developed for dwelling houses. The beer has dried up and the inn which survived from coaching days has finally closed. But the rooms are still there where the colliery manager, Hewitt, drank his whisky, where the Ingleton miners held their celebrations and where landlord John Dumoney hanged himself.

THE CRAVEN HEIFER

> When you have lost your Inns drown your empty selves
> for you have lost the last of England.
>
> Hillaire Belloc.

The Craven Heifer was a beer-house founded in the 1840s in a miner's cottage by John Tomlinson, a miner from Ingleton Colliery. John's wife, Eleanor, was the daughter of John Harling landlord of the Bay Horse and so was capable of running the inn while her husband was at work. The name was taken from the famous Craven Heifer reared at Bolton Abbey by the Rev. William Carr.

The Beerhouse Act of 1830, brought in by the Duke of Wellington, made it possible for people to open a room in their cottage for the sale of beer for a two guineas licence fee. The idea behind the act was to slow the sale of gin and spirits and promote the drinking of beer which was considered a far healthier drink and also a drink that would encourage agriculture by the increased use of barley. They could open every day except Sunday, but only beer and cider could be sold. There were three beer-houses in Ingleton in 1876, the Oddfellows, The Craven Heifer and the Masons Arms – only the last two of these remain today.

In 1861 George Hathersall and his wife were running the Craven Heifer. By 1871 John Tomlinson had gone to his last resting place, but his nephew had returned to Ingleton to run the inn with the help of his wife and one servant. It is interesting to note that the young John still continued his occupation as a miner. Once again his wife Ellen was able to help as she was the daughter of Joseph Gawith an innkeeper from Ulverston. In 1881 Ellen was running the Craven Heifer with the help of her widowed father. In the early days the beer-house would be kept to one room of the cottage. In 1867 the inn was refused a spirits licence but later became fully licensed. In 1891 John Tomlinson handed over to William Philips and after only two years in occupation he handed over to William Clapham.

Very little of a dramatic note ever seems to have taken place at the Craven Heifer. No one threw dynamite on the kitchen fire, no one fell to their deaths down the cellar steps and no landlord hanged himself in the bar. However, it is recorded in 1876 that a servant girl, Jane Thexton, knocked herself unconscious on a large iron pan while bending down to get coal to put on the fire. The Craven Heifer was one of the last inns in Ingleton to offer the warmth and attraction of a coal fire.

Eventually the inn was bought by Yates and Jackson in 1897 and extended to the neighbouring cottages as it is today.[6] Betsy Ann Clapham, the first woman licensee, was landlady from around 1896. From time to time she had trouble with drunks especially miners. In December 1913 she refused to serve Herbert Hayes with a drink and asked him to leave. He said there was no man in Ingleton who could turn him out. He assaulted her by banging her on the head with a spittoon and finished up in court. Her youngest son, Joseph Robert, who served in the 9th Duke of Wellington's was killed on the Somme in July 1916. Later the rest of the family emigrated to Canada. Betsy Ann Clapham died aged eighty in May 1927.

In 1922 William Arkwright Longton handed over the Craven to William (Billy) Routledge and he left it to go back to Ingleton Colliery as train driver. The inn was nearly closed in 1924 when there were objections to the renewal of the license at the Brewster Sessions. Yates and Jackson appealed against the closure and the appeal was allowed.[7] For many years in the 1970s two miners lamps stood on the bar at the Craven Heifer. It was an accidental symbolism, but the Tomlinsons who founded the inn would have been pleased to know these mementoes of their occupation as miners were being displayed.

Masons Arms with Percy and Winifred Matthewman holding their new tricycle c.1890.

THE MASONS ARMS

Beer! happy produce of our isle
Can sinewy strength impart,
And wearied with fatigue and toil
Can cheer each manly heart.

The Masons Arms opened as a beer-house in the 1840s, it wasn't there in 1841 but is registered in the 1851 census return. It began as a single room in a cottage on the New Road and was founded by Joseph Gillbanks, a stone mason. Joseph Gillbanks used the field behind the inn to store his stone and carve his gravestones and other masonry. Joseph was born on November 20th 1801 and died on November 28th 1886. He is buried in Thornton churchyard.

By 1881 Tom Matthewman who was born at Huddersfield was the landlord at the age of 32 and his employment was given as Marble Mason. Tom Matthewman had married Joseph Gillbanks' daughter, Elizabeth. He was still landlord in 1891, but his main employment was given as 'monumental mason'. Tom Matthewman advertised regularly in the Lancaster Press and his advert was usually used to head the notes on what was going on at Ingleton.

INGLETON
TOM MATTHEWMAN
MONUMENTAL SCULPTOR

Monuments, tablets, Tombs, Headstones, in Granite, Marble, and Stone, in the imperishable Lead Letters. Designs and estimates on application. Agent for Aberdeen Red, Grey, and Blue Granite.

In 1886 Tom Matthewman, Gillbank's son-in-law took over as landlord of the inn. Tom Matthewman would have done better if he had kept to selling ale rather than chipping stone as he succumbed to silicosis and died at the age of 47, on May 14th 1894. He is also buried in Thornton Churchyard and lies under a stone which he made himself. His wife Elizabeth continued to run the Masons Arms from 1894 and was soon applying for a spirits licence in September 1894 which was refused. The inn at this time occupied three cottages and had three entrances, one to the drawing room, one to the smoke room and a third to the commercial room. The inn contained four bedrooms of which two were for visitors. There was also a large room at the back for the use of visitors for dinner and tea parties. There were no stables and the only outbuilding was a water closet at the extreme end of the back garden.[8] Elizabeth Matthewman's tenure came to an end when she fell down the cellar steps at the Masons and was seriously injured in August 1900.

John Wignall, known as 'Jam Belly Wignall' took over the inn and was there for many years. Over the years the Mason's beer house gained a full spirits license. In May 1900 the inn was sold to Yates and Jacksons of Lancaster, but John Wignall continued as landlord. In May 1922 Arthur Hanwood became landlord. Yates and Jackson's owned other inns in Ingleton apart from the Mason's Arms and they held them until 1984 when they sold out to Thwaites of Blackburn.

ODDFELLOWS ARMS

The Oddfellows Arms first gained a beer-house licence on May 13th 1848. By this time there were many Oddfellows in Ingleton and brother John King who became the first landlord was a leading member of the Ingleton lodge.

William Taylor was landlord of the Oddfellow Arms in 1851. Later John King's son, John King, took over as landlord and he served until his death in1891 when John Tomlinson moved from the Craven Heifer to take over. When John Tomlinson was older and complained of being unwell his wife was far from being sympathetic. On one occasion she was heard to remark, 'Thous been deein for long enough, if thous gooin to dee get thysel deead!!' John Tomlinson died on October 15th 1915.

The Oddfellows Arms was more or less on the same site as the old Cross Keys Inn which went back to the seventeenth century. It stood on the topside of the little square at Ingleton. In September 1887 the Oddfellows Arms gained a licence to sell wine and the word 'wine' could long be seen painted over the door. The inn had been taken over by Yates and Jackson by 1904 and finally closed in 1910. At the Brewster session on February 18th 1909 'The magistrates gave notice that having regard to the character and necessity of the neighbourhood, and the number of licensed houses in the immediate vicinity, the license now held for the Oddfellows Arms, Ingleton, is unnecessary. The house is not so well adapted... and they had instructed the Clerk to give the requisite notice in the proper quarter.'

At an adjourned Brewster Sessions George Jackson applied for a review of licence for the Oddfellows. The licensee was John Tomlinson and the registered owners Messrs Yates & Jackson. The inn had a beer license from May 13th 1848 and wine from 30 September 30th

The Oddfellows' Arms is on the right, with wines written on the door lintel.

1887. The present tenant came on July 3rd 1891. The licence was provisionally renewed until meeting with the Compensation Authority. H.D. Wilson on behalf of the owner, George Jackson of Lancaster applied for renewal of the licence of the Oddfellows Arms Ingleton, but the police objected to a renewal:-[9]

PC MacDonald said he had known the Oddfellows Arms since 1905. It stood at right angles to the Main Street, in the centre of the village, and was an old house similar in size to two cottages. It had a frontage of 31 feet 6 inches, and a width at the end next to Main street of 16 feet 6 inches. It covered an area of about 71 square yards. The licensee was John Tomlinson and the registered owner were Messrs Yates and Jackson, Lancaster. There was very little made of ordinary living and the average number of customers, when he had looked in, was about two or three per night, the kitchen being the room generally used. There was also a little out trade. The estimated population of the village proper was 1,210 and there were four fully licensed houses and three beer-houses, giving 173 persons to each licensee. The number of dwellings nearer to it than to any other licensed house was 31. The distance to the Wheat Sheaf Hotel, which was fully licensed, was 171 3/4 yards; to the Craven Heifer Inn, which was a beer-house 445 yards; to the Bridge Hotel, fully licensed 932 yards; and to the Masons Arms beerhouse 1,016 yards. In his opinion the licence might be discontinued without inconvenience. The house was not so well adapted for a licensed house as others in the place. There was only a small place in front for vehicles, and there was no stabling. There was a backyard, which was jointly used with three other tenants. The present tenant had been there since July 3rd 1891, and on June 6th 1895 he was summoned for allowing domino playing for beer, and was ordered to pay costs of 6s:6d. The house had been licensed since May 13th 1848, and a wine licence was added September 30th 1887.

147

At the time of closing the rent was £45 per year. The inn was a tied house and the tenants were elderly people. The land in front of the inn was private property and it was railed off once a year at the November Fair. At the Brewster Sessions in 1910 the Bench sitting at Ingleton Court House decided to refer the house for compensation. The licence was provisionally renewed until the meeting of the Compensation Authority. Eventually the compensation was paid and the Oddfellows closed it doors.

INGLEBORO' HOTEL

Stupendous mountain, my hy, my hy,
I never see'd anything half so high;
Was it contracted for ? or did it grow ?
Or was it made out of a volcanoh ?

Anon.

Planned to be the Victoria Hotel, but changed to the Ingleboro' Hotel.

Unlike the mountain it was named after, the Ingleboro' Hotel was contracted for and there hangs a story. It all began in 1867 when John Kidd decided that Ingleton needed a new large and impressive hotel to meet with the needs of the growing number of visitors who now came to the area by train. He decided to desert his old coaching inn, the Bay Horse, build a new hotel across the road and transfer the license. The hotel would be called the New Victoria. The only reason Ingleton didn't ever have a New Victoria Hotel is that John Kidd changed his mind during the planning and building stage and the building became the Ingleboro' Hotel.

In November 1867 John Kidd made the announcement that the Bay Horse would be closed and the new hotel built. Workmen demolished the old buildings on the new site and dug out the foundations for the new hotel and then work stopped. People were told that there were 'defects in the plans' and nothing was done for over two years. In August 1869 new plans were drawn up, contractors were selected in March 1870 and building work began again. Joseph Bentham of Ingleton was the main contractor and the building was ready for occupation early in 1871.

The first licensee, Miss Ellen Powell, opened the hotel on Saturday night April 6th 1872. However, even though the hotel was opened, furnished and running, litigation went on between the owner, John Kidd, and the builder, Joseph Bentham, over the final payments for building costs. Miss Powell died around 1879 and Thomas Redmayne took over at the Ingleboro' until he retired in 1882. John Slinger came to the Ingleboro' in 1882 and was landlord for twenty one years and handed over to William Fisher in 1902. When John Slinger was landlord the hotel was extended to have large assembly rooms on the west side of the building. This was opened on January 27th 1883 with a free supper and dance. Three-hundred Ingletonians attended and it was said 'it was such an opening as never took place in Ingleton within the memory of the oldest inhabitant'. John Slinger died in April 1908.

In the 1880s the Court Baron met here when the Lords of the Manor of Ingleton dealt with manorial business and followed the business meeting with a lavish meal. When John Kidd died in 1888 the ownership of the hotel passed to James Kidd and he was the owner until he sold to Yates and Jackson of Lancaster in 1907. The inn finally closed in the 1970s and after considerable building work, was turned into a nursing home.

HILL INN

It's good to leave the dust and glare
Of city streets and noisy mills,
And revel in the sweeter air
Amid the glory of the hills.
Visitors' book, Hill Inn

The Hill Inn was the home of the Proctor family who lived there in the seventeenth century. Built in 1615 it became an inn in the eighteenth century and still serves as such today. It served the outlying Ingleton Fells district for many years and then became very

Hill Inn Chapel-le-Dale.

popular to outside visitors during the late nineteenth century after the arrival of trains. Its visitors book contained entries by well known people as Geoffrey and Eleanor Winthrop-Young, Edith Summersgill, Lord Tweedsmuir, better known as John Buchan the author of *Thirty-Nine Steps* and Tom Stobart who was photographer on the successful British assault on Everest. Many came to walk the Three Peaks and later to join the Three Peaks' Race.

Marie Hartley and Joan Ingleby wrote 'The inn naturally takes its name from Ingleborough, whose dominant shape, so close now, draws the eye.'[10] But it is not so, the Hill Inn was named after a much smaller hill, as it stands on the part of Chapel-le-Dale long known as the Hill. The Hill Inn saw some riotous occasions during the building of the Settle Carlisle Railway. W.R. Mitchell in his book on the building of the railway, *Seven Years Hard*, records that Mary Ann Lee was charged with dancing in an indecent manner with drunken navvies at the Hill Inn.

When the inn was undergoing repairs many years ago the writer was called in to see a shoe which had been found built into the wall of the chimney breast. It was a well worn, woman's black shoe. The Kilburns were landlords here and were burned to death in a road accident in 1928. Tom Kilburn the son of John Kilburn landlord of the Station Inn came to Hill Inn with his wife Isabella. They were well known for their good food and hospitality. Fred Riley records, 'Near the church door is the grave of Tom and Isabella Kilburn of the Hill Inn, whose tragic death in 1928 robbed the dale of two of its most popular and highly respected inhabitants'.[11] The Kilburns gravestone is near the Church door at Chapel-le-Dale, and elaborate stone cross and anchor. It reads, 'in loving memory of Tom and Isabella Ellen Kilburn of Hill Inn died 11 January 1928.'

GEARSTONES

For centuries there was a trade in Scottish cattle, with huge droves being driven from north to south of the country. Ingleton lay on the old drovers' roads and great herds of cattle passed through the township. In 1792 John Byng, 5th Viscount Torrington, passed through Ingleton on his travels and noted in his diary. 'At Ingleton I saw vast droves of Scottish cattle passing to the south' Torrington also described how he came to Ingleton from Askrigg. He came along the route of the old Roman road from Bainbridge meeting the present Hawes to Ingleton Road at Gearstones. He wrote:-[12]

> I was much fatigued by the tediousness of the road where we met two farming men, with whom we conversed about the grouse, and their abundance. Crossing a ford, Mr. Blakey led me to a public house - called Geirstones, the seat of misery in a desert; and tho filled with company, yet the Scotch fair held upon the heath added to the horror of the curious scenery: the ground in front crowded by Scotch cattle and the drovers; and the house crammed by the buyers and sellers most of whom were in plaids, fillibegs etc. The stable did not afford hay. The only custom of this hotel or rather hovel is derived from the grouse shooters, or from two Scotch fairs; when at the conclusion of the days squabble the two Nations agree in mutual drunkenness. The Scotch are always wrapped up in their plaids – as a defence against heat, cold or wet; but they are preventions of speed or activity: so whenever any cattle stray'd, they instantly threw down the plaid, that they might overtake them. All the Yorkshire around, though black and frightful seems of small account in the comparison of Ingleborough – at whose base we now travel.

So Gearstones Inn lay the extreme north eastern part of the township of Ingleton. In 1816 the inn came up for sale and was described as, 'All that Inn or Public House, called the

Gearstones, consisting of five good rooms upon the ground floor, with cellar underneath the whole, five excellent lodging rooms in the second storey; and an attic over the whole; also two barns, Brewhouse, Chaise house, and stables, with hay chambers over the same. With a good cottage and necessary offices and gardens.'

The Inn also had thirty-two acres of land attached to it and at the time a grain market was held at Gearstones every Wednesday throughout the year. Stagecoaches to and from Lancaster and York called at Gearstones every Monday, Wednesday and Friday. William Lister was the landlord at the time the inn was put up for sale by auction on 18 September 1816. Every January railway men and the grouse shooters had their annual dinner at the Gearstones and this tradition continued until the inn was closed.

Our last story of Gearstones occurred in 1873 during the building of the Settle Carlisle railway. One quiet May evening George Young, a railway worker, who had been drinking at the inn, threw a packet of Nobel's Patent safety Dynamite onto the kitchen fire. 'The oven was blown out, the boiler front was broken to pieces, and the fire place driven out. The kettle which was hanging over the fire was smashed to fragments'. Fifteen window panes were broken, the clock was shattered and the hearthstone was lifted up. The report in the *Lancaster Guardian* was headed 'Dangerous Larking' – but George Wright of Dent Head who was seriously burnt about the face would have thought it more than any lark. Francis Yates was landlord at the time and his daughter Alice was working in the inn at the time of the accident, but was not injured. The newspaper of the day gave no hint as to the motive for the outrage. Young was committed to Leeds Assizes to stand trial.

Gearstones was almost entirely re-built around 1880 after which it was reported that 'It is a quiet comfortable place, and from the sitting room window there is a delightful view of the mountains and valley southwards'. The inn was closed and the license surrendered on June 30th 1911. It was all part of the JP's trying to close little used inns in outlying areas because they were a problem for the police to control and gave them extra work.

NEWBY HEAD INN

The inn at Newby Head was a Drovers' Inn and roadside inn for travellers on the Lancaster Richmond turnpike Road. Here drovers, packmen and other travellers called for a drink and to stay the night. The lodgings were basic and not only were rooms shared, but beds were shared as well, as was often the custom of past centuries. In January 1843 an inquest was held at Newby Head Inn by the Skipton coroner Thomas Brown. Isaac Mason, a native of Kendal, had been found dead in bed. According to the landlord and the person who shared the bed he went to bed appearing in good health. During the night he became ill and his bedfellow went downstairs to get a candle for light. When he returned he found Isaac Mason dead. The verdict was 'died by the visitation of God'.

The inn stood at one thousand-four-hundred feet above sea level in desolate countryside. Thomas Guy was innkeeper in 1821. Edmund Thistlethwaite was landlord in 1841 and by 1851 John Swinbank had taken over. In 1905 the landlord changed from Christopher Swinbank to Simeon Parker. The Swinbanks had been at Newby Head at least since 1851 when John Swinbank was 'victualler and farmer' with 170 acres of land. It was one of the outlying inns which the magistrates were keen to close around the turn of the century mainly because it was too far out from the towns to supervise and they saw no real need for it. It was always a farm and after its closure as an inn in 1919 it returned to full time farming.

THE WELCOME HOME

> How oft doth man, by care oppressed,
> Find in an inn a place of rest!

The Welcome Home Inn was opened at Ribblehead near Batty Wife Hole in 1870 by James Mathers. It was one of the inns that sprouted up during the building of the Settle Carlisle Railway through the area. The other inns were the Travellers Rest, the Brewery Inn, the Railway Inn and the Station Inn: the latter two appear to have been the same establishment. At Ribblehead the shanty towns of Jericho, Jordan, Sebastopol, Batty Green and Batty Wife Hole were built to accommodate the railway workers. Alongside them sprang up inns and shops to serve the workers and their families. The people of Ingleton complained of traffic through the village day and night taking supplies to the railway workings. When those supplies were barrels of beer they questioned the emergency of the supply. One reporter said, 'One might think that drink was the principal commodity for sustaining navvy life.'

The Welcome Home is the only one with a clear story from opening to closure. James Mathers was born in Bolton, but before coming to Ribblehead he had lived for some years in Wales where several of his children were born. He was forty-three years old and settled in the timber built Welcome Home with his wife Mary and six children, Jane, John, Ellen, Mary, James and Martha. The magistrates had been generous with licences at the railway shanty towns at Ribblehead as they knew it would cut out illicit drinking houses. James Mathers' wife, Mary, also ran a small pawnbroking business at the inn.[13] She would advance money on goods left with her and naturally most of the money went on drink.

Coroners' Courts were held at the Welcome Home on more than one occasion. In July 1872 James Sherman was bringing a loaded wagon and horse out of Blea Moor tunnel when he slipped and the wheels of the wagon ran over his ankles. John Stirzaker came to his aid and brought him down to Batty Green in a cart. Sherman refused to have his wounds bound to stop the bleeding and when he reached Batty Green blood was trickling out of the cart and he had bled to death. The inquest at the Welcome Home recorded a verdict of 'accidentally killed by a railway wagon running over his ankle'.

James Mathers collected many of his supplies in the village of Ingleton and he frequently made the journey by horse and cart. On April 29th 1872 he was in Ingleton for supplies and left his horse and cart outside the Wheat Sheaf Inn. Before returning home he gave his horse some meal and water and for this purpose took off the head collar. Before he could replace the head collar the horse took fright at something in the street and dashed off at a brisk pace. James Mathers ran after it and in making an attempt to stop it was knocked down and one of the iron cart wheels ran over his neck and killed him on the spot. His body was taken into the Wheat Sheaf ready for the inquest. On the afternoon of May 1st an inquest was held by J.P. Brown the deputy coroner and a verdict of accidental death was recorded. On another occasion a railway worker laid down on the line for a rest after drinking at the Welcome Home Inn and the first train in the morning decapitated him.

James was buried in the churchyard at Chapel-le-Dale and there his memorial leans against the far wall. His grave with its curious verse has puzzled many visitors and also writers on the Dales who did not know the story which you have just read.

IN AFFECTIONATE MEMORY
of
JAMES MATHERS
WHO DIED APRIL 29TH 1872
AGED 45 YEARS

WHEN I WAS IN THE PRIME OF LIFE,
IT WAS THROUGH A FALL I LOST MY LIFE,
NO MAN IN THE WORLD NEED BOAST OF HIS MIGHT
HE IS ALIVE IN THE MORNING AND DEAD AT NIGHT.

For a while James Mathers' widow ran the Welcome Home and then his brother, Samuel, came to take over the inn and continued as landlord until the inn was closed. At Ingleton Petty Sessions on September 24th 1876 the Welcome Home Inn had its licence withdrawn and was closed down. Today no trace of the inn remains where James Mathers once sold his beer at 2d a quart.

TRAVELLERS REST
BREWERY INN

There is confusion over the inns at Ribblehead during the railway construction. When the census was taken in 1871,Thomas Moore, the enumerator was not very efficient in recording the premises. He classed all the properties in the area as Batty Wife Hole. Batty Green was across the road from Batty Wife Hole and it got no mention in 1871. Not only did Thomas Moore record Batty Green as Batty Wife Hole but in recording the inns he simply gave them a number without any name. At 71 Batty Wife Hole George Jackson was innkeeper; at 73 James Mathers lived with his family; the third licensed premises were next door at 74 Batty Wife Hole where John Garlick was innkeeper.

Now we know that these inns are most likely to have stood on Batty Green at the side of the turnpike road going from Ingleton to Hawes as the correspondent of the *Lancaster Guardian* writing about the area in August 1870 said, 'From Batty Green, which is a wayside waste on the west of Batty Wife Hole on which most of the wooden huts are built… Most of the huts, which number more than forty and are increasing, are made of wood, with roofs covered with waterproof felting. Amongst the huts we noticed a saddler's shop, a grocer's shop, a shoemaker's shop, a green grocer's and a bookseller's and stationers shop.' He also tells us that there was a brewery opposite Batty Green, but does not mention any inns. However, he does end his article by advertising Settle Temperance Society and saying that many men have 'signed the pledge' with Mr Tiplady, the railway missionary, so we can understand his reluctance to mention the drinking houses. John Garlick was not only an innkeeper, but he also kept a shop at Batty Green. We know that the shop had a front window because Thomas Jones, a Welsh navvy, was charged with stealing an oil lamp and five pieces of scented soap from it.

George Jackson gained a licence for the Travellers Rest in 1870 and was soon supplying the railway workers with beer. He not only sold beer but brewed his own on the spot. He was only a young man of twenty-one years in 1871, but he was well settled as an innkeeper at Ribblehead. Trade was brisk at Batty Green and the business set up George Jackson for the rest of his life. He prospered well during the building of the railway and later founded Yates and Jackson's Brewery at Lancaster. He became a councillor and was several time mayor of Lancaster. George Jackson himself acquired several inns at Ingleton over the years and Yates and Jackson held some of them until they sold their brewery business in 1984.

George Jackson was the only known brewer at Ribblehead and the Brewery Inn may well have been his. The Brewery Inn at Batty Green was still there in 1875 for in January it was the venue for a pigeon shoot. The contest was between Robert Stavely, gamekeeper for James Farrer, and George Holt, timekeeper on the Settle Carlisle Railway. The innkeeper at the time is not mentioned but Robert Stavely won the contest. In the list of licensed inns given in 1876, the Travellers' Rest is listed with George Jackson as landlord. This is a puzzle, as the only inn to survive long after the end of the railway works was the Station Inn.

RAILWAY INN
THE STATION INN

The Railway Inn is mentioned in September 1871 when David Davies had a fatal accident and his body was taken to the Railway Inn ready for the arrival of the deputy-coroner Thomas P. Brown who held an inquest there on Wednesday September 27th. In February 1872 Peter Miles, a worker on the section of line at Batty Wife Hole had been drinking in the Railway Inn and then left for Sebastopol. He was drunk and in the dark he wandered into the tramway tunnel where he laid down to rest and was run over by an engine. The inquest was held at the Railway Inn where the verdict was 'Accidentally killed by being run over by a railway engine.'[14] It was natural at first that the inn was known as the Railway Inn as there was no station in the early days. Later the Railway Inn probably became the Station Inn and remained so until this day.

Following the completion of the Settle Carlisle railway works the authorities were keen to close down the licences which had been granted when building began. The Brewery Inn had gone and the Welcome Home was closed. The only survival was the Railway Inn which probably later became the Station Inn. However in 1877 it was still referred to as the Railway Inn Tavern. [15] In 1877 the owner of the Railway Inn was given as George Jackson.

John Killburn schoolmaster and publican was innkeeper at the Station Inn at Ribblehead for many years. He was born in 1815 and was a schoolmaster for thirty-five years at Chapel-le-Dale and before that taught at Bruntscar Hall. Speaking of the inns at Ribblehead Speight says, 'The one near the station was built when the line was being made about twenty years ago. Since 1876 it has been tenanted by old John Kilburn, who for 35 years was master of the little school at Chapel in the Dale. He was six years shepherd on Ingleborough, and though now near 80 (1892) is still hale and able, and regularly attends Bentham market, ten miles off.' He did part time work as a butcher and vet and local physician. John Kilburn was still running the Station Inn at the age of 76 in 1891 and died in 1900.

THE BLACK BULL

That there was a Black Bull Inn at Ingleton there is no doubt and evidence seems to show that there were two. A Black Bull stood at the corner of Main Street and Church Street. Balderston in his *Ingleton Bygone and Present* tells us, 'Close to the church is a house, formerly called the Black Bull Inn, with memorial stone above the door of considerable age'. This date-stone, which has long since gone or been covered, recorded R B A 1710. However, the date-stone can be clearly seen on post cards from the beginning of the twentieth century. In 1797 the deeds record the transfer of the property from Richard and Elizabeth Balderston to Robert Chapman so that it may well have been B for Balderston on the date-stone, 'That messuage & Dwelling House with a Brew House, Stable, Hayloft, Bake-house with a dwelling house over same and Necessary House ... adjoining to the Churchyard...commonly called or known as the sign of the Black Bull Inn and in the occupation of John Ellershaw.' This information comes from a deed in possession of Ralph Tomlinson, whose family ran the premises as a bakery for many years.

In the Craven Muster Roll of 1803 John Ellershaw senior is shown as a landlord, and his son John Ellershaw as landlord's son. By 1812, John Ellershaw, junior, had taken over as landlord of the Black Bull. In May of that year his eldest son was killed in a road accident in the main street. A loaded cart ran over him and the Coroner came to Ingleton for the inquest. In 1857 a second deed records that following death of Robert Chapman and his will made in 1841, the Black Bull adjoining the churchyard at Ingleton passed to the Rev. Roger Chapman of Burton. This is the property at the bottom of Church Street fronting into the main street. Once Tomlinson's bakery it has been for many years a newsagent's shop. The floor is covered with smooth old slate flags typical of many eighteenth century inn country inns of the area. Now for the second Black Bull. Joseph Carr tells us in his memoirs, 'In 1836 I began to visit Ingleton more frequently, and thus became acquainted with most of the people. I visited some of the Methodist meetings which were held in a room in the centre of the village, connected with a detached house once known as the 'Old Black Bull.' Carr's description puts the Black Bull firmly in the main square and it seems appropriate as the old bull ring is in the square. Here was the place where bull baiting was carried on until well into the nineteenth century as a village entertainment. Tradition has it that the license was taken away from the Old Black Bull around 1820 on the instigation of the Rev. William Waller.[16] The house had a date-stone of 1752 before the extensive Victorian renovations.[17]

In 1839, the Tithe Award shows that Thomas Green owned the Black Bull Inn and paid one penny Church Land Rent to the Rector for it. The tithe schedule shows that the occupier at the time was J. Oddie. There is a suggestion that it was re-opened as a beer-house for a short time. The old inn then became Thomas and Margaret Green's grocer's shop and post office during the 1840s. Baines Directory for 1822 lists no Black Bull at Ingleton. The answer to the dates of the second, and possibly third Black Bull, lies in deeds deposited with a Bentham solicitor which the author has been unable to research.

THE CROSS KEYS

The Cross Keys was the sign of St Peter and the Cross Keys at Ingleton was only round the corner from the Church. This was probably the favourite spot for the bell-ringers and churchwardens. The Cross Keys is mentioned in the deeds of a shop in the little square at Ingleton and it tells us that the inn was in the corner of the square.

At Ingleton Manor Court on December 1st 1766 it was recorded that John Wilkinson passed to Thomas Wildman 'a messuage or Tenement known by the name of Cross Keys near Seedhill in Ingleton with a Brewhouse and other appurtenances thereto belonging as by deed dated the 27th of January 1766'. There was a well and pump between the house and brew-house. In March 1778 the building was passed from John Wildman to Marmaduke Morton. This inn disappeared not many years afterwards.

BELL HORSE INN

In their book *The Yorkshire Dales* Marie Hartley and Joan Ingleby wrote, 'Bell Horse Gate, the present steep road to the rivers, commemorates by its name the leader of a pack-horse train, and it once had an inn of the same name on it'. The Bell Horse Inn has been often mentioned in Ingleton and was supposed to have stood in Bell Horse Gate. One of the cottages has a small upstairs window where some have said the landlord was able to watch for approaching customers. However, no such inn appears in the records – in fact it never existed. Common sense also would be against it, for Bell Horse Gate, being half the width it is today, had no space for carriages to stop and park. It is the first of what can be termed Ingleton's phantom or ghost inns - inns that never existed at all!

THE RING O'BELLS

There is a story that an inn named the Ring O'Bells stood near the church – well it would have to be for the bell ringers to quench their thirst after the hard work of pulling the bell-ropes. But once again there is no record of such an inn. The early bell ringers took their beer at the Cross Keys Inn, which was genuine enough, but the Ring O'Bells appears to be just another of Ingleton's ghost inns.

THE COCK INN

The Cock Inn was reputed to be in the Back Gate and was supposed at one time to have been the site of cock-fights when that sport was popular in this country. Stories are also told of a murder taking place there and blood stains on the floorboards. There are also stories of a ghost and hauntings. Writing about Ingleton's inns Speight tells 'But the oldest is probably that known as the Cock inn, on the Ingleton Hall road, below the railway bridge. It was formerly a well-known trysting place of cock-fighters, and it is said that more than one dark deed of crime has been perpetrated within its rooms. One of the old floors showed many ominous blood stains, which no amount of scrubbing could ever remove. The house of three gables was probably built in the time of James I, but it has been much altered and improved. A carved oak partition inside bears the date 1616'.[18] Balderston tells us a similar story calling it Cock Inn House. Once again this house was never an inn. The house was simply Cockin or Cocking House named after John Cockin and his family who lived there and it stood in Cocking Croft. The house has been long demolished. All the Cock Inn stories are fiction and that is a fact.

HOLLY PLATT

Once again it is Hartley and Ingleby in their book *The Yorkshire Dales* who describe another inn at Ingleton that never existed. Holly Platt, a farm on the old Clapham road out of Ingleton has been described as an old coaching house in various books on the Ingleton area. Writing about the old Clapham road from Ingleton Hartley and Ingilby record. 'On the old road we pass a farmhouse, Holly Platt, a former coaching inn. It has a raised platform from which coaches were boarded and where luggage was unloaded, and a two-storied porch supported on columns, whose upper storey acted as a look-out for traffic'.[19] Sadly once again this is a myth which mainly appears to have arisen because the farmstead has a porch with windows in the side which over-imaginative persons have interpreted as look out for coaches coming along the road. No-one would stay at such a place when the inns of Ingleton were so close with all the village's facilities. To give the story a final blow it never appears in the licensing or any other records which a genuine inn most certainly would have done.

In August 1802 Holly Platt estate was advertised to let, in the *Lancaster Gazette*. 'All that valuable Estate or Farm, pleasantly situated at Holly Plat, about one mile from Ingleton on the highway to Clapham; consisting of a capital dwelling house, barn, stable and shippon. 80 acres of customary measure of rich arable, meadow and pasture land, with an unlimited right of common on Ingleborough. This estate is well watered and fenced, and it is now the most desirable sheep farm in the county, and now in the possession of Messrs Wildman and Foster as tenants'. There is no mention of a coaching inn or brewhouse – it was purely a sheep farm and so it continued.

This chapter had shown that Ingleton's inns have a fascinating past. When you enter one of these old inns think for a while of the thousands who have passed through the door before you. They came on foot, on horseback, with packhorse, by coach and carriage, stagecoach, railway and finally by car and motor coach. To think of them is to imagine the whole range of historical costume, Elizabethan leather jerkins and puffed out knee breeches, Stuart cloaks and feather hats, then came the Georgians, the Victorians, the Edwardians and the rest.

They trod the same floors and came for the same reason, men and women of all walks of life, the Lord of the Manor, the doctor, constable and tradesman. To Ingleton's Inns came Lord Torrington, the poets Southey and Gray and the artist Turner who painted in the township. But mostly they were working men, packmen and drovers, farmers and labourers, miners and joiners.

REFERENCES

1.   *Lancaster Gazette,* November 6th 1802.
2.   *Lancaster Gazette,* July 17th 1809.
3.   *Lancaster Guardian,* September 7th 1872.
4.   Recordings by Maggie Tomlinson 1975. (Author)
5.   *Lancaster Guardian,* March 26th 1889.
6.   *Ingleton Manor Court Books, NYRO, ZUC (MIC) 1558.*
7.   *Lancaster Guardian,* February 9th & June 7th 1924.
8.   *Lancaster Guardian,* September 18th 1894.
9.   *Lancaster Guardian,* March 13th 1909.
10. *The Yorkshire Dales,* M. Hartley & J. Ingilby, Aldine, 1963, p.134.
11. *The Attractive Charms of Chapel-le-Dale,* F. Riley, Settle Undated. P.11.
12. *The Torrington Diaries,* ed. B.W. Andrews, Eyre & Spottiswood 1936.
13. *Shanty Life on the Settle-Carlisle Railway,* W.R. Mitchell, Castleberg, 1988, p.30.
14. *Lancaster Guardian,* March 17th 1872.
15. *Lancaster Guardian,* April 28th 1877.
16. *Lancaster Guardian,* October 24th 1891.
17. *Lancaster Guardian,* April 30th 1892.
18. *The Craven and North-West Yorkshire Highlands,* H. Speight, Smith Settle,1989, p.215
19. *The Yorkshire Dales,* M. Hartley & J. Ingilby, Aldine, p.128.

AGRICULTURE

EARLY AGRICULTURE

The native Brigantes were settled when the Romans came to Yorkshire and they bred cattle and grew corn in what became Ingleton. Ingleton has the remains of Brigantian, Romano-British and Viking settlements and they have left a mark on the Ingleton landscape. The trouble at Ingleton is that the landscape has been severely marked by centuries of mining, quarrying, and road and railway workings. In Ingleton township much of the land lies above the 200 metre contour and the soils on the hillsides are thin. However, the alluvial soils of the valleys and lowlands provide a rich herbage.

ABBEY LANDS

In the middle ages monasteries came to own and lease a great deal of land in the Pennines. Furness Abbey farmed and owned considerable tracts of land across Ingleton and the neighbouring townships including Horton and Dent. Ingleton's connection with Furness Abbey is well illustrated in the Furness Abbey Coucher Book which registers all titles and deeds to the property of the monastery. In January 1250 Alice, the daughter of Adam of Staveley, granted to the monks at Furness her pasture at Southerscales. This grant of land was confirmed by her son Henry on November 30th 1255. The extent of this pasture is described in the Furness Coucher Book and the pasture takes us from present day Southerscales across into Chapel-le-Dale and covers Scales and on to Ellerbeck. The document mentions the cliffs at Weysdale called Scales and Lower, Middle and Upper Scales are there to this day. Alice Staveley's father was sub-lord of several manors including Ingleton. He held the land under the Mowbrays who were chief lords in that they held the land from the king.

In September 1303 William son of Adam de Twyselton recovered common pasture in an action against the Abbot of Furness. This was land at Southerscales in 'Ingelton in Lonesdale' as Ingleton was termed in this account. In 1343 there was a dispute between the Abbot of Furness and the rector of Bentham over rights of land at Ingleton. The abbot had rights through land purchased and the rector had rights by his position. The land in question was two vaccaries called Burbadthwait and Quernsyd. Vaccaries were cattle farms and these two were in Ingleton Fells. In 1344 the Abbott of Furness was claiming five-hundred acres of moor and pasture in Ingleton and he succeed in his claim.[1] Gearstones in Ingleton Fells was in the Manor of Newby the third manor to which parts of Ingleton township belonged. It was also a possession of Furness Abbey and this may well be the origin of the weekly corn and oatmeal market which was held there. The properties of Furness Abbey are recorded in the *Liber Regis* of Henry VIII and include Gearstones, Cam House and many other places in the Ribblehead area.[2]

> Redd'et firmis in Lonsdall, viz.: Kesden £10 12s 4d, Thynook et Hardacre £2 9d 0d, Hesyllhaw or Greynclose £3 6s 8d, Villa de Newby £6 5s 11d, Newby Coote £4 1s 7d ob', Clapham Towne £2 7s 0d, Stakhouse £5 6s 8d, Selffed £13 3s 4d, Southouse £8 2s 8d, Souterscale £13 6s 8d, Brunt Skarre £3 6s 8d, Wyntersckayll £8 0s 0d, Raneskall £2 8s 0d, Camhouse £3 3s 4d, Lynghyll et Byrkwith £6 19s 0d, Netherlonge £3 18s 8d, Thorns £2 10s 4d ob', Geerstons et Coltparke £5 9s 2d, et Yngman Lodge £6 6s 8d. In toto £110 18s 4d.

The abbey sheep granges were out at Twistleton and Ingleton Fells and little affected the villagers at Ingleton, although Ingleton provided monks for several Yorkshire abbeys and local shepherds looked after the monastic sheep. From around 1340 to 1366 William of Ingleton was Abbott of Sawley Abbey in Lancashire.[3]

Furness Abbey had contact with wool dealers in St Omer in 1212, and Florence 1294 and so wool from Ingleton sheep was taken to Furness and from there probably ended up in France and Italy. The abbeys had problems with Scottish raids, but in good years the wool clip was safely stored in the abbey before being either collected or sent on to foreign markets and the abbeys profited well. All this ended with the dissolution of the monasteries in 1536.

The Metcalfe family of Fell End sheep shearing.

MEDIEVAL STRIP FARMING

Ingleton with its mountainous landscape and river valleys did not have the simple strip field system that most midland and southern villages had, but a system was there. Land was divided into strips as near to the village as possible in the early days and then new fields were added as the call for land became greater. These strip fields were in operation before the Norman Conquest and continued for centuries. There was a three year cycle of crop rotation with each strip being left fallow for one year in three. The land in the fields was divided by grassy banks called balks which were left unploughed. A villager held strips in a number of fields so that he got some good and some bad. However it was far from an efficient system as the farmer had to travel from place to place to farm his separate strips.

Fields was a word originally denoting open country, but then was applied to unenclosed land used for village agriculture. These were great fields divided into furlongs and sub-divided into strip or doles. Each furlong usually had a name, but the individual strips did not. The modern day meaning of field came later by which time they were smaller and enclosed by wall or hedge.

After the crops had been harvested the land was used for pasture, but the village had plenty of common pasture land or waste where sheep and cattle could be put to graze. Farmers were allotted so many 'beast gates' 'cattle gates' 'cow gates' or 'sheep gates' on the commons so that the land did not become over stocked. But healthy cattle were mixed with diseased cattle and the tendency was for many farmers to overstock the commons and there was over-grazing When the commons were over-stocked the more ruthless farmers would 'dog off' the animals of rivals. By using his dogs to drive neighbours sheep onto higher ground he could gain the better grazing for his own animals.

Over the years the system became more lax and owners swapped strips to have more land together. Buying and selling of strips also was allowed and some built up larger land holdings. Wills frequently record the transfer of land. Henry Lamb in 1671 left, 'a parcel of ground lying on Heslay', and land in the 'Townefields'. In 1626 John Balderston of Moorgarth left, 'my over close, a little parcel of meadow ground lyinge at Guyeninge Gap, a Rood and a halfe of ground lyinge on Hardbacke be it more or lesse. A ten fall of ground lying at Hesley end, and a calfe gate, or there abouts in the new Close'. This shows how by the early seventeenth century the land had been broken up.

No one has left us any records of these early fields so we have to look at the evidence - land, early maps, later documents, and conjecture. Lime lands, Hardback and many other names had disappeared by the time the Tithe Award Commissioners listed all fields in Ingleton in the 1840s. Hesley had also become Hasler and Harsler. However, we can see the irregular fields on the map which were likely the large open fields divided into strips. The only surviving ones to be shown on a map were shown on the plan of Edward Parker's lands made in 1765. Plan XXII[d] clearly shows Bracken Bottoms divided out in long strips and the schedule on page 38 records, 'Bracken Bottom consisting of 5 Dales'. If other strips were evident in the landscape at the time they were not noted or marked on any maps.[4]

TUDOR FARMING

Elizabethan inventories show that the farming in Tudor times was closely related to that of today. The farming was mainly pastoral, the livestock cattle and sheep. Much of Ingleton was rough moorland and fit only for sheep grazing. Breeds of sheep are not mentioned as they are listed as wethers, ewes, hoggs or lambs. Wethers were the male castrated sheep bred for mutton and hoggs were year old female sheep. The main breed in the hilly areas of the north was the black-faced heath sheep. These black-faced or scotch sheep have their descendants in the modern Scotch black-face, Rough Fell, Swaledale and Dalesbred sheep. Another likely breed was the Herdwick sheep which was a white-faced horned breed. It was the smallest of the hill sheep and agile in mountain areas. It was reputed to produce good and tasty mutton.

If sheep were the most numerous stock, cattle were the most valuable. There was only one bull recorded in the inventories and that belonged to Alexander Guy of Yarlsber. Bulls were of prime importance in breeding, but only a few could afford the cost and upkeep of a bull. Alexander Guy also had the most numerous and varied stock. He had ten oxen and stotts, four twinters, ten stirks, ten steers, a herd of twenty one cows, a bull and eight calves. The stock of this one farm, the most substantial yeoman's farm in the township well illustrates the cattle stock and practice in Ingleton.

Oxen were used as draught animals for ploughing and carting and could still be at their peak at seventeen or eighteen years. Many were worked until they were around ten years old when they were fattened and sold off for meat. In the Elizabethan period Ingleton farmers said that there were, 'above four-score Draught oxen upon their said Tenements'.[5] Oxen survived through the eighteenth century and into the nineteenth century in Yorkshire. The question of ox versus horse was a common one, the main argument being that the ox cost little in grazing and provided meat at the end of its working days, while the horse needed extra food, was more prone to health problems and provided only hide at the end of its day.

Ingleton was on the old drovers routes bringing cattle from Scotland to the south. Many passed through Gearstones at Ingleton Fells then took the Horton road while other herds coming from Kirkby Lonsdale came through Ingleton. Ingleton had a spring fair and a November fair, both traditionally cattle fairs. Cattle were also kept for their dairy produce and the lower down the social scale the more important this was to survival. In the surviving Ingleton will inventories only a few spinsters, the village miller and a few labourers had no cattle at all. There is no doubt that cattle, in providing beef, hide, horn and tallow, as well as milk, cheese and butter were of great importance to the Elizabethan farmer.

Whereas only nine inventories listed oxen, forty listed horses. A horse was more sure-footed in hilly country and were needed in such an extensive parish as Ingleton to visit family, neighbours, the village centre and markets. Alexander Guy had twelve horses and was probably breeding horses. As Alexander Guy also was the collector of the tithe corn for both Ingleton and Bentham, Alexander's horses would be used for much carting and carrying. William Hird's six horses at Twistleton could well have been pack-horses for Twistleton was on the old pack horse route from Dent to Ingleton. The inventories list horses and mares, foals and fillies and colts and stags. The presence of young horses and stags, which were unshod and unbroken horses, further suggests horse breeding.

From horse flesh to the pig is a wide gap, but pigs played an important part in Elizabethan farming. The pig was a successful producer of meat, turning waste and swill, acorns and beech mast, into good meat with speed and efficiency. What is more, pig meat kept better than most other meat. Ingleton farmers also kept hens and a few kept geese. Bee hives were common as honey was the main sweetener before the days of imported sugar. Bee keeping was relatively cheap and so the poor were not debarred by the cost of equipment.

Land was under the plough and cereal and root crops were grown. The evidence is in the inventories where corn is mentioned both in the barn and growing on the ground. There is also the evidence of ploughs and plough gear which many farmers had. Agnes Sproat (1589) had, the Croppe on the earthe being corne Growing upon vij roddes of ground,' valued at £2 6s 8d. Christopher Craven (1558) had his crop within the barn and upon the ground. Both these were July inventories before the harvest was completed. Thomas Guy had five acres of growing corn valued at £4 3s 4d.

After harvest inventories show wheat, oats corn and barley. Bigg, a course variety of barley, is more often mentioned that barley. Bigg produced a reasonable crop even on poor ground and was used mainly for brewing beer and was also used in boiled mash for cattle food. Wheat rarely appears in inventories, but oats are common. It was the only cereal that would succeed in the poorest and wettest soil and the Ingleton soil could be poor and wet. Where oats were grown it was used for oat cakes and haver bread was a common part of Ingleton diet. Almost all homes had a backstone to bake oatcake. The tithe corn at Ingleton was collected and stored by Alexander Guy and is listed as bigg and haver that is barley and oats which confirms that they were the main cereal crops.[6]

Farming in Ingleton was subsistence farming; they hoped to produce enough food to carry both humans and animals from one harvest to the next. When they had problems it usually began with the failure of crops and this often brought the villagers to food shortage and sometime to starvation. Haymaking was very important as the amount and quality of the hay was a critical factor in the ability of a farmer to keep his livestock through the winter, especially his horses. His horses had to work the whole year through. Hay was also important for the diet of cattle and sheep. Sunny weather was essential for good haymaking: unsettled weather led to poor hay.

Haymaking at Goat Gap with the Metcalfe family.

PINFOLD & PINDER

Ingleton had a pinder in 1297 who looked after the pinfold and stray animals which were kept there. Henry Pinder lived in the village and the pinfold was probably at the top of the Back Gate where it still remained in 1920. In 1379 Robert Pinder and his wife are shown in the Poll Tax of that year. The pinder had an important job from manorial times as he kept stray animals safely until their owners collected them. Of course they had to pay a small fine to regain their animals. This sometimes caused annoyance and occasionally the pinfold was broken into by irate farmers trying to get hold of their animals without paying the fine.

The pinder at Ingleton was a manor court appointment right up to the end of the nineteenth century. In 1821 the Manor Court was annoyed at the number of stray animals on the local roads and streets and decided to reaffirm its authority:-

We the Jury of the Manor of Ingleton with the consent of the steward of the said Manor do here empower the Pinder to Impound Horses, asses, cows, sheep, Geese and Piggs that shall be found in the highways and lanes within the said Manor and also cattle that shall be found grazing in the wastes or Commons of persons that hath no right to herbage and shall charge the following sums and no more for impounding the same. For an Horse and Cow one shilling each, a Calf 6d, for each sheep 6d, for Geese 1/6d a dozen, for each Pigg 2/- and each ass 6d and for every person bringing Goods to the Fold 4d as well for each persons Cattle.

Joseph Dowbiggin came into court and was sworn into the office of pinder for the Manor of Ingleton and was expected to keep the streets and roads clear of stray animals. In Dec 1828 Thomas King was sworn as pinder for the Township of Ingleton which consisted of Ingleton, Moorgarth and Coldcotes. He was given a list of fines which he had to impose:-

For every Head of Chattele, Horse, Mares, geldings, Foles, asses and mules, Cows and calves the sum of 6d per Head and for every Pig the sum of 6d per Head and for every Sheepe sixpence per Head and for every goose Two pence per head. To be impounded out of the Streets, Lanes and Highways within the village of Ingleton and Coldcotes. The said Pinder to impound all goods and Chattles that may be found trespassing on the wastes, Commons of persons that hath not right of Common in the said Township.

In Aug 1834 Samuel Moor was made pinder for the ensuing year. In 1840 Thomas Borrowdale served as pinder. In 1854 the pinder was William Yates and the pinfold was noted as being at the top of Back Gate. William Yates was still pinder in January1865 when he had trouble with William Thistlethwaite who broke the lock on the pound door. Thistlethwaite though taken to court was let off with payment of 6d as he was an old man.

In 1913 the pinfold needed a new two part gate, one six feet and the other three feet. It had not had much use for many years but in March 1920 it was brought back into use as straying animals were causing extensive damage.[7] Ingleton applied for a licence for a pinder. Many villages have made an historic monument of their pinfold, but at Ingleton it has almost disappeared and survives only as part of the garden and drive of a cottage in Upper Gate.

ENCLOSURE & ENCLOSURE AWARD

Land was enclosed from prehistoric days, with small fields for cattle and cereals. From medieval times the lord of the manor was keen to enclose his land and slowly did so. The Cholmleys, Lowthers in Ingleton Manor and the Shireburnes in Twistleton Manor all pushed for enclosure in the sixteenth century. When enclosures took place farms, which had previously been in the village, moved out to stand in the fields they farmed. This early enclosure enclosed much of the open fields and some commons or waste as it was more readily known.

On June 22nd 1767 a meeting was held at the Bay Horse Inn at Ingleton to plan the enclosing of three thousand acres of Ingleton and Bentham Moor. It became known as the Ingleton and Bentham Moor Enclosure Award. It covered commons and waste and included land in the parishes of Bentham, Ingleton, Wennington and Burton. The Commissioners were John Moore, Thomas Hawkshead, Robert Lacy, Thomas Goss, Henry Ellershaw and John Foster and they produced a massive plan and a three hundred page document.[8]

Landowners were given a portion of land in relation to the land they already owned and the church received land as did the Lords of the Manor. At the same time as enclosing, the Commissioners determined the tithes which would be due to the Rector of Bentham. Routes over the commons were restricted to the new roads which were laid out. Exception was made for Ingleton Colliery who had the right to mine in the area and cart coal across the land where necessary. This enclosure changed the look of the land considerable and changed people's routes in the countryside. No longer could they wander at will, but were confined to the enclosure roads. It was an agricultural improvement, but there were some who lost out.

TITHE AWARD

The Tithe Award reminds us that early farmers paid tithes to the Church in the form of animals and grain. In theory this was meant to be a tenth of the farmer's income. This was changed to a cash payment with the passing of Tithe Commutation Act of 1836. However, in practice, many places had already changed their payments 'in kind' to cash payments long before the act. The Tithe Schedule, dated 1839, which accompanies the map shows the owners and occupiers of every farm, field and cottage and the amount of rent due.

The Tithe Schedule also names every field in the township of Ingleton and shows its usage and acreage. Copies of Ingleton's Tithe Award can be found in the Public Record Office in London, the North Yorkshire Record Office at Northallerton and a third copy can be found in Sheepscar Archives at Leeds.

DROVERS AND CATTLE FAIRS

Drovers played an important part in agriculture for many centuries moving cattle around the country mainly from north to south. Drovers were also employed in cattle movement in the local area especially bringing cattle to and from local cattle fairs and markets. Ingleton's St Leonard's Day Fair had become mainly a cattle and livestock fair by the eighteenth century. The Ingleton Fair was centuries old and was one of the largest cattle fairs in the neighbourhood. In 1884 the show of cattle were reported as extremely large, so much so that some of the oldest inhabitants could not remember anything like it.

There was a weekly calf market at the Bridge Inn for many years and in 1851 farmers decided to hold a cattle market in addition. The first was held on Thursday May 12th 1851 and was held every alternate Thursday. The market was held in the Bridge Inn Croft behind the inn. Butchers came from as far away as Wigan, Leeds, Bradford and Huddersfield.

CHEESEMAKING

Cheese was made on many farms in Ingleton through the ages. As there was less sale of milk in the country the milk could be turned into butter and cheese and kept for long periods. Writing about local cheese in his memoirs Anthony Hewitson said, 'Cheese of a really good kind was a rarity in and about the village. Much of that consumed went by the name of 'whangby' – a tough, leathery article, dense enough almost to require an axe or saw in the cutting of it, and in some instances so extremely hard that I have been tempted to fancy if a specimen was rolled down say the brow of a steep pasture it would break or send flying whatever it came into contact with and would dash through any wall there might be at the bottom like a runaway boulder stone'.

Much cheese made in the township would surely have been better than Hewitson described, but when it was made in the farm dairy the quality would vary considerably. Gerald Tyler in his book *Farming Life in Chapel-le-Dale,* tells us, 'Old cheese press stones are still to be found. Frederick Riley found one at Broadrake weighing over 500 pounds with a lifting ring fashioned from a horse shoe. At Ivescar he found another weighing over 1000 pounds. But, as Riley recorded, cheese making had virtually ceased by the 1930s'.[9]

FIELDS AND FIELD NAMES

Field names have been in use since medieval farming. The large open fields at Ingleton had more interesting names than South Field, West Field and North Field. They included Town End Field, Crooklands, Skinner Crooklands, Thackmire, Cringlemires, Thacklands, Flatts and others. Many names dropped out of use and when the Tithe Award map was made in the 1840s the present names were registered. Similarly go to Ingleton's farms today and you will often find it difficult to match the field names given in the Tithe Award as new names have arisen.

Annums denote land recently taken into cultivation and Ingleton has its Annums, Far Annums, Low Annums, High Annums and Little Annums all behind. Yanhams house probably has the same name origin. At the rear of the other side of the main street are crofts, Far Croft, Middle Croft, Tenter Croft, and a dozen others all denoting the small fields which were attached to the early cottages and well protected in centuries gone by.

The Clod was the large field where the two rivers met in Twistleton. In 1671 it was owned by Henry Lamb, a cooper. In 1772 John Oddie, Lord of the Manor of Twistleton bought land 'called the Clod and on which a dwelling house has been lately built'. A large refreshment room was built on the site in Victorian times and later Clod Villas were built.

HARVEST HOME

The importance of harvest in the calendar up to the end of nineteenth century can not be overestimated. It was vital and a good harvest was worth a good harvest festival service in church and a good harvest supper. But during the twentieth century harvest home became meaningless to most. Fruit and vegetables were brought into church, usually the produce of every country from France to New Zealand. In 2008 the people in Ingleton rely on the Co-op in Ingleton or the super market at Kirkby Lonsdale and whether there is a good harvest or not does not have the slightest effect on them: in previous centuries it meant life or death.

The old barn at Ingleton Hall.

REFERENCES

1. *The Furness Coucher Book*, Vol.II, ed. J. Brownbill, Chetham Society, 1919.
2. *Craven and the North West Yorkshire Highlands,* H. Speight, Smith Settle, 1989, p.178.
3. *Historical Account of the Abbey of Sawley,* ed. J. Harland, London 1854, p.42.
4. *A Survey of Lands lying in several Townships* in the Counties of York and Lancaster Belonging to Edward Parker Esqr, R. Lang, 1765, LRO DDB 84/1.
5. *Elizabethan Ingleton,* J.I. Bentley, Ingleton Publications, 1980, p.28.
6. id, p,34.
7. *Lancaster Guardian,*Mar 13th 1920.
8. WYAS Wakefield, Enclosure Awards, 84 Ingleton & Bentham Moor 1767.
9. *Yorkshire Dalesman,* May 1975, p.20.

INGLETON MILLS

MANORIAL CORN MILL

Ingleton's manorial corn mill was a few hundred yards up river from Ingleton Bridge on the village side of Ingleton Beck. It stood near the site of Ingleton swimming baths. The mill was also called the Wheat Mill or the Upper Mill. It was called the Upper Mill as opposed to the lower Meal Mill on the Twistleton side of the river close by Ingleton Bridge. Ingleton Corn Mill was certainly up and running in 1306 when it is mentioned in an inquisition post mortem as belonging to the Lord of the Manor and had probably already been in existence for a couple of centuries. The mill was run by water power and the mill race came from a weir at a bend in the river upstream. The mill race came across open ground and around the edge of Sammy Croft before reaching the mill wheel.

Richard Coop was Ingleton's miller who died in 1588. Apart from on old blanket his sole possessions were his few clothes. He either lived in the mill or in lodgings in the village. The next miller noted in Ingleton's records is Henry Foster who died in 1650. He owned a house in Ingleton which he left to his wife Agnes for her lifetime and then to son John. The manorial connection was strong in that most of the money he was owed was by members of the Lowther family; Gerrard, Robert, Richard and Lancelot. John Harrison was a widower and miller at Ingleton when he married in July 1722. Stephen Eglin of Ingleton is mentioned as a miller in his will when he died in 1740. Stephen Carr was miller at Ingleton in 1765 and is shown in Edward Parker's Estate Book as occupying all the mill sites in Ingleton, the Corn Mill, the Meal Mill in Twistleton and Walk Mill in the Bottoms. In October 1789 John Marsden miller, married Betty Wildman at Ingleton.

The Ingleton Corn mill is shown on Edward Parker's estate map of 1765 and Thomas Jeffry's map of 1767.[1] In 1769 the jury at Ingleton Manor Court acted against Thomas Redmayne for building a wall which stopped carts passing between the mill and Bell Horse Gate and he was ordered to remove it by the next court or face a heavy fine: he moved it. The mill is again mentioned in the court rolls in 1782. Then in November 1800 when a deed was made for the transfer of land on the Strand from Matthew Carter to the owners of Ingleton Mill it stated, 'near the place where the Upper Mill formerly stood' showing that the old corn mill had been demolished by 1800.[2] This means we can be certain that the corn mill was demolished between 1782 and 1800. The most likely time was during the building of the new mill and the reorganising of the mill races.

WALK MILL OR FULLING MILL

> Clooth that cometh fro the weyvng is nought comly to were
> Til it be fulled under foot or in fullyng stokkes,
> Wasshen wel with water and with teasels scracched,
> Ytowked and yteynted and under taillours hande.

> Langland, Piers Plowman, c.1350.

William Langland in his Piers Plowman tells us that cloth is not comely until it has gone through several processes after weaving and the first process was fulling. Fulling was the beating of the cloth until the warp and weft were fully meshed to make as smooth dense cloth. The process was originally done by treading under foot and the man who did it was called a walker. Walking cloth gave way to the fulling stocks where water power raised great wooden hammers to fall on the cloth. There was a fulling mill at Ingleton in 1306 most probably with fulling stocks.[3] It would have most likely not have been in place for long as the 1300s saw the rise in fulling mills throughout the country. The fulling mill was in the bottoms by the side of the river Greta: this is now roughly the site of Ingleton Pottery. On his death in 1711 Robert Wilkinson senior left the Walk Mill to his son Thomas with sons Robert and another to have free use, except for 2s per year which they had to pay towards repairs.[4]

The fulling mill at Ingleton lay 'under the Brow', that was how Robert Wilkinson the owner, put it in his will when he wrote it in 1709. People brought their pieces of cloth in rolls either on horseback or over their shoulder down to the mill in the Bottoms. Water from the river came into the premises and drove a wheel which turned a single wooden axle. As the roller turned it threw up the hammers in turn raising them and then allowing them to drop onto the cloth in the trough beneath. The Wilkinson family of weavers had the Walk Mill to full their own cloth, but they would also full for others who brought their cloth from Ingleton, Thornton, Westhouse and further afield. The fuller in charge, paid by the owners, recorded and dealt with the cloth coming into the mill.

In the centre arch is the site of Ingleton's ancient fulling mill or walk mill.

When the cloth had been pounded and meshed it was taken up to be stretched on tenters to dry. Tenter Croft where this was done was a large croft on the Bank just above the mill. Tenter Croft is now the site of the car park and Ingleborough Community Centre. Here there were rows of frames with hooks top and bottom to which the cloth was attached to dry. Across the river in Thornton parish was Tenter Bank, near Holme Head Farm, and perhaps cloth was also taken to be stretched and dried on tenter frames there.

In 1765 on Parker's Estate map the building doesn't seem to appear as a mill but as a house and there is no mention of a fulling mill or Walk Mill. 'The Hall House Garden & Backside near the River below the Bridge.' Stephen Carr was a miller and at this time occupied all the mill sites. We know he was a miller from his marriage on August 7th 1769 when he married Agnes Dixon at Ingleton. He died in 1802 and was buried at Ingleton. His family had certainly been in the area for several generations as is shown by local parish registers.

The existence of a fulling mill and fulling stocks suggests that woollen cloth was being produced in Ingleton from medieval times. William Day was a weaver in Moorgarth and in

167

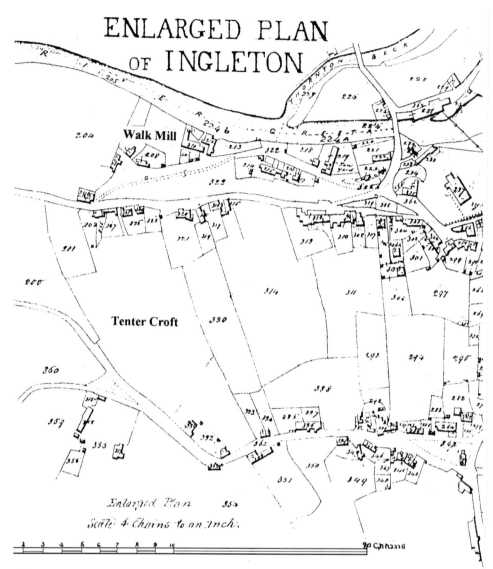

Walk Mill

Tenter Croft

Enlarged Plan
Scale 4 Chains to an inch.

The area of Walk Mill and Tenter Field from the Tithe Map.

1583 he left his weaving equipment to son-in-law Richard Balderston. His will says he was a weaver and he had a 'pair of studdles' meaning a loom. Looms like trousers were usually termed a pair. Thomas Armitstead is named in his will in 1702 as a 'woolenwebster' and the inventory of his goods includes, 'Loomes, sheares and other warke towels.' Few people are mentioned as weavers at Ingleton, but there were probably many who had a loom and wove as a second occupation.

Much of the area in the Bottoms was known as Walk Mill or Walk Miln well into the nineteenth century when the Preston family owned it. In August 1827 the Court Rolls record that Walk Mill was in the occupation of John Preston, 'all of which said premises are situate in the bottom of the Brow in Ingleton.' From that time the name Walk Mill gradually dropped away and it was eventually completely forgotten. The tithe Map of 1847 recorded the building simply as a factory.

INGLETON COTTON AND FLAX MILL

George Armitstead, a cotton spinner from Clapham; Ephraim Ellis, a joiner from Ripon; William Petty, a bridle bit maker; and Thomas Wigglesworth, a flax-dresser, jointly paid £120 for the old Mill Barn at Ingleton. They bought the property from Thomas Redmayne and after demolishing everything on the site, old mill, kiln and cottages, they built a new cotton spinning mill in 1791. Previously the old Twistleton meal mill had stood on the site along with an old kiln. The meal mill was centuries old and run by a wooden water wheel and was just inside the Manor of Twistleton.[5] Bridge End House was later built as a manager's house alongside the mill. An insurance policy no 147505 was registered with the Royal Exchange by Mary Armitstead & Co in September 1795 covering the mill, smithy and joiner's shop for £2,000.[6]

These partners had already been responsible for turning Clapham Corn Mill into a cotton spinning mill around 1786. Although the original Ingleton Mill deed stated that Ephraim Ellis was a joiner from Ripon he had a share in both Clapham and Ingleton mills and a house in Ingleton. He died in 1802 and his will mentions, 'All his share in Cotton Mill situated within the Manor of Twistleton with all buildings and Out Houses, Frunts, Yards, Water, Watercourses, Heriditaments and Appurtenances thereunto belonging.' His wife Anne got a seventh part and his children John, Benjamin, Ephraim, Nancy, Mary and William also shared in his property including the mill.[7]

TO BE SOLD BY AUCTION,

At the house of Mr. RICHARD BROWN, innkeeper, at Ingleton, in the county of York, on MONDAY, September 18, 1809, between the hours of six and eight o'clock in the evening (subject to such conditions as will be then and there produced)

THAT large FACTORY, known by the name of INGLETON MILL, situate in the Manor of Twistleton, adjoining the turnpike-road from Leeds to Kendal, with or without the MACHINERY. This Mill is very well adapted for spinning flax. There are two good STREAMS belonging to the premises, which turn a wheel 18½ feet diameter, and 9 feet wide.

Also, TWO COTTAGE HOUSES, situate in Ingleton aforesaid.

The Machinery in the above-mentioned Factory is as follows:

Five Breaking Engines, twenty inches wide, with Cards—Six Finishing Engines, twenty inches wide, with Cards—Two Stretching Frames—One Hundred and Twenty-four Spindles—Eleven Boxes of Drawing—Thirteen Drum Frames, forty-eight spindles each—Three Double Reels, eighty hanks each—Two Double Carding Engines, one thirty and the other thirty-six inches wide—Two Billies, with one hundred and sixteen spindles—Seven Jennies, one hundred and thirty-two spindles in each—One Cutting Engine, by water—and other articles, too numerous to mention.

Should the Machinery not be sold on the same day with the Mill, it will be SOLD by AUCTION, on the succeeding day, viz. September 19, 1809.

For further particulars, in the mean time, apply to Mr. JOHN ELLIS, of Ingleton.

§ Time for payment will be fixed on the day of sale.

INGLETON, AUG. 28, 1809.

Sale notice of Ingleton Mill from the *Lancaster Guardian* of 1809.

Thomas Wigglesworth of Padside Hall in the parish of Hampsthwaite, sold his share of Ingleton Mill to the others in June 1806. The mill must not have been very successful for the partners, who since the death of Ephraim Ellis had now grown to over ten. In 1809 the mill was put up for sale by auction at the Wheat Sheaf Inn at Ingleton. John Ellis of Ingleton, one of Ephraim Ellis' sons was noted as the person to apply to for further information. George Burrow of Westhouse bought the mill from the partners William Petty, John Armitstead, Mary Armitstead, John Ellis, Benjamin Ellis, Ephraim Ellis the younger, Henry Hutton and Nancy his wife, Thomas Russell and Mary his wife and Anne Ellis. George Burrow worked the mill, but he did not hold it for long as in February 1813 he sold it to James Coates, a linen manufacturer of Kirkby Lonsdale for £710. The agreement was made with the proviso that George Burrow remain as tenant of the mill for a further year.[8]

In 1800 the mill owners acquired land on the other side of the river from the mill, on the Strand. It was a small piece of land adjoining Matthew Carter's garden and the Church and was used to build the stone supports for a water trough to carry water from the old corn mill race across to the new mill. The deed stated that it was, 'near the place where the Upper Mill formerly stood containing in length thirty three yards and in breadth twelve yards.' The trough had major repairs about 1921 and was later demolished in 1942. The timber from the water trough was used to floor one of the upstairs rooms in the mill. The base on the pillars can still be seen on the river bank. In this way the mill used water from both the Doe and the Twiss.

The Coates family ran the mill under the name of John Coates & Son and were listed in the Baines Directory of 1822 as 'Flax & Tow Spinners'. John Coates manufacturer, nephew of James Coates, married Betty Dent at Ingleton in February 1813 and their son John Thomas Coates was born in November 1813. The mill appears to have changed from flax and tow to cotton between 1822 and November 1832, when the company became bankrupt and the mill was put up for sale. The auction sale was held at the mill itself, and it would appear there was no sale as it continued in the Coates family ownership. However, a new partner, Henry Davis, a linen manufacturer from Kirkby Lonsdale, came along who probably saved the company financially. Henry Davis was only involved with Ingleton Mill for a few years for he gave up his share of the mill in 1836.

John Thomas Coates came into ownership in several stages, in 1835, as the only son and heir, he inherited a third share on the death of his mother, Elizabeth Coates. He bought a further third share from Henry Davis of Kirkby Lonsdale in 1836.[9] His final share probably came from either his father who died in 1842 or his great uncle who died in 1851. John Thomas Coates was then in full control. In 1841 he was living at Bridge End House adjoining the mill, but later he moved to Holme Head House just out of Ingleton in Thornton-in-Lonsdale.

On December 1st 1842 the Ingleton Manor Court Rolls record. 'We the Jury consent to the lords of the said manor granting to John Thomas Coates of Ingleton aforesaid Cotton Manufacturer leave and Licence to erect a weir across the Stream called Ingleton Beck otherwise Greeta at a certain place called Ingleton Force for the purposes of Damming the water and make a Mill Dam for the use of Ingleton Mill for such Terms as the Lords shall think fit, upon condition that the said Weir is so constructed and the Water so managed as to occasion no inconvenience to the Public and no Damage to any property.' Previous weirs had been washed away by the power of the river and little remains today of the new weir John Coates built.

In 1851 John Thomas Coates was a twenty-six years old married man still living at Bridge End House and noted as a cotton spinner employing seventy-two persons, twelve men, fifteen women, twenty boys and twenty-five girls. He was married to Margaret Greenwood, the daughter of James Greenwood, at Ingleton Church on December 3rd 1838 by the Rev. Richard Hodgson. At the same time his sister Agnes Stockdale Coates married the Rev. Richard Hodgson. John and Margaret Coates had no children.

Then came the fire. On April 1st 1854 Ingleton Mill burned down. The *Lancaster Gazette* fully reported this historic blaze on April 8th.

INGLETON COTTON MILL TOTALLY DESTROYED BY FIRE

On Saturday evening last, the inhabitants of Ingleton were thrown into considerable state of alarm by the breaking out of a most awful fire in the cotton mill belonging to John Thomas Coates Esq., cotton spinner of this place. It was discovered between seven and eight o'clock, the fire having originated in one of the upper stories, and in a short time it was evident from the progress of the flames, that the whole of the building was doomed to destruction. A messenger was despatched with all haste to Bentham Mill for a fire-engine and until its arrival all hands were employed in endeavouring to prevent the fire communicating with the house adjoining, as it was plain that all that could be hoped for was to save this part of the premises, and which for some time was in imminent peril. Some delay occurred in getting the fire-engine from Bentham Mill owing in a great measure to the absence of Mr. R.W. Waithman Esq., from home, and upon its arrival at the scene of disaster all probability of saving any part of the mill and machinery was at an end, as the building at that time was completely gutted, and scarcely anything remained but the blackened walls. Its services were therefore applied to prevent the burning of the house, and we may add that its assistance, being fitted up with Mr. Waithman's excellent patent linen hosepipe, which answered exceedingly well from its lightness and pliability. It was also instrumental from saving the steam engines from injury. The mill was fitted up with the best machinery that could be procured, and no pains or expense was spared to render it one of the most perfect of its kind. For the origin of the fire no cause can at present be assigned, as the mill had not been running for a few hours. Mr. Coates, in person along with one of his workmen, went through the premises a short time before, and as far as they could see everything was in perfect safety, the cause therefore, remains enveloped in mystery. The estimated damage is from £7,000 to £8,000. The scene is described by eye witnesses to have been awefully grand, the flames bursting forth from every window, and the falling of burning timbers in the interior, the crackling and giving way of the roof, the flames shooting up towards the sky, made the most minute object visible for a great distance. Too much praise cannot be given to the neighbours for their praiseworthy endeavours to save the property and buildings, and we may add, that Messrs Leak, Hodgson, Sisson, Saul and others were unremitting in their efforts to subdue the flames. Most of the household furniture was carried into the fields and neighbours houses. We are happy to say that Mr. Coates was in great measure insured in the Sun and Norwich Union Fire Offices, there being £3,150 in each office.

Following the fire the mill it was several years before a new mill was built. But a new mill was built and completed by William Atkinson and Sons. It was advertised to be let for ten years in the *Lancaster Guardian* in November 1861:-

INGLETON MILL. Mill with Steam Engines, Water Wheel, Gas Works, Warehouse, Dwelling House, Outbuildings and Cottages. **TO BE LET** For ten years, and may be entered upon immediately, all that newly erected and substantial **STONE BUILT MILL**…The Mill contains four floors, exclusive of the attics and cellars and measures one hundred feet in length, by forty-two feet in width, inside the different rooms being from ten to twelve feet in height, and will be fitted up with the main shafting and gearing, Steam pipes etc., to meet the wishes of a tenant. The Engine House adjoining, is also four stories in height and entirely fire proof. These fire proof rooms are thirty-seven feet long, by twenty feet wide, inside measures. The Steam Engines are by Peel, Williams & Peel. The water wheel is entirely of iron, thirty feet in diameter, and twelve feet wide, with an excellent supply of pure water. There are also gas works, warehouse, Smith's shop and Other outbuildings…

From the time of the mill fire on the 1st of April 1854 the Ingleton mill was closed for twelve years. After re-building it was empty until William Bracewell of Barnoldswick and Eli Towler of Burton-in-Lonsdale took it over, but for years they seemed to do nothing. The people in the village were concerned that this was a great loss of employment in the village.

In May 1867 they complained, 'About four or five years ago large quantities of machinery were brought from Barnoldswick near Colne, and there appeared every prospect of the mill being soon in full operation; but hitherto the machinery had been lying useless on the mill floor. Had this mill been run for the last twelve years, how much it would have added prosperity to the village and the domestic comforts of both work and trades people'.

Again the *Lancaster Guardian reported* on November 23rd 1867:-

When Messrs Bracewell and Towler took possession of the new mill, it was no more than a mere shell, consequently there was much to be done, by way of flagging, putting up shafting, repairing the weirs and watercourses, before even the machines could be put up. Progress is being made for fitting the mill for running, but no doubt the depression in the cotton trade has a tendency to retard the work in hand. On Tuesday and Wednesday a new boiler of between fourteen and fifteen tons weight was being removed from the station to the mill by means of a windlass and rollers. The mill will be worked by steam and water power. This shows that the preliminary works for running the mill are going on, though it may be but slowly. The long standing of this mill has been a serious loss in the way of business to the village and neighbourhood, but it is hoped that the present occupiers will shortly be able to give remunerative employment to the population.

It must be remembered that part of the time was the time of the American Civil War, 1861-1865, when supplies of cotton were cut off from the southern states. John Thomas Coates retained ownership of the mill and it was leased to Bracewell and Towler. Bracewell and Towler gave employment to many men and boys and girls as they worked the mill for several years with some success. William Bracewell soon had other interests in Ingleton when he bought the colliery and a farm. However, through depression in trade and other reasons the mill ground to a halt around 1883. The stoppage of the mill was a serious blow to those employed and also to Ingleton's tradesmen. Much machinery was sold and in June Mr Ford of Bentham and Mr Delaney of Settle came to examine the mill and unsold machinery. It was rumoured that Mr Delaney and some neighbouring manufacturers were considering running the mill, but nothing came of it.

In September 1897 after many years of standing empty, the people of Ingleton saw the mill race being cleaned out. On November 20th the *Lancaster Guardian* reported. 'A young man called John Bragg had an accident at Ingleton Mill. After being idle for twenty years the mill has been taken over by Messrs Carter and Sons of Blackburn for the purpose of making acetylene gas. Bragg had been told to bar the water wheel as it stuck in one place. Instead of using a bar he jumped on it setting it off. It broke his leg and crushed his foot'. The water wheel is thirty-three feet in diameter and fourteen feet across and is made or iron. It is driven by the combined waters of the Doe and the Twiss supplying about 160 horse-power. As this source is not always reliable there is a compound tandem engine of some 400 horse power. The finished product of the mill was carbide of calcium. When water was added to this it produced a light which was considered equal if not superior to gas.

In September 1898 the people of Ingleton were invited to an exhibition of acetylene gas in the old cotton mill which caused considerable interest in the village. There were soon complaints of the smoke that poured out of the mill chimney. However, the business did not last long and once again the mill stood idle.

On October 7th 1898 the owner of the mill, John Thomas Coates, died at Holme Head House in Thornton aged eighty-four years. He was a JP and well respected in Ingleton, he was a Captain in the Ingleton Volunteer Rifle Corps for many years and also served as a

Ingleton mill fire on Thursday October 13th 1904.

governor of the National School. By his will dated April 25th 1896 he left everything to his housekeeper Elizabeth Slee.

In July 1904 Mr P. Middleditch of Halsteads, who used to run the hemp mill at Bentham, leased the mill and fitted up the second floor of the mill with machinery and announced plans to start hemp production and initially employ twenty people. Then on Thursday afternoon, the 13th of October 1904 Ingleton Mill once again burned to the ground. The fire originated

The mill remains after the fire.

in the middle storey about 3 o'clock and the mill was speedily a mass of flames. Within an hour the roof fell in and soon afterwards the west wall fell with a crash. The Ingleton fire brigade was soon on the spot, but was unable to cope with a fire of such magnitude. The damage was estimated at £8,000, but was covered by insurance.

During severe storms later in the year the gable end collapsed and tons of stone fell doing considerable damage to neighbouring property. The following February further parts of the mill walls collapsed due to frost. In April 1911 two steeplejacks from Manchester were engaged to demolish the mill chimney and there was some sadness at the disappearance of a familiar landmark. In July 1905, John Charles Walker of Glenholme in Ingleton, bought from Elizabeth Slee for £300, 'All that Mill or Factory situate at Ingleton aforesaid and known as Ingleton Mill and the water wheel house and chimney and the land forming the side thereof. Together with the rights of water, watercourses, springs, weirs, dams, races, reservoirs, and water wheel'. John Walker tried without success to get some business to begin operations at Ingleton Mill. Then following the death of John Walker the mill passed to his wife Mrs Annie Walker. The part of the mill saved from the fire was leased by the Ingleton Electric Lighting & Power Company and used as a generating station and battery house.[10] The mill was acquired by Thomas Redhead in the 1930s and used during the war for storing skins from the tannery. Anthony Brown leased it for a workshop and then bought it from Thomas Redhead in 1961. After 1963 the mill was later let to a hay and straw merchant. The end of the mill story came when W.A. Brown & Partners demolished it and built Mill Wood development which was opened in 1987.

The mill had a fitful history of bankruptcies, long closures, auction sales and fires over its near two hundred year existence. Changes of use were a regular event and few businesses seemed to work for very long partly due to Ingleton being so far removed from the centres of Yorkshire industry.

MILL RACE ACCIDENTS

For centuries there were open mill races at Ingleton and from time to time children fell into them and were swept away and drowned. In June 1850 John Darwen's son fell into the mill race when crossing a wooden plank placed over the mill race at the cotton factory. As the water was swollen by heavy rain he was carried a distance, but fortunately other children ran to another plank across the race and pulled him out. Mr Sellars was quickly on the scene and brought the young boy round.

In October 1873 Mrs Hutchinson went out to shop and when she returned home one of her young sons was missing. He had followed her out of the house, but in crossing a narrow flagstone that spanned the mill race he had fallen in. Robert Hutchinson was three years old and his body was found at the end of the water trough that crossed the river by John Ford, the engineman at the mill. The boy had been stopped by a gate and was dead. In February 1875 another child of the same family, Philip, fell into a tan pit at the tan-yard and was drowned.

In July 1902 two girls were playing near the mill race and stood on a plank which crossed it. The daughter of John Hird, shoemaker in Ingleton, fell in and was washed away. The body was found the following day two miles downstream. There were calls for the village to cover the mill race, but nothing was done as the council considered that it was not their business. However, part of the mill race along the land up river of the Strands was run in a large ceramic pipe right to the trough which carried the water across the river.

DENT'S MILL

Dent's mill is shown on the map of the Ingleton bypass produced in 1823. It is also shown on the first six inch Ordnance Survey map of 1851. The early mill was on the site of Lytham

Terrace in what is now Laundry Lane. John Thomas Coates owned buildings on the site according to the Tithe Map and he also occupied the two adjoining fields of Malt Dubs and Little Dubs. In 1852 when James Coates of Ingleton mill died, his will mentioned that he owned a third share in Dent's Mill. The mill was turned into a brewery in 1866 and the press report said, 'It is a long time since the whirr of wheels, the clatter of spindles, and the loud shout of workmen and children ceased in this mill'. It would appear to have had been in existence from around 1820 to around 1860.[11] John Coates had married Elizabeth Dent at Ingleton in 1813 and the name Dent's mill most likely comes from this source.

RICHARD BROWN AND HIS MILL

Richard Brown was a prominent Ingletonian. His family had been landlords of the Wheat Sheaf, butchers, blacksmiths and carpenters and were quite well off. He lived on the Bank and was a Cotton Manufacturer. In 1851 he employed 68 men, 57 women, 39 girls and 37 boys. In 1871 he was still employing over a 100, but most probably in Settle and not Ingleton.

Richard Brown's mill at Ingleton was most likely Dent's Mill of which he was the occupier but not the owner. Richard Brown owned the field across the road from Dent's Mill which was called Between Gates. It could not have been part of Ingleton Mill as that mill was closed after the 1854 fire for ten years and Richard Brown's mill had a small fire on February 23rd 1856:-

About two o'clock in the morning on the 2nd inst., a fire was discovered in the blowing room adjoining the cotton mill occupied by R. Brown of Ingleton, which was consumed in a short time, but owing to the exertions of the persons present, combined with a plentiful supply of water, the other parts of the building and machinery were saved. How the fire originated is not known, as all was safe when the workpeople left the place the night before.

REFERENCES

1. LRO, DDB 84/1, 1763.
2. Deeds Ingleton Mill, Conveyance dated November 29th 1800. Anthony Brown.
3. *Yorkshire Inquisitions,* Vol 4, YAS Record Series, Ed. W. Brown, 1906, LXXVII. John son of Hugh, IPM, p.98.
4. LRO, WRW/L, Robert Wilkinson, 1711.
5. Deeds Ingleton Mill, Conveyance of Land in Manor of Twistleton, April 1st 1791. Anthony Brown.
6. *Yorkshire History Quarterly ,* Vol.2, Issue 2, Nov. 1996, The Watermills of Ingleton Pt.2, Phil Hudson, p.74. (The Watermills of Ingleton Pt I was published in *Yorkshire History Quarterly* Vol. 2, Issue 1. The present author provided illustrations and some information for these articles.)
7. LRO, WRW/L, R629 111, Ephraim Ellis, 1802.
8. Deeds Ingleton Mill, Conveyance Burrow to Coates, Indenture between George Burrow of Westhouse Cotton Spinner & James Coates of Kirkby Lonsdale Linen Manufacturer, Anthony Brown.
9. NYRO, ZUC/1/3/2, (MIC 1557) Ingleton Manor Ct Books & Papers 1820-1939, Aug.18th 1836.
10. Deeds Ingleton Mill, Conveyances July 12th 1905. Anthony Brown.
11. *Lancaster Guardian,* December 29th 1866.

COALFIELD AND COLLIERIES

In 2005 *Ingleton Coalfield* was published by the Northern Mine Research Society.[1] This chapter on Ingleton coalfield is a very condensed version of that history, and as Mike Gill and Bernard Bond assisted me in producing that volume some of their contributions will also appear in the following pages.

The Ingleton Coalfield lies to the south-west of the village in a wide area of scattered farms and enclosed fields, which cover some four square miles. The coalfield is thirty miles from the nearest Lancashire coalfield area of Burnley and about forty miles from the Yorkshire coalfield area around Wakefield. It is a little known and isolated coalfield which looked to Burnley in Lancashire for its engineering repairs, and over the years imported miners from coalfields throughout the north and midlands.

In spite of some five centuries of coal-mining at Ingleton there is little evidence to make the present day inhabitant or visitor aware of this. Walking the old Coal Pit Road, which crosses the coalfield almost at its centre from the New Road to Brook House, the sites of the old mines are readily surveyed. At Newfield House you can see the site of Newfield pits and look across the fields to the New Winning Colliery. Barker's Old Ingleton Colliery at Dolands and the Moorgarth colliery site in the distance also come into view. The old pits on the outcrop are visible to the west and the site of New Ingleton Colliery, near the main road, is clear to the north. It is all surprisingly close and compact in this pleasant, green, rolling countryside.

THE BEGINNINGS

Richard Lowther's inventory drawn up after his death in 1646 lists a coal mine and work tools worth £3 6s 8d.[2] This is the first mention that Richard Lowther had a coal mine at Ingleton. As his son, Gerard Lowther, was in debt after the Civil War and needed money he leased all coal mines and rights to mine to his aunt, Francis Walker. He also leased the manor to his uncle Anthony Bouch. The relationship can be seen on the Lowther pedigree illustrated in this chapter. The lease of the colliery, dated 1648, was for one hundred years and the amount £2,100. Francis Walker was already a widow and this was an investment for herself and her family.

As well as owning land around their manor house the Lowthers owned land at Parkfoot and Faccon Farm on Bentham Moor. There is little doubt that this land was selected and retained because of its known coal measures and the fact that the coal there was at a shallow depth and readily mined. The Lowthers mined coal at Ingleton from around 1610 to 1650, but unfortunately, mainly due to the Civil War, they had no great success and the Ingleton branch of the family never recovered financially. We know from legal documents of 1678 that little or no coal had been extracted in the manor of Ingleton itself.

IN CHANCERY COURT

Frances Walker enjoyed the income from the colliery at Ingleton from 1648. The coalfield was put in the hands of an agent and Frances and her four children, George, Eleanor, Frances and Jane, took little interest in the day to day running of the business. In 1660 Anthony Bouch of Cockermouth, to whom Ingleton Manor had been mortgaged, not having been paid his mortgage by the Lowther family, foreclosed and took possession of Ingleton Hall. He claimed that he had lost £500 in loans and mortgages in his dealing with the Lowthers. The Walkers continued their mining operations and four years later, in 1664, Frances Walker died and left a quarter share in Ingleton Colliery to each of her children.

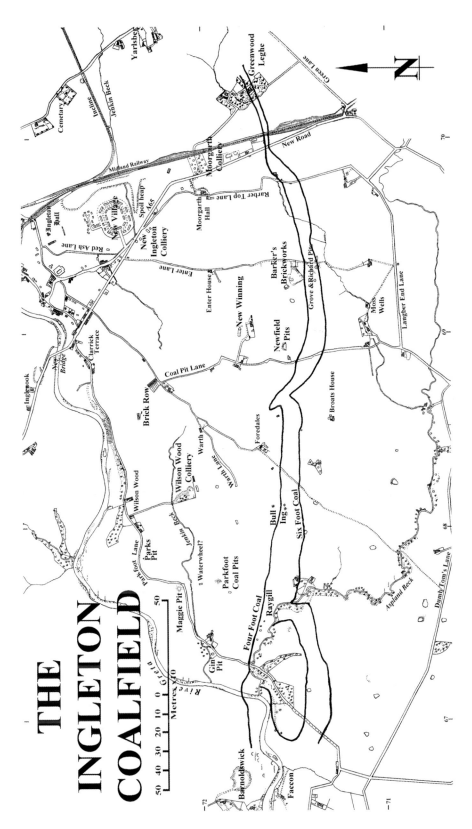

THE INGLETON COALFIELD

Metres 50 40 30 20 10 0 50

N

Greenwood Leghe

Green Lane

New Road

Moorgarth Colliery

Barber Top Lane

Midland Railway

Cemetary

Incline

Jenkin Beck

Yarlsber

Ingleton Hall

New Village

Spoil Heap

Moorgarth Hall

New Ingleton Colliery

Red Ash Lane

Enter Lane

Enter House

New Winning

Barker's Brickworks

Grove & Richard Pits

Moss Wells

Langber End Lane

Inglenook

Craven Bridge

Carrick Terrace

Brick Row

Coal Pit Lane

Newfield Pits

Broats House

Foredales

Wilson Wood

Wilson Wood Colliery

Warth

Wenth Lane

Jenkin Beck

Bull Ing

Six Foot Coal

Aspland Beck

Dumb Tom's Lane

Parks Pit

Park foot Lane

Waterwheel?

Parkfoot Coal Pits

Four Foot Coal

Raygill

Maggie Pit

River Greta

Gin Pit

Barnoldswick

Faccon

70

69

68

67

72

71

177

Anthony Bouch, Lord of the Manor, died at Ingleton Hall in February 1673 and his son Henry succeeded him. For five years the colliery agent, Leonard Wharton, who had an eleven year lease of the coalfield in return for paying £70 per year, mined at Ingleton without any problem. Then, in 1677, he sank two new shafts in the Bull Ing field and Henry Bouch began a dispute with him. Bouch claimed that all mining had previously been restricted to Raygill and the commons of Bentham Moor, and that though these mines were in the Manor of Ingleton and Bentham no-one had ever sunk pits on the demesne lands of the Lord of the Manor before.[3] Bull Ing, a seven acre meadow, was part of Henry's freehold demesne lands.

Henry Bouch sued Leonard Wharton for trespass in the local courts and gained forty shillings damages. Henry stopped access to miners and harassed them and those who were coming from the surrounding area to buy coal. The fact that the Bouches and Walkers had been sisters and brothers-in-law meant nothing to Henry Bouch. His father and aunts and uncles were all dead and his was a new generation. Although Leonard Wharton had only worked the colliery for five years out of his eleven year lease, he surrendered it in 1678, deciding that he had suffered enough harassment and was ready to leave Ingleton.

The colliery owners realised that as Lord of the Manor, Henry Bouch had influence in the local courts and at Quarter Sessions. They knew that the only way to get a just solution to their problem was to take their case to a higher court. Luckily for the Walkers, Eleanor Walker had married William Knipe, who was a solicitor. William Knipe approached the other shareholders in the colliery with a plan to take the case to the Chancery Court in London. Collins and Watkins refused to contribute to any costs saying that they were not going to throw good money after bad. Because of this, William Knipe pursued the case in Chancery alone, but on behalf of all the shareholders and Leonard Wharton, leaseholder of the mines.

The case against Henry Bouch claimed that:-[4]

> The plaintiffs having sunk two shafts in a place called the Bulling being parcell of the lands mortgaged but the Defendant to ruin and destroy their plaintiffs work and to drown the same on purpose that the Plaintiffs may take no advantage thereof hath sunk another shaft near thereunto betwixt them and their Mine field of coal and hath also preferred Indictments of forceable entrys against the Plaintiffs' servants and workmen for sinking and digging and for using necessary ways to the Plaintiffs Pitts and sometimes stops up the ways and does dayly bring actions at law against the Plaintiffs servants and also against the Country who used to fetch coals at the Pitts so that the works are like to be unemployed and the whole filed of coals lost altho' it hath cost the Plaintiff near five hundred pounds very lately to dreyn the field of coals with engines and waterworks and unless he is prevented will render the Plaintiffs Collieries altogether useless and unprofitable.

In November 1678 William Knipe won his case for the mine owners. The court restored their right to dig coal mines where they wished and to have access to those mines for their wagons and carts. The defendant, Henry Bouch, was denied the right to mine anywhere in the area covered by the Lowthers' lease. However, it added 'But within Lower Ragill the said Defendant may work at his pleasure the said lands being never in the Lowthers' possession but always a distinct colliery from the Lowthers'. At this point George Walker's son Anthony, agreed to contribute to the costs and continue his share in the colliery, but the Collins and Watkins families still refused to pay any of the court costs, saying that they did not consider it a worthwhile proposition as the lease had not so long to run.

The Knipes and Walkers handed the job of restoring the colliery to a local manager, Cuthbert Kidd, who lived in Burton-in-Lonsdale. The colliery was let to him without payment for two years. The pit at Bull Ing was restored and made productive and a roadway was completed across the field to the coal road which ran down by Fourdales Farm to meet Warth Lane. Local carts and pack-horses were soon back at the Ingleton pits to collect their coal. The aerial photograph of Bull Ing shows that the field was extensively mined in the following years and amongst the many shafts are the ones which caused the court case. The pits at Raygill and Faccon also continued production, as they were to do for a further century and a half. Once freed from harassment, the coalfield owners were again able to distribute Ingleton coal throughout the neighbourhood, to Burton and Hornby, to Clapham and Giggleswick, and further afield to Kirkby Lonsdale and Kendal. In the years that followed from 1678 to the end of the century Ingleton colliery flourished.

Aerial photo showing shafts in Bull Ing field.

THOMAS MOORE - DOCTOR OF PHYSICK

In May 1701 Doctor Thomas Moore, of Lancaster, married Marianne Walker in the Parish Church of St Wilfred at Melling. She was the widow of Edward Walker and daughter of Isaac Knipe of Holling Hall in Giggleswick. They soon went to live in Wakefield, where they had two daughters, Anne and Susannah. Thomas set up a successful medical practice in Kirkgate, and in 1722 he built a fine new house with a stable, coach house, garden and croft.

Thomas Moore knew of his wife's first husband's links with Ingleton colliery and of William Knipe's chancery case and the ensuing family wrangles, which were still going on. He had money, and coal had become a popular investment, so between 1702 and 1711 he

179

bought out the other shareholders. They were no doubt glad to see the back of Ingleton colliery and to get their hands on some money after thirty years of problems.

Cuthbert Kidd continued to run the collieries and in 1728 Thomas retained him with a lease for a further seven years at £160 per annum. In 1732 following the death of Cuthbert Kidd the lease went to George Foxcroft, for eleven years at £68 per annum. This new lease states that Thomas Moore's colliery was called Bull Ing or Balderstone Close. It adjoined Parker's coal mines on Raygill and the lease gives details of the care needed to be taken with coal carrying and water courses.[5]

The large drop in the value of Foxcroft's lease suggests that Thomas Moore found it difficult to get a new lessee. Perhaps this was because the colliery had become run down and unproductive as a result of Cuthbert Kidd's ill health. Foxcroft, who lived at Halsteads in Thornton-in-Lonsdale, administered collieries on each side of the river Greta, both in Ingleton and in Burton, and their main workings were closest at Faccon. This arrangement continued throughout the rest of Moore's ownership.

Thomas Moore died at Wakefield in 1733. His will, dated December 11th 1732, arranged that after the provision of an income of £40 per annum for his wife, all his property including the Ingleton colliery should go in equal shares to his two daughters, Anne and Susannah.

THE SERJEANTSON FAMILY

The Serjeantsons, from Hanlith near Malham, also had a house in Wakefield. It was Wakefield where William Serjeantson married Susannah Moore in 1736. William would have known that the colliery's ownership would come into his family's hands because Thomas Moore had left each of his daughters, Susannah and Anne, a half share in it. Susannah gave him her share in November 1737. William and Susannah had two sons and two daughters before William died, at the age of 43, on September 27th 1759. Their eldest son, William, was born at Wakefield in 1738 and, when he came of age, he ran the collieries jointly with his mother, who had inherited her sister Anne's half share in 1766.

There were three William Sergeantsons, William 1716 to 1759, William 1738 to 1782, and William R.L. 1766 to 1840. Throughout this period, coal from the various pits at Ingleton was dispersed throughout the area by packhorse and wagon. The centre of activity was on Ingleton and Bentham Moor at Faccon, by the river Greta. Writing in 1780, the Rev John Hutton referred to the Ingleton coalfield and said that a 'fire-engine' was working in the Black-Burton collieries.[6] He also commented that:-

> The number of small carts laden with coals, and each dragged by one sorry horse, that we met, was astonishing. Many of the smaller farmers betwixt Kirkby Lonsdale and Kendal, earn their bread with carrying coals, during most part of the year, from the pits at Ingleton, Black-Burton, or Burton in Lonsdale, to Kendal, and the neighbouring places, for fewel, and burning lime in order to manure their land. These beds of coal we were informed, are six or seven feet in thickness.

In 1743 the colliery was leased to George Foxcroft of Halsteads, and Robert Lawson for twenty-one years at £91 per annum. Lawson was a Lancaster merchant who had become joint Lord of the Manor of Burton with Foxcroft. The latter man died in 1749 and in 1757 a further lease for twenty-one years was agreed with Edward Foxcroft and Robert Lawson. This lease was for £340 per annum, suggesting that more coal was being mined and sold and the colliery was on a better footing.

In 1771, at the expiration of fourteen years of the lease, the Serjeantsons gave notice to Foxcroft and Lawson that they wished to take advantage of a proviso in the lease to end it.

MOORE & SERJEANTSON PEDIGREE

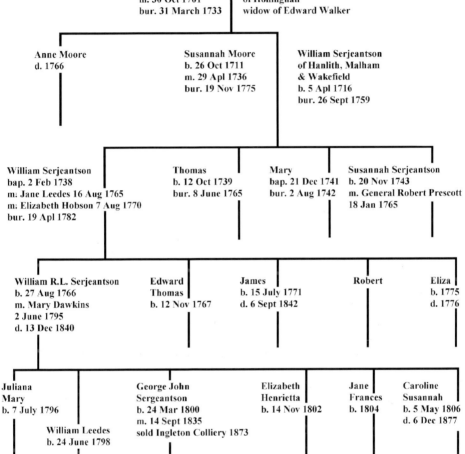

Thomas Moore 'Doctor of Physic' b. 1675 m. 30 Oct 1701 bur. 31 March 1733	**Marianne Walker** (née Knipe) dau. of Isaac Knipe of Hollinghall widow of Edward Walker	

Anne Moore d. 1766

Susannah Moore b. 26 Oct 1711 m. 29 Apl 1736 bur. 19 Nov 1775

William Serjeantson of Hanlith, Malham & Wakefield b. 5 Apl 1716 bur. 26 Sept 1759

William Serjeantson bap. 2 Feb 1738 m: Jane Leedes 16 Aug 1765 m: Elizabeth Hobson 7 Aug 1770 bur. 19 Apl 1782

Thomas b. 12 Oct 1739 bur. 8 June 1765

Mary bap. 21 Dec 1741 bur. 2 Aug 1742

Susannah Serjeantson b. 20 Nov 1743 m. General Robert Prescott 18 Jan 1765

William R.L. Serjeantson b. 27 Aug 1766 m. Mary Dawkins 2 June 1795 d. 13 Dec 1840

Edward Thomas b. 12 Nov 1767

James b. 15 July 1771 d. 6 Sept 1842

Robert

Eliza b. 1775 d. 1776

Juliana Mary b. 7 July 1796

William Leedes b. 24 June 1798

George John Sergeantson b. 24 Mar 1800 m. 14 Sept 1835 sold Ingleton Colliery 1873

Elizabeth Henrietta b. 14 Nov 1802

Jane Frances b. 1804

Caroline Susannah b. 5 May 1806 d. 6 Dec 1877

The family name was Serjeantson, but
George John spelt his name Sergeantson.

They had not been at all happy with they way things were being run at Ingleton. Lawson and Foxcroft left the mines and they were taken over by a new steward, Mr Atkinson, who became very well trusted by the Serjeantsons. After being given notice to quit the former lessees had employed more men and had worked day and night shifts to raise as much coal as possible. They were also accused of sinking an extra shaft in their own manor, of Burton, and tunnelling from it under the Greta to extract coal on the Ingleton side. In 1775, four years after closing the lease, Serjeantson took legal advice as to whether he should prosecute Foxcroft and Lawson for illegally mining his coal. He was told that, whilst he had a strong case even though four years that had elapsed, it might cause him some embarrassment if he pursued the matter. From then on, there was rarely any goodwill between the Ingleton and Burton Collieries even when, at one point, the Serjeantsons bought a half share of the Burton coalfield.

When Susannah Serjeantson died in 1775, she left her colliery to her only surviving son, the second William Serjeantson, but he survived his mother by only seven years. On William's death in April 1782, the ownership of the collieries passed to William's widow, Elizabeth, and their son, William Rookes Leedes Serjeantson, when he came of age. W.R.L. Serjeantson was born on August 27th 1766 and was only sixteen when his father died. He became a captain in the Dragoon Guards and after leaving the army, he bought Badger Hall, at Bedale, in August 1799 and, having renovated and extended it, renamed it Camphill. The Serjeantsons now owned property at Hanlith, Wakefield, and Camphill. They also had a house in Marylebone, where they spent the London season and where several of their children were born. The profits from Ingleton Colliery helped considerably to maintain this wealthy lifestyle. W.R.L. appears to have spent little, if any, time at Ingleton overseeing his collieries and relied on Mr Atkinson, who was both steward and lessee. When the latter retired, Mr R. Preston was appointed as agent at Ingleton. The Burton Colliery was in two parts and, in 1792, W.R.L. Serjeantson bought one of them from Edward Foxcroft for the sum of £1,600. In 1820 he also bought Faccon, which included the farmhouse and 20a 3r 2p of land, from James Farrer for £850. In 1828 he bought Faccon Close for £100 from Robert Lawson. Both Faccon and Faccon Close were in the Parish of Bentham. The agent for the Burton Colliery was Thomas Hodgson and he was to become a thorn in the Serjeantsons' flesh, especially that of George John Sergeantson, W.R.L's son and heir.

It is in this period that we have the first evidence of children working in the Ingleton mines. The family of John Hodgson, who died aged 93 in 1874, recounted in the *Lancaster Guardian* how he had worked at Ingleton Colliery from being four years old. His mother, a poor widow from Bentham with two children to support, was allowed only one shilling a week by Bentham Parish. She managed to get her son, John, taken on as an errand boy by Leonard Atkinson, the steward of the colliery. When he was six years old John Hodgson began the arduous work of a trailer, or puller, of coal and worked underground. He said that there were girls of the same age working underground at the same time. At the age of fifteen John Hodgson changed his occupation to colliery wright, a trade which he continued until his retirement at the age of eighty-two. We shall see later that boys, though not girls, continued to work in the mines at Ingleton into the twentieth century. The Muster Roll for Ingleton in 1803 lists all men between the ages of seventeen and fifty-five. In this list of 229 men thirty-four were miners.

GEORGE JOHN SERGEANTSON & JOSEPH HUNTER

George John Sergeantson was born in 1800. He graduated at Oxford in 1822, but he did not return to the family home at Hanlith, in Yorkshire, until May 1826, when he found his estate and business neglected. He took an interest in the family's coal pits at Ingleton, which his father had also neglected. W.R.L's agent at Ingleton, a Mr R. Preston, often left Leonard Hodgson, a carpenter, in charge of the colliery. In 1844 Sergeantson wrote an account of the coalfield for his own use and this has been invaluable. In these memoirs he outlined the history of the colliery's ownership, as he knew it, and then recorded what was going on when he took charge.[7]

George persuaded his father that Preston and Hodgson were both unworthy of the trust placed in them, and Preston was dismissed in December 1828. George took the advice of Mr Blenkinsop of Middleton Colliery, at Leeds, who recommended a young colliery manager by the name of Joseph Hunter. Joseph Hunter was only twenty-three years old, but he came to Ingleton with such enthusiasm that George Sergeantson was impressed and with his father's agreement appointed him agent. Mr. Preston was dismissed in December 1828 and Joseph Hunter appeared in Ingleton in January 1829. He soon showed his competence in management by firing Leonard Hodgson in April for his incompetent and expensive engineering. On first coming to Ingleton Joseph Hunter lodged at Yarlsber as his predecessor had done.

Joseph Hunter found everything in a bad state of management and it took time to get things organised. Time and money had been wasted in many areas especially in starting to drive an adit from below Burton-in-Lonsdale cotton mill to the gins at Parkfoot. This level had been driven as far as the bridge which crosses the river Greta to the pottery at Barnoldswick. This laborious and extensive work had been mismanaged and several times the roof had collapsed. When Mr Hunter became the colliery agent this work was abandoned and steam power employed to pump the water from the mines as well as to raise the coal. Joseph Hunter brought the first steam engine to Ingleton to drain the mines and got rid of the old water wheel at Parkfoot which was a massive and unsightly affair. The race came all the way from the low side of Ingleton Bridge where it connected to the river Greta. It passed on the low side of the Brow through the Springs and other fields, after which the water was conveyed through wooden troughs raised on lofty stone pillars to the gin-wheel. Such an unsightly construction was considered an eyesore to the green meadows of Wilson Wood and the whole district was said to appreciate its removal.[8] Much of the line of this water course can still be traced across the fields.

JOSEPH HUNTER AND THE NEW WINNING PITS

From the time that George Sergeantson took a personal interest in Ingleton Colliery and from the time that he appointed Joseph Hunter as colliery agent, Ingleton Coalfield took a turn for the better and developed considerably. Steam was brought to the coalfield, new areas were tested for coal and mining became more systematic rather the haphazard sinking of small shafts. The Faccon area was phased out and the new developments were in Ingleton. A new colliery was opened at the Winning.

The New Winning pit employed nearly a hundred men and boys, far more than had been previously employed on the Ingleton Coalfield. It was the mine long remembered as the beginning of a 'golden age' at the colliery. This was the place where it was frequently recounted in the press that:-

At this time it was no unusual thing to see in the early morning, and especially in winter, more than a hundred carts waiting to be supplied. It was common for persons at a distance to start with their horses and carts the night before to reach the pit on time to be sped with coals as soon as the men started work. If reports be correct sometimes a thousand loads or two-hundred tons of coal, was pulled a day. Carts came from Kendal and neighbourhood, Kirkby Lonsdale, Hornby, Wray, Bentham, Clapham, Austwick and Settle.

Carts used a raised embankment across Marl Pit field, through Enter Farm into Enter Lane, or Coal Pit Lane as it was also called. John Simpson JP, 1782-1858, who lived at Lane Farm, near Crooklands, Kendal, recorded in his journal that: 'I went also sometimes with two carts to near Ingleton Coal pits, going all night to be in time, as it was first come first served, and it was almost night the next day when I got home'.

By 1853, however, Sergeantson and Hunter had decided that the New Winning workings had become too extensive and it was necessary to begin sinking new shafts on the nearby Wilson Wood Estate. This new mine had begun raising coal by 1856 and the New Winning was closed in 1857 after working twenty-three years.

New Winning House built by Joseph Hunter. Later lived in by James Barker.

MOORGARTH COLLIERY

Though the coal at Moorgarth was quite shallow, the ground there was heavily faulted and very disturbed because of its proximity to the Hollintree and Craven Faults. Sergeantson's memoir shows that the area was already being mined by the late 1820s and confirms the difficult geology. It is likely that these pits closed in the 1830s and there is no sign of mining at Moorgarth on the first edition Ordnance Survey map, of 1850-51. Sergeantson and Hunter worked a number of pits at Moorgarth, which covers a wide area, but what was known as the Moorgarth Colliery was half a mile out of Ingleton on the left hand side of the New Road to Clapham. From 1849 the main reason for choosing this site was because of its close proximity to the railway line. There were many problems with this site, but it produced coal over many years.

In 1863 a shaft nine feet in diameter had been dug to a depth of seventy-seven yards when in August a feeder burst into the shaft and flooded it to a depth of sixty yards. It was thought that the water had come from old mine workings, as so often was the case. Pumps were put down in June 1864, but it took until February 1865 to drain the water and resume work. It is said that Joseph Hunter made little profit from Moorgarth Pit because it was troubled by numerous faults in the coal and occasional outbursts of water from old workings. The colliery manager's house at Moorgarth was built by Joseph Hunter.

WILSON WOOD COLLIERY

Wilson Wood was the main colliery at Ingleton in the nineteenth century and it was worked over several decades. The pit was begun by Joseph Hunter on the Wilson Wood Estate in 1853 and struck coal in 1855. Wilson Wood was a replacement pit for the New Winning which closed in 1857.The *Lancaster Guardian* reporting on the Winning, on December 17th 1853, said that, 'The colliery is at a standstill in consequence of the pumps being out of repair. The effect is very much felt by the area'. The Winning only came back into partial production in May 1854 and was never really in full production again.

Sinking was begun at Wilson Wood in the Autumn of 1853 and the six foot seam of coal was struck in 1855 at a reported depth of 120 yards. Engine house and chimney were completed and the mine came into operation. Cottages and a blacksmiths forge were also constructed on the same site. The Six Foot seam was also known as 'Deep Coal' or 'Bottom Coal'. Depending on location it was composed of between three and five separate seams, or leaves of coal separated by thin partings of shale, called dirt bands. The thickest of these leaves was near the middle of the seam and in 1897 was classed as 'steam coal'. The leaves above and below were classed as 'house coal'. Presumably it was possible to keep much of the dirt separate when the coal was cut by hand, but it had to be well screened, especially when the railway began importing better quality coal. It was often mixed with Four Foot coal to improve its quality.

Four Foot coal was mined at Wilson Wood from July 1858 as there had been some difficulty of getting at the seam. The Four Foot seam was of regular thickness, with no dirt bands, and was often called the 'Main Coal'. It was said to burn with a bright flame and make a very hot fire, though it burned rather quickly. It was the principal objective of the later collieries and commanded a higher price than the Six Foot coal. However, the coal which was of good quality was very welcome once it was in production as the Six Foot coal had a poor reputation. Differing depths are reported for the Wilson Wood mine shaft, but was certainly the deepest mine which had been sunk in the Ingleton Coalfield up to that time.

All went quite well at Wilson Wood apart from the usual run of accidents. Then in December 1865 a lodgement of water burst into the drift from the Four Foot seam and entered the shaft about fifty yards from the bottom. The flow of water was such that men and ponies were brought to the surface. The pumps gained upon the water and the miners were able to return to work in about twenty-four hours. However, this was only a foretaste of much worse to come.

FLOOD AND HARDSHIP

On January 6th 1866 the Ingleton Colliers' Club held their annual meeting at the Bay Horse Inn. After an excellent supper, George Willis, the viewer of the colliery, gave the usual toasts which included, 'Success to the Ingleton Collieries'. However, before the end of the year, disaster struck Ingleton twice. One Sunday night in late October 1866 a feeder at Wilson Wood burst into the mine shaft and began to flood the mine. On Monday one of the pit ponies swam to the bottom of the shaft and then went back to the stable which was on a higher level. On Tuesday some of the miners descended a narrow shaft and gave the horses hay. However, the water continued to flow so copiously that in spite of the two engines pumping day and night, by Thursday the water had risen ten yards in the shaft, the two pit ponies had been drowned and the pit given up for lost.

On October 27th a reporter from the *Lancaster Guardian* visited the site and gave the following melancholy report:-

A VISIT TO THE COLLIERY

What a change has come over the place in one short week – the puffing of the steam, the hissing of the boilers, the rattling of chains, the clang of shovels, the banging of the furnace doors, the rushing noise of sliding coals into empty carts, the clanking of the pumping and pulling engines, the running banter and chatter of then men with blackened faces and garments, the clamour of sonorous voices, the leaping flames of the perpetual fires, and the dense columns of curling smoke have disappeared and left silence to reign around. As to the cause of the disaster there are a variety of opinions. Some think it was a lodge of water from an old working, some the water from the river, some a feeder, some say that there was an increase in water, and that the engine was to blame for it only pulled five inches of water at a stroke instead of nine inches. The stoppage of the colliery will be a bad affair for some old hands, some of whom have been connected with it for fifty years, as the time is gone for them seeking employment in other districts. Some of the old hands and some of the younger men were occupied drawing out the pumps, which with other jobs may fit them a week or two. The stoppage of the colliery will tend to make Ingleton a duller place, and to diminish the trade of shopkeepers. It will also increase the cost of making pots and lime, as railway coal is much more expensive than Ingleton coal. It is hoped that ere long the coal beds at Ingleton will be worked with profit to the proprietor and the country.

By November some colliers had already left Ingleton and found work in Burnley on the Lancashire coalfield. Other miners left their families in Ingleton and went to work in the Yorkshire coalfield at Barnsley – where they signed up at Oaks Colliery. Some who stayed at Ingleton were reduced to poverty. But if Ingleton folk thought that their bad luck had ended that November they were sadly mistaken as tragedy was about to strike again.

On Wednesday December 12th 1866 one of the greatest mining disasters in the history of this country occurred at Barnsley. It was the Oaks Colliery where the Ingleton miners had signed on that blew up killing three hundred and sixty men and boys. On Friday December 14th members of the Oaks Branch of the South Yorkshire Miners Federation came to Ingleton to visit the homes of all members of the branch in the district to discover who was dead and the number of widows and orphans. In the list of dead were the following from Ingleton; James Barker, aged fifty-one years, who left a widow and six children; his son Thomas Barker, aged twenty-six, who left a widow and one child; his two sons Andrew Barker, aged nineteen, and William Barker aged sixteen years, both unmarried. Also killed was Robert Remington, but his father Richard who was also thought to have been killed had been absent from the pit through illness on the day of the accident. Andrew Barker, aged forty-six and his son Richard, aged fifteen were also killed; the father left a widow and seven other children. The devastation to the Barker family is plain to see.

The two shafts at Newfield Colliery are included at this point as they were planned by Joseph Hunter and George Sergeantson in the emergency following the flooding of Wilson Wood. They were sunk in 1872 and one had just begun production when the colliery ownership passed to William Bracewell. They were sunk by William Metcalfe, Robert Lindsay, Thomas Lindsay, Robert, Jos and John Tomlinson. The road to the pits into the old Coal Pit Road was made by William Metcalfe senior. The first shaft was sunk to the four foot or 'main' coal and the first coal was brought up in the spring of 1872. The Four Foot coal was at a depth of 82 feet. A second shaft was sunk a short distance south of the first shaft to mine the Six Foot seam which was struck at 156 feet deep. The Six Foot coal was reached in November 1872 and first mined in December of the same year. A double cylinder pulling engine was used to raise the coal.

The remains of the two spoil heaps can be seen near Newfield House. The Four Foot seam was put in operation first as that coal always had a good reputation in the locality as it burned with a bright flame and made a hot fire. People said it burned quickly, but it was always in demand. The coal from these two seams was often mixed for sale.

END OF THE SERGEANTSON AND HUNTER PERIOD
The Sergeantsons had owned Ingleton Collieries for four generations and now this was coming to an end. After the flooding of Wilson Wood and the troubles in mining at Moorgarth neither

of these two men had the inclination to undertake a complete reorganisation of the colliery on an extensive scale. George Sergeantson had been looked on by many as a generous employer as he frequently paid a small pension to his old miners and allowed many to stay on doing surface work into their eighties. He also made a substantial subscription, of around half the cost, to the new Ingleton National School which was built in 1848.

Both Sergeantson and Hunter were responsible for building much cottage property in Ingleton. On March 5th 1864 the *Lancaster Gazette* reported. 'Mr Joseph Hunter has built a row of ten neat airy, and comfortable dwellings for the men employed at the colliery which must add much to the domestic convenience of those whom he gave employment'. The row of cottages was Clarrick Terrace. In 1872, George Sergeantson at the age of seventy-two was ready to retire to his agricultural pursuits. Joseph Hunter, the agent at Ingleton, was sixty-seven years of age, but his sight was failing and retirement in the peace and quiet of his own home was very welcome. Sadly Joseph only lived a further two years and died in September 1874 at the age of sixty-eight. His grave is at the rear of Ingleton Parish Church and there are stained glass windows to the Hunter family inside the church. George Sergeantson lived on to a ripe old age and died on December 21st 1889 at the age of eighty-nine and was buried at Burneston.

At this time it was acceptable for the gentry to take an interest in agriculture, to collect paintings and to serve in the militia, but to be concerned with coal mines and industry was considered rather unpleasant. The revenues were welcome, but the source of the revenue was not advertised. When the Serjeantson family history was written there was no mention of Ingleton Colliery in its pages although the family had owned the colliery for four generations and it had provided them with a considerable income.

WILLIAM BRACEWELL – OWD BILLYCOCK

William Bracewell was described as a man of drive, undaunted courage and untiring energy. He was the largest single-handed manufacturer on the Manchester Cotton Exchange and owned mills in Barnoldswick near Colne, as well as others in Lancashire. He also owned a foundry and engineering factories in Burnley, a corn mill in Barnoldswick, considerable land and hundreds of houses. Local people in Lancashire called him 'Owd Billycock' because of the hard hat, similar to a bowler, which he invariably wore.

As an entrepreneur with a growing industrial empire he was in need of coal. William Bracewell already had business ventures in Ingleton with the Ingleton Mill and had contacts in the village. Learning that the colliery owners at Ingleton were having problems it seemed to him they might be bought out at a reasonable price. The opening of the Barnoldswick Railway Company's branch line to Barnoldswick from the Skipton to Colne line at Earby in 1871, made the venture possible. Bracewell became full owner of Ingleton Colliery in 1872 buying it outright for £15,000.[9] William Bracewell began work on the coalfield at once and that he lived up to his reputation as a man of drive and energy can be seen by the press reports from Ingleton. However, he did not put his time and money into Ingleton Colliery without first assessing the situation and the main source of his

William Bracewell.

information was not George Sergeantson or Joseph Hunter, but Edmund Danson. Edmund Danson had worked at Ingleton Colliery for around eighteen years and was colliery clerk. Danson had married the daughter of George Willis, the colliery manager in 1865. In 1872 George Willis was aged sixty-eight and still manager. With the re-opening of the colliery William Bracewell retired George Willis and gave the job of manager to Edmund Danson. The *Lancaster Guardian* reported the changes on the coalfield on 17 August 1872:-

INGLETON COLLIERY

A short time ago the works at the colliery were all tending to decay, and there was no immediate prospect that anyone of an enterprising spirit would come forth to check time's dilapidations and put things in working order... When visiting the works on Wednesday the 14th inst., all was life and activity, where recently all was silent desolate and dreary. Windows broken, walls cracking, shops, and engine sheds, and other buildings sinking quietly into decay. Today bricklayers, excavators, blacksmiths, painters and carters, were all busy carrying on the preparative works, which will require no small amount of time and money. Much rubbish has been carted away, and the beds for the boilers have been excavated. Bricklayers were busy making the walls for the boilers, so that shortly all will be ready for pumping the long accumulated waters from the old works.

The old pumping engine has been taken down, and though at first it was considered that with a little improvement it would be fit for future use, still now it has met the doom of old iron, and its successor will be a new engine of better and more economic construction. The iron horse, which was never in good repute with the colliers, has long merited its fate, for its consumption of coal was so great that the yield of coal scarcely met expenses. Should no unforeseen impediment occur blacksmiths will shortly be at work, and a new and powerful engine will be employed day and night to draw the water off the works.

When Bracewell took over the colliery about twenty miners were employed. They were the miners listed in the Ingleton Census Return of 1871 as follows: Thomas Barker, John Tomlinson senior, John Tomlinson junior, Joseph Tomlinson, Thomas Tomlinson, Robert Lindsay, Thomas Lindsay, John Scott, William Scott, William Singleton, Anthony Singleton, Richard Mason senior, Richard Mason junior, Henry Mason, George Howson, William Howson, John Slinger Howson, William Metcalfe senior, William Metcalfe junior, John Metcalfe, Joseph Metcalfe, Christopher Hodgson, John Wadeson, Edmund Danson colliery clerk and George Willis colliery manager. It is interesting to note that from the late eighteenth century there had been several notable colliery families at Ingleton and of special note were the Lindsays, Tomlinsons, Metcalfes and Barkers. The Barkers at this time were represented by only one miner as so many of them had died at Oaks Colliery in 1866. Members of these few families developed a knowledge of the Ingleton Coalfield that marked them as elite among the miners, even if they held no official rank or position. They were holders of generations of inherited experience. They were consulted on new sinkings, new roadways and were indispensable to the colliery owner and manager.

From the time that Bracewell came to Ingleton coal was being produced at Newfield pits and once Moorgarth and Wilson Wood were back in production more miners were needed. Had this been a colliery in the Yorkshire or Lancashire coalfield then colliers could have been brought from a short distance, but Ingleton was an isolated coalfield. In view of this it was necessary to recruit locally and it was said that there was never such a motley group of miners as those at Ingleton in 1873. Formerly the colliers were men who had been trained up to mining from their earliest youth, and grandfathers, fathers and sons worked together in the same pit. With colliers in the area being few, men of a wide variety of occupations were drawn into the industry especially with the prospect of regular employment and good wages. Shoemakers, carters, masons, gardeners, footmen, stone-getters, and mill workers were among those who deserted their old occupations and found employment in the Ingleton pits.

The Moorgarth Colliery on the Clapham road also had a remarkable renewal. Brick offices were erected, the old chimney repaired and extended and the whole site put in working order. It is surprising that this site was redeveloped as it was the one mining site at Ingleton which seems to have given the worst trouble. It was worked with great difficulty because of both many faults and water. Before Bracewell renewed the colliery, its deserted ruins had been pointed out as the place where engineering skill had met insurmountable difficulties. However, Moorgarth colliery eventually produced quality coal for many years. In the period than William Bracewell ran the Ingleton Coalfield no main new mine was sunk, but those already existing were re-opened and run with great efficiency.

William Bracewell worked the Ingleton coalfield with enthusiasm. He was soon employing around one-hundred-and-twenty men and thirty horses at the colliery. Twenty horses and carts were employed, from early morning to evening, to transport coal to the Midland Railway sidings. There it was loaded into the railway wagons which he had specially provided and shipped to Barnoldswick. This export of coal by rail amounted to about half the total production at the colliery.

Bracewell had a one way system for coal carts. Empty carts went from the Bridge Inn along the road past Clarrick Terrace to Wilson Wood. At Wilson Wood they turned up the back of the cottages and travelled on a raised embankment towards the colliery passing over a brick arched bridge as they came into the colliery premises. Having been loaded with coal they passed the colliery buildings up into Warth Lane and then down to the old coal road which came out at the Mason's Arms. This one way system was necessary due to the narrowness of the lanes and roads. This information came from the Tomlinson family who had worked in the coalfield for generations.

The success of the colliery showed itself in the growth in the number of Ingleton's cottages, the increase in rents and the benefits to the village's shopkeepers. In January 1875 a large gathering of miners and officials met at the Bridge Inn to make a presentation to Edmund Danson the colliery manager. Over a hundred guests sat down to an excellent dinner and after dinner speeches were made. John Wadeson, the under-viewer, was chairman and he praised Edmund Danson for the important part he had played in bringing about the prosperous state of the colliery. After mentioning his twenty years of service at the colliery, he added. 'The difficulties of a colliery manager are uncommon, for on the one hand he has to discharge his duties to the employer and to see that the workmen do not fail in their work, and on the other hand he must consider the interests and feelings of the men and see that they get a fair day's wage for a fair day's work. If in addition to this he can keep up a good feeling amongst the men, one towards another, and a good understanding between them and their master, he will prove himself a manager of rare ability and one who will deserve well of both parties. Mr. Danson has tried to come up to this description of an efficient manager and there is no one in the company who will not be ready to say that he has succeeded. Mr. Danson, by impartially doing his duty, has won out good opinions, and we all know how highly he was esteemed by our late employer, Mr Hunter, and we are proud to think that he stands equally as high in the esteem of our present employer, Mr Bracewell'.

John Wadeson also praised Edmund Danson for his work as both secretary and treasurer of the Ingleton Colliery Sick Club. The presentation of a mantel clock was made by William

Marble clock presented to Edmund Danson.

Metcalfe, underground viewer, who told how he had known Edmund Danson since he was a boy and had followed his promotions in the colliery with interest. The clock was inscribed, 'Presented to Mr. Danson, colliery manager, by the officials and workmen of the Ingleton collieries, as a token of respect. Jan. 9th 1875'. There is no doubt that because of his education Edmund Danson had been one of a very few people capable of doing the secretarial work for the Sick Club and that he had done the work well. This clock, retaining its inscription, is still in use at Broats House Farm in the centre of the old coalfield.

One of the first things that Bracewell did at Ingleton was to produce bricks on the site at Wilson Wood and use them for his own work as well as sell them locally. He built Brick Row, sometime called Bracewell Row, but now known as Beech Terrace. Here twelve houses were built for miners and their families. The manager lived in the house at the end of the row which was four feet longer than the rest and had a cellar. William Bracewell also owned Clarrick Farm, which provided hay and grazing for the many colliery horses; three farms at Wilson Wood, Parkfoot Farm and other farms in Ingleton and branched into dairy farming. Warth Farm was also used for producing hay for the horses.

The Ingleton Collieries ran relatively smoothly for many years. Occasionally there was some excitement on the coalfield

Edmund Danson colliery manager.

when there was a minor flooding, an accident, or a breakage of the pumping engines. There was some excitement on Saturday November 7th 1874 when pit ponies and a mule went down Wilson Wood pit. Being Saturday a crowd of men, women and boys gathered to see the ponies and a mule be netted and let down the shaft where they had to labour for many years before they again saw the light of day. The crowd were assured that there were comfortable stables in the mine and that the ponies would have ample food and bedding. On Saturday October 12th 1878 the miners were on their way to work when they were informed that their old coal shaft at New Winning was on fire, and they were ordered to return to their homes for buckets. As, in 1877, the shaft at New Winning had been made into a ventilation shaft for the

Wilson Wood pit a fire was kept constantly burning at the bottom to encourage the flow of air and this fire had ignited old timber in the shaft.

When the *Lancaster Guardian* dated 21 March 1885 was delivered at Ingleton there was one article that the local people read with sadness. Most had heard by word of mouth, but now they could read the facts.

DEATH OF THE OWNER OF INGLETON COLLIERIES

The death is announced of Mr. William Bracewell, of Barnoldswick, near Colne, manufacturer and proprietor of the Ingleton Collieries, which took place on Friday last, in the 72nd year of his age. Owing to failing health Mr. Bracewell had for a considerable time been unable to make a personal inspection of these collieries.... During Mr. Bracewell's proprietorship the work was carried on with unabating energy, and very much to the material prosperity of Ingleton. The briskness of the coal trade has been kept up chiefly by the consumption of Ingleton Coal at Mr. Bracewell's mills in Barnoldswick... It is with real sorrow that we have to report his death, knowing that the way he carried on his collieries at Ingleton has been so largely beneficial to both workmen, tradesmen and others. The interment of the late Mr. Bracewell took place at Bracewell Church on the 18th inst.

The people of Ingleton were worried as to who would take William Bracewell's place and they were right to be so. Mr Bracewell's trustees were far less efficient than he was and his empire began to collapse. It was in the spring of 1887 when the seriousness of the situation was realised at Ingleton, and in July 1887 the *Lancaster Guardian* announced 'Evil times have fallen on these ancient coal mines, and their altered condition will prove disastrous not only to the Inhabitants of Ingleton but to the whole country around'. The colliery slowly ground down and the output of coal was so low that the carters had only one day's work in a week. An effort to sell the colliery as a going concern at Lancaster in July met with failure – there was not a single bid. Many of the miners had already been given their notice and had left to seek work in either the Lancashire coalfield or collieries in Yorkshire.

PROPOSED FORMATION OF A NEW COMPANY

By the end of July 1887 the seriousness of the situation brought a public meeting to the Ingleboro' Hotel on Wednesday the 27th. The purpose of the meeting was to prevent the Ingleton Collieries being closed. Joseph Carr was chairman and he told the meeting bluntly. 'Were the collieries to collapse it would be disastrous to Ingleton. Workmen would have to leave the neighbourhood, a large number of cottages would be unoccupied, the cottages and other property would be depreciated. It would be a serious loss to shopkeepers and other tradesmen. Indeed the closing of the collieries would be the most disastrous event that had ever taken place at Ingleton'.

The scheme to form a new public company had the support of the leading men of the village and most offered their services. The idea was to form a limited liability or co-operative company in which all including the workers themselves could buy shares. Edmund Danson the manager produced figures for the meeting to show that the idea was feasible. The meeting heard that the Chancery Court had ordered that the colliery plant had to be broken up and sold, piece-meal. The meeting was advised to buy the plant, coal and what was absolutely necessary for working it. The motion to carry on Ingleton Collieries was carried without any opposition.

On Friday August 5th those interested in the proposal to purchase the Ingleton Colliery was held at the Ingleboro' Assembly Rooms. Joseph Carr was chairman and told the meeting that they met that night under more hopeful circumstances. Their deputation had met with a favourable reception at Barnoldswick although they had done nothing that was binding. The railway wagons, Clarrick Farm, Brick Row cottages and other items not needed were not to be included in the purchase. The horses, carts, horse-gears, plant, a four acre field, two cottages, sheds, workshops connected with the colliery and the coal would be included in the purchase.

Adjournment was made to a private room in the Ingleboro' Hotel for those wishing to take shares. The shares were brought down to £1 so that working men in Ingleton could become involved. The chairman broke the ice by taking the first fifty shares. Mr Cragg took fifty, Mr Ford took a hundred and Mr T. Coates of Barbon took a hundred as well. Within half an hour over a thousand shares had been taken up and there appeared no doubt that the purchasing money would be raised as well as a good floating capital.

On Saturday morning August 6th the promoters of the scheme met Mr C.G. Bracewell, the Receiver of the Court, Mr Smith his co-trustee, and their solicitors Mr Weeks and Mr Beaumont. After lengthy discussion the trustees provisionally agreed to sell the colliery plant for £1,500, and when the possession was taken of the purchase the output of coal on bank should be taken at a valuation made by Edmund Danson, the colliery manager. Messrs Carr, Cragg, Coates, Slinger, and Worthington made themselves responsible for the purchase money. The matter then came before the Registrar of the Court of Chancery at Manchester on Tuesday August 9th and he refused to sanction the bargain. Mr W. Bracewell had protested that £1,500 was a ridiculous sum and that the royalty alone was worth far more.

The Chancery Court having set aside the bargain which had been provisionally made with the trustees of the Bracewell Estate for the sale of the colliery and plant, the private piece-meal sale of the colliery plant went ahead on Thursday August 11th at Ingleton. It was a 'break up sale' with a very large attendance. The sale commenced at one pm. and closed about eight; engines, pumps, horses, carts and railway wagons were bought by dealers from a wide area and Ingleton colliery plant was stripped and dispersed to destinations throughout the country. The colliery plant brought £1,089 13s 6d which was considerably less that the £1,500 which had been offered by the Ingleton rescue committee, and the total was only £1,876 6s 6d.[10]

The twelve brick houses of Bracewell's Row brought only £160 as many were standing empty and there were no forthcoming tenants. Pemberton cottages brought only one bid of £160 for the same reasons. Had the colliery continued the cottages would have been worth a great deal more. The pumps were stopped and Wilson Wood was flooded and sank into decay for all time. In his memoirs Joseph Carr, who did so much to save the colliery, stated that, 'this was a noble industry absolutely thrown away'.

JAMES BARKER

Following the failure of the attempt to form a new colliery company at Ingleton and the second flooding of the Wilson Wood pit, the man who stepped in to save the coalfield from extinction was James Barker. James Barker was born in Ingleton and most of his working life was connected with the Ingleton Collieries. We have seen that many of his relations had been killed in the 1866 Oaks Colliery disaster. In spite of the many Barker family deaths at Oaks Colliery and his own father's death in Ingleton Colliery, James Barker became a miner at Ingleton and worked in the coal trade with enthusiasm throughout his working life.

Beginning as a miner, James Barker soon became a deputy. Injured several times he led a charmed life and always seemed to make a swift recovery. In March 1887 when he was underviewer, he was working underground when 'an immense stone slipped out of the roof of the passage and fell upon him in a way as to break one of his thighs. It required four men to lift the stone off him and it was with great difficulty that he was raised to the bank'. He was attended by Dr Bradley and was making a good recovery by the end of March.

After the stopping of the pumps at Wilson Wood and the sale of the colliery plant, James Barker approached the trustees and gained rights to mine on a small scale. At this time, following the flooding of the mines no one seemed to be showing any interest in the coalfield and the trustees were pleased to have some income. Barker was able to take advantage of the situation to get started without a great deal of capital. Before 1887 he had worked under colliery manager Edmund Danson, but from 1889 to 1890 they worked as partners under a lease from Bracewell's Receiver. Their partnership was short-lived, however, and on September 3rd 1890 they were in court to dissolve it.[11] Barker took a lease on his own in 1890 and, on February 28th 1893, he bought the royalty from Bracewell's two surviving Trustees, Smith Smith and Joseph Henry Threlfall, for just over three hundred pounds.

James Barker invested his knowledge of the coalfield and its miners more than he invested cash. Although in 1895 he did take a partner, Joseph Haigh, who was able to provide good financial support. James Barker knew all the Ingleton miners, the sinkers and road-makers and they were glad to come and work for him and continue some employment in the coalfield. He certainly would not have been able to finance a mining company or run a deep mine such as Wilson Wood, but he was able to sink hand pits and continue a supply of Ingleton coal.

In 1900 James Barker drew up a list of all the present and previous pits in the Ingleton Coalfield and tried to locate and date them. It was a difficult task, but with the aid of the Tomlinsons, Lindsays, other miners and mining records he produced a few sheets of notes for his own personal use. He wrote, 'The present pit now working commenced to sink on May 16th 1889. The pit was sunk by James Barker, Robert Tomlinson, Joseph Hodgson and John Tomlinson (Driver) & Richard Dobson. This was Barker's main pit at Dolands, Grove Pit, and it continued well into the next century. A shaft was sunk to the east to air this pit by Joseph Hodgson, Richard Dobson and John Tomlinson in 1889.[12] Dolands was the name of a field at Moorgarth sometimes called Dorlands.

Even with the working of Dolands coal output was relatively small compared to Bracewell's day and there were only about a dozen miners working and sometimes not even that number. The 1891 census return for Ingleton shows only eight miners, not counting colliery engineer and clerk. In 1881 the cottages at Pemberton, Bracewell's Row and Clarrick Terrace were full of miners, but by 1891 half of the dozen houses in Bracewell's Brick Row were uninhabited, their collier occupants had long gone.

Jimmy Barker also built brick kilns in Dolands and produced his well known bricks inscribed, 'Barker Ingleton'. He named several pits after members of his family including Nellie Pit and Richard or Dick Pit. In 1899 James Barker built a tramway across the Keighley to Kendal road to take his coal from Dolands to the Midland Railway. The layout of the tramway from Dolands was across the fields to the Kendal road and then through the old Moorgarth Colliery site to the railway. The Greenwoods of Greenwood Leghe complained that they constantly used the Keighley to Kendal road both on foot and with horses, carts and carriages and that the proposed tramway was a danger to

A 'Barker Ingleton' brick.

them. Shortly before James Barker began to build the tramway the Greenwoods served him a writ to stop construction. However, Barker went ahead and constructed the tramway across both Rarber Top Lane and the Keighley Kendal Road.

William Norman Greenwood, Percy Greenwood and Oscar Greenwood then took Barker and his partner Joseph Haigh to court to compel them to remove the tramway, to restrain

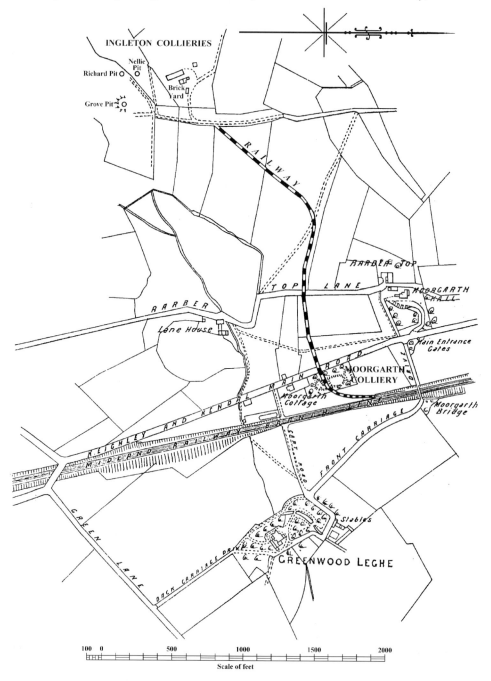

BARKER'S TRAMWAY

them for laying any tramway across the local roads and to claim costs. In defence Barker quoted the history of Ingleton coalfield and recited his right to mine coal and to enjoy full access to and from the pits, tracing it back to the original lease of 1648. However, the Greenwoods did not question his mining rights, but simply claimed that the tramway crossing was a danger. The landlord of the Three Horse Shoes gave evidence that the tramway had frightened his horses and so too did Dr Griffiths, George Padgett and others. The action took place in the Chancery Division of the High Court in London in June 1900. In spite of witnesses from the County Council having passed the crossing and declared it quite safe, James Barker lost the case. The Greenwoods as local 'squires' certainly had influence and money to pay for the best lawyers and to secure influential witnesses.[13] According to local tradition James Barker 'lost a fortune' in costs and the village was split between the two camps creating a lot of hard feeling. One witness, Dr Griffiths, who went to London to give evidence on behalf of the Greenwoods collapsed in court and never fully recovered. It was a sad case and James Barker's grandson, Gordon Barker, recalls that later one of the Greenwoods said that they should never have gone to court over the matter and wasted so much money. It is also said that one of the Greenwood family turned up at Barkers coal yard for a cart of coal shortly after the court case and is reported to have said, 'No hard feelings'! What James Barker said is not recorded.

The Greenwoods' court case was the death knell to James Barker's business. The effect of losing the case is reflected in the numbers employed. In 1896 there had been nineteen men underground and seventeen on the surface. In 1901 this had fallen to twelve below and eleven above, and in 1903 there were only six men underground and three on the surface.[14]

In 1903 James Barker sold his mining rights to a syndicate, but continued as manager for a couple of years. A new company called Inglenook was formed. Apart from undertaking some prospecting, Inglenook's principal purpose was to acquire the mining rights and pave the way for another, larger company, which would sink a new colliery and work the coal.

On Saturday November 6th 1915, James Barker set off from his home at the Winning to go to Leeds. Probably because he was a little late, he climbed over the wall and up the embankment instead of going to the station by the proper footpath. As he passed the goods warehouse, he was seen to stumble onto his knees and then fall on his face. Being a stout man he fell heavily and his face was badly cut. He was carried into one of the waiting rooms, where he died a few minutes later from the heart attack he had suffered. The funeral was conducted by the Reverend J. Llewelyn at Ingleton cemetery. It was a well attended service and his ten sons, three of whom were serving in the forces, and one daughter attended.

NEW INGLETON COLLIERIES

The New Ingleton Colliery Company was registered in October 1909 with a capital of £37,500 in £1 shares, 'to acquire certain collieries and seams of coal, cannel and fireclay, and certain seams and beds of clay in Yorkshire, to adopt an agreement with Inglenook Limited, and to carry out the business of a colliery proprietor, manufacturers and dealers in, pottery, earthenware, bricks, tiles, pipes, china, terra cotta, and ceramic wares of all kinds'. There were 11,400 A shares and 26,100 B shares.[15] To celebrate the formation of this New Ingleton Colliery Company a dinner was given by the directors at the Bridge Hotel in December.

As early as 1887 George Barker, mining engineer, had strongly suggested that two new shafts be sunk nearer to the village by the New Road. His advice was eventually taken and these were sunk in 1913. This George Barker was James Barker's son. Another of James Barker's sons continued the Barker influence in the coalfield as manager of the New Ingleton Colliery Company.

The New Ingleton Collieries Ltd undertook the last phase of mining in the Ingleton Coalfield. It continued working Barker's shafts on Dolands and after work began on the new colliery, alongside the A65, the shafts at Dolands became known as the Old Pit. Work on sinking the No.2, or downcast, pit of the New Ingleton Colliery began in the late summer of 1912 and by early November the 14-foot-diameter shaft was reported to be 33 yards deep. Sinking continued and in June 1913 the sinkers found what became known as the Ten Foot Seam, which was 10 feet 6 inches thick, at a depth of about 124 yards. Less than two weeks later, another seam of coal, the Nine Foot Seam, was found at a depth of about 131 yards.

Neither the Ten nor the Nine Foot Seam had been seen elsewhere in the coalfield. Nor had they been detected by borings. Not surprisingly, therefore, their discovery caused great

Early activity at New Ingleton Colliery.

optimism. Nevertheless, sinking continued with the intention of proving the Four Foot and Yard Seams, but because a fault crossed the shaft, they were absent at the expected horizon. In early March 1914, therefore, the sinkers reached the Six Foot Seam, here seven feet thick, at a depth of 257 yards. A few weeks after finding the Ten Foot Seam, the first sod of the No.1, or upcast, shaft was cut in July 1913. Unfortunately, however, the desperate need for coal on the outbreak of World War I meant that sinking at this shaft was stopped at a depth of 156 yards and work concentrated on winning coal quickly from the Ten Foot Seam.

The opening of the colliery was attracting families to Ingleton and causing a housing shortage. So with the New Ingleton Colliery came the New Village. It was also known as the Model Village and it is still referred to as 'the model' by many locals. In December 1913 the New Ingleton Colliery bought 34,623 yards of land off the New Road at Ingleton from Emily B. Greenwood for £757 11s 6d. The Colliery then sold the land at the same price to the Ingleton Estates Company Limited in October 1914 with the intention that they should erect one hundred-and-two dwelling houses on the land. This deed, and others, were recorded in the Wakefield Registry of Deeds.[16]

The Ingleton Estates Company, with head office in Chesterfield, then took out a mortgage from George Alexander Calder of the Public Works Loan Office, under the Public Works

Loan Act of 1875. They applied for £12,750 under the Housing of the Working Classes Act of 1890, 'for or towards the defraying of the cost of erecting one-hundred-and-two houses for the working classes.' The first instalment of the loan was £2,966 and further instalments followed. The loan was to be repaid over forty years and on October 14th 1949 it was duly recorded that the principal money had been duly repaid. The Ingleton Estates Company erected one-hundred-and-two houses between 1914 and 1916. As the houses were completed they were leased to the New Ingleton Collieries by a series of twenty-three leases.[17]

The impact of the colliery on Ingleton's economy was further highlighted in January 1916, when it was reported that the minimum day's wage for a collier was 9s 9d, but many were earning as much as sixteen shillings per day.[18] Surface workers were paid in proportion and this meant that around £600 per week was going into the local economy. In *Ingleton Coalfield* all known Ingleton colliers were listed using parish registers, muster rolls and census returns and other sources. More men who worked New Ingleton colliery have been found since and include Samuel Preston, who was a filler, James Guilliam, Fred Lynn and Dick Lynn who started work as a pony boy at the colliery on his 14th birthday, April 23rd 1926. The Lynn family came from the Doncaster Coalfield.

The colliery now had an air compressor, which drove an underground haulage engine, and a steam-driven fan for ventilating the workings. Output was about 1500 tons per week, but they hoped to reach 2000 tons shortly. Screens had been built, at a cost of £11,000, on the colliery sidings next to the Midland Railway Company's Ingleton branch line.

The Ten Foot and the Nine Foot Seams 'only occurred over a very limited area'. It is also worth noting that if the shafts had been sunk a little over 100 yards to the west, then probably

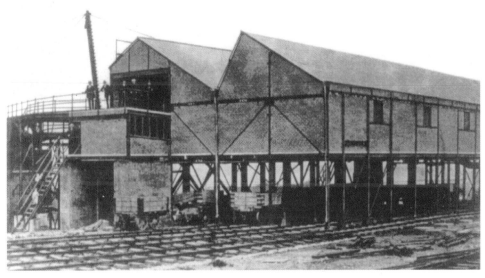

New Ingleton Colliery screening plant in 1916.

neither seam would have been found. The Ten Foot Seam was described as a first-class house and steam coal, so a circular pillar of coal, with a diameter equal to the depth at that point (130 yards), was left to support the shafts and the remaining twelve and a half acres of the seam were removed by September 1918.[19] A major customer was Vickers, Maxim & Co's coke works at Barrow in Furness. Coal was also being sent to Liverpool and Southampton, as well as to the Midland and the London & North Western Railway companies. By 1921, slack coal was also being exported to France, and Ingleton coal was sent to Fleetwood, Hull and Barrow for use on trawlers and other vessels. The Nine Foot Seam, which was classed as a moderate steam and house coal, was developed by driving a number of cross-measures drifts down from the Ten Foot workings. Nevertheless, only two small patches of coal were removed before that seam, too, was abandoned in 1918.

As well as delaying shaft sinking, government wartime regulations, especially restrictions on raising capital, hindered planned developments and probably shortened the colliery's life. It certainly had serious consequences for the mine in the immediate post-war years. Faced with the loss of output from the Ten and Nine Foot Seams, the company began developing the Six Foot Seam as rapidly as wartime conditions allowed. In January 1917, however, the sinking of No.1 Shaft had been resumed and it was then 180 yards deep. This shaft found the Four Foot and Yard Seams in their expected positions at 233 and 236 yards from the surface respectively.

The Six Foot coal was said to be good, average quality, suitable for locomotives and general steam-raising. It was developed by driving a main haulage road westwards along the strike of the seam, and a series of feeder gates at forty-five degrees to it, both up and down dip, served the tubbing stalls where the coal was cut. By 1919 output was about 2,200 tons a week, and the seam was worked until September 1921.

The Hollintree Fault, which became the mine's effective northern boundary, was soon discovered. It threw the coal down an unknown distance to the north and no workings went beyond it. To the south, what was described as a 'roll, of unknown width' was encountered. This was a local thickening of the roof or floor strata which caused thinning of the coal seam, and it might have been associated with the fault, seen in No.2 Shaft, which crosses that area.

Soon after sinking began, a single, standard-gauge, branch line was laid to the colliery from the Midland Railway Company's up line. This line began 275 yards south of Ingleton station and ran round the northern and eastern side of the New Village until it reached the A65 near Jenkin Beck. The line originally stopped at the wall by the A65, but by early 1914 it had been extended across the A65 into the colliery yard. Once in the pit yard, the line passed the weigh office and ran to a set of points which led to the locomotive shed.

The colliery was linked to the screens on the colliery sidings by a double, two-foot gauge track. At first, coal and spoil were taken on this line across the road and the tubs which ran on it were hauled by an endless wire rope. Later the road crossing was replaced by a brick-lined tunnel which ran under the road, and the railway became horse drawn. One branch of the line ran onto the spoil heap and the other ran to the screens, where coal was graded into different sizes by being shaken about on perforated plates. It was a dusty and noisy process as the coal passed from one plate to another, with the smaller lumps and slack dropping through on to other plates, where the process was repeated. The graded coal was carried on endless belts, after being hand-picked for stone, to the waiting railway wagons. The screens, which could handle 500 tons a day, produced steam coal, screened coal, cobbles, nuts, double screened nuts, rough and fine slack, and nutty slack.

For many years William Routledge drove New Ingleton Colliery's two locomotives. The first of these was named Victoria, after the Queen. It was built in 1901, by Peckett & Sons of Bristol, and he described it as a beautiful and powerful little engine of twenty tons. The dome was always kept well polished. When it retired in the early 1930s, Nowells of Lancaster cut it up for scrap at the top of the sidings. Victoria's replacement, called King George V, was hired from Thomas Ward, of Sheffield. The colliery company was offered the engine for £400, but it was short of money and so opted to hire it for £7 per week. After the mine closed in 1936, Mr Routledge was ordered to run the engine up to the top of the sidings, draw the fire and leave it there. Ward's fitters then removed the connecting rods, which linked the

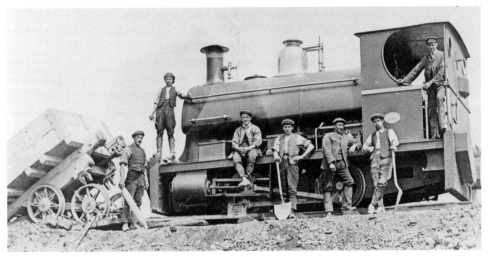

Queen Victoria engine tipping spoil. From the left: John Thomas Bradley tip end man, Joe Walker, greaser, Billum Wilcock, labourer, Thomas Whitham, labourer, Anthony Noble, Jack Gott, ganger, Billy Routledge, loco driver.

Engine King George with Ingleton Colliery wagons on the sidings at Ingleton goods yard.

locomotive's driving wheels to the slide gear and cylinders, and greased up other parts before hooking it onto a train and taking it back to Sheffield.[20]

The Ingleton Coalfield saw numerous accidents, many of them fatal. On November 1st 1918, two colliers were killed by a roof-fall. George Smith of Brighouse aged twenty-seven, Nicholas Andrews aged thirty-five of Castleford, and Henry Turner of Ingleton, were lowering an empty tub, on rails, to the coal face. This was down a slope, estimated at 1 in 4, and they had used a rope to lower the tub part of the way, and then let it down by hand the remainder. They had a locker (a wood or iron rod stuck through the spokes to stop the wheel turning) in the wheels, and Turner was at the front with the other two holding the tub back. On entering the stall, the tub caught and dislodged a prop, causing the roof to fall on Smith and Andrews, crushing them to death. It took two hours to free their bodies. The length of the props was given as 6 feet 6 inches, suggesting that they were in the Six Foot Seam.

The colliery's principal seam was the Four Foot Seam, but its development was delayed by the outbreak of war. In 1918, however, the impending exhaustion of the Ten and Nine Foot Seams forced development of the Four Foot and Three Foot Seams. Because they were very close together, it was decided to work the Four Foot Seam first.

Although it was a small, isolated coalfield, Ingleton was not immune from national events. The price of coal on the export market soared after the war and the government, which still controlled the mines under war-time legislation, enjoyed very high profits. In January 1919, therefore, the Miners' Federation of Great Britain demanded a substantial wage rise, a six hour day and nationalisation of the mines. The government responded by setting up a Royal Commission, to be chaired by Lord Sankey. This recommended a seven hour day and increased wages, which the government accepted, and, after further debate, nationalisation, which the government rejected.

When the high prices ruling on the export market collapsed in 1921, the government quickly relinquished control and returned the mines to their owners, with disastrous results. Many collieries were losing money and, in a labour-intensive industry, the owners sought to cut wages in order to reduce their costs. The men rejected this and were locked-out from April 1st until early July, when they resumed work, having accepted substantial reductions. For the Ingleton men, however, this truce did not last long because, following an agreement between the owners and the men, the wage rates payable in Cumberland and Lancashire, with which counties the company was competing, became materially less than Yorkshire. The company, therefore, decided to stop mining the Six Foot Seam, unless the men would accept 'a reduction in wages sufficient to enable competition with the adjoining counties to be maintained'.[21] No such agreement was reached, however, and the colliery was closed in September 1921. The men were laid off, except for a skeleton crew, which kept the principal roadways etc in repair.

Trade had improved by January 1924 and wage rates in the adjoining counties were much nearer parity. The company felt that such conditions would allow a local trade in house coal without undue disadvantage, so it circulated the shareholders and proposed that the

Ingleton Colliery Officials

Officials at New Ingleton Colliery. Front row L to R:- George North, under manager; A.B.Hewitt, manager; unknown; Joseph Burke, deputy.

Demonstration by the Ingleton Colliery first aid team.

mine be reopened. It also sought their agreement to restructure the company in order to raise money by selling £50,000 of First Preference Shares and reducing the number and status of other types of share. By 1924 the company's lease, which had an unexpired term of forty-seven years, covered an area of 3,407 acres, of which an estimated 2,250 acres of coal would be workable. Royalties, payable on the coal raised, varied from 3d to 4d per ton, and the minimum rents amounted to £460 a year until October 1st 1925, when they would rise to £525 a year until October 1st 1928, and subsequently to £825 a year. With the optimism which is customarily found in prospectuses, this was said to be enough to 'last for considerably more than 100 years' at the projected annual output of 200,000 tons. In fact, that was about twice the level of output ever achieved.

It was intended to open the Four Foot Seam and it was estimated that a weekly output of 2,000 tons could be achieved within nine months of reopening. The board's proposals must have been acceptable because, on March 8th, the *Lancaster Guardian* reported that Ingleton Colliery had reopened the previous Thursday after being closed for two and a half years. The Six Foot workings were never reopened, however, and, having stood since September 1921, they were abandoned in 1928 after a total area of forty five acres of coal had been removed.

Poor trading conditions had returned by 1925, and the owners demanded further cuts in pay and an increase in the hours worked, from seven to eight per day. The miners' leader, A.J. Cook, responded with the famous 'Not a penny off the pay, not a minute on the day', and the owners issued lock-out notices. The latter expired on May 4th 1926, when the TUC supported the miners by calling a General Strike which lasted for nine days. The lock-out continued, however, and by the end of July the strike committee at Ingleton had been feeding 150 children for some weeks past. The lock-out continued through a long, hot summer until the miners were beaten and voted to return to work in late November. As in other areas, some men returned to work early. At Ingleton, thirty men were back at work and raising coal by September 11th. This had risen to 150 men, or 43% of the pre-strike workforce, on October 23rd, and 200 men were back at work on November 6th. Work now concentrated on getting coal from the Four Foot Seam and, in April 1930, one consequence of this was the closure, because of subsidence, and the eventual replacement in 1933, of the New Bridge over the River Greta. The area of Four Foot Seam worked is bounded to the north by the Hollintree Fault and to the south by an un-named fault.

Following the Wall Street Crash in 1929, the early 1930s was a time of severe economic depression. In an effort to protect trade, a national quota was imposed on the coal industry. This regulated the monthly output of coal from each colliery and meant that orders for coal could not always be met and income was restricted. As part of its efforts to increase efficiency, the company had introduced electrical power to the colliery by 1926. This allowed a change from compressed-air to electrically-driven coal-cutters and the introduction of endless-rope haulage on the main haulages. The last change reduced the number of horses employed and made their handlers available for other work. Nevertheless, the number of men employed remained fairly constant until February 1932 when, owing to a reorganisation of working methods underground, seventy-five men and boys were given a week's notice, which expired on March 1st.[22] Early that September, over one hundred more men were given notice and the rest were put on short time. Not all of them finished, however, because the *List of Mines* for that year shows that the numbers employed on the surface and underground had been reduced by one hundred and twenty-one from the total in 1931.

In 1934 the New Ingleton Collieries went into liquidation and by arrangement with the Receiver appointed by the National and Provincial Bank Ltd, the Ingleton Estates Company resumed the collection of the house rents as from April 19th 1934. There were now strong rumours that the colliery would close. The colliery had enough orders for it to work six days a week, but it was impeded from doing so by the quota. A new seam, the Yard Seam, was being developed and it was expected to yield high quality coal. On the surface the Receiver saw the boilers which made steam to drive the winding engines, but he also saw signs of modernisation, under which the mine had become 'electrified'. The mine generated its own electricity, which went down the pit at 3,300 volts to a transformer, where it was reduced to 550 volts and distributed throughout the mine. Electrical power had taken over from pit ponies by driving the engines which pulled the tubs on the haulages. It also drove the coal cutters and the fan which sucked air from the upcast shaft.

The Four Foot Seam was nearing exhaustion by late 1934 and some 140 acres of it had been removed when the mine closed. In the meantime, however, another seam was to be tried. A report to the shareholders in 1924 described the 'yard coal' or Three Foot seam as an excellent house and gas coal as well as being a coking coal. Nevertheless, it was 'somewhat irregular in thickness, and being separated from the Four Foot Seam by only one or two feet of fireclay' it was felt 'desirable to concentrate working on the Four Foot, and leave the Three Foot for a later period'.[23] The Three Foot was said to be of good quality and burned brightly, leaving a red ash. It was worked at Wilson Wood, Old Ingleton and Moorgarth Collieries, and now preparations were being made to work it at New Ingleton Colliery.

That time came in 1935, when a roadway in the Four Foot Seam was dinted, to remove the rock which separated the two seams, and a face was developed. The face, which was ready for turning coal in early September, was to be mechanised, with an electric coal cutter, face conveyor and gate conveyors. The coal would be taken from the face and loaded into tubs on the main haulage road. In August 1935 the colliery was said to be in better condition than it had been for some time and many more years of coal production at Ingleton were predicted. Coal was being produced on one shift, from 6.30am to 2 pm, five days per week during the summer, and six in winter, when demand was higher. There was very little water, and only one pump, discharging thirty gallons per minute, was needed.[24]

This optimism was dealt a serious blow when during the night of Sunday October 20th, about twenty-five yards of the new face collapsed. The fall was estimated to be two thousand tons. Two hundred and fifty men were thrown out of work the following day. The four pit ponies, Dandy, Bill, Don and Prince, were brought out of the pit and two of them were sold. The other two were kept for working with the skeleton staff.

In early November, F. Middleton, one of the colliery company's directors, met with miners and the Yorkshire Miners Association to offer new terms. It was proposed to reopen the mine using hand getting instead of mechanised cutting. The wages would also be reduced for certain classes of work and the company sought assurances that, should there be a national or county stoppage (strike), the miners would continue to work. The men refused these terms and further talks took place, leading to an agreement which allowed a few men to return to work in late November 1935. All was not well, however, and no Yard Seam was worked after February 10th 1936 and the mine was closed for good in March 1936.

The *List of Mines* shows that a small number of men, kept on to salvage machinery from the workings and on the surface, were employed until 1940. During this period, the colliery was managed for the receiver by H.L. Hirst. Ingleton Colliery was formally abandoned on August 16th 1940.[25] The New Ingleton Collieries Ltd, was dissolved by the Registrar of Companies under section 295 of the Companies Act 1929 by notice in the *London Gazette* dated September 17th 1946. Following the closure of New Ingleton Colliery, negotiations took place between Mr G. Rickards, MP for Skipton, and Mr Ernest Brown, the Minister of Labour. The result was that Ingleton was placed on the list of distressed areas.

The New Ingleton Colliery rescue team with under-manager George North. Centre front row Bob Pollard. (photo Celia Pollard)

REFERENCES

1. *Ingleton Coalfield*, J. Bentley, B.R. Bond & M.C. Gill, NMRS British Mining No.76, 2005.
2. LRO, WRW/L , Probate Inventory Richard Lowther 1649.
3. YAS DD123 (Knipe & Others against Bouch November 4th 1678.) p.5.
4. id, p.3.
5. YAS DD123, Lease Moore to Foxcroft 1732.
6. *A Tour to the Caves,* Rev. J. Hutton, London 1780, p.12.
7. G.J. Sergeantson's Memoirs, 1844.(The original held by Ord & Maddison of Darlington, is now lost, but there is a copy in the NMRS Records.) Hereafter called Sergeantson's Memoirs.
8. *Lancaster Guardian,* July 20th 1872.
9. *Industrial Archaeology,* Vol. 5 No.4, The Ingleton Coalfield, Harris A., 1968, p.321.
10. *Lancaster Guardian,* August 13th 1887.
11. *Lancaster Guardian,* September 13th 1890.
12. Barker MSS. J.Barker's handwritten draft of his statement for the 1900 court case, Attorney General V Barker & Haigh, p.2.
13. *Lancaster Guardian,* June 23rd 1900.
14. *List of Mines in the United Kingdom of Great Britain & Ireland*, 1896, 1901 & 1903.
15. *Lancaster Guardian,* October 30th 1909.
16. West Riding Registry of Deeds December 2nd 1914. Vol 48. P.1220. No.442.
17. Deeds of 118 New Village, Ingleton. (D.E. Starkie, 1980)
18. *Lancaster Guardian,* January 15th 1916.
19. Abandonment Plan 6842, January 18th 1919. Abandonment plan of Ten Foot Seam at New Ingleton Colliery.
20. Information from the late William Routledge, Honey Cottage, Ingleton.
21. Barker MSS. New Ingleton Collieries Ltd; Report by the Administrative Director to the shareholders, January 4th 1924.
22. *Lancaster Guardian,* February 26th 1932.
23. Barker MSS. Report of the Administrative Director, Jan. 4th 1924.
24. *Lancaster Guardian,* August 23rd 1935.
25. Abandonment Plan 12811, (formally abandoned August 16th 1940) and plan received December 23rd 1940. Abandonment Plan of Yard Seam at New Ingleton Colliery.

QUARRIES

INGLETON SLATE QUARRIES

While staying at Ingleton around 1780, John Hutton took an evening walk with friends to the slate quarries about a mile above Ingleton. 'Here we had both objects both of art and nature to amuse ourselves with: On one hand was a precipice ten or twelve yards perpendicular, made by the labour of man, being a delve of fine large blue slate, affording a useful cover for the houses in the adjoining part of Yorkshire, Lancashire and Westmorland. On the other hand was the river rolling down from rock to rock into a narrow deep chasm, where there was no room for human foot to tread between the stream and the rugged, high, steep rocks on the other side'.[1] John Hutton had walked out of the village by Thacking Road and seen the slate quarries on the river Twiss. This is now part of the falls walk, but in the eighteenth and nineteenth centuries was always a right of way.

The slate quarries at Ingleton were on both rivers, the Pecca slate quarries by the Doe on the Twistleton Hall Estate and the quarries in Quarry Wood on the Twiss or Ingleton Beck. Slate quarries were worked on both sides of the rivers. They were worked extensively in the eighteenth and nineteenth centuries and probably earlier. Hutton mentions that Ingleton slate was well known in his time and it was used for flooring, roofing, partitions in shippons and a variety of other uses.

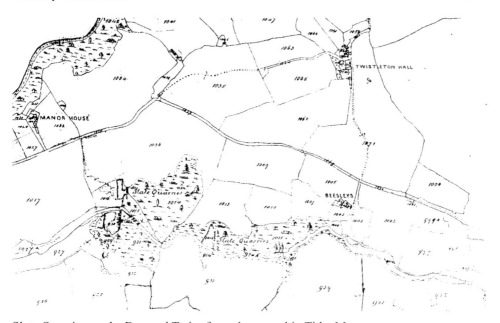

Slate Quarries on the Doe and Twiss from the township Tithe Map.

Speight mentions these quarries especially the ones on the Twiss near Baxenghyll Gorge. 'A little further on we descend round the lofty old slate quarries where the walls of rock, going vertically upwards to a great height, present a wonderfully interesting spectacle. The slates, says Prof Sedgwick, are coarser than the fine greenish-blue slates of the central group of Cumberland, but resemble them in colour. Some of them are marked with 'beautiful dendritic coverings of pyrites, and occasionally studded with large, bright cubes of that mineral'. They are co-extensive with those at Pecca, on the Thornton Beck, but the latter are spoiled with joints and fractures, and have long since been abandoned'.[2]

Speight's first mention of the slate quarries comes in his survey of the river Doe around Pecca Falls. He says, 'A short distance above we reach the Pecca Falls, which unquestionably form the grandest water scenes along the river course. The old Pecca slate quarries here, where the fractured rock is brought into striking prominence by the tremendous Craven fault, enunciated in the last chapter, will arrest the attention of the geologist'.[3] In March 1810 the *Lancaster Gazette* announced, 'Blue Slate quarries near Ingleton. To be let by private contract. The slate quarries in the estate at Twistleton Hall, near Ingleton, belong to James William Farrer and in the occupation of John Walker. The tenant or John Nicholson will show the same. Further particulars from Robert Waddington, of Crow Nest, or J. Hartley, solicitor Settle.

Sometimes the slate is termed blue and sometimes considered green and related to Lakeland slate. Speight, as we have seen, terms the slate 'bluish-green'. Professor Phillips in his *Illustrations* observed, 'In the extensive quarries above Ingleton the cleavage planes present one constant course to the South East, dipping slightly to the South West; cross joints run vertically to the North and oblique joints dip North East. The stone is mostly of a fine texture and green colour within, though often purple on the surfaces'.

William Green worked a slate quarry at Ingleton for many years. He was born in Grasmere in 1776 and had worked with Lakeland slate before coming to Ingleton and setting up as a slate merchant. He worked the slate quarry on the eastern side of Ingleton Beck.[4] However, the other side of the river was also worked and there are remains of a ford in the river where the slate was brought across to the eastern side to be taken down to Ingleton. Robert Smith who was born in Ingleton in 1817 and his brother both worked for William Green in the slate quarries. Robert Smith went to America in 1847 and started a quarry business there.[5] There was always a difficulty in getting the slates out of the quarry and Green's quarry had a road out along by the river through the Skirwith Farm lands and down Thacking Road into Ingleton. This road is now part of the waterfalls walk which passes through the quarry. He was retired by 1851 when the census return for Ingleton show him aged seventy-five and note him as 'retired slate merchant' However, his son William Green aged thirty-five was still listed as a slate merchant and was still working the slate quarries. Both father and son lived in the Bottoms at Ingleton. When William Green senior died in 1851 his will showed that he owned at least nine properties in Ingleton, a shop in the village and eight cottages in the Bottoms. William Green had prospered well in working Ingleton slate.

Slabs of slate rock were got ready for splitting or 'riving'. Skill not brute strength was needed for this. A 'river' split the rock with hammer and chisel for the required thickness. A dresser would then shape the slate into a tile. The green rock was harder and would not cut so easily into thin courses. The Ingleton census returns show slate merchants and slate rivers. In 1841 William Green aged twenty-eight, who lived in the Back Gate, is shown as a slate river. Christopher Smith, living in the Bottoms, is recorded as a slater; John Guyers also living in the Bottoms is a slate river and his near neighbour George Coward aged thirty is a slate merchant. By 1851 William Green was seventy-five and had retired and his son William Green aged thirty-six, was still a slate merchant, but the only slate worker in Ingleton. The parish registers show that Thomas Carr, a slater, married Elizabeth Brown at Ingleton July 8th 1764. Christopher Smith, another slater, married Elizabeth Battersby at Ingleton in 1806.

Thomas Guyers was also a slater when he married Esther Smith in 1794. John Guyers, his son, was also a quarryman and native of Ingleton. He left Ingleton and found work at Catlow Quarries in Nelson, Lancashire. He died there following a heavy bout of drinking, aged sixty-four. John was baptised at Ingleton on Mar 20th 1814, son of Thomas and Esther. Another member of the Guyers family was also a slater. Ingleton registers record that George Guyers, a slater, and his wife Isobel Guyers had a daughter, Esther, baptised in 1819.

The Pecca slate quarries stopped working around 1850 and Green's slate quarry in 1853. Joseph Carr writing in his 1865 guide said, These ancient quarries long ago fell into desuetude in consequence of cheaper slate, of a lighter and better quality being brought by rail from other districts.' The railway which arrived at Ingleton in 1849 allowed the easy transport of Welsh blue slate which helped to kill the local trade. However, much of the Ingleton slate was a good colour and quality and slabs on the walls near Quarry Wood have been there for near two hundred years.

NUTGILL FLAGSTONE QUARRY

Nutgill Flag Quarry was a subterranean quarry and some might call it a stone mine. However, though most quarries are worked as a surface pit others remain completely underground. Nutgill flag and slate quarry worked from the eighteenth century supplying flagstones and green slate. In September 1804 the quarry was advertised to be let for a 'term of years'. The stone was used for hearths, fireplaces, tomb stones and flags. The flagstones from Ingleton had even been exported as far as the West Indies where they were used in stores, probably as stone shelves. As there was a problem with water it was suggested that it might be necessary to have a water wheel and an engine to take off the water and if so the owner would be willing to share the costs.

In February 1816 notice was given in the *Lancaster Gazette* that the Lords of the Manor of Ingleton, who had previously held a share in the opening and working of Nutgill Quarry, had relinquished their interest. Their partner was John Howson and he was in financial trouble. The press announcement also said that all those who owed for slate or stone sold and delivered from the quarry should pay their debts to Jonathan Stordy of Bentham Mill as soon as possible. By June the following year those acting for John Howson were organising a payout to creditors at the Bay Horse in Ingleton.

In December 1887 the *Lancaster Guardian* recounted:-

Nutgill flag quarry lies about two miles from Ingleton, at the south eastern boundary of the township…The quarry has been worked at intervals from time immemorial. Within the memory of some of some older inhabitants it was carried on behalf of the Lords of the Manor. After being for a considerable time unoccupied, Mr B.C. Robertshaw, of Bingley became the lessee of the quarry. When he took possession of it was in very rough condition, so much so that it would have been greatly to his advantage that the ground had been in its primitive state. Previous occupiers had dug a spacious opening down into the rock, and then worked out the flags beneath the earth. On this account useless debris had been cast on heaps or thrown aside without any regard for future operations. The mouth of the ancient drift or tunnel was so choked with earth and stones that Mr Robertshaw, to prevent the quarry from being flooded had to make a new course for a streamlet.

A steam engine was employed and more efficient system organised. Fourteen men were working there in December 1877 and they were fully employed as there was a great demand for flags. Flags of great hardness were being quarried. At one time flag sales were limited and local, but later they found a market in Liverpool, Blackpool, Southport, Adlington, Lancaster, St Anne's on Sea, Leeds and Keighley. The flags were useful for floors, foundations, slating and general purposes. Balderston recorded that only five men were still working there in 1888. The underground flag quarries lay forgotten for many years until 1970 when a lorry travelling to Nutgill sank into the ground. Local cavers exploited the situation and explored the man-made underground caverns.

LIME INDUSTRY

HENRY ROBINSON - STORRS LIME KILNS
INGLETON LIME WORKS

Henry Robinson took the lease from the Lords of the Manor to work Storrs Common for limestone and lime burning. There were kilns on the eastern bank of the Twiss, the low kilns, and the higher Storrs kilns near to the road to Chapel-le-Dale. Henry Robinson took these over and developed a substantial lime industry on the Storrs at Ingleton. He was a native of Skipton who lived in Settle where he titled himself a coal merchant. Although he only stayed at Ingleton for short periods, he worked the limestone on Storrs extensively and provided considerable employment for local workmen for two decades. The 1851 census return shows Henry Robinson living at 29 Chapel Street in Settle where he was recorded as a coal-agent.

Henry Robinson came to Ingleton in 1861 and invested considerable money in building new lime kilns at Storrs and experimented with new methods of lime burning. By August 1863 he had built his new patented lime kiln. The *Lancaster Guardian* of August 15th 1863 recorded:-

> The old method of working lime was to lay a strata of coal and stone alternatively on account of which there was a serious loss in lime ashes as they have but a slack market at one ninth the price of lime. The object of the improved method is to do away with lime ashes, by means of converting the stone into lime by means of internally heated air…The kiln hill has been raised 48 feet and pierced near its centre with two thoroughfares in each of which there are four fireplaces each having two flues into the kiln which divide the interior into eight equal parts, so that the heat is equally distributed throughout the limestone. Small steam jets are in constant use to prevent the loss of the grates melting in the white heat, and a large steam jet is used in the chimney to produce a continuous draught as this is the great secret of success.

However, his new system failed, but Henry Robinson was described by Joseph Carr as, 'a persevering commercial gentleman… who in the face of difficulties of no ordinary character, has been scheming, planning, inventing, building, pulling down and re-building, at a cost of much money, time and physical and mental toil, to find a way a superior and less expensive way of making lime'.[6] In August 1869 two horses were found dead in their stable which adjoined the lime kiln at Storrs. Carbonic acid gas had passed into the stable due to a change of wind and the horses had been gassed.

Eventually Henry Robinson had success with his new kilns at Storrs. The two old kilns which were a few yards apart and thirty feet deep, were first arched over. Then a new kiln with a massive opening on its summit, and forty feet deep was erected on top. On the level of the two old kilns, two circular holes were made, one each side, for passing fuel into the kilns. The kiln took about sixty tons of limestone at a time. This plan of feeding the fuel in at a lower level than the top made a great saving in fuel and a cheaper product.[7] Around this time Henry Robinson blasted large quantities of limestone rock at Storrs. On August 21st 1869 300 pounds of powder brought down around four thousand tons of rock. The explosions shook houses in Thacking road.

Henry Robinson not only produced lime, but he also carried on a large business in supplying limestone for road works and smelting and often sent off a hundred tons a day from Ingleton Station. His men were paid 9d per ton to quarry the stone and the carters received the same for transporting it to Ingleton station. He had a machine for breaking stone and for crushing limestone to powder for agricultural use. Many local farmers tried his lime, but found its fertilising properties were small and it soon fell into disuse.

Henry Robinson's lease from the Lords of the Manor came to an end in 1882 and due to a dispute the Storrs lime works came to a standstill. Henry Robinson claimed £500 compensation for the working kiln at Storrs which the Lords considered excessive. They made a counter claim saying that Henry Robinson had let the old kiln go to ruin and that he had worked limestone rock contrary to the covenant. The case went to arbitration and the enquiry took place at the Ingleboro' Hotel on the 15th of November 1882.

In view of the dispute and other problems Henry Robinson bowed out of Ingleton and returned to Skipton where he lived in Newmarket Street with his family. He died the following year of 1883 and was buried at Skipton. Henry Robinson was also annoyed that his wish to build an overhead tramway from Storrs to Ingleton station met with such opposition that he had to abandon it.

His lease was taken up by Richard Atkinson who continued working Storrs lime kilns for some years. In 1878 Henry Robinson had bought land on Storrs called Storrs Garth to extend his works and this also was bought by Atkinson from Henry Robinson's son, John Walker Robinson. In 1884 Richard Atkinson was brought to court by the Ingleton Angling Association for pollution of the river near the Storrs lime kilns. Partially burned lime which had been tipped by the edge of the river found its way into the river and fish were killed for a mile downstream. He had been cautioned about tipping lime so near to the river, but had done nothing about it. Atkinson was convicted and fined.

Richard Atkinson continued burning lime at Storrs until he sold out to W. George Perfect of Stainforth. Perfect was secretary of the Craven Lime Company and the Storrs kilns were worked by Craven Lime. On Perfects's death his widow transferred the Storrs works to the Craven Lime Company. Later Robinson's kilns were demolished and plant erected for producing tarmac for the roads. The large plant at Storrs worked for many years.

MEAL BANK QUARRY

Meal Bank quarry is tucked away at Ingleton and many village folks never really ever went there, or in fact knew the entrance. Yet it was close to the village and they certainly were aware of that from the numerous blasts which shook their cottages on a regular basis. Meal Bank was first worked on a small scale by Richard Brown of Ingleton, but eventually it became one of the largest producers of lime in the Yorkshire dales.

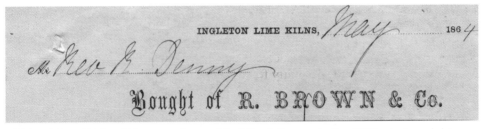

INGLETON LIME KILNS, *May* 186 4

Mr *Rev R Denny*

𝔅𝔬𝔲𝔤𝔥𝔱 𝔬𝔣 R. BROWN & Co.

Bill head from Richard Brown, who ran Meal Bank Quarry in the 1860s, to the minister the Rev. Richard Denny. Denny as well as being minister and magistrate was also tenant of one of the Greenwood Estate farms. The bill was for lime for his fields.

Joseph Bentham had worked an old lime kiln at Lennie Wood close to Meal Bank. However, the kiln was abandoned and collapsed in 1893. Joseph Bentham continued in his trade of builder and timber merchant. Richard Brown worked the Meal Bank kiln in the 1860s. The Browns had been solid commercial figures in Ingleton since the eighteenth century working as carriers, butchers, innkeepers, carpenters and blacksmiths. Richard's father George was a carpenter and wheel-right based at the Wheat Sheaf and Richard was also a cotton manufacturer. John Berry Darwen managed the kilns for Richard Brown and the Darwens were connected with Meal Bank over many years.

In 1860 John Darwen's son, Martin aged eleven, ran away from work and home having stolen and sold a knife belonging to his father. Being afraid to go home for fear of his father's anger he took shelter at the lime kiln. He was found dead on Friday January 7th close to the opening of the kiln. He was burned down his left side from head to foot. The verdict at the inquest was, 'Died of starvation'. Two sons of John Darwen were to die at Meal Bank and records show that he was regular, drunkard, wife-beater and poacher and caused considerable mayhem in Ingleton.

In 1864 Clark & Wilson first came to Meal Bank and for a few years worked the old kilns there. They then took a twenty-five year lease of the site in November 1868 from James Farrer lord of the Manor of Clapham. So began Clark & Wilson's Ingleborough Patent Lime Works, although it was always known locally as Meal Bank. In 1868 they began work building a new extensive Hoffmann kiln. By June the new kiln, oval in shape and 160 feet long by 76 feet wide, was about completed. It covered an area of 1,350 square yards. It was reported

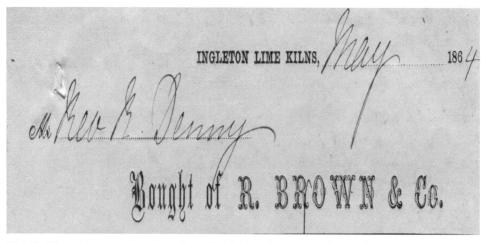

The Hoffmann kiln at Meal Bank built in 1868 and photographed before a tramway was built to encircle it in 1892.

that an old lime burner of eighty two years of age was amazed at the development of this new system. The *Lancaster Guardian* reported on January 23rd 1879:-

> The kiln which is of an oval shape and covered with a sloping wooden roof, has a regular and neat appearance from a distance…The distance round the kiln is 450 feet. At a height of four feet from the foundation a platform, of the breadth of 6° feet runs round the kiln, from which the stone is wheeled into the chamber to be converted to lime. There are fourteen chambers 9 feet high in the centre arch and 18 feet wide on the floor, and the passage from the platform to each chamber is 6 foot at the centre of the arch. Each chamber holds about 100 tons of stone, which is packed in or piled, with openings for fuel and draught; and as it is calculated that two fifths of the stone passes off in moisture and carbonic gas one chamber should yield about 60 tons of lime, which is the quantity taken from the kiln every day.
>
> From the platform to the feeding chamber is 11 feet perpendicular, and as the wall slopes it is 14 feet. Above the kiln in the feeding chamber, which is 150 feet in length, 6 feet in width and 14 feet from the floor to the ridge… In this chamber there are 424

holes through which the fires are kept up. The workmen whose place it is to feed the fires, wheel the fuel in a barrow, put a funnel in each hole, and then with a small scoop carries on the operation with more comfort, cleanliness, and ease than the old system of lime burning.'

Donkeys were used as well as horses. The packers filled the chambers and then they were sealed with road scrapings to make them air tight. The press report gave all the costs and the method of disposing of the carbonic acid gas through a flue built into the side of Meal Bank and then passing out of the large brick chimney as white vapour. Once the new Hoffmann kiln was in use over fifty labourers were employed at the quarry and although output grew they could not keep up with orders. This led to an increase in blasting to bring down greater quantities of rock. The *Lancaster Guardian* of October 9th 1869 under the heading 'Dangerous Blast' reported that, 'the explosion last Monday made things dance in the shop windows of Ingleton.' Houses were shook to the foundations and there were many complaints.

About 1873 a massive blasting operation was planned and Dr Watts of Giggleswick School was asked to set off the charge. Well over two tons of gunpowder was used. Ingleton folks came to watch the operation, but many were nervous about the whole affair. Many people gathered around Dr Watts feeling that at least they would be safe near him. An experiment was made with new explosive in June 1875. At the close of the successful experiment the explosive agent said he would show them a new way of catching fish. The river ran close to the quarry and they selected a deep pool under the limestone cliffs. A portion of a cartridge was thrown into the pool and the water flew out in lofty jets and trout came stunned to the surface. When it was tried in shallower water both water and stones were thrown out of the river.

In 1872 the old company was dissolved and the Craven Lime Company Ltd was formed. The new company appointed Messrs Clark & Wilson to manage their lime works at Ingleton and Stainforth. In 1873 kiln packers were paid five shillings a day and stone getters, who were paid by the ton, earned from twenty-five to thirty shillings a week. This method of payment probably led to the taking of risks and the considerable accidents to stone-getters at the quarry.

There were many accidents at Meal Bank, three in 1869 alone. On Thursday September 16th Thomas Darwen was loosening a large block of limestone with a crowbar when it fell upon him and killed him. It took twelve men to remove the stone from his body. This was the second son of John Darwen to have died at Meal Bank. Also in September a twelve year old boy was knocked unconscious by falling limestone rock and a man drilling rock caused a fall of rock which injured him. In January 1875 George Sellars, while boring rock in preparation for blasting, was crushed and cut to pieces when around fifteen tons of rock fell on him. It severed his leg and scattered his body in parts. His workmates collected his body in a sack.[8]

In January 1885 John Darwen had a serious accident. While preparing to blast rock the charge exploded and he was lucky not to have been killed. However, his hand was badly injured and he was permanently blinded by the blast. It was not recorded whether this was John Darwen senior or junior, but by 1891 the Darwen family had disappeared from Ingleton. Sadly they were not missed at Ingleton, as apart from John Darwen senior's fighting, drunkenness and wife beating, John Darwen junior's dog had on one occasion bitten out the cheek of a young girl in the village disfiguring her for life.

Horses were used to cart the lime from the quarry up Mill Road past the mill and then over Thornton Bridge and up the hill to Thornton Station. It was expensive work and was heavy on the horses. Most of the carters provided their own horses for this work although the company kept a few horses themselves. A tramway was proposed, but the landowner, Mr

Looking over Meal Bank Quarry to the village, a sketch by F.C.Tilney around 1900.

Foxcroft, would not allow it. Hopkinson also thought that the tramway would interfere with his scenery walk and cut down the number of visitors. Joseph Carr eventually persuaded everyone that a railway would be good for the economy of Ingleton, stop cruelty to horses, and not affect the tourists in any way.

Eventually the absentee landlord, Mr Foxcroft, was persuaded and the tramway went ahead. The contractor was John Atkinson of Ingleton and the first sod was cut in Broadwood on April 10th 1892. The line left Meal Bank, ran through a tunnel and then over the viaduct and up the hill to Thornton. On March 13th 1893 the line was opened for the passage of one of the London and North Western railway engines. Joseph Carr was proved right, the Craven Lime Company flourished, more men were employed, and there was no falling off of visitors to the falls walks.

Lime was in great demand for building in the growing towns and cities of Lancashire and Yorkshire in the late Victorian period and Meal Bank thrived. There was a great demand for it in Bradford and Halifax. The quarry supplied Widnes Chemical Works with an average of three rail trucks a day of lime containing six to seven tons each. In 1901 it was reported that Meal Bank was, 'doing brisk trade'. However, by 1908 that trade had considerably diminished and in 1909 most workmen at Meal Bank were laid off and by January 1910 only six men were being retained. Orders for lime were probably being placed elsewhere in the company. The Great War came with a great demand for lime for munitions and blast furnaces, but Meal Bank did not re-open. The *Lancaster Guardian* of January 15th 1916 reported 'This quarry once the staple industry of Ingleton continues to be closed down, but optimists still hope and think they will re-open it some time or other'. Ingleton was pleased for people to come in and develop industries, but in the case of the Craven Lime Company, although this was good in the beginning, at the end it proved bad: the company supplied lime from their other quarries and the Ingleton economy suffered.

RIBBLEHEAD LIMESTONE QUARRY

Ribblehead Lime Quarry was worked by the Craven Lime Company during the nineteenth century, but abandoned in 1900. It was in a remote place where the weather was often atrocious and where it was difficult to get labour. In the 1940s Adam Lythgoe of Warrington bought the quarry and worked it to produce powdered limestone for agricultural use. Much high quality lime was also sent for the iron industry in Durham. A powder plant at the quarry produced lime for toothpaste, cosmetics and scouring powders as well as for agriculture. The quarry was again abandoned in the late 1960s until ARC bought the site in 1973.

The new owners saw the potential of millions of tons of good limestone to replace their Middlebarrow Quarry at Silverdale. Had the quarry been re-opened it would have seen a massive expansion. However, it never happened and the quarry lay inactive until 1998 when Hanson's, who were then the owners, announced their intention never to work the quarry again. Hanson's assisted in making the site into a nature reserve. Some levelling and landscaping was done and then gradually the harsh landscape began to be reclaimed by nature. Hanson's handed the site to English Nature in 2001 and due to their decision acres of limestone pavement were saved.

PRESTON'S LIMESTONE ROCK

Thomas Preston took a crowbar and inserted it under a limestone clint on the slopes of Ingleborough. He found that he could lever it gently from the ground and he did so. The year was 1870 and he began a limestone company that lasted for three generations and removed hundreds of thousands of tons of limestone from the fells around Ingleborough for ornamental walls, rockeries, and general garden use. Thomas Preston obtained leases from landowners to remove the limestone pavements from their land. He had to loosen the weather-worn stone, manhandle it and load it onto horse and cart. It was then carried to the railway station at Ingleton or other local stations. From there it was carried all over the country and even overseas.

The work done by Thomas Preston, his son John and his grandson, Richard, changed the landscape around Chapel-le-Dale and Ribblehead. Once the limestone pavement had been removed fields could be made by clearing the rubble left and much land was gained for agriculture as the ground quickly healed and became covered in vegetation. Today many would say that the removal of the limestone was desecration and spoiled much of the natural look of the countryside. Eventually because of extensive quarrying many areas had to be marked for preservation or limestone pavements could have disappeared from the region.

John Preston not only worked limestone on the fells but ran a successful fish and fruit business in Ingleton. He died in February 1927 and was buried in Ingleton cemetery. Richard Preston took over from his father after the WWI and his largest job was to supply 20,000 tons of limestone to just one large house in London. On another occasion a Scottish visitor called and took away a hundredweight of limestone in the boot of his car. The art in laying limestone rock gardens was to so position the stone that it gave the impression of being the natural strata of rock. Reginald Farrer of Ingleborough Hall used estate labour to transport rock for his own ornamental gardens, but later ordered his stone from Prestons.

In May 1936 Richard Preston had a display of limestone ornamental rocks at the Chelsea Flower Show. King Edward attended and the fame of Ingleborough limestone was brought to the notice of royalty. The king asked about the interesting rockery stones and was told by one of the men on the stand that it was 'a lump of Ingleborough'. The King ordered some of the typical weather worn limestone brought from the terraces below Ingleborough. The king was told it was hundreds of years old – a considerable understatement. In 1951 an order came from the organisers of the Festival of Britain. This work kept Richard Preston and his

Prestons removed thousands of tons of limestone pavements from Ingleton township.

men busy for six months at the South Bank site in London. There one thousand tons of limestone were used, most of it forming a huge wall at the entrance of the 'Origin of the Land' pavilion. The wall was twenty five feet high, about forty yards long and a yard wide, at the bottom, tapering to two feet at the top.

In the 1950 five lorries were still used for the work and Richard Preston employed five men, three at Ingleton and two at Orton in Westmorland. The lorries were mostly ex-army and needed to be tough for the heavy work on the fells. Work was carried out up to 1,200 feet above sea level and was be a strain on both men and vehicles. He was taking between eight and fourteen thousand tons of limestone from the fells annually. The workers always kept their eyes open for interesting shapes which brought a higher price. Very occasionally a remarkable piece of natural sculpture was discovered. A piece of weathered limestone was found in the shape of a cross standing on a ball. The only flaw was that one of the arms of the cross was shorter than the other by less than an inch.[9]

THE GRANITE QUARRY

Adam Sedgwick is reputed to have told Walter Scott, a railway contractor, about the special qualities of the rock around Skirwith at Ingleton. Walter passed the information to his son John Scott and eventually John Scott and Company, a small syndicate, began work on a quarry in 1886. There is a long period between Adam Sedgwick's survey in Yorkshire in 1822 and the beginning of operations in 1886, but whatever the truth of the matter Adam Sedgwick certainly surveyed the area. When Adam Sedgwick became a geologist he said, 'Hitherto I have never turned a stone: henceforth I will leave no stone unturned'.

The 'Granite Quarry' in the early twentieth century.

The quarry was always called 'Ingleton Granite Quarry' by the locals, but in fact it is not granite, but an extremely hard metamorphic rock which is excellent for railway ballast, road stone and aggregate for concrete. No doubt the word 'granite' was used by the quarry company to stress the strength and quality of their product.

The company came fully into John Scott's hands in the 1890s and he worked it for many years mainly providing railway ballast, road stone and crushed stone for concrete work. An overhead system took the stone to be crushed and sorted on the opposite side of the road to the quarry. A railway line was constructed down to Ingleton station in 1887 by John Hewitson a local contractor. The embankments were built from waste at the quarry and can still be seen today. Heywood's guide to Ingleton said, 'It is a novel sight to see the small locomotive and its train of wagons moving slowly along the hill sides, now disappearing in an hollow, and now rising on the crest of a hill top, and finally arriving at a point some 600 yards above the Midland railway, where the wagons are let down the incline by an endless chain – one full wagon in descending pulling an empty one up'. At this time the quarry employed about thirty men and boys.[10]

G. Hollinghead, Assistant Keeper of Technology at Bradford Industrial Museum, wrote in the 1970s that the quarry locomotive was called the Northumbria and was dumped at the end of the works and left to rust.[11] He played on it when he was a boy around 1922. Also Robert Western in *The Ingleton Branch* dated 1971 states that, 'From the quarry there was a single track which passed the stock yard, the reservoir, the White Scar Caves, around the hill at Skirwith, close to Crina Bottom and ended above Easegill. This section of the line which was about a mile long was worked by a saddle-tank named Northumbria'.

However, the engine Cyprus was also said to have worked at the quarry. The Cyprus, an 0-4-0 engine was manufactured in Leeds by Manning & Wardle in 1878. It worked in Birmingham and then was said to have come to Ingleton to work at the Granite Quarry. A works document seems to confirm that the engine was sent to Ingleton. It may well be that it preceded the Northumbria.

It was always a problem to get workers for the quarry especially in times of good employment as it was at a distance from the village and the work was arduous. In 1890 a number of men came from Guernsey to work at the granite quarry. They were members of the Guernsey Society of Stone Workers and their departure for Ingleton was marked by a fraternal celebration. These men had been in contact with the quarry at Ingleton after seeing an advertisement. The management at Ingleton quarry sent a representative to the Channel Islands to interview them, engage them and pay their passage back to Ingleton. The men, six stone workers from St Samson, sailed on board the SS Gazelle to England. The men named Allen, Tristrum, Burnley, Langbois, Pugh, and Carr, arrived safely at Ingleton and settled well into their quarry work.[12]

Unfortunately a mysterious explosion occurred just before the men left and it was suspected that they had done it. The Guernsey men denied that they had caused any explosion saying that 'they would never do such a sly trick'. The men were said to be well behaved and were welcomed to Ingleton. However, many believed that the explosion had been their way of saying goodbye to a disliked employer.

The census return for Ingleton taken in March 1891 only a few months later shows that only one or two of the men had stayed. Henry Pugh was still working at the granite quarry, but he had been born at Taunton in Somerset. Henry's wife, Emily was born in Guernsey as was his one year old daughter. There was a William Langley and Edward Langdon from Guernsey, one of whom may have been Langbois in an Anglicised form. However, there were more quarrymen from Guernsey, Jersey and Alderney including Charles Jolly, Michael Hafner and Henry Goman. By the census of 1901 there is no mention at Ingleton of anyone born in the Channel Islands: they had all returned to their homeland or moved on elsewhere.

During the Great War the quarry was temporarily closed but opened again in 1920. After the war, ex-war department petrol driven trucks were used to transport the stone down to Ingleton as there had been problems with the rail wagons, especially after a long closure. The quarry was later sold to a syndicate of Newcastle gentlemen who passed it to John Brooks of Lightcliffe near Halifax, who was also the owner of Shap Granite Quarries. John Willie Tate was manager of the quarry for thirty-one years. He left in February 1921 to take employment in Leeds.

The new owners replaced the old steam railway with an aerial ropeway. The ropeway was second hand according to one of the installers, Tom Wilson, of Ingleton. It was set on twenty-six towers and set off straight up the hill from the crushers and then followed the old rail line to the old drum head at Ease Gill. The aerial ropeway closed at the end of World War II when lorries were used for transport.

The original quarry was closed in September 1957, but other areas of the same rock are still quarried at Skirwith closer to Ingleton. The quarry was owned in turn by the Ingleton Granite Company to around 1944, XL Granite (Ingleton) Ltd, to 1960, and later Amalgamated Roadstone and Amey Roadstone Corporation. It is now owned by Hanson Aggregates UK who are the world's largest provider of crushed rock.

REFERENCES

1. *A Tour to the Caves,* Rev. J. Hutton, London, 1780, p.18.
2. *Craven and the North West Yorkshire Highlands,* H. Speight, 1989, Smith Settle, p.232.
3. id, p.228.
4. *Guide to Ingleton,* A. Hewitson, 1896, p.9.
5. *Lancaster Guardian,* January 16th 1892.
6. *Lancaster Guardian,* October 23rd 1869.
7. *Lancaster Guardian,* August 15th 1863.
8. *Lancaster Guardian,* January 22nd 1876.
9. *Yorkshire Dalesman*, 1956, pp.341, 342.
10. *Heywood's Ingleton Guide,* 1898, pp.8,9.
11. *Yorkshire Dalesman,* October 1974, p.559.
12. *Lancaster Guardian,* November 8th 1890.

Ingleton slate in Beezley Glen.

ROADS

EARLY ROADS

There were tracks in the Ingleton area in prehistoric times and these became more defined during the Bronze Age and Iron Age. In the Iron Age there was a settlement on the very top of Ingleborough and the area would be well supplied with trackways. When the Romans came to this country, road building was developed and a good system of roads was planned and constructed, but the Roman roads in the area of Bainbridge and Ingleton were still relatively primitive.

The Roman road came from Bainbridge Fort through Ingleton. It crossed Cam Fell and then came down via Chapel-le-Dale and round the lower slopes of Ingleborough. It has been suggested that it came down through Chapel-le-Dale and into Ingleton via the Meal Bank. We have already said this route is unlikely to have ever been considered by military road builders for several reasons. It might have been used by the Romans, but it was unlikely to have been a Roman built road.

When Adam Fothergill came along as surveyor for the new Richmond Lancaster Turnpike in 1751 he had no hesitation, he came straight down past Chapel-le-Dale seeing the route down through Twistleton as what it was, a narrow and difficult pack horse track for Twistleton Hall and the other farmsteads on the Twistleton promontory. A good road was not cut through Twistleton until 1795 when the Ingleton Vestry minutes record, 'We agree to purchase as much land of James Greenwood so as to make a Sufficient Road within Twistleton in the Parish of Ingleton'. The road was planned to be five yards wide and to be built within stone walls.[1]

It has been said that the Hawes Road out of Ingleton to Chapel-le-Dale was a new cut road by the Richmond to Lancaster Turnpike, but this is unlikely to have been so. There was a settlement at Skirwith on that road from at least the thirteenth century and those who lived and worked there did not go all the way round via Chapel-le-Dale to get to Ingleton, they had a road into the village.

PACK HORSES & PACK HORSE ROUTES

The use of pack horses and pack horse trails goes back to the middle ages and beyond. The pack horse man could lead his animals on the narrowest and most hilly routes, and his aim was always for the shortest route. The pack horse carriers generally went over the hills to avoid the wet lowlands as these trackways over the hills were quite hard even in wet weather. Strings of from six to forty horses travelled together, usually well loaded, on which ever route they took. The leading horse usually carried a large bell on its neck, and the others too might have bells, leading to the children's song:-

> Bell-horses, bell horses,
> What time o'day ?
> One o'clock, two o'clock,
> Off and away.

Children would follow the pack horses as they came up Bell Horse Gate in Ingleton interested to see the animals, to enquire what they were carrying and where they were going. Each horse had a rough wooden saddle called a pannier onto which merchandise was strapped in sacks or bags. Other pack horses had wicker baskets to carry their goods. Pack horses also took slate from Ingleton slate quarries, coal from the pits and lime from the lime kilns and wool on its way to Kendal and other places. 'In the procession there were sometimes from thirty to forty travelling in a single line up Bellhorse-gate, through the Main-street and on by the old road to Clapham'.[2] Dr Arthur Raistrick describes the old pack horse route from Dent to Ingleton in his *Green Tracks on the Pennines*:-

From Dent there are two other pack-horse roads of great age and interest. The one that is now least used but very attractive, leaves the old road on the south side of the Dee at Deepdale foot, and from Dike Hall rises rapidly as a walled lane up the northwest shoulder onto the Great Wold. After climbing to over 1,600 feet OD., it becomes an unfenced road and soon mounts onto the firm, dry limestone terrace that forms the ridge of Great Wold. Turning more to the south it crosses a highest point at just over 1,700 feet OD., and then drops to the head of Force Gill. In this part of the road the old name of Craven's Old Way is given on some of the older maps while in the dispute over the Dent-Newby boundary it is called Craven's Wath or Little Green Wald, the road from Dent to Ingleton.

Down Littledale it reaches the hamlet of Winterscales then keeps to the lower flank of Whernside past Ivescar and Bruntscar to Ellerbeck, turning abruptly at the latter point down the hillside to Chapel-le-Dale. From Chapel-le-Dale it continues as the walled green road on the west side of the Greta to Beezleys, and down the tongue of land between the two sets of falls to Ingleton. This part of the road from Chapel-le-Dale to Beezleys may in fact be much older and be part of the Roman road from Bainbridge to Casterton, being a direct continuation of the Cam Fell road line.

The pack horses were usually Galloways, long in the back and short in the legs and something about thirteen hands in height. Robert Southey (1774-1843) noted them in his book *The Doctor*. 'The whole carriage of the Northern Counties, and indeed of all the remoter parts, was performed by pack-horses, the very name of which would have been long since been as obsolete as their use, if it had not been preserved by the sign or appellation of some of those inns in which they were accustomed to put up. Rarely, indeed, were the roads about Ingleton marked by any other wheels than those of its indigenous carts'. Interesting to note that this Victorian Poet Laureate took notice of Ingleton's roads. Southey also noted that stage coaches went about ten miles an hour.

Southey appears to suggest that the pack horses had disappeared in his later years around 1835, but there are reports of pack horses being still used in the hilly areas of Yorkshire and Lancashire for at least thirty years after that date. The pack horses were often referred to as 'gals' probably short for Galloways. If they carried slate they were 'slate gals' and if they carried lime they were 'lime gals' and if they carried coal, as they did from Ingleton pits, then they were 'coal gals'. 'When the pack horse trade collapsed through the roads being made better fit for carts there was for some time a brisk trade carried on in pack horse bells, which were sold for old metal, and each weighed about two pounds'.[3]

TURNPIKE ROADS

The development of Ingleton as a village was very much due to its position at the crossing point of two important roads whose origins went back to medieval times. These roads brought foot, horse and wheeled traffic through Ingleton and some of it was induced to stop and spend time and money in the village. Blacksmiths shoed horses and repaired wagons and coaches: the local inns provided food and refreshment and a night's rest.

These roads were the Richmond to Lancaster road and the Keighley to Kendal road. These two routes had shared a common route through Ingleton for centuries, but in the eighteenth century an entirely new system of road administration came into being called turnpike roads. Since Tudor times villages had been responsible for the roads passing through their townships and local people had to provide labour when required. When these turnpike roads came turnpike trusts were set up and roads surveyed and repaired by money raised from collecting tolls at toll bars along the new turnpike roads. However, local people still had to provide free labour for several days each year.

Jeffrey's map of 1775 highlighting the crossing of the two turnpike roads

Local gentry and others got together to form a turnpike trust by Act of Parliament. Thus empowered they appointed surveyors and brought the road up to turnpike standard. Toll bars were erected to collect cash and this paid for materials for repairing the road as well as paying interest to those who had invested money in the trust. Both the Keighley to Kendal and the Richmond to Lancaster roads were turnpiked in the eighteenth century and they brought prosperity to Ingleton. Turnpike trusts were a great impetus to road making and repairing and were responsible for a great increase in traffic. Roads which had been in ruinous condition were repaired without landowners or local authorities having to put their hands in their own pockets to find the money. The Richmond to Lancaster Turnpike was authorised by Act of Parliament in 1751 and the Keighley to Kendal Turnpike Trust was formed two years later in 1753.

THE LANCASTER-RICHMOND TURNPIKE

The Lancaster to Richmond Turnpike was created by Act of Parliament in 1751.[4] The Richmond to Lancaster road had as its principal aim the linking of the Irish Sea with the North Sea. This road linked Lancashire with Yorkshire across the Pennines. Like other turnpike roads this road joined together many old roads already in existence, repairing them and attempting to make them uniform in breadth and quality. Goods from the growing port of Lancaster could be taken across the country, wine, flax, and timber was transported through Lancashire and Yorkshire and butter, cheese and other country products came in the opposite direction.

When the petition to Parliament was made the state of the old road was described as, 'so bad, ruinous, narrow and rocky that it is totally impassable at some Times of the Year for any kind of Wheeled Carriages; nor can the same, by the several Days Works on the Highway, and the ordinary Course and Provision of the Law, be so effectually amended and kept in good and sufficient Repair, as to make the same passable for Wheel Carriages; and that the said last mentioned road is now dangerous to all Persons travelling thereon'. The road was probably very bad in places, but the petitioners always exaggerated the situation to some extent to further their case.

The road left Lancaster and passed through Caton and alongside the Lune through Hornby, Melling and Burton to Thornton-in-Lonsdale. At Thornton it dropped down into Ingleton entering Ingleton over Thornton Bridge and Ingleton Bridge before running up Bell Horse Gate and through the village. Passing over Storrs Common it ran through Chapel-le-Dale and just beyond Gearstones, still in Ingleton township, it turned over Cam Fell following the route of the old Roman Road to Bainbridge. A later deviation in 1795 took the road from Gearstones to the extremity of Ingleton at Newby Head and from there down Widdale and on to Hawes and Bainbridge. The changed route was less hilly and brought Hawes onto the Lancaster Richmond Turnpike Road.

The first general meeting of the trustees was held in the Red Lion in Askrigg on June 19th 1751. At this meeting Alexander Fothergill was appointed surveyor of that part of the turnpike road from Brompton near Richmond to Ingleton Bridge. Alexander was a surveyor, attorney, farmer, and Quaker, but he was also a diarist and the fact that several years of his diaries have survived has given us a great insight into the building of this road.[5] Fothergill was busy at once organising work on the road, both contract work and free statute labour and ordering materials for building the toll bars. He rode daily on horseback in all weathers over Cam Fell and down to Ingleton stopping to check work and pay wages. He lodged at many places including Gearstones, Ingleton and Settle.

He had trouble in getting local people to supply free labour for the road as they were liable to do under the Highways Act of 1555: this labour Alexander referred to as 'statute work' and he meant to enforce it. The Turnpike Act had empowered the surveyor to access this free labour through the Quarter Sessions. On July 23rd 1754 he wrote. 'The inhabitants of Ingleton make complaint that serving 3 days upon our road is an oppression &c.: Mr Fenton directed the surveyor to make application to me upon that account &c. After the meeting I gave Christopher Holm orders to repair some bad places in the Storrs road. I also ordered Thomas Carr to get his bargain done on Bleamoor as soon as possible.' Bleamoor was a particularly difficult stretch of road because of bogs.

Alexander kept his eye on Ingleton closely. On August 5th he wrote that, 'Christopher Holm had then bein 3 days repairing the Storrs road. In the morning I spoke to severall persons to open and clean the sides of the road in their fronts in the town to give passage for the water and sent William Hardy, John Hunning and Richard Balderston & James Sharp notices in writing to remove the rubbish from their fronts on or before the 10th of this month and also Robert Balderston to make up his fence laying down in the road at this time.' This meant that the roadsides down through the village from Upper Gate to Bell Horse Gate were well drained and cleared of obstructions. On November 7th 1754, a cold morning with sleet and rain , Alexander had problems when they were short of labourers to do the work in Bell Horse Gate. He contracted with Thomas Carr, 'to make and pave a good sufficient channel for the watter all along close to Dr Thornbeck garth wall at 1s. 2d. per rood'.

When Alexander surveyed the road down through Chapel-le-Dale he knew there was only one sensible route into Ingleton and that was on the east side of the river Wease. The stretch of the river through Chapel-le-Dale was known as the Wease at this date and the

Chapel had been Weasedale or Wisedale Chapel for centuries before Chapel-le-Dale was ever thought of. The road continued down the shoulder of Ingleborough. However, he had a problem in that to keep the road on the level ground near to the river, where he wanted it for the comfort and safety of passengers, he needed to acquire land through four fields. On August 4th Alexander Fothergill measured up for the road finding it to be 960 yards. He needed a way eight Yards wide for the road which brought the land to 7,680 acres. He reckoned the land to be worth 4d per square yard making a total of £8 3s 4d. However, On September 14th when he met with John Metcalfe, Robert Metcalfe and Jeffrey Tennant, three of the four landowners, and offered £20 for the land and damages he met resistance and commented in his diary, 'They refused to set any price until they had consulted Mr Fenwick and each other but I found by their talk that no reasonable price will be accepted.' Eventually a price was agreed, but Alexander had to wave an order signed by the West Riding JP's before things were settled.

Before the road was completed tolls bars were erected on the route to collect money from those who used the road. The turnpike tolls were let to the highest bidder at auction. The owner of the tolls bought the tolls as an investment and then usually put in a toll collector to collect the pence from passing traffic. In 1803 the Greeta Bridge Gate on the Richmond Lancaster road was let by auction at Lancaster on January 19th. The previous year it had taken £91. In 1809 Bulk Gate, Greeta Bridge Gate and Thornton Gate, also known as Ingleton Gate, were let at the Town Hall in Lancaster. The previous year, after collecting expenses, the gates had made £120, £91 and £171 respectively. The Ingleton Gate was actually in Thornton just a couple of hundred yards from Thornton Bridge over the Doe. The Greeta Bridge was between Melling and Hornby and not to be confused with the Greta Bridge on the New Road at Ingleton. By 1850 the tolls taken at Ingleton Gate were only £51. In 1854 the tolls were auctioned at the Castle Inn at Hornby. Tolls produced the previous year were Bulk Gate £105, Farleton Gate £120, Greeta Bridge £160 and Ingleton Gate £32 14s.

The toll bar keepers of Ingleton Gate at Broadwood from 1822 were recorded in the *Lancaster Guardian* in October 1894. They were Thomas Lindsay, Jennings, Thistlethwaite, Middlebrook and C. Harrison. The Thornton or Ingleton Gate bar was demolished in 1868 and stood on the roadside almost under the Ingleton railway viaduct.

The Lancaster Richmond Turnpike Road was thrown open to free use in 1878. By the 'Highways and Locomotives Act' of 1878 all roads disturnpiked since 1870 became 'main roads' and the cost of maintaining them was to be shared equally between the district through which they passed and the County magistrates in Quarter Sessions. Then by the Local Government Act of 1888 the powers of the Quarter sessions were passed to new County Councils and they had to find the full cost of maintaining the main roads.

KEIGHLEY KENDAL TURNPIKE

The second turnpike road through Ingleton was the Keighley to Kendal road. Around 1750 there was a movement in Yorkshire to put roads under Turnpike trusts and in 1753 a private Act of Parliament was obtained for the road between, 'Keighley in the West Riding of Yorkshire and Kirkby in Kendal in Westmorland'.[6]

This was already an important highway between the manufacturing districts of Yorkshire and Kendal, not only for the exchange of agricultural produce and manufactured goods, but also for the traffic in half-manufactured material such as combed wool sent to be spun in the farm houses and villages, or warp and weft for the handlooms. The width of the road was agreed upon as seven yards of which five yards would be fully surfaced. The landowners along the road rarely showed any generosity in selling the land necessary for improving the road, but where there were difficulties arbitrators were called in to fix a price.[7]

The Keighley-Kendal road came into Ingleton from Clapham via Yarlsber and the Cross. It left Ingleton by Bell Horse Gate, across the river Doe into Thornton and then up the hill where it passed close to Halsteads and Thornton Church Stile, also known as the Marton Arms, before continuing on its way to Kendal via Cowan Bridge and Kirkby Lonsdale.

There was a stone cross where the old road came into Ingleton from Settle to join the Richmond Lancaster road which gave it the name of the Cross and also the name Cross Farm. The cross disappeared centuries ago, but later an eighteenth century finger post was placed there. This tall slender milestone gave the miles to Kirkby Lonsdale, Hornby, Clapham and Hawes and Richmond. In the nineteenth century it was stolen, reportedly by the lord of the Manor of Twistleton, who kept it as a trophy. Ingleton made no great fuss and those who did were told they would not get it back. It wasn't as though they prided it at Twistleton, but simply used it as a gate post where it still stands today. It is time this historic artefact was re-instated where it belongs. It would make an interesting project for the Parish Council or other interested body.

The Ingleton toll bar house and gate on the New Road of the Keighley to Kendal turnpike c. 1875. (Drawn from faded photo)

Toll bars were built along the road, but the situation at Ingleton was complicated by the fact that the two turnpike roads both passed through Ingleton and shared a common route for a couple of miles. The 1847 OS map shows Thornton Gate near to where the railway viaduct now stands. Another Toll gate is shown on the same road above the site of the Court house and Police Station. A further toll bar, the Greta Bridge Toll Bar, was constructed following the building of the Ingleton bypass on the Keighley to Kendal road. This toll bar cottage still stands near to the iron bridge crossing the river Greta. Toll gate keepers sometimes had a second job. In 1851 Christopher Harrison kept the Greta Bridge Toll Bar on the New Road and lived in the toll house cottage with his wife. In 1871 the census shows that James Atkinson kept the Greta Gate. It is a very small cottage yet he lived there with his wife, four children and two lodgers.

THE INGLETON BYPASS
No improvement work had been done for nearly twenty years after work at Settle in 1804. Then following a renewal of the Turnpike Act in 1823 four new sections of work were planned

Bell Horse Gate a steep and narrow road.

for the Keighley to Kendal road. The one to affect Ingleton was a stretch of new road from Clapham to Westhouse. This improvement was proposed as early as 1792, but not carried out until 1823. The main purpose was to bypass the village of Ingleton because of the problems wheeled vehicles, especially coaches, had in negotiating Bell Horse Gate. It is said that horses from local inns had to come to assist stage coaches climbing Bell Horse The situation had become worse from around 1814 when stage coaches became larger and more frequent. The Union Coach started running to Ingleton in 1807 and ran to the end of its coaching days. For the first sixteen years it ran through Broadwood up Bell Horse Gate, through the main street and out on the old Clapham Road.

The new road took a new route from the lower end of Clapham over Newby Moor, past Whinneymire and Goat Gap, through several fields to join the Ingleton to Bentham road and then followed that road a short distance before cutting through further fields and crossing the river Greta by a new stone bridge.

224

The Ingleton contracts were advertised in the *Lancaster Gazette* on December 6th 1823:-

TO ROAD-MAKERS, WALLERS AND BRIDGE-BUILDERS.
KEIGHLEY AND KENDAL ROAD.
TO BE LET BY TICKET,
At the House of Mr. J. Brown, the Wheat Sheaf Inn, in Ingleton, On
Monday, the 15th day of December next at twelve o'clock at noon;

THE FORMING, MAKING, STONING and
FENCING of that part of the Diversion of
the Yorkshire District of the Keighley-Kendal
Turnpike-Road, commencing at or near Westhouse, and extending Eastwards, as the same is
now staked out, to a farm called Whinny-
mire-Hall, being in length 630 roods, or upwards.

Also to be Let at the same Place.
At two o'clock in the afternoon on the same day,
The GETTING and LEADING Materials for,
and BUILDING of a BRIDGE over the River
Greet, below Ingleton, with the Filling up,
Forming and Making the road &c. at each end of the same.

And also to be Let.
In like manner, at the House of Mr. W. NEALE,
the New Inn, in Clapham, on TUESDAY the
16th day of the said month of December, at
twelve o'clock noon.
The FORMING, MAKING and FENCING, of
The remaining part of the above mentioned Diversion
of the said Road, commencing at Whinneymire Hall,
and extending Eastward, as the same is now staked out,
to the village of Clapham
being in length 700 roods and upwards.

A plan of the above mentioned diversion and specifications for the work will be
left at the various places of letting, and at the offices of Messrs J. & W. Hartley
Solicitors, Settle. Settle November 17th 1823.

The plans for the new road were made by Mr Swire and his assistant Mr Russell of
Kendal. The Greta Bridge was designed by Thomas Anderton of Gargrave and the valuer for
the land through which the road passed was Richard Ayrton of Rylstone. The road was duly
built and completed in 1826 and the final report issued by the trustees stated that it had been
delayed 'owing to several unforeseen and in some cases unavoidable delays arising in some
degree from what no human foresight could prevent, and in part from the indefinite manner
in which our engineer had made his original levels and estimates, and also for his want of
punctuality in appearing on the line of road at the times requested by your committee and
agreeably to his engagement' Regret was expressed at the heavy outlay of near £11,000
partly due to the cost of the Greta Bridge. The bridge cost £2,548 1s 0d which included a
culvert on Newby Moor.

The 'New Bridge' at Ingleton erected in 1825 and demolished in 1933.

The old road from Yarlsber to the Cross at Ingleton became a side road when the New Road was completed in 1826. Soon after 1826 travellers discovered that they could turn off the side road into Ingleton and by making a detour through the village avoid the Greta Bridge Toll Bar. The turnpike trustees then put a chain across the side road at Three Nooked Field, which is where traffic now turns off the main road into Laundry Lane. The problem at Ingleton was that there were so many side roads than most locals could avoid the toll bars if they put their mind to it and most of them did. The problem arose again in 1868 when the Richmond to Lancaster Turnpike removed its Ingleton Gate, the toll gate near Ingleton railway viaduct in Thornton. It was then easy for travellers to turn off before the New Bridge and pass through the village, down the Rake over the rivers and then join the main road again at Thornton without paying any toll. Once again the turnpike authorities put up a chain to block people doing this and charged a toll at the chain.

This chain caused an outcry in the village. The problem was that the innocent suffered with the guilty and many people were having to pay twice. One Sunday night in April 1868 someone sawed one of the chain posts off at the ground and pulled the other post up. The police were unable to find the culprit and most people in Ingleton were pleased both that the chain had been removed and that the culprit had not been discovered. The chain was replaced, but then on July 14th a meeting of the Turnpike Trust decided to remove all trace of the chain and posts and it was removed the same day. As the chain bar had caused so much trouble in the neighbourhood there was considerable rejoicing especially among those who used their carts in the area.[8]

Other problems arose from time to time and the builders of the railway into Ingleton had problems in May 1847. A chain toll bar had been put up near to Ingleton to catch the wagons and horses bringing stone down from the quarries into Ingleton for the railway viaduct. The sub-contractor, James Smith, angered by the heavy charges being placed on the stone decided to work his railway builders day and night to bring the railway down to Ingleton as fast as possible. Then the stone was loaded onto railway wagons and brought down his own line so avoiding the toll gate. With the coming of the railway into Ingleton material rolled into the township bypassing the turnpike road and all its toll bars, for the turnpike roads it was the beginning of the end.

In 1878 the Keighley and Kendal Turnpike Trust expired and the road they had controlled since 1753 became free to public use. At a meeting of the trustees held on October 30th 1877 instructions were given to Mr Bradley, the surveyor, 'to refuse no reasonable offer for the toll-gates and that the gates must be taken off their hinges at 12 o'clock on the 1st of November and put aside and sold as soon as possible.' The roads had not been well repaired in the last years and with competition from the railway had produced less income. Several local gentry lost money when the trust was wound up including Robert Ingleby of Lawkland and the Farrers of Clapham.

DROVERS' ROADS

Drovers moved their cattle along green roads and across open fields and moorland so that grazing was at hand as well as to save wear and tear on the cattle's hooves. Later they also did this to avoid payment of tolls. It must be remembered that Ingleton and Bentham Moor was not enclosed until after 1787 and so they could take whatever route they wished over the land and their route depended on the dryness of the land. When people asked the way to Dent from Ingleton in earlier days they would be told to take any way they chose. Before Kingsdale and Thornton Fell were enclosed travellers walked over the moorland as others had done since the country was first inhabited. Thornton was not enclosed until 1812 and Kingsdale valley was open and access to Yordas cave was unrestricted.

Droving was a hardy life in open air open to all weathers, often sleeping out with their cattle and only occasionally sharing a bed in some drovers' inn. The droving routes and tradition were many centuries old and probably go back before the Norman Conquest. Scotland relied on the sale of its cattle in England and Yorkshire saw droves of them year after year. Drovers continued to bring their cattle the old way until the railways came and cattle were able to be carried to fairs and markets by cattle wagons.

LOCAL ROADS

Ingleton has many local roads, more than most Yorkshire villages, and there are several reasons for this. In medieval times Ingleton was linked with Burton-in-Lonsdale and its castle, and roads were necessary to get there. Then for centuries Ingleton was linked to Bentham in a joint manor – the Ingleton and Bentham Manor. Also until the end of the nineteenth century Ingleton was a chapelry of Bentham Parish. The Ingleton coalfield which certainly produced coal through five centuries was responsible for many coal roads being made to get coal from the mine shafts and away to neighbourhood towns and villages by pack horse and cart. Over the centuries different roads were known as Coal Pit Lane and the Old Coal Road.

In May 1911 there was a question as to whether Coal Pit Lane was a continuation of Red Ash Lane. There is little doubt that it was, for at one time coal carts regularly went that way. However, around 1882 Red Ash Lane was deliberately narrowed. It was done before Ingleton gained its Parish Council. In 1896 a complaint from Councillor Bentham at a Parish Council meeting was recorded in the *Lancaster Guardian,* 'It is not fourteen years since Red Ash Lane was narrowed. He watched it done and there was a waywarden there at the time who should have known better.'[9] Now Red Ash Lane, also known as Graberty Lane, is reduced to a footpath.

The roads in early days were extremely dusty and many places had water carts to spray the roads in summer to keep the dust down. Then tar began to be used as a road covering, but that was expensive and when it was first suggested at Ingleton the decision was made to use water which was cheaper. It was in May 1915 that the first roads were tarred in Ingleton. The High Street, Main Street, the Bank, Hollin Tree Road, West End and the New Road were

Schofield's the first garage in the New Road.

tarred at a cost of £23 7s. This was not tar and chippings put down by steam roller, but simply tar sprayed onto the road from a horse drawn boiler or brushed onto the road surface. At least this stopped the clouds of dust, but in hot weather the tar itself could become a nuisance. Eventually the tar-macadam system was used where tar and chippings were put down by steam roller.

Roads in and around Ingleton were at their worst during the building of the Settle Carlisle Railway. In July 1870 the press reported:-

As there is so much traffic on the roads between Ingleton Station and Batty Wife Hole, on the Settle and Carlisle Line, more men ought to be employed in keeping the highways in a proper state of repair. It is annoying to hear the never ceasing complaint 'the roads at Ingleton have never been so dirty, and in so bad a state of repair as they are now.' After a good shower of rain the streets and roads are thick puddles so that it is difficult for pedestrians to pick their way with daylight. Thacking Road leading to the Storrs limekilns, is so broken up and worn into hollows, that it is reported that axeltrees are broken and carts in other ways injured. The road through the dale to Ingleton Fells was never in so bad state of repair within the memory of the oldest inhabitant living. Having passed over it a few days ago after a little rain one may bear witness to its condition. Pools of water, loads of mire, deep and long cart ruts and bends across the road for miles, greeted ones eyes and caused such thumping and jumping in the vehicle that one ran the risk of breaking the springs or sustaining some other injury. To use the mildest words, roads in such a wretched state are neither creditable to the skill and management of the district surveyors, the discerning eye of the waywarden, nor the township whose duty it is to see that their roads are kept in a good state of repair. The immense traffic over a good part of the road in question is no excuse.

BRIDGES

The two bridges over the river Twiss and the Doe are about a hundred yards apart. Up to the eighteenth century they were only about nine feet wide, about half their present width, which made it difficult for carts to pass, but as there were few carts and most goods were carried by pack horse that was no real problem. However, with the coming of the turnpike road and more four wheeled vehicles the roads had to be widened. Viewed from below each arch looks like two and the join in the middle can be seen where there is a gap. In the centre of Ingleton bridge the left side drops a couple of feet lower than the right. One bridge was widened on the right and the other on the left which had the effect of helping to straighten the road. The Ingleton bridge appears to have more regular stones on the upstream side and this is most likely the newest section.

Anthony Hewitson noticed the road widening as a boy living in Ingleton and noted it in his guide book. 'The duplication has been made conversely – one enlargement being on the higher and the other on the lower side; so that the roadway here, anterior to the alterations named, must have been very crooked, and probably the additions to the bridges were made contrariwise with the view of getting it straighter'.[10]

The West Riding Quarter Session 1611-1642, note 'Ingleton Bridge, on 16th of July, 10th of James (1612) 60li ordered to be estreated on ye West Riding. It was not known who were to repair itt'. The Quarter Session record:- 'That the Bridge commonly called Ingleton Bridge over the water of Greta, and between the market town of Wakefield and the market town of Kirkby Lonsdale in Co. Westmorland, is now in great decay for lack of repair so that the King's lieges cannot pass over it without great peril to their lives. Wit. John Condor, Wm Wood, Leonard Procter'.

The Quarter Sessions meeting at Skipton in 1638 mention the bridges again:- 'Thorneton and Ingleton bridges - Forasmuch as this Court is informed of the great ruyne and decaye of two bridges situate within the parish (sic) of Ewecrosse, commonlye called Thornton and Ingleton bridges, which said bridges are usually repaired at the equal charge of both the Wapentakes of Staynecliffe and Ewecrosse, and for that information is given that the sum of viij li will but repair the same. Ordered that the sum of eight poundes be forthwith estreated upon the said wapentakes and collected by the high constable there and paide over unto William Lowther Esq, one of his Maties Justices, who is desired to see the same bestowed for the repair of the said bridges'.

The third bridge at Ingleton is the New Bridge built in 1824 or 1825 when the Keighley to Kendal turnpike road bypassed Ingleton village. In the 1920s this stone bridge taking the New Road over the river Greta began to subside and pieces broke off the abutments. The damage was so bad by September 1929 that the road was closed and all traffic re-routed through the village. The County Council, which believed that mining subsidence was the likely cause, sent Professor Fearnside, of Sheffield, to investigate. He had already advised the colliery company on geological matters and so the manager, A.B. Hewitt, took him underground. When the subject of the bridge's subsidence was raised, however, Hewitt denied that the problem was caused by mining subsidence and quickly got Fearnside out of the pit.

The colliery company, which by then was financially weak, suggested that it might go into liquidation should the County Council claim for the cost of re-building the bridge. Eventually, the County Council paid for building a new iron bridge, slightly downstream from the old stone one, which was demolished. According to Fearnside, this cost around £50,000 and J.L. Eve & Co. began the work in January 1933. The foundations of this old stone bridge can be seen upstream of the steel bridge that replaced it and it crossed the river at a different angle to the present bridge.

STREETS

The streets and roads within the village itself tell us a lot about the settlement of the place. With the Front Street and Back Gate we know we have a village settlement in a square. Between Front Street, the Bank and Back Gate were the crofts and grass garths of the villagers. It was Front Street in 1841 and Main Street in 1851. Of course names changed. Originally they were mostly called gates, the Middle English name for road. There was Upper Gate, Back Gate, Foregate, Nether Gate, Lower Gate and Bell Horse Gate - names all recorded in Ingleton's past. Foregate was up by the Wheat Sheaf and Lower gate was the lower area of the main village street in the eighteenth century. Back Gate and Upper Gate have always been a contentious subject. Upper Gate was the top area where the road joined the turnpike road and Back Gate was lower down. Back Gate was the rough area of impoverished cottages and a place of overcrowding and poverty. But Poverty itself, and Poverty certainly existed as a street, a notoriously filthy one that ran alongside the Churchyard. It was Poverty long enough and had to fight hard to clean up its image and become today's Church Street. Nether Gate was the lower portion of the village by the Ingleboro' Hotel, a venerable name, but one which fell into misuse and was forgotten. It is good to see that Bell Horse Gate, Upper Gate and Back Gate are still in use after at least six centuries.

The Victorians wanted to get away from the old fashioned 'gates' and brought in High Street which was popular and a purely Victorian introduction. Then from Poverty we went to Comical Corner, a very suggestive name of which we know little, but it is recorded in the census returns which makes it as official as anything ever was. Then there was Bridge Street which we know now as the New Road. It was generally known as the New Road from its building but Bridge Street does appear from time to time. On November 18th the *Lancaster Guardian* commented under 'Summer Improvements' that, 'The Masons Arms in the New Road, looks quite a new place since it was renovated by its owner Mr Matthewman. In every way in its improved appearance it is a credit to Bridge Street.'

In 1915 people complained that no one was certain which was Main Street and which was High Street and that other streets and roads were known by different names. This led to the Parish Council announcing an official list of street and road names in the press on December 11th 1915. The Council's sub-committee recommended the adoption of the following names:-

The Square, both the inner and outer Square; High Street from the Square to the Cross; Flatts from the Cross to Yarlsber; Storrs Road from the Cross to Granite Quarries; Thacking Road from the Square to Beezley Grange; Strands from the Square to the Strands; Sammy Lane from Thacking to the Strands Road; Oldfield Lane from the Square to Strands; Main Street from Square to Bell Horse Gate; Church Street, from the Square to Main Street; the Bank, from Bell Horse Gate to Hollin Tree Road; Hollin Tree Road, from the Bank to Tansey Terrace; West End, from Hollin Tree Road to New Road; New Road, from New Bridge to Skew Bridge; Bentham Road, from New Road to Bentham boundary; Tatterhorn Road, from New Road to Bentham boundary; Westfield Road, from New Road, to Tansey Terrace; Landry lane, from Tansey Terrace to New Road; Upper Gate, from High Street, to Tansy Terrace; Red Ash Lane, from Upper Gate to Laundry Lane; Bell Horse Gate from Main Street to Richmond Road; Richmond Road from Broadwood to Bell Horse Gate; Twistleton Road, from Richmond Road to Twistleton; Strands from Richmond Road to Strands; the Rake from Richmond Road to the Bank. There are only two changes from the old names. Brewery Lane changed to Laundry Lane and Back Gate and Upper Gate have been merged into Upper Gate. Eventually the suggestions of the sub-committee were adopted.

Demolition of the old stone bridge.

Construction of the iron bridge in 1933.

The completed iron bridge.

Now the Parish Council may have adopted the changing of Upper Gate and Back Gate into simply Upper Gate, but the people of Ingleton did not. They saw Upper Gate as slightly snooty and Back Gate as solid, working class and historic and it continued to be Back Gate to the majority, as it still is to this day. The street names came from the people of the village and they will only be acceptable when they are in line with their wishes. There was no mention of Moore Lane, Merton Terrace in the Back Gate, the Bottoms, Paul's Fold and others, perhaps this was because they caused no problems. However, these were serious decisions for the council and those decisions have been mainly adhered to.

REFERENCES

1. Vestry Minutes 1795. (Deposited NYRO 2007)
2. *Lancaster Guardian,* October 6th 1894.
3. ibid
4. Richmond-Lancaster, 1751 24 Geo II c.xvii.
5. *Alexander Fothergill and the Richmond to Lancaster Turnpike Road,* NYRO, 1985
6. Keighley-Kendal 1753, 26Geo II c.lxxxvi.
7. *The King's Highway in Craven,* J.J. Brigg, Reprint, S.R. Pubs., 1968.
8. *Lancaster Guardian,* April 18th 1868.
9. *Lancaster Guardian,* June 5th 1896.
10. *Guide to Ingleton,* A. Hewitson , 1896, p.5.

RAILWAYS

THE 'LITTLE' NORTH WESTERN

Ingleton was affected by the coming of the railways in two ways. Firstly there was the rail link from Skipton that served the village and the surrounding area and then later there was the coming of the Settle Carlisle line which passed through the outlying areas of the township and brought a station to Ribblehead. Our first consideration is the building of the railway that first put Ingleton on the rail map of Great Britain.[1] The first railway line came from Skipton. In September 1845 railwaymen came to Ingleton and took account of the traffic on all the roads leading from the township for a railway company survey. On June 26th 1846 the North Western Railway Bill received Royal Assent after which work began and the railway soon approached Ingleton. In May 1847 the line was crossing Newby Moor and wagons and horses were carrying stone down into Ingleton from the quarry for building the viaduct across the valley at Ingleton. At this time it was intended that the railway should go beyond Ingleton to Lowgill.

The Commissioners of the Keighley Kendal Turnpike put up a chain toll-gate and charged the contractors quite heavily on the stone being brought down into the township. Annoyed by this, the sub-contractor, James Smith, immediately employed his men to work day and night on the line between Newby Moor and Ingleton so that all the stone required at Ingleton could be brought down the line and escape any charges.

By August 1847 a good number of workmen were employed on the railway line above Ingleton. The first pay day took place at the Bay Horse Inn Ingleton on Wednesday August 18th 1847. In September a temporary bridge which had been erected over the river Greta at Ingleton for foot passengers was washed away by floods. Luckily the accident took place during the night otherwise many people may have been injured as from the time it was built to its destruction it was daily covered with workmen or people attracted from curiosity.

Many other accidents occurred during the work. A horse was killed when large stones were being unloaded at the viaduct and there were three accidents to men in May 1848. In March 1849 a tip driver, John Murphy, had to have his leg amputated after an accident at Ingleton. In April William Winder of Ingleton, a railway labourer, had his shoulder dislocated and his right arm crushed when a stone fell from one of the wagons. John Annan was seriously injured when two rail wagons broke loose and ran over his legs. He had only been working at Ingleton for a day and a half. The people of Ingleton were also well-aware of the presence of the railway men as many lived or lodged at Ingleton and spent a good amount of their spare time in the village inns consuming beer. Occasionally there was a pitched battle between railwaymen. In June 1849 a fight took place at Ingleton between Denis McKeaney, alias 'Ginger' and McLyn. After bruising each other for about twenty-five minutes McLyn was declared the victor.

Early in 1849 the work was coming to an end and railway labourers were being paid off. In July an engine and two carriages came down the line of the North Western Railway as far as Ingleton carrying the government inspector and a party of directors and contractors. A large crowd of locals came to view the engine and carriages. The opening celebrations took place on September 26th and the twenty-five miles of line from Skipton to Ingleton was duly inaugurated.

By the end of 1847 the North Western Railway Company was in financial difficulties and had to cut spending. In August 1848 it was decided to end the Lowgill line at Ingleton and complete the Lancaster line from Clapham. Further work beyond Ingleton on the proposed Ingleton to Lowgill line was cancelled although £18,500 had already been spent. When the line opened to Ingleton in 1849 the Ingleton viaduct had been left with only its foundations completed and in the countryside beyond, railway works had been abandoned some never to be worked on again. However, several years later the scheme was taken up again, money raised and the line continued from Ingleton to Lowgill.

The press reported in November 1858 that workmen were busy preparing for resuming the works on the North Western Railway at Ingleton. They were erecting stables for horses and doing other work. By January 1859 scaffolding was being erected for completing the railway viaduct over the river Greta. This was an immense undertaking which was completed in October 1859 without accident, although some timbers were blown down during terrible spring storms. Not only was all the scaffolding in place by October, but eight piers had already been finished and the remaining two were predicted to be finished by the end of October.

On May 8th 1860 the keying of the last arch in the viaduct took place. After the keystone had been ceremoniously fixed by the engineer, Mr Campbell, he stated, 'We have crowned this work so far as putting in the last keystone and making a completion of the arches. This important undertaking has been carried out and executed in a superior and workmanlike manner, and it affords me great pleasure that the work has so far been clear of any accident. I am extremely well satisfied with the noble structure, and I know it will stand as an honour to the builder, and as a monument of industry and skill to succeeding generations'.

At the end of his short address three cheers were given for the viaduct, three cheers for the engineer and three cheers for the builders. The viaduct which was carried out under the superintendence of Mr Woodiwiss crossed the Greta just below the confluence of the Doe and Twiss. It not only crossed the river Greta, but it joined two parishes, that of Ingleton and Thornton-in-Lonsdale. The length of the viaduct is 800 feet, and the breadth 27 feet 4 inches. It contains 1,100 cubic yards of ashlar stone, 5,100 cubic yards of stone blocks, 3,000 cubic yards of rubble and 2,600 cubic yards of brick. There are eleven arches of fifty seven feet span, the highest of which is eighty-four feet. There is a girder bridge over the road, which is a continuation of the viaduct of twenty-five feet span. A parapet of ashlar stones four and a half feet high top off the viaduct on both sides. The first stone was set on April 4th 1859 and the last keystone on May 8th 1860. At any one time an average of forty men had been working on the viaduct over the year.

On Monday evening May 14th a hundred workmen and officials sat down to a supper at the Wheat Sheaf to celebrate the keying of the last arch. The contractor, sub-contractor's engineer, local gentlemen and workmen were all present on the occasion. There was good food followed by speeches and Ingleton Brass Band was engaged for the event. On January 18th 1861 the viaduct was damaged by frost. The ballast of clay and ash expanded and began pushing off the large stone parapets. About seven-hundred feet had been removed on the north side when about one hundred and twenty feet on the south side fell with a tremendous crash. It was fortunate that no one was injured as some stones fell onto the road near the toll bar which stood between Holme Head Farm and Broadwood. A great deal of work had to be repaired.[2]

The railway viaduct at Ingleton crosses to Thornton-in-Lonsdale and takes us out of Ingleton, but it is interesting to follow the development of the line from Ingleton at least to Barbon. The work went on as the viaduct was built and from time to time there was trouble on the line. The first occasion was in March 1859 when the navvies working on the cutting between Ingleton and Westhouse went on strike because they were having to work an extra half an hour without pay. Some were discharged and others left before the strike was settled. The men eventually agreed to work the extra half an hour so long as they were paid for it.

A more disturbing development came in October of the same year when a large number of navvies stopped Mr Taylor's carriage on the hill near Halsteads. The carriage was carrying money to pay Mr Taylor's men at Casterton, but the crowd was so large and fierce that Mr Taylor agreed to return to the office near the railway viaduct. The men were under the impression that the money was their pay and was being taken away. Superintendent Exton and four constables were called and tried to remove the money, when they did the crowd became threatening and they were driven back to take refuge in the office. Eventually a messenger was sent to Casterton to bring Mr Heys, Mr Taylor's representative, and he explained that their employer had been paid the money for their wages that morning.

Following the riot, Mr King, the contractor, and two of the ring leaders were arrested and sent for trial at Leeds Quarter Sessions and were charged with riot and assault at Thornton-in-Lonsdale. The events caused much excitement in the village and some said there had been a thousand men in the crowd. Because of the riot the works under the management of Mr King, which extended from the viaduct to Byber Mill, was suspended for a time. Then the section was split into two, the first becoming a new contract and the second part being added to Mr Taylor's contract. From this time the railway works proceeded without problems. Mr Taylor's contract extended for thirteen miles and by early December 1860 six miles of line had already been laid and by the end of December the rails were completed to Barbon.

There was a sad accident in May 1861 when Mr Nicholson, the inspector for the Lune Valley Railway was injured near the railway bridge between Halsteads and Thornton Church. He lost the toes on both feet and being seventy-five it was difficult to operate and he died of his injuries. Mr Nicholson had worked on the Stockton and Darlington Railway from its beginning, which was the first public passenger railway in the world.

By August 1861 the line to Lowgill was completed and opened for goods and minerals on August 24th. The following week Colonel Yolland, the Government Inspector, passed over the line and found it satisfactory. The line was opened for passenger service on September

One of the first trains crossing Ingleton viaduct in 1861.

16th from Ingleton to Lowgill. On the day of the opening the first train from Leeds arrived at Ingleton Station about five minutes after the train for the North had left Thornton Station. On the following day when the first train was coming in, the other was going out. The result of this mutual awkwardness of the two companies was that the passengers who were travelling north had to walk the long route from Ingleton Station to Thornton station carrying their luggage. Then they had to wait five hours for the next train. This was a bad start and lack of co-operation between the two companies eventually led to the Midland Railway, who controlled the LNWR planning a route of their own through to Scotland – the Settle Carlisle route. Two stations had only been built in the first place because the two companies could not agree terms for sharing Ingleton.

The first station at Ingleton had a wooden platform and wooden buildings. There was no waiting room for gentlemen apart from an open shed. These wooden buildings were entirely removed by May 1885 and rebuilt in stone. The press reported, 'There are few country stations on any of the great railway lines that will in anyway now compare with the Ingleton LNW Station.' The new stone platform appeared to impress people the most, 'The new platforms are of considerable length and edged with substantial coping stones'.

Ingleton station around 1900.

The railway brought vast numbers of visitors to Ingleton in the Victorian and Edwardian periods. Then the motor car brought a new form of transport. With the growth of the motor car and the motor bus railways went into decline and the 1950s saw many closures including Ingleton. The last train came to Ingleton station on January 30th 1954. The station buildings slowly turned to ruin and the station yard was used as a car park. Then came the Ingleborough Community Centre and this added a new dimension to Ingleton.

THE SETTLE CARLISLE RAILWAY
The Settle Carlisle Railway only passed through the wildest parts of Ingleton Township at Ingleton Fells or Chapel-le-Dale. However, for a few years it had considerable effects on the life and prosperity of the village. The railway also left Ingleton a legacy in the form of a magnificent viaduct, and the station at Ribblehead, which are still in use. The Settle Carlisle Railway came late in the railway age. George Stephenson, his son Robert and many of the

Last passenger train at Ingleton station on January 30th 1954. William (Billy) Routledge, wearing a flat cap, is the centre figure.

Ingleton's derelict station in 1965. (H.L. Holland)

other early railway engineers were dead. But the Midland Railway wanted a direct route to Scotland and so in the 1860s their engineer, Charles Stanley Sharland, was sent to survey the route for the proposed railway. He walked the seventy mile route from Settle to Carlisle in ten days. An oft' repeated story tells that at one time Sharland and his men were snowed up at the Gearstones inn for days or even weeks and had to tunnel through snow to the local water trough. Sharland withdrew from the railway project in November 1870 due to ill health and died of tuberculosis at Torquay the following March: he was only twenty-six.

The Railway Bill received Royal Assent on July 16th 1866. The L.N.W.R was quite disturbed at the revenue it might lose and started talks with the Midland to reach an agreement which would save the Midland, having to spend a vast amount of money on their new project. However, work on the new railway had begun and to abandon it would need Parliamentary agreement. Abandonment plans were put to Parliament but were rejected and the Midland had to go ahead and build. This meant the end of any prospect of Ingleton becoming part of a main route to Scotland: it would become a quiet rural branch line.

How did all this affect Ingleton? For a start the population almost doubled in 1870 and this is shown in the census return. In 1861 the population was around 1,600, in 1871 when the Settle Carlisle railway was under way the population was 2,541 and in 1881 it was back to 1,625. Most of these people were railway workers living in the Shanty towns of Batty Green, Batty Wife Hole, Sebastopol, Jericho, Jerusalem, Belgravia and others. The name Sebastopol came from the Crimea where British navvies under Peto had built a railway which was important to the success of the campaign and had helped in the capture of Sebastopol in September 1855. However, there were also those who came to the village itself. Horse dealers moved in to supply the horses needed, and dealers in beer and other goods which came into Ingleton station and had to be carted up the Hawes Road to Ribblehead.

Everyone appears to think that the majority of the navvies working on the Settle to Carlisle line were Irish, but this is a complete myth. Irish navvies were a rarity and the exception and were often picked on and bullied by the other men. The 1871 Ingleton census shows that the first twenty men shown in the shanty towns came from a wide variety of counties including, Derbyshire, Yorkshire, Middlesex, Sussex, Lancashire, Dorset, Surrey, Oxfordshire, Somerset, Herefordshire and Northamtonshire. It would be difficult to find a county in England and Wales not represented at Ribblehead. A great deal that has been written on the Settle Carlisle line is second and third hand. The following material is mainly taken from what was written in the press at the time, and though the language might be Victorian and antiquated, it is what the people were thinking, saying and doing.

In May 1870 a ganger called Frank Taylor showed signs of bad feeling towards an Irishman, John O'Neil. He incited other men to hatred and about forty of them made their way to John O'Neil's hut near Winterscales. Frank Taylor shouted, 'I give you notice that if you are not out of this hut by tomorrow night, I shall either pull it down or burn it over the top of you'. William H. Ashwell, the contractor, took the man to Ingleton for police safety and to report the situation. The police superintendent and two constables went to the railway workings where they found that Frank Taylor had already absconded after which all quietened down'.

About the same time a navvy working on Mr Woodiwiss' site went up to young Mr Woodiwiss and used insulting language to him. The engineer of the line was also present and they told the man to go away. On his way the navvy met an Irishman and beat the unoffending man with a crowbar. The engineer intervened and had just given the navvy a good thumping when Mr Woodiwiss senior arrived on the scene and instantly discharged the man.

The press recorded. 'One might think that drink was the principal commodity for sustaining navvy life, for men are rushing from all quarters to the petty sessions aided by their several layers to get the magistrates to recommend their applications to the Honourable Commissioners of Inland Revenue for permission to sell beer and other excisable liquors till the ensuing Brewster Sessions. As there has been so much illicit trade the magistrates have been generous with applicants'.

The Hawes road to Batty Green became rutted and worn with the constant traffic which left Ingleton day and night to keep the railway and railway workers going. Ingleton felt the navvies had become all important and a press correspondent wrote:-

Ingleton's streets are kept alive nearly night and day by the rattling of wheels, the cracking of whips, and the shout of men travelling with their brand of goods for the navvies at Batty Wife Hole. Tailors and drapers, shoemakers and grocers, bread-bakers and butchers, green grocers and beersellers, may be seen carrying their wares to supply the varied and ever recurring wants of the men who are working the Settle and Carlisle Railway. Beer is an important item in the wants of navvies. And there is no lack of well filled beer barrels. Indeed beer is considered so necessary an article in the daily want of navvies that at times it may be seen on its transmission route at three o'clock in the morning. One might think that the navvies were the most important men in the neighbourhood for men and goods are coming from every quarter for their advantage. It is evident that tradesmen in every department are vying with each other to make the most of them. *Lancaster Guardian,* June 25th 1870.

On Monday, August 1st 1870 Mrs Powell and her niece, Annie Wall aged seven, arrived in Ingleton to go to Sebastopol, near Batty Wife Hole, where they lodged. The day afterwards they continued to Blea Moor where they were to live. An engine and trucks derailed on a temporary line and Annie Wall was buried in earth and killed: Mrs Powell was badly scalded.

One of the many wonderful results of railway making is that of bringing in a short time a large population into a locality, where men never from the beginning of the world had thought of pitching their tents. Batty Wife Hole and Blea Moor are places so bleak and dreary, that had it not been for the making of the Settle and Carlisle railway, they might have remained unnumbered ages before they would have been selected sites for human dwellings. Only a few months ago scarcely anything was heard on these moorland wastes but the bleating of sheep, the barking of shepherd's dogs, and the discordant notes of the grouse, but now all is life and bustle and human dwellings have sprung up like mushrooms. The clang of pick and spade, the rumbling wheels of railway wagons, the shrill whistle of locomotives, well-fed horses with their loads of coal, timber, rolls of felt, household furniture, wives, mothers, and children on their way to their new homes, iron rails and other materials, are things of daily occurrence.
There is a brewery on the opposite side of Batty Green and a large Tommy shop and other dwellings are being built near Batty Wife Hole. One of the dwellings in this little wooden town is differently constructed to all the rest, as from its appearance it must have served as a caravan. It was said that it was brought all the way from London, and that it was the first dwelling fixed on Batty Green. Mr H. Ashwell's spacious railway yard is at the west end of Batty Green. Here was noticed a blacksmith's shop, saw mills, carpenter's shed, stable, pay office and stores. There are about 132 huts, each capable of supplying accommodation for eight lodgers, from Batty Wife Hole to the end of Mr Ashwell's contract at Dent Head. The population of Batty Green is from 300 to 350, at Sebastopol 200 to 300, and at dent Head etc. near 300.' *Lancaster Guardian,* August 20th 1870.

At Batty Moss there was a limekiln for burning lime and a brick making machine which in full operation made between around 20,000 bricks each day. The clay for the bricks came of the moss and was ideal for brick-making and was free for the digging. The two major works in the Ribblehead area were the Ribblehead Viaduct and the Blea Moor Tunnel. You will still hear it told how the viaduct was built on bales of wool. If someone tells you that just laugh: the viaduct was built on deep foundations of concrete and masonry. It is amazing how the stories of bridges being built on bales of straw and bales of wool survive. The Ribblehead viaduct has twenty-four arches, is 440 yards long, and is 104 feet high at the highest point. The first stone was laid by the contractor, William Ashwell on October 12th 1870.

Blea Moor Tunnel is 2,629 yards long and was started in 1870 and completed in November 1874. The tunnel is half in Ingleton township and half in Dent. The most dramatic events took place at the north end of the tunnel when several men were trapped by floodwaters and Thomas Bell was drowned on July 9th 1870.

The only way to get engines up to the railway works was via Ingleton. In taking such heavy loads up to Ribblehead horses were often changed or extra added on the route: the spare horses were kept at farms along the way. When an engine was due to be moved it caused a considerable stir in the village:-

On Monday night the street was crowded with spectators, carters and horses, so that the Queen's highway was greatly obstructed. The cause of this unusual gathering was a monster steam engine which was on its way to Batty Wife Hole. The engine was brought to the station by the Midland line, and then drawn by horses to its destination. It required fourteen strong horses and the assistance of a large number of men to get it above Storrs that night. To the credit of Mr Moody who was in charge of Mr Ashwell's horses, he would not allow a whip to be used. The horses with the assistance of the men whose exertions had been stimulated by the promise of a pint of beer each, drew the monster machine up the hill in fine style. On the following day they managed early on in the forenoon to get the engine to the summit of the steep hill on the other side of Chapel-le-Dale. Up this hill the team consisted of twenty-four horses. *Lancaster Guardian,* June 4th 1870.

Much excitement was caused at a very early hour on Monday morning, as it was generally known that a railway engine would be drawn by horses up the Storrs Brow on its was to Mr Ashwell's contract, Batty Wife Hole. About 3am the tramp of Mr Ashwell's sleek-skinned and well fed horses warned many of the people that if they wished to see the removal of the engine from the Back Gate their snug quarters must be quitted without delay. Thirty or more horses were yoked up to the locomotive, as they drew it in fine stile up the Storrs, which was one of the most difficult ascents of the journey. It was a fine sight to see so many horses willingly exert themselves to draw the ponderous machine. Though the hour of departure was early, many women as well as men accompanied the lengthy team to above the Storrs. It was well for both man and beast that the weather was so fine, or the imperfect state of the road would have made the transit of the engine a difficult matter. *Lancaster Guardian,* June 3rd 1871.

You may have read that hundreds of workers died building the Settle Carlisle Railway in the Ribblehead area which is quite untrue. The number in the Ingleton section was quite small. The majority of deaths in the railway shanty towns were women and young children. The burials mainly took place at the little church at Chapel-le-Dale and the small burial

Name.	Abode.	When buried.	Age.	By whom the Ceremony was performed.
William Dean No. 233.	Sebostopool	Jan. 22	11 month	Wm Harpur
John Hollerenshaw No. 234.	Sebastopool	Jan 24	40 years	Wm Harpur
Charles Bibby No. 235.	Sebastopool	Jan. 31	9 months	Wm Harpur
Louisa Annie Thompson No. 236.	Jericho	Feb. 1	3 years	Wm Harpur
Fredrick Little No. 237.	Inkerman	Feb. 5	4 years	Wm Harpur
Tom Atkinson Little No. 238.	Inkerman	Feb. 9	1 year & six month	Wm Harpur
Thomas Smith No. 239.	Jericho	Feb. 12	10 months	Wm Harpur

BURIALS in the Parish of Chapel le Dale or Ingleton Fells in the County of York in the Year 1871

Extract from Chapel-le-Dale Church burial register for 1871.

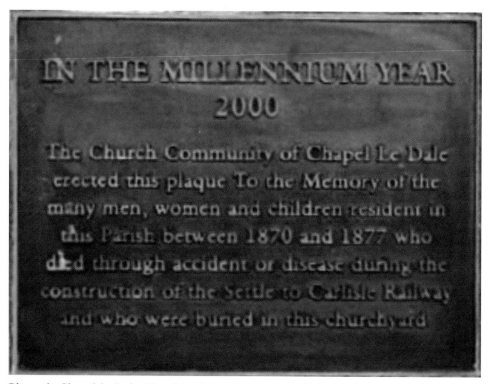

Plaque in Chapel-le-Dale Churchyard to commemorate all the Settle Carlisle Railway
dead who lie there - men, women and children.

organising a series of concerts in the school. Smallpox caused many deaths and a smallpox
isolation hospital was built. Many deaths to navvies were caused by drunkenness and
recklessness. Men when drunk laid down on the railway line to rest and were run over while
in an unconscious state.

The memorial plaque in Chapel-le-Dale Church commemorates only the railway workers
who died in the building of the Settle Carlisle Railway. This in spite of the fact that by far the
greater number who suffered and died were wives, children, domestic servants, tradesmen
and visitors: these camp-followers had no mention. However, this was put right in the year
2000 when a stone pillar and plaque was set up in the churchyard to commemorate all the
men, women and children who had died during the construction of the railway.

On Friday morning the 9th inst, another fatal accident occurred on the tramway between
Batty Wife Hole and the south entrance of the tunnel on Bleamoor. About 6am the
engine left Sebastopol with six earth wagons attached to it, when John Lee, the
deceased, and other railway workers were on the train. When the engine entered one
of the cuttings about a hundred yards beyond Winterscales huts, the driver shut off
steam, when Lee who was sitting on the front of one of the wagons towards the end of
the train, fell off and two wagons passing over his arm and leg broke them. William
Lang who was riding in the same wagon called to the engine driver, he immediately
stopped the train, when Lang and Thomas Barker ran at once to Lee's assistance and
got him from under the wagon. After Barker had staunched Lee's wounds, as well as
he could, they carried him to his lodgings at Sebastopol and sent for the railway
doctor. When the doctor arrived about an hour later, Lee had sunk so far from the loss

of blood that he was unable to rally. He was sensible to the last, and a short time before his death occurred at 10am he dictated the name and address of his sister who lives in Wiltshire. T. Brown Esq held an inquest on the body of the deceased on the 12th inst., at the Viaduct Inn near Batty Wife Hole, when the jury gave the following verdict; died from mortal injuries by an accidental fall from an earth wagon in motion, on the Settle and Carlisle railway. The deceased was interred at Chapel-le-dale. *Lancaster Guardian,* September 17th 1870.

Another fatal accident by falling from a wagon happened in September 1871. George McConnel was a travelling razor grinder and rag gatherer who visited the railway shanty towns:-

In this occupation he visited the huts at Bleamoor on Saturday the 23rd. Every Saturday afternoon a train starts at the tunnel to take the work people who wish to go buy their week's provisions at Batty Green. The train is known as the 'market train.' James Oldfield, the guard of the train, who was the principal witness at the inquest, said that the market train, which had started from the tunnel about 2pm consisted of two wagons and an engine. On arrival at Jericho about 2.30pm George McConnel was allowed to ride to Batty Green. There were about ten passengers on the train who were all requested to sit down at the bottom of the wagons. The deceased, who disregarded this caution, sat on the far end of the first wagon. When they had travelled about a quarter of a mile, as the guard saw that the points were wrong, he called out to George Dudley, the driver, to pull up, when he at once threw off the steam and reversed his engine. On the points being adjusted the engine was started when the passengers were again cautioned to sit down and hold tight. At starting the trucks gave a jerk, when George McConnel fell from his seat onto the line. The guard called out to the driver 'stop the engine, a man has fallen overboard,' The engine was stopped and reversed. The guard who ran to the assistance of McConnel found him under the second wagon in the centre of the tramway. After giving him some water to revive him, he got him into the wagon when he was conveyed to Mr Mather's Welcome Home. After he had been seen by Dr Green and his assistant Dr Heighton, he was conveyed in Mr Ashwell's spring cart to his home in Ingleton. It appears that the deceased in his fall had been caught at the lower part of his body and right thigh between the buffers. On Sunday 24th about 2.30pm George McConnel died, in the 86th year of age. *Lancaster Guardian,* September 30th 1871.

The two main problems at Ribblehead were the weather and the ground itself. The weather was frequently wet and the area was well known for its strong winds. Much of the land around Batty Moss was sphagnum moss and bog where a worker could sink knee deep into the morass and horses had great difficulty in working. 'Once when four horses were dragging a telegraph pole over such a swamp the exertion became so great that one of the beasts tore a hoof off'.[3]

Bog carts were made which ran on a large revolving barrel rather than wheels and did not sink into the ground. However, the clay they had to deal with was often so hard that it had to be drilled or blasted. Yet after rain it turned to the consistency of thick porridge, sticking to everything it came in contact with from tools to wagons.

One cutting was made to take wagons through it and rail lines were laid. It rained in the night and by the following morning the cutting had collapsed and the rail lines had disappeared in the mud. Two years later when another cutting was being made the railway line appeared again. 'A splendid discovery for a geological fellow,' said the engineer. 'He could prove lots from this. Here is a railway in the glacial drift, in the glacial period, rails, sleepers and all. Then the world must have been inhabited then; there is nothing new under the sun'.[4]

One of the saddest occasions during the period occurred in September 1871 following the deaths of twins Emma and Miriam Wardle. The girls survived only four days and arrangement were made to bury them at Chapel-le-Dale cemetery. The story was told in the *Craven Weekly Pioneer* under the title Singular Funeral:-

> A funeral of a strange character took place in the graveyard at Chapel-le-Dale, on the 6th inst. Notice of interment of twin children had been given by a working man on the Bleamoor Railway Works, to the curate in charge of the parish during the winter absence of the Rev. E.Smith, fixing the time at 2.0 pm on Wednesday 6th inst. On the day named, the funeral cortege arrived at the Chapel yard about five minutes before the time mentioned, when it was found the gate was fast, and that there was no appearance of either clergyman or sexton. At length the parson arrived, when he coolly told the bereaved father that he had quite forgotten that the funeral was to take place, consequently no grave was made, as no notice had been given to the sexton. Under the circumstances, the father had to borrow tools, dig the children's grave, toll the bell, act as clerk, and then to complete the sad and melancholy affair, he had to fill up the grave he had made.

Luckily the Court House and police head quarters for the whole of Ewecross were at Ingleton and Superintendent Exton and his police were able to keep in close touch with activities at Ribblehead. Most of their problems were petty crime and drunk and disorderly charges, although more serious crime occurred from time to time. There was also a mission at Batty Wife Hole run by James Tiplady, aged twenty-six who titled himself as 'Home Missionary for the Midland Settle & Carlisle Railway Company,' Church services were regularly held. In 1871 a school was opened at Batty Green and children of the railway workers were given a basic education. Jane Herbert, the teacher, who was twenty-one years

The Station Inn and Ribblehead viaduct. The sender of this post card complained of the noise the trains made at night as they slept at the inn.

old shared a hut with James Tiplady and a sixteen year old domestic servant. The school was also used for concerts. By the time the railway works came to a close there was mission hut, school, reading room and hospital.

In September 1875 there were objections to renewing the licences at Ribblehead and this was a sign that things were coming to an end as far as Ingleton township was concerned. Some licenses were renewed but the following year of 1876 there was only one licence renewed at Ribblehead and that was for the Travellers Rest. By September 1875 the press were reporting that most of the huts on the moor have been removed, and many of the working people had left. Eventually all the sites were cleared and the area returned to its rural calm. On December 4th Ribblehead station was opened. Now you will find only the Ribblehead Station, the Station Inn, and the Ribblehead viaduct standing in magnificent isolation.

REFERENCES

1. Much of the information in this chapter came from: *The 'Little' North Western Railway*, D. Binns, Wyvern Publications, 1982; *The Lowgill Branch* R.G. Western, Oakwood Press, 1971 and *The Ingleton Branch, A Lost Route to Scotland,* R.G. Western, Oakwood Press.
2. Where dates are given the material is most probably from the Lancaster press.
3. *The Railway Navvies,* T. Coleman, Book Club Ass., 1965, p.193.
4. id, p.194.

TOURISM

In *Portrait of the Dales* Norman Duerden describes Ingleton as 'a Beauty Spot without Beauty.' Joseph Carr the Victorian Ingleton writer said that his first impressions of Ingleton village were far from favourable. 'It was so unshapely and out of line in its streets, and many of its houses had been put up without the least regard to order or harmony. Some of them were built to the very edge of the street, while others stood some distance back, and I thought it was the queerest village I had ever seen'. Carr tells us that there was an old saying that 'Ingleton was the last thing God created and he left it unfinished'. Well if there is not great beauty in the village of Ingleton there is character; and as for beauty there is plenty of that in Ingleton's surroundings, you only have to lift your head and look. Jessica Lofthouse, who wrote profusely of Lancashire and Yorkshire, stated in her book, *Country Goers North,* that, 'Within a five mile radius of Ingleton are more wonders to the square mile than anywhere else in England, a fact that tourists have been aware of for over two centuries'.

The first tourists to Ingleton came in the late eighteenth century. They were usually writers, artists and fairly wealthy travellers coming to explore the mountainous areas of Yorkshire which were becoming quite popular. The Poet Gray came to Ingleton, Southey wrote here and the world famous artist, Joseph Mallord William Turner, painted in the township. Lord Torrington passed through on his travels as did others. The caves in the Ingleton area also achieved popularity in the eighteenth century and the Rev. John Hutton describes his visit to the scenery and caves in the Ingleton area in his book *A Tour to the Caves*, which was published in 1780.

He stayed at Thornton Church Stile and visited Yordas Cave in Kingsdale. Leaving Yordas he went via Twistleton to Ingleton. While staying at the Bay Horse Inn at Ingleton he took an evening walk to view the slate quarries and river scenery. John Hutton is one of the first to record and publicise Ingleton's scenery. Having described the steep slate quarries on the one hand he continued:-

> On the other hand was the river rolling down from rock to rock in a narrow deep chasm, where there was no room for human foot to tread between the stream and the rugged, high, steep rocks on each side. Several pieces of the slate were bespangled with yellow marcasites of a cubic form, and different sizes, and others were gilded over with various foliages of ferns, pines, oaks, and other vegetables. We crossed the river by means of broken fragments of rocks, which afforded us their rugged backs above the surface of the water to tread on. Here we met with a fine field for our entertainment as botanists. There was the lady's slipper, the fly orchis, rarely to be met with elsewhere, and many other scarce and curious plants. We crossed over to take a second view of Thornton Force, on the south side of the Kingsdale river, and followed its murmuring stream down a deep glen, fortified with high precipices on each side, to Ingleton.

Joseph Carr who was born in Bentham, but who came from an old Ingleton family, wrote *Rambles about Ingleton,* a guide book on Ingleton scenery in 1865. It was the first of its type, but similar guide books have been produced continuously since that date to the present time. Joseph Carr, a well-built, nonconformist preacher, was also a press correspondent with a lively interest in the Ingleton area. He was especially interested in the scenery of the river valleys of the Doe and Twiss and he explored it regularly. The valley of river Doe which forms the boundary between Ingleton and Thornton was most inaccessible. There was a rock barrier at Creepingsteads which blocked access into Swillabottom. Joseph Carr said that in his early rambles he never met with a fisherman, tourist or even a farmer through whose land the rivers ran.

Joseph Carr spread the word of the interesting river scenery in Ingleton and others offered to join him including Frank Kidd, Edward Thistlethwaite the village postmaster, George Smith of Storrs Hall and others. Meanwhile Joseph Carr's guide books spread through the area. The railway had come to Ingleton in 1849 and a few people came to see the area. By 1858 cheap trips from Leeds were ending at Ingleton station bringing some visitors to Ingleton, although most had already got off the train. The ones who came climbed Ingleborough, walked to Thornton Force and visited Weathercote cave. Then after Carr's 1865 publication more people came to visit Ingleton.

The people of Lancashire and Yorkshire town were eager to get into the countryside now that the railways made this possible. With growing leisure-time and money they were eager to find places that would give them attractive countryside and fresh air and Ingleton certainly offered these. Churches and chapel folk came on day trips and were welcomed by their fellow chapel folk in Ingleton. On July 3rd 1875 the *Lancaster Guardian* recorded:-

SUMMER RAMBLES

Ingleton, on account of its fine scenery and health-promoting mountain breezes, is becoming increasingly popular as a place for summer rambles. On Saturday last the choir of Salem Chapel, Nelson, visited the neighbourhood for a day's out. After taking breakfast in the Sunday School department of Bank Chapel, they sang with good effect some of Sankey's melodies in different parts of the village to the delight of the villagers. On Tuesday 29th ult., the choir of the Wesleyan Chapel, Colne, visited the neighbourhood and took refreshment at the same place as the Salem choir. It may be to the advantage of choirs and Sunday schools to be informed that the Bank Chapel is open free to all religious sects, either for rest or refreshment. The Colne choir, after the example of the Nelson choir, sang many select pieces both in the village and at the station before their departure. Their singing was highly appreciated and much talked about by the people. Both choirs took the same route through Swilla Bottom by the Pecca Waterfalls and to Thornton Force. The bold and diversified scenery was much admired and especially at that point where four or five waterfalls can be seen from one standpoint. The leaping white streams and deep dark pools where their foaming for a time was checked, were scenes of mountain grandeur surpassing anything they have previously witnessed.

On July 30th 1878 a long excursion train brought visitors from Leeds, Bradford, Shipley and Keighley. Though the passengers had the choice of getting off at stations before Ingleton, around four hundred came to Ingleton. On this occasion problems arose when the visitors were charged for walking over the fields to Thornton Force, a route which had previously been open to free access. Visitors expressed their annoyance, but the tenants said the charge was made to compensate for damage done by tourists. Over the next few years tourists continued to come to Ingleton and the Midland Railway provided more excursion trains as they saw that Ingleton was providing more accommodation and making refreshments available. Whit Monday 1883 saw six hundred visitors arrive at Ingleton station. These developments led Joseph Carr and other Ingleton men to form the Improvement Committee and open out the falls walks in a more organised manner.

THE IMPROVEMENT COMMITTEE

The early explorers at Ingleton waterfalls needed ropes and ladders to make a safe journey through the river scenery and then they had many hair-raising moments. Joseph Carr wrote regularly in the *Lancaster Guardian* and slowly over the next twenty years more people came to hear of the attractive scenery at Ingleton. In March 1885 Joseph Carr met Thomas Moore in the street at Ingleton and they discussed the need to make an easy entry to the Ingleton scenery at Broadwood into Swillabottom. Thomas Moore, one of the most well-known men in the village, agreed to see some of the local hotel keepers and others and arrange a public meeting. Joseph Carr agreed to have a notice printed and displayed in the village.

Edwardian tourists on the Bank.

The public meeting was held on March 14th 1885 at the Ingleboro' Hotel. There was not a large attendance and many who attended had not even seen any of the scenery. However, an Improvement Company was formed and a committee appointed. Joseph Carr was appointed chairman and secretary and T. Bonnick treasurer. The committee were comprised of the Rev. J. Turner, R.B. Ellershaw, Dr. Grime, J. Hewitson, John Slinger, landlord of the Ingleboro' Hotel, A.S. Kirk of Greenwood Leghe, Sam Worthington of the Wheat Sheaf, and John Kidd of Blue Hall.[1]

The committee and others gave money to get the work started and Joseph Bentham was appointed to plan the roads and employ the necessary men to do the work. As the weather was fine the roadways were soon constructed and the entrance at Broadwood tidied up. The Improvement Committee received great praise and many more people contributed money to the project while others donated timber for fences, posts, seats and wooden foot-bridges.

Arrangements were made with the tenants who held the land and they were mainly happy to be paid for any damage to their grass. However, the Rev. Fisher of Hornby refused permission for a foot-bridge to be built across the river at Beesley. A report was sent to the Lancaster Press and *Leeds Mercury* and the resulting articles prepared for the opening which took place on Good Friday April 11th 1885. The opening was a great success with five excursion trains bringing in visitors from Leeds and other towns.

The success enabled the committee to further improve the walks by making seats, fixing wooden bridges and steps where the ground was rocky and steep. Visitors came into Ingleton in such large numbers that many houses provided refreshments and some offered accommodation. The first season was a great success and the farmers were happy with the arrangements for compensation as they were given a share in the profits made. As the walks extended from the north end of Swillabottom to the Pecca waterfalls, Thornton Force and Ravenwray through the Glebe land, an agreement was made with the tenant, Thomas Maudesley. The glebe was Church land under the Dean of Worcester and the tenancy was yearly.

The Ingleton area was a favourite place for botanists because of its wild flowers and especially its rare ferns. One problem with opening up the falls was the digging up of plants and ferns. The dealers in ferns did the most damage. Some of them stayed for weeks and sent large crates of ferns to different parts of Lancashire and Yorkshire. Tables were set out on the falls walk with ferns and plants for sale and boys and girls sold ferns from baskets in the streets of Ingleton. There was an outcry against this as rare plants began to disappear. Boards had to be erected to warn against damaging the plant life, but problems with fern gatherers lasted for years.

The Improvement Committee were keen to stress that the improvements were not only being done for people coming by train from a long distance, but also for local people. Many of the inhabitants of Ingleton and the villages around were ignorant of the natural scenery on their own doorstep.

On Saturday August 8th 1885 the first fatal accident occurred at Pecca falls. Alice Parker, the wife of Bentham postmaster, John Parker, fell onto rocks and into a pool below. Benjamin Holroyd, of Accrington, threw off his coat and plunged into the seething water, but he could not get within a yard of the body which was being swirled round in the centre of the pool. He became exhausted and had to withdraw before being in danger of drowning himself. A second man, Ebenezer Berry, from Over Darwen went into the water with a rope round his body and eventually with the help of others the body was recovered. The pool was thought to be sixteen feet deep at the time. The body was taken to the Marton Arms. It was thought a wound on her head caused her death and the inquest found a verdict of 'accidentally killed'. Alice Parker had been given a stick by her husband to help her walk up the hill. She put the stick on a loose stone which caused her to overbalance and fall into the pool below. The Parkers had been part of a Bentham Church Choir trip arranged by the rector Rev. Joy.[2]

The Improvement Committee continued their work in the village and in the river valleys. The first problem came when there was a claim for increased compensation for the right of way over the Glebe Allotment on the Thornton side of the river Doe. This became a fear for the committee that as they had only a yearly agreement, some of the farmers would demand more compensation than the committee could pay. In 1885 funds were raised by concerts and a gala. The committee hoped for help from the trades-people and farmers, but they deluded themselves into thinking they were running things effectively and could continue to do so. In their own public service they had overlooked the jealousy and financial temptation of many in the village. Some, though working on the committee, were ready to take over for their own benefit

In a letter to the press and signing himself as Johnie at Crinabottom, and written in mock local dialect, someone noted the problems of lack of food and services at Ingleton with the influx of visitors. He advised people only to make reasonable charges for food and drink or visitors would be driven away. He ended, 'Another thing sud be kept back, and that's jealousy o'yan another. We sud remember that ivery yan hes as mich reight as another to mak' an honest penny, and that it's a mark of covetous disposition an bad breedin when there's a feelin o'envy and yan gits mear custom than another.'

Visitors rolled into Ingleton by rail at Whitsuntide 1886 and records were broken. The first train on Whit Monday left Blackburn at 5am and arrived at Ingleton around 7am with eight hundred passengers, or excursionists, as they were often called. On Whit Monday around two thousand came, on Tuesday five thousand and on Saturday near six thousand. The local folk were astounded at the number of visitors who flooded the village as well as fanning out into the falls and surrounding countryside. The church was being rebuilt in 1886 and many skulls were found under the floor. On one occasion the police had to go to Ingleton station in an attempt to recover skulls about to be taken home by tourists on their excursion train to Bradford.[3] On another occasion so much cutlery disappeared from the Wheat Sheaf that the landlord, Sam Worthington, went to the station himself to recover it. In 1885 around sixty thousand visitors came to Ingleton and in 1886 the number reached around one hundred thousand.

However, all was not well at Ingleton. There were rumours that the Improvement Committee were using the money from the walks for their own gain and lining their own pockets. The stories spread to the press and the Rev J. Turner, Joseph Carr and Alfred Kirk, who were among the most honest men in Ingleton had to suffer much abuse. It made it worse as they were sincerely working for the good of the public. Perhaps one or two of the Improvement Committee such as Sam Worthington and John Slinger made money from the increased tourist business in Ingleton, but the majority did not.

The Improvement Committee became the Ingleton Improvement Company so that they could raise funds and carry on their work more efficiently. At their meeting in August 1886 the Committee decided that instead of taking any dividend they would provide a new church clock for the village and they also make a gift to the Wesleyan Sunday school. The new church clock arrived from Potts of Leeds in December 1886, but the face of the old clock was reused. The Improvement Company had a difficult task in dealing with six tenants and their landlords and this led to their downfall in 1887 after a short but active life.

In the spring of 1887 some tenants on the falls walk took over the walks without any formal notice, ignoring written and verbal agreements made with the Improvement Company. The Company had spent a great deal of money making roads and they were offered no compensation.[4] The Company went to court to get compensation for work done between 1885 and 1888. It was the Ingleton Improvement Company v Makinson and others. Mr Drinkall, the tenant at Thornton Hall had let the paths to Joseph Hopkinson of Huddersfield. The tenancy of Thornton Hall was deliberately changed so that agreements could be broken by a new tenant. Hopkinson had offered the tenant £40 per annum and the landlord £10 and took over that section of the falls walk. He was a carpet-bagger from Huddersfield and a financial opportunist. Hopkinson, who ran the Britannia Works in Huddersfield had originally been asked to make signs for the walks and had offered to provide some free. There is no doubt that he saw the financial opportunity and was one of the plotters against the Improvement Company.

In 1887 Joseph Hopkinson, in partnership with Messrs Downham and Denny on the other river, charged 3d entrance to all the scenery. Then in 1888 farmers Sutton and Downham joined up with Sam Worthington and opened the road through the old slate quarries on the Twiss and charged 2d entry. Joseph Carr recorded in his memoirs, 'As to the owners of the Skirwith estate, they took our bridges and everything we had done without saying, 'Thank you gentlemen for increasing the value of our estate to a very considerable sum'. They would not even give us the opportunity of taking the walks at any rent, and let them to a person by the name of Denny'.

A problem came as Hopkinson's tickets still gave the impression that all the scenery could be viewed for 3d. Articles were written in the press advising visitors to avoid this trap, but the problem continued. In August 1894 a group of around 1,200 visitors from Blackburn came to Ingleton on two special trains. They hired the Low Demesne and a brass band for recreation. They walked the fall run by Sutton and company for 2d per person, but ignored Hopkinson's scenery as he would give them no discount. In 1896 Joseph Hopkinson leased the Skirwith estate part of the walks and began to charge 6d for both walks whether people wanted both or not. The press advised visitors as follows, 'Go in parties and offer 3d each, be firm and give no more. If the offer is rejected, without any more parleying walk forward on the footway, which is plain enough and after walking a short distance turn left up a slight ascent, and then forward to Thornton Force and Ravenwray, then cross the river to Twistleton, and go on to the entrance to Beezley walks, and all this for 3d each.'

The question of rights of way became a contentious one. Many in Ingleton were worried about losing the right of way through Broadwood and over the Helks to Thornton Force. They were also worried about losing their right of way to Quarry Wood on the Twiss. There is no doubt that the scenery owners were closing rights of way and would have closed others but for the outcry. The Parish Council reminded those who complained that all the people of Ingleton had the right of way through the falls. The scenery owners had guaranteed free access for all Ingleton people and there was no cause for complaint.[5] In 1899 a further enquiry was held at Ingleton about rights of way in the scenery area. Mr Procter said, 'that a complete round of the entire scenery was now an established fact, and he would advise them to let well alone. Ingleton people were now admitted free, but if they did not let the matter drop, they might have to pay in the future. The thanks of the Council was given to Dr Waller, Dr Whittingdale, and Messrs Downham, H. Brown and G. Mattocks for their evidence'.[6] There was a considerable outcry from Ingleton people who thought the Parish Council had sold them out by not insisting on their rights of way. They said it was a matter of principle not 6d for a scenery walk.[7]

Once the railway arch was built across Broadwood the scenery company blocked the rights of way beyond to the Helks and Thornton Force. Then they built their pay box in front of the arch and all but a few courageous people were intimidated. The man at the ticket office would ask, 'Have you a ticket sir?' 'No this is a public footpath'. 'Where to sir?'. 'Thornton Force'. No it isn't sir'. But of course it was and the worry was that if people accepted a charge on the road that could be later presented in court.[8] Years before when Anthony Holgate, tenant of the Glebe Allotment blocked up the stiles on the public footpath Joseph Gillbanks, landlord of the Masons Arms, went to clear them and threatened to clear them again if necessary. Hopkinson's men would take the name and addresses of local people even on a right of way and threaten them with court action. Joseph Hopkinson died suddenly on Sunday October 6th 1895. He had married into the family of Richard Brown at Ingleton and for a time lived in Broadwood cottage. He was a Liberal member of Huddersfield town council.

Unpleasant rivalry continued at Ingleton for many years as the rival scenery companies vied for custom. On one occasion the village bellman was engaged to meet excursion trains and announce that all visitors were requested to enter the walks by the Broadwood entrance as the walks on the other side were closed. This was completely untrue. Men were also sent round the falls to divert people to their own walks and away from their rivals.

Eventually the falls came under one ownership and the situation became more stable. The Worthington family ran the falls walks for many years. William S. Worthington worked in the falls walks from 1919 and was in charge for many years, taking over from his father Sam Worthington, and continuing until around 1960. Then his nephew Dennis Worthington took over. Dennis was an ex- Yorkshire policeman and sadly an alcoholic who left bottles in the roots of trees around the walks so that he was never far from a drink wherever he was working. He built up debts at the Three Horse shoes and other places in Ingleton. He used his Ingleton postcard collection as part of a debt repayment to Tommy Sydney, landlord of the Three Horse Shoes. Many of these photos have been used in this volume as the author bought the collection from the Sydney family.

Had the Improvement Company been supported by Ingleton's farmers and landowners then today there could have been a source of income for the village to pay for amenities and improvements. Sadly however it was lost to commercial enterprise and now the village has little control over its scenic walks and the prices charged for viewing them.

THE LAKE SCHEME

Several schemes were promoted at Ingleton both to beautify the area and to encourage visitors. One such scheme was

BAXENGILL GORGE, INGLETON.

BEAZLEY FALLS, INGLETON.   1204

to make a lake between the Craven Lime Works and Quarry Wood. It first came to light in July 1891 when it was heralded in the local press. The promoters said that nature had already done most of the work. The Lords of the Manor were said to be in favour of the scheme and it had already been costed by John Hewitson and R. Atkinson. At a public meeting at the end of July, chaired by Joseph Carr, everyone appeared to be in favour and many tradesmen promised to donate seats.

By February 1892 the area had been well surveyed by Messrs Hall and Baker. Mr Seddon, Lord of the Manor of Twistleton was in favour of the lake as was the Craven Lime Company. Bath and boat houses were being proposed and many looked forward to skating on the lake in winter. The promoters felt sure that a lake would make Ingleton more attractive as a summer resort.

A company was proposed to carry out the work and Mr T. Seddon, who owned part of the site selected for the lake, and Mrs J. Seddon lady of the Manor of Twistleton had made a promise to take up shares. The lake was proposed at a time when the waterfalls walks had been open for seven years. At a public meeting in April 1892 a report by Messrs Harrison, Hall and Moore was read out:-

GENTLEMEN – We have carefully considered the proposition as to making an artificial lake on the site pointed out to us. The site is admirably adapted to such a purpose both from an engineering point of view and from the beautiful natural surroundings. It seems as if nature had intended it to be a lake at the southern end, for at this point the rocks on both sides converge, and the channel of the stream is reduced to less than one half its width, and the strata as far as could be seen from a superficial inspection is well calculated to support without risk of fracture any strain that might be placed on or against it. It seems to us that a large area of water might be embanked at a relatively small cost, and without much or any risk to owners further down the stream. We have been advised that your Committee before proceeding with this construction of the lake must get consent in writing of the owners of, if any, mills below the proposed lake as they could stop the Committee by injunction from completing the lake, probably after considerable expense had been incurred. The danger of the bank bursting is very small owing to the strength of its position, and if a good strong job is made we could not see how it would be possible for the bank to give way.

The drawbacks to the scheme are to some extent its advantages. It has rock on all sides even at the bottom. It has been found that water escapes through the various fissures, rents, and caverns which are always found in a district like Ingleton; and there is a possibility that when the lake is completed, the water would gradually but certainly be forced through these fissures, and in a dry summer the lake might become dry ground.

Something was mentioned about making the lake four or five feet deep over the whole area. This we cannot advise. The money required in the first place for this purpose would be about £1,500; much better to spend a little more on the strengthening of the bank and beautifying the banks of the lake. We think that it is not improbable that ere many years have elapsed, the winter floods will of their own accord have filled the deeper portions of the lake with rocks, boulders and gravel, and ultimately the Committee would have to go to some expense excavating or removing the same. Sometimes in situations like the intended one, where winter floods assume considerable proportions, the filling up is very rapid.

It is impossible with the limited information at our disposal to give accurate information as to the costs of an embankment with fish-pass, and by-wash, but it would not be safe to put it down at less than £1,500, although from the proximity of good material and the natural advantages that the rise gives for a strong bank, a very considerable saving might be effected. Nevertheless this is one of those cases where economy must be a secondary consideration. If there is any other matter that you think of, kindly write, and we shall be pleased to assist you in any way in our power to bring to a successful issue what must, in the very nature of it, be a very great additional attraction to your already beautiful neighbourhood – We are, yours faithfully, Harrison, Hall and Moore.[9]

Delays came in the plans for the lake and they were mainly due to the difficulties in arranging terms with the owners of Skirwith and Manor House estates. Land from both estates was needed and the ground being of little value for pasture it was thought it might be rented on moderate terms. Skirwith Estate finally agreed to lease the land for a hundred years at £10 per year. The committee considered that two or three acres would be needed from the Seddon's land and began negotiations with them. However, in December 1893, due to the sudden death of Thomas Seddon, heir of John Seddon, Lord of the Manor of Twistleton and Ellerbeck, negotiations stopped. Following this loss Mrs Seddon announced that she did not wish to be involved any further in the scheme and that put an end to the proposed lake at Ingleton.

Youth Hostel at Greta Towers.

YOUTH HOSTEL-GRETA TOWER

The house was built by John Kidd of Ingleton. For many years it was a private residence and then it became a guest house for visitors as so many of Ingleton's residences did. It was run for some time by proprietors Barratt and Fenton. When Margaret Lowcock had the house she considered turning it into a cinema. Around 1937 it was taken over by the Youth Hostel Association. Previously the youth hostel had been at Storrs Hall. A report in April 1936 said that, 'In spite of the weather the number of campers at Ingleton was more than usual and the Youth Hostel at Storrs Hall was full'.[10]

CARAVANS

At a meeting of the Dales Tourist Association in 1955 one reason given for the drop in stays at guest houses and hotel was the increase in caravans. There certainly had been an increase in touring caravans enabling tourists to move from one spot to another. At this time static caravans are only mentioned as being used by site engineers and such for living away while working. However, static caravans were soon to become an important part of Ingleton's tourist scene.

When Frank Greenwood took an interest in caravans in 1958 there were only ten caravans in the Ingleton area. He first called his business Broadway Caravans and then it became Broadwood. By 1968 there were 297 caravans. Frank Greenwood had several sites at

Broadwood, Marton Arms and the Trees, but although commonly called Ingleton they were in Thornton-in-Lonsdale and Westhouse. A large caravan park was also developed at Greenwood Leghe and a small one on the site of New Ingleton Colliery. As well as contributing to local rates, caravans have brought visitors to Ingleton and contribute to trade in the village.

CAVES

About half of all the known caves and pot-holes in the country are in the Ingleton area. Ingleton has been a centre for caving for around two hundred years, although many of the caves are actually outside the Ingleton boundary. Yordas Cave, one of the caves visited in the eighteenth century, is in Kingsdale in the parish of Thornton-in-Lonsdale and there are many other caves in the same valley. There were caves in Chapel-le-Dale which were fashionable to visit in the nineteenth century. Weathercote Cave was a popular cave, but has always been on private land.

The nearest show cave to Ingleton village was Storrs Cave on Storrs Common. A short opening among the rocks of Storrs Common had long been termed Storrs Cave. In Victorian times there had been an attempt to supply Ingleton with water from this cave, but the supply was too small. However, there were a few men in Ingleton who considered that if the entrance was opened out it might prove an important and interesting cave. In 1884 a fund was raised for this purpose and work began. Workmen soon had the cave explored to a distance of seventy yards. The chief promoters of the scheme were Messrs, Hopkinson, Hewitson, Bonnick, Slinger, Worthington, Bentham and Boyd: John Hewitson was in charge of operations.

By July 1884 the entrance had been made secure and the cave opened out and made ready to be a show cave. Blasting work was still going on and the walkways were laid with timber. After being open for several years in the Victorian period it was closed because it became dangerous due to the timber flooring becoming rotten and slippery.

WHITE SCAR CAVE

The main show cave at Ingleton and the one with the most interesting story is White Scar Cave which lies on the slopes of Ingleborough on the road from Ingleton to Chapel-le-Dale. White Scar Cave now claims to be the longest show cave in Britain and contains one of the largest caverns in the country. This cave system was said to have been first discovered by Christopher Francis Drake Long in August 1923. Long had visited Cheddar show caves as a boy and seeing people paying to visit the caves made him determined to find a cave of his own in the hope that he also could open it to the public and make some money.

However, the cave entrance had been known for centuries and John Playfair noted it in his travels through Ingleton in the late eighteenth century, but he did not explore it and in reality did not know that it was a substantial cave of any note. However, as he was a noted geologist, it became known as Playfair's Cave. Reg Hainsworth of Ingleton along with friends actually explored the entrance in the early 1920s. They were stopped only because of a decomposing sheep and although they said they would return to explore further they never did. So in reality it was Christopher Long and his friend John Churchill who first explored and opened up the cave.

Christopher's father was a doctor in York and in 1921 Christopher went to Cambridge University to read medicine. Here he set up the first caving club in Cambridge called the 'Troglodytes'. As they were a considerable distance from any caves, Christopher had his fellow cavers practising caving by crawling through the sewers of Cambridge. Whenever he had time he came north where along with his friend John H. Churchill he spent much time exploring Stump Cross Caves.

Long and his companion Churchill came to Ingleton on August 9th 1923. The pair sat on the hillside at Scales Moor and looking across the valley they saw the possibility of there being a cave behind one of the rock fissures in the hillside opposite. Eventually they explored the hillside and discovered the entrance to what is now White Scar Cave. The first thing the explorers found was the skeleton of a sheep not far inside the crevice. This was probably the decomposing sheep Reg Hainsworth had encountered at an earlier date. Long and Churchill then negotiated a long wet crawl and all this with only candles for light. On this first journey they found the first waterfall and then the second waterfall before they returned to the outside.

Christopher Long outside his newly discovered cave in 1923.

They were thrilled by their first explorations and returned again the next day. They were soon resolved to blast the narrow entrance and open it up as a show cave for others to explore and enjoy. Work began and good progress was being made until money ran out. Then in September 1924 Christopher Long was found dead after taking an overdose of chloral hydrate, which he used as a sleeping medicine. As Long suffered from manic depression and was known from his school and college days as an emotionally disturbed young man, it was assumed by many that he had committed suicide. However, the Coroner's inquest said that there was no evidence to show whether he had taken the overdose accidentally or with the intention of causing death.[11]

Christopher Long was buried in the graveyard at Chapel-le-Dale where there is a gravestone in the form of a Celtic cross. The inscription records, 'In loving memory of Christopher Francis Drake Long. Born 12th August 1902. Died September 3rd 1924. In the light of all lights we see the light'. After many years the grave became much neglected and complaints led to its renovation, but many have said that Long's best memorial is White Scar Cave itself.

The work was continued and of course needed considerable capital investment, which was mainly supplied by Geoffrey Swift, a solicitor from York and friend of the Long family. The cave was opened to the public on April 10th 1925. Soon after the opening John Churchill left the country to work in Nigeria. Swift was left as sole proprietor and appointed Tom Greenwood as manager. Having taken over the management of White Scar Cave it became

Work to open White Scar Cave to the public.

Tom Greenwood's main interest in life. Ever since it has prospered with regular improvements being carried out, and extensions being made to allow visitors to travel further into the mountain. On the death of Geoffrey Swift, who died on active service in July 1942, Tom Greenwood became lessee and managed the cave until his death in April 1947. His grave in Chapel-le-Dale churchyard reads, 'In loving memory of Tom Gordon Greenwood of White Scar Cave who died April 18th 1947'.

The cave passed to Tom Greenwood's widow and daughters. Daughter Mabel Sharp continued to run the cave as both owner and manager. During the time she managed the cave further exploration was allowed. Following Mabel Sharp's announcement that she would retire in 1970 family disputes led to a High Court judge ordering that the cave be sold by auction on February 20th 1975. The family had killed the goose that laid their golden egg! The cave brought £23,000 which was far less than expected. Many local business men at Ingleton thought of buying the cave, but did not attend the auction considering that the price would be beyond their means. The cave, being underground, came under the mineral rights of Amey Roadstone Corporation who leased it for a fixed rental plus a percentage of takings.

The cave was bought by Anthony Bagshaw of Marchington Hall Uttoxeter. Bagshaw installed Julian Barker as manager and Julian, as Mabel Sharp before him, lived in the bungalow which stood on the site. Bagshaw being a businessman was keen on publicity and erected a large flagpole and flew the Union Jack. The Yorkshire Dales National Park objected to this although most in Ingleton were happy with this and flew flags in support. Then the flagpole disappeared one night and was found on Ingleborough – it all gave excellent publicity for the cave owner.

In 1982 the owner bought a twenty foot green dinosaur and fixed it in front of the cave. This contravened planning regulations and Ingleton parish Council, the North Yorkshire County Council and the National Park all protested. Then one night the dinosaur was decapitated and more publicity was gained. Eventually following the threat of litigation by the National Park the dinosaur was taken away.

Exploration and development of the cave proceeded under the management of both Mabel Sharp and Julian Barker and the cave was fully surveyed. A great chamber was discovered in

1971 by a caving group led by John Russon. They called the massive cavern which is over 330 feet long, Battlefield Chamber because its boulder-strewn floor looked to the first explorers as if it had been the site of a battle of giants.[12] It was this chamber that Anthony Bagshaw planned to open to the public in 1986, but due to various problems was not opened until May 1991.

In 1995 the cave did have a major setback when seven tourists were locked in the cave after closing time without light or means of getting out. The group which included an eight year old child had strayed from the main party. They managed to get back to the entrance and smash their way out with a sledge hammer which they found. The management then had no method of counting visitors in and out of the cave and no one noticed the cars left in the car park. White Scar Caves of Uttoxeter were fined £10,000 at Skipton Magistrates' Court. The incident reported in the *Craven Herald* and Lancaster press brought adverse publicity.

Following the death of Anthony F. Bagshaw in 1999 his son Anthony took over. It is possible to find full details of the cave on the internet and even take a 'virtual tour', but there is nothing like visiting the cave in person and experiencing the real thing.

PHOTOGRAPHERS AT INGLETON

Ingleton attracted artists and photographers following the opening out of the river scenery in 1885. Valentines of Dundee, Friths of Reigate, Vaughans of London, Parkinsons of Bolton and other national concerns sold albums of photographs and single photos for a long period before the coming of the post card era.

THOMAS MOORE

Thomas Moore was the first photographer in Ingleton and was the first to take photographs of the waterfalls. In connection with the early development of photography he used to visit Manchester, Blackburn, Lancaster, Windermere, Durham, Skipton, Hawes and different towns in Westmorland. He was a Jack of all trades, rate collector, newspaper correspondent, sign

The Wheat Sheaf hired carriage, horses and driver too.

painter, fiddler, brass engraver, artist, photographer and more. The 1871 census return shows him living in the main street aged forty-nine and recorded as a photographer. One of Thomas Moore's daughters married a Capstick and he had a grandson Thomas E. Capstick who by 1891 was eighteen and his assistant photographer. The family lived in Moore's Lane.

TOM CAPSTICK

Thomas Capstick was the grandson of Ingleton's first photographer, Thomas Moore. He was born at Dent but lived most of his life at Ingleton. He took over Sawdon's studio in Broadwood. He produced many post cards of the Ingleton area. In 1901 he was living in Main Street with his wife Alice and young son Norman. He was twenty-eight and was noted as a photographer working from home. He had a photographer's shop in Main Street Ingleton and also sold china and fancy goods.

WILLIAM HENRY SAWDON

William Sawdon worked at Ingleton for many years. He was born in Pickering in Yorkshire about 1860. In 1891 he was aged thirty-one and living on the Bank at Ingleton with his wife Fanny and family. In 1892 he bought Prospect Cottage at Ingleton and lived there until 1901. His employment is given as photographer and artist. He later moved to live at Bentham. Carr in his memories of Ingleton tells us that he had a shop in the village. We also know that he had a wooden built studio in Broadwood itself to catch the tourists. William Sawdon painted in oils as well as being a photographer.

WILKINSON

In 1891 Joseph Wilkinson was working as a photographer in the main street at Ingleton. He had come from Trawden in Lancashire. He lived with his wife Annie and a boarder who worked as a photographic printer. Joseph Wilkinson eventually moved to live in Burton-in-Lonsdale. Joseph Carr in his memoirs says that, 'Messrs Sawdon and Tom Capstick of Ingleton and Wilkinson of Burton-in-Lonsdale, late of Ingleton, have done much by their wonderful art to make Ingleton known as the land of the waterfalls'.

REFERENCES

1. *Recollections of Ingleton*, J. Carr, 1896. ed. J.I. Bentley, 1991, pp, 44,45.
2. *Lancaster Guardian*, August 16th 1885.
3. *Recollections of Ingleton*, J. Carr J., 1896, ed. J.I. Bentley, 1991, p.87.
4. *Lancaster Guardian,* May 7th 1887.
5. *Lancaster Guardian,* September 4th 1896.
6. *Lancaster Guardian,* April 8th 1899.
7. *Lancaster Guardian,* April 15th 1899.
8. *Lancaster Guardian,* August 20th 1898 & January 7th 1899.
9. *Lancaster Guardian*, April 16th 1892
10. *Lancaster Guardian ,*April 17th 1936.
11. *Craven Herald,* September 12th 1924.
12. White Scar Cave, Chapel-le-Dale, North Yorkshire, *Cave and Karst Science,* Vol 33, No.2, 2006, Stephen A. Craven. (This is the most comprehensive article on White Scar Cave.)

INGLEBOROUGH

The first of England
These eyes to fill
Was the lifted head
Of that proud hill.
Lawrence Binyon

Ingleborough was a Beacon Hill from time immemorial and there is little doubt that beacon fires have been lit there from prehistoric times to the present day. It is specifically mentioned in the 1588 list of beacons in the West Riding of Yorkshire drawn up when the Spanish Armada was threatening. 'Yewcrosse Beacon. There is but one beacon in Yewcrosse standing upon a high mountain called Engleborough, which standeth in the way from Skipton to Kendall or Wharton in Lancashire and so to the next sea.' Dr Whitaker, writing in his Craven history in 1805, tells us, 'that within living memory fires were lit on the Craven Hills every 9th of August, St Laurence's Eve, as a memorial to the beacon fires, of which Ingleborough was the chief, kindled by the Saxons to alarm their countrymen on the approach of the Danes'.

On the night of Queen Victoria's Jubilee, June 21st 1887, a huge bonfire was lit on Ingleborough, the illumination of which was seen beyond Leeds a distance of some forty miles. Many people contributed to the expenses of the bonfire including the Rev. J. Turner minister of Ingleton, Rev. M.T. Farrer of Clapham, Major Foster of Hornby Castle, T.F. Fenwick of Burrow Hall, and C.M. Saunders of Wennington Hall. The cost of the bonfire was £11 10s 10d :-

Expenses

	£	s	d
Paraffin, 18 gallons(Co-op)	0	13	6
Paraffin barrel (Co-op)	0	3	0
Four barrels (Co-op)	0	10	0
Coal and timber (Ingleton collieries)	0	13	10
Carting materials from Ingleton, 3 tons 6 cwts at £1.5s per ton.	4	2	6
Getting peat	0	8	0
Taking peat up	0	5	0
Pulling heather	0	10	0
Taking heather up	1	0	0
Carting timber given by Rev. M.T. Farrer	1	5	0
Carting timber given by Mr Hewitson	1	0	0
Total	£11	10	0

In addition Mr John T. Coates gave two barrels of gas tar for the fire. Mr Foster of Yarlsber and Mr Ormrod of High Leys carried all the material to the summit and six Ingleton volunteers were chosen to sustain the fire during the night. Upwards of sixty fires were visible from the summit of Ingleborough that night, June 21st 1887, ranging mostly on the south and west from Pendle Hill to Skiddaw. The above is just one instance of a beacon fire on Ingleborough and many were known to have taken place in the last two centuries.[1]

HEIGHT

Whernside, Ingleborough and Penyghent
Are the highest hills 'twixt Tweed and Trent.

This is an interesting rhyme, but it is not true. Scafell Pike, Scafell and Helvellyn have this distinction. In 1786 Thomas Hurtley of Malham gave the height of Ingleborough as 5,280 feet quoting Jefferys.[2] Whernside was given as 5340ft and Penyghent as 5220ft. This would have made Ingleborough considerably higher than Snowdon at 3571 feet and Ben Nevis at 4406 feet. In 1810 Ingleborough was given as 3,987 feet high by Houseman. *A Geographical and Historical View of the World* by John Bigland in 1810 states, 'The mountains of Craven in Yorkshire, especially Whamside, Pennygant and Ingleborough are the highest in England'. The Ordnance Survey of the area wasn't done until after 1840, so publications such as this could account for the often quoted rhyme. Bigland quotes Houseman's tables of the heights of the principal mountains in Great Britain, measured by Donald & Waddington.

John Bigland concludes 'But great precision, as well as skill, is requisite for measuring the height of mountains. A late excellent mathematician, Mr Ewart of Lancaster, having measured the height of Ingleborough with select instruments and the greatest amount of care, found the results to be as follows: Height of Ingleborough above the level of the sea by barometrical measurement 2,375.12 feet; by trigonometrical measurement 2,380.79 feet'. Ewart's measurements are quite remarkable for their time as the modern Ordnance Survey map gives the height of Ingleborough as 2,373 feet.

There was a series of articles and letters in the *Yorkshire Dalesman* in the 1960s on the heights of Yorkshire mountains.[3] Ingleborough stands an isolated and solitary well defined mass, so easily identifiable from many parts of Lancashire and Yorkshire. Perhaps it was this commanding and imposing aspect that made early writers greatly overestimate its height. Having quoted the heights of Ingleborough, Whernside and Penyghent from the 1786 figures the writer in the Dalesman comments with Yorkshire humour, 'But I am willing to concede that they may have worn down a little since then!'

Ingleborough mountain.

HORSE RACING ON INGLEBOROUGH

Around 1760 a reader of the *Gentleman's Magazine* requested to hear something of the mountain of Ingleborough in Yorkshire. As nothing was published a reader sent an article on Ingleborough which was published in 1761.[4] The writer who signed himself Pastor was probably a minister living in the area as his information was very detailed. In the article there is just a short mention that within the memory of those living horse races were held on the summit of Ingleborough in the eighteenth century. But for this article in the *Gentleman's Magazine* we would probably have never known of it. It is said that on the last occasion a horse and rider were killed and the practice was ended.[5]

HOSPICE

The building and opening of a tower on Ingleborough was a memorable event in the history of the Ingleton. It was called the Ingleborough Hospice indicating that it was for the benefit of all who climbed the mountain. Hornby Roughsedge of Bentham House, and one of the Lords of the manor of Ingleton, was the main promoter of the scheme. He obtained subscriptions and was the main subscriber himself. One man who was there at the opening was John Thomas Coates who said that he was sixteen years old at the time, and as he was born in 1814, this would make the event about 1830.[6] He also said that many local gentlemen, as well as Hornby Roughsedge, contributed to the building fund.

The Hospice on Ingleborough, built c.1830.

The tower was a circular and substantial building with a dome roof. A round stone table for refreshments was fixed in the centre. It looked as though it would resist winter storms for many years and with occasional repair last for ages. Over the door of the tower were the word 'Pro Bono Publico'. Many people looked upon the project as a waste of time while

In 1890 the cairn on the summit of Ingleborough still showed several courses of the old Ingleborough Hospice at its base.

others were keen to see the edifice built as an attraction to the area and especially to those who climbed the mountain. During its erection people watched with telescopes from miles around and proclaimed it one of the wonders of Lunesdale. The promoters decided to make the opening of the tower a memorable event.

The opening took place in the summer and people came from all the villages around. The chief features of the day were feasting, racing and drinking. The racecourse was round the summit of the mountain, which was about a mile. In one race twice round the summit, Smith, a well known Ingleton miner, won the first prize, Kit Foster of Yarlsber the second and a Clapham man the third. A collection was made from the spectators to meet expenses.

At night it is said that drunkenness and mischievous rowdiness led to the desecration of the tower and much damage was done. The stone furniture was smashed and some of the ornamental copingstones were thrown down. Hornby Roughsedge and his friends who had planned and carried out the building of the tower were so angry they vowed to do no repairs. The blame was put on Ingleton's miners and if they were to blame it was most likely because they had no liking at all for Mr Roughsedge, the Lord of the Manor; they found him patronising, aloof and unsympathetic to their situation. However, the Hospice Tower did stand for many years before it was reduced to a complete ruin. A drawing of the hospice by Miss Jarry of Settle showing it in a partially ruined state is dated August 21st 1839. The ruins lay near to the south-west of the mountain's edge. William Routledge of Ingleton had a framed drawing of the hospice and in the back was an article entitled, 'The Hospice on Ingleborough.' The writer concluded his account, 'In the writer's opinion it might be replaced by some simple windshield for the benefit of those who climb the peak – Nov. 1923.' This was in fact carried out thirty years later.

STINTING INGLEBOROUGH

In August 1802 Holly Platt estate was let by ticket for two years. The farm consisted of eighty acres and 'unlimited rights of common on Ingleborough.' In 1848 meetings were held in Ingleton with the intention of applying to the Enclosure Commissioners for power to stint Ingleborough.[7] Stinting is a term little used today and needs explanation. The number of cattle a farmer could put on the common pasture were known as stints, but in Yorkshire the term was usually cattle or sheep gaits. However, when it came to allocating those sheep gaits the term stinting was used.

However, the efforts were frustrated. Farmers drove their sheep in unreasonable numbers upon the commons which caused many complaints of overstocking. A Parish meeting in 1850 resolved to get notices printed warning farmers that if they should turn more sheep and cattle onto the commons than they were allowed then they would be prosecuted. The farmers considered that as long as the 'unlimited right' remained in force the smallest farmer could put as many sheep and cattle on the commons as the largest farmer.

In 1877 a meeting was held in the National school at Ingleton to again consider the stinting of Ingleborough. There was an estimated 1,700 acres on common which was mainly around ten farms whose farms were on the borders of the commons. The farms were Chapel House, Dale House, Skirwith, Fell End, Yarlsber, Slatenber, Cross, Holly Platt, Dry Gill and High Leys. The two main opponents at that meeting were Mr Gill of Holly Platt and Mr Jackson of Dale House who proposed an amendment not to stint. They claimed that they took their farms with unlimited rights of common and had no wish for that to be changed. The steward of the Lord of the Manor was present and it was explained that a two thirds vote were needed to enclose land and a third to stint. A resolution was passed that Ingleborough be stinted and that Storrs and Cold Cotes commons be enclosed, if it can be done on application to the Enclosure Commissioners'.[8]

However, no progress at all was made over the next few years. In 1881 the subject was brought up again. This was done because the rights were confined to only a few farmers and that unlimited right to Ingleborough caused over stocking. There was also ill-will caused by some farmers moving neighbour's sheep from the best pastures. This illegal act was usually known as 'dogging' as dogs were used to drive off the sheep. Time passed once again before a meeting of those landowners who had right on Ingleborough met in 1883 to consider stinting the waste lands of Ingleton.

Unless the landowners of Clapham-cum-Newby would join in fencing off their areas, the expense for Ingleton would be excessive. If both areas joined, only one Commissioner would need to visit for both groups. Mr Bateman, steward of the Ingleborough Estate, represented M.T. Farrer. He said that Mr Farrer was in favour of the scheme and he owned three quarters of the Parish of Clapham-cum-Newby. They talked of the walling needed and a proposal to find if Clapham-cum-Newby would join Ingleton and enter into an agreement was carried unanimously.[9]

In May 1884 the Rev. M.T. Farrer, lord of the manorial rights to the east side of Ingleborough, was asked to join the Ingleton Committee to get the whole of Ingleborough stinted. A deputation visited him, but still no progress was made. Meetings went on for years but in spite of resolution after resolution nothing happened. After another long delay of five years a meeting was held in December 1889. A new special committee was appointed consisting of Messrs, Kirk, Carr and Ellershaw, but they were unsuccessful and the attempt collapsed. Joseph Carr's final comment was, 'To fail, after twelve years agitating by public and committee meetings, corresponding with widely scattered commoners and numerous visits to Settle, was enough to make the most energetic committee give up in despair. If equal justice cannot be done to a useful portion of the community without so much trouble and expense, it is time that some reform should take place in the method of stinting commons.'[10] There is no doubt that forces were working against the stinting committee and they probably knew it. Through their stewards and solicitors the lords of the manors pretended to be interested, but in fact they appear to have deliberately instituted delays and probably never intended to let the scheme go ahead.

INGLEBOROUGH MOUNTAIN RAILWAY

In 1895 a new scheme came to the notice of Ingletonians – the building of a mountain railway to the summit of Ingleborough. The idea had been suggested a few years before, but it was not until after a railway had been opened to the top of Snaefell in the Isle of Man that the idea became popular. The line was to be something less than four miles long and would climb to the summit of the mountain. The promoters said that it would be a great attraction and addition to Ingleton's tourist facilities. There was also the consideration of 'mountain treasures ready to be won' as it was proposed that limestone and millstone grit could be quarried and the bog or turf moss be worked.[11]

By 1898 plans had been made for the Ingleborough tramway and much support raised. 'There is a fair prospect, unless insurmountable opposition should arrive, of grand old Ingleborough doing greater service to the public than that of a site for sightseeing. What advantage will a tramway be to the public? It is impossible to tell in how many ways. There are millions of tons of good building materials, which if quarried could be of great service to a rising town like Ingleton'.

The promoters gave no thought to environmental problems claiming that the idea of marring the scenery was nonsense. However, opposition began to mount and one writer wrote, 'Thank God there are enormous difficulties in the way of this precious project for one thing the bog between Crina Bottom and the summit is calculated to swallow some thousands of pounds alone. The writer was T. Harrison of Carlisle who was a native of Ingleton.' His comments appeared under the title, 'Outcry against tramway'.[12]

A committee was formed and activity towards the building of the tramway pushed ahead. John Hewitson prepared plans and estimates and a limited liability company was launched. It would go to within seventy feet of the summit and would be four miles long. It was to start from the Hawes road half a mile out of Ingleton and would run up Fell Lane for a quarter of a mile. A passing place for trams going the other way was marked on the plans. Near Red Gait Head the line would cross the bog lands for a distance of forty yards, where the bog is only from two to four feet deep. There would be one level crossing over an accommodation road and about eight culverts. The estimated cost was from twenty to twenty-five thousand pounds. The steepest gradient would be one in thirteen and the sharpest curve towards the summit of the hill of an eight chain radius. Specimens of stone and slate from the summit were exhibited in aid of the project.

Fifty landlords supported the scheme as did Ingleton's magistrates and many local people. However, the promoters did not get all their own way, a defence committee was formed to stop 'the proposed mutilation of Ingleborough.' But meanwhile Mather & Platt of Manchester were involved in detail planning for the railway and on March 10th 1898 Dr Hopkinson, the managing director of Mather and Platt of Manchester visited Ingleton. Dr Hopkinson having surveyed the route for the electric railway approved the scheme and said that his company would take up a large number of shares in the project. People in Ingleton were also considering taking up shares and a possible prospectus had been drawn up.

Then the Lords of the Manor decided against the scheme, and as important landowners, they were able to put an immediate stop to development. The committee members were most indignant and threatened to get an Act of Parliament if necessary. However, enthusiasm slackened and people in the area turned their thoughts and energies to providing electric light and power for the village and the Ingleborough railway scheme came to nothing, while the Ingleton Electric Light and Power Co was formed and flourished.

A MOUNTAIN TO CLIMB

For visitors to Ingleton, Ingleborough was always the mountain that had to be climbed. As tourism grew in the nineteenth century people climbed Ingleborough from many directions, but from Ingleton the usual route was via Fell Lane and Crina Bottom.   For several years, on Whit Monday, the Methodists in Ingleton held 'love feasts' on Ingleborough. These meetings were held in the morning and people came from all directions. On these occasions there were several speakers on what Joseph Carr termed 'that lofty platform'. At the close of the service some people walked around the summit to admire the view before descending to Ingleton to join the old people's tea.

CRINA BOTTOM

On the occasions when it was felt members might not reach the summit, open air services were held at Crina Bottom. In July 1860 the promoters stated, 'Crina Bottom is on the west side of Ingleborough and is one of the most secluded and lovely spots in creation. The scenery at this season of the year is enchanting. There is a lovely Swiss-looking cottage, sheltered by the rugged limestone scars- the spruce in its richest green, growing amongst the fantastic rocks - the Foal's Foot on the side of the majestic hill, with its piles of broken rock- the flat on which the meeting will be held with a green sward surpassing that of the most carefully attended lawn'.

Crina Bottom on the slopes of Ingleborough is a farmstead that many have found a step too far from the village of Ingleton. Some have enjoyed the isolation for a while, others have occupied it as a summer residence, but some have come to grief there. Edward Burrows of Yarlsber left, 'one close called Crinabotom,' to his daughter Alice in his will made in 1647. In 1780 the farmstead passed from Francis Kidd to John Metcalfe. It was described as an 'Inclosure with dwelling house and barn' and was recorded by a deed of February 19th 1780.

The next known inhabitants of Crina Bottom were the Guyers family. George Guyers owned cottages in the Back Gate and a small field on the north side of the river Greta. He cut hay in that field and carried it home to Crina on his back as he needed it. Crina Bottom was a lonely place to live especially as the couple grew older. About the end of January 1815 Jenny Guyers went out to get some meat from High Lees and never returned. Her husband raised the alarm and the village constable and many folks in Ingleton came to help in the search for the old lady who was eighty-two. Eventually the woman's body was found on the mountainside by a shepherd's dog, but in the meantime the husband, aged seventy-eight, had fallen sick and died on Sunday February 26th. On the following Wednesday, March 1st, the couple were buried together in the same grave in Ingleton churchyard.[13]

Crina Bottom.

In December 1823 the Ingleton Court Rolls show that Lawrence Lambert of Wrayton passed Crina Bottom farm with three enclosures to Martin Kenyon of Ingleton. Martin Kenyon was perhaps nicknamed Tibby as the *Lancaster Guardian* of December 25th 1897 records that Tibby Kenyon and his sister occupied the farm, and that once two men tried to rob the sister after the sale of a cow.

About 1830 the Overend family of Bentham bought Crina Bottom and made a small mountain retreat of it for the summer months. Then about 1840 they left and moved to Darlington. They added to the front of the house and they put the curious rockery stones in place.[14] Crina Bottom is spelled Cryne Bottom on the Tithe Map of 1847. At that time there was the farmhouse, garden, and two enclosed fields, Near Meadow and Far Meadow, consisting of four acres of land. Mrs Overend was still the owner, but the occupier was William Coates. In 1841 twenty year old Martin Coates lived at Crina with a female servant Mary Hey.

In 1851 John Dinsdale was living there with his wife Ann and eight year old daughter Elizabeth. He was listed as a farmer of ten acres. In 1854 John Overend formerly of Bentham

266

flax spinner passed Crina Bottom to Thomas Garbutt of Stockton on Tees who was a wine merchant. At this time it was recorded that there were three closes of ground and just over three acres of land. In 1861 thirty-four year old Matthew Dinsdale was farming Crina and living there with his wife, Agnes, and five children.

1871 saw Isaac Brayshaw living at Crina Bottom with his wife Ann, daughter Sarah, and son Isaac. In December 1872, aged fifty-nine, he was taken ill and died. He was due to be buried at Clapham Church on the 17th but there had been snowstorms and a heavy fall of snow. Telegraph poles had been blown down and in places snow drifts were level with the walls. As the road to Crina Bottom was snowed up, alternative plans were made. A hearse was brought from Westhouse and parked at Skirwith and then friends and family carried the deceased over allotments, rocks and mountain walls often wading through deep snowdrifts until they reached the road at Skirwith. Eventually Isaac Brayshaw was conveyed to his last resting place.[15]

In the 1881 census return, Crina Bottom is reported as uninhabited. By 1891 Thomas Marsden, a fifty-seven year old Lancashire farmer from Accrington was established in the farmstead. He was living there with his wife Margaret, a daughter and a grandson. In 1901 the census shows that William Wilson a quarryman at the granite works was living there with his wife Agnes five children and a nephew. William Wilson complained of the condition of Fell Lane which at times he claimed was almost impassable. He claimed that the Lords of the Manor received a shilling a cart for all the limestone coming down, but did little in repairs. The Wilsons bought Crina for £200 in 1903 and William Wilson sold it to Mary Moore of Burley in Wharfedale in 1919 for £250, as shown in the Ingleton Manor Court Rolls.

In April 1887 there was an outcry when a charge was made for visitors to go up Fell Lane from Storrs. On April 16th the *Lancaster Guardian* published an article entitled 'Taking Toll for an Ancient Road:-

> The road for which the toll of one penny is made upon all persons who use it, is from the Storrs or waste on the east side of Ingleton. It is the ancient road to Crina Bottom, Ingleborough, the peat mosses and other places. Another ancient road from Cold Cotes to Slatenber goes into it. From time immemorial this road has been used without let or hindrance by horses, carts and vehicles, and pedestrians. Such a thing as charging tourists or anyone else a penny each was never heard of before last year. The visitors had a right to complain, and it is to be hoped that someone versed in the public rights of way will look into the matter. If visitors are to be thus charged for making use of our waste land it will soon come to pass that they will desert the neighbourhood in disgust.

Following this complaint and others the charge was dropped. In Victorian times some of the residents at Crina Bottom served food to people climbing Ingleborough. Ann Brayshaw was one, but her work was made difficult as there was no water on the premises and it had to be carried a fair distance. Often the visitors would order food on the way to the summit and collect it on their return. Another problem for the caterers at Crina Bottom was that they had a long trip down to Ingleton to get food when their stocks ran out.

Several people have been lost on Ingleborough over the years and searches were sent out from time to time. On Sunday evening September 23rd 1888 a woman and child were lost on Ingleborough. The Riddle family was staying at Ingleton Hall Boarding House at the time. Richard Foster, the village bellman, and Miss Riddle's uncle went by cart on the old road to Crina Bottom. The bellman had been asked to take his bell, but he refused. He said that he could shout loud enough to be heard all over the south west side of the mountain where he was sure the lost ones were. Sure enough he was correct, the woman heard his calls and the woman and child were rescued. The church bells of St Mary's were rung about midnight to celebrate, but this disturbed and alarmed many villagers who wondered what was going on.[16] Tom and Teresa Barnes rented Crina Bottom during World War II. As Tom was in the army, a relative and her children moved in with Teresa. Then they were joined by a family of evacuees making a total of eight. They used a horse and cart to travel up and down to the village.

INGLEBOROUGH SHELTER

The Ingleton Fell Rescue Team decided in 1952 to commemorate the coronation of Queen Elizabeth II by erecting a cross-wall shelter on the summit of Ingleborough. The idea had come from Reg Hainsworth and the man in charge of construction was Andrew Brown. The secretary, Clifford Humphries, dealt with the question of permits. To cover the building costs and providing a bronze plaque, subscriptions were invited from the public and assistance was received from home and abroad. The team began by carrying all the sand and cement up the mountain in quantities which could be placed in a rucksac, often making several journeys each during a week so that they had material for a week-end building session.

The stone was collected from below the summit so as not to damage any archaeological remains. Water was collected from the tarn down towards Swine's Tail. To get this it was necessary to climb down five hundred feet to Swine's Tail and then climb back with a five-gallon drum of water. As the work progressed the group were able to get a tractor to the summit on several occasions and this made the task much easier. On the evening of Coronation Day a service of consecration was conducted on the summit by the vicar of Ingleton, the Rev H.J. Croft. Violet Farrer of Clapham unveiled the indicator. Sadly since the building of the shelter, vandals have done quite considerable damage to the stone seats.

In May 1937 this car took old tyres to the summit of Ingleborough for the coronation bonfire of George VI. Getting stuck on the mountain helped Reg Hainsworth, the organiser of the bonfire, to gain extra publicity for the event..

REFERENCES

1. Printed Jubilee Balance Sheet & Bonfire account 1887. In possession of author.
2. *Yorkshire Dalesman,* November 1960, p.542.
3. *Yorkshire Dalesman,* 1960 June, p.175, 1961 January, p.739, September, p.440.
4. *Gentleman's Magazine,* Vol xxi 1761, p.126.
5. *The Craven & North West Yorkshire Highlands,* H. Speight, Smith Settle, 1989, p.238.
6. *Bygone Bentham,* J. Carr, Landy Publications 1997, p.131.
7. *Recollections of Ingleton,* J. Carr, 1896, ed J.I. Bentley, 1991, p.28.
8. *Lancaster Guardian,* June 30th 1877.
9. *Lancaster Guardian,* January 13th & Feb. 3rd 1883.
10. *Recollections of Ingleton,* J. Carr, 1896, ed J.I. Bentley, 1991, p.31.
11. *Lancaster Guardian,* November 16th 1895.
12. *Lancaster Guardian,* January 22nd & 29th 1898.
13. *Lancaster Gazette,* March 18th 1815.
14. *Lancaster Guardian,* December 25th 1897.
15. *Lancaster Guardian,* December 21st 1872.
16. *Lancaster Guardian,* September 29th 1888.

LITERARY CONNECTIONS

This chapter shows that Ingleton is rich in its literary and artistic connections. Southey, Gray and Turner came here. There are connections with Wordsworth and Ruskin and Conan Doyle knew Ingleton well. Over the years many writers and artists came to Ingleton to write, to paint and to relax. Most came because of the caves, the river scenery and Ingleborough mountain. Some came because it was on their route to somewhere else and noted the village as they passed through: a few lived here. The characters in this chapter range from Drunken Barnaby travelling in the seventeenth century to Victorian Poet Laureate Robert Southey, who took great delight in Ingleton in the nineteenth century. Conan Doyle, the famous writer of detective stories knew the village and married at Thornton Church across the valley. While here he plucked the name Sherlock from the church minister and made it world famous as Sherlock in Sherlock Holmes. Many of those noted here were national figures, while others were purely local writers.

ROBERT R. BALDERSTON 1848-1928 & MARGARET BALDERSTON.

Robert Balderston was born at Hawes in 1848 and came to live in Ingleton where his family had lived for many generations. As a young man he was a teacher at Storrs Hall School, a boarding school for girls at Ingleton. His aunt, Elizabeth Smith, had founded the school. He was a well known figure in the village and spent his spare time on varied scientific experiments with atmospheric electricity. With the assistance of his wife he published *Ingleton Bygone and Present* around 1888. The book is undated, but the new church opened in 1887 is shown in the frontispiece. The book is written in the old-fashioned antiquarian style which tends to deride the quaint spellings in old documents and to list historical items without any attempt to explain or evaluate them. A great deal of the book concerns itself with folklore, caves, scenery, geology and flora and fauna. However, it is a sought-after antiquarian book and commands a high price.

There is something of a puzzle about Robert Balderston as throughout his life he appears to have been over qualified, but under employed. He is firstly employed by his aunt as a teacher and in the 1871 census gives his employment as, 'Undergraduate of Cambridge', but meaning teacher. By 1881 he is living in Ravenstonedale and unemployed but enters himself as 'Late Natural Science Professor and Journalistic Writer'. His supporting aunt at Storrs School had died and obviously the new owners of the school had dispensed with his services. In 1891 he is back at Ingleton where he entered his employment as, 'Professor of Natural Sciences, Botany, Geology, Chemistry & Zoology, Schoolmaster & Author'. In 1901 he was living in the Horsemarket in Kirkby Lonsdale alongside manual workers and labourers and his employment was 'Sewing Machine Repairer'. Old men of Ingleton in the 1970s remembered him coming round the village in a long untidy coat to repair sewing machines: rather a come-down for a distinguished professor.

RICHARD BRAITHWAITE ALIAS DRUNKEN BARNABY (1588-1673)

Richard Braithwaite, known as drunken Barnaby, was an odd character and his book *Drunken Barnaby's Journal* is certainly an unusual book. He was also known as Barnaby Harrington. He toured Yorkshire writing verses about all the places he visited, including Ingleton. Westmorland born and educated at Oxford University, he was a churchman, country gentleman and prolific writer. He was known for his four great passions; classical scholarship, local history and folklore, drinking, and fondness for the opposite sex. Indulging in his latter two passions frequently got him into trouble. In his journal he describes his adventures on

Engraving taken from *Drunken Barnaby's Four Journeys to the North of England* printed in 1805. The artist J. Harding had obviously not been told that Ingleton Church had a tower and not a spire.

his journey from Oxford to Kendal by way of Rotherham, Aberford, Wetherby, Doncaster, Wakefield, Bradford, Keighley, Giggleswick, Clapham and Ingleton. At Ingleton he tells us he was stoned by angry women for injuring a blacksmith.

On leaving Clapham Barnaby says:-

> *Veni Ingleton ubi degi*
> *Donec fabri caput fregi,*
> *Quo peracto, in me ruunt*
> *Mulieres, saxa pluunt,*
> *Queis perculsus, timens laedi,*
> *His posteriora dedi.*

> Thence to Ingleton, where I liv'd
> Till I brake a blacksmith's head,
> Which done, women rush'd in on me,
> Stones like hail shower'd down upon me,
> Whence astonish'd, fearing harming,
> Leave I took, but gave no warning.

Another translation is given by Balderston in *Ingleton –Bygone and Present.*

> I came to Ingleton, where I dwelt
> Until I brake a blacksmith's pelt,
> There rush on me, when that was done,
> The women-kind, down rains stone;
> With which, dumb-foundered, fearing hurt,
> I showed to them my hinder part.

A footnote under the Ingleton verse in the 1805 edition notes the following:-

> *Pirgus inest, fanum sub acumine collis;*
> *Collis ab elatis actus & auctus aquis.*

> The poor man's box is in the temple set;
> Church under hill, the hill by waters beat.

271

JOHN BYNG - VISCOUNT TORRINGTON 1743-1813

John Byng, later fifth Viscount Torrington, was one of the most celebrated travellers of the late eighteenth century. He was born in 1743 and made his career in the British Army. When he retired as Lieutenant-Colonel he went to work in the Inland Revenue at Somerset House, a position that allowed him to make extensive tours of England and Wales between the years 1781 and 1794. His visit to Ingleton came in 1792 when travelling from Askrigg he arrived at Gearstones and described the masses of Scottish cattle in the area and the Scottish drovers accompanying them. His comments about the area have already been quoted in the article on the Gearstones Inn.[1] We are indebted to visitors like Byng who give us such precise insights into activities which took place in the past within the boundaries of Ingleton Township.

ROBERT BALDERSTON CRAGG 1854-1906

Robert B. Cragg, born in Kirkby Lonsdale, became a solicitor in Ingleton and later in Skipton. He wrote *Legendary Rambles – Ingleton & Lonsdale.* The book is not dated, but the frontispiece is labelled 'Ingleton in 1898,' which is most likely the year of publication. He claimed that the object of his book was to preserve a few of the legends that still linger around Ingleborough. However, he wrote his accounts as stories and, in most cases, invented characters, dates and dialogue which must be almost entirely fictitious. He does not record where he got his original legends from before he embellished them. The value of this book to the historian is almost nil and it must be read mainly as a work of fiction. Robert Cragg served on various committees in Ingleton including the Improvement Committee. In 1887 he presented a carved wooden reredos depicting the Last Supper to the new church. He died at Skipton in April 1906.

SIR ARTHUR IGNATIOUS CONAN DOYLE 1859-1930

Sherlock Holmes, or at least part of him, was born at Ingleton. Conan Doyle knew Ingleton well. He regularly visited his mother when she lived at Masongill near Ingleton and married his first wife at Thornton-in-Lonsdale. He was born in Edinburgh in May 1859, the son of Charles Doyle and Mary Foley. His family was Catholic and he went to Hodder, the prep

school for Stonyhurst College, and then, when he was eleven, on to Stonyhurst College itself, which is a Jesuit college near Clitheroe. However, his stay there put him off Catholicism for life and he married a Protestant and became a spiritualist. He went to Edinburgh University where he obtained his MB in 1881 and MD in 1885.

His marriage to Louisa Hawkins took place at St Oswald's Church Thornton-in-Lonsdale on August 6th 1885. By this time his mother had moved to Masongill Cottage. She had moved there through friendship with Dr Waller, who had been a lecturer at Edinburgh University and whose family owned Masongill House. There is no other explanation for the Doyles coming to Masongill and living near

Portrait of Conan Doyle who found his Sherlock at Ingleton.

to the Wallers: it was no coincidence, Dr Bryan Charles Waller must have known the family well. That friendship is reputed to have ripened into something more intimate and this is understandable as Mary Doyle was as good as a widow, in fact she let it be known that she was a widow. However, her husband, Conan's father, who was an alcoholic and epileptic had been quietly locked away.   It is said that Charles Doyle was committed to Crichton Royal Institution, a mental hospital near Dumfries, but stories circulated in Ingleton that he was locked away in a cottage at Masongill and looked after by a keeper. Conan Doyle's sisters, Jane Adelaide Rose Doyle, and Mary Josephine Doyle both married at Thornton Church and the registers were signed by Bryan Charles Waller. On Conan Doyle's visits to Ingleton the minister there was the Rev. Sherlock. The Rev. Sherlock had several uncles, one the Rector of Bentham, another Cornelius Sherlock, the architect of Ingleton's new church built in 1886, and a third Randal Hopley Sherlock a newspaper proprietor from Liverpool. Conan Doyle reversed the surname Sherlock making it the forename for his new super detective, Sherlock Holmes, whose first story came out in 1887. The surname Holmes is said to have come from Oliver Wendell Holmes, the US poet, who was a favourite of Conan Doyle's.

The Doyles crop up in the local press from time to time and one such occasion was in July 1905. Conan Doyle's mother came to the station at Ingleton to collect some items. Following her visit the horse bolted and the horse and trap got onto the railway line and headed off across the viaduct. Fortunately no trains were coming and no real damage was done either to the horse, trap or Mrs Doyle herself, and she was able to return home unscathed.[2]

EMMELINE GARNETT

Emmeline Garnett, teacher, has written many books on the area of Wray, Bentham and Ingleton as well as a wide variety of other works. Her book *Hills of Sheep* written in 1955 tells the story of a young boy, Will Appleby, who experienced the changes at Chapel-le-Dale during the building of the Settle Carlisle Railway. Though a story for children, it has been read and enjoyed by children and adults alike for half a century. Other works include *The Wray Flood of 1967: Memories of a Lune valley Community*, 2002, *The Railway Builders* 1952, *Dated Buildings of Bentham* 2000. All her works are well researched, informative and a pleasure to read.

THOMAS GRAY 1716-1771

The poet Gray came to Ingleton in the autumn of 1769 and in describing his journey from Morecambe to Ingleton he commented, 'Now, our road began gradually to mount towards the Apennine, the trees growing less and thinner of leaves, till we came to Ingleton. It is a pretty village, situated very high, and yet in a valley at the foot of that huge monster of nature, Ingleborough.' He had refreshments at an inn and noted that he met, 'Sir Bellingham Graham, and Mr. Parker, lord of the manor - one of them six feet high, and the other as much in breadth!' It was this Edward Parker who demolished the old Ingleton Hall and built the present structure. Parts of the old hall were taken to Browsholme and used in ornamental stonework.

Gray lived a scholarly life in Cambridge and in the summer he travelled to the north of England looking for inspiration in nature. He stayed at Ingleton and noted the scenery. He called Ingleborough, 'that huge creature of God and the rivers he called 'two torrents' where great stones rolled along the river beds instead of water. He admired the two bridges at Ingleton calling them 'two handsome arches flung over the streams'. Gray is most well known for his poem 'Elegy Written in a Country Church-Yard'.

ANTHONY HEWITSON, 'ATTICUS & INGLE' 1836 – 1912.

Anthony Hewitson's parents were born at Ingleton, but they moved to Blackburn and Anthony was born there on August 13th 1836. However, as a young boy he was sent to live at Ingleton with his grandparents, Thomas and Dorothy Moore. There is no doubt Anthony enjoyed his childhood in the village and his time at Ingleton National School, for in later life he was always keen to return to the Ingleton and Dent area to visit family and friends and enjoy the rural delights.

Anthony was a bright child and took in all he saw in the village and noted more than most. His own personal account of his childhood in Ingleton was written for the *Lancaster Standard* in a series of articles in May and June 1896 under the pen name 'Ingle.' These memoirs were published in 1982 as *The Story of My Village-Ingleton 1840-1850*. Parts of his story is used in various chapters of this book from education to the church. He returned to live with his parents in Lancaster around 1850 and it was there that he began his career in journalism. He was apprenticed to Mr Clarke, printer and proprietor, of the *Lancaster Gazette.*

In 1857 after completing his apprenticeship he became a reporter at the *Kendal Mercury.* He later worked in the office of the *Brierley Hill Advertiser* in Staffordshire and then in Wolverhampton. He then returned nearer home to Preston, where in 1868 he became proprietor of the *Preston Chronicle.* He remained with the paper until it changed hands in 1890. In 1893 he helped to establish and was managing director and editor of the *Lancaster Standard.*

Hewitson wrote a *History of Preston Ad 705-1883* in 1883 which was republished in 1969 by SR Publications Ltd. Under the pen name 'Atticus' he also wrote *Northwards* which covers the history of most townships from Preston to Lancaster. The book was reprinted by Landy Publishing in 1993. No local history book had a greater reputation than *Northward.* He also wrote *Stonyhurst College Past and Present* around 1878. Hewitson also wrote a guide to Ingleton which was revised over the years. Unlike most other guides to the village it contained much interesting history. There is more solid factual history in Hewitson's twenty page Ingleton Guide than in the 369 pages of Balderston's *Ingleton, Bygone & Present.* Hewitson's books are still read and sought after.

Anthony Hewitson.

Throughout his life Anthony Hewitson kept in touch with his roots. He regularly visited the Ingleton and Dent area both to enjoy the countryside and to meet up with relatives and old school friends. He wrote a series of diaries which are now deposited with the Lancashire Record Office. A few extracts are given below.[3]

June 7th 1865   Went with wife, mother and two aunts, by rail to Clapham; there got conveyance; drove through Ingleton. Saw the house wherein I was brought up and fields wherein I often played. Drove on to Dent by Kingsdale- a most terrific and unpardonable road. Found uncles, aunts and cousins therein profusion-one nearly drunk. Came to Lancaster same night. A tremendous ride and a rapid ride. Scenery compensated for all.

August 31st 1884 I to Lancaster by 8.20 train. Then with me, wife, my sister and her husband to Ingleton by train having to wait at Clapham junction 1˜ hours. On reaching Ingleton were met by my cousin Thomas Moore. Went to see the scenery in Swilla Bottom. Very romantic and beautiful. At night met with some Preston people (Councillor Hale etc) at Wheatsheaf and had some whiskey. Slept, I and wife, at cousin's.

September 1st 1884. I, my wife, and six of the Preston lot to Dent by Ribblehead. Fine. Went to and examined source of the Ribble, a small spring running from a rocky hole on south west side of Gearstones. Then to Dent where we inspected the church and saw grave of my grandfather and grandmother (Thomas and Dorothy Moore) and had dinner at the Sun Inn – once my grandfather's property. His grave is at east end of the church… At night in Ingleton. Had a good time with cousin Thomas Moore. Tom Boyd (an old companion) and one Hewitson (stepson of my uncle Bob Hewitson).

March 15th 1887. Off to Ingleton by 8.10 morning train. Had a first class free pass. Hills lined with snow. Got some information for second edition of my Ingleton Guide. Good dinner and tea at Broadwood Cottage – Mr J. Hewitson's. Had a chat with Tom Boyd.

March 22nd 1887. To Ingleton per 8.25 morning train. Had foot warmer under my feet. Revising my guide to Ingleton. Called at my cousin's T. Moore – not in. Went to Ingleborough Hotel – soda and gin, Wheatsheaf where I had a bottle of ginger ale. Called on Aunt Prudence. Had a look at the old house (Bows House, Pan Well House) where I lived with my grandfather. Had dinner with my cousin Tommy Moore.

July 30th 1906. This forenoon about 10.30 I, my wife, son Ethelbert and his wife and child, daughter Rose and her husband and two children (Billy and Molly) started for Dent in a big four wheeled conveyance, drawn by two horses hired at the Wheatsheaf, Ingleton, from which place the driver was also supplied. We went up Chapel-le-Dale and by Gearstones Inn, turning near Newby Head Inn for Dentdale. The dale very pretty. Got to Dent putting up at the Sun Inn-about 2pm. Ordered dinner. Looked about-mainly up Flintergill, passing old Tommy Middleton's house on the west side. Tommy used to pop in at the Sun Inn every forenoon for a 'drop' in my early days when I used to walk over from Ingleton to Dent with my grandfather old Tommy Moore who owned the Sun, which was kept by his eldest son Peter for numerous years.

REV. JOHN HUTTON c. 1740-1806

John Hutton made a name for himself by writing about the caves and scenery around Ingleton in the eighteenth century. There were many travellers at the time writing of their experiences, but none wrote about the caves and scenery in such detail as John Hutton. He actually visited the caves, describing them and recording his experiences. John Hutton was a local man who knew the area well. His book *A Tour to the Caves* was published in 1780 and re-printed in 1781. It was later republished this century in 1971.[4] Hutton set off on the tour described in his book from Kendal as he lived in the area at the time.

John Hutton was minister at St James Burton-in-Kendal between 1764 and 1806. He was also closely associated with the Ingleton township and in 1790 he became joint Lord of the Manor of Twistleton with John Oddie. John Hutton and his book are highly regarded in caving circles. The importance of the book is that it was the earliest to give detailed descriptions of the caves. T.R. Shaw wrote about his important position in the history of caving in the *History of Speleology* in 1971.[5]

THOMAS HAYTON MAWSON 1861-1933

Thomas Mawson was born at Scorton in 1861, but about 1868 his father came to live and work at Ingleton as a warper in the local mill. At first the family rented an old cottage, but then in 1870 his father, John William Mawson, bought a small plot of land from Joseph Carr for twelve pounds and had a cottage built on it – Prospect Cottage. In 1876 Prospect Cottage was sold and the Mawsons went to live at Langber Villa where they started a market garden.

Sadly the difficult work and financial worry led to the early death of John Mawson and the boys were left to run the market garden themselves. At the age of nineteen Thomas was running the business with his younger brothers Robert and Isaac. In the 1881 census they were termed 'Common Gardeners.' They struggled on, but after nearly two years had to give up because of debts and other problems. Later Thomas and his brothers set up the Lakeland Nursery in Windermere. They were very successful and Thomas turned to garden design work. His first commission was Graythwaite Hall at Newby Bridge. Here his designs were a blend of architecture and gardening which became a feature of his future work.

Thomas went on to work alone and design gardens at Langdale Chase Troutbeck, Cleve How, Heathwaite, Brockhole and many other gardens in Windermere. He worked at Holker Hall and in 1909 designed the formal gardens at Rydal Hall. He eventually worked not only throughout Britain, but throughout the World. He became the leading landscape architect of his day. His clients included Queen Alexandra, Andrew Carnegie, the Maharaja of Baroda and Lord Leverhulme. He was involved with town planning schemes in Ottawa, Vancouver and Calgary. He was commissioned to plan the gardens of the Palace of Peace at the Hague and the royal gardens in Athens. He lectured widely and wrote several books, the one of interest to us being his autobiography in which he mentions Ingleton.

This world famous landscape architect tells us, 'The view down the valley of the river Greta was one of the finest prospects I have ever seen and thus early I was taught the value of a fine panorama.' He tells us that he received great encouragement from his schoolmaster at the National School in Ingleton and that his Sunday school teacher was Joseph Carr. Of him he says, 'I wonder if any other Sunday school was ever presided over by such a genius for the work? An entire absence of monkish, religious sentimentality, and recognition that what was needed was not so much theology as an expansion of our powers of observation, were his dominant characteristics…when he addressed us in the simplest language on the great creator's work he was entrancing. He was also inspiring, creating for the boys great visions of what they might be and do in the world. Altogether I think this Sunday school did much to fire my imagination and prepare me for my life-work.'[6] Certainly Thomas Mawson seems to think Joseph Carr deserved his monument of the Bank at Ingleton. Thomas Mawson died at Hest Bank in November 1933.

FREDERICK RILEY 1878-1960

Frederick Riley was brought up in Preston in Lancashire, but he spent the greater part of his life working in Settle. For many years he was engine driver at the Langcliffe Paper Mill. He was a keen lecturer on natural history and the antiquities of the Yorkshire Dales. His first book was *The Ribble from its Source to the Sea*. His second book was also topographical, *The Settle District and North-West Yorkshire Dales* which was published in 1923. The only real comment on Ingleton is, 'Ingleton, where good accommodation may be had, is a capital centre from which to explore this romantic portion of Yorkshire'. Riley also gives an account of the building of the Hospice on Ingleborough in the nineteenth century. When the Langcliffe Mill was burned down in 1940 he continued to run the family bookshop in Settle.

His main interest in the Ingleton area was Chapel-le-Dale and he wrote *Gleanings from a Yorkshire Valley-The Attractive Charms of Chapel-le-Dale*. The book which is undated was probably written around 1930. On returning from a night on Ingleborough he wrote, 'So once again I left the hill whose familiar form keeps guard over the district which we love, and though as old as time itself, bears all the freshness of eternal youth.' He concluded his book on Chapel-le-Dale with this last paragraph. 'And now for a while I must leave this valley of many charms, a valley one hopes will long remain unspoiled. The days spent in Chapel-le-Dale have been very pleasant, and through the gateway of memory one will often picture this wonderland of nature where there is so much to please the eye and to enrich the mind. Yet even more than the dale's natural attractions will be the treasured memories of happy friendships, and of kindly hospitality received even from those to whom I came as a stranger within their gates.'

ELVI RHODES

The cover of Elvi Rhodes' novel, *The Mountain,* shows the half- constructed railway viaduct at Ribblehead in the background, while the foreground depicts a scene from the shanty town life of the railway workers. The mountain of the story is Whernside and it was to the railway works in its shadow where Jake Tempest was drawn. His mother had left him a picture of Whernside in Yorkshire and when he heard that men were needed to build the Settle to Carlisle Railway he went along with hundreds of other men and their families from all over the country. He settled in to the harsh climate and rough living in the shanty towns and then met the woman who gave light to his life.

This is at least the second novel written about the construction of the Settle Carlisle Railway. Elvi Rhodes is a native of the West Riding of Yorkshire educated at Bradford Grammar School. Her other novels include *Opal, Dr Rose, Ruth Appleby, Cara's Land, The Bright One, Midsummer Meeting and The House of Bonneau.* Elvi Rhodes now lives near Brighton Sussex and says, 'A storyteller is how I would describe myself. That's what I am'.

ROBERT SOUTHEY 1774–1843

I have sought in vain for Richard Guy's tombstone in Ingleton church-yard. That there is one can hardly, I think, be doubted; for if he left no relations who regarded him, nor perhaps effects enough of his own to defray this last posthumous and not necessary expense; and if Thomas Gent of York, who published the old poem of Flodden Field from his transcript, after his death, thought he required no other monument; Daniel was not likely to omit this last tribute of respect and affection to his friend. But the church-yard, which, when his mortal remains were deposited there, accorded well with its romantic site, on a little eminence above the roaring torrent, which with the then retired character of the village, and with the solemn use to which it was consecrated, is now a thickly-peopled ground. Since their time, manufactures have been established in Ingleton, and though eventually they proved unsuccessful, and were consequently abandoned, yet they continued long enough in work largely to increase the population of the church-yard. Amid so many tombs the stone which marked poor Richard

Robert Southey, Poet Laureate 1813-1843.

Guy's resting-place might escape a more diligent search than mine. Nearly a century has passed since it was set up … Time corrodes our epitaphs, and buries our very tombstones.

Returning pensively from my unsuccessful search in the church-yard, to the little inn at Ingleton, I found there, upon a sampler, worked in 1824 by Elizabeth Brown, aged 9, and framed as an ornament for the room which I occupied, some lines in as moral a strain of verse as any which I had that day perused among the tombs. And I transcribed them for preservation, thinking it not improbable that they had originally been composed by Richard Guy, for the use of his female scholars, and handed down for a like purpose, from one generation to another. This may be only a fond imagination, and perhaps it might not have occurred to me at another time; but the many compositions have been ascribed in modern as well as ancient times, and indeed daily are so, to more celebrated persons, upon less likely grounds. These are the verses:-

> Jesus permit Thy gracious name to stand
> As the first effort of an infant's hand:
> And as her fingers on the sampler move,
> Engage her tender heart to seek Thy love;
> With Thy dear children may she have a part,
> And write Thy name Thyself upon her heart.

These words were written by Robert Southey in his book *The Doctor*.[7] Southey, a prolific writer of prose and poetry, was born at Bristol, but lived much of his life at in Keswick. He knew the Lake District well and became one of the 'Lakeland Poets,' he also much loved and admired the scenery and history of Ingleton. His book *The Doctor* is a lengthy production which is not in print today. Though a novel it is a mixture of fact and fiction, in which Southey packs in most of his experiences and a lifetime's knowledge of local history and stories. It has been called a novel, but it is hardly that; in fact no one description would cover this work. The book has been called intolerably dull and yet people have also said there are many delightful pages, and some of those delightful pages are about Ingleton.

The Doctor was Doctor Daniel Dove of Chapel-le-Dale and Southey tells us of Daniel Dove's home and his upbringing. In the excerpt in which Southey tells us of the search for Richard Guy's grave at Ingleton we have a mixture of fact and fiction. Richard Guy, the schoolmaster of Ingleton, is most probably a fictitious figure, but history records that Richard Jackson, schoolmaster of Ingleton, did write or transcribe the poem on the battle of Flodden Field. When Southey writes about leaving the church-yard and going back to his room in the inn at Ingleton and reading the sampler written by nine year old Elizabeth Brown we are surely entering the world of fact. The Ingleton parish registers show that an Elizabeth Brown was baptised in 1814, the daughter of Joseph Brown who in Southey's time was the landlord of the Wheat Sheaf Inn at Ingleton. She would have been nine years old in 1824 which Southey tells us was the date on the sampler. In all probability Southey did see that sampler in the Wheat Sheaf. Robert Southey held a fascination for Ingleton and he knew its stories and history.

Chapter XXII of *The Doctor* is entitled 'Rowland Dixon and his Company of Puppets.' The story of Rowland Dixon, the puppet master from Ingleton who died in 1788, will be told in the last chapter. Southey was made Poet Laureate in 1813 and was most popular in his day. His fame tends to have been eclipsed by his contemporary 'Lake Poets' such as William Wordsworth. Some of Southey's poetic works are still popular today though most are left unread.

THE STORY OF THE THREE BEARS

In his novel, *The Doctor*, Robert Southey tells us that William Dove, Dr Dove's brother, had a favourite story which he told to his nephew and others at Ingleton Fells – it was the story of the three bears. *The Doctor,* published in 1837 is the first time the story of the three bears appears in print. Southey wrote the story and he set its origin in the township of Ingleton.

'Once upon a time there were Three Bears, who lived together in a house of their own, in a wood. One of them was a Little, Small, Wee Bear; and one was a Middle-sized Bear, and the other was a Great, Huge Bear.' You will note that they are not father bear, mother bear and baby bear, as this version came later. However, they all had their porridge bowls, their chairs and their beds. Continuing his story Southey tells us that after making porridge the bears had gone for a walk in the wood while it cooled. 'And while they were walking a little old Woman came to the house. She could not have been a good honest old Woman; for first she looked in at the window, and then she peeped in at the keyhole.' When the three bears returned to their house and found the old woman on the little bear's bed, 'Up she started; and when she saw the three bears at the side of the bed, she tumbled herself out of the other and ran to the window…Out she jumped; and whether she broke her neck in the fall; or ran into the wood and was lost there; or found her way out of the wood, and was taken up by the Constable and sent to the House of Correction for a vagrant as she was, I cannot tell. But the Three Bears never saw anything more of her'.

Later the old woman in the story was changed to a girl called Silver hairs. Then in the 1904 edition of *Old Nursery Stories and Rhymes* Goldilocks came into the story and had remained there since.

HARRY SPEIGHT 1855-1915

Harry Speight was born in Bradford in 1855. He worked for a Bradford export business, but in his spare time wrote articles for local magazines and newspapers. From 1884 he concentrated on his literary career. He had a strong interest in archaeology, geology and natural history and for over fifteen years he dedicated himself almost entirely to the study of the history of his native Yorkshire. His *Craven and the North-West Yorkshire Highlands* published in 1892 established his name as a Yorkshire historian. He also wrote *Nidderdale and the Garden of the Nidd, Upper Wharfdale and Lower Wharfdale* and several other books.

It is the Craven volume which concerns the Ingleton area and was advertised as, 'Being a complete account of the history, scenery and antiquities of that romantic district.' There is a vast amount of material on Ingleton and the surrounding villages and it has been a great help in preparing this book. Speight tends to fall for romantic tales and tells of the cock fighting and drinking at the Cock Inn at Ingleton which never existed. He even tells of bloodstains on the floor which no amount of scrubbing could remove. His historical writing also tends to be over concerned with the lords of the manor and the gentry as was most antiquarian writing of the Victorian period. However, his books have been reprinted and he is still read and studied. There is still no better book to gain a picture of the Ingleton area and surrounding villages than his *Craven and the North West Yorkshire Highland.* Harry Speight lived much of his life at Bingley where he died in 1915.

Chapel-le-Dale church.

God's lowly temple! Place of many prayers!
Grey is thy roof, and mossy are thy walls,
And over old green graves thy shadow falls,
To bless the spot where end all human cares!

The humble hearted, and the meek and pure
Have, by the holy worship of long years,
Made thee a hallowed place, and many tears,
Shed in repentance deep, have blessed thy floor.

Lowly thou art; but yet when time is set,
Will He who loved what wicked men despise-
Who hears the orphan's voice, that up doth rise
In deep sincerity – not thee forget!

                                        Robert Southey

The grammar school at Hawkshead where Robert Greenwood of Ingleton became a school friend of William Wordsworth.

WILLIAM WORDSWORTH 1770-1850

Wordsworth comes into our story as a school friend of Robert Hodgson Greenwood of Bank Hall in Ingleton. William and Robert attended Hawkshead Grammar School together. Wordsworth was there with his two brothers, John and Christopher, and they lodged with Ann Tyson in the village of Hawkshead, as did Robert Greenwood. Sadly although writing about Bolton Abbey, Gordale Scar and other local Yorkshire beauty spots Wordsworth doesn't appear to have written one verse on Ingleton. However, Robert Greenwood was portrayed as the boy who played the flute in Wordsworth's Prelude Book 2. In the following section Wordsworth recounts one of their night escapades when they took a boat on the banks of the Lake Windermere and explored the islands.

Prelude Book II
When in our pinnace we returned at leisure
Over the shadowy lake, and to the beach
Of some small island steered our course with one
The Minstrel of the Troop, and left him there,
And rowed off gently while he blew his flute
Alone upon the rock-oh, then, the calm
And dead still water lay upon my mind
Even with the weight of pleasure, and the sky
Never before so beautiful, sank down
Into my heart, and held me like a dream!

The boy with the flute, whom he calls 'The Minstrel of the Troop' was Robert Greenwood from Ingleton. This we know from Christopher Wordsworth's *Memoirs of William Wordsworth*.[8] It is interesting that Robert Greenwood was also involved with Wordsworth's first attempt at writing poetry, in fact he may well have been the one to stimulate him to do this. When Mary Wordsworth wrote to her nephew Christopher Wordsworth in August 1854 she said, 'Your uncle used to speak of a sonnet which, coupled with one from his schoolfellow Greenwood, he once sent to the Gents Magazine from Hawkshead'.[9] It was traditional for boys who went to university to donate a book to the school library. When Wordsworth and Greenwood left Hawkshead for university the book they presented bears their signatures and those of two other students leaving at the same time.

The young men went to Cambridge University and took degrees there. William Wordsworth, who studied at St John's Cambridge, we are told, only just managed to pass his degree due to spending time on other interests. Robert Greenwood from Ingleton and Christopher Wordsworth, William's brother, both became distinguished academics and spent most of their lives at Cambridge. Christopher Wordsworth was Master of Trinity College from 1820 to 1841 and Robert Greenwood was a Senior Fellow of the same college. Wordsworth and Greenwood followed each other's progress in life and kept in touch. In a letter to William Matthew, written on August 3rd 1791 Wordsworth writes, 'I have heard from Greenwood,' he says 'for the first time the very day I received your last. He is in Yorkshire with his father, and writes in high spirits, his letter altogether irregular and fanciful. He seems to have much of Yorick in his disposition; at least Yorick, if I am not mistaken, had a deal of the male mad-cap in him, but G. out mad-caps him quite'.[10]

When William Wordsworth visited his brother, Christopher, at Cambridge he was also able to see his old friend Robert Greenwood. We know that members of Trinity College at Cambridge came to Ingleton to see Robert when he was staying at the old family home of the Greenwoods. On one occasion a Trinity don who Robert Greenwood didn't like very much, being on a northern tour decided to call in at Ingleton and visit Robert. 'His reverence is out' the farmer's wife told him, helping my husband with the hay and there's no time to loss as its blowing like rain.' The visitor made a later call in the evening and this time he was luckier. 'I'll go and tell his reverence you're here, sir,' the farmer's wife said. 'He's in the cow'us now helping with the milking astead o'me.' The visitor went with the farmer's wife and greeted Robert. 'Why Greenwood you look as if you'd been doing this all your life.' 'And as you know I haven't', said Greenwood. 'But my father being a statesman I was born and bred to it.' The visitor was puzzled by Robert Greenwood's use of the word statesman, which he used in the northern sense of a statesman, being the owner, or customary tenant, of a small landed estate which he farmed himself. This story was a favourite with William Wordsworth.[11]

The Greenwood connection with the Wordsworths continued over many years until Robert Greenwood's death. In April 1839 John Wordsworth wrote to his uncle, William Wordsworth, giving him news of Robert Greenwood. 'Poor Greenwood still continues in much the same state, and may remain so for months or even years. His legs have entirely failed him, he cannot rise from his chair without assistance. The lower part of his body in short seems to be totally disabled, but the upper retains its energies, his intellect is perfectly clear, he is glad to receive a visit from a friend, and he can read even the smallest print without spectacles.[12] Robert Greenwood died in December 1839 and was buried in front of the church at Ingleton: William Wordsworth died in 1850 and was buried at Grasmere.

JOSEPH MALORD WILLIAM TURNER 1775-1851

William Turner painted at Ingleton during his travels in Yorkshire. He painted Chapel-le-Dale church and Weathercote Cave and made many sketches. His painting of Chapel-le-Dale church can be seen in *The Chapel in the Fells* by Gerald Tyler. Turner illustrated the *History of Whalley* and the *History of Richmondshire* for the Lancashire author Thomas Dunham Whitaker.

REFERENCES

1. *The Torrington Diaries,* ed. B.W. Andrews, Eyre & Spottiswood 1936.
2. *Lancaster Guardian,* July 22nd 1905.
3. LRO, DP 512, Diaries Anthony Hewitson
4. *A tour to the Caves,* Rev. J. Hutton, S.R. Publishers 1970.
5. *History of Speleology,* T.R. Shaw, John Hutton, 1740? – 1806, His Tour to the Caves and his place in History of Speleology, Vol. 2 Parts 3-4, pp.109-128.
6. *The Life and Work of An English Landscape Architect*, T.H. Mawson, Richards Press London, 1927.
7. *The Doctor*, Southey Robert, (Newly edited and abridged from John Wood Warter's edition of 1848 by Maurice Fitzgerald) G. Bell & Sons, London, 1930.
8. *Wordsworth Prelude I.II & V and XII,* H. Derbishire H., OUP, 1928, p.60.
9. id, p.80
10. id, p.79.
11. id, p.80.
12. id, pp.79 & 80.

One of the Ingleton views that Thomas Mawson admired.

OTHER INDUSTRIES

INGLETON TANNERY & SKINYARD

For many years there were open tan pits in the Bottoms at Ingleton and the stench from them was frequently an irritation to the villagers. When tourists began to come to Ingleton in greater numbers it became even more of a nuisance. They had been dug out by the riverside and each had its own name, but a plan showing their location and names has probably been long since lost. Around 1882 the old tan pits were filled in and a new building made for the tannery and skin-yard.[1] A tannery was far from a pleasant place to work. Processes involved handling rotting flesh, as hides came straight from the butcher and slaughterhouse. The most noticeable characteristic of a tannery was the smell, an overpowering stench. In hot weather the smell was almost unbearable and in winter the open sided sheds could be freezing. To make conditions worse the tannery could be alive with rats.

The tan yard in the Bottoms c. 1885.

John Preston was a tanner and fellmonger at Ingleton for many years. He married at Ingleton in April 1818 and lived at Howes House in the Bottoms at Ingleton until his death. He was born at Hanlith about 1785 and came to Ingleton in the second decade of the nineteenth century. He was well known by butchers from Lancaster to Kirkby Lonsdale from whom he got his skins. In John Preston's time the hides were scraped to remove hairs and flesh and then immersed in the various pits, first lime pits and finally pits with oak bark solution. It was a long and skilled process.

By 1823 the Court Rolls show that John Preston occupied most of the area in the Bottom tan-yard, skin-yard, fulling mill and other premises and all came under the name Walk Mill. In 1851 John Preston was living with his wife Mary, his son James aged thirty, his son Robert aged twenty and also in the household was Matthew Redhead a seventeen year old servant from Lancaster. John's sons were noted as tanners, but Matthew Redhead was recorded as a skinner. Matthew was the first Redhead, the first of many, to be recorded at Ingleton and the

Redhead family eventually took over the business. The Preston family were also involved in similar businesses at Lancaster and Settle.

After John Preston's death the business was carried on by his son, James Preston, but sadly James died at an early age, on September 18th 1868, and before his sons were of age to learn the business. James Preston's will dated September 4th, 1868, and proved December 15th states, 'I give and bequeath all that my tan yard at Ingleton in equal shares to children.'[2] When the boys reached a suitable age they were sent to learn the business and eventually came back to Ingleton to take over the tannery. In the meantime the tannery was run by others. A notice in the *Lancaster Gazette* announced that the Tannery at Ingleton was to be let with possession in November 1875. It was said to have convenient tan and skin-yard, with drying sheds and garden.

On their return, John and James Preston were the ones who made extensive alterations to the yard and premises and built up an extensive business in skinning and tanning. In 1894 the Prestons sold out to Thomas Redhead who had come to Ingleton to join his brother Matthew. Thomas Redhead died March 19th 1906 in his 68th year. He left three sons and four daughters. Apart from his business as a fellmonger he was also a director of Ingleton Gas Company and a member of the Oddfellows.

The Redhead family continued the business although eventually the business became only that of fellmongers. One of their most expert fellmongers was known as 'Skinner Jackson.' The family, at one time, sent out leather greeting cards at Christmas. The business closed down in the 1960s.

INGLETON BREWERY

The Ingleboro' Brewery was opened at Ingleton by Wignalls' Brewery of Skipton. They also had a brewery at Barrowford in Lancashire. The brewery was set up in the premises of Dent's Mill which in 1866 had been out of use as a mill for many years. In 1866 the building underwent a thorough re-construction and renovation by William Wignall of Skipton, and late of Wignall and Thompson, Barrowford Brewery. The road running by the new brewery was soon known as Brewery Lane. In 1871 William Wignall was living in Brewery House next to the brewery with his wife Hannah and three children.

The brewery was flooded in September 1874 when the brewery horses had to be removed from the stables. On Thursday June 13th 1878 the brewery was put up for sale by auction at the Wheat Sheaf. Mr Hogg of Skipton was the auctioneer and William Wignall who occupied the brewery was present. Mr Pagett solicitor for the sale was present, but the sale, or rather the attempt at a sale, was a complete failure. The correspondent of the *Lancaster Guardian*, who was a nonconformist gloated that, 'The failure to effect a sale was conclusive proof that the brewing business is not one that will thrive in Ingleton!'[3]

INGLETON LAUNDRY

A laundry opened on Brewery Lane in 1905 and Brewery Lane became Laundry Lane and though the laundry has long since gone Laundry Lane remains today. The laundry was opened by Messrs Ellis and Boys on a field site known as Between Gates. Local Christians, especially chapel folk, were pleased to see the brewery go and as cleanliness is said to be next to Godliness what better to eventually take its place than a laundry. The New Ingleton Sanitary Laundry did more than keep clothes clean, it brought many young girls to work in Ingleton who later married local men. 'I first came to Ingleton to work in the laundry when I was a young woman' has been said by many. The company collected and delivered laundry over a wide area in horse drawn vans.

Laundry vans and laundry girls in the Edwardian era c. 1906.

As the years passed the laundry became known as Ingleton Steam Laundry and also advertised as Ingleton and District Laundry Limited. It was reported to be doing well in 1907 and 1908. In 1913 the press reported that Ingleton's steam laundry had another successful year. In May 1915 Henry Cockerton, one of the partners in the steam laundry, died. He had lived in Ingleton for eleven years. The laundry ball became one of the great events of the year in Ingleton. In 1933 it was held in the assembly rooms at the Ingleboro' Hotel and proceeds were given to the Royal Lancaster Infirmary. In October 1935 about eighty of the laundry staff went on an outing to Blackpool. This number appears quite large and probably included partners and friends. The Ingleton laundry does not appear to have survived long after World War II.

The Laundry Ball an event of the year.

VICTORIA SAW MILLS

Victoria saw mill was named in honour of Queen Victoria by Joseph Bentham. In 1849 Mr Bentham succeeded Brown in the old joiner's shop near the Wheat Sheaf Inn. He worked alone till 1850 and by 1853 had two journeymen, two sawyers and two apprentices. By 1870 there were eight joiners and eighteen men and boys working in the sawmill. There were also eight masons, six labourers and twelve horses working in the business which brought added prosperity to Ingleton.

The saw mills had five circular saw, two blocking machines, two boring machines, one rougher, and two finishing machines. All these were worked by two engines combining thirty horsepower. At the saw mills 1,200 cubic feet of timber was used weekly for felloes, ash planks, bobbins blocks, bobbins, chair wood, wagon wood and many other uses.[4] The other uses included coffins and these were frequently needed during the building of the Settle Carlisle Railway through Ingleton Fells.

Sadly by 1877 Joseph Bentham's timber business was in financial difficulties. He had over-stretched himself and became bankrupt. His goods and property were sold by auction at the Wheat Sheaf on Wednesday 27th of June 1877 by Richard Turner. His joiner's shop in Main Street sold to J.Howson for £161, and Howson also bought the blacksmith's shop adjoining for £121. A house in the centre of the village brought £105 and the villa residence called Church View brought £360. Sammy Croft containing one acre with an eight-stalled stable, built of stone with a large granary over it, a large wooden shed, a good piggery and a loose box was sold to Robert Wilkinson for £210. In May 1879 Joseph Bentham's creditors met to wind up his estate. The first and final dividend was set at 4s 2d in the £1, the money to be paid by June 25th. Joseph Bentham lived at Yanhams House

The Victoria Saw Mills were taken over by Robert Wilkinson in November 1877. Robert Wilkinson eventually moved to Clapham and then to Gargrave, where he carried on a similar business. The Ingleton business was taken over by Mr Procter, but business declined due to foreign timber merchants supplying turned wooden items such as bobbins at a lower cost. By the end of 1896 much machinery had been removed from the Victoria Saw Mill and the business was never successful again.[5]

REDHEAD'S MINERAL WATER FACTORY

A mineral water factory, or ginger beer factory, was opened in the Bottoms in September 1886 for the manufacture of sweets and mineral drinks. It was started by the Redhead family. In 1891 it was being run by George Redhead whose employment was registered as, 'Aerated Water Manufacturer,' and in 1901 the proprietor was Clarke Redhead. The old glass bottles marked Redhead Ingleton turn up from time to time, but are quite rare.

GRETA PRINTING WORKS

John Heywood's Guide to Ingleton around 1887 tells us that:-

Ingleton has its newspaper which is published weekly, on Wednesday. It is issued by Mr J. Brookes, printer and stationer, who settled in Ingleton in 1875, and is one of the oldest tradesmen in the place. He has a well-stocked shop of books, stationery, and newspapers, also a lending library, and is always willing to advise or assist visitors in want of apartments or requiring information about the scenery.[6]

John Heywood's Guide to Ingleton and District was itself printed in the village by John Brookes. He originally came from Warwickshire and set up business and home in the Main Street at Ingleton where he lived with his wife Mary and young family. John Brookes later took premises in the Bottoms for his printing works which he shared with the Liberal club. However, John Brookes and his family left Ingleton and settled in Ontario in Canada around 1895.

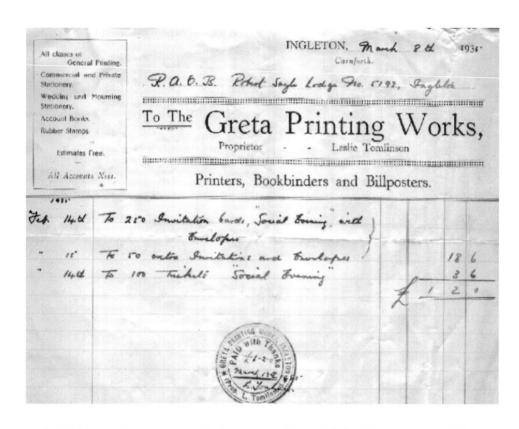

In 1895 Jos. A. Fletcher was on the letter head of Greta Printing Works as printer, billposter and bookbinder. The Howson family later ran Greta Printing Works and bill heads for F. Howson can be found. Moses Frederick Howson also followed as a printer and stationer and is said to have used Redheads old mineral water factory in the bottoms. Charles E. Clark became proprietor in the 1920s and in the 1930s the business was run by Leslie Tomlinson. Leslie Tomlinson ran the printing works with machinery which was becoming quite obsolete and in the end the business closed.

INGLETON CINEMA

For many years Ingleton had a cinema. From the early days of cinematography film shows were shown at Ingleton by visiting film makers and this was usually done in some village assembly room. Then a cinema was started in the Ingleboro' Hotel and there silent black and white movie films were shown. Eventually Ingleton acquired its own cinema opened by J.T. Marsden in May 1930. The cinema advertised, 'After seeing the outside views visit the cinema.' Special programmes were arranged for visitors on wet days at short notice. Johnny Marsden was manager in the 1920s. Times of showing were Monday, Tuesday, Wednesday and Thursday 7.30 and Fridays 6.30. Four changes of film per week were advertised.

Advertisement from a local guide.

Later the cinema became one of four owned by Arthur Graham and became the Nuvic Cinema. Every week Tommy Robinson collected four films at Leeds and these were then circulated between Ingleton, Settle, Kirkby Lonsdale and Sedbergh. Arthur Slinger was the projectionist for many years. Arthur Bateson became his assistant and then took over and was projectionist for several years until he went in the army in 1951. Seats at that time were 7d, 10d and 1s 6d. There were evening shows Monday to Friday with two shows on Saturday night. The growth of television brought the end to Ingleton's cinema.[7]

REFERENCES

1. *Lancaster Guardian,* December 22nd 1882.
2. *Ingleton Manor Court Rolls* 1820-1939, NYRO ZUC/1/3/2/, MIC 1557.
3. *Lancaster Guardian,* June 15th 1878.
4. *Lancaster Guardian,* September 10th 1870.
5. *Recollections of Ingleton* 1896, J. Carr, ed J.I. Bentley, 1991, p.24.
6. *Heywood's Guide to Ingleton & District c. 1888,* pp.12,13.
7. Information on cinema mainly from Arthur Bateson of Ingleton.

POST OFFICE AND SHOPS

The post office and shops run naturally together as the post office in Ingleton was always associated with some shop in the village. There is a problem with shops in that they were frequently opening and closing in various premises throughout the village. Some lasted a short time and others for years. Then shop owners came and went, moving into other towns and villages, or vacating their shops on retirement or death. Again so many letters and articles mentioning shops in Ingleton's past never accurately said where they were. So this is an account of some of the shops and shop owners who have been traced.

POST OFFICE

From the beginning of country postal services, Ingleton occupied the first place in the district. In the early 1800s it was the chief post office before there was a post office at Bentham. Charles Parker of Bentham Mill had to send a boy three times a week to Ingleton Post Office to collect mail. At that time the post office was in Blue Hall along with a general store. It was kept by the Marriner family for many years, first by William Marriner and then his son John. In October 1806 the Ingleton slate quarries late in the occupation of William Marriner were let at the Bay Horse on Saturday November 1st showing that William Marriner had other interests apart from shop-keeping. He died in October 1806 aged forty-five.

The next post office at Ingleton was kept by the Chapman family who occupied the premises in the main street later occupied by Thomas Baines as a draper's shop. When the Chapman family moved to Burton the post office was moved to a small grocer's shop on the east side of the Wheat Sheaf where it was run by Miss Jane Brown. From this shop it was removed to Thomas Green's shop in the square in the centre of the village in 1843. This was a large shop with a frontage on the north side of the street. During the time of this post office the mail gig used to arrive in the small hours of the morning. A man called Tomlinson drove the mail gig from Settle to Kirkby Lonsdale. When he arrived at Ingleton he woke up the post master who let down a letter bag from the upstairs window to collect the letters which he had to deliver in the morning. The area of delivery was very small at that time and those living at Hollin Tree and beyond had to collect their own mail. After Thomas Green's death his wife continued as post master for two years.

In May 1847 the new post master to be appointed was Robert Danson who was also the schoolmaster of the Churchyard School and later the National School. As a schoolmaster's salary was low a schoolmaster often needed other employment to gain a reasonable living. In Robert Danson's case he was schoolmaster, shopkeeper, post master and also did some debt collecting: members of his family would run the shop while he was at school. Robert Danson moved to a house on the west side of the Three Horse Shoes where the Post Office was again combined with a grocer's shop. When Robert Danson was appointed as postmaster it was reported in the *Lancaster Gazette* that 'The appointment is in accordance with the wishes of the clergy and the most respectable and principal inhabitants'.

A tradition says that the postmistress of that time had such an inquisitive state of mind that she was in the habit of detaining certain letters that she might pry into their contents. It is said that the owner of Dent's mill on one occasion took a letter and told her 'I have brought this letter unsealed that you might read it, for it is important that it goes today!'[1]

Mrs Danson carried on the Post Office for a good many years, but then following her husband's untimely death, she married William Remmington of Twistleton and gave up the business. Edward Harling Thistlethwaite was the next Post Master and he took over around 1866 and added the business to his grocery business in the Main Street. After having the

The Post Office in 1908. It was opened in 1897.

business for many years Edward Thistlethwaite died suddenly in June 1885 aged sixty-seven. On the day of his death to enquiries about his health, his answer was, 'I am somewhat better'.

Mrs Thistlethwaite took over as post mistress helped by her daughter, Annie. Annie continued the position after her mother's death. When Annie Thistlethwaite retired to get married she was presented with a valuable testimonial for the efficient way in which she had run the Post Office. J. Lumb, who moved to Ingleton from Bradford, was appointed the next postmaster and occupied the same house and office that Annie Thistlethwaite had vacated.

There were complaints that the premises were far too small for an efficient post office and were not central enough. Mr J. Lumb resigned as post master in October 1895 due to ill health. A fine new Post Office was made from the Liberal Club and the village Coffee Tavern which stood at the centre of the village near the church gates. Richard Brown had built the property in 1891 on the site of his old barn and stable. The Liberals were left out in the cold and their library and furniture had to be stored in the mill.

This new post office was opened on June 21st 1897 with Fred Howson as the new post master. Fred Howson was followed by Mr Slinger and then Thomas Nuttall. Thomas Nuttall had been post master at Ingleton for

Billy Saul post man at Ingleton outside Prospect Cottage.

many years when he died in August 1920. His wife continued from 1920 to 1924. Mark Ireland who had been postmaster at Arkholme succeeded Mrs Nuttall in October 1924.[2] The post office has been in the top shop on the old Bay Horse site at least since 1930. For many of those years Jim Coates was post master.

Before leaving the subject of the post office we remember one of Ingleton's most well known postmen, Tom King. Thomas Foster King was postman between Ingleton and Ribblehead for thirty-three years. As well as being postman he also did errands for dales folk and was rewarded by produce such as butter. He retired in November 1912 and was presented with a clock inscribed, 'Presented to Tom King, by the whole of Chapel-le-Dale and district and a few friends, as a mark of respect after 33 years service as postman between Ingleton and Ribblehead 1879-1912'.[3] His grand-daughter told the story that he was occasionally offered a lift on the footplate of Lord Henry Bentinck's coach. One day Lord Bentinck said to him. 'Don't you feel proud to be travelling with a Lord?' 'Nay' said my grandfather 'Boot's on t'other foot, it's thee riding with a King'. Tom died around 1935.

SHOPS

We know of several people who kept shops in Ingleton because of their wills. Sadly in most cases there was no information as to what kind of shop they kept. Even when there is an inventory it usually says simple 'shop goods' without a hint as to what they were. Richard Babthorpe's will of 1672 tells us that he had goods in the shop worth £12 and debts owing in the shop book for £7. William Allanson's will in 1719 tells us that he was a shopkeeper at Ingleton and his inventory lists 'Shopp Goods', 'Debts in the Shopp Book' and 'More Shopp Goods', but once again there is nothing to tell us the nature of the goods or his shop.

Thomas Redmayne was an early Ingleton shopkeeper in 1707 and in 1711 it is noted that he had a shop at the east end of a dwelling house at Seedhill. In 1787 a note in the court rolls tells us that Elizabeth Thornbeck, heir to Christopher Thornbeck, had a dwelling house in Bell Horse Gate which included a shop with rooms over it. As Christopher Thornbeck was an apothecary perhaps this was Ingleton's first chemist's shop. Many shopkeepers died young. To be a shopkeeper was not a good trade in times of plague, typhus or smallpox. Everyone came shopping and the shopkeeper met them all and took their money and he had a good chance of taking their germs as well.

SHOPS ON OLD BAY HORSE SITE

Three shops were built on the site of the Bay Horse Inn by John Kidd. Mrs Wilkinson sold glass, china and toys at the top shop. John Slinger ran his game and poultry business from the second, while the third was Walter Bonnick's bakery and confectioner's shop. Thomas Bonnick and his wife Mary ran a confectioner's shop. Their son Walter took over the business for some time and was a corn and flour dealer as well as a confectioner. The Bonnicks took an interest in many village activities and Thomas was a member of the Improvement Committee. They used their shop window to show trophies at competition times and when the church clock was not working in 1884 the Bonnicks put a clock in their shop window and lit it at night with two gas jets.

WILLIAM BOARDMAN-BAKER & CONFECTIONER

William Boardman had a shop in the High Street and was followed by his son George. George added the bakery and confectionery business. George later opened a shop in Bell Horse Gate. In 1891 George Boardman was forty-five years old and a grocer and his wife Lydia was a confectioner and together they ran the shop. William Boardman was a pauper barber from Rotherham, where he was born about 1820. In 1851 he was living on the Bank,

Shops on the old Bay Horse Inn site. The top shop has been the Post Office for around eighty years.

William Boardman baker and confectioner in Bell-Horse-Gate.

a pauper with a wife, five children and a pauper mother-in-law. His family had only just arrived at Ingleton, as the youngest child Mary, aged one, was born in Rotherham. The family had most probably been removed from Rotherham due to being paupers.

Perhaps the overseers of the poor at Ingleton did try to return the eight of them back to Rotherham. However, the family had earlier connections with Ingleton as William Boardman's father, Richard Boardman, a skinner, had married Dorothy Hewitt at Ingleton Church on July 2nd 1816. This would certainly explain how a pauper family were allowed into the village. However, once their shop business was founded the Boardman family never looked back.

MARY HODGSON - GROCER

Mary kept a shop in the Back Gate at Ingleton for many years. Following the victories at Inkerman and Alma during the Crimean War, her mother had taken her and her sister along with a donkey and climbed Ingleborough. There they planted a flag in honour of 'our victorious soldiers'. Mary last climbed Ingleborough about 1912, when she was seventy years of age. Mary married John Hodgson an Ingleton blacksmith who also opened a grocer's shop in the Back Gate. When Mary became a widow in the 1890s she continued to run the shop. In May 1920 Mary was charged with selling underweight bread. Thirty-six of her loaves were tested and thirty-two were found to be light weight.

Mary Hodgson in front of her small shop in the Back Gate.

JAMES TOMLINSON GROCER

Carr tells us that, 'Amongst the departed trades people of Upper Gate were Mrs Metcalfe, Miss Foxcroft, and James Tomlinson. The last named began business on the Bank, now occupied by Thomas Walker. Meeting with a serious accident at the colliery which incapacitated him from hard work, his mates clubbed up their contributions to set him up in a shop which they patronised. This clannish humanity set him on his feet and opened the path of prosperity to him'.

James Tomlinson was thirty-three in 1851 and running a grocer's shop on the Bank. He lived with his mother, aged seventy-seven who is recorded as housekeeper. By the 1871 census, twenty years later, he had married, moved to premises in the Back Gate and died, but his widow, Mary, was still running the shop in the Back Gate.

RACHEL QUINLAN DRAPER

Mrs Rachel Quinlan came from Bentham where she ran a draper's shop and bought several old cottages in the main street at Ingleton. Demolishing them she built a large three-storeyed shop on the site and opened the largest drapery business in the district. Following her death in 1876 the business was run by her son Robert and then taken over by Samuel Leach. Her son Robert was also a shopkeeper and oil dealer in Ingleton for many years.

Quinlans shop in the Main Street.

SAMUEL LEACH DRAPER & BOOT & SHOE DEALER

Samuel Leach was a school master from Earby who having visited Ingleton to see the scenery decided to stay. He settled and took over Quinlan's drapery shop in the main street which thrived. He advertised his shop as a 'Drapery Establishment & Boot Warehouse'. He sold drapery and boots and shoes and also produced his own albums of Ingleton scenery photographs and sold Ingleton guides which helped to bring tourists into his shop. The ground floor was later converted into a bank.

BUTCHERS AND AMERICAN BEEF

The first butcher mentioned in the parish registers is Robert Procter in 1609 when his wife was buried. When John Redman was buried in 1699 his occupation was recorded as butcher. John Wilson was a butcher in 1759 when his son Edmund was baptised and Thomas Battersby when he married in 1784. Benjamin Ellis was also a butcher in Ingleton when he married in 1809. Butchers shops were of importance to those who could afford much meat in their diet apart from what they bred or caught themselves. The butchers in Ingleton always seemed to prosper. In 1770 Richard Vipond passed a house, stable and garden and two butchers shops, 'all upon the Seed Hill in Ingleton,' to Thomas Brown. The Browns were butchers in Ingleton before they took over the Wheatsheaf, the joiner's shop and the blacksmith's.

American beef first came to Ingleton in February 1875. The beef was supplied by Mr Slinger and auctioned in the village. John Dumoney, landlord of the Bridge Inn, became an agent of the American Fresh Meat Company and sold American beef and mutton in a shop at the Bridge Inn. The shop opened on March 3rd 1877 with a fine show of juicy beef and a large quantity was sold at prices varying from 6d to 9d per pound.

THE SHOP IN THE SQUARE

George Lumb from Burton-in-Lonsdale bought the large premises in the Square at Ingleton in 1891 and enlarged the building on the north side. He made it into the largest grocer's shop in the district as well as a boarding house. He became a well-known local figure and ran the shop for many years. The building had previously been the old Black Bull Inn. The Lumbs' vans were a well known sight in Ingleton well into the twentieth century. The Lumbs also had a shop in New Road.

Lumb's shop in the New Road.

THE CO-OPERATIVE STORE – THE CO-OP

In November 1875 a Co-operative Society was formed at Ingleton following a public meeting at the National School. The Rev. T.D. Sherlock was chairman and he 'expressed his desire to do all in his power to promote the welfare of the working classes'. Mr Bibby, and Mr Knowles from the co-operative society at Bentham came to explain how the society had been started there and the benefits that it had brought. Joseph Carr was there and when it got down to forming a society he was asked to take over as chairman. The rules of the Bentham society were read over and adopted with the addition of a new rule relating to the reserve fund. Between forty and fifty people paid deposits for shares and a committee was formed to get the Ingleton Co-operative Society Ltd well and truly launched.[4] The shop was opened on New Years Day 1876 by which time £300 had been invested by village people. Joe Thornton was the first manager and Thomas Redhead had the number 1 co-op check number. When the fourth quarterly meeting was held the total income for the year was recorded as £3,187 9s 8d. The first anniversary was celebrated by a meal at the National School where seventy members gathered.

After two years trading the society's first problem was credit. Too many goods were being sold on credit and the management was always short of cash and involved in extra book keeping. One of the rules, the 24th rule, said that members could get credit at the shop to the limit of three quarters of their capital of £5. In March 1878 a meeting was held and the rule was abolished from July 1878. Credit could still be obtained but a lower amount and it had to be paid by the end of a fortnight. A second meeting was called for on March 9th when other problems were discussed. It appears that members were not happy with the running of things. For several quarters a dividend of up to 2s 6s had been paid in the pound, but then in the last quarter there had been no dividend and there was a loss of £6 which could not be explained after stocktaking and checking the books.

In 1880 the co-op bought the premises it had been renting for £531 and this was raised from members' shares. William Colton presided at the first quarterly meting in April 1880 and reported income of £1,536 10s 6°d. A second meeting was held on the 28th to discuss the new premises which were on the main street across from the Parish church. It was planned to add a third storey to the building to make a large room suitable for society meetings as well as public meetings. When the premises were completed they were said to have improved the appearance of that part of the village. The press reported that 'The working men of Ingleton have shown much spirit and what can be accomplished by united self help.'

It was 1881 before the new premises were completed and open. They adjoined the old shop which was then opened for drapery goods. George Coward who was in charge of the building of the store died before it opened and a presentation was made to his only daughter Emily. In January 1882 the annual meeting recorded a good year with growing sales and a membership of 190. It was reported, 'that the stores were well stocked with flesh meat, fresh and cured, with drapery goods and all things usual in a good general provision establishment. The Society has proved an excellent investment for the working men of Ingleton'.

Looking down the street to Ingleton's Co-operative Society shops.

This chapter has been an overview of shops in Ingleton over several centuries. The villagers always had a basic need for food, clothing and household goods and there was always someone ready to supply that need. At first shops were very basic, but in the nineteenth century they began to provide more in the way of luxury goods to those who could afford them. In the late nineteenth century Ingleton attracted more shopkeepers when it became a tourist centre. As with its innkeepers many of Ingleton's shopkeepers came from out of the village. So many of Ingleton's shopkeepers were here for only a few years and left little trace.

1. *Lancaster Guardian,* October 7th 1876.
2. *Lancaster Guardian*, October 18th 1924.
3. *Lancaster Guardian,* November 16th 1912.
4. *Lancaster Guardian,* November 13th 1875.

DOMESTIC BUILDINGS

This is not a chapter on vernacular architecture as the author is certainly not an expert in that subject and so often those said to be experts on local architecture have made such a mess in interpretation. When the County Council architects surveyed Ingleton for its listed buildings in the 1970s they made countless errors, putting buildings in the wrong century, giving buildings the wrong name and even copying date stones incorrectly: the survey for Ingleton was quite hopeless. This work is due to be renewed, but has not yet been done. Ingleton's listed buildings lie in a conservation area which according to the North Yorkshire County Council is, 'The older part of the settlement situated generally to the south-east of the river valley being centred on St Mary's Church, Bell Horse Gate, Main Street and the Square…' However, this is not really true for the oldest part of Ingleton centres on Ingleton Hall and its demesne lands.

This chapter then is a record of some of Ingleton's domestic buildings giving whatever information has been discovered during many years of research. It tells, where known, not only about the buildings themselves, but also something of the people who built them and lived in them. Firstly most of Ingleton's cottages were rough and rubble built. The cottages of the eighteenth and nineteenth centuries were often built to rent and built cheaply. Even in the nineteenth century most did not have a toilet, few had water and many had no ceilings upstairs and were open to the roof. A writer of local jottings in the *Lancaster Guardian* on November 27th 1869 commented:-

> Though Ingleton is so favourably situated for stone and lime, there still are too many cottages so constructed and in such a state of repair, that they are not convenient and comfortable. Most of the bedrooms of such cottages are open to the roof, the slate and flags of which are so far from being weatherproof, that in winter it is no unusual thing for the occupiers to have snow coverlets for their beds.

Fine snow will blow under many roof coverings today, but then for many it blew straight onto their beds. The winters for most Ingleton folk were cold and dark and that was in the discomfort of their own homes. In past centuries toilets were a problem and often there was only one toilet for several cottages. Water had also to be brought for the nearest well or pump and only lucky ones had a well in the house or garden. Cottages were often shared and a whole family would share one bedroom and then many would often take a lodger in addition. 'Few cottages have more than one sleeping room each, yet strange to say, there are families who have so little regard for common decency, that they take in lodgers'.[1] Cottages were often lit by rush lights made from oil and rushes as many could not afford candles which were much more expensive. Hundreds of rush lights could be made for a few farthings. Cottagers were left to dry their clothes in any field or over hedges. The wooden clothes driers were winter hedges to many folks.

The first buildings we look at are the halls. Only one was a true hall and that was Ingleton Hall, the seat of the Lord of the Manor for around eight hundred years. The rest were pseudo-halls, grander houses of grander folk, the lesser gentry and top yeoman farmers.

INGLETON HALL

Ingleton Hall appears not to be a listed building only the barn was listed as a grade III building. The official listing reads, 'Ingleton Hall (Barn only) The old house has completely disappeared, replaced by a C.19 farmhouse of no interest. A large C.17 barn with moulded

Ingleton Hall the site of Ingleton's ancient Manor House.

segmental headed doors is all that remains and this is in poor condition'. A couple of lines on the most important buildings in Ingleton next to the Church is ludicrous and it is not even true. Ingleton Hall has not completely disappeared it is in part preserved in the present building. The barn though scheduled as an historic building was nevertheless demolished. The Hall should certainly be fully listed in the next survey.

Bank Hall the original home of the Greenwood family.

The site of the hall probably dates back over a thousand years. An early wooden hall would have been replaced several times before the stone cased building lived in by the Lowther and Bouch families in the seventeenth century was completed. However, this was partially demolished in the eighteenth century by the Parker family and some ornamental stonework was removed to Browsholme Hall. The hall was a moated hall for many centuries and part of the dried up moat still survives.

Lancaster Parish Registers show the burial of Mr William Walker of Ingleton Hall on March 16th 1668. The entry says 'for debte' suggesting that he was at the time imprisoned at Lancaster for debt. He was most likely a Walker relative of the Lowther family. On March 12th 1758 Bentham Parish Registers record the marriage on Joseph Smith and Margaret Oddie of Ingleton Hall.

In the nineteenth century Ingleton Hall had fallen into a very dilapidated condition and was greatly improved in its outward appearance by T. Burrow. The hall was sold in June 1901 to G.H. Padgett for £5,300. This was in two lots. The first lot was house and garden and thirty-seven acres of land. The second lot was twenty-nine acres of land on the east side of the railway. Sadly Padgett died in Feb 1903 having only just bought Ingleton Hall, but having resided at Ingleton for five years. He came from Menston Hall and was Chairman of Ingleton Electric Light and Power Co.

Richard Bradley lived and farmed at Ingleton Hall for many years and is shown in the 1881 and 1891 census returns. His daughter Elsie May Bradley married Ernest Oscar Boardman the youngest son of George Boardman of Ingleton. The Boardman family are still living at Ingleton Hall in 2008.

BANK HALL

This is listed as a grade II building. The house was probably first built in the seventeenth century and re-fronted in 1765 when David Greenwood and his wife Jane came to live here following their marriage in 1764. The interesting date-stone for 1765 is inscribed with the initials of David and Jane Greenwood. The Greenwood family came from the Halifax area. Isaac Greenwood who was baptised at Luddenden on May 18th 1699 was the first Greenwood to come to Ingleton and he settled on the Bank. As the Greenwood family acquired more land and property they moved away from the village as their neighbours included miners and labourers and built the imposing Greenwood Leghe a mile or so out of the village.

The building became Slingers Temperance Hotel in the nineteenth century and the front was stuccoed. Slinger's Private Hotel also had a garage attached which sold petrol and hired out cars. The hall is now divided into two properties. The removal of the stucco from one property shows clearly where Bank Hall was extended in the early nineteenth century.

BLUE HALL

Blue Hall according to its date stone was built in 1668. However, we know from Anthony Hewitson that the original date stone was covered in rendering during restoration and a new one carved in the nineteenth century.[2] Blue Hall was a post office and general store around 1800 run by the Marriner family. The hall was much altered and the gardens laid out in the style of a gentleman's residence by the Kidd family who lived there in the nineteenth century. A maternity and child welfare centre was opened in the Blue Hall in September 1931. Blue Hall is now divided into three dwellings.

WHITE HALL

White Hall stands off the High Street and is a substantial house. White Hall was to be sold by auction at the Bay Horse in Ingleton in September 1826. 'A comfortable family mansion house called White Hall, situated in High Street Ingleton, consisting of an entrance hall, two parlours, two kitchens, and other offices, a number of lodging rooms and attics, a large wagon house, with an excellent granary over it; barn stable and yard…The house was lately in the occupation of William Fairbank'. The hall also came up for letting and sale again in 1837 and 1839. It was much renovated by Mrs Greenwood and in 1864 reported as a very respectable dwelling. For many years it was a guest house attracting visitors from a wide area.

BUG HALL

Bug Hall stood in the Back Gate and was demolished in the mid nineteenth century. It was reported to have been 'an old barn with appurtenances, known by the unenviable name of Bug Hall'. It was bought by Mr Foxcroft of Skipton who demolished it and built a grocer's shop and some neat cottages on the site. Very little is known of it.

STORRS HALL

The origin of Storrs Hall was Ingleton's Poor House built in the eighteenth century. Because of its elevated position and extensive views it was long known as Mount Pleasant. When the Poor House at Ingleton became obsolete with the building of the new workhouse at Giggleswick by the Settle Union, Mr and Mrs George Smith of Keighley bought the premises. They used it as a holiday cottage until they decided to enlarge the buildings and move their school from Keighley to Ingleton. Joseph Carr reported that the architect was one of the finest in Yorkshire, but did not name him. Certainly Storrs Hall, now split into several dwelling houses is quite impressive and far from its lowly origins as a poor house.

MOORGARTH HALL

Moorgarth Hall was built by Alfred S. Kirk and became known as the Hydro. In the 1920s it was an hotel advertising itself as, 'Pleasantly situated in two acres of Wooded Grounds, on the Keighley and Kendal Road. Tea Gardens, Summer Camp, Tennis courts, and Apartments, Breakfasts, Luncheons, Teas and Light refreshments at any time. Large and Small parties.' The proprietor was J. Hainsworth.

TWISTLETON HALL

Twistleton Hall was described in a sale notice of August 1803 as 'Most advantageously situated near Ingleton, consisting of a good mansion house, with convenient barns and outbuildings, all in good repair; and of about one hundred and seven customary acres of very rich arable, meadow and pasture land, divided into convenient fields, and all lying nearly contiguous; now in the occupation of John Parker under a yearly rent of £203'.

BEECH TERRACE (BRICK ROW, BRACEWELL'S ROW)

Beech Terrace was built in 1875 by William Bracewell the proprietor of Ingleton Colliery. He used the clay from the mine at Wilson Wood to set up a brick making works and the row was built from these bricks. There are twelve houses in the row and the one at the end by the road, slightly larger than the others and with a cellar, was the manager's house. When they were sold in 1887 following the death of William Bracewell they were advertised as, 'Twelve brick-built messuages or dwelling-houses and shop, known as Brick Row, situate adjoining the turnpike road from Ingleton to Bentham'. The rents were paid fortnightly and the total rents for the year were £79 6s.

BEEZLEY FARM

Named from the Beesley family who were in Ingleton in the seventeenth century. The spelling of the name has varied over the years and the spelling given here is from the Electoral Register. In 1691 Richard Beesley and his wife Agnes were registered as Catholics.

BELL HORSE GATE

The property in Bell Horse Gate was probably originally one large dwelling. Then it was divided into three cottages. The large porch to the second cottage was added long after the original building was erected. In 1787 a dwelling house in Bell Horse Gate was registered in the Ingleton Court Rolls when it was passed from Elizabeth Thornbeck to Oliver Farrer. The property had belonged to her father, Christopher Thornbeck, an apothecary in Ingleton. The property was composed of a house and a shop with rooms over the shop. There was a croft and garden and 'Well Garth with a draw well therein'. Perhaps the shop was the first chemists shop in Ingleton. If the well, a deep one with rope and bucket, was in the lower Bell Horse Gate area then the water in it would have drained through the graveyard with all considerable health hazards. In 1919 the three cottages in Bell Horse Gate were all bought together by Samuel Worthington for £350.

CHURCHYARD VIEW

This building was erected on the site of the old Churchyard School and probably used some of the materials from the old building. The house was built by Joseph Bentham timber merchant of Ingleton. In June 1877 the house was put up for sale by auction and sold to Mr Yates of Kirkby Lonsdale for £360.

CLOD VILLAS

Clod Villas were so named because they were built on the Clod. They were not the first buildings to be built there as buildings are shown on the Tithe map of 1847. In 1897 the Clod came up for sale, 'The Clod situate on the South West side of Ingleton and Thornton bridge and measures about half an acre. For building purposes this is a chance rarely met with in the district'. The two Clod Villas also came up for sale, one in the occupation of Miss Everett and the other lived in by the owner Miss Ellershaw. Each house was said to contain two cellar kitchens, two sitting rooms, three good bedrooms, pantry and all the necessary outbuildings. There was also a large refreshment room standing on the site which could accommodate one hundred and fifty people at one sitting.

In December 1921 Clod Villas with the land adjoining sold to John Downham of Bentham for £725. John Downham died in May 1927at the age of eighty-three, having only occupied the premises for a few years. He had been churchwarden and school manager and had previously lived at Beesley and Twistleton Hall.

COCKING HOUSE (COCKIN)

Cocking House was for sale with a barn, stable and croft in July 1808. There was an old malt kiln nearby and the land around was called Cocking Croft. It was named after the Cockin family and John Cockin lived there for many years in the eighteenth century. James and Stephen Hammerton lived there as tenants in 1808. This was one of Ingleton's fine old houses which gradually fell into disrepair and was demolished in the early twentieth century.

CROSS FARM

Cross Farm on the Hawes road out of Ingleton was the site of Ingleton's first poor house. There old men, poor widows and orphaned children were put together to keep down the cost of maintaining the poor. They were given a very basic diet and where possible put to work to help pay for their keep. Later the poor house moved to the site of Storrs Hall and Cross Farm became simply a farm again. In 1808 the farm was in the occupation of John Herd. It was described as a substantial farmhouse, with barn, stabling and other outbuildings.

GREENWOOD LEGHE

This large house was built around 1875 in a commanding position on a fine elevation with extensive views by William Norman Greenwood. It was built on the site of Riggs Hill and was named after Greenwood Leghe in Heptonstall near Halifax the family home and origin of the Greenwood family. It stood empty for many years and was finally demolished in the 1970s.

HARLING HOUSE

Harling House was originally built as Rock House by William Metcalfe in 1875 and the name was later changed to Harling House. The plot of land on which Harling House now stands was bought by Robert Atkinson for £51 at a sale held in the Three Horse Shoes in June 1875. The *Lancaster Guardian* recorded it as, 'a plot of ground where Harling Barn once stood on the south side of the New Road leading to Moorgarth Colliery'. It was soon passed to William Norman Greenwood of Greenwood Leghe. The Court Rolls record the passing of the land on August 11th 1875, 'William Norman Greenwood to William Metcalfe Collier, land formerly site of Harling Barn'. The date stone over the door shows the house was built in 1875 and the initials M, W & M stand for Metcalfe, William and Margaret. The census return of 1881 records the house as Rock House and shows that William Metcalfe, mining engineer, was living in the house with his wife and one servant.

By 1891 Robert and Annie Winder were living in the house. Robert Winder was a stonemason and part of the firm Newsholm and Winder. In May Annie Winder of Harling House died. The Winder's daughter, Gwendoline died of pneumonia in New York on May 9th 1928 at the age of thirty-three. Their second daughter Sally George, a former teacher at Chapel-le-Dale, also went to the USA and had a family there. Sally's son, Carl George, became a Professor of Biology in New York.

IVY COTTAGE

In 1901 there were three Ivy Cottages in Ingleton. One in the Bottoms, one on the Bank next to Ivy Mount and one in the Back Gate. The Ivy Cottage mentioned here is the one in the Bottoms. It is built onto the old Fulling Mill. In April 1926 it was bought in auction by Harold Redhead for £185. The occupier at that time was T.Heselton. In July 1927 Thomas Preston, tanner, died at Ivy Cottage at the age of 58. He had been a member of St Mary's Church and had served on the Parish Council. He was a member of the Oddfellows, Ingleton Brass Band and at one time had been landlord of the Station Hotel at Ribblehead. By May 1928 the Fletcher family were living in Ivy Cottage and their three year old son lost one eye when boys were throwing stones.

LONG CHIMNEY

In *Ingleton Bygone & Present* the Balderstons recount, 'On the Twistleton promontory at Long Chimney, between Twistleton Hall and the Manor House, may be seen the groundwork and walls of some ancient ruins; they certainly are but vestiges of what we believe formerly occupied the same place, and their history does not generally appear known; still it is understood that a considerable part of the original building was subterranean or consisted of vaulted chambers below ground'. The building's date stone of 1667 is initialled B A & M.

It is often said that this was earlier a nunnery, but there is not one scrap of evidence to prove this. All religious houses were listed with their contents at the dissolution and this is not listed in any records. The story appears to be pure fabrication: there is no evidence whatever of a nunnery on Twistleton promontory. The story most likely came from Robert B. Cragg who wrote *Legendary Rambles – Ingleton and Lonsdale.* The problem with Cragg is that he tells his legendary stories in a fictional manner and never tells us where he got his original legend from. The following account comes from the story, the Helks Lady.

One day after another the monasteries fell, and on the Corpus Christi Day following the death of Dame Redmayne, Sir Thomas Cromwell's minions were coming to take possession of the revenues of the small nunnery at Twistleton ... The mid-day bell at the nunnery rang out its silvery tones to call the nuns to their prayers, as quietly as if there was no raging tempest without, and no trouble in store for them ... Here Major Burrow showed his commission and orders signed by Sir Thomas Cromwell himself, and asked for possession in the name of the King. The nuns' possessions were poor indeed, scarcely anything but a relic of St. Agatha, which they were allowed to keep.

The chapter ends, when Sir Guy tells the nuns they all can have a home at Halsteads, 'and placing his long lost bride before him on his saddle, he rode proudly down the valley. The bells of St. Oswald's rung their merriest peals, and the sorrow of the nuns turned into joy, and the Ingleton bells took up the joyful strain'. The above account and the pages from which it is taken are one hundred per cent pure fiction.

So Long Chimney was simply an old farmhouse from the seventeenth century. By 1888 when the Balderstons published *Ingleton Bygone and Present* they tell us that Long Chimney was in ruins. There is no mention of anyone living at Long Chimney in the early census returns from 1841 so that this farmhouse must have been a ruin for around two centuries.

COTTAGES AT MOORE LANE

Moore Lane is inscribed on the cottages and Moor Lane in the official Electoral Roll. Good to see there are still some confusions and everything is not cut and dried in twenty-first century Ingleton. Even the Moor family changed their name spelling from generation to generation. The three cottages in Moore Lane were built by Thomas Moore who died in 1895. As the Moore family benefited from money from the Sill family of Dent, and as the Sill family of Dent were involved in sugar plantations and the slave trade in the West Indies, then these cottages are Ingleton's tangible link with the slave trade.

The three cottages are mentioned in the press in 1894. 'Opposite the printing office up a yard are three workmens' cottages built by Thomas Moore'. When in his will he left one of the cottages to his grandson, Tom Capstick, he also left him, 'a share in the privy and ashpit in respect of the said house'. This shows that they shared one toilet and ashpit in 1895.

PAUL'S FOLD AND STRAND COTTAGES

The cottages by Ingleton Bridge and the cottages by the river were all called Paul's Fold. Then the cottages facing the river were rebuilt around 1874 and renamed Strand Cottages. Joseph Carr tells us that, 'In addition to the many new houses mentioned there are the Strand Cottages, which are built on the site of the old cottages at the foot of the churchyard, once known as Paul's Fold, named after Paul Berry, the old parish clerk of sixty or more years ago'. Descendants of Paul Berry have come to Ingleton and not realised that Paul Berry probably lived in what are now Strand Cottages and not what is now called Paul's Fold. The Strand cottages were rebuilt by Richard Brown who had bought them from the Berry family. In 1921 the Court Rolls recorded, 'All those five dwelling houses in Paul's Fold at Ingleton Bridge known as Strand cottages'. It is interesting that they used both names in this case. The

Blue Hall has served as a gentleman's residence, post office, Holiday Fellowship guest house, school and clinic.

The old Paul's Fold rebuilt and renamed Strand Cottages in 1874.

house by the bridge in Paul's Fold has the date stone 1668 with initials R & B and surname A. It is difficult to find the names of those initialled even with the help of parish registers, although in this case the surname could well have been Allen or Atkinson.

PEAR TREE COTTAGE

Pear Tree Cottage is a two-story eighteenth century rubble stone grade III listed building As with most of Ingleton's old cottages the original windows have all be altered. At the east end is an external chimney breast. At the rear of the building is a round staircase turret. A. Howson, who served in the Royal Air Force during World War I lived here in the 1920s and ran the cottage as a guest house.

PROSPECT COTTAGE

Prospect Cottage was built in 1870 by William Henry Mawson, father of the world famous landscape gardener, Thomas Mawson. The Mawsons lived there several years before selling to William Atkinson. In 1892 Atkinson sold the property to William Sawdon one of Ingleton's noted artists and photographers who lived there around ten years. Thomas Mawson wrote, 'The site was well chosen, because although it stood at the end of a row of old cottages, it had a southern exposure, overlooking a valley through which ran the river Greta, with wooded slopes and panoramic distances... The view down the valley of the river Greta was one of the finest prospects I have ever seen, and thus early I was taught the value of a fine panorama'.

SEED HILL

The house is mentioned in a deed of 1760, 'All that Messuage or tenement known as Seed Hill or Seedy Hill, lately rebuilt wherein Francis Procter did lately live.' Francis Procter was buried at Ingleton in 1760. So in 1760 Seed Hill was rebuilt, but it was not a complete rebuilding. Ancient side doors from previous centuries were filled in and substantial alterations made to make it an acceptable Georgian house for a gentleman.

Seed Hill with a history of many centuries.

Slated Mansion on the left, with view of viaduct and train c1875.

Seed Hill house was auctioned at the Bay Horse Inn in September 1802. The house consisted of 'a dining room, parlour, kitchen etc, on the ground floor, four bedrooms, a dressing room with garrets over them; a detached brew-house, with good gardens, well stocked with fruit trees'. John Barlow lived there for many years in the eighteenth century and died there in March 1801. There has probably been a house on the site from the fifteenth century and certainly from the sixteenth. One interesting feature of the house is the deep well in the corner of kitchen.

The Redmayne family lived here from around 1620 to well into the eighteenth century. The Hearth Tax of 1672 shows that the house, lived in by Richard Redmayne and family, had three hearths and few in Ingleton had more. His son Thomas Redmayne died there in 1725 leaving daughters Margaret and Ellen. In the nineteenth century William Hodgson, farmer, lived at Seedhill Farm from the 1830s to the 1860s followed by Thomas Hodgson a farmer of twenty-nine acres who was still living there in 1901 at the age of sixty-nine. The house was split into two cottages around 1930, but has now been fully restored into one property by the present occupier.

SLATED MANSION

Slated Mansion lies at the bottom of the Brow. Originally it is said that the house was thatched and became known as the Slated Mansion when the thatch was replaced by a new roof of local slate. Originally it had mullioned windows which were replaced about 1865. It has a date-stone with the inscription 1717 T, I & M. The initials are most likely Thirnbeck J & M. That is James and Margaret Thirnbeck. James Thirnbeck married Margaret Chamley at Ingleton on July 12th 1714. *Ingleton Bygone & Present* tells us that a doctor once lived there and James Thirnbeck was a doctor. When he married again at Thornton in January 1734 the register recorded him as 'Christopher Thornbeck of Ingleton practitioner in Physick and Surgery widower.'

GRETA GATE TOLL HOUSE (GRETA BRIDGE)

This was the toll house on the Keighley Kendal turnpike built when Ingleton bypass was constructed in 1823. It served as a toll bar until 1877 when the Turnpike Trust was abolished, the gate removed and the house sold. The last toll collector was James Atkinson who lived there with his family.

YANNAMS HOUSE

Appears to have been named from the field it was built on the Annams meaning intake or new intake. Joseph Carr lists it as one of the few 'substantial and genteel houses' in Ingleton in 1896. Carr also mentions it among the 'old dwellings of the long departed yeomanry' which have undergone a considerable change, thus suggesting nineteenth century modernisation of an older house.

Minister T. Burrow Pooley lived there and in 1851 the minister of Ingleton, the Rev. Richard Denny was in residence. It later became the home of Joseph Bentham who was a timber merchant.

LITERARY INSTITUTE OR VILLAGE INSTITUTE

This building is included here as it finished up as partly residential accommodation. There had been a Reading Room at Ingleton from February 1888. It began with a cottage in Church Street, but eventually a plot was bought close to the Wheat Sheaf and the foundation stone of a new Literary Institute was laid in May 1900 by Hector Christie JP of Settle who for many years was chairman of the Craven Lime Works. There was a library and maps and a collection of artefacts of local interest was eventually gathered together including bronze age axe heads. Funding was always a problem and eventually the collection was broken up and the building turned into a surgery with residential accommodation above.

Foundation stone laying for the Literary Institute in May 1900.

GENERAL

About 1958 when James Newhouse asked Ingleton mason, Alan Storey, to install a new fire place at Chapel House Farm an oval oven was discovered. Inside was an old legging made of leather. An old local lady said she remembered the oven being in use. It was blocked up again with the leather legging left inside. Mrs & Mrs Newhouse were at Chapel House farm, Chapel-le-Dale twenty-eight years. When they rented a cottage in the Back Gate at Ingleton they again asked Alan Storey to install a new fireplace. Another oven was found and this time it contained a miner's union card made out to Hector Walker. The latest oven was in the shape of a beehive, and apart from the door, which measures 12 in x 9 ins there is no other opening, the old red bricks were handmade and in perfect condition.

Joseph Carr used to comment on the inappropriate names which some Ingleton folks of his time used for their houses. Beezley Grange, he commented – where is the grange? What he would have said if confronted with The Hyning, Floriana, Rosebec, Pomarez, L'Abri, Elsinore, Juno, Lemon Cottage, Fron-y-Felin, Wynstay, Loen, and Schiehallion heaven only knows. They have no relation to Ingleton and district at all, but that is the way of things today and people have the right to call their house whatever they wish. Most would seem more appropriate on a Morecambe caravan estate. Good to see Inglefalls, Three Peaks House, Rock View, Dalescroft, Moorlands, Burnside, Ingleholme, the Old Dairy, Pinecroft, Croftland, Linton Cottage and Greengarth, for these certainly seem at home in the area.

REFERENCES

1. *Lancaster Guardian,* November 27th 1869.
2. *Guide to Ingleton*, A. Hewitson, 1893, p.3.

PUBLIC SERVICES

WATER

From early days Ingleton relied on a few wells and the river for water. One of the wells was Pan well just off the Back Gate where in spite of local building the well survives. It was called Pan well due to the large iron basin into which the spring ran and which looked something like a large pan. Several houses had their own well such as the one at Seed Hill which was revealed again some years ago in one of the rooms. Neatly stoned to a depth of fourteen feet it ran with clear fresh water. Objects found in the base of the well showed that it was probably flagged over in the Victorian period. Some of the old houses had a well in the cellar. There were also a few pumps scattered around the village including one by the Bridge Inn. Joseph Carr was so proud of his pump at Hollin Tree that even when water was piped through Ingleton, he tried to resist having to pay water rates for water he did not want.

As the population grew so did pollution and some wells became tainted. The worst problem was where people took their water from the river, as they did on the Strand, even in Victorian times. As rubbish and sewage was being tipped into the river higher up the valley it became a health risk. In November 1874 a Vestry meeting was called in the National School at Ingleton to consider a proper water supply for the township and to realise the importance of providing a clean and plentiful supply of water for the inhabitants. Joseph Carr was the chairman of the meeting on that evening.[1] Dr Symes the Medical Officer for the Settle and Skipton Unions attended the meeting and he spoke of the filthy water used by the inhabitants of Poverty and the premises all around the church area. They used water from the river or the mill-race, which was usually polluted by the town sewage. He pointed out that this was an area where typhoid fever had been prevalent and that there was no wonder people suffered from much sickness.

Attempts had been made to supply Ingleton with water from a natural reservoir at Storrs, but the supply failed in dry weather. Some distance beyond Skirwith there was an abundant and constant supply of wholesome water which was reliable in all seasons. This was a powerful flow from the north side of Ingleborough. As there was a rapid descent from the source they would need no reservoir and the pipes might be connected to the source as it issues from the hillside. The cost of the work was estimated at £1,000, interest £35 at 3° per cent. It was explained that the installation cost and costs for collecting water rates would have to be raised by a water rate which could pay for the system in thirty years. The meeting proposed and passed a resolution, 'That the Rural Sanitary Authority and the Settle Union be requested to provide a supply of pure and wholesome water for the use of the township of Ingleton, and other purposes, and it be recommended that the cost of contracting the necessary waterworks should be borrowed by the Sanitary Authority from the Public Works Loan Commissioners, and the payment should be spread over a term of thirty years'. This was one meeting where the resolution was passed without any dissension.[2]

By January 1876 little had been done. The people in Ingleton were getting annoyed as one thing that Ingleton had in abundance was water with many springs in the area on every hand and yet the inhabitants were insufficiently supplied with water. The initial plan had been abandoned and a new plan was made to have a storage tank on the road leading to Chapel-le-Dale. Then came a legal problem as the lessees of Ingleton Mill claimed all water from Swarbeck. The water scheme would not have needed all the water from the stream as a tank of 6,000 gallons was planned and water would be conveyed from the tank by service pipes of four inch bore. It was pointed out that employees of Ingleton Mill would benefit greatly from the new water supply, but the mill owners and lessees made heavy claims for water losses and the case had to go to arbitration.

The greatest barrier to getting water to Ingleton was the excessive charges being made by the mill for loss of water rights. At first they asked £200 and then £500 in compensation. Parliamentary powers had to be applied for as the parties could not agree and come to reasonable terms. The arbitrator awarded the owners of Ingleton Mill £23 18s and the lessees £54 5s.[3] The delay had one good result in that the cost of the iron pipes needed had been reduced in price by nearly a half. It was July 1879 before tenders were put out for the waterworks and Phoenix Foundry's tender of £419 8s 6d was accepted for 3,045 yards of four inch iron pipe and 550 yards of three inch pipe.

When the work was completed the bill was near £3,000 which caused complaints, but everyone was pleased to have a good supply of fresh water. Once the village's water supply was running then the Sanitary Authority began dismantling local pumps to ensure that the new water supply was used. Some who had the town water put into their house swore never to use it and continued with their old wells and pumps. Joseph Carr accused the Inspector of Nuisances of being 'bent on smashing up my pump and those of a few other persons.'[4] Joseph Carr complained that he had to pay for the town's water when he had a plentiful supply of good spring water. The inspector came to Hollin Tree and tested Carr's water supply hoping to find some pollution, but he did not. In spite of much fuss that was made by many who wished to retain their pumps and well Joseph Carr himself praised the new water supply in his memoirs, 'I very willingly bear this testimony, that it is by far the very best improvement for the health, comfort, and convenience that was ever made for the benefit of the inhabitants of Ingleton'.

Of course Ingleton's water supply has needed considerable work since its initial installation in 1879. There were numerous extensions to the mains and pressure had to be increased as supply was poor when visitors came in summer. Then the growth of the population necessitated a better supply when the New Village was built. A new scheme costing around £3,400 used springs on Southerscales Moor which, even in the driest period yielded fifty-five thousand gallons in twenty-four hours. New pipes conveyed the water to the old workings and this work was done urgently in 1915 as forty-four houses were already completed in the New Village and becoming occupied.[5]

GAS

In September 1866 a few of Ingleton's forward-looking inhabitants planned to have the village lit by gas during the coming winter. Messrs Humphray, Brown, Bentham, Preston, Hartley and Dent met in the National School on the evening of August 31st for the purpose of forming a Gas Company. The £5 shares were speedily taken up once the inhabitants were convinced of the benefits and the scheme quickly got off the ground. John Thomas Coates was appointed the managing director as he had gas works adjoining Ingleton Mill and leased his gas-making equipment for a term of twenty years, with the proviso that the lease may expire at the end of seven or fourteen years. The lease came into effect on November 1st 1866.

Better days were predicted for Ingleton once the streets were lit by gas. People would no longer have to hold events on moonlight nights or stumble home in the dark. By October 1866 a contract had been made with Jefffrey Moorhouse of Kirkby Lonsdale to lay gas pipes in the streets of Ingleton. The gas company also advertised for contractors for the excavating so that the work could proceed quickly. By January the first street gas lamp was set up on the Hill and lit in the evening by John Thomas Coates the Managing Director of the gas company. Everyone proclaimed it a great success.

The gas works at Ingleton, now demolished.

In August 1868 there was a public meeting at the National School to determine whether the provisions in an Act of William IV entitled, 'An Act to repeal an act of the 11th year of his late majesty George IV, for the lighting and watching of the parishes in England and Wales, and to make other provisions in lieu thereof,' or so much thereof as relates to lighting, be adopted and put into practice to light the streets of Ingleton more efficiently.

The main body of the meeting was in favour of adopting that part of the Act which would empower them to light up the streets with gas. Mr J. Bentham was the chairman and told the meeting that it was contemplated having three lamps in addition to the lamp at Seed Hill, and that the four lamps for gas, lighting and cleaning would cost thirty shillings each or £6 for the lighting expenses for the year. This would mean that it would only be a penny in the £ and the following year °d in the £.

As usual many Ingleton folks were against anything that would cost a great deal of money. They had done without street lights for centuries why bother now? To meet the arguments of those who objected to the expense it was agreed that none of the officers that might be appointed would have any salary. Eventually most people saw the advantages of lighting the streets of Ingleton. The inhabitants and visitors would be able to transact business after dark, it would check those deeds of mischief often carried out in the dark and it would modernise the village. G.S. Homfray, G. Smith and G. Coward were elected inspectors for the ensuing year. It was also proposed by G. Coward and seconded by Rev R. Denny that the sum of £15 be expended the first year.

Farmers objected to the street lighting on the grounds that it led to heavy parochial rates and the street lighting died out through lack of support. Ingleton folks had hardly become accustomed to the streets being lit by gas before they were again plunged into the dark. However, many had gas put in their own homes, but once the novelty had worn off there were growing complaints that the gas was both expensive and of poor quality. One inhabitant wrote to the press in December 1869 stating, 'Sir, the gas as at present supplied is inferior, and such an exorbitant price as to prevent myself, as well as many more of my standing from using it…The gas company are charging 7s 6d per 1000 feet, which I think you will agree is very high compared with the charge of 4s at other places with fewer inhabitants than Ingleton'. There were also problems with the gas lamps in the village in the winter of 1869 and someone complained, 'Now the streets are as much doomed to darkness during the winter months as they were in the reign of Henry the Eighth'. Due to lack of upkeep the Ingleton lamps were out most of the time over the following ten years.

However, the Gas Company continued, although the increase in consumption was slow during the 1870s and there were still complaints of dear gas. On Monday January 22nd 1877 only four people turned up to the shareholders' meeting of the Ingleton Gas Company. In 1880 there was new agitation for street lighting. Ingleton had become noted for the darkness of its streets. In wet weather and when there was no moonlight it was a difficult task for people to move about the village especially in wet weather when the streets had patches of mud. The churchwardens made a good start by having two lamps fixed up at the church gates during the winter season and this was a great advantage to those who lived in that area. New action resulted in twelve street lamps being set up for the winter of 1880 and this time they were much appreciated.

In 1885 the Ingleton Gas Company laid gas mains down to Holly Tree, to the New Road and Tansy Green to light the streets there. The lamps in those areas had been oil lamps which had blown out on windy nights and been useless. The Gas Company also reduced the price of gas as many householders and particularly shopkeepers had discontinued to use it. The following new lamps were put up in 1885; one at the bottom of Upper Gate near Cocking House, one at the Cross below the Storrs, one at the back of Church Gate, one at high Wood Cottage New Road and another at the bottom near the viaduct. The lighting of the streets which for many years was delayed by opposition now became a permanent amenity.

Complaints of poor street lighting cropped up again in 1887 and then in March 1889 when the gas lighting failed for several nights. A press report stated, 'On Sunday night last, when the church and chapel closed the night was densely dark and the rain was pouring down so that many people could scarcely grope their way home. Many collisions took place in the streets between persons going in the opposite directions, some of them with such force that the weaker ones were knocked down'.

Much depended on the lamplighter who went round lighting the gas lights in the village and things became better when William Harling was appointed in the autumn of 1889. However he had to obey instructions and could not light the lamps when told not to do so. He was instructed not to do so on nights when the moonlight would be sufficient. This was done to save money. In October 1889 there was a public meeting on street lighting. At this meeting street lighting was extended to Fell End, Yarlsber, Greenwood Leghe, New Winning, Pemberton, Wharf and Wilson Wood. There was also a petition to put up an extra lamp in the Bottom which was granted.

When electric lighting came to Ingleton in 1900 the Gas Company had to review its workings. They replaced obsolete equipment with a new retort and purifier. This not only gave the people of Ingleton a better quality gas, but the company also reduced their gas charges from 6s 8d to 5s per thousand feet.

In May 1915 the Gas Company sold the plant at Ingleton to Mr Ellis of Heckmondwyke as a going concern for around £700. The last charge of coke at the retorts was on February 25th 1956. After standing for several decades the gasometer and buildings at Meal Bank were finally demolished or changed to domestic use.

ELECTRICITY

Ingleton was one of the first places in the country to get the benefit of electric lighting. This is rather surprising as Ingleton was only a relatively small village in the Yorkshire Dales. However, the inhabitants had become fed up with the problems of gas lighting. They were annoyed with the supply, the quality and the cost of the gas at Ingleton. Some complained that the gas stank them out of their houses. Several public meetings were held and at a meeting in February 1899 twelve rate payers were selected to canvas the village and discover whether people would prefer electricity to gas. A new century had just begun and the people of Ingleton were seventy-five percent in favour of getting the new and up-to date method of lighting – electricity. John Brookes of Ingleton, termed it 'the most beautiful and perfect light in existence – God's own light'. He also said having watched Ingleton's river power for thirty years that the river could supply the new electric power.

A company was formed and registered, with William Metcalfe, as chairman; John Brookes as secretary; and Mr Brotherton as manager. The Directors acting on the advice of engineering experts decided on a capital of £4,000 in £1 shares, and over 3,500 of these shares were taken up almost at once. Water power would be obtained from up river where there was a weir forty feet wide. The water was conveyed to the generating house through wrought iron pipes thirty inches in diameter. The pipes were laid on the bed of the stream and then forward in a wooden launder. The water was strained at a pen-trough fixed outside the power house.

In the generating house there were two vortex turbines each being capable of developing fifteen to twenty horse-power, with an effective head of twenty-five feet, and run at a speed of 320 revolutions per minute. Each turbine drove a dynamo which had a maximum output

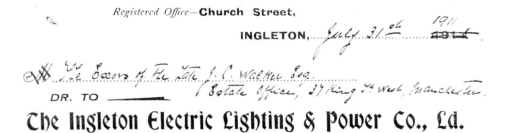

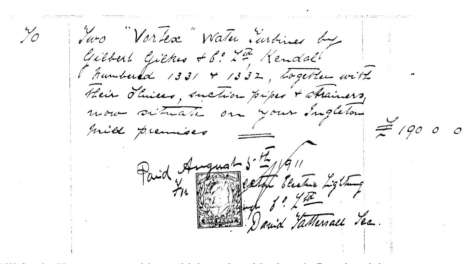

Bill for the Vortex water turbines which produced Ingleton's first electricity.

of thirty-five amperes, three-hundred and thirty volts. The current was conveyed through insulated cables from a switchboard in the centre of the power house to the battery house situated in Church Street in a central position. The battery house was three storied and altogether there were one hundred and sixteen accumulator cells, the capacity of the battery being some 750 ampere hours. Sufficient current could be stored so as to meet any accident which might be experienced at the power house. In the basement of the battery house was fitted the main switch-board, at which the current was measured and regulated. The principal streets of the town were wired with three-core lead covered armoured distributing cables laid in the ground. There were thirty-two street lamps each of thirty-two candle power, giving a good light. The old gas standards were used but the wood standards and brackets were replaced by up-to-date lamps. The electric lighting company charged 6d per unit and as a consequence of the public lighting, there was a lighting rate levied by the Parish Council to bring in £70. Ingleton was on 200 volts DC lighting until 1933.

THE ELECTRIC LIGHT *Lancaster Guardian*, January 20th 1900.
The Ingleton Electric Light and Power Company Ltd, have nearly finished laying down the necessary plant for the illumination of Ingleton and have fixed the opening ceremony for Wednesday, 24th ult. Major J.A. Farrer of Ingleboro' Hall has kindly consented to switch on the light, and the occasion is to be celebrated by a banquet at the Wheat Sheaf Hotel, to which the leading inhabitants of the district are being invited. The ratepayers of Ingleton will be glad when the work is satisfactorily accomplished as the state of darkness into which the streets have been plunged during the winter has proved very annoying and inconvenient.

ELECTRIC LIGHTING 'SWITCHING ON' CEREMONY AND DINNER

Both towns and villages are frequently asking for more light, and on Wednesday, Ingleton, which has been in darkness practically throughout the winter, emerged from its difficulties and is now rejoicing in a system of electric lighting. The growth of the West Riding village as a health resort has made the inconvenience arising from insufficient lighting very keenly felt, and matters reached a climax last

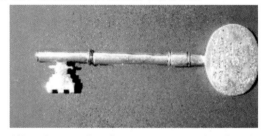

Silver key used at the Battery House in Church Street on the evening of turning on Ingleton's electric lights.

winter, when complaints were rife against the quality and quantity of the gas. Although they may have been almost lightless this winter, the effect of the floating of the company has been beneficial to the ratepayers in this sense, it has been an incentive to the Gas Company to replace some obsolete plant, which was responsible for the defective lighting, with a new retort and purifier. Not only have Ingleton people in their house had better gas, but the price, an important point was reduced from the proverbial lawyer's fee - 6s 8d, down to a simple crown. It remains to be seen what the effect of the competition will be.

To return to the scheme we may state that contracts were let, amounting to about £3,300, for the supply and erection of generator, storage and distribution plant, and Wednesday saw the culmination of the efforts of the workmen connected with the various firms who have been busy for some months past. The contractors were as

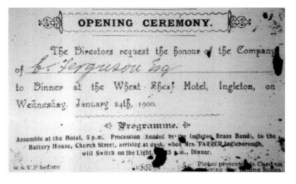

Invitation to the opening ceremony and dinner at the Wheat Sheaf on January 24th 1900.

follows: Water power, Messrs G. Gilkes and Company Kendal; electric current, Messrs Drake and Gotham, King-street, Manchester; sub-contractors for the street lighting and cables, Messrs Callenders, London; local contractors for the building of the power house. Messrs Thistlethwaite and Kettlewell, Ingleton; local sub-contractor for the battery house, Mr Mackay, Ingleton; local contractors for street trenching, Messrs Thistlethwaite and Kettlewell; engineers for the whole project Messrs G. Gilkes and Co., Kendal.[6]

ELECTRIC POWER FROM WATER *Lancaster Guardian,* **February 24th 1900**
This article, fully illustrated, appeared in the national magazine *Electrician* for last week:-

Ingleton is a picturesque little Yorkshire village of some 1,600 inhabitants. Its chief attraction is its healthful situation on the hill slopes of the West Riding; its principal trade apparently, granite quarrying. This sequestered spot has recently presented to electrical engineers an unusually instructive object lesson in the utilisation of water power for the village electric lighting. Out of all proportions to the size of the hamlet or magnitude of the undertaking, the Ingleton electric supply works merit careful consideration and study on the part of electric light engineers; and we make no apology therefore for devoting to so small a scheme such a large proportion of our space this week.

The attitude of electrical engineers towards water power utilisation in this country has been very diversified. While some have held the extreme view that the rivers and coastal tides of Great Britain afford a prolific source of power for electrical supply, others have proclaimed the opposite extreme view, that coal, and coal alone, is the source of our energy, and that all attempts to utilise water power were a delusion and a snare. In both extremes there is lack of reason; for while it is demonstrably true that there is no very widely distributed nor large amount of water power commercially available in this country, it is equally patent that here and there throughout the land there are specially favoured spots, affording a sufficiently abundant and steady supple of water power to work, either entirely in part, electrical works large enough for local demands.

Unfortunately electrical engineers have not always been happy in the selection of these spots. At Worcester, for example, the utilisation of the Tene has not met with qualified approval, but has been on the contrary, much lamented locally. At Buckingham a small electrical supply works was originally run from the Ouse, but steam power subsequently re-placed the energy of the stream. Better success, however has attended other efforts in this direction; and we may cite the presently re-modelled works at Carlow, Ireland, and the water power plant at Laxey, as evidence of this.

The neighbourhood of Ingleton would appear to afford reasonably good means for running electrical supply from water power. The river Greta flows through the

317

village, and the sharp declivity of its course immediately above Ingleton has enabled an effective fall of some 30 feet to be obtained, with only a moderate capital outlay, on retaining works and conduits. At a point above 900 ft, above a convenient location for the power house, a weir was thrown across the stream; the principal dimensions include a width of 40 ft and a height of 5 ft. Near the right bank, the weir has a sluice admitting of a 30 in., wrought iron pipe line which follows for a short distance the course of the stream. The lower end of this pipe discharges into a wooden chute, by which the head water is conveyed the remainder of the distance to the penstock above the power house. At the present moment the iron hand of winter has been laid on the works, but, we may add, severe as the frost has been, it has not interfered with the maintenance of electric supply.

Our readers will have been enabled by the forgoing brief account to perceive how thoroughly Messrs Gilbert Gilkes and Co., of Kendal, the contractors for the entire undertaking have developed all the possibilities of this mill site. The result of the construction work thus far described has been to create an effective working head of 27 ft at the turbines. We will now enter the power house and see how this is utilised. It seems almost absurd to dignify the simple little structure, with its one room with the lofty name of 'power house', yet in design and equipment the building is amply adapted to all present requirements. Within the machinery room are two 'Vortex' turbines, each provided with a separate intake from the penstock and a separate draught pipe leading to the tail race. The turbines run on horizontal shafts, each developing from 15 to 20 h.p. according to condition of the water supply at the time. Each turbine drives its own continuous-current dynamo by means of rope gearing. The dynamos are shunt wound, to give either 45 amperes at 250 volts or 35 amperes at 330 volts, as required for charging cells. A simple switchboard is erected near the centre of the room, facing the dynamos, and it is equipped with the necessary switches and instruments.

Such are the provisions for generating electric current by means of water power at Ingleton. So simple, indeed are these provisions, that probably no power house in the world requires less attention. Beyond the fact that the manager calls once a day to oil up and see that all is in order, it is found quite practicable to leave the place locked up. All other necessary regulation is done at the battery house, which is situated at about 500 yards from the power house and nearer the centre of the village. The battery house is a three storied structure, and is equipped with 116 cells of 780 ampere - hours capacity by Messrs Drake and Gorham. In this ample storage battery the Ingleton Electric Lighting Co., have wisely provided themselves with a strong bulwark against the evils of breakdown of the power house; and it cannot be doubted that the security of an installation of this description is greatly increased by abundant storage capacity.

Distribution is effected on the three-wire system by means of Callender three-cored lead covered and armoured cable. There are three feeding points, fed by Callender triple-concentric lead-covered and armoured cable. The entire system has been designed for about 2,000 8cp lamps. A considerable amount of public lighting has already been carried out, some 32 gas lamp posts having been fitted with 32 c.p glow lamps, one lamp in each post. Formerly street lamps were not lighted when the moon was supposed to be shining over Ingleton, and even on dark nights all lamps were extinguished at 10p.m. The advent of electric light has made the moonlight a superfluity, and has added half-an-hour to the time when the village folk are expected to have turned indoors.

The whole plant was completed and in operation by February 1900. The 3,150 shares offered to the public were quickly taken up. Unfortunately the company was seriously handicapped by the effects of spring frosts and autumn droughts. At these times when the river was so low the turbines only gave off a few horse power and were insufficient to supply all consumers. The company then installed an oil engine to cope with such emergencies.

CEMETERY

The churchyard at Ingleton had been full for generations, but as most graves had few gravestones the ground could be used again and again and there was no great problem. However, in the nineteenth century with the growth of population and with the spread of vaults and larger tombstones the churchyard did become overcrowded and by then it was considered that it could become a health risk. Until 1852 most people in the country were buried in church graveyards. By the middle of the nineteenth century many places in England were in a worse situation than Ingleton, especially those places which had experienced large population growth. To solve this problem the government passed the Burial Acts of 1852 and 1853. The 1852 Burial Act was for London and the 1853 Burial Act was for the rest of the country. The acts allowed local authorities to set up and administer their own cemeteries. In 1880 Dr Barry was commissioned by the Settle Rural Sanitary Authority to look at the burial grounds within the Settle Union, which of course included Ingleton. He produced a report which said that a new cemetery at Ingleton was urgently needed. In October 1880 a township meeting was held in the national school to discuss Dr Barry's report.[7] The chairman, R.B. Ellershaw began the meeting by reading the following extract from the minute book of the Poor Law Board Settle of October 13th 1880. 'With reference to Dr Barry's special report of the burial grounds in this Union the Guardians of the Union acting as the Rural Sanitary Authority, are satisfied that a new cemetery for Ingleton, excluding Chapel-le-Dale, is an urgent necessity'.

Mr Danson proposed that Dr Barry's report be adopted and the resolution was carried. The meeting was told that if the people of Ingleton did not provide a site for the cemetery and make a cemetery, then the sanitary authority would take the matter in hand and do the work at the expense of the parish. About one and a half acres of land was needed and the first suggestion was that the cemetery should be made on the Storrs. If the Storrs was used then it would save Ingleton much expense as the Storrs Common was waste land and only the consent of the Lord of the Manor would be needed.

The problem with Storrs was that it was at the wrong side of the village and the road leading to it from the Cross was steep. John Kidd suggested that five gentlemen should be appointed to look for a proper and fitting site and should report back to a later meeting of ratepayers. If Storrs was decided upon then they should contact the Lord of the Manor at once for permission. Joseph Carr seconded the motion which was passed. The five men appointed were Messrs Danson, Ellershaw, Metcalfe, Holden and Bentham.

The second meeting was duly held in November and the committee reported that they had found three sites. The first was the Storrs site, the second was the Low Flatts on the south side of the village and the third was at Yarlsber. A vote was held between the two most popular sites, the Storrs site and the Flatts, and resulted in nineteen voting for the Flatts and twenty-one for the Storrs. This immediately raised objection and there was a great argument. Some demanded a wider poll to get the opinions of more of the inhabitants. It was pointed out by one person that the Storrs site was totally unsuitable for a burial ground being seventy five per cent rocks and boulders, apart from the long and steep road which led to it. However, tests made at the Storrs found that test pits could be dug to eight or nine feet in good soil and were dry. The Flatts site was said to be water logged and test graves filled with water. The Storrs site was said to be 1,223 yards from the Church gates and the Flatts site 1,067 yards.

A poll was held at the National School on November 11th 1880 and the Flatts site was chosen by a majority of forty. The town crier announced the results to the village in drenching rain. It appears that the reason most farmers were in favour of the Storrs site was that it would be cheaper and would be less of a burden on the rates. It was estimated that the Storrs site would cost £400 and the Flatts site £700. However, in the long run the Sanitary Authority at Settle would have the last say in the matter.

In December a deputation came from Settle to examine the two sites selected by the Ingleton Township. Accompanied by Ingleton men they soon came to the conclusion that the Storrs was an unsuitable site and moved to the Flatts. They also came to the conclusion that the Flatts was not a suitable site. A third site was then looked at, the Yarlsber Flatts, beyond the vicarage on the old road to Clapham. One problem with the Low Flatts site was that the rent had been left to three churches, Horton in Ribblesdale, the Chapel of Ease at Lowgill and Chapel-le-Dale. The rent was equally divided between the three ministers of those churches. It was considered that problems and delay might be caused with having to deal with the Ecclesiastical Commissioners. The local folks at Ingleton were more than a little annoyed that their officials were not considered competent to select a proper burial ground for their dead.

As the question dragged on, complaints arose again about the excessively crowded churchyard. It was reported, 'The churchyard is excessively crowded and the remains of our fathers and other relatives have again and again been disturbed from their resting place, and their remains been mangled and broken with the sexton's hack and spade. It is a scandal and sacrilege to all concerned to allow such a state of things to exist. Excluding family ties and friendships it is discordant to common decency to break up undecayed coffins and human remains.' The writer pointed out that if the High Flatts site on the old Clapham Road was chosen the owner had offered to sell as much land as was necessary at £200 per acre and the work could be started at once.[8]

Eventually a government inspector, Mr Smith, came to Ingleton and held a session at the Court House on Friday June 10th 1881 to hear what the ratepayers had to say about the chosen sites. The majority still wanted Low Flatts, but the medical officer Dr Atkinson said the Yarlsber Flatts were much more suitable. The Local Government Board then let it be known that they would not lend money for work on the Low Flatts site. This was the final blow to the Low Flatts supporters and the Yarlsber High Flatts site was settled upon.

Work began in 1882 and by December although not fully completed the new cemetery was ready for burials. Everything was finished apart from the planting of trees, shrubs and ornamental gardens which were to be left until the spring of 1883. The cemetery was divided into parts so that church people and nonconformists could be buried in their own section, but they shared the same cemetery chapel. The cemetery occupied an acre and a half of a portion of the Yarlsber estate owned by the Rev Farrer of Clapham. The plans for the chapel, walls and grounds were all drawn up by John Hartley, land agent at Clapham. The contractors for the whole works were William Atkinson and Sons and R.B. Ellershaw acted as unpaid clerk of works. The site cost £300 and the total cost was slightly over £1000. The general opinion was that the new cemetery was charmingly situated on a quiet side of the village, where it commended extensive views. The laying out of the ground was also considered to be in harmony with the situation.

The closing of Ingleton churchyard for burials and the opening of the new cemetery brought about a very sad event. On Sunday the 17th of December 1882 a young child was the first to be buried in the new cemetery. The child's mother had been buried only three months before in the churchyard and the father wished them to be buried together. The whole village was sympathetic as this was the usual practice when a child died soon after its mother. However, the Rev Pughe was adamant, the churchyard was closed for burials and that was that. He was blamed for refusing the burial and though some supported him saying that he had no choice, others held it against him during his stay at Ingleton. The Rev Pughe could have allowed the child to be buried with the mother without any real problem as it was done in other places. A very large number of people from the village gathered to see this first funeral service in the new cemetery and the Wesleyan choir came to sing a hymn at the close of the service.

Although the cemetery had a licence for burials it was not finally consecrated until April 28th 1883 by Bishop Ryan when he consecrated the section set apart for burial of members of the Church of England. A considerable portion for burial of nonconformists was left unconsecrated. It was not until Thursday August 23rd that Dr Hoffman with the authority of the Local government Board closed the Ingleton churchyard as a common burial ground. The churchwardens came to give him information on the vaults in the churchyard, but as they could not be exact they made an estimate of twenty.

An Order in Council at the Court at Osborne, dated December 31st 1883 ordered that:-

Forthwith burials at Ingleton Church, and also in the churchyard shall be entirely discontinued, with the following modifications, viz:- a. In such wholly walled graves as are now existing in the churchyard, burials may be allowed on condition that every coffin buried therein be separately enclosed by stonework or brickwork, properly cemented. b. In such partly walled graves as are now existing in the churchyard provided that the earth above them can be opened to a depth of five feet without exposing coffins or disturbing human remains, burials may be allowed of so many of the following relations of those already interred viz: widows, widowers, parents and children as can be buried at or below that depth.

SEWAGE

Ingleton was well favoured for carrying out an economical and effective system of sewage as the natural drainage to the river in the valley was excellent. For centuries during the hours of darkness toilet waste was thrown into the street and left to drain or rot away. On the Bank sewerage used to flow across the road and be absorbed down the Brow. Carr wrote in his memoirs, 'The street which is now called Church-street, was at one time when it was known as Poverty far from being in an ordinary sanitary condition. It required much care to pass through it on a dark night without being contaminated'.

For much of its history the people of Ingleton used a toilet at the bottom of their garden or at the end of the row of cottages. A privy usually housed the toilet with its wooden tub and seat. It was only in the late nineteenth and twentieth century that modern toilets made their appearance. These were then connected up to the drains but a disposal system was needed as a great quantity of raw sewage could not be put into the river. In 1892 when Thomas Moore left a cottage in his will he also left, 'a share in the privy and ash pit in respect of the said house.' It appears there was one toilet for all the cottages in Moore Row. In 1896 the sanitary situation at Ingleton was still poor and Councillor Bentham brought the subject up at a Parish Council meeting in May. He said it was not likely that Ingleton would ever attain a good position as a summer resort until something was done about sanitation. 'He thought the ash pits should be periodically cleaned, and water closets substituted for some of the old fashioned closets where the night soil had to be wheeled through a passage and in some cases through the houses.' Dr Griffiths said that Ingleton was supposed to be a health resort, but that unless the toilet facilities and ash pits were bettered it could be a death trap.

A township meeting in June 1878 considered the proposals for sewering the village. Making the sewers in the village was done under the Settle Sanitary Authority and the builder, Richard Atkinson, was told that as they had full powers they could dig their trenches on anybody's land without asking for their consent. They thought they had law on their side and so strong was their opinion that they cut through John Kidd's property at Blue Hall when they could have gone along the roadside. They also cut through Joseph Carr's land in the Springs breaking down walls and damaging the ground. However, both John Kidd and Joseph Carr took the authorities to court for compensation and the Sanitary Authority had to pay a high cost for their high-handed methods.[9]

On Thursday September 18th 1879 a ratepayers meeting in the National School met to arrange the acquiring of the Bull Land at Ingleton for disposing of drainage and sewerage under the Land Claims Consolidation Act. Following this the Settle Sanitary Authority built the sewerage works on the Bull Lands by the River Greta in 1880. It was known as the Irrigation Field. From around 1884 the Irrigation Field was let by the Settle Sanitary Authority and brought a few pounds per year in rent. On April 24th 1909 the *Lancaster Guardian* recorded the cost of Ingleton's sewerage works in Ingleton's parish debts. In 1880-1882 they had borrowed £1,915 for the sewerage works which would be paid off by 1910.

For centuries there was no waste collection at Ingleton as elsewhere. Individual households got rid of their own rubbish. They either burned it on the house fire, burned it in their gardens, scattered it on the fields or tipped it into the river. The river was the great favourite as it carried all away. It was only in the late nineteenth century when more things began to be sold in bottles and jars and tinned foods came into production that a real problem arose and arrangements had to be made to collect ash and waste and tip it in some central location. At first the riverside near the present-day outdoor swimming pool was used and then the bank of the river Greta on the Bentham Road. Here Victorian and Edwardian rubbish still lies ten or twenty feet deep. Many other places in the village where there was a convenient depression were levelled off with tipped rubbish and grassed over leaving no trace.

REFERENCES

1. *Lancaster Guardian,* November 21st 1874.
2. id
3. *Lancaster Guardian,* August 3rd 1878.
4. *Recollections of Ingleton,* J. Carr, 1896 ed J.I. Bentley, Ingleton Pub., 1991, p.106.
5. *Lancaster Guardian,* March 6th 1913.
6. *Lancaster Guardian,* January 27th 1900.
7. *Lancaster Guardian,* October 23rd 1880)
8. *Lancaster Guardian,* May 21st 1881.
9. *Recollections of Ingleton,* J. Carr, 1896 ed J.I. Bentley, Ingleton Pub., 1991, pp.112,113.

MILITARY SERVICE

If I should die think only this of me:
That there's some corner of a foreign field
That is forever England........
Rupert Brooke.

Ingleton men served throughout the centuries in English and British armies throughout the world. We know that they were represented at Waterloo, in Spain fighting the French in the Peninsula War, in the Crimea fighting the Russians, in Africa during the Boer War, in France and Belgium in World War I and throughout the world in World War II. They would also fight at Flodden Field, Agincourt, Crecy, and in the Civil War. Most came back to tell their story, but few were ever recorded. We have already seen the list of men from Tudor Ingleton ready to serve in time of war, but it sadly does not tell us which of them had seen military service. Many were bowmen and kept their long bows by them at home as their fathers and grandfathers had done before them.

In 1868 an Ingleton born blacksmith, turned soldier, died on April 2nd aged 79 years. Luckily his obituary in the press noted that he had served with the Royal Scots Fusiliers at Quatre Bras, Hougoument and finally at Waterloo. He passed through without a scratch and returned to London with his regiment. However, while serving in Spain he was seriously injured and had to have his right leg amputated which finished his military career. For the rest of his life he enjoyed his pension of one shilling a day. A little research showed that he was born at Ingleton in 1789 the illegitimate son of Ellen Howson.

The Crimean War came in 1854 when British forces, along with the French and Turks, went to fight the Russians. When victory was announced in the Battle of Alma in 1854, and when the final victory came in May 1856 the bells of Ingleton church were rung to celebrate. John Thomas Coates took two cannon to the top of Meal Bank and continued to fire them off until nearly midnight on both occasions.[1,2] Of the men who served in the war nothing is said at the time. However, in June 1880 Thomas Buck a labourer at Storrs lime kilns died after collapsing at work while helping to put a quarter of a circular iron plate over the mouth of a kiln: the portion weighed over two tons. In his obituary we are told that he aged fifty-seven, was born at Dent and served in the Crimean War.[3]

When seventy-three year old Mrs Thomas Marsden died in 1911 her short obituary mentioned that she had followed her first husband to the Crimea where he was a soldier.[4] She was there for two years and had worked as a nurse. Sadly so little information is given that we do not know her Christian name, her maiden name or the name of her first husband who served in the Crimean War. It is likely that this Ingleton woman did her nursing service on the spot in the Crimea and not in the Turkish hospital at Scutari where Florence Nightingale served.

A stirring scene took place at Ingleton when Thomas Calverley departed for South Africa in January 1900. He was a signalman at Ingleton, but being a reservist, was called to serve in the Boer War. The man was accompanied by railwaymen from his house to the station and following them were the Ingleton Brass Band playing 'Soldiers of the Queen' and a crowd of two hundred people. At the station several patriotic songs were sung and there were loud cheers and a fusillade of fog-signals as the train pulled out. Some people in the village collected funds for those serving in South Africa. Collections were made in the Volunteers Drill Hall and other places to supply the West Riding regulars, 'The Havercake Lads' with tobacco, notepaper and other materials.

Only a few Ingleton men served in the Boer War the most well-known of them being William Norman Greenwood of Greenwood Leghe. He served in the Duke of Cambridge's Yeomanry as a volunteer and many in Ingleton were amazed that 'he had paid to be shot at'. He was captured by the Boers and spent some time in a Boer prison, but was liberated and returned home in November 1900. He was given a great welcome at Ingleton where the streets were decorated with flags. Greenwood was met at the Bridge Inn by a procession, which escorted him to a banquet at the Wheat Sheaf served in the pavilion. The procession was headed by the Ingleton Brass Band, followed by Superintendent Haynes of the police, then a landau containing William Greenwood in uniform accompanied by his mother. The local volunteers came next led by Lieutenant Tate and finally other Ingleton folk who wished to join the procession.[5] Cpl. Mullen, Cpl. Clapham and Pte. Birkbeck also served in the Boer war and returned to Ingleton at the war's end in 1902 and they were given an enthusiastic welcome at Ingleton Station.

VOLUNTEER RIFLE CORPS

In 1859 Rifle Volunteers Corps were raised across the country when there was a fear that the French were about to invade. The Volunteer Rifle Corps survived just under fifty years and were the forerunners of the Territorial Army. At Ingleton a public meeting was held on the 17th of January 1860 for the purpose of forming a volunteer rifle corps. Moving spirits of the meeting were the Rev. Richard Denny, T. Leach, Nicholas Waller, John Thomas Coates, Joseph Hunter, Richard Brown, and W.I. Whittingdale. Volunteers had been formed across England, and Ingleton did not want to be left out. It was too far to travel regularly to Kirkby Lonsdale for those willing to train to defend their country. It was considered that a Corps should be formed from the Bentham, Burton and Ingleton district and the following resolutions were passed. First it was necessary that a Rifle Corps be formed in the district: secondly that Joseph Hunter, Richard Brown and John T. Coates should be appointed as a working committee to carry out the purposes of the meeting; thirdly that Nicholas Waller Esq should be appointed secretary and treasurer of the Rifle Corps.

The meeting had not been all that well attended and it was thought that the spirit of national defence might take some rousing in Ingleton. However, many donations to support a Rifle Corps were given on the night and by February forty-seven members had signed up for service. On February 3rd they attended a Petty Sessions at the Ingleton Court House and there they all took the Oath of Allegiance. There was a hitch in the proceedings when W.A.F. Saunders JP was missing and had to be sent for from Wennington Hall. Only when he arrived could the ceremony be completed.[6]

Once the Ingleton Rifle Corps was formed, a meeting was called at the National School later in February to elect officers. Nicholas Waller of Masongill chaired the meeting and John Thomas Coates was elected Captain, Richard Brown Lieutenant, and Samuel Hartley, Ensign. The Rev. Richard Denny was elected Chaplain. The number of volunteers had passed fifty and by April 1860 there were over seventy members. In March the officers were approved by the Lord Lieutenant of the County and Captain Harvey of the 25th King's Own Borderers came to Ingleton to inspect the practice grounds.

Once the rifle corps got going Non Commissioned Officers were chosen. Joseph Bentham was appointed Sergeant Major, and Samuel Hartley, R.W. Elletson, Richard Bennett and W.K. Kilburn were promoted Sergeants. Giles Bateson, John Taylor, William Mansergh, Edward Thistlethwaite and William Dixon became Corporals. Lance Corporals were James Armstrong, Thomas Middleborough, Richard Barrett, Thomas Barker and John Harrison was appointed bugler. In August the Ingleborough Rifle Corps of the 26th Yorkshire Rifles held their first dinner given by their officers, Captain Coates, Lt. Brown and Ensign Hunter.

Local gentry took an interest in the Ingleborough Rifle Corps to encourage good shooting. Oliver Farrer of Ingleborough Hall gave a silver cup for first prize and Felix Slade of Halsteads gave one for second prize. Oliver Farrer also provided a new rifle range at Crina Bottom. The range was on the western sheltered side by a high range of cliffs, extending above a mile to the south, and on the east by a spur of the mountain running in a parallel direction. The target was placed at the head of the valley and the different firing points are in the same straight line of a gentle and uniform slope stretching upwards of a thousand yards to the south.

This range was some distance from the village and another was used on Storrs common. An article headed 'Dangerous rifle practice' appeared in the *Lancaster Guardian* on August 31st 1872. It appears that at this time they were taking up a firing position near the boundary wall of the common not far from Bull Copy and thirty or forty yards on the east side of the public road running from Ingleton to Hawes. However, the target was placed across the valley on Meal Bank and the riflemen fired across the public road. 'On this road there is a great deal of traffic and foot usage, and to say the least it cannot be pleasant for man or beast to be passing to and fro while members of the rifle corps are firing over their heads at a target on Meal Bank.' The article was keen to point out that as yet no one had been shot, but horses and men had been considerably frightened. The article ended, 'Whether such practice is dangerous or not, it is now lawful to fire over a public highway, to the alarm of the Queen's loyal subjects'.

The Ingleborough Rifle Corps held contests with other corps and defeated the Settle riflemen at Settle. A return contest was held in December 1862 at Ingleton when Settle were defeated again. To receive their capitation money the War Office required all members to pass a course of drill and the Ingleborough corps did so on December 28th 1862 when inspected by Major Cookson. A celebration dinner at the Bay Horse Inn followed the inspection. The corps was officially the Ingleborough Rifle Corps but it soon became generally known as the Ingleton Rifle Corps.

The cups presented by Oliver Farrer, Felix Slade and Joseph Hunter were eagerly contested by the riflemen. Money prizes were also given by Oliver Farrer and Felix Slade and equally contested. In July 1864 the following Ingleton men were among those winning prizes, George Boardman, Thomas Moore, Samuel Hartley and Thomas Boyd.

In 1870 there was considerable excitement in Ingleton when on Monday November 28th it was announced that telegrams had been received by two local gentlemen that England had declared war on Russia and that the members of the rifle corps were to be called out.[7] Some of the wives of rifle corps men heard the news with alarm, while others hearing the news looked forward to separation from their husbands. Some suggested that the Ingleton riflemen might run in the face of the enemy, other suggested that their looks would be sufficient to frighten the Russians, but the main feeling was that the Ingleton men would display as much courage as any other group of volunteers. Some young men were reported to have been keen to rush into battle.

The following morning the newspapers, which were eagerly read, had no news of the emergency and they realised it had been a false alarm. It appears that a man from Ingleton being told in Bentham that a telegram had been received that the militia were going to be called out spread the information when he returned to Ingleton. Spreading from person to person the story soon the whole village became certain that war had been declared on Russia. Such rumours were spread so easily in the days before telephone, radio and television

From time to time the riflemen paraded in the village headed by the Ingleton Brass Band. The volunteers had their ups and downs and around 1881 they were amalgamated into larger units and they became the Ingleton Detachment of I Corps of Volunteers, 3rd Duke of

Ingleton Volunteers at camp in 1904. Back row l to r, Sgt. J.W.Lambert, G.Pooley,
H.Birkett, Bell, A.Booth and Cpl. W.J.Routledge. Front J.Vickers and T.Fletcher.

The war memorial at Ingleton.

Wellington's. At that time twenty-eight men enrolled. From time to time they showed their presence by marching round the village as they did on Sunday the first of July 1896 led by the Giggleswick Brass Band. Lt. Tate was now in charge and the Colour Sergeant was Sgt. Bell.

In 1891 there was a military exercise in the area and eight large guns were placed around the Bridge Inn. Soldiers were billeted at the Bridge Inn and the Wheat Sheaf. The locals were disappointed that the war games did not last longer. This had no connection with the local volunteers. In 1897 the Ingleton Volunteers took part in the Diamond Jubilee celebrations for Queen Victoria. A detachment of the volunteers was in charge of two cannon, which were fired from the top of Meal Bank. It was intended to fire a twenty-one gun salute from Meal Bank, but as it rained the gunners were only able to fire three times.[8]

In May 1908 the Ingleton Volunteers were disbanded following the Territorial Army and Reserve Force Act of 1907. In December 1908 a public meeting was held at the Wheat Sheaf to enlist men into the new Territorial Army. An Ingleton Detachment was formed under Lt Mackenzie and Ingleton cadets under Lt. A. Barker and 2nd Lt. J. Barker. The Ingleton Territorials had not been serving for many years before World War I began. The Ingleton men were called up in August 1914 with orders to report to Skipton. There were a total of forty men including reservists. Charles Littlefair, the postman between Ingleton and Chapel-le-Dale, turned up for work at 6 am and found his calling up papers to go to the Tower of London to join his regiment.

It was reported in the Lancaster press that Ingleton had the first place in Yorkshire villages and the fifth place in the country in its response to the war effort. One hundred and twenty-seven men from Ingleton were serving in the forces by January 1915. In May 1915 the Duke of Wellington's Regiment from Skipton paraded in the village in a recruiting drive.[9] However, already one Ingleton soldier, Thomas Metcalfe, had returned home without a leg, which he lost at the battle of Mons. The story of those men, especially those who died serving their country is given in Andrew Brooks' excellent book, *The Ingleton War Memorial 1914-18 1939-45*. This book published in 2005 is a fascinating account not only of the men who died in two world wars, but also the story of the village of Ingleton during the two wars. It should be read by everyone with an interest in Ingleton's history. This chapter can be concluded by stating that Ingleton men have distinguished themselves in military service through many centuries.

REFERENCES

1. *Lancaster Guardian*, October 7th 1854.
2. *Lancaster Guardian*, May 24th 1856.
3. *Lancaster Guardian*, June 26th 1880.
4. *Lancaster Guardian*, October 28th 1911.
5. *Lancaster Guardian*, November 17th 1900.
6. *Lancaster Guardian*, February 18th 1860.
7. *Lancaster Guardian*, December 3rd 1870.
8. *Lancaster Guardian*, July 3rd 1897.
9. *Lancaster Guardian*, May 29th 1915.

FRIENDLY SOCIETIES

Friendly societies existed in England from the eighteenth century and were generally a means of banding together to provide financial assistance for illness and death. The risks of injury were high in the Ingleton mines and quarries and few employers gave any sickness payments. Working men along with their wives and children could easily become paupers. Those who joined a friendly society paid a subscription and could call on the society for help when they needed it. On top of this they enjoyed the social side of the society with its meetings, suppers and marches. The friendly society gave a feeling of security and belonging.

In 1887 Ingleton had a grand procession for the Queen's Jubilee and Ingleton's friendly societies formed an important part of that procession. They consisted of the Independent Order of Oddfellows, the Grand Order of Oddfellows, the Druids, the Meal Bank Club and the Colliery Sick Club. These were days before the Department of Health and Social Security had even been thought of and the National Health Service was a thing of the distant future.

ODDFELLOWS

The Oddfellows go back to the eighteenth century. The society spread over the country and men banded together both for the ritual of the society and the mutual assistance in times of sickness and death. The Oddfellows were a force to be reckoned with in Ingleton where they developed quickly during the nineteenth century. There were two Oddfellows societies in the village, the Independent Order of Oddfellows of the Manchester Unity and the Grand United Order of Oddfellows, which was a breakaway group.

The Ingleton Lodge of the Grand United Order of Oddfellows was established in December 1841 when a considerable number of members were enrolled. The initial meeting were held at the Bay Horse Inn which in 1841 was the house of John Hodgson.[1] In 1855 the Grand United Order of Oddfellows met at the house of John King, the Bay Horse, who was innkeeper and surveyor of highways for Ingleton township.

The main members were usually working men, but in Ingleton the society was well supported by the church minister and other leading citizens. They encouraged members to join because they knew it was for the workers' good. They also knew that if workmen were providing for their own illness and burial then there would be less call on the poor rates of the township. At the Oddfellows second anniversary in November 1843 the Rev W. Waller said that being a member of the Oddfellows saved men 'crying at the door of the parish officer, to receive the doleful pittance of the parish board'.[2]

The Loyal Heart of Oak Lodge no 665 of the Independent Order of Oddfellows was formed at Ingleton in 1842 and held their first anniversary dinner at the Wheat Sheaf on Christmas Day 1843. They held a procession which was joined by brothers from other lodges in the area. In November 1844 the Grand United Order held a march to mark their anniversary. Led by the Ingleton Brass Band they marched to Halsteads and back to hold their dinner at the Bay Horse. The ministers of Ingleton, Thornton and Chapel-le-Dale were present and eighty sat down to the meal.

The Loyal Heart of Oak Lodge followed the same procedure in May 1845 marching to Halsteads and then back to Ingleton church to hear prayers by the Rev S.B. Pooley the Vicar of Thornton and a sermon by the Rev. R. Denny curate of Ingleton. They also hired the Ingleton Brass Band and carried colourful flags. This again all shows that they were well supported by the clergy for their benevolent work in the village. In an address in November the same year the Rev. Richard Denny said, 'that they had bound themselves together to stand by each other, to bear each others burdens, to encourage and comfort, as necessity might require, which was praiseworthy; that they had formed themselves into a society, the object of which was to lay up a proportion of their incomes to be expended in the relief of any members who might stand in need according to the regulations of the club. He said it was surely better, at such times, to have some resources of their own, to which they could apply with credit, than to be obliged to go with cringing importunity, and throw themselves on the providence of those who relieve with a grudging hand'.[3]

In May 1845 two members of the Ingleborough Lodge No.578 of the Grand United Order of Oddfellows, Leonard Ellison Huck and Thomas Green, were buried on the same day in Ingleton church-yard. On the day of the funeral the lodge members assembled at their lodge room in the Bay Horse Inn before proceeding to the church. According to the press report 'the church was decorated to excess' and upwards of a hundred attended the service.

In May 1847 two Ingleton miners fell to their deaths in a mining shaft in the fields above Wilson Wood. One of them, Thomas Harrison, was a member of the Oddfellows and was given a full Oddfellows funeral on May 10th. Many members of the Oddfellows Lodge joined the funeral procession and other people in the village came to witness the procession and burial. The friendly societies organised impressive funeral ceremonies partly as a means of encouraging other people to join them.

The Ingleton Oddfellows swore an oath similar to the one below:-

I AM AN ODDFELLOW

I believe in the Fatherhood of God, and the Brotherhood of man.

I believe in Friendship, Love and Truth as basic guides to the ultimate destiny of all mankind.

I believe my home, my church or temple, my lodge and my community deserve my best work, my modest pride, my earnest faith, and my deepest loyalty, as I perform my duty 'to visit the sick, relieve the distressed, bury the dead and educate the orphan' and as I work with others to build a better world, because, in spirit and truth, I am and must always be, grateful to my Creator, faithful to my country and fraternal to my fellow-man:

I AM AN ODDFELLOW

DRUIDS

The Ancient Order of the Druids was founded in 1781 in London. They flourished in Victorian times and are first noted in Ingleton in May 1873 when the Ingleton Druids met at the Ingleboro' Hotel. Much of their ritual was based on the Freemasons with a mixture of Druidical legend and symbolism. At Whitsun they walked dressed in their society's regalia, which one reporter termed 'peculiar paraphernalia'. In May 1875 one hundred and thirty members walked in the Druids procession.[4] The Druids, as most friendly societies, had their splits. In 1833 one section became a registered friendly society known as the United Ancient Order of Druids while the rest were called the Ancient Order of Druids. In 1858 a section of the United Ancient Order of Druids became the Order of Druids. The various groups were usually welcome at each others lodges. Although the original Druids were pagan, the friendly society Druids were Christianised and there was no paganism in any of their rituals unlike the 'mystical' Druids who celebrate at Stonehenge in modern times.

A Druid funeral at Ingleton was an event that brought many people to watch the specific ritual of the society. The druid mourners came dressed in their regalia and oak leaves were place on the coffin. Oak leaves were an important symbol, as the word 'druid' contains the Celtic word 'dru' meaning oak. It also symbolised that the original Druids met and performed their rituals in sacred oak groves. How long the Druids survived at Ingleton is not known.

The Ingleton Oddfellows carry their banner on the Bank.

ROYAL ANTEDELUVIAN ORDER OF BUFFALOES – RAOB

The RAOB is one of the largest surviving fraternal organisations in the country. It grew out of a meeting in the Harp Tavern in London in 1822 and initially it was purely social and its ritual, regalia, and ceremonies were deliberately frivolous. The name came from a musical hall song of the time called, 'Chasing the Buffalo'. By 1866 the order had spread and became a Grand Lodge and its ceremonies became much more serious. To a great extent it followed the Masonic structure.

In Ingleton the Sir Robert Sayle Lodge number 5193 was formed which was a subordinate of the Province of Lancaster. The lodge was usually referred to as the Robert Sayle Lodge. This Ingleton society is the only one where documents, books and letters have survived in the village. These had belonged to John Walker, who was the society's secretary, and were for many years stored in the base of a long case clock. They were used for writing this chapter and then deposited in the North Yorkshire Record Office at Northallerton.[5] The first date mentioned in any of the documents is April 19th 1924 when several names are entered in the record as having attained their 'First Degree'. The first named are brothers F. Slinger, W. Ely, L. Ash, George Fleming, W.A. Longton, J. Burke, J.T. Sharpe, J.R. Wilson, R.J. Jackson, C.H. Redhead, T.E. Redhead, Fred Ireland and R.W. Gee. Other names follow up to the year 1934. Many of the names have comments opposite them such as expelled, left, bad or deceased. Many well-known Ingleton families were represented including Robinson, Tomlinson, Barker, Slinger, Redhead, King, Walker, Howson, Royston and Metcalfe.

The lodge held its meetings at the Wheat Sheaf and there members were initiated or had their 'First Degree Ceremony'. The initiate was told, 'You are about to become a member of one of the most ancient and honourable Orders ever formed by man. Ancient no doubt it is, having existed from time immemorial,' and so an amount of doubtful history followed. The candidate swore an oath which began, 'I hereby solemnly declare that I will never divulge the Secrets, Signs, and Passwords which may be given to me in this or any other lodge of the Royal Antediluvian Order of the Buffaloes under the Grand Lodge of England'. He was then told that he would now seal the obligation by kissing the emblem of purity and symbol of peace. That symbol was a clay pipe which he held to his heart. The members were required to support the British Crown and Constitution and were encouraged to be friendly, truthful and to help other brothers.

The governing authority for the Ingleton Lodge was at Lancaster where the Provisional Grand Lodge met at the Castle Hotel. The Ingleton lodge regularly sent funds, monthly reports and general correspondence. Applications were made to Lancaster for grants for medical treatment, access to the society's convalescent home at Harrogate and for RAOB sashes and regalia. There was only one major clash with the Lancaster Lodge when the Ingleton Lodge went to Lancaster for church parade and found that other groups apart from the RAOB were marching. For many years James Tomlinson served as 'Funeral Marshall' and William Dodd and J. Monks served as treasurer.

In December 1935 the secretary of the Lancaster Lodge in writing to Joseph Walker at Moor Lane Ingleton concluded his letter, 'Many thanks for putting the matter so concisely and clearly. The Robert Sayle Lodge is to be congratulated in that their affairs are in such good hands.' The book recording lodge meetings stops in 1940 and the lodge may well have closed because of the Second World War.

INGLEBOROUGH INDEPENDENT MOUNTAINEER FRIENDLY SOCIETY

This little known friendly society formed a lodge at Ingleton in 1878. They held their third annual supper at the Three Horse Shoes on January 8th 1881.[6] There were twenty-four members of the society at that time. The chairman for the evening was William Briscoe and during the meeting eight new members were initiated. The name suggests that the friendly society was very local and very little survives to show its existence. It was a short-lived society as it did not appear in the list of friendly societies who marched to celebrate Victoria's Jubilee in June 1887.

MEAL BANK CLUB

As well as the national friendly societies, Ingleton also had its local ones and the Meal Bank Club was one of them. It was a yearly benefit society in that all remaining cash at the end of the year was shared between members and a new start was made for the following year. The club was first instituted by the workmen of the Meal Bank Lime Works and took its name from the business and the place where the lime works were carried on.

Although the club was based at the Craven Lime Works it was always open to other men in the village if they wished to join. The members contributed one shilling each month and a further shilling on the death of a member or member's wife. In the year 1876 the sum of £44 18s 6d was collected and the expenditure was only £10 15s 6d which meant that the balance of £34 3s was shared among the seventy-two members and each received 9s 4d.

The club was also known as the Meal Bank Sick & Burial Society and held its annual meetings at the Wheat Sheaf. The meetings were usually held in the few days after Christmas and before the new year. The club gave help to the sick as well as providing for burials. By 1878 the number of members had grown to eighty-five. When the club held its annual supper at the Wheat Sheaf the landlord applied for an extension of hours. After the supper the club's surplus money was divided amongst the members. Perhaps this was a bad time to share out the cash as much of it probably went over the bar to pay for beer. After the supper there were toasts, speakers and entertainment usually in the form of singing. For many years Robert Chamley was chairman and treasurer, C. Bentham was the secretary and T. Walker the visitor of the sick.

Members who had been on the sick list and received benefit were still entitled to their share of any money left in the club's account. In 1884 Mr Bentham read the balance sheet after the Christmas meal. During the year nineteen members had been on the sick list and the total days they were unable to work were 339. At 1s 2d per day the expenditure was £23 5s 6d. The expenses for funerals were £9 3s. The income for the year was £75 16s 4d leaving a balance of £41 11s 3d to be shared amongst the ninety-two members giving each of them nine shillings.[7] The largest number of members appears to have been in 1896 when 117 were recorded.

Many well known village people served on the committee of the Meal Bank Club. In 1894 Sam Worthington, landlord of the Wheat Sheaf, was treasurer, J.T. Wignall was secretary and John King served a visitor of the sick. There was a supporting committee of F. Walley, J. Thornton, R. Chamley, F. Lambert, W. Burbridge and John Slinger. Though the club was principally for workmen they needed men like landlord Sam Worthington and other business men to serve as treasurer and secretary as many workmen were still illiterate. By 1910 only half a dozen men were retained at Meal Bank and the Meal Bank Club faded into history.

THE INGLETON COLLIERY SICK CLUB

Colliers in Ingleton formed the Ingleton Colliery Sick Club in the early nineteenth century. The club, which supported sick miners, their widows and orphans, was run by the men. Such clubs often shared any surplus money amongst the members at the end of the year. The Ingleton club did the same, but in some years the money was carried forward. Meetings were held at the Bridge Hotel and in January 1874 Edmund Danson, the colliery manager, was in the chair. The previous year's income was £79 2s 0d and the £65 3s 0d spent on sickness and funerals left a surplus of £13 19s 0d, which was carried forward. After the meeting, around one hundred members sat down to dinner.

A year later, over a hundred miners and officials thanked Edmund Danson for his work as both secretary and treasurer of the club. William Metcalfe, the underground viewer, said he had known Danson since he was a boy and had followed his promotions in the colliery with interest. He then presented him with a mantel clock, which was inscribed 'Presented to Mr Danson, colliery manager, by the officials and workmen of the Ingleton collieries, as a token of respect.[8] The colliers' supper for 1876 was told that the club had collected £80 3s 0d during the year and £8 2s 0d was paid out. The main toasts drunk at the dinner were 'Success to the Ingleton Collieries' and 'Success to the Ingleton Colliery Sick Fund'. In 1881, at the annual supper held on January 1st, it was reported that there was a nice balance to divide amongst the members. Over the years, village dignitaries were invited to be chairman or to give speeches and make toasts. In 1888 the Rev. J. Turner, the vicar, was in the chair and Alfred S. Kirk, of Greenwood Leghe was vice chairman. The Colliery Sick Club appears to have been suspended for some years after the closure of Wilson Wood, but was revived as the New Ingleton Colliery Sick and Dividing Society. It made donations to Lancaster and Leeds Infirmaries and other hospitals. In 1932 a twelve shilling dividend was paid to each member. At this meeting it was announced that any workmen in Ingleton was now welcome to join the colliery sick club. The Colliery Sick Club ended with the closure of New Ingleton Colliery in 1936.

REFERENCES

1. *Lancaster Gazette,* January 1st 1841.
2. *Lancaster Gazette,* November 25th 1843.
3. *Lancaster Gazette,* November 29th 1845.
4. *Lancaster Guardian,* May 22nd 1875.
5. RAOB Documents donated by Mrs Ann Pybus, daughter of John Walker, Deposited NYRO Northallerton 2008.
6. *Lancaster Guardian,* January 15th 1881.
7. *Lancaster Guardian,* January 7th 1884.
8. *Lancaster Guardian,* January 9th 1875.

Ingleton Church, 1851, by W.J.E. Rooke.

STORIES, PERSONALITIES AND OLD CUSTOMS

Many stories turn up during historical research on a village. Some are funny, some tragic and others just full of interest. They often don't fit into the neat headings of education, inns, politics or railways, but are worth recording. In fact some will say these are the most interesting part of a village history. There are also many notable characters who come into the Ingleton story who are worth a special mention. Because of the growth of the press and better record-keeping it is mainly those of the nineteenth century who have been best recorded. This chapter tells the story of a few of them who made an impression on the village or on the places to which they moved to live. Some like teacher and long serving village constable, William Thompson, have had their stories told in previous chapters.

THE INGLETON LION HUNT

Have no fear, no lion has been seen in Ingleton for many a year. Our story goes back to the year 1875. One Wednesday evening in June of that year a messenger brought the astounding news that a young lion had escaped from Bentham and as it had run in the direction of Ingleton it was necessary for parents to keep their children out of harm's way until the beast had been recaptured. The village was in great alarm that night and the next morning, when the news was circulated that the lion had been heard roaring in the streets during the night, everyone was further alarmed. During the day the whole village talked about the escaped lion and the need for its recapture.

The excitement was not only confined to the village, but the news travelled by rail and by pedestrians and carters to other districts in the area so that the lion at large and the hunt for it became a well known event. After the lion escaped it was pursued by men armed with guns and other weapons of defence and destruction. It took refuge for a time beneath the long spreading branches of a roadside elm tree near Fourlands Inn and there its pursuers fired four shots, but in their haste they missed and the lion somehow escaped.

Having made good its escape the lion crossed the fields in the direction of New Winning where it was said to have made a detour, running in the direction of Fell End Farm and for a time taking refuge in one of the shippons. After a short rest it made for the limestone crags of Storrs Common and then ran down the sloping banks of the river and plunged into the water by the Craven Lime Works. It eventually took refuge in the thickets of Lennie Wood. The shouting of pursuers, the fright of cattle and sheep, the desire to have the honour of slaying the monster, and the dread of being torn to pieces can more easily be imagined than described.

The alarm was increased in the village when a stranger mounted on horse with hunting knife and pistols in his belt passed over the bridge by the mill and headed for the wood where the lion had found shelter. Some of the courageous youths of the village who were fond of adventure armed themselves with suitable weapons and made for the outskirts of the wood. The uncertainty of knowing where the lion might be lurking made them move very cautiously. The hairbreadth escapes and disasters of the chase were detailed to the watching crowd. Some of the young men who were too anxious to be a lion slayer committed blunders highly characteristic of their lack of experience in lion hunting. Through their haste, or poor vision, a sheep and two lambs rushing out of Lennie Wood met with a painful and speedy end. They were upset by the blunder, but then anyone in similar circumstances might have taken a bleating sheep for a roaring lion!

Towards night there was much anxiety and little groups in the street discussed the event of the day. Then news arrived that eventually the lion had been shot after repeated firing. Everyone was pleased and relieved and some who heard the news were intent on securing a

The leading men of Ingleton around 1905. They are Back row l to r: George Walling, schoolmaster, R.Atkinson, Joe Thornton, John Slinger, and Frank Lambert. Middle row, Robert Chamley, Anthony Brown, unknown, Dr Mackenzie, John Metcalfe, Superintendent Haynes, Sam Worthington and J.Drinkall. Front row, K.C.Rass, F.Howson, Mr Maudsley, W.Boyd, Richard Collett, station master, Ed Ayrton, J.P.Procter, Sam Leach, Rev J.Turner, and John Slinger.

piece of its tufted tail or mane or skin as a memorial to such a chase that had brought excitement to the village. For a time conflicting statements perplexed the people. There were reports that it had caused havoc with a Midland passenger train and had caused the death of a neighbouring farmer, but this seemed too absurd for belief. A more reasonable account set the matter right. An heroic Westhouse man had rushed into the field gun in hand and given the lion a fatal shot or so they said. It all depends if 'they say' is a reliable witness.

Eventually the whole story was explained. It appeared that a stranger of somewhat doubtful sanity had met a villager and his wife at Ingleton on Wednesday night and told them a young lion had escaped from Bentham, and the rest was all village gossip and the result of imaginative and over-excited minds. When in the future you hear of lions, leopards and other large cats being sighted in the English countryside, think that even if people say they have seen them or even smelt them it is most likely only a return of the 'Ingleton lion'.[1]

A VICTORIAN CARRIAGE ACCIDENT

During the Victorian period members of the Rowntree family of York frequently visited Ingleton and were so attracted by the fresh clean air and beautiful scenery of the dales that in 1875 they rented a part of Storrs Hall as a holiday residence. John Stephenson Rowntree, his wife Elizabeth, their numerous children and servants all enjoyed the change from the flat countryside around York.[2] The Rowntree family were the owners of the Rowntree Chocolate factory in York where they were well known. John was the eldest son of Joseph Rowntree and was born in 1834. He was a director of the family company. The family were also well known Quakers and when in Ingleton the family visited the Friends Meeting House at Bentham. On Monday July 5th 1875 Mr Rowntree and his three oldest children set off on foot to climb Ingleborough. They left Mrs Rowntree to take the remaining children and two nurses for a drive to Chapel-le-Dale. Having enjoyed their visit to Chapel-le-Dale it was on their return journey that tragedy struck. As the carriage neared Storrs Hall the horse took fright and bolted off at full gallop, and at tremendous speed began to descend the hill towards Cross Farm. At a short distance from the farm the four wheeled phaeton came into contact with the wall adjoining Fell End Farm. Mrs Rowntree, the four children and the two nurses were all thrown out of the vehicle onto the stony road. Both horse and humans were terribly cut and bruised and the blood in the road was said to have given the appearance of a place of slaughter.

Edward Slinger, who was breaking stones opposite Storrs Hall when the accident occurred, said that he heard the carriage coming and seeing it go past so fast realised it was out of control. When he heard the smash that followed he ran quickly to the site where he found one of the nurses leaning against a wall, a child running about screaming, a baby in the nurse's arms and the others lying at the roadside. After a quick glance he ran down the road to the Court House where he found Superintendent Horn. A boy was immediately sent for Doctor Griffiths. Then Superintendent Horn dealt with the victims on the road as best he could before the doctor arrived. Several of the victims were unconscious and they were all made as comfortable as possible. Soon all the injured members of the family were taken back to Storrs Hall and their wounds were treated by Dr Griffiths.

After the accident the horse was standing facing towards the carriage. The carriage was right side up, but one of the wheels was completely broken off. The horse was taken to the Wheat Sheaf and whether it was shot or recovered is not recorded. As soon as possible a telegram was sent to York to call the Rowntrees' own doctor. He arrived on Tuesday, but only in time to see Mrs Elizabeth Rowntree die of a fractured skull.

The boy of five had extensive scalp wounds and a fracture of the skull. The little girl had wounds on her face, but the youngest boy and the little girl received only slight injuries. On Wednesday J.B. Brown, the deputy coroner, held an inquest at the Ingleborough Hotel. Before leaving York the carriage had been fitted with a special brake knowing that it was to be used in hilly country. However, from an examination of the carriage after the accident it appeared that the brake had not been used. A verdict of 'accidentally killed' was recorded. Elizabeth Rowntree was forty years old. For some time there was concern for the five year old, but eventually all the surviving victims made good progress and returned to York. From that time the Rowntree family did not return to Ingleton which held such tragic memories for them. John Rowntree married again in 1878.

Horse, woman and child. This photo taken c 1890 on Thacking Road tells of a day when horses reigned supreme for labour and transport.

A DIRECT HIT AND A NEAR MISS

The Victorians had a quaint way of referring to lightning as 'electric fluid', but lightning or electric fluid, it can prove fatal, as the following story shows. The Sherlock family were well known in Ingleton as the Rev. T.D. Sherlock was the vicar of the St Mary's Church. It was announced that his father, Randal Hopley Sherlock, who had recently retired as proprietor and editor of the *Liverpool Mail* was coming from Liverpool to live at Ingleton. Randal Sherlock's brother was Edgar Sherlock, Rector of Bentham and another brother Cornelius Sherlock was to be the architect of the new St Mary's Church at Ingleton.

Randal Hopley Sherlock was coming to Ingleton in the hope that the clean and bracing air and relaxing atmosphere would help to cure the various complaints which had forced him into retirement. He arrived in August 1875 and settled in at the vicarage. On a Tuesday evening not long after his arrival he walked to the Midland Station to enquire about some luggage he was expecting from Liverpool. Having made his enquiries and seeing that the skies were darkening and threatened a storm, instead of taking the usual road by the station gates, he took a shorter route for Upper Gate and home walking between the railway lines. Witnesses stated that just at this time, 'the dark cloud that was casting a pitchy hue over the village, opened and shot down a mass of electric fluid which divided in its descent.' Another witness stated that 'The electric fluid in its descent was terrible beyond description, and it passed in two directions eastwards and westwards.' As the lightning flashed one fork struck near the Three Horse Shoes Inn while the other fork felled Randal Sherlock striking him on

337

the head and killing him instantly before he had gone thirty yards from the station. As the 5.35 train was almost due many people saw the lightning strike Mr Sherlock and saw him fall. Mr Cousins, the station master, took charge of dealing with Mr Sherlock who was pronounced dead on the spot.

Mr Sherlock's hat was torn to shreds and his shirt collar and tie were in tatters. His gold watch and chain were partially melted and the end of his umbrella was knocked off. For Randal Hopley Sherlock Ingleton proved to be a place of short retirement. Mr Sherlock who was sixty-eight years old was buried at Chester. A stained glass window was placed in St Mary's Church with a brass memorial plaque. It read 'In Loving Memory of Randolph Hopley Sherlock of Liverpool, killed by Lightning at Ingleton, August 9th, 1875. This window was erected by his widow'.

A more fortunate story of lightning comes from just up the road at Thornton-in-Lonsdale. On September 3rd 1817 the Rev. T.H. Foxcroft of Halsteads and his family received a near miss when lightning struck the house. The minister was so delighted at his deliverance that he not only composed a poem about it for the occasion, but also had the poem painted on a board and nailed to a tree by the house for all to see. The poem read:-[3]

> Almighty parent, God of love,
> Teach us our gratitude to prove,
> By praise unfeigned and warm;
> Filled with electric fire, the ball
> Did here in awful grandeur fall,
> Hur'ld by Thy mighty arm.
> Shielded by Thee our circle dear,
> Though filled with agonising fear,
> All trembling, pale we stood,
> Yet still survive, our praise to give
> To Thee by whom alone we live
> Our Saviour and our God.

The house at Halsteads still stands not far from Thornton Church, but the vicar's thanksgiving has long since fallen from the tree.

THE THIEVING ELEPHANT

Our next story concerns the elephant that robbed the Wheatsheaf Inn. Ingleton had a name for attracting wild beast shows, circuses and freak shows. They were mostly held in the Bridge Inn Croft behind the Bridge Inn and people not only came from Ingleton but surrounding villages. One Sunday in December 1894 Bostock's Menagerie arrived in Ingleton and as usual put up at the Bridge Inn. However there was no room for the elephant they had brought and so it was arranged that the elephant would be settled for the night in one of the carriage houses opposite the Wheat Sheaf Inn. It appears that the beast was restive in its lodgings as firstly they were not very large and secondly it was very cold frosty night. The elephant took out the door with one push of its head and walked out into the road. The animal had the street to itself as by now all the inhabitants of the village were asleep and the village had its usual midnight silence.

The elephant wandered through the wood yard to Mr Worthington's back door, the back door of the Wheat Sheaf, and began to force an entrance. The animal broke open three doors and dragged out a chair and a table, but it was food the animal was after and eventually it found a basket of onions and made a meal of them. Sam Worthington had by now heard

338

noises downstairs and went to investigate and discovered the elephant. The problem then was to find the keeper and a man was sent to the only common lodging house in the village. The keeper was found and came to take charge of the elephant. News of the midnight escapade was soon spread through the village and induced more people to attend the show on Monday night.

TALLY JACK – A PAUPER'S FUNERAL

> Some were born to rule
> Some were born to slave.
> Some were born to riches. . .
> And some to a Pauper's grave.
> Ian E. Kaye

Tally Jack was a drover. His real name was John Leeming, but he was Tally Jack to most who knew him. He was a native of Leck, but for many years lived at Ingleton. His life was a hard one driving cattle from place to place in all weathers. In October 1884 returning to Ingleton on foot after driving cattle he met with Mr Bracewell's wagons near Ireby. He was glad of a lift and was getting on the front wagon when he slipped and fell and one of the wheels passed over his ankle. His ankle and foot were badly crushed and he was under the care of Dr Griffiths at Ingleton for some time. However, he recovered and was back driving cattle from place to place.

His last cattle drive was from Milnthorpe Fair to Thornton-in-Lonsdale and the weather being wild and wet he caught a cold. He rested up in the common lodging house at Ingleton and there he died one Friday morning in May 1886. He was given a pauper's burial at Ingleton cemetery on May 26th, but the way he was hurried to his grave without any humanity caused considerable agitation in Ingleton. On his death he was laid out as he had died, but a neighbour woman had pity on him and brought a clean shirt for him to be dressed to give some decency to the corpse. The mistress of the lodging house did not know until a coffin was taken into her home at 2pm on Saturday that he was to be buried that day. He was rolled into a pauper's coffin just as he died. There was no 'winding' as it was locally termed, or flowers to show that a human being was about to be carried to his final resting place. Some of the neighbours begged that the funeral be put off until the Sunday when a funeral might have been conducted with more decency. The command was stern and no delay could be given which was taken by many as a reflection on the humanity and sense of decency of the vicar, churchwardens and overseers. No relatives were informed of his death or funeral, and no friends at Leck were informed, who said had they known they would have buried him with decency amongst his own kindred at their own expense.

A few men followed him to the grave and the *Lancaster Guardian* reported that, 'Those men felt keenly the indecencies which attended the burial, and gladly would have made any effort, if it had been put off until the Sunday, to have secured a respectful funeral. It is a disgrace to the village that such a thing should have happened in it, though the villagers could not prevent it. Let those who feel it so subscribe for a plain stone to mark the spot where poor Jack rests from the bitter colds, rains, and long fastings which helped to make up his chequered life and hasten him to a premature grave'. Sadly there was no response to the call and Tally Jack's grave remains unmarked to this day.

THE GERMAN GUN FROM WORLD WAR ONE

One of the mysteries of Ingleton is the great gun that stood at the Cross. At the end of WWI the Ingleton War Committee asked for some trophy in recognition of the gallant part that Ingleton played in the Great War and it was considered a great honour to be awarded one. A German gun was offered and a public meeting decided to accept it. It was placed at the Cross where the old road went off to Clapham. However, after a time with children playing on it and with the effects of the weather, it got into a shabby state. Some people said that it should be put behind spiked railings, while others said it just needed a coat of paint.

The Ingleton public became tired of the German gun and wanted to be rid of it, but the Parish Council decided to keep it. It was proposed at one time that it should be put on the Brow and some said that was a good idea as someone might push it down into the river. Others suggested that the village institute should find a place for it and that if not it should be placed on Storrs Common out of the way. In November 1925 the Parish Clerk submitted several letters to the Parish Council from the inhabitants of the Bank protesting about the suggestion that the gun should be put on the Brow. They wished it to remain at the Cross. It was agreed to call another meeting to discuss what should be done with it.

In 1935 the gun was still standing at the junction of the Hawes Road and the old road to Clapham. It also still occupied the attention of both the local folk and the Parish Council. In March 1936 the chairman of one meeting said it was a pity there was no Ingleton museum to put it in. A vote was taken and the result was that twenty-six wished to get rid of it and only six wished to keep it. It was suggested that they sell it for scrap iron and put the money to the Jubilee fund. The clerk to the council warned them that they might have to pay someone to take it away.

Finally in September 1936 the German gun was taken from its sixteen year old resting place and deposited in a scrap iron merchant's yard. Since being brought to Ingleton it had caused regular problems and arguments. An offer to buy the gun for ten shillings brought the Parish Council's problems to an end. And so the German gun quietly disappeared at a time when thoughts of war had long since turned to thoughts of peace. The remarkable thing is that no one appears to have photographed it in all its years at Ingleton.

POLICE SUPERINTENDENT GUNN

Superintendent Gunn was the least popular of all the police who were ever based at Ingleton. The superintendents before him had all been well liked and respected, but Gunn was the exception. When he arrived at first he was considered reasonable and friendly, but things soon took a turn for the worse. With a name like Gunn he was soon called Pop-Gunn and when troubles began with the people of Ingleton it was said that 'Gunn should be fired' or that 'Gunn should be shot'.

It all began in 1894 when Superintendent Gunn took an exception to ornamental limestone rockery stones in the street. According to him they were all encroachments and he would get rid of them. Unfortunately many of the decorative stones were on private property, but Gunn would not listen. Up to the arrival of Gunn the street stretched from the houses on one side to the houses on the other. Most folks didn't fence off every part of their property and sometimes extensions and bay windows were built which were encroachments in the true sense of the word. Some thought that Superintendent Gunn had been pushed to do this by higher authority, but he would never say.

Several cases were brought to Ingleton Court House in October 1894. Ingleton had been in a state of excitement over the police orders for shopkeepers, innkeepers and others to remove their rockeries from the unenclosed land at the front of their premises. The first case was against Sam Worthington of the Wheat Sheaf. He was summoned for obstructing the highway by placing a large quantity of rockery stones in front of his house. Supt Gunn said that it was an encroachment on the highway and an obstruction. Richard Brown in defence stated that the recess had once been the site of a building and was private property. PC Tomlinson said that the stones were not there in 1887. The summons was under the Highways Act of 1835. The defence showed Ordnance Survey maps and brought other evidence, but to the surprise of the court the magistrates decided in favour of Superintendent Gunn. Later the police measured up the Wheat Sheaf's railings and they were removed by workmen from the County Council in spite of the fact that people with common sense thought them an improvement to the street.

This was a clear instance where the law was in complete error but the fine had to be paid. The area in question, and more, is now completely walled off and no-one would question that it was the property of the Wheat Sheaf. Mr Baines was the second to be summoned for a similar case. Richard Brown was able to prove that where the rockery now was there used to be an outbuilding and water pump and so the area must be private. The court accepted the evidence and dismissed the case. The case was also dismissed against the Temperance Hotel and the Ingleborough Hotel. The Coffee Tavern was fined as were others and the court cases took several hours.

When Superintendent Gunn was asked if telegraph poles were encroachments and if so would he summons the Postmaster General? He replied to the effect that he would think about it. Then Superintendent Gunn set his sights on vending machines and started prosecuting the owners of those. Gunn said, 'there are a large number of those machines in Ingleton and they have become an intolerable nuisance, causing horses to shy and thus a source of danger.' The Ingleton Post Master was summoned and replied in the press accusing Gunn of having too fertile an imagination. He pointed out to the superintendent that he might use his time better by trying to catch thieves or in stopping vandalism. He ended his letter, 'In the Gilbert and Sullivan opera the policeman bemoans his lot and sings – Taking one consideration with another, the policeman's lot is not a happy one – this may be so, but much depends on themselves and how they make it. Yours Truly, J. Lumb, Post Master Ingleton June 10th 1895'.

The prosecutions went on against rockeries, fences, vending machines and stalls until the inhabitants of Ingleton were completely fed up. They knew Superintendent Gunn could have not done all this without the support of the magistrates and so they turned on them, especially, T.B.T. Ford, Mr Farrer and T.E. Fenwick who was chairman of Ingleton Bench and along with Gunn they became figures of ridicule. When Superintendent Gunn began the same tactics in Bentham the people had seen what had happened in Ingleton and were prepared. They fought against the police action and made an appeal to the Court of the Queen's Bench and won. The police and magistrates took no further action. When in July 1897 it was announced that Mr Gunn, Superintendent of Ewecross Division of the West Riding Constabulary, was about to resign there was a sigh of relief in Ingleton.

I'LL SHOOT THEE NEAT

Esther Robinson was a rather odd woman who lived at Ingleton in Victorian times. She had been charged with begging at one point in her life and in 1866 she was fined for letting a horse stray on the road. She had the nickname of 'Neat'. Now Esther Robinson had a special dread of firearms and had got the idea into her head that one day she would die of gunshot wounds. The local lads all knew of this and they took every opportunity to play on the old woman's feelings and fears.

On February 2nd 1867 she went to Mrs Clapham's house in the village with some vegetables. There were several people in the house and there was a double-barrelled shotgun hanging on the wall. One of the company, Mathias Carr, who was seventeen, walked up to the shot-gun and said, 'Neat I'll shoot thee'. Mrs Clapham warned him not to touch the gun which might be loaded. However, ignoring her he stood on a chair to get the gun down and it fell on the floor. He picked it up and pointing it at Esther repeated, 'I'll shoot thee Neat' Esther ran at him and struggled with him and then turned to leave the house, but as she did so the gun went off and the contents blasted the back of her head and she fell dead on the floor, her brains being scattered round the room. Mathias Carr was arrested and charged with manslaughter, but was eventually discharged with only a caution. In prophesying her own death by a firearm Esther Robinson had surely brought it about.

HAROLD GREENWOOD – A FAMOUS POISONING CASE

In June 1920 some people in Ingleton took notice of an inquest held in Kidwelly in Wales. The inquest was on the body of Mabel Greenwood who had died a year earlier and whose body had been exhumed due to the suspicious circumstances of her death. The reason that the event roused interest in the village of Ingleton was because the woman was the wife of Harold Greenwood, a member of the well-known Greenwood family of Greenwood Leghe in Ingleton.

The coroner's court lasted two days and many witnesses were examined. The coroner's summing up lasted three quarters of an hour following which the jury retired. Within an hour, and after a consultation in private with the coroner, the foreman of the jury returned into court and handed in the jury's verdict. 'We are unanimously of the opinion that the death of the deceased, Mabel Greenwood, was caused by acute arsenical poisoning, as certified by Dr Wilcox, and that the poison was administered by Harold Greenwood'.

Harold Greenwood was born in 1874, the second son of William Norman Greenwood of Ingleton. In July 1896 he married Mabel Bowater, daughter of William Vansittart Bowater of Bury Hall, Edmonton in Middlesex. He had qualified as a solicitor and gone to practice in Wales, firstly in Llanelly in 1898 and then in Kidwelly. The family lived in several houses in the area, finally settling in a large residence called Rumsey House. There in 1919 he lived with his four children Irene, Eileen, Ivor and Kenneth, although two of the children Eileen and Ivor were mainly away at boarding school. Rumsey House employed three maids and a gardener. Mrs Greenwood's sister, Edith Bowater, also lived in the house although she was not popular with Harold Greenwood who considered her an unwelcome intruder and called her 'the Kidwelly Postman' because of the gossip she delivered to everyone.

Mabel Greenwood had been a semi-invalid for some years and suffered from a variety of health problems which had been put down to a weak heart. As the coroner's court had found that she died of arsenic poisoning, investigation showed that it was most probably administered to her in red wine which she drank prior to her final collapse. Harold Greenwood was arrested and brought to trial in Carmarthen. He had not helped himself by marrying again only four months after his wife's death. He married Miss Gladys Jones, a woman he had known since childhood. Not only this but it was known that he had also proposed to yet another woman.

The trial was held in the Guild Hall at Carmarthen. Harold Greenwood was defended by Sir Edward Marshall Hall one of the most famous advocates of the day. Marshall Hall was known as 'the Apollo of the Bar,' and 'the Great Defender,' because of his reputation of successfully defending notorious alleged murderers. Marshall Hall was able to cause doubts when witnesses disagreed on many points of the case. One of the main setbacks for the prosecution came when Greenwood's daughter said that she had also drunk from the bottle of red wine and not been affected.

Harold Greenwood made a poor witness and contradicted himself many times. However, he had the support of Marshall Ward who easily dealt with the prosecution's flimsy evidence.

342

The jury took two and a half hours to return their verdict. The words handed to the judge read, 'We are satisfied on the evidence of this case that a dangerous dose of arsenic was administered to Mabel Greenwood on Sunday, June 15th, 1919. But we are not satisfied that this was the immediate cause of death. The evidence before us is insufficient and does not conclusively satisfy us as to how and by whom the arsenic was administered. We therefore return a verdict of not guilty.'

Harold Greenwood tried to continue at Rumsey House in Kidwelly but the local folk made it quite obvious he was not welcome by completely shunning him. Even his family doctor took him to court for unpaid bills. Driven out of the society he knew, he changed his name to Pilkington and moved to Herefordshire. There he died nine years later on January 17th 1929 at Rose Cottage in the village of Sellack. His death went almost unnoticed at Ingleton. It is often said that Oscar Greenwood was the last of the Greenwoods of Greenwood Leghe, but Harold's two sons, Ivor and Kenneth, lived to continue the Greenwood Family of Greenwood Leghe.[4]

ROWLAND DIXON c.1720-1788

Rowland Dixon was born around 1720 and was brought up in Ingleton where his family had resided for at least a couple of centuries as witnessed by the parish register which records that a Rowland Dixon was baptised on May 29th 1662 and the name Rowland Dixon occurs many times from that date. The subject of our story became a miner at Ingleton and when he began to make puppets for display he made some out of pit props, and the puppets were almost life size. Rowland Dixon began to travel with his puppets and was soon able to make a good living from it, at least better than the hard life in the Ingleton coal mines.

We owe much of our knowledge of Rowland Dixon to Robert Southey, for Southey having spent time researching in Ingleton, recorded the story of Rowland Dixon in his book *The Doctor*. Southey heads one of his chapters 'Rowland Dixon and his Company of Puppets' and tells us that he was known as the 'Puppet-show-master-general, of the North'.[5] The life size puppets needed a large covered wagon to transport them round the country. In town and village he gave his performances which were founded on popular stories and ballads such as Fair Rosamund, who was a mistress of Henry II; Jane Shore, the mistress of Edward IV who was later charged with witchcraft and forced to walk the London streets in penance as a harlot, and Bateman who hanged himself for love. He had scriptural subjects for Easter and Whitsuntide such as the Creation, the Deluge, Susannah and the elders, and Nebuchadnezzar. These had been handed down from the time of the old mysteries and miracle-plays.

We are also indebted to Anthony Hewitson for telling us something of Rowley Dixon in his memories of his childhood in Ingleton.[6] Hewitson tells us that in his boyhood Roland Dixon's puppets were stowed away in a cottage at the centre of the village. 'These were the double set of puppets or marionettes – one being life size and the other of less proportions.' Hewitson tells us that they were known as Rowley Dixon's puppies and that at one time he had the honour of performing before the Royal Family. According to Hewitson:-

The puppets, when their show days were over, passed into the possession of Dixon's son-in-law; they were packed away in big boxes at the cottage referred to; and at that cottage I once saw a box open, and noticed on a chair or table some of the dresses of the puppets- the garments were of full adult size, they looked like female dresses, and appeared to be made of silk or satin, one or more of them being of a very rich colour. Between thirty or forty years ago (c.1860), such of the puppets as were then left – they chiefly belonged to the bigger sized lot, were sold to Thomas Moore and subsequently disposed of to an itinerant showman.

Rowland Dixon died in 1788 and his will was proved on September 25th of that year. However, his burial did not take place at Ingleton and so he may well have died on his travels. On his death he owned two cottages at Ingleton which along with all his possessions were left to his children Jane, Stephen and Ann. His scenes, machinery and puppets were left to his daughter Ann, wife of John Sedgewick. Ann Dixon had married John Sedgewick, a yeoman of St John's Parish York, on June 10th 1768. In spite of his profession Rowland Dixon was still unable to write his name when he witnessed the marriage register.

THOMAS MOORE 1771-1854

Thomas Moore was born in Dent in 1771, the eldest child of Peter and Margaret Moore. His father Peter Moore was cousin to Adam Sedgwick the noted geologist. Thomas married Dorothy Harling and the couple lived at Bruntscar and Coltpark in Ingleton Fells. However, not been keen or farming Thomas eventually settled in Ingleton and it was there he made a name for himself. He was a shoemaker as many of his family were and the trade seems to have been a second employment for many farmers in Chapel-le-Dale. He was also a fiddler of great repute in days when the fiddle was the principal source of music for dancing, for weddings and in church services. Thomas was also an engraver of coffin plates and a small brass box, engraved and made by him c.1820, in the possession of his descendants, is engraved 'amicitia amor et veritas'. As this is the motto of the Oddfellows 'friendship, love and truth' he was most probably an Oddfellow.

William Harling, Dorothy Moore's father, was a relative of Ann Sill of Dent. The Sills were a wealthy family with an estate at St Thomas in south-east Jamaica. There they ran a sugar plantation with negro slave labour. Miss Ann Sill inherited the estate on the death of her brothers. The Sills brought negro slaves to Dent and one is known to have married locally and another, Thomas Anson, ran away from Dent in 1757. Ann Sill was financially helpful to William Harling during his lifetime and then befriended his daughter Dorothy.

Thomas and Dorothy Moore received financial help from Ann Sill during her life time. Due to this money from the Jamaican sugar plantation, and thus the slave trade, the Moore family were able to lead a financially secure life. Then following Anne Sill's death, Dorothy Moore benefited further as she was one of the thirteen legatees in Ann Sill's will. The Moore's received £100 per annum from the trustees until the estate was sold and settled and they were then due for a £500 share. Adam Sedgwick was one of the trustees of the will which owing to the abolition of the slave trade in Jamaica took a considerable time in settling.

When Thomas died in 1854 he was still waiting for the legacy which was due to his wife from the estate of Ann Sill. Thomas' wife Dorothy died on April 18th 1841 and was buried in the churchyard at Dent. Thomas Moore died in February 1854 aged eighty-four he was buried in the same grave. In the obituary column of the *Lancaster Gazette* was the following:- 'Died Ingleton, February 25th, Mr Thomas Moore, yeoman, aged 83 years. Much respected'. Today there are many descendants of Thomas and Dorothy Moore in this country and throughout the world. Several of them have been helpful in supplying information for this book and still take a keen interest in the history of the Ingleton area.

THOMAS MOORE 1822-1895

This Thomas Moore was the grandson of the above. Thomas Moore senior had a son Thomas Moore who lived in Ingleton and then moved to Darwen in Lancashire where he died in 1879 and was buried in Burnley. He was something of a rake in his youth and was not as notable as his nephew Thomas. Thomas Moore the subject of our second study was the son of Peter Moore one time landlord of the Sun Inn at Dent. He was born in Ingleton and appears to have all the talents and traits of his grandfather. He was a fiddler, shoemaker, sign-writer, artist and much else. He built three cottages in Ingleton off the main street known as Moore Lane. He was Anthony Hewitson's cousin and we shall leave Anthony to give his details as he did in writing his obituary in the *Lancaster Observer* on September 20th 1895:-

Death of Mr. Thomas Moore. – Early on Tuesday morning (September 17th) after a series of paralytic attacks, Mr. Thomas Moore quietly departed this life. He was a native of Ingleton though his fore elders came to the place from Dent. The various branches of trade in which he occupied himself were so numerous that it would be difficult to enumerate them all. Before surpliced choirs were introduced into country churches, he was the leading chorister at the Ingleton parish church. When a string band was formed at the same church, he was one of the leading violinists, and occasionally he presided at the American organ. He would play on nearly every kind of wind instrument and some of these instruments he made himself. He was a member of the old Ingleton brass band, and many years ago he had the training of the juvenile drum and fife band. In his younger days he was very popular at all the country dances in a wide district, and always went by the name of 'Tommy Moore, the fiddler'. When photography came into public use, he was not long before he was able to undertake it with advantage to his family. In carrying out his craft he used to visit Manchester, Blackburn, Lancaster, Windermere, Durham, Skipton, Hawes and different towns in Westmorland. He was the first photographer who took photographs of the beautiful and long hidden waterfalls at Pecca ravine and the quarry woods. Though a native of Ingleton he was ignorant of those falls until they were popularised in the columns of a Lancaster journal. Some of his negatives were lent to the Midland railway Company for reproduction for advertising at their several stations. He occasionally gave attention to oil painting. For many years he had been employed as a rate collector for the Settle Sanitary Authority. He also formerly did much in sign painting and lettering coffin plates. In addition to the crafts mentioned, he took time to act as correspondent for many ratepayers. In 1877 he became correspondent of the *Lancaster Observer* , and sometime afterwards in the same capacity he was of a friendly and cheerful deportment, and as to religion he was a member of the Church of England, and in politics a Conservative. In these matters he had the good sense never to carry out his views with asperity. He was widely known and respected and will be much missed in the village.

JOSEPH CARR 1812 – 1899

If anyone could ever be called Mr Ingleton it was Joseph Carr. Not only did Joseph Carr influence the history of Ingleton, but as a press correspondent and a writer of lengthy memoirs he recorded it. He has been mentioned in many parts of the book and so here he will have just a short biography. Born in Bentham on December 3rd 1812 in spite of what his gravestone says. That was engraved in 1920 on his daughter's death. He couldn't have been born in December 1813 as he was baptised in Janury 1813, as the parish registers record. He came from an old Ingleton family. His grandfather, Joseph Carr, was born in Ingleton in 1739 and married Isabel Armistead at Ingleton in 1762. His father Richard Carr born in 1778 moved to Bentham to work as a flax-dresser. Joseph was brought up in High Bentham where the family lived on Main Street.

After being educated at Bentham Grammar School, Joseph was apprenticed in the woollen trade and spent time in France, where he had problems with Frenchmen who thought he was spying for his firm back home. He returned to England, but later returned to Boulogne as a missionary in charge of a small church there. He was in Boulogne in the summer of 1840 when Louis Napoleon staged an attempted coup and saw the fight in which Louis Napoleon

Railwaymen at Ingleton with Richard Collett, station master. The man in the centre of the front row is said to be Joseph Carr.

was taken prisoner. Not only that, but with others, he was compelled to dig graves in the sand for the burial of those killed in the encounter. Several days later he was in the market square in Boulogne when Louis Phillipe came to thank the people for helping to capture his enemy.

Joseph became a very religious person at quite a young age and at twenty-three became a total abstainer from alcohol. He first came to visit Ingleton in 1824 for a church service with his family. Then from 1836 he was a more regular visitor to attend Methodist meetings. He spent some time teaching, as many Grammar School educated boys did without taking any further qualifications. He was recorded as a schoolmaster when he married at Bentham Parish Church on October 18th 1843. He married Alice Balderston of Ingleton and through her influence came to live at Ingleton. From 1843 to 1854 Ingleton was his occasional home, but from 1854 it was his permanent home and remained so for the rest of his life.

In his memoirs of 1896 he said, 'I was once a weakling, and twice I have been at the point of death, and now in my eighty-fourth year of age I can jump off my knees with my hands in my pockets, jump three steps at a time, run up two flights of stairs two steps at a time, and climb fruit trees. This speaks much for New Testament teaching, total abstinence from drink and tobacco, constant moderation in living, and a long residence in a healthy locality'.

As a preacher he travelled a wide area, but it was in Ingleton that he had most influence. He was liberal and nonconformist and opposed the more powerful Tories and church people. He was a master in taking the chair at public meetings, and at organising and promoting new ideas and schemes for the good of the village. The greatest surprise came when on his death his burial service was held in St Mary's Church and the Rev. James Turner of the Church of England took the service both in the church and at Ingleton cemetery where he was buried. He was held him in such admiration that a memorial was raised to him on the Bank.

JOSEPH HARRISON 1804-1880

The personalities in this chapter were men who made a name for themselves in Ingleton. This short biography is about an Ingleton man, but one who made a name for himself elsewhere. Joseph Harrison was baptised at Ingleton Church on November 27th 1804, the son of William Harrison. He was educated at Ingleton and began work in the village as a blacksmith. He had heard that there was a great demand for iron work in Blackburn in Lancashire, especially in the mills. So in 1826 he walked from Ingleton to Blackburn with little more than his bag of tools and rented a small smithy in Dandy Walk. As he was skilled in ironwork he soon found plenty of work, from making iron railings and gates for the many new houses being built to casting lamp posts and bollards.

Then he began casting parts for textile machinery and the demand became so great that he went to Bank Foundry off Bolton Road. He became one of the most successful business men in the Blackburn area. He was an iron founder, cotton spinner, and manufacturer. He took out many patents and improved looms to both ease labour and increase production. He took part in the Great Exhibition at Crystal Palace in London in 1851 where his sons assisted him. One year after the exhibition Messrs Harrison and Sons received an order to fit out a textile factory in Sweden. It is said they completed the order in eight days and the machinery left Blackburn in one consignment for Liverpool filling forty railway wagons.

He was one of the councillors returned at the first municipal elections in Blackburn on November 1st 1851 and he served for twenty years. He was a JP and served as Deputy Lieutenant for the county. He was joint Lord of the Manor of Samlesbury and spent thousands of pounds on restoring the manor house which is today one of the most interesting examples of early domestic architecture remaining in the north of England. Joseph Harrison, of Galligreave Hall, died in February 1880 at the age of seventy-six. Many in Ingleton had watched his success and his obituary was recorded in the Ingleton news of the *Lancaster Guardian*.[7] Joseph's son Henry Harrison born in 1834 went on to become a successful business man like his father and was also a Mayor of Blackburn.

WILLIAM TOMLINSON 1801-1858

William Tomlinson was born at Ingleton in 1801 into a family of coal miners. As a youth he began work at Ingleton Colliery and it is probably there that he had a serious accident which led to the amputation of a leg. At this time this would have cut his means of continuing employment as a working man and thrown him on to his family or the parish for support. However, William Tomlinson was extremely fortunate, for the minister of Ingleton Church, the Rev William Waller, took a personal interest in him. It is likely that minister William Waller saw promise in the youth for during the time he was minister at Ingleton he had taken a great interest in Ingleton's school and even taught there. It is possible that he had seen William Tomlinson's potential when he was a boy, either in Sunday school or day school.

At William Waller's instigation William was sent to be educated at a local public school, most probably Giggleswick. There William Waller financed William's education and his training as a teacher. William's first teaching post was at Rathmell Day School in the village of Rathmell which lies between Settle and Long Preston. On the 5th of March 1831 he married Margaret Bannister of Lancaster at St Mary's Church Ingleton. The couple moved to Westhouse and both taught school there. William and Margaret's children were all born at Westhouse and baptised at St Oswald's Church in Thornton in Lonsdale. As the children grew up William provided them with a good education and three sons, William Bannister, Anthony Thomas and Joseph went to private boarding schools. William Bannister Tomlinson is shown as a boarder at Giggleswick in the 1851 census return.

William's elevated social position as a teacher influenced him into becoming a supporter of the temperance movement. The *Lancaster Gazette* of February 10th 1844 records, 'On Friday evening last, a meeting of the members of the Temperance Society was held in the Wesleyan Chapel at Ingleton. Mr Tomlinson, of Westhouse, was called to the chair. After which several discourses in advocacy of teetotal principles were delivered to a numerous audience, not withstanding, the signatures obtained were few.' William's Tomlinson relations, who were mainly miners in Ingleton, regularly frequented the village inns and beer-houses. William must have become quite detached from his family as his father and brothers were very much working class with habits of drinking and poaching: they were also mainly illiterate.

William died at Westhouse aged fifty-seven and is buried in St Oswald's churchyard, at Thornton in Lonsdale. There is no memorial to him which appears strange considering his respected position in society and his thirty years of dedicated service to the community.

Here is an excellent example of how education could raise a man into a new professional and social life. Education in William's time was neither free nor compulsory and few miners' children ever attained much even if they went to school as they usually started work in the mines around the age of ten. William's children mainly progressed well: the daughters marrying successful business men. Eldest son, William Bannister Tomlinson, obtained his B.A degree and was ordained Deacon in 1858 and Priest in 1865. He became headmaster of Horton Grammar School and was also curate of the church there. He was curate of Chapel-le-Dale 1867-1868 after which he became curate of Stainforth. From 1874 to 1877 he was curate of Settle and chaplain to the Settle Union Workhouse at Giggleswick.[8]

JOHN TOMLINSON 1854 – 1882.

John Tomlinson was a blacksmith at Ingleton Colliery when he had a fatal accident in June 1882. However, the accident was at Ingleton Midland Station where he was repairing a coal wagon. Having examined one side of the wagon he went under the buffers to examine the other side. While doing this his right leg was run over by another railway wagon carrying six tons of pig iron. The shunter moving the second wagon was not aware that John Tomlinson was near the wagon. The seriously injured man was taken by special train to Leeds Infirmary and died there at 7.30pm.

John Tomlinson was buried in Ingleton churchyard and most of the miners from Ingleton colliery attended the funeral as did many more people from the village for he was a very popular man. Such was his popularity that his work colleagues erected a memorial to him over his grave. The grave is situated on the left at the top of the main path to St Mary's Church. William Tomlinson the teacher and John Tomlinson the colliery blacksmith were distant cousins and part of a large Tomlinson clan who lived in Ingleton from the eighteenth century to the twentieth century.

BODY SNATCHERS - RESURRECTION MEN.

One mystery of the churchyard at Ingleton was the disappearance of a potter's child. A family of potters were travelling through Ingleton in 1846 when one of their children, a girl of near two years, was taken ill. The mother asked for shelter and Margaret Shepherd, a kind-hearted woman, who lived in the New Road allowed the mother and child to rest in her house. During the day the child became worse and died in a convulsive fit. The family had to remain for the burial and John Hartley made a small coffin for the child. The potter's family were going to Leeds and on their return gave Margaret Shepherd a present for her help.

The event was forgotten until about ten years later the sexton uncovered the coffin while cutting another grave. The plate was still readable on the coffin. 'Ann Swales, died February 15th, 1846 aged 1 year'. The lid was split in the attempt to move the coffin and out of curiosity he examined it and found it to be empty. This caused consternation in the village as they had not before considered that they had suffered from body-snatchers or resurrection men as they were called. The *Lancaster Guardian* had reported on February 29th 1868, 'However the coffin was empty and there is no doubt that the child was taken out by a resurrectionist after its interment and this painful disclosure cannot but lead to the conclusion that there are many empty coffins in our quiet churchyard'.

In the 1820s the Lancaster press recorded several instances of bodies being found in cellars, on a stage coach coming into Lancaster, and in one case several bodies were found packed in salt when a large barrel fell onto the docks and broke open. All the bodies, removed from their graves shortly after burial, were on the way to medical schools in Scotland where bodies were bought without questions being asked. However, the Anatomy Act of 1832 legalised the use of certain corpses and was said to have made body-snatching redundant, yet Ingleton's case was ten years later. What other explanation could there be for the body of the young child being missing from its coffin?

BULL BAITING

Hewitson recorded an account of bull baiting in the *Story of My Village*:-[9]

Bull-baiting formed part of the recreational programme. I once saw a bull subjected to the baiting process. The animal, a very ponderous one, was rope-fastened, to a heavy ring in the ground – in the centre of the village on the hill where there is now (1893) a large ring fixed to a stone – and a crowd stood around whilst two or three dogs tackled the bovine gentleman. There were children as well as men – women also to the best of my recollection – in the crowd, and nobody appeared to think that there was anything at all cruel or improper in the proceedings. We all looked on very earnestly – sometimes quite close to the bull, owing to the shortness of the rope by which it was fastened to the ring. Now and then it seemed to get a longer tether – no doubt the man in charge of the rope purposely allowed this – and then it made the crowd sway back very quickly and excitedly out of reach of its big, minatory head-piece; but the bull was soon drawn in again and not until thus limited in range were the dogs, as a rule, set at it. The bull horned the dogs, low down, pretty considerably, the object not being so much to crush or gore as to get its horns under their bellies, and then to toss them into the air.

Hewitson then quoted Henri Misson who wrote about bull-baiting in England in the eighteenth century. Misson said that the dogs could be thrown thirty feet into the air and injured on falling if the dog's owners were not ready beneath him to give him a soft landing. Hewitson continued:-

But there was no danger of this sort to be mitigated or obviated in the encounter I witnessed. I saw one of the dogs pitched up ten or a dozen feet, but it dropped unhurt. Owing to the way the rope was tightened in, when close quarters were reached, the bull was precluded from tossing the dogs beyond the harmless altitude mentioned. The baiting performance lasted altogether about half an hour, and at its close the dogs, considerably hair-ruffled and dirty, but not perceptibly injured, were drawn off, whilst the bull, much bitten about the neck and bleeding at the nose, was led away, probably to a neighbouring slaughterhouse. The old bull ring, fixed to a large stone embedded in the ground, may now be seen, in the centre of the village where the baiting took place.

MAYOR CHAIRING

In the early years of the nineteenth century Mayor Chairing was a custom celebrated in Ingleton as in many other towns and villages. According to Hewitson the action took place at Shrovetide. Hewitson tells us that, 'A stumpy, reckless, drink-loving working man usually figured as the hero of the affair – the Mayor. His face was blackened with soot and he sat on a chair placed upon two or three light, short planks. Then he was carried shoulder high on this platform by a number of men to where money was likely to be got or drink given. A halt was made immediately opposite each house.' A speech was made by the Mayor praising those who lived in the house and especially the head of the household. The hoped for result was a gift of money or a drink. Although Hewitson tells us that Mayor Chairing was carried ut at Shrovetide a writer in the *Lancaster Gazette* in 1851 ended his report on Ingleton fair by saying, 'In the evening the assembly rooms were crowded, and the following morning a new mayor was elected and chaired, and thus the conclusion of Ingleton Fair'.

One Ingletonian described the scene of a Mayor Chairing from his youth. He told how a procession started from the Bay Horse Inn. 'The 'Mayor' of that year was the village toper, old Bob Stackhouse – old Bob Staggers we called him, from his normal condition, who with his face daubed with red paint, and I think with straws stuck in his hat band, was seated in a chair and carried on the shoulders of two brawny colliers. And then I suppose they perambulated the village'. Robert Stackhouse was an agricultural labourer who was born in Ingleton in 1806.[10]

RIDING THE STANG

Riding the Stang was a village practice which may well have begun in Saxon times and survived to the nineteenth century. This custom had no fixed time or season, but was set in motion by the occurrence of wife-beating or adulterous activity. Once the news had spread round the village action was taken. The victim was tied to a pole and carried through the village on the shoulders of two hefty men, where he was subjected to both ridicule and assault. In some place there are records of the person being so badly beaten that he later died: there are no such records at Ingleton. Because of this danger it became more usual for effigies of straw to be used to represent the victim.

In the 1880s a stout little Ingleton man who had been showing too much regard for the wife of a local collier was tarred and feathered and fastened to a long stout pole. He was then carried through the village. Often effigies were used as in November 1891 at Ingleton when the effigies of a married man and a single woman were taken through the village on a cart. A youth stood between them and rang a bell to attract public attention. Afterwards the effigies were taken to a neighbouring hill where they were blown up with gunpowder and then set on fire.

Another form of the custom at Ingleton is described by Hewitson:-

A couple of long poles or cart shafts were procured and upon these, which were opened out parallel, a chair was fastened by cords. A blustering care-for-nothing sort of fellow was got to sit on the chair. Then a move was made to the house of the objectionable or guilty party – the man riding above perhaps holding in one hand an old can and brandishing a thick stick with the other, whilst the surrounding crown of youths and adults would be in possession of innumerable din-making articles in the form of pan lids, kettles, broken tin canisters, fire-shovels and pokers. When the house was reached, there arose shouts and yells, followed by a distracting deafening outburst of noise made by means of the afore-mentioned articles. A denunciation or proclamation of the offending person, by the man in the chair, immediately supplemented all this; and then the crowd withdrew, along with the stang-riding apparatus to different parts of the village. They went to street corners and open spaces and there all the original din was repeated and the guilty individual re-proclaimed and condemned.

Riding the Stang was not only associated with gong clanging and shouting, but usually a doggerel rhyme was chanted beginning with something like, 'Here we come with a ran tan tan' and in the rhyme the victim was named and his supposed sins were revealed.

REFERENCES

1. *Lancaster Guardian,* June 26th 1875.
2. *Lancaster Guardian,* July 10th 1875.
3. *Recollections of Ingleton* 1896, J. Carr, 1896 ed. J.I. Bentley, Ingleton Pub., 1991, p.89.
4. *Famous Trials, Harold Greenwood,* W. Duke, Ed J. Hodge, Penguin Books, 1954.
5. *The Doctor,* Robert Southey Ed. and Abridged version by M. Fitzgerald, from John Wood Warter's ed of 1848. London Bell & Sons 1930, p.78-83.
6. *Story of my Village,* A. Hewitson, Ed. J.I. Bentley, 1982, p.12.
7. *Lancaster Guardian* February 21st 1880.
8. *The Ingleton Tomlinsons,* T. Tomlinson, 2006, pp.187-190.
9. *The Story of my Village,* A. Hewitson, Ed. J.I. Bentley, 1982.
10. *Lancaster Guardian,* Dec. 20th 1902.

RIVER NAMES AT INGLETON

There is no better way to begin this chapter than quoting the words of Alfred Wainwright in *Wainwright in the Limestone Dales*:-[1]

> If there is in the north of England a more beautiful walk than the tour of the glens and waterfalls of Ingleton I have yet to discover it. In the space of four enchanting miles there is a rapid succession of lovely vistas of river scenery, of bewitching cascades and waterfalls in a woodland setting of great charm. For visitors from an urban background here is a foretaste of paradise .... Two streams come down from a hilly hinterland and after a sedate infancy suddenly leap into a happy frolic through verdant surroundings to reach the village where they converge as the River Greta.

> It is a little unfortunate that there are differences of opinion about the names of the two streams. In my young days, the western stream was known as the River Doe and the eastern the River Twiss: there was no apparent reason for the name Doe, but the name Twiss seemed to be derived from Twistleton Scar and Twistleton Hall below which it flowed. But by the time I had reached middle age the Ordnance Survey had switched the names after an inconclusive local census, and for a few years the eastern stream appeared on their maps as the River Doe before being changed again – this time to the River Greta, having no doubt decided that the eastern stream was the principal of the two and really the source of the parent river. Confusion was compounded by local guide books and publications, the western steam being named therein as Kingsdale Beck with some justification, since it is a continuation of a stream of that name in its higher reaches; and the Twiss/Doe/Greta now appeared as Dale Beck.

This wrangling over river names at Ingleton has gone on for well over a hundred years. In June 1887 the Ingleton correspondent to the *Lancaster Guardian* wrote an article entitled, 'Confusion in the River Names at Ingleton'.[2] The writer explained that with there being so many maps and guides to Ingleton it was most confusing to tourists. It was also confusing to local people. The writer explained that most visitors took the Ordnance Survey as their authority. This was the problem, for when the Ordnance Survey officers produced the first OS map of the Ingleton area they got the river names wrong. The Irish Ordnance Survey men looked at older maps and talked to old folks in Ingleton, but they made their main mistake of incorrectly naming the main river, the boundary of Ingleton and Thornton.

This boundary river was the Doe or Daw and had always been so in official records. The Court Rolls prove this and the first surviving record of the boundary of Ingleton is dated 1592. This boundary description was given in full in Tudor Ingleton and here the section is given that proves the Doe ran from the Greta up through Broadwood to Ravenray, the boundary then continuing to the top of Whernside:-

& then to the water of Greeta and up the water of Greeta North to the water of Daw to ravenrath & then to a place called the Nabbe of the Shawe & then to Miafould and so to a Stone called Mossy Stone & then to the standing stone & up the ffoulsike north east to the Hole in the ff(?) and then to the height of Whernside & as the Heaven water divideth.

From the Greta into the Doe and to Ravenwray, there is nothing clearer than that. The problem was that this record from the court rolls was tucked away in colliery records and is now in the Yorkshire Archaeological Society Archives at Leeds, the original court rolls of this period had not survived. If the map makers had looked at the surviving court rolls they could have followed the Lord of the manor, Edward Parker's riding of the boundaries in 1754. Once again they would have seen that the Ingleton Thornton boundary river was the Doe without any question of doubt.

The river Doe is the boundary between Ingleton and Thornton and always has been.

When Edward Parker, Lord of the Manor, led his men to ride the boundaries in September 1754 the Ingleton Court Rolls record began, '**Beginning where Thornton River called Doe runs into and meets Ingleton River called Greet and down said river until Parks on an old Watercourse there to the river again.**' And they ended, '**in a direct line to the Standing Stone through Green Barn to Ravenray and then down the River Doe where it runs into and meets the Ingleton River where began.**' Once again nearly two centuries later there is no problem with the river name. Not only that but the document is signed by William Carus the long serving Steward of the Court, Edward Foxcroft, Richard Balderston and most other leading men of the village.[3]

Having clearly and probably legally established that the river Doe is the boundary between Ingleton and Thornton we must look at what other names it has been called. It has correctly been called Thornton Beck as this was colloquial. It has been also called the Greta and the Twiss, but these names are totally incorrect. Higher upstream it has been correctly called Kingsdale Beck as after all it does run through the valley of Kingsdale.

Let us now go to the river bounding Ingleton from Twistleton and what more natural name than the Twiss. This river has also been called colloquially Ingleton Beck especially where it ran through Ingleton. Further up the valley in Ingleton Fells this river was know as the Wease or Weasedale Beck and we know that in the sixteenth century the church at Ingleton Fells was known as Weasedale or Wisedale Chapel. John Brockbank, minister at Ingleton in 1667, wrote to a neighbouring church to apologise for not being able to visit because, 'I have already promised to be at Weasedale Chappell then which is a Chapple belonginge to us'.[4]

353

With things so clear how have things been so messed up? The main reason is that the people discussing and making decisions on the problem, whether the Balderstons in their *Ingleton Bygone and Present*, Hewitson in his Guides, Carr in the press, or even the OS were simply not in possession of the facts. In view of this they have come to many and varied conclusions and they might have well as tossed a coin to make their decision.

The Balderstons in *Ingleton Bygone and Present* entitle a section of the appendix, 'The Disputed Nomenclature of the Rivers, Greta, Twiss and Doe'. Many pages are spent in getting nowhere. They quote Dr Whittaker and then old men of the village. One old man of the village had told them that one river was the Dee and the other the Doe. The Balderstons accuse the Township of 'culpable negligence' for not marking the names on the Township Map. Finally through lack of historical evidence the Balderstons settled nothing and came down on the wrong side. They have the Wease on the Thornton boundary though Weasedale was the old name of Chapel-le-Dale. Their historical knowledge and historical research capabilities were very limited.

Joseph Carr had the river Doe as the Thornton Ingleton boundary, but had the second river as the Greeta. He recognised that the confusion over river names must be very perplexing to visitors. Joseph Carr's final comment in his article in 1887 was. Though the writer does not decide which are the correct names of the two rivers, still he thinks it is time for publishers of maps and guides to Ingleton to avoid the confusion of names.' Writing again in 1892 Joseph Carr says that, 'he never heard the old inhabitants of that date call Thornton Beck any other name than the Doe'.[5]

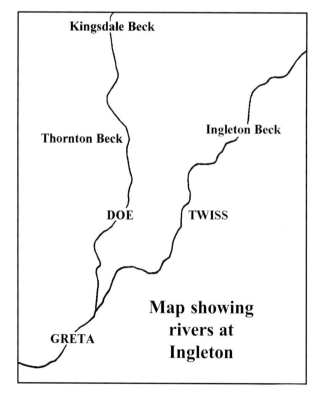

Map showing
rivers at
Ingleton

Speight in his *The Craven and North-West Yorkshire Highlands* discusses the problem at length.[6] He begins:-

A word now as to the nomenclature of these streams, which has given rise to much confusion, and not a little unfortunate wrangling as to what really are their proper names. In legal documents relating to the neighbourhood, in the Ordnance Survey Maps, and other Government publications, as well as in local guide books, the greatest variance prevails. In the oldest map procurable on the district, namely Saxton's (A.D.1577), the western beck is called Kinesdale, and the eastern or Chapel-le-Dale, the Greeta

Speight goes on at length, but the main point is the fact that Saxton marks the Ingleton beck as the Greeta thus continuing the Greeta up through the township. This has also been done by the OS and sadly this creates a question that cannot be simply solved. The Doe and the Twiss have always been taken as twin rivers and not the same river, therefore at some time the name Twiss must have been applied to the Ingleton beck. Speight does say that, 'there is no doubt that the Kingsdale stream is the River Doe.'

For the OS and many others it is now decision time. The western river must be named the Doe. The eastern river must be named either the Greeta or Twiss. If the Greeta is chosen then we lose an important Ingleton river name - the Twiss. If the Twiss is chosen then we keep the twin rivers Doe and Twiss and the Greta is still there at their confluence. The Ingleborough Archaeological Group and the Ingleton Angling Association are for the Doe and Twiss for the western and eastern rivers respectively as is the author of this history. It is interesting to note that Ingleton Angling Club issue a map to their members and the rivers are clearly marked. The club have been consistent over a hundred and fifty years.

Just before publication the OS wrote to say they found no reason to change the names back to what they were some forty years ago. The unaccountable Ordnance Survey quango continues to be obtuse up to this day, but the campaign for accuracy will continue.

REFERENCES

1. *Wainwright in the Limestone Dales,* A. Wainwright, Michael Joseph, 1991, p.60.
2. *Lancaster Guardian,* June 11th 1887
3. NYRO, Ingleton Manor Court Rolls 1692-1801 ZUC 3/1, MIC 1181.
4   Private collection of Bill Dootson.
5. *Lancaster Guardian,* March 26th 1892.
6. *Craven and the North West Yorkshire Highlands,* H. Speight, Smith Settle, 1989, p.225, 226.

General Index

I

Ingleboro' Assembly Rooms 191
Ingleboro' Brewery 285
Ingleborough Mountain Race 73
Ingleborough Patent Lime Works 210
Ingleton Angling Association 209
Ingleton Brass Band
    72, 128, 304, 323, 324, 325, 328
Ingleton Cinema 288
Ingleton Co-operative Society Ltd 296
Ingleton Electric Light & Power Co. Ltd
    174, 301, 316
Ingleton Electric Lighting Co. 318
Ingleton Estates Company Ltd 196, 202
Ingleton Fire Brigade 69
Ingleton Gas Company 285, 314
Ingleton Improvement Company 250, 252
Ingleton Rifle Corps 325
Ingleton Steam Laundry 286
Inns/Hotels
    Bay Horse Inn
        48, 53, 137, 138, 142, 144, 163,
        185, 207, 233, 246, 290, 292,
        301, 307, 328, 329, 350
    Bell Horse Inn 155
    Black Bull Inn 48, 154, 155, 296
    Brewery Inn 152, 154
    Bridge Inn
        62, 68, 86, 142, 144, 189, 195, 295,
        311, 324, 327, 332, 338
    Castle Inn 128
    Cock Inn 279
    Craven Heifer 48, 86, 144
    Cross Keys Inn 109, 155
    Gearstones 86, 150, 158, 221
    Hill Inn 86, 149
    Horse Shoe Inn 141
    Ingleboro' Hotel
        59, 60, 85, 138, 142, 148, 191,
        209, 230, 248, 286, 288, 336
    Marton Arms 63, 74, 223, 249, 255
    Masons Arms
        48, 86, 141, 144, 145, 189,
        230, 251
    Newby Head Inn 151
    Oddfellows Arms 48, 86, 146
    Railway Inn 152, 154
    Red Lion 221
    Ring O'Bells 156
    Royal Oak 138
    Station Inn 67, 150, 152, 154, 245
    Sun Inn 344
    Temperance Hotel 301

    Three Horse Shoes Inn
        40, 48, 60, 85, 109, 117, 141, 195,
        252, 290, 304, 331, 337
    Travellers Rest 86, 152, 245
    Wheat Sheaf Inn
        40, 48, 53, 58, 63, 67, 70, 82, 85,
        102, 116, 118, 121, 138, 152, 169,
        175, 209, 234, 248, 250, 278, 285,
        286, 290, 309, 316, 324, 327, 331,
        336, 338, 340
    Welcome Home 139, 152, 243
    Woolpack 138
Ivy Cottages 304

J

Jenkin Beck 198
Jericho 56, 238
Jerusalem 238

K

Keighley to Kendal Turnpike Road
    194, 222, 233
Keighley to Kendal Turnpike Trust
    220, 227
Kirkby Lonsdale 59, 169, 170
Kirkham 58
Kirksteads 138

L

Labour, Minister of 203
Lancaster Richmond Turnpike 222
Laundry Lane 17, 67, 175, 285
Lennie Wood 209, 334
Lightcliffe 216
Literary Institute 309
Llanelly 342
Local Government Board 64
Locomotives:
    Cyprus 216
    King George V 198
    Northumbria 215, 216
    Victoria 198
Long Chimney 304
Lowgill 233
Luddenden 42

M

Manning & Wardle 216
Marl Pit Field 183
Masongill 60, 272
Masongill House 272
Mayor Chairing 350

Meal Bank 212
Melling 179
Midland Station 337, 348
Mill Barn 169
Mill Wood 174
Mills
      Bentham Mill 207, 290
      Byber Mill 235
      Clapham Corn Mill 169
      Dent's Mill 290
      Fulling Mill 304
      Ingleton Mill 311, 312
      Langcliffe Paper Mill 276
      Upper Mill 166, 170
      Victoria Saw Mills 286, 287
      Walk Mill 167
      Wheat Mill 166
Miners' Federation of Great Britain 200
Moorgarth 4, 16, 39, 160, 167, 184
Mount Pleasant 302

N

National & Provincial Bank Ltd 202
Nelson 206
New Bridge 73, 202
New Ingleton Sanitary Laundry 285
New (Model) Village
      69, 73, 196, 198, 312
New Road 195
New Road Bridge 73
New Zealand 54
Newby Head 86
North Field 164
Northern Mine Research Society 176
Nutgill 119
Nuvic Cinema 289

O

Old Coal Road 227

P

Pan Well 311
Parkfoot 74, 176, 183
Parkfoot Bridge 49
Parkfoot Farm 190
Paul's Fold 305
Pear Tree Cottage 307
Pecca Falls 247, 249
Peckett & Sons 198
Pemberton 193
Phoenix Foundry 312
Pit Ponies 203

Port Lyttleton 54
Post Office 290, 291
Poverty 321

Q

Quarries
      Catlow Quarries 206
      Craven Lime Works 252,
      309, 331, 334
      Granite Quarry 67, 70
      Granite Works 68
      Green's Slate Quarry 207
      Ingleton Granite Quarry 215
      Ingleton Slate Quarries 290
      Meal Bank Lime Works 331
      Meal Bank Quarry 63, 69, 70, 209
      Middlebarrow Quarry 213
      Nutgill Flag Quarry 207
      Pecca Slate Quarries 205, 207
      Ribblehead Lime Quarry 213
      Shap Granite Quarries 216
      Storrs Quarry 111
      Wellhead Quarry 108
Quarry Companies
      Amalgamated Roadstone 216
      Amey Roadstone Corporation
      216, 257
      Craven Lime Company (Ltd)
      64, 67, 68, 209, 211, 212, 213
      Hanson Aggregates UK 216
      Ingleton Granite Company 216
      Storrs Lime-works 128
      XL Granite (Ingleton) Ltd 216
Quarry Wood 205

R

Railway Companies
      Midland Railway Co. 198, 242
      North Western Railway Company
      233
Railways
      London & North Western Railway
      197, 238
      Lune Valley Railway 235
      Midland Railway
      189, 193, 197, 215, 238, 247
      North Western Railway 233
      Settle Carlisle Railway
      53, 56, 74, 154, 228, 236, 240
Rarber Top Lane 194
Raygill 119, 178, 179
Rechabites 69

Surname Index

Battersby, Benjamin 46
Battersby, Christopher 40
Battersby, Elizabeth 206
Battersby, John 22
Battersby, Nicholas 44
Battersby, Richard 36
Battersby, Stephen 37
Battersby, Thomas 17, 18, 24, 93, 295
Batty, Anthony 40
Batty, John 39, 40
Batty, Leonard 20
Batty, Richard 32
Batty, William 32
Bayliff, James 44
Baynes, Lawrence 45
Baynes, Richard 49
Baynes, Thomas 89
Baynes, William 46
Baytman, Anthony 22
Baytman, Thomas 22
Beamonde, James 23
Beamonde, John 23
Beamonde, Thomas 23
Beaumond, Joan 26
Beaumond, John 93
Beck, Charles 111
Beesley, Mr 38
Beesley, Richard 37, 89, 90, 303
Bell, Thomas 240
Bell, W.G. 84
Bell, William 54, 55
Bennett, Richard 324
Bentam, Richard 101
Beezley Grange 310
Bentham, C. 332
Bentham, Ellen 101
Bentham, J. 313
Bentham, John 40, 47, 79, 113
Bentham, Joseph
    45, 85, 105, 141, 149, 209, 248,
    286, 303, 309
Bentham, Thomas 44, 101, 131
Bentham, William 37, 47
Benyson, Ranold 21
Benyson, Thomas 23
Berry, Ebenezer 249
Berry, Hannah 80
Berry, Paul 46, 81, 102, 103, 126, 305
Beverley, Christopher 117
Birket, Daniel 45
Blackamore, Richard 114
Bland, John 138
Blenkinsop, Mr 182
Boardman, Ernest Oscar 301
Boardman, George 64, 142, 292, 301, 325

Boardman, Richard 294
Boardman, William 77, 292
Boddy, Symon 40
Bond, Bernard 176
Bond, John 44
Bonnick, T. 248
Bonnick, Thomas 292
Bonnick, Walter 292
Borrowdale, Thomas 47, 163
Bostock's Menagerie 338
Bouch, Anthony 33, 34, 35, 37, 38, 176
Bouch, Henry 42, 113, 115, 124, 178
Bouch, Mary 34
Bowater, Edith 342
Bowater, Mabel 342
Bowater, William Vansittart 342
Bowes, Thomas 91
Bowker, John 43
Bowker, William 46
Boyd, Thomas 325
Bracewell, C.G. 192
Bracewell, William
    118, 128, 130, 171, 172, 186,
    187, 189, 191, 302
Bracken, General 59
Bradley, Dr 193
Bradley, Elsie May 301
Bradley, J.T. 133
Bradley, John 113
Bradley, Richard 113, 301
Bradley, Robert 119
Bragan, James 72
Bragg, John 172
Braithwaite, Richard 270
Braithwaite, Thomas 37
Bramley, William 115
Brayshaw, Ann 267
Brayshaw, Isaac 267
Brennand, Richard 49
Bricke, Andrew 37
Briscoe, Gamaliel 45, 85, 141
Briscoe, James 118
Briscoe, John 130
Briscoe, John James 130
Briscoe, William 331
Brockbank, John 90, 94
Brocklehurst, Albert 72
Brontë, Charlotte 134
Brontë, Patrick 133
Brontë sisters 133
Brookes, John 315
Brooks, Andrew 327
Brooks, John 216
Brotherton, Edward 40
Brotherton, Mr 315

Brown, Adam 44
Brown, Agnes 135
Brown, Andrew 268
Brown, Anthony 174
Brown, Elizabeth 206, 278
Brown, Ernest 203
Brown, Francis 125
Brown, H. 251
Brown, J.B. 336
Brown, James G. 131
Brown, Jane 135, 290
Brown, Joseph 44, 80, 104, 138, 278
Brown, Margaret Greenwood 135
Brown, R. 60
Brown, Richard
    59, 64, 128, 131, 135, 138, 175, 209,
    210, 251, 291, 305, 324, 341
Brown, T. 243
Brown, Thomas 151, 295
Brown, Thomas P. 154
Brown, W.A. 174
Brown, William 124
Brunton, James 104
Bryan Dugdale 44
Bryans, Wm 49
Buchan, John 150
Buck, Thomas 323
Buckham, Edward 141
Bullock, Francis 103
Bullock, James 44
Bullock, William 77
Burbridge, W. 332
Burke, J. 330
Burrow, George 169
Burrow, T. 301
Burrowe, Thomas 29
Burrows, Edward 266
Burton, James 37
Burton, John 37
Butterfield, Richard 37
Byng, John 150, 272

C

Calder, George Alexander 196
Calverley, Thomas 66, 323
Calvert, Anthony 37
Calvert, Leonard 37
Calvert, Thomas 32, 36, 79
Calvert, Widow 89
Calverte, William 22
Campbell, Mr 234
Canncefield, Leonard 22
Cansfeild, John 36
Cansfeld, Roger 29

Cansfield, Elizabeth 79
Cansfield, Richard 40
Capstick, Thomas 259
Capstick, Thomas E. 259
Capstick, Tom 305
Caractacus 2
Cardew, A. 115
Carpenter, John 9
Carr, Edmund 43
Carr, Elizabeth 113
Carr, Joseph
    1, 56, 84, 97, 104, 117, 118, 128,
    131, 155, 191, 192, 207, 208, 212,
    246, 250, 252, 264, 247, 276, 296,
    302, 305, 309, 310, 311, 312, 319,
    322, 345, 354
Carr, Mathias 342
Carr, Matthias 342
Carr, Richard 345
Carr, Stephen 44, 45, 166, 167
Carr, Thomas 206, 221
Carr, William 45, 144
Carter, Grace 79
Carter, Matthew 43, 126, 166, 169
Carter, William 79
Cartimandua 2
Carus, Wm 49
Caton, Thomas 78
Cerialis, Petillius 2
Chamley, Margaret 308
Chamley, R. 332
Chamley, Robert 332
Chapman, R. 60
Chapman, Robert 47, 125, 126, 154, 155
Chapman, Roger 155
Charles, Bryan Waller 273
Charneley, Thomas 32
Charnley, Thomas 130, 131
Chernley, Thomas 114
Child, Robert 62
Cholmley, Richard 24, 25, 29, 92
Christie, Hector 309
Churchill, John 255, 256
Clapham, Anthony 44
Clapham, Betsy Ann 144
Clapham, Joseph Robert 144
Clapham, William 77, 144
Clapham, William Thomas 67
Clark, Charles E. 288
Clark, Marmaduke 44
Clarke, Robert 91
Clarke, Robort 35
Clegg, Kenelm Vivian Sigismund 68, 143
Clerk, Robert 101
Coates, Agnes Stockdale 170

363

Coates, Elizabeth 170
Coates, James 169, 175
Coates, Jim 142, 292
Coates, John 170, 175
Coates, John T. 260, 324
Coates, John Thomas
    85, 128, 170, 172, 175, 262, 312,
    323, 324
Coates, Martin 266
Coates, T. 192
Coates, Thomas 109
Coates, William 266
Cockerton, Henry 286
Cockin, John 35, 75, 156, 303
Colton, William 297
Comeinge, Willm 32
Condor, John 229
Conyers, Christopher 13
Cook, A.J. 201
Cookson, Roger 43
Cookson, T. 59
Coop, Richard 20, 166
Cosyn, William 23
Cousins, Mr 338
Coward, G. 313
Coward, George 77, 82, 84, 297
Cowburn, George 128
Cragg, Francis 44
Cragg, James 44
Cragg, R.W. 59
Cragg, Robert Balderston 67, 272, 305
Craven, Christopher 22, 161
Craven, Elizabeth 35
Craven, Isabel 20, 36, 37
Craven, James 100
Craven, John 32, 49
Craven, Leonard 17, 29
Craven, Willm 36, 49
Cravyn, Christopher 22
Cravyn, Gyles 22
Cravyn, John 21, 23
Cravyn, Leonard 21, 22
Cravyn, Richarde 22
Cravyn, Thomas 22
Cravyn, William 22
Croft, ffrancis 35
Croft, H.J. 268
Croft, Harold John 91
Cromwell, Thomas 99, 305

D

Danson, Edmund
    59, 131, 188, 189, 191, 192, 332
Danson, J.M. 131
Danson, Mr 118, 319
Danson, Robert 127, 128, 131, 290
Darwen, John 174, 211
Darwen, John Berry 210
Darwen, Thomas 211
Davies, D.J. 91
Davies, David 154
Davis, D.T. 99
Davis, Henry 170
Dawbikin, Lancelott 35
Dawson, Joseph 44
Dawson, Miles 80
Day, William 16, 167
Denny, R. 128, 313, 328
Denny, Richard 56, 91, 96, 309, 324
Denny, William 88, 89
Dent, Betty 170
Dent, Elizabeth 175
Dent, Jane 126
Dent, William 43
Deny, John 22
Deny, William 22
Dernaly, A. 111
Dewhirst, Jane 130
Dickenson, R. 49
Dickinson, Robert 143
Dinsdale, John 266
Dinsdale, Matthew 118, 267
Dinsdale, Norman Vincent 91
Dixon, Agnes 167
Dixon, Ann 344
Dixon, Jonas 79
Dixon, Miles 49
Dixon, Rowland 278, 343, 344
Dixon, Rowley 343
Dixon, W. 59
Dixon, William 46, 324
Dobson, Richard 193
Dodd, William 331
Dodgson, Nurse 72
Domoney, John (see Dumoney)
    143, 144, 295
Dootson, Bill 94
Douthwaite, Thomas 47, 48
Dove, Daniel 278
Dove, William 279
Dowbiggin, Joseph 162
Dowbigging, Lawrence 40
Down, Christopher 45
Downey, Simon 37

Downham, John 303
Downham, Messrs 251
Downham, Stephen 83
Dowthwaite, Thomas 138
Doyle, Charles 272, 273
Doyle, Conan 97, 272
Doyle, Jane Adelaide Rose 273
Doyle, Mary 273
Doyle, Mary Josephine 273
Dring, George 70
Drinkall, Mr 250
Dudley, George 243
Duerden, Norman 246
Dumoney, John, 86

E

Edmund Lund 44
Edmundson, John 44
Eglin, Stephen 166
Ellershaw, Henry 47, 163
Ellershaw, Jenny 135
Ellershaw, John 44, 48, 154, 155
Ellershaw, Miss 303
Ellershaw, R.B. 118, 248, 319, 320
Elletson, R.W. 324
Ellis, Anne 169
Ellis, Benjamin 43, 169, 295
Ellis, Charles 91
Ellis, Ephraim 169
Ellis, John 46, 169
Ellis, Samuel 44
Ely, W. 330
Eve, J.L. 229

F

Fairbank, William 44, 302
Farraday, Richard 43
Farrar, James 58
Farrer, Captain 74
Farrer, J.A. 316
Farrer, James 154, 182, 210
Farrer, James William 206
Farrer, John 124
Farrer, M.T. 260, 264
Farrer, Mr 341
Farrer, Oliver 303, 325
Farrer, Reginald 213
Farrer, Richard 143
Farrer, Violet 268
Farthwaite, Michael 24, 90, 92
Fawcett, Nathaniel 47
Fawcett, William 46
Fearnside, Professor 229
Fenwick, T.E. 341

Fenwick, T.F. 260
ffalscrofte, Thomas 22
ffalsecrofte, James 21
ffirbanke, Thomas 35
ffirthbanke, Geffray 22
ffoster, Thomas 23
ffoxcroft, Gyles 36
ffoxcroft, Isabel 79
ffoxcroft, John 113
ffoxcroft, Leonard 36
ffoxcroft, Miles 36
ffoxcroft, Richard 75
ffoxcroft, Thomas 36
ffoxcroft, William 36
ffregleton, John 22
ffregleton, Thomas 22
Fieldhouse, Richard 92
Fieldhouse, Thomas 90, 92
Filburn, John 141
Firbank, John 124
Fish, Robert 16
Fisher, William 142
Fishwick, Arthur 63
Fitzhugh, Henry 10
Fleming, Daniel 34
Fleming, George 330
Fleming, William 34
Fletcher, Jos. A. 288
Fletcher, Walter 59
Foley, Mary 272
Forbes, Jemmy 64
Ford, John 174
Ford, T.B.T. 341
Foster, C. 116
Foster, Christopher 139
Foster, Henry 166
Foster, John 44, 163
Foster, Kit 263
Foster, Major 260
Foster, Peter 32
Foster, R. 110
Foster, Richard 39, 267
Foster, Samuel 46
Foster, William 45, 141
Fothergill, Adam 218
Fothergill, Alexander 221, 222
Foxcroft, Edward 180, 182
Foxcroft, Edwd 49
Foxcroft, George 180
Foxcroft, Giles 100
Foxcroft, John 18, 91
Foxcroft, John Morton 44
Foxcroft, John 49
Foxcroft, Miss 294
Foxcroft, T.H. 338

Foxcroft, Thomas 16, 18, 25
Frankland, Christopher 90, 93
Fregylton, William 22
Fry, Roger Joseph Hamilton 91

G

Gambles, Robert 1
Garbutt, Thomas 267
Garlick, John 153
Garnett, Emmeline 273
Garnett, John 125
Gawith, Joseph 144
Gee, R.W. 330
Geldart, Robert 35
Gent, Thomas 277
Gibbons, Annie 144
Gibson, John 78
Gibson, Richard 24, 35
Gilkes, Gilbert 317, 318
Gill, Mike 176
Gill, Thomas 143
Gillbanks, George 54, 55
Gillbanks, Joseph 86, 111, 128, 145, 251
Gillbanks, Joseph George 54
Glover, Rowland 37
Goman, Henry 216
Goss, Thomas 163
Gott, John 107
Graham, Arthur 289
Gray, Alex 22
Gray, Thomas 43, 273
Greaves, W. 116
Green, Margaret 155
Green, Ralph 44
Green, Thomas 155, 290, 329
Green, William 43, 126, 127, 206
Greenbank, John 32, 46
Greenbank, Leonard 32, 37
Greenbank, Thomas 32, 37
Greenbank, William 17, 32, 40
Greenwood, Christopher Jackson 42
Greenwood, David 42, 60, 301
Greenwood, Emily B. 196
Greenwood, Frank 254
Greenwood, Harold 70, 342
Greenwood, Henry 37
Greenwood, Isaac 42, 301
Greenwood, Isabella 61
Greenwood, James 46, 170, 218
Greenwood, Jane 42, 301
Greenwood, Mabel 70, 342, 343
Greenwood, Margaret 170
Greenwood, Oscar 62, 73, 194, 343
Greenwood, Percy 73, 194

Greenwood, Robert 281, 282
Greenwood, Robert Hodgson 42, 281
Greenwood, Tom 256, 257
Greenwood, William 43, 60, 61
Greenwood, William Norman
    60, 66, 109, 141, 194, 304, 324, 342
Gregory, A. 133
Gregson, John 23
Gregson, Richard 22
Gregson, Thomas 37
Gregson, William 22
Griffiths, Dr 59, 195, 336, 339
Grime, Francis 46
Grime, Joseph 45
Guilliam, James 197
Gunn, Superintendent 340
Gurdon, R. 33
Guy, Alexander 26, 160, 161
Guy, John 40
Guy, Margaret 26
Guy, Richard 277, 278
Guy, Thomas 35, 39, 151, 161
Guy, William 19
Guye, Alex 23
Guye, John 21, 23
Guye, Thomas 21, 23
Guyers, George 206, 266
Guyers, Isobel 206
Guyers, Jenny 266
Guyers, John 206
Guyers, Thomas 46, 206
Gybson, Christopher 23
Gybson, John 22
Gybson, Richarde 21
Gybson, Roger 22

H

Hafner, Michael 216
Haigh, Joseph 193, 194
Hainsworth, J. 302
Hainsworth, Reg 73, 255, 268
Hall, Edward Marshall 342
Hall, John 36
Hall, Thomas 36
Hambleton, Thomas 79
Hammerton, James 46
Hammerton, Stephen 43, 303
Hammerton, Thomas 43
Hanwood, Arthur 146
Hardy, William 221
Haresnape, John 46
Haresnape, William 43
Harling, Dorothy 344
Harling, John 16, 18, 89, 138, 144

Harling, William 344
Harlyn, John 21
Harlyn, Matthewe 21
Harlyn, Richard 21, 23
Harrington, Barnaby 270
Harrison, C. 222
Harrison, Christopher 46, 223
Harrison, Edmund 43
Harrison, Henry 347
Harrison, John 46, 83, 166, 324
Harrison, Joseph 347
Harrison, Mary 78
Harrison, Richard 45, 46, 77
Harrison, T. 131
Harrison, Thomas 329
Harrison, William 18, 347
Hibbert, Harry 67
Hartley, George 77
Hartley, J. 206
Hartley, John 137, 138, 320, 348
Hartley, Marie 150, 155
Hartley, S. 131
Hartley, Samuel 59, 128, 131, 324, 325
Hartley, William 138
Haslem, Richard 78
Hathersall, George 144
Haulay, John 13
Hawkins, Louisa 272
Hawkshead, Thomas 163
Hayes, Herbert 144
Hazlam, John 35
Heaton, John 131
Hebden, John 44
Herbert, Jane 244
Herd, John 46, 304
Herd, Leonard 49
Herd, Lodge 46
Herd, Marie 32
Herd, William 44, 126
Heselton, T. 304
Hewitson, Anthony
    102, 120, 131, 135, 164, 229,
    274, 301, 343
Hewitson, J. 248
Hewitson, John 215, 252, 255
Hewitson, Mr 260
Hewitt, A.B. 72, 229
Hewitt, Dorothy 294
Hey, Mary 266
Heys, Mr 235
Higson, Alf 68
Higson, Jack 68
Hird, Alexander 40
Hird, Christopher 36

Hird, John 174
Hird, Leonard 36
Hird, William 17, 24
Hirde, John 22
Hirde, William 22
Hirst, H.L. 203
Hodgson, Brian 40
Hodgson, Christopher 47, 188
Hodgson, John 43, 45, 117, 294, 328
Hodgson, Joseph 102, 193
Hodgson, Leonard 45, 182
Hodgson, Richard 170
Hodgson, Robert 42, 49, 91
Hodgson, Samuel Butler 126
Hodgson, Thomas 35, 182, 308
Hodgson, William 82, 308
Hoffman, Dr 321
Hogg, Mr 285
Holden, Isaac 106
Holgate, Anthony 251
Hollies, Elizabeth 60
Hollinghead, G. 215
Holm, Christopher 221
Holme, John 138, 143
Holmes, Oliver Wendell 273
Holmes, Sherlock 273
Holroyd, Benjamin 249
Holt, George 154
Homfray, G.S. 313
Hone, William 97
Hopkinson, Frank 70
Hopkinson, Joseph 250, 251
Hornby, Charles Edward 59
Hornby, Henry Hugh 59
Hornby, Hugh 58
Hornby, Hugh Frederick 59
Hornby, Joseph 58
Hornby, Richard Cortazzi 59
Hornby, Thomas Dyson 59
Horsfall, Richard 32
Houghton, William 45
Howson, A. 307
Howson, F. 288
Howson, Fred 291
Howson, George 188
Howson, John 113, 126, 207
Howson, John Simpson 46
Howson, John Slinger 188
Howson, Joshua 142
Howson, Moses Frederick 288
Howson, Richard 46
Howson, Thomas 37
Howson, William 118, 188
Huck, Leonard Ellison 329
Hugganson, Nic 78

Huginson, Geo 37
Humphries, Clifford 268
Hunning, John 221
Hunter, Joseph
    116, 128, 182, 184, 186, 188,
    324, 325
Hunter, Mr 97
Husband, Robert 37
Hutchinson, John 43
Hutchinson, Mrs 174
Hutchinson, Robert 174
Hutton, Agnes 60
Hutton, Henry 169
Hutton, John
    43, 59, 60, 180, 205, 246, 275
Hutton, William 72

I

Ingleby, Joan 150, 155
Ireland, Fred 330
Ireland, Mark 292
Ireland, Mr 128
Iveson, Roger 20

J

Jackson, Christopher 43, 113, 114
Jackson, Ellen 60
Jackson, George 86, 146, 153, 154
Jackson, J. 91
Jackson, James 124
Jackson, John 49, 78
Jackson, Matthew 77
Jackson, Percy 73, 133
Jackson, R.J. 330
Jackson, Richard 118, 278
Jackson, Thomas 23, 126
Jackson, William 45
Jarry, Miss 263
Jeffry, Thomas 166
Jenkins, John 72
Jenson, Roland 91
Johnson, George 46
Johnson, John 36, 40, 60
Johnson, Marmaduke 36, 39
Johnson, Richard 22
Jolly, Charles 216
Jones, Gladys 342
Jones, Thomas 153

K

Kay, Charles 47, 125
Kenyon, Martin 266
Kenyon, Thomas 125

Kenyon, Tibby 266
Kenyon, William Thomas 63
Kidd, Abraham 115
Kidd, Cuthbert 44, 179, 180
Kidd, Francis 78, 113, 266
Kidd, Frank 247
Kidd, John 44, 148, 248, 292, 319, 322
Kidd, Robert 43, 142
Kidd, Thomas 78
Kilburn, John 150
Kilburn, Tom 150
Kilburn, W.K. 324
Killburn, John 154
King, J. 59
King, John 86, 138, 146, 332
King, Thomas 45, 162
King, Thomas Foster 292
Kirk, Alfred 109, 250
Kirk, Alfred S. 61, 248, 302, 332
Kirk, Gerald 61
Kirkham, Richard 70
Kitchen, James 138
Kitchen, John 77
Knipe, Isaac 179
Knipe, William 179

L

Laburne, Robert 37
Lacy, Robert 163
Lamb, Anne 79
Lamb, Edward 35
Lamb, Henry 39, 164
Lamb, John 39
Lamb, Leonard 35
Lamb, Thomas 35, 38
Lamb, William 36
Lambert, F. 332
Lambert, John 47
Lambert, Lawrence 43, 266
Lambert, Thomas 47
Lang, William 242
Langdon, Edward 216
Langland, William 166
Langley, William 216
Langstrath, John 37
Langstroth, Edward 43
Langstroth, John 43
Langstroth, William 47
Langton, Edmunde 22
Lawson, Robert 180, 182
Layfield, Myles 39
Leach, Samuel 295
Leach, T. 324

Leak, Anthony 89
Leak, Thomas 89
Leake, Agnes 90
Leake, Anthony 37
Leake, Jeffrey 37, 89
Leake, Thomas 90
Leaks, Anthony 79
Lee, Mary Ann 150
Lee, T. 72
Leech, Alice 79
Leeming, David 46
Leeming, Edmund 43
Leeming, James 77, 131
Leeming, John 339
Leslie, Harriet Ann 60
Lindsay, Robert 186, 188
Lindsay, Thomas 44, 138, 186, 188, 222
Lister, Anthony 45
Lister, J. 128
Lister Parker, T. 109
Lister, William 47, 48
Littlefair, Charles 69, 327
Litton, Edmond 37
Livesey, S.N. 91
Llewellyn, John 91, 99
Llewelyn, J. 195
Lockett, Henry J. 91
Lodge, Edmund Foxcroft 46, 125
Lodge, Edward Foxcroft 117
Lodge, John 89, 90
Lodge, Ottuel 45
Lodge, Richard 86
Lofthouse, Jessica 246
Lond, Thomas de 13
Long, Christopher Francis Drake 255, 256
Longton, W.A. 330
Longton, William Arkwright 145
Lord, James 118
Lowe, H. 55
Lowther, Christopher 34
Lowther, Elizabeth 33
Lowther, Gerard
    29, 30, 31, 33, 34, 39, 176
Lowther, John 30, 34
Lowther, Lancelot 39
Lowther, Richard
    31, 32, 33, 34, 39, 40, 176
Lowther, Robert 32, 39
Lowther, William 30, 31, 39, 229
Luke, Yvonne A. 1
Lumb, George 296
Lumb, J. 291
Lund, Christopher 44, 47, 48
Lund, James 47, 49

Lund, John 43, 44
Lund, Richard 43
Lund, William 83
Lupton, Christopher 20, 23, 90
Lynn, Dick 197
Lynn, Fred 197
Lytham Terrace 174
Lythgoe, Adam 213

M

Mackenzie, Dr 72
Madden, Matilda Theresa 59
Mansergh, William 324
Margerison, Robert 91
Marriner, William 46, 290
Marsden, J.T. 73, 288
Marsden, John 45, 166
Marsden, Johnny 288
Marsden, Thomas 267, 323
Marsden, William 77
Marshall, Robert 78
Marshall Hall, Edward 70
Martindale, George 130, 131
Mason, Henry 188
Mason, Isaac 151
Mason, Richard jnr 188
Mason, Richard snr 188
Mason, Rowlyn 23
Mason, Thomas 119
Mathers, James 139, 152, 153
Matthew, William 282
Matthewman, Elizabeth 146
Matthewman, Mr 230
Matthewman, Mrs 54
Matthewman, Tom 145
Mattinson, James 143
Mattocks, G. 251
Maudesley, Thomas 249
Maudsley, John 131
Maudsley, Richard 78
Maudsley, Stephen 78
Mawson, John 276
Mawson, John William 276
Mawson, Thomas 276, 307
Mawson, William Henry 307
McConnel, George 243
McKeaney, Denis 233
Melbourne, Clement 68
Mercer, Nicholas le 9
Merry, George 63
Metcalf, Anthony 44
Metcalf, George 45
Metcalf, James 43

Peel, James 46
Peers, Thomas 143
Perfect, W. George 209
Petty, Robert 23
Petty, William 169
Petye, Edmonde 23
Philips, William 144
Picard, J.R. 59
Pickard, Richard 37
Pickering, William 24
Pinder, Henry 9, 162
Pinder, Robert 162
Playfair, John 255
Pooley, S.B. 328
Pooley, T. Burrow 309
Pounder, Jacob 44
Pounder, Thomas 43
Powell, Ellen 85, 149
Powell, Mrs 239
Prctor, Geffray 22
Preston, James 63, 77, 285
Preston, John 168, 213, 284, 285
Preston, R. 104, 182
Preston, Richard 213
Preston, Robert 119
Preston, Samuel 197
Preston, Thomas 213, 304
Price, Barrington 60
Prockter, Alexander 36
Prockter, Anthony 36, 37
Prockter, John 37
Prockter, Leonard 36
Prockter, Thomas 35, 36, 37
Prockter, Willm 35
Procter, Agnes 113, 115
Procter, Alexander 32, 40
Procter, Ann 79
Procter, Christopher 75
Procter, Francis 307
Procter, James 16, 20
Procter, Jennett 29
Procter, John 82, 117
Procter, Joseph Thomas 141
Procter, Leonard 32, 229
Procter, Peter 21, 40, 113, 114
Procter, Richard 21, 44
Procter, Robert 40, 45, 295
Procter, Thomas 40, 114
Procter, William 44, 92
Proctor, John 23
Proctor, Leonarde 23
Proctor, Thomas 22
Proctor, William 22
Prospect Cottage 307

Pugh, Henry 216
Pughe, Charles 98, 106
Pughe, Charles Reay 91, 98
Pynder, Robert 12

Q

Quinlan, Rachel 295
Quinlan, T.T. 59

R

Radcliffe, Joseph 46
Raine, James 89
Raistrick, Arthur 219
Raws, John 47
Ray, J. 116
Redhead, C.H. 330
Redhead, H. 72
Redhead, Harold 304
Redhead, Matthew 284
Redhead, T. 59
Redhead, T.E. 330
Redhead, Thomas 67, 174, 285, 296
Redman, Alexander 39, 40
Redman, Ann 40
Redman, Anne 36
Redman, Christopher 23
Redman, Giles 80, 124
Redman, Gyles 21, 36
Redman, James 80
Redman, John 23, 35, 37, 40, 295
Redman, Leonard 22, 35
Redman, Marmaduke 37, 40
Redman, Richard 22, 35
Redman, Thomas 37
Redman, William 21, 90, 91
Redmayne, Agnes 79
Redmayne, Isobell 90
Redmayne, James 91, 101, 125
Redmayne, John 12
Redmayne, Richard 308
Redmayne, Thomas
    45, 85, 139, 140, 149, 166, 169, 292, 308
Redmayne, William 31, 79
Remington, James 125
Remington, Robert 186
Remmington, Christo 37
Remmington, Elizabeth 79
Remmington, James 37
Remmington, W. 60
Remmington, William 290
Remyngton, Robert 23
Renison, Richard 47
Renshaw, Charles 143

371

Wetherhead, John 91
Wetherhead, Leonard 16, 79
Wetherhead, Richard 19, 92
Wetherhead, Thomas 26, 39, 40
Wetherhead, William 36
Wetherhird, Leonard 92
Whaley, Francis 45
Whaley, William 47
Wharton, Leonard 178
Whitaker, Dr 260
Whitaker, Thomas Dunham 109
Whitham, Anne 139
Whittingdale, Dr 251
Whittingdale, W.I. 324
Whytton, Matthewe 22
Wigglesworth, Henry 35
Wigglesworth, Thomas 169
Wignall, J.T. 332
Wignall, John 146
Wignall, William 285
Wilcock, Edward 43, 138
Wilcock, Richard 35, 47
Wilcock, Robert 44
Wilcock, William 35, 47
Wildman, Betty 166
Wildman, Charlotte 78
Wildman, Christopher 47
Wildman, Edward 45
Wildman, John 155
Wildman, Peter 77
Wildman, Richard 47, 125
Wildman, Septimus 46
Wildman, Thomas 75, 155
Wildman, William 47
Wilkinson, John 46, 155
Wilkinson, Joseph 259
Wilkinson, Mrs 292
Wilkinson, Robert 36, 68, 101, 167
Willan, J.W. 78
Willan, John Whaley 47
William Carr 44
William Knipe 178
William Scott 44
William Serjeantson 182
Williamson, George 16, 90, 93
Willis, George 47, 185, 188
Willis, William 59, 83
Wilsman, James 47
Wilson, Carus 133
Wilson, Christopher 46
Wilson, Edward 94
Wilson, Esther 80
Wilson, H.D. 147

Wilson, J.R. 330
Wilson, James Richard 141
Wilson, John 125, 295
Wilson, Richard 29
Wilson, Thomas 36, 40
Wilson, Tom 216
Wilson, W. 112
Wilson, William 267
Winder, Annie 304
Winder, May Annie 304
Winder, Robert 304
Winder, William 233
Windle, Robert 33
Windle, William 77
Winn, William 46
Winthrop-Young, Eleanor 150
Wise, Christopher 45
Witham, John 36
Witton, William 35
Wombwell, George 62
Wood, John 37
Wood, William 32, 229
Woodiwiss, Mr 234, 238
Worden, John Henry 141
Wordsworth, Christopher 281, 282
Wordsworth, John 282
Wordsworth, Mary 281
Wordsworth, William 42, 278, 281, 282
Worthington, Dennis 251
Worthington, Samuel
    63, 68, 70, 140, 248, 250, 251, 303,
    332, 338, 340
Worthington, William S. 251
Wray, Christopher 91
Wright, George 151
Wyldemen, William 22
Wylson, Thomas 21

Y

Yates, Francis 86, 151
Yates, Mr 303
Yates, William 163
Yeadon, George 46, 141
Yeadon, Joseph 46, 117
Yeadon, Richard 45
Yeadon, Thomas 126
Yeatts, George 94
Yolland, Colonel 235
Young, George 151